CODIFICATION OF ADMINISTRATIVE LAW

This open access book presents the first comparative study on the legal sources of administrative law. Every modern legal order needs a set of general rules to apply and enforce administrative law; the rules impose principles of action, of procedure, and of organisation of the authorities. The legal basis of these rules may be quite diverse. Some countries have tried to codify administrative law, whilst others work with few rules or unwritten rules.

The book considers the consequences that arise from the different degrees of codification of general administrative law. It presents answers to important questions including:

- Does codification increase predictability and legal certainty?
- Does codification lead to a 'petrification' of administrative law?
- To what degree does the constitution shape administrative law?
- Which areas of administrative law are suitable for codification, which are not, and why not?

The book answers these questions by presenting 13 country reports, covering both civil and common law traditions, a chapter on the EU, and a comparative analysis.

This book is available as open access through the Bloomsbury Open Access programme and is available on www.bloomsburycollections.com.

# Codification of Administrative Law

*A Comparative Study on the Sources of Administrative Law*

Edited by
Felix Uhlmann

•HART•
OXFORD • LONDON • NEW YORK • NEW DELHI • SYDNEY

HART PUBLISHING

Bloomsbury Publishing Plc

Kemp House, Chawley Park, Cumnor Hill, Oxford, OX2 9PH, UK

1385 Broadway, New York, NY 10018, USA

29 Earlsfort Terrace, Dublin 2, Ireland

HART PUBLISHING, the Hart/Stag logo, BLOOMSBURY and the Diana logo are trademarks of Bloomsbury Publishing Plc

First published in Great Britain 2023



Open Access was funded by the Faculty of Law of the University of Zurich.



A catalogue record for this book is available from the British Library.

A catalogue record for this book is available from the Library of Congress.

Library of Congress Control Number: 2023932648

ISBN: HB: 978-1-50995-492-6
ePDF: 978-1-50995-494-0
ePub: 978-1-50995-493-3

Typeset by Compuscript Ltd, Shannon

# CONTENTS

# LIST OF CONTRIBUTORS

**Tom Barkhuysen**, Professor at the University of Leiden

**Ariane Berger**, Private Lecturer at the University of Berlin

**Janina Boughey**, Associate Professor at the University of New South Wales

**Roberto Caranta**, Professor at the University of Turin

**Delphine Costa**, Professor at Aix-Marseille University

**Stéphanie De Somer**, Associate Professor at the University of Antwerp

**Markus Heintzen**, Professor at the University of Berlin

**Pierre Issalys**, Professor Emeritus at the University of Laval

**Konrad Lachmayer**, Professor at the Sigmund Freud University (Vienna)

**Sarah Nason**, Senior Lecturer at Bangor University

**Jon Christian Fløysvik Nordrum**, Associate Professor at the University of Oslo

**Ingrid Opdebeek**, Professor at the University of Antwerp

**Willemien den Ouden**, Professor at the University of Leiden

**Jane Reichel**, Professor at Stockholm University

**Michaela Ribbing**, Professor at Stockholm University

**Edward L Rubin**, Professor Emeritus at Vanderbilt University

**Ymre E Schuurmans**, Professor at the University of Leiden

**Felix Uhlmann**, Professor at the University of Zurich

# Introduction

FELIX UHLMANN

Every modern legal order needs a set of general rules to enforce administrative law. These rules are 'general' because they apply regardless of the specific subject area. They impose principles of action, of procedure and of organisation of the authorities, and form the core of administrative law.

The legal basis of such rules may be quite diverse. Common law is obviously an important legal source in countries with a common law tradition, but, despite common perceptions, legislation is central to administrative law too. In typical civil law countries but also the EU, there is a mixture between judicial development and selective interventions by the legislator. In Switzerland, for example, substantive principles of administrative action are strongly influenced by the case law of the Federal Supreme Court and other courts, while procedural law has largely been codified, both at the federal level and the cantonal (state) level. There are also countries in which principles of general administrative law have been converted into a comprehensive codification – in particular, the Netherlands (Algemene wet bestuursrecht (General Administrative Law Act)).[1]

Which rules are codified at which level depends rarely on a conscious systematic decision. What is codified and on which level can be explained in part by tradition, but in some cases, it appears rather random. For example, in Switzerland the institute of revocation of administrative law decisions has largely been developed based on court practice, while the related institute of revisions has been regulated in procedural Acts; still, there are also cantons which have expressly legislated on the revocation of administrative law decisions and a right to a revision is accepted by courts under specific conditions even in the absence of an expressive legal provision. Similar examples can be found in the areas of state liability for false official information or for the delegation of administrative tasks to private persons.

To date, there has been hardly any research on the practical consequences that arise from the different degrees of codification of general administrative law. Does codification increase predictability and legal certainty? Does codification lead to a

[1] The GALA (English translation) can be found on the websites of various public authorities with a partly international audience, such as the tax authorities (www.belastingdienst.nl). The English version contains all tranches, but is not totally up to date. All Dutch legislation and regulation can be found on the governmental website: wetten.overheid.nl. All parliamentary papers on the codification of the GALA can be found at: www.pgawb.nl.

'petrification' of general administrative law? To what degree does the Constitution shape administrative law? Which areas of general administrative law are suitable for codification, which are not, and why and why not?

This book encompasses answers to these questions from 13 countries and the EU. The findings are summarised in an overall analysis. We hope that these insights may help legislators and other state actors to think more consciously about the benefits but also the challenges of codifying general administrative law. For scholars, this book might be useful as a basis for further analysis on the sources of administrative law. And, finally, we hope to encourage other scholars to undertake similar projects; comparative research on administrative law is still relatively rare – wrongly, I believe.

International projects are often burdensome, both for editors as for contributors. This book seems to be the exception to this rule. The contributors were extremely disciplined and I like to thank for the cooperative effort. The publisher was most helpful and diligent. There was also luck. The workshop for this project took place in Zurich only weeks before the outbreak of the pandemic. I would also like to express my gratitude for the financial support of the Swiss National Science Foundation for the workshop and for the financial support for the open access of this book by the Faculty of Law of the University of Zurich. Last but not least, I am extremely thankful to my assistant Rico Tanner. Without his tireless efforts, this book would not have been possible. At the end of the works we were assisted by Lucile Pasche whose support was also greatly appreciated.

# 1

# The 'Codification' of Administrative Law in Australia

JANINA BOUGHEY

## I. Introduction

In the 1970s, Australia was a leader in administrative law amongst common law, Westminster systems. Following recommendations set out in the 1971 Kerr Report,[1] the Commonwealth Government led the way in establishing a generalist merits review tribunal (known as the Administrative Appeals Tribunal), a public sector Ombudsman (copied from the Swedish model), and in 'codifying' and simplifying aspects of the procedures, 'grounds' and remedies of judicial review of administrative action in the Administrative Decisions (Judicial Review) Act 1979 (Cth) (hereinafter 'ADJR Act')'. These developments were designed to make it easier for individuals affected by administrative decisions to make complaints and obtain remedies for improper and unlawful administrative action. Together with freedom of information laws and constitutional and common law avenues of judicial review, they are often said to form a 'package' or 'system' of institutions and laws which attempt to ensure that governments are transparent and accountable.[2]

For the most part, the reforms were, and continue to be regarded as, a success.[3] States and territories copied the Commonwealth model of amalgamating specialist tribunals, and eventually went further to confer judicial powers on these tribunals (which is possible at the state and territory level due to the less strict separation of judicial power).[4] The separate Commonwealth migration and social security tribunals

[1] Commonwealth Administrative Review Committee, *Commonwealth Administrative Review Committee Report*, Parliament of the Commonwealth of Australia Paper No 144 (1971) (Commonwealth) ('Kerr Report').

[2] See generally M Groves and J Boughey, 'Administrative Law in the Australian Environment' in M Groves (ed), *Modern Administrative Law in Australia: Concepts and Context* (Melbourne, Cambridge University Press, 2014) 3.

[3] Though there are growing gaps. See: JJ Griffiths, '50th Anniversary of the Kerr Report' (2021) 28(4) *Australian Journal of Administrative Law* 224; J Boughey, 'A Call for Ongoing Political Commitment to the Administrative Law Project' (2021) 28(4) *Australian Journal of Administrative Law* 242.

[4] See generally J Boughey, E Rock and G Weeks, *Government Liability: Principles and Remedies* (Sydney, LexisNexis, 2019) ch 6.

were finally amalgamated into the Administrative Appeals Tribunal (AAT) in 2015.[5] This suggests that the creation of generalist merits review tribunals has generally been thought to be successful, though there are certainly challenges in particular tribunals, particularly relating to the politicisation of appointments, resourcing and overly legalistic cultures.[6] Likewise, the states and territories have each established Ombudsmen and enacted freedom of information laws, which tend to be similar to the Commonwealth model. Reforms have been made to each of these institutions and laws over the past five decades, in response to challenges that have arisen, such as outsourcing,[7] and to strengthen the administrative law framework.[8]

The success of the codification of judicial review in the ADJR Act is less clear. It was initially heralded as a leading innovation, but, in recent decades, the ADJR Act has attracted considerable criticism for the longer-term impact that it has had on judicial review in Australia. It has also become less influential as a model for reform in the states and territories. The central criticisms of the ADJR Act are as follows:

- Its narrow jurisdictional formula has meant that the common law and Constitution[9] remain important sources of judicial review jurisdiction, resulting in a complex, dual system of review at the federal level.
- It lacks any guiding purpose or principles and so has contributed to the 'formalism' of Australian administrative law.[10]
- By codifying the 'grounds' of review, the Act has stunted the development of the common law.[11] Along similar lines, it is possible that the inclusion of a duty to give reasons in the Act has prevented the need for the development of such a duty at common law.

[5] Tribunals Amalgamation Act 2015 (Cth).

[6] See, eg, in relation to the AAT: R Creyke, 'Amalgamation of Tribunals: Whether 'tis Better …?' in S Nason (ed), *Administrative Justice in Wales and Comparative Perspectives* (Cardiff, University of Wales Press, 2017) 316; IDF Callinan AC, *Review: Section 4 of the Tribunals Amalgamation Act 2015*, 19 December 2018, https://www.ag.gov.au/legal-system/publications/report-statutory-review-tribunals-amalgamation-act-2015. The politicisation of the AAT due to the previous Government's political appointments led the Australian Government to announce in December 2022 that the AAT would be abolished and replaced with a new federal administrative review tribunal.

[7] See, eg, Migration and Ombudsman Legislation Amendment Act 2005 (Cth), inserting s 3BA into the Ombudsman Act 1976 (Cth).

[8] See, eg, Freedom of Information (Reform) Act 2010 (Cth). But note that these reforms have been weakened significantly by the Coalition Government's decision to starve the Australian Information Commissioner of funds. See J McMillan, 'Transparent Government – Are We Travelling Well?' (2021) 28(4) *Australian Journal of Administrative Law* 259.

[9] Constitution of the Commonwealth of Australia 1901.

[10] M Aronson, 'Is the ADJR Act Hampering the Development of Australian Administrative Law?' (2004) 15 *Public Law Review* 202, 203. The issue was also raised by a number of submissions to the ARC's inquiry into federal judicial review: see Administrative Review Council (ARC), *Federal Judicial Review in Australia*, Report No 50 (2012), 130–32.

[11] *Re Minister for Immigration and Multicultural Affairs; Ex parte Applicant S20/2002* (2003) 198 ALR 59, 94–95 [156]–[168] (Kirby J).

Each of these criticisms will be analysed in section IV below.

In more recent decades, the Commonwealth Parliament has focused on a different type of 'codification' of judicial review principles: the creation of purportedly exhaustive codes of procedure in the migration context. These codes raise some of the same issues as the codification of judicial review procedure, as well as some different ones. These will be also be analysed in section IV below.

Sections II and III briefly explain the background context of Australian administrative law against which these 'codification' attempts operate. Section II defines administrative law and 'codification', and section III sets out the legal sources and principles of judicial review of administrative action in Australia. As noted, section IV then analyses the Australian experience of the codification of judicial review principles.

## II. The Definition and Delimitation of Administrative Law

It is impossible to neatly map the boundaries of 'administrative law' in Australia, as I am sure it is in most jurisdictions.[12] For example, each of the major textbooks on administrative includes a slightly different set of laws and institutions within its scope. All agree on four central components:

- judicial review;
- merits review (tribunals which sit within the executive branch and are usually empowered to conduct a *de novo* review, and determine the correct and preferable decision);
- ombudsmen; and
- freedom of information laws.

Beyond this, there is no consensus. Most major texts include anti-corruption and integrity bodies and whistleblower laws.[13] Some include auditors general[14] and parliamentary scrutiny,[15] and a few add human rights,[16] public service codes

[12] See, eg, in this book P Issalys, 'A Persistent Taste for Diversity: Codification of Administrative Law in Canada', section I.

[13] See, eg, R Creyke et al, *Control of Government Action: Text, Cases and Commentary*, 5th edn (Sydney, LexisNexis, 2019); J Bannister, A Olijnik and S McDonald, *Government Accountability: Australian Administrative Law*, 2nd edn (Melbourne, Cambridge University Press, 2018); R Douglas et al, *Douglas and Jones's Administrative Law*, 8th edn (Sydney, Federation Press, 2018).

[14] J Bannister, A Olijnik and S McDonald (n 13); R Douglas et al (n 13).

[15] J Bannister, A Olijnik and S McDonald (n 13); P Cane, L McDonald and K Rundle, *Principles of Administrative Law*, 3rd edn (Melbourne, Oxford University Press, 2018).

[16] R Creyke et al (n 13).

of conduct[17] and royal commissions.[18] All additions are defensible, as each of these laws and institutions contributes to the administrative law enterprise of government accountability and transparency. However, if administrative law is defined broadly as any law or institution concerned with government accountability and transparency, then this list should be even longer – indeed, endless. It could, for instance, also include private law as it applies to government[19] and the media (both traditional and new forms).

In Australia, all of the institutions and laws said to form part of 'administrative law' are entirely creatures of statute, with the exceptions of judicial review of administrative action and parliamentary scrutiny. The Constitution entrenches judicial and parliamentary scrutiny of administrative action to some degree at the federal, state and territory levels, but in most there are also statutes which interact with this constitutionally entrenched oversight. In other words, 'administrative law' in Australia is largely statutory. The institutions and principles that regulate merits review, access to information and ombudsmen are all found entirely in legislation, though, of course, courts play a crucial role in interpreting this legislation.

It would be an impossible task to attempt to cover all of this statute law in this chapter. Instead, the focus in this chapter is on the Australian statutes which 'codify' principles of judicial review of administrative action, and their interaction with common law and constitutional principles. These do interact with other administrative law institutions in various ways. For example, the High Court of Australia appears to be more inclined to permit Parliament to limit the availability of judicial review where alternative accountability mechanisms are provided by statute or the Constitution.[20] However, the most interesting answers to the questions regarding the effects of codification are yielded through a focus on judicial review principles.

## A. 'Codification'

I have used quotation marks when referring to the 'codification' of administrative law principles because of the different meaning that the term has in common law jurisdictions and related debates about whether true codification is possible in that context.[21]

[17] R Creyke et al (n 13).
[18] J Bannister, A Olijnik and S McDonald (n 13).
[19] See generally J Boughey, E Rock and G Weeks (n 4).
[20] See J Boughey and G Weeks, 'Government Accountability as a Constitutional Value' in R Dixon (ed), *Australian Constitutional Values* (Oxford, Hart Publishing, 2018) 99, 115 f.
[21] For a summary, see C Skinner, 'Codification and the Common Law' (2009) 11 *European Journal of Law Reform* 225, 227 ff.

In the Australian context, the ADJR Act and other statutes to which I refer in this chapter are not truly 'codes' in the sense used in civil law jurisdictions. Rather than providing an exhaustive statement of the law, the codification of administrative law in common law jurisdictions has usually involved consolidating judicial precedent into statutory form, often leaving scope for continued development of the law by the judiciary.[22] Australia's statutes rely on established common law concepts and interpretive presumptions, and interact with common law and constitutional principles. They were not intended, for the most part, to be a comprehensive and exhaustive statement of the relevant rules. However, there have been some recent, more limited attempts to exhaustively set out the 'fair hearing' requirement of natural justice in the migration context, which I will address below in section IV.D.

## III. Legal Sources of the Principles of Judicial Review of Administrative Action in Australia

The function of courts in reviewing administrative action is to determine and enforce the legal limits of administrative powers. These legal limits may be sourced expressly in the statute that confers power on the relevant administrative body or they may be implied. In the increasingly rare situations where the executive exercises non-statutory powers, limits may be found in the Constitution or, perhaps, common law.[23]

As in other common law jurisdictions, there was a protracted and largely fruitless debate throughout the 1980s and 1990s about whether the limits on administrative action articulated and enforced through judicial review are sourced in common law or statute.[24] The High Court has recently resolved this debate, largely

[22] TH Jones, 'Judicial Review and Codification' (2000) 20 *Legal Studies* 517, 518. For a discussion of the US experience, see in this book EL Rubin, 'The United States: Systematic But Incomplete Codification'.

[23] This is unsettled. See A Sapienza, 'Interpreting the Limits of Non-statutory Executive Power: What Role for the Grounds of Judicial Review?' in J Boughey and LB Crawford (eds), *Interpreting Executive Power* (Sydney, Federation Press, 2020) 222. On the High Court of Australia's approach to constitutional limits on statutory executive powers see: J Boughey and A Carter, 'Constitutional Freedoms and Statutory Executive Powers' (2022) 45 *Melbourne University Law Review* 903.

[24] This began in the UK with D Oliver, 'Is the Ultra Vires Rule the Basis of Judicial Review?' [1987] *Public Law* 543. Major contributions to the debate include: J Laws, 'Law and Democracy' [1995] *Public Law* 72; J Jowell, 'Of Vires and Vacuums: The Constitutional Context of Judicial Review' [1999] *Public Law* 448; C Forsyth, 'Of Fig Leaves and Fairy Tales: The Ultra Vires Doctrine, the Sovereignty of Parliament and Judicial Review' (1996) 55 *Cambridge Law Journal* 122; P Craig, 'Competing Models of Judicial Review' [1999] *Public Law* 428; C Forsyth and M Elliott, 'The Legitimacy of Judicial Review' [2003] *Public Law* 286; TRS Allan, 'Constitutional Dialogue and the Justification of Judicial Review' (2003) 23 *Oxford Journal of Legal Studies* 563. In the Australian context, the debate largely played out

in favour of the latter, statutory view, but acknowledges that the principles and presumptions of statutory interpretation are sourced in common law.[25] Thus, in each case, the limits of an administrative power are specific to the power being exercised rather than general rules that apply to every administrative power in all circumstances.

However, there are some common principles that are presumed to apply to administrative powers, unless the statute expressly or impliedly limits them, including a duty to afford procedural fairness and an obligation to act reasonably. These are often referred to as the 'grounds' of judicial review, and form the substance of texts and commentary on administrative law in Australia. The term 'grounds' suggests that the limits are free-standing causes of action, which is not accurate. They are, in fact, simply common express and implied legal limits on administrative power which interact and overlap with one another, and are highly context-specific. Nevertheless, this nomenclature of 'grounds' is still used (albeit less frequently) and is one of the ways in which the codification of judicial review principles in the ADJR Act has shaped Australian law. These common limits are listed in sections 5 and 6 of the ADJR Act, which provide that review may be sought 'on any one or more of the following grounds …'.

## A. 'Grounds' of Review

There are myriad ways of conceptualising the 'grounds' of review. Each major textbook categorises them differently. My preferred approach is, unsurprisingly, the one that my co-authors and I take, which groups the grounds thematically into four broad categories:[26]

- errors as to whether the decision-maker has authority to decide;
- fact-finding errors;
- breaches of procedural fairness; and
- errors in the exercise of discretion.

For the most part, the grounds available under the ADJR Act and common law are the same, and this was the intention of the drafters of the ADJR Act.[27] There are a few exceptions, which I will explore in section IV.

in the judgments of Mason J and Brennan J in a series of procedural fairness cases, beginning with *Kioa v West* (1985) 159 CLR 550. See generally M Aronson, M Groves and G Weeks, *Judicial Review of Administrative Action and Government Liability*, 6th edn (Sydney, Thomson Reuters, 2017) 412 ff.

[25] See *Plaintiff S10/2011 v Minister for Immigration and Citizenship* (2012) 246 CLR 656, 666. See generally W Bateman and L McDonald, 'The Normative Structure of Australian Administrative Law' (2017) 45 *Federal Law Review* 153.

[26] J Boughey, E Rock and G Weeks (n 4) ch 4.

[27] *Kioa v West* (1985) 159 CLR 550, 567 (Gibbs CJ), 576 (Mason J), 625 (Brennan J).

## *i. Acting without Authority*

The first and most basic concept that underpins judicial review is that every government action must be sourced in law.[28] This is usually legislation, but may be a non-statutory source of power such as prerogative-type[29] powers or the non-statutory power to contract.[30] This is a straightforward idea, but determining whether a particular action is lawful is rarely simple, because it will frequently require the interpretation of complex statutory provisions.[31]

An administrative body may have acted without authority if it fails to comply with a procedure that the law requires it to follow before making a decision, such as a requirement to consult.[32] Commonly, these are notice or consultation requirements, which are sometimes designed to codify the requirements of the hearing rule of procedural fairness. The relationship between such procedural codes and procedural fairness is complex and unsettled, and is discussed in section IV below.[33] A breach of process may or may not invalidate the actions of a decision-maker, depending on whether Parliament can be taken to have intended for invalidity to result from the breach.[34]

Other ways in which an administrative decision-maker may act without authority are if there is a defect in their appointment, or in the delegation of powers to them,[35] or if they misconstrue the scope of their statutory powers.[36]

## *ii. Fact-Finding Errors*

Fact-finding is generally regarded as the 'merits' of an administrative decision, and courts will usually not review alleged fact-finding errors. There are good policy and constitutional reasons for this position.[37] However, where Parliament has provided that a particular fact must exist in order for the decision-maker to have authority to act (or to act in a particular manner), then the existence of the fact becomes a question of law, and so can be reviewed by a court.[38]

[28] *Entick v Carrington* (1765) 19 St Tr 1030; *Church of Scientology v Woodward* (1982) 154 CLR 25, 57–61 (Mason J), 70–72 (Brennan J). Under the Administrative Decisions (Judicial Review) Act 1977 (Cth) ('ADJR Act'), an argument that an administrative decision was not authorised by statute would be made under s 5(1)(d).

[29] I say 'prerogative-type' powers because the High Court has indicated that s 61 of the Constitution is the source of executive power, and has been careful in the way it explains the relationship between s 61 and historical prerogative powers at the federal level. See, eg, *Williams v Commonwealth* (2012) 248 CLR 156, 184 [22] (French CJ).

[30] See generally N Seddon, *Government Contracts: Federal, State and Local*, 6th edn (Sydney, Federation Press, 2018).

[31] See, eg, *Independent Commission Against Corruption v Cunneen* (2015) 256 CLR 1.

[32] A breach of such a procedure is a ground of review under s 5(1)(b) of the ADJR Act.

[33] *BVD17 v Minister for Immigration and Border Protection* [2019] HCA 34.

[34] *Project Blue Sky v Australian Broadcasting Authority* (1998) 194 CLR 355. See generally J Boughey, E Rock and G Weeks (n 4) 105 f.

[35] See generally J Boughey, E Rock and G Weeks (n 4) 107 f.

[36] See, eg, *Independent Commission against Corruption v Cunneen* (2015) 256 CLR 1.

[37] See M Aronson, M Groves and G Weeks (n 24) 195 ff.

[38] See, eg, *Plaintiff M70/2011 v Minister for Immigration and* Citizenship (2011) 244 CLR 144.

There are several grounds recognised under common law and under the ADJR Act through which these arguments can be made. The common law ground has historically been quite narrow, and the drafters of the ADJR Act sought to expand it by expanding the facts which could be reviewed and relaxing the standard of review.[39] However, the relevant provisions of the ADJR Act have largely just proven to be complex and confusing.[40] Their application remains unclear, and Parliament has failed to respond to the recommendation that the ADJR Act's no evidence grounds be amended.[41]

### *iii. Procedural Fairness*

Procedural fairness[42] places two requirements on decision-makers: they must give a person who will be affected by their decision a fair hearing; and they must not be, or appear to be, biased. These requirements are presumed to apply 'in the absence of a clear, contrary legislative intention'.[43] Such an intention may be found in the express language of a statute or may, in rare cases, be implied.[44]

The duty to give a fair hearing only applies where a decision affects a person (including a company) or small group of persons 'in his individual capacity (as distinct from a member of the general public or a class of the general public)'.[45] The way in which courts draw this line has not been articulated, but is probably a question of pragmatism as much as anything else.

The content of the fair hearing rule is highly flexible. The High Court has said that it depends on 'what is required in order to ensure that the decision is made fairly in the circumstances having regard to the legal framework within which the decision is to be made'.[46] It generally requires that a person has a fair opportunity to present their case and rebut credible, adverse evidence.[47]

What will amount to bias in a given administrative context is similarly flexible. The test is: might 'a fair-minded lay observer … reasonably apprehend that the [decision-maker] might not bring an impartial mind to the resolution

[39] Committee of Review of Prerogative Writ Procedure, *Report of the Committee of Review of Prerogative Writ Procedure*, Parliament of the Commonwealth of Australia Paper No 56 (1973) 9–10 ('Ellicott Report').

[40] M Aronson, M Groves and G Weeks (n 24) 259.

[41] ARC, *Federal Judicial Review in Australia* (n 10), Recommendation 8.

[42] This term is used interchangeably with 'natural justice', although this is not the universal position; see, eg, A Robertson, 'Natural Justice or Procedural Fairness' (2016) 23 *Australian Journal of Administrative Law* 155. The distinction is frequently immaterial: *Re Minister for Immigration and Multicultural Affairs; Ex parte Lam* (2003) 214 CLR 1, 14 [37] (Gleeson CJ) ('*Lam*').

[43] *Minister for Immigration and Border Protection v WZARH* (2015) 256 CLR 326, 335 [30] (Kiefel, Bell and Keane JJ) ('*WZARH*').

[44] See, eg, *CPCF v Minister for Immigration and Border Protection* (2015) 255 CLR 514, 541–42 (French CJ); 558–59 (Hayne and Bell JJ), 607 (Kiefel J), 322–23 (Gageler J). For a more in-depth discussion, see M Aronson, M Groves and G Weeks (n 24) 457 f.

[45] *Kioa v West* (1985) 159 CLR 550, 632 (Deane J).

[46] *WZARH* (2015) 256 CLR 326, 335 (Kiefel, Bell and Keane JJ).

[47] *Kioa v West* (1985) 159 CLR 550, 628 (Brennan J).

of the question'.[48] This test developed in the judicial context. In the administrative decision-making context, the case law makes it clear that the reasonable lay observer's *expectations* of different administrative decision-makers will differ from their expectations of judges.[49] The degree of impartiality expected of an administrative decision-maker will depend on their position, the nature of the powers they exercise and the statutory context.[50]

### *iv. Legal Errors in the Exercise of Discretion*

Although Dicey was concerned that administrative discretion was antithetical to the rule of law,[51] courts have long recognised that even very broad discretionary powers have legal limits.[52] Over the course of the twentieth century, these principles have been extended to all categories of decision-maker and all types of administrative decisions.[53] As noted above, Australian courts continue to locate these limits in the empowering statute, explaining, for instance that:

> The common law principle of construction … establishes a condition of reasonableness as a default position. Absent an affirmative basis for its exclusion or modification, a condition of reasonableness is presumed.[54]

Thus, in order to determine whether a decision-maker has exercised a statutory discretion lawfully, a court must closely examine the relevant statute. As with the 'grounds' of review generally, the limits on discretion are not fixed and no exhaustive list is possible,[55] but several key, interrelated and overlapping principles commonly arise in interpreting the scope of administrative discretions.

The first is that administrative powers may only be exercised for the purpose for which they were granted.[56] The purposes for which Parliament has granted a power can be ascertained by through the interpretation of the statutory context and the objects of the statutory scheme as a whole.[57]

[48] *Ebner v Official Trustee* (2000) 205 CLR 337, 344.

[49] See, eg, *Minister for Immigration and Multicultural Affairs v Jia* (2001) 205 CLR 507, 531 (Gleeson CJ and Gummow J).

[50] *Isbester v Knox City Council* (2015) 255 CLR 135, 146–50 (Kiefel, Bell, Keane and Nettle JJ).

[51] AV Dicey, *Introduction to the Study of the Law of the Constitution*, 8th edn (London, Macmillan, 1915).

[52] See, eg, *Rooke's Case* (1598) 5 Co Rep 99B; *Webb v Manchester and Leeds Railway Co* (1839) 4 My & CR 116; *Sharp v Wakefield* [1891] AC 173, 179–81.

[53] See, eg, *Roncarelli v Duplessis* [1959] SCR 121; *Padfield v Minister of Agriculture, Fisheries and Food* [1967] AC 997; *R v Toohey; Ex parte Northern Land Council* (1981) 151 CLR 170. See generally, J Boughey, *Human Rights and Judicial Review in Australia and Canada: The Newest Despotism?* (Oxford, Hart Publishing, 2017) ch 5.

[54] *Minister for Immigration v Li* (2013) 249 CLR 332, 371 [92] (Gageler J) ('*Li*').

[55] *Minister for Immigration and Border Protection v SZVFW* (2018) 264 CLR 541, 567 [59] (Gageler J) ('*SZVFW*').

[56] See, eg, *Brownells Ltd v Ironmongers' Wages Board* (1950) 81 CLR 108, 119–20.

[57] R Creyke et al (n 13) 574.

Second, decision-makers must consider all matters that the statute requires them to take into account, and cannot take into account matters which the statute prohibits them from considering.[58] Again, the determination of whether a matter is one which must, or cannot, be considered is a question of law which depends on the proper construction of the empowering statute.[59]

Third, the person on whom a statute confers discretion must be the one to exercise that discretion: they cannot fetter their discretion by applying a policy at the expense of the merits, or acting at the behest of another person.[60] Australian law takes a relatively rigid approach to delineating hard law and soft law, such as policies, and the legal consequences of each, due to its strict separation of powers. For this reason, the High Court has rejected a doctrine of substantive legitimate expectations as applies in the UK.[61]

Fourth, there is a presumption that decision-makers must exercise discretionary powers in a way that is reasonable and rational.[62] While the test for unreasonableness has undergone some shifts in recent years, it is said to still be a 'stringent standard', which preserves the line between judicial and administrative power.[63] What is unreasonable in each case 'is inherently sensitive to context; it cannot be reduced to a formulary',[64] and will depend 'upon the context, including the scope, purpose, and real object of the statute'.[65]

## B. Constitutional Influences

Australia's Constitution has had an enormous impact on the development of judicial review principles, and indeed administrative law more broadly. Two features of the Constitution have been particularly important: the strict separation of judicial power; and the entrenchment of the High Court's judicial review jurisdiction.[66]

The Constitution has been found to require a strict separation of judicial power from the powers of the legislature and executive branches (which are not strictly separated under the Westminster model). The effect of this on administrative law is that courts attempt to draw a strict line between the judicial function of interpreting the law and determining whether it has been breached, and the administrative function of applying the law. In Australia, this is referred to as the 'legality/merits

[58] These are often misleadingly referred to as the 'relevant' and 'irrelevant' considerations grounds.
[59] *Lo v Chief Commissioner of State Revenue* (2012) 85 NSWLR 86, 89 (Basten JA).
[60] See generally M Aronson, M Groves and G Weeks (n 24) 300 ff.
[61] *Lam* (2003) 214 CLR 1.
[62] *Li* (2013) 249 CLR 332.
[63] *SZVFW* (2018) 264 CLR 541, 551 [11] (Kiefel CJ), 728 [52], [54], 729 [58] (Gageler J), 734 [88]–[89] (Nettle and Gordon JJ).
[64] *SZVFW* (2018) 264 CLR 541, 567 [59] (Gageler J).
[65] *SZVFW* (2018) 264 CLR 541, 586 [135] (Edelman J).
[66] See S Gageler, 'The Constitutional Dimension' in M Groves (ed), *Modern Administrative Law in Australia: Concepts and Context* (Melbourne, Cambridge University Press, 2014).

distinction', and it has been pivotal to the way in which courts explain and justify the legal limits on administrative power. The High Court frequently repeats Brennan J's seminal explanation from *Attorney-General (NSW) v Quin* that:

> The duty and jurisdiction of the court to review administrative action do not go beyond the declaration and enforcing of the law which determines the limits and governs the exercise of the repository's power. If, in so doing, the court avoids administrative injustice or error, so be it; but the court has no jurisdiction simply to cure administrative injustice or error. The merits of administrative action, to the extent that they can be distinguished from legality, are for the repository of the relevant power and, subject to political control, for the repository alone.[67]

The legality/merits divide has influenced the way in which courts justify the scope and limits of the 'unreasonableness' ground of review, in particular, as this is often regarded as the 'ground' most at risk of impinging on the merits of a decision.[68] However, it has also had several other consequences, which differentiate Australian administrative law from the law in other common law jurisdictions.

One is the rejection of any doctrine of deference to the executive branch on questions of law.[69] The High Court has wholeheartedly accepted the proposition from *Marbury v Madison* that 'it is emphatically the province of the judicial department to say what the law is', but has rejected later US case law which reaches a pragmatic compromise through which courts may defer to the interpretations of expert agencies in certain circumstances.

Another manifestation of the separation of powers has been the rejection of any principles which give substantive protection to a person's legitimate expectations of government induced by government promises or policies.[70] The broad rationale for this is that policy-making is an administrative function and that policies do not form part of the law. As the judicial role is limited to determining whether an administrative official has breached the legal limits of their powers, courts have no legitimate role in assessing either the merits of a policy or the weight which should be given to a policy in a particular administrative decision. Governments must also be free to change their minds about policies, and to apply them and not apply them, in order to reach the most appropriate balance between competing public and individual interests in each case.

The second aspect of the Australian Constitution which has been important in shaping administrative law principles is the entrenchment of the supervisory jurisdiction of superior courts. The Constitution expressly entrenches the High Court's jurisdiction to hear matters in which certain remedies are sought against

[67] *Attorney-General (NSW) v Quin* (1990) 170 CLR 1, 35.

[68] See generally *Li* (2013) 249 CLR 332 and *SZVFW* (2018) 264 CLR 541.

[69] See J Boughey, 'Re-evaluating the Doctrine of Deference in Administrative Law' (2017) 45 *Federal Law Review* 598; S Gageler, 'Deference' (2015) 22 *Australian Journal of Administrative Law* 151. On the US doctrine of deference see in this book EL Rubin (n 22) section V.

[70] *Lam* (2003) 214 CLR 1. See generally G Weeks, *Soft Law and Public Authorities: Remedies and Reform* (Oxford, Hart Publishing, 2016) chs 6 and 7.

Commonwealth officers,[71] and has been held to impliedly entrench the jurisdiction of state supreme courts to determine whether state administrative officials have acted within the lawful limits of their authority.[72]

This entrenched jurisdiction has been described as 'secur[ing] a basic element of the rule of law'[73] and ensuring that there are no 'islands of power immune from supervision and restraint'.[74] The full extent of what the Constitution entrenches remains somewhat unclear,[75] but what is clear is that there is *something* of substance that is protected. Parliament cannot prevent superior courts from effectively performing their supervisory function by, for instance, legislating to prevent courts from having access to the information on which an administrative decision was based.[76] It is less clear whether Parliament can authorise an administrative decision-maker to act in a way which breaches a fundamental 'norm' of administrative law – such as to act unfairly, unreasonably or irrationally. The High Court has said that Parliament could not authorise decision-makers to act in bad faith,[77] but beyond that, the parameters of what the Constitution entrenches and prohibits Parliament from doing are somewhat unsettled.

A third aspect of Australia's constitutional landscape (and indeed law more generally, for the most part), which has had some influence on administrative law is the absence of a bill of rights. Australia is now alone amongst common law, Westminster systems in having no federal human rights bill, charter or Act. This is not to say that Australian law does not protect rights. It simply does so in a rather ad hoc manner, and mostly through targeted legislation (such as privacy laws and anti-discrimination laws).[78] One effect of this is that Australian administrative law has been framed in a way that is not about individual rights. This is evident in the quote from Brennan J above: courts have no stand-alone power to cure administrative injustice; their role is limited to determining whether the executive branch has acted within the lawful limits of the powers conferred on it by statute and the Constitution. This does not necessarily mean that Australian judicial review is less rights-protective in the substantive outcomes it reaches compared with other jurisdictions, but it has influenced the way in which courts justify their role and the ways in which they reason.[79]

[71] Australian Constitution, s 75(v).

[72] *Kirk v Industrial Court of NSW* (2010) 239 CLR 531 ('*Kirk*').

[73] *Plaintiff S157/2002 v Commonwealth* (2003) 211 CLR 476, 482 [5] (Gleeson CJ) ('*Plaintiff S157*').

[74] *Kirk* (2010) 239 CLR 531, 581 [99] (French CJ, Gummow, Hayne, Crennan, Kiefel and Bell JJ).

[75] LB Crawford and J Boughey, 'The Centrality of Jurisdictional Error: Rationale and Consequences' (2019) 30 *Public Law Review* 18.

[76] *Graham v Minister for Immigration and Border Protection* (2017) 263 CLR 1.

[77] *Commissioner of Taxation v Futuris* (2008) 237 CLR 146, 157 [25], 164–66 [55]–[61].

[78] See generally, M Groves, J Boughey and D Meagher (eds), *The Legal Protection of Human Rights in Australia* (Oxford, Hart Publishing, 2019).

[79] J Boughey (n 53) chs 6 f.

# IV. The Codification of Judicial Review

## A. The Rationale for and Forms of Codification

The codification of various aspects of judicial review has been an enduring law reform issue in common law jurisdictions for most of the past century.[80] By the late 1950s, the common law system, which centred around the prerogative writs, had come under considerable criticism from commentators in both the UK[81] and the US[82] for its complexity and lack of certainty. In the first edition of his *Administrative Law Treatise*, published in 1958, Kenneth Culp Davis famously wrote of administrative law under the common law:

> An imaginary system cunningly planned for the evil purpose of thwarting justice and maximising fruitless litigation would copy the major features of the extraordinary remedies. For the purpose of creating treacherous procedural snares and preventing or delaying the decision of cases on their merits, such a scheme would insist upon a plurality of remedies, no remedy would lie when another is available, the lines between the remedies would be complex and shifting, the principal concepts confusing the boundaries of each remedy would be undefined and undefinable, judicial opinions would be filled with misleading generality, and courts would studiously avoid discussing or even mentioning the lack of practical reasons behind the complexities of the system.[83]

These now familiar arguments about the deficiencies of the prerogative writs and the potential benefits of codification have since been considered by law reform bodies in virtually every common law jurisdiction[84] – often multiple times – and are an ongoing issue in law reform in Australia.[85]

[80] The issue was considered as early as 1932 by the Donoughmore Committee: *Report of the Committee on Ministers' Powers*, Cmd 4060 (1932) 62, discussed in DGT Williams, 'The Donoughmore Report in Retrospect' (1982) 60 *Public Administration* 273, 286 f.

[81] Evidence of SA de Smith to the Franks Committee: *Report of the Committee on Administrative Tribunals and Enquiries*, Cmnd 218 (1957) Minutes of Evidence, Appendix 1, 10; SA de Smith, *Judicial Review of Administrative Action* (London, Stevens & Sons, 1959) 17, 29.

[82] K Culp Davis, *Administrative Law Treatise*, vol 3 (St Paul, West Publishing, 1958) 388; K Culp Davis, 'English Administrative Law – An American View' [1962] *Public Law* 139, 149 ff.

[83] K Culp Davis, *Administrative Law Treatise* (n 82) 388.

[84] See, eg, Australia: Kerr Report (n 1); Electoral and Administrative Review Commission, *Report on Judicial Review of Administrative Decisions and Actions* (1990) (Queensland); Canada: Royal Commission Inquiry into Civil Rights, *Report Number One* (1968) vol 1 ('McRuer Report') (Ontario); Institute of Law Research and Reform, *Judicial Review of Administrative Action – Application for Judicial Review*, Report 40 (1984) (Alberta); Law Reform Commission, *Administrative Law: Judicial Review of Administrative Action*, Report 69 (1987) (Manitoba); New Zealand: Public Administrative Law Reform Committee, *Fourth Report* (1971); Law Commission, *Mandatory Order Against the Crown and Tidying Judicial Review*, Study Paper 10 (2001); South Africa: South African Law Commission, *Administrative Justice Report*, Project 115 (1999); UK: Law Commission, *Remedies in Administrative Law*, Report 73 (1976); Committee of the JUSTICE – All Souls Review Committee, *A Review of Administrative Justice, Some Necessary Reforms* (Oxford, Clarendon Press, 1988); Law Commission, *Administrative Law: Judicial Review and Statutory Appeals*, Report 226 (1994).

[85] For example Australia's (now defunct) peak advisory body on administrative law considered whether Australia's federal judicial review legislation should be scaled back or redrafted in 2012 (among a range of other options) in order to address problems that have emerged as a result of the legislation: see ARC, *Federal Judicial Review in Australia*, Report No 50 (2012).

Statutory reform to the common law is supported by those with a range of philosophical views about the role of administrative law.[86] Some theorists have argued that codification simplifies and clarifies the law, making it easier for people to bring successful applications.[87] Others have argued in favour of codification as a method of controlling judicial discretion.[88] In response to these arguments, many common law jurisdictions, including a number in Australia, have codified various aspects of judicial review. Broadly these statutes have attempted to do one of two things: set out a single, simpler procedure for making judicial review applications to the courts; or codify the rules of natural justice.

The first category encompasses a broad spectrum of laws. The most minimal simply create a single judicial review application procedure – often called an 'order for judicial review' – to replace the processes governing applications for prerogative writs under the common law. This is usually achieved through amendments to court rules or civil procedure legislation. At the other end of the spectrum are statutes which codify, and in some instances reform, the common law more extensively. For instance, these more ambitious statutes may provide that administrative decision-makers are under a general duty to give reasons,[89] codify standing or jurisdiction requirements,[90] or set out some or all of the grounds on which applications for review may be made.[91] These more comprehensive reforms are usually achieved through the enactment of separate legislation, such as the ADJR Act.[92] However, they do not necessarily need to take the form of separate legislation.[93]

The second category of administrative law statutes – which codify the requirements of natural justice – may apply to administrative decision-makers generally, including government departments, tribunals, boards, commissions

[86] TH Jones (n 22) 518 f.

[87] See, eg, JUSTICE – All Souls (n 84) 157 f (recommending codification of the grounds of review along Australian lines in order to make the law 'as clear as possible and to make it accessible and intelligible to ordinary people').

[88] See, eg, J Griffith, 'Constitutional and Administrative Law' in P Archer and A Martin (eds), *More Law Reform Now: A Collection of Essays on Law Reform* (Chichester, Barry Rose, 1983) 55 ff. Similar arguments were made by Republicans and conservative Democrats leading to the introduction of the US Administrative Procedure Act of 1946, Public Law 79-404, 60 Statute 23. For a discussion of this, see GB Shepherd, 'Fierce Compromise: The Administrative Procedure Act Emerges from New Deal Politics' (1996) 90 *Northwestern University Law Review* 1557.

[89] See, eg, ADJR Act s 13; Administrative Procedures and Jurisdiction Act, RSA 2000 c A-3, s 7; Promotion of Administrative Justice Act 2000 (South Africa) s 5.

[90] See, eg, ADJR Act s 3 (limiting the Federal Court's jurisdiction under the act to 'decision(s) of an administrative character made under an enactment'), ss 5 and 6 (requiring that a 'person who is aggrieved' by a decision to which the Act applies may seek judicial review under the Act); Judicial Review Act, RSPEI 1988, c J-3, s 5(b) (Prince Edward Island) (allowing a judge to dismiss an application for judicial review on the ground that the person is not someone who would be 'adversely affected' by the relevant act).

[91] See, eg, Federal Courts Act, RSC 1985, c F-7, s 18.1(4) (Canada); ADJR Act ss 5 and 6; Judicial Review Procedure Act, RSO 1990, c J 1, s 2.

[92] South Africa's Promotion of Administrative Justice Act 2000 is another example.

[93] See, eg, Federal Courts Act RSC 1985, c F-7, ss 18–18.5, 28.

and ministers,[94] or just to certain categories of decision-maker (typically 'quasi-judicial' tribunals).[95] The procedures set out may apply automatically,[96] or they may be opt-in, requiring the legislation empowering decision-makers to expressly require compliance with the statutory procedures.[97] This type of legislation has been particularly popular in North America and has dominated the attention of Canadian law reformers since the US-enacted Administrative Procedure Act of 1946.[98] There are no examples of this type of general procedural code in Australia, probably due to the fact that the focus of Australian policy-makers has been on amalgamating tribunals rather than developing procedural codes of general application to tribunals.[99] However, in recent decades, the Australian Parliament has made numerous attempts to codify the rules of natural justice that apply to migration decisions, many of which have been undermined through judicial interpretation. I consider these provisions briefly below because of the light they shed on the effects of codification more generally in Australia.

## B. The ADJR Act: Overview

The cornerstone of Australia's statutory judicial review framework is the federal ADJR Act. The ADJR Act was introduced on the recommendation of two committees established by the Commonwealth Government to inquire into aspects of administrative law. The first, the Kerr Committee, was established in October 1968

[94] For example, Ontario's Statutory Powers Procedure Act, RSO 1990, c S 22, s 1 applies to 'any person or persons on whom a statutory power of decision is conferred by or under statute'.

[95] For example British Columbia's Administrative Tribunals Act, SBC 2004, c 45, which only applies to 'tribunals', although aspects of its procedural code have been applied to other 'entities'. See the discussion below.

[96] For example, Statutory Powers Procedure Act, RSO 1990, c S 22.

[97] For example, Administrative Procedures and Jurisdiction Act, RSA 2000 c A-3.

[98] Public Law 79-404, 60 Statute 237. On the APA, see in this book EL Rubin (n 22), especially sections III and IV. The issue continues to attract the attention of Canadian law reform bodies. For example, in 1996 the Canadian Department of Justice released a report recommending that a comprehensive procedural code be adopted as 'opt in' legislation applicable to all administrative decision-makers: Department of Justice, *Proposal for a Federal Administrative Hearings Act*, September 1996, reprinted in Robert W Macaulay and James LH Sprague, *Practice and Procedure before Administrative Tribunals*, vol 4 (Toronto, Thomson/Carswell, 1988) [38.2]. In 2004 British Columbia enacted the Administrative Tribunals Act, SBC 2004, c 45, which sets out uniform procedures that apply to selected tribunals in the province and is discussed below. Similar 'model codes' of tribunal procedure have been recommended in Alberta and Saskatchewan: see Alberta Law Reform Institute, *Powers and Procedures of Administrative Tribunals*, Consultation Memorandum No 13 (2008); Law Reform Commission of Saskatchewan, *A Model Code of Procedure for Administrative Tribunals*, Consultation Paper (2003).

[99] See, eg, Administrative Review Council, *Better Decisions: Review of Commonwealth Merits Review Tribunals*, Report No 39 (1995) 136–46; Victorian Attorney-General's Department, *Tribunals in the Department of Justice: A Principled Approach* (1996) Discussion Paper; Queensland Parliament, Legal, Constitutional and Administrative Review Committee, *The Accessibility of Administrative Justice*, Report No 64 (2008) ch 9 (including discussion of previous reform suggestions in Queensland).

with the mandate of considering and reporting on the judicial review jurisdiction to be given to the proposed new Federal Court. In addition to the new court's jurisdiction, the Kerr Committee was directed to inquire into the 'procedures whereby review is to be obtained', 'substantive grounds of review' and 'desirability of introducing legislation along the lines of the United Kingdom Tribunals and Inquiries Act 1958'.[100]

In its 1971 report, the Kerr Committee discussed the 'complexity' and 'technical limitations' of the common law in this area, which it saw as diminishing the effectiveness of judicial review.[101] The Committee recommended a package of reforms to administrative law, of which a statutory form of judicial review was one element. With respect to statutory reform, it recommended that the federal legislation establish a single application procedure for judicial review which was not remedy-dependent and codify the grounds on which review could be sought.

The Kerr Committee's approach to statutory reform of judicial review took a relatively 'red light' view of judicial review: one which sees the principal role of courts as constraining the executive state.[102] The Committee's report made it clear that the principal purpose of the proposed legislation was to achieve 'more comprehensive review of administrative decisions' and facilitate access to the courts.[103] The Committee's approach to other aspects of reform to administrative law was more deferential towards the executive.[104]

Following the Kerr Report, the Australian government established two further committees to examine aspects of the proposed reforms. The Ellicott Committee was charged with the judicial review legislation and agreed with the Kerr Committee's recommendations[105] and the Bland Committee with the other proposals.[106] During the course of the Ellicott Committee's inquiry, Professor Wade visited Australia from Oxford and expressed concerns about the proposed codification of judicial review. Wade's particular concern was that specifying the grounds of review 'could have the effect of excluding the possibility of judicial development of additional grounds'.[107] He suggested that if the legislation were

[100] Kerr Report (n 1) 1.

[101] Kerr Report (n 1) 9 f, 16 ff.

[102] C Harlow and R Rawlings, *Law and Administration*, 3rd edn (Cambridge, Cambridge University Press, 2009) ch 1.

[103] Kerr Report (n 1) 3, 6.

[104] See, eg, A Cassimatis, 'Judicial Attitudes to Judicial Review: A Comparative Examination of Justifications Offered for Restricting the Scope of Judicial Review in Australia, Canada and England' (2010) 34 *Melbourne University Law Review* 1, 16, who notes that the Committee's recommendations relating to the AAT were more concerned with balancing efficient administration and individual justice. See also L Blayden, 'Designing Administrative Law for an Administrative State: The Carefully Calibrated Approach of the Kerr Committee' (2021) 28(4) *Australian Journal of Administrative Law* 205, 216 f.

[105] Ellicott Report (n 39) 5, 11.

[106] Committee on Administrative Discretions, *Final Report of the Committee on Administrative Discretions* (1973).

[107] Ellicott Report (n 39) 9.

to go ahead, it should include an open ended ground to allow the legislation to adapt to developments in the common law. The Ellicott Committee did not accept Wade's warning, but did accept his advice with respect to the inclusion of an open-ended ground. As a result, the ADJR Act contains two open-ended grounds: that a decision is 'otherwise contrary to law';[108] or was an 'exercise of power in a way that constitutes abuse of the power'.[109]

In addition, the Ellicott Committee recommended that a new ground of review be added to those available at common law permitting the Federal Court to grant relief:

> [W]here the fact which the officer relied upon for his decision did not exist or where the officer or tribunal was required to act on evidence admissible before it or on facts of which it might take notice and there was no evidence or no such facts to support findings of fact made by the officer or tribunal in exercising his or its discretion.[110]

It was envisaged that this statutory ground would go beyond the common law 'no evidence' ground, which was only available to challenge jurisdictional facts. This was another of Wade's suggestions, although the Ellicott Committee did not elaborate on why it was recommending this expansion in the common law 'no evidence' ground of review.

The ADJR Act today is substantially the same as when it was first enacted in 1977. The Act confers judicial review jurisdiction on the Federal Court of Australia and the Federal Circuit Court of Australia. Its key features are as follows.

## *i. Establishing a Simplified Review Procedure*

The ADJR Act establishes a single procedure for applying for an 'order of review', which applies regardless of the remedy being sought.[111] It also sets out a single test for standing – 'a person aggrieved' – which has been interpreted as 'almost identical' to the common law 'special interest' test.[112] The courts are empowered to make orders with the same effect as the prerogative writs to remedy unlawful administrative action, but may provide whichever remedy they deem appropriate, rather than being restricted by the grounds on which review is sought, type of error or class of decision-maker.[113]

[108] ADJR Act s 5(1)(j).
[109] ADJR Act s 5(2)(j).
[110] Ellicott Report (n 39) 10.
[111] ADJR Act s 11.
[112] R Douglas, 'Standing' in M Groves and HP Lee (eds), *Australian Administrative Law* (Melbourne, Cambridge University Press, 2007) 170. See, eg, *Tooheys Ltd v Minister for Business and Consumer Affairs* (1981) 36 ALR 64, 79; *Re Australian Institute of Marine and Power Engineers v the Secretary, Department of Transport* (1986) 13 FCR 124, 132–33.
[113] ADJR Act s 16.

### *ii. Providing a Right to Reasons*

Another recommendation of both the Kerr and Ellicott Committees was that a person with standing to seek review of a decision should have a right to obtain reasons for that decision.[114] There is no general common law right to receive reasons for an administrative decision in Australia.[115] Accordingly, the inclusion of such a right in the ADJR Act is an important distinction between common law and statutory judicial review in Australia. The right to seek reasons applies to all decisions to which the ADJR Act applies, unless it is expressly excluded by statute.[116]

### *iii. Codifying the Grounds of Review*

The ADJR Act codifies the grounds of review, setting out 17 specific grounds on which the courts can review administrative decisions. These cover all of the 'grounds' of review under common law, discussed in section III above, as well as the ground of failing or refusing to make a decision. Many of the grounds are expressed in highly specific terms. For example, review may be sought for an 'improper exercise of power',[117] which includes (among many other things): 'taking an irrelevant consideration into account'; 'failing to take a relevant consideration into account'; 'an exercise of a power for a purpose other than a purpose for which the power is conferred'; and 'an exercise of a personal discretionary power at the direction or behest of another person'.[118] For the most part, the statutory grounds restate the grounds available under the common law.[119] The exception is the statutory 'no evidence' ground which goes beyond the common law ground as discussed above, although the precise extent to which it does so has not yet been settled by the courts.[120]

In addition, there are the two open-ended grounds mentioned above, added to address Professor Wade's concern that specifying the grounds of review may hinder the development of additional grounds at common law.[121] Aronson has described the provisions as 'invitations to the Federal Court to add different or newer common law grounds' to the 17 listed.[122] Yet neither ground has been widely used by applicants, nor have they been the subject of any analysis from the courts. In fact, 'these grounds are so underused and under-theorised that they may fairly be described as "dead letters"'.[123]

[114] Kerr Report (n 1) 78–79; Ellicott Report (n 39) 8.

[115] *Public Service Board v Osmond* (1986) 159 CLR 656.

[116] The legislature may exclude decisions-makers from this statutory duty to provide reasons by listing them in sched 2 to the ADJR Act.

[117] ADJR Act s 5(1)(e).

[118] ADJR Act s 5(2)(a), (b), (c) and (e).

[119] *Kioa v West* (1985) 159 CLR 550, 567 (Gibbs CJ), 576 (Mason J), 625 (Brennan J).

[120] M Aronson, M Groves and G Weeks (n 24) 259.

[121] Ellicott Report (n 39) 9.

[122] M Aronson (n 10).

[123] M Groves, 'Substantive Legitimate Expectations in Australian Administrative Law' (2008) 32 *Melbourne University Law Review* 470, 518.

## C. The ADJR Act: Effects and Effectiveness

For at least a decade after its introduction, the ADJR Act was considered a leading innovation. It became the primary avenue for judicial review applications, improved access to the courts and resulted in a surge in judicial review applications.[124] Aronson, Groves and Weeks have suggested that the Act's codification of the grounds of review may have contributed to the increased number of applications by advertising the grounds of review to the legal profession.[125] Twelve years after the ADJR Act was enacted,[126] Sir Anthony Mason, then Chief Justice of the High Court of Australia, concluded that the legislation may have:

> [A]chieved more than mere simplification and clarification of the grounds and remedies for judicial review. It may have played a part in assisting the judicial elaboration of the common law principles of review.[127]

However, more recently the ADJR Act has attracted considerable criticism for the longer-term impact that it has had on judicial review in Australia. It has also become less influential as a model for reform in the states and territories in recent years, with Victoria and Western Australia rejecting proposals for similar acts in 1999[128] and 2002[129] respectively.[130]

Three main criticisms have been made of the ADJR Act: that it has not achieved its objective of simplifying the procedure for applying for judicial review; that it lacks a guiding purpose; and that it has ossified the law. I examine each of these below. I argue that there is a fourth effect that the ADJR Act seems to have had on Australian judicial review principles, which is methodological rather than substantive. By listing the 'grounds of review' in specific and narrow terms, I suggest that the ADJR Act has resulted in Australian courts continuing to reason by reference to these narrow grounds instead of adopting the more flexible and less structured approach to reasoning as courts in the UK and Canada have done.

[124] P Billings and A Cassimatis, 'Australia's Codification of Judicial Review: Has the Legislative Effort Been Worth it?' in M Groves (ed), *Modern Administrative Law in Australia: Concepts and Context* (Melbourne, Cambridge University Press, 2014) 180, 181 f; M Aronson, M Groves and G Weeks (n 24) 66 f; A Mason, 'Administrative Review: the Experience of the First Twelve Years' (1989) 18 *Federal Law Review* 122, 123.

[125] M Aronson, M Groves and G Weeks (n 24) 67. Justice Basten agrees: JJ Basten, '50th Anniversary of the Kerr Committee Report: Judicial Review' (2021) 28(4) *Australian Journal of Administrative Law* 269.

[126] Although only nine years since the ADJR Act had come into operation. The Act was assented to in 1977, but did not come into effect until 1980. The delay has been ascribed to 'bureaucratic objections' to the requirement to give reasons: see D Pearce, *Commonwealth Administrative Law* (Sydney, Butterworths, 1986) 143.

[127] A Mason (n 124) 125.

[128] See Peter Bayne, *Judicial Review in Victoria*, Expert Report No 5, Victorian Attorney-General's Law Reform Advisory Council (1999).

[129] Law Reform Commission of Western Australia, *Report on Judicial Review of Administrative Decisions*, Project No 95 (2002) 26.

[130] As Nason's chapter in this book details, the ADJR Act model was also rejected in the UK's recent inquiry into whether judicial review should be codified, with the Report concluding that it would make

### i. It has not Simplified the Process of Applying for Judicial Review

The central criticisms of the Act relate to the narrow scope of its jurisdictional formula.[131] For a range of reasons, some deliberate choices,[132] some a reflection of the state of administrative law at the time the ADJR Act was drafted[133] and others the result of narrow judicial interpretation,[134] the scope of the Federal Court's jurisdiction under the ADJR Act is narrower than the scope of the High Court's jurisdiction under the Constitution. In the early years of the ADJR Act, this resulted in some applications for review still needing to be heard at first instance in the High Court. Expressing concern about the High Court's 'heavy work load', the Federal Parliament conferred an additional source of judicial review jurisdiction on the Federal Court in 1983, which matched the High Court's original jurisdiction under section 75(v) of the Constitution.[135]

The result is that there is now a dual system of review at the federal level, which has ironically introduced a new set of complex, technical issues into Australian administrative law of the very same nature that the ADJR Act was enacted to resolve. The ADJR Act is now used by litigants less often than the

little difference. See in this book S Nason, 'Codification of Administrative Law in the United Kingdom' section IV.C.

[131] For a detailed analysis, see P Billings and A Cassimatis (n 124) 183 ff; ARC, *Federal Judicial Review in Australia* (n 10) chs 4 f in particular; M Aronson (n 10) 204 ff; M Groves, 'Should We Follow the Gospel of the Administrative Decisions (Judicial Review) Act 1977 (Cth)?' (2010) 34 *Melbourne University Law Review* 736; C Mantziaris and L McDonald, 'Federal Judicial Review Jurisdiction after *Griffith University v Tang*' (2006) 17 *Public Law Review* 22.

[132] The Parliament can exempt decisions from the scope of the ADJR Act by listing them in Schedule 1. It has chosen to do so with respect to many decisions which may be non-justiciable in any event (eg, defence and national security) as well as with a range of others that have their own separate statutory review schemes (eg, workplace relations, migration and tax). See Administrative Review Council, *The Scope of Judicial Review*, Discussion Paper (2003) 17, 44–46.

[133] For example, the requirement that decisions be made 'under an enactment' may be explained by the fact that when the Act was drafted, the common law judicial review principles and remedies only applied to decisions made under statutory power. It was not until the 1980s that the common law expanded to encompass decisions made under prerogative power and by the Crown: see *Council of Civil Service Unions v Minister for the Civil Service* [1985] AC 374; *Minister for Arts, Heritage and Environment v Peko Wallsend Ltd* (1987) 75 ALR 218, 223 (Bowen CJ), 227 (Sheppard J), 246–49 (Wilcox J); *R v Toohey; Ex parte Northern Land Council* (1981) 151 CLR 170; *FAI Insurances v Winneke* (1982) 151 CLR 342.

[134] See, eg, *Griffith University v Tang* (2005) 221 CLR 99, 130 [89] (Gummow, Callinan and Heydon JJ) (interpreting the ADJR Act's requirement that decisions be made 'under an enactment' as requiring a close nexus between the rights and obligations affected by a decision and legislation as the legal source authorising the decision impacting on those rights and obligations); *NEAT Domestic Trading Pty Ltd v AWB Ltd* (2003) 216 CLR 277, 296–300 [47]–[64] (McHugh, Hayne and Callinan JJ) (holding that the AWBI, which had a statutory power to effectively veto a government authority's approval of bulk wheat exports, was not subject to review under the ADJR Act as the AWBI 'does not owe its existence to the [empowering] Act', but to corporations law. As a result, the majority reasoned that AWBI was required to act in the interests of its shareholders and that imposing public law obligations on the company would, in many cases, be inconsistent with those interests).

[135] Commonwealth, *Parliamentary Debates*, House of Representatives, 21 September 1983, 1046 (Lionel Bowen, Minister for Trade), discussing the Statute Law (Miscellaneous Provisions) Act (No 2) 1983 (Cth) which inserted s 39B into the Judiciary Act 1903 (Cth).

Judiciary Act,[136] but it has not been completely dispensed with by applicants because it remains useful for other reasons. In particular, one of the major technical and difficult issues associated with the prerogative writs – the need to demonstrate jurisdictional error – is not a limitation under the ADJR Act.[137] Accordingly, judicial review applicants need to make careful, technical strategic choices.[138] The Administrative Review Council (ARC) recommended that the ADJR Act be amended to fix some of these problems so that litigants could benefit from the clear, express statements of principle in the ADJR Act.[139] However, to date, the Federal Government has not proposed any such amendments to the ADJR Act and has ceased funding the ARC.[140]

### *ii. It Lacks a Guiding Purpose*

A second complaint about the ADJR Act is its lack of any guiding purpose or principles.[141] The criticism is actually one that has been levelled more generally against Australian administrative law, with a number of commentators arguing that Australian administrative law has, to a greater extent than its counterparts in the UK and the US, struggled to locate itself within any set of organising principles or framework.[142]

It is contended that the enactment of the ADJR Act provided an opportunity for legislators to express a more general set of principles to guide the development of Australian administrative law and its failure to do so left judicial review in Australia without any 'organising themes which might give some shape and direction to each particularised ground'.[143]

Others, including the ARC, reject the suggestion, arguing that an objects clause may further narrow the scope of judicial review under the Act[144] and 'create more uncertainty about the grounds of review' without having 'any real benefit for decision-makers'.[145] Furthermore, the High Court's focus on the Constitution as

[136] ARC, *Federal Judicial Review in Australia* (n 10) 65 ff.

[137] See JJ Basten (n 125).

[138] B Tronson, 'The Practical Impacts of the *ADJR Act* on Judicial Review Applications', *AUSPUBLAW Blog*, 22 October 2021, auspublaw.org/2021/10/the-practical-impacts-of-the-adjr-act-on-judicial-review-applications.

[139] ARC, *Federal Judicial Review in Australia* (n 10) 72 ff.

[140] J Boughey and G Weeks, 'Comment from Australia: Australian Government Scraps Peak Administrative Law Advisory Body', *UK Constitutional Law Association Blog*, 20 May 2015: ukconstitutionallaw.org/2015/05/20/janina-boughey-and-greg-weeks-comment-from-australia-australian-government-scraps-peak-administrative-law-advisory-body.

[141] M Aronson (n 10) 203. The issue was also raised by a number of submissions to the ARC's inquiry into federal judicial review: see ARC, *Federal Judicial Review in Australia* (n 10) 130 ff.

[142] S Gageler, 'The Underpinnings of Judicial Review of Administrative Action: Common Law or Constitution' (2000) 28 *Federal Law Review* 303; B Selway, 'The Principle Behind Common Law Judicial Review of Administrative Action – the Search Continues' (2002) 30 *Federal Law Review* 217.

[143] M Aronson (n 10) 203.

[144] M Aronson (n 10) 218.

[145] ARC, *Federal Judicial Review in Australia* (n 10) 132. See also M Groves (n 131) 760 ff.

the centre of administrative law principles and its preparedness to interpret the ADJR Act differently from the common law where statutory language requires suggest that an ordinary Act of Parliament may not ever have been capable of fulfilling this guiding role.

### *iii. 'Ossifying' the Common Law*

The third set of criticisms of the ADJR Act are those relating to its effect on the development of the common law, and the 'grounds of review', in particular. As discussed above, when the Act was first being designed, a major concern was that the statutory grounds would not be able to keep pace with developments in the common law, resulting in a fracture between the common law and the ADJR Act. But this has not occurred. The codified grounds of review available under the ADJR Act have proven sufficiently flexible to accommodate substantial changes in the scope of the common law, including, for example, considerable changes to the application of the rules of natural justice.[146] For the most part, the grounds of review available under the ADJR Act are the same as those available under the common law. The High Court has held that the ADJR Act grounds should be read as a summary of the common law grounds, except where the language of the Act requires otherwise.[147]

Furthermore, and as noted above, the Australian courts have not found it necessary to rely on the two catch-all grounds inserted at Professor Wade's urging, which indicates that the other codified grounds have been sufficiently malleable to accommodate developments that have occurred in the common law. However, this may change following recent developments in the scope of the unreasonableness ground of review under common law. In *Minister for Immigration and Citizenship v Li*,[148] the High Court expanded the unreasonableness ground at common law beyond the traditional formulation articulated by Lord Greene in *Associated Provincial Picture Houses v Wednesbury Corporation*.[149] However the ADJR Act entrenches the *Wednesbury* formulation, providing that an application for review may be made on the ground that an 'exercise of a power … is so unreasonable that no reasonable person could have so exercised the power'.[150] Thus, it may now be necessary for applicants to rely on one of the catch-all grounds in making certain arguments regarding the unreasonableness of an administrative decision.

The only settled differences between the grounds of review available under the ADJR Act and the common law are the result of deliberate policy choices

[146] *Kioa v West* (1985) 159 CLR 550.

[147] *Kioa v West* (1985) 159 CLR 550, 576–77 (Mason J), 594 (Wilson J), 625 (Brennan J).

[148] *Minister for Immigration and Citizenship v Li* (2013) 87 ALJR 618.

[149] *Associated Provincial Picture Houses v Wednesbury Corporation* [1948] 1 KB 223, 230. For an overview of the changes to the unreasonableness ground in the past decade, see J Boughey, 'Legal Unreasonableness: In Need of a New Justification?' (2022) 45 *UNSW Law Journal* 113.

[150] ADJR Act s 5(2)(g).

on the part of the ADJR Act's drafters. The ADJR Act's grounds are broader than the common law's grounds in two ways. The first, which has already been discussed, relates to the 'no evidence' ground of review. The second way in which the ADJR Act grounds of review are wider than the common law grounds is due to the fact that the Act draws no distinction between jurisdictional errors and errors within a decision-maker's jurisdiction. While this removes one of the most complex areas of the law from the ADJR Act, Aronson argues that by severing of the link with jurisdictional error, the ADJR Act's grounds of review 'offer no readily apparent principles to keep the court on the path of judicial review and away from merits review'.[151] I disagree. The grounds of review listed in the ADJR Act are still errors of law, even if they need not be errors of law that go to jurisdiction. Perhaps more problematic is the fact that common law judicial review in Australia is very much concerned with jurisdictional error, and the concept has become increasingly important over the past 20 years.[152]

Neither of the reports by the Kerr and Ellicott committees contained any discussion of the reasons for the abolition of the distinction between jurisdictional and non-jurisdictional errors in the ADJR Act, although the Kerr Report did briefly discuss the difficulties inherent in the distinction.[153] The practical effect of this difference between the common law and the ADJR Act is that the ADJR Act's grounds of review are broader than the common law grounds as they are not limited to jurisdictional errors or non-jurisdictional errors of law on the face of the record. This means, for example, that all procedural errors may be remedied under the ADJR Act[154] regardless of whether Parliament intended that a failure to follow certain procedures would take a decision-maker beyond their authority.[155] These two differences between the grounds of review available under the ADJR Act and common law may result in some additional complexity and technicality in Australian administrative law. Yet, unlike those aspects of the ADJR Act which restrict the scope of statutory review compared to the common law, there have not been any calls to amend the statutory grounds of review so that they fall into line with the common law grounds.

A more troubling criticism of codification of the grounds of review was articulated by Kirby J in *Re Minister for Immigration and Multicultural Affairs; Ex parte Applicant S20/2002*.[156] His Honour argued that while the ADJR Act has been 'overwhelmingly beneficial', its codification of the grounds of review had 'retarded' the development of the grounds of review under common law in Australia.[157]

[151] M Aronson (n 10) 203.

[152] See JJ Spigelman, 'The Centrality of Jurisdictional Error' (2010) 21 *Public Law Review* 77; LB Crawford and J Boughey (n 75).

[153] Kerr Report (n 1) 13 f.

[154] Which provides that the court may review a decision on the ground that 'procedures that were required by law to be observed in connection with the making of the decision were not observed'.

[155] See, eg, *Muin v Refugee Review Tribunal* (2002) 190 ALR 601, 640 [169] (Gummow J).

[156] *Re Minister for Immigration and Multicultural Affairs; Ex parte Applicant S20/2002* (2003) 198 ALR 59, 94 [157] ('*Applicant S20*').

[157] *Applicant S20* (2003) 198 ALR 59, 94–95 [156]–[168] (Kirby J).

He pointed to developments in the grounds of review under the common law in England since the enactment of the ADJR Act and argued that the common law in Australia had not kept pace. Specifically, he noted that the 'no evidence' ground had expanded to include factual errors made within a decision-maker's jurisdiction,[158] and that English courts would also now review jurisdictional facts which were only required to be met to the decision-maker's satisfaction on all grounds, not just whether the state of mind was logically formed.[159] He argued that:

> The common law in Australia might have developed along similar lines. However, it was at about the time of Lord Wilberforce's exposition in *Tameside* that the ADJR Act was enacted in relation to federal administrative decisions. The somewhat arrested development of Australian common law doctrine that followed reflects the large impact of the federal legislation on the direction and content of Australian administrative law more generally.[160]

Similar arguments have since been made by commentators regarding the unreasonableness ground of review in Australia.[161]

The Australian High Court has since followed the English approach to subjective jurisdictional facts.[162] It has also recently expanded the unreasonableness ground from its traditional, narrow *Wednesbury* formulation, so that it now has much in common with the flexible Canadian standard of reasonableness.[163] However, the 'no evidence' ground at common law remains stricter in Australia than in England.[164] Wade and Forsyth have suggested that the expansion of the

[158] *Applicant S20* (2003) 198 ALR 59, 97 [165] (Kirby J), citing *R v Criminal Injuries Compensation Board; Ex parte A* [1999] 2 AC 330, 344–45 (Lord Slynn of Hadley).

[159] *Applicant S20* (2003) 198 ALR 59, 96 [162] (Kirby J), citing *Secretary of State for Education and Science v Tameside Metropolitan Borough Council* (1977) AC 1041 ('*Tameside*'), 1047 (Lord Wilberforce).

[160] *Applicant S20* (2003) 198 ALR 59, 97 [166] (Kirby J).

[161] See M Taggart, '"Australian Exceptionalism" in Judicial Review' (2008) 36 *Federal Law Review* 1, 12; J Pennel and Y Hui Shi, 'The Codification of *Wednesbury* Unreasonableness – A Retardation of the Common Law Ground of Judicial Review in Australia?' (2008) 56 *AIAL Forum* 22.

[162] A majority of members of the High Court now seem to have accepted that facts dependent on the subjective satisfaction of a decision-maker may be jurisdictional, and may be reviewed for 'irrationality' and 'illogicality': see *Minister for Immigration and Multicultural and Indigenous Affairs v SGLB* (2004) 78 ALJR 992, 998 [34] (Gummow and Hayne JJ); *Minister for Immigration and Citizenship v SZMDS* (2010) 240 CLR 611, 624 [37]–[39] (Gummow ACJ and Kiefel J), 647–48 [129]–[130] (Crennan and Bell JJ); *Plaintiff M70/2011 v Minister for Immigration and Citizenship* (2011) 244 CLR 144, 179–81 [57]–[59] (French CJ indicated that it does not matter whether discretion is within jurisdiction or goes to jurisdiction, as in either case the Court will still be asking whether the power was properly construed by reference to all of the ordinary grounds of review).

[163] See *Li* (2013) 249 CLR 332 and *SZVFW* (2018) 92 ALJR 713.

[164] See discussion in M Aronson, M Groves and G Weeks (n 24) 259 ff. In Australia many recent decisions have continued to restrict the common law 'no evidence' ground to jurisdictional facts or 'particular facts' which the legislation requires a decision-maker to find: see, eg, *Minister for Immigration and Multicultural and Indigenous Affairs v SGLB* (2004) 207 ALR 12, 21 [39] (Gummow and Hayne JJ, with whom Gleeson CJ agreed at 13); *SZAPC v Minister for Immigration and Multicultural and Indigenous Affairs* [2005] FCA 995, [47]; *SZWFB v Minister for Immigration and Citizenship* [2007] FCA 167, [32]. By contrast, English courts have gone well beyond this traditional concept of the 'no evidence' ground to find that decision-makers have erred when they have made a mistake with regard to material facts, regardless of whether the statute requires the facts to be established: *E v Home*

'no evidence' ground in the ADJR Act may have obviated the need for the courts to expand the ground at common law:

> To find facts without evidence is itself an abuse of power and a source of injustice, and ought to be within the scope of judicial review. This is recognised in other jurisdictions where the grounds of judicial review have been codified by statute. In Australia the Administrative Decisions (Judicial Review) Act 1977 expressly authorises review on the ground that there was 'no evidence or other material' to justify the decision where some particular matter has to be established, and a somewhat analogous provision has been enacted in Canada.[165]

The Canadian provisions to which Wade and Forsyth refer have not prevented Canadian courts from developing the common law ground along the same lines as the statutes. However, in Australia, Kirby J's argument finds some support in the fact that the Australian High Court has only been asked to consider expanding the common law 'no evidence' ground along English lines on one occasion, where the majority found it unnecessary to consider the issue.[166]

It is possible that if given the opportunity to consider the scope of the ground, the High Court would also expand the no evidence ground, but that the ADJR Act coupled with the Federal Court's alternative jurisdiction under section 39B of the Judiciary Act has prevented these opportunities from arising. Yet, it is equally possible that the Australian High Court would be reluctant to expand the 'no evidence' ground at common law because to do so would risk encroaching on the merits of the decision and thus offend the constitutionally entrenched separation of powers. This has been the High Court's reasoning for refusing to follow English decisions expanding another common law principle – substantive legitimate expectations, as discussed in section III above. However, Canada's Supreme Court has likewise declined to follow the English expansion of legitimate expectations for similar reasons, though without the express link to any separation of powers doctrine.[167]

Therefore, while it is possible that the ADJR Act may have prevented the High Court from needing to consider whether to expand the 'no evidence' ground under common law, it is far from clear that the Act has generally had the effect of stifling the development of the grounds of review. Restrictions in the Australian High Court's approach to review, where they exist, appear largely to have continued because of constitutional constraints – particularly Australia's constitutional separation of powers. Furthermore, the High Court actually relied on the ADJR Act to justify extending natural justice obligations to administrative (as opposed to

*Secretary* [2004] QB 1044, 1071 (Carnwath LJ); W Wade and C Forsyth, *Administrative Law*, 10th edn (Oxford, Oxford University Press, 2009) 232 ff.

[165] W Wade and C Forsyth (n 164) 232 (references omitted).

[166] *Re Minister for Immigration and Multicultural and Indigenous Affairs; Ex parte Applicant S134/2002* (2003) 211 CLR 441, 458–59 [35]–[37](Gleeson CJ, McHugh, Gummow, Hayne and Callinan JJ).

[167] *Mount Sinai Hospital Center v Quebec (Minister of Health and Social Services)* [2001] 2 SCR 281, 303–04 [27]–[30] (Binnie J for McLachlin CJ).

quasi-judicial) decision-makers in *Kioa v West*.[168] While the reasoning used by the Court was dubious in that respect, it does further illustrate that the codification of administrative law principles has not impeded their development.

Another feature of the ADJR Act, which was widely heralded as one of its most innovative and important elements, but which may ultimately have hindered developments in the common law, is the duty it places on decision-makers to give reasons. The High Court of Australia has maintained its position that:

> There is no general rule of the common law, or principle of natural justice, that requires reasons to be given for administrative decisions, even decisions which have been made in the exercise of a statutory discretion which may adversely affect the interests, or defeat the legitimate or reasonable expectations, of other persons.[169]

This contrasts with the approach in Canada and the UK, where, although there is no right to reasons in all cases, the common law has been held to require decision-makers to give reasons for most decisions.[170] The ADJR Act imposes an obligation on federal decision-makers whose decisions are reviewable under that Act to give reasons for their decisions, on request by a person with standing to seek review. Other federal, state and territory statutes do likewise with respect to other administrative decisions.[171] The effect is that most Australian decision-makers are under a statutory duty to give reasons for their decisions.

It is clearly arguable that this may have obviated the need to Australian law to develop along the same lines as it has in Canada and the UK to expand common law natural justice requirements to include a duty to provide reasons in most cases.[172] Yet, once again, the High Court's recent changes to the unreasonableness standard somewhat undermine this argument. *Li*, and the cases which follow it, emphasise that a decision may now be legally unreasonable if a decision-maker has failed to provide an adequate justification for it.[173] In other words, a decision may not meet the legal threshold of reasonableness if a decision-maker has failed to provide an adequate justification for it. As I have argued elsewhere, this development seems to undermine the position established in *Osmond*.[174] But it also demonstrates that

[168] *Kioa v West* (1985) 159 CLR 550, 578–79 (Mason J), 596–97 (Wilson J), 360–61 (Deane J).

[169] *Public Service Board of NSW v Osmond* (1986) 159 CLR 656, 662 ('*Osmond*'). Affirmed (in *obiter*) in *Wingfoot Australia Partners Pty Ltd v Kocak* (2013) 88 ALJR 52, 61 [43].

[170] *Baker v Canada* [1999] 2 SCR 817, 848 [43]. For a discussion of the English position, see M Elliott, 'Has the Common Law Duty to Give Reasons Come of Age Yet?' [2011] *Public Law* 56. See generally M Groves, 'Reviewing Reasons for Administrative Decisions: *Wingfoot Australia Partners Pty Ltd v Kocak*' (2013) 35 *Sydney Law Review* 627, 640.

[171] See, eg, Administrative Appeals Tribunal Act 1975 (Cth) s 28; Administrative Decisions (Judicial Review) Act 1989 (ACT) s 13; Judicial Review Act 1991 (Qld) pt 4; Judicial Review Act 2000 (Tas) pt 5; Administrative Law Act 1978 (Vic) s 8. See also NSW Supreme Court Practice Note (CL) 3 cl 23.

[172] J Boughey (n 53) ch 4.

[173] See *Li* (2013) 249 CLR 332, 367 (Hayne, Kiefel and Bell JJ); and *SZVFW* (2018) 92 ALJR 713, [10] (Kiefel CJ), [82] (Nettle and Gordon JJ).

[174] J Boughey, 'The Reasonableness of Proportionality in the Australian Administrative Law Context' (2015) 43 *Federal Law Review* 59, 86.

reasoning'.[184] With the exception of an activist period during the early 1990s, Australia's High Court has adhered to what has variously been described as a strict 'legalist', 'formalist' or 'literalist' approach to public law.[185] This approach has been influenced by Sir Owen Dixon, who famously stated that: 'There is no other safe guide to judicial decisions in great conflicts than a strict and complete legalism.'[186] Under Dixon's influence, the High Court has generally tended to develop the common law via small and incremental rules rather than being guided by broad principles such as 'community values', human rights and international law.[187] Furthermore, the fact that Australian courts have largely adhered to the list of legal errors set out in the ADJR Act has not prevented the scope of judicial review in Australia from expanding in recent decades. This expansion has simply occurred via a different, more 'formalist' methodology than in similar jurisdictions.[188]

It is noteworthy that this too seems to be changing in light of the recent broadening of unreasonableness in Australia. In *Li*,[189] the High Court applied unreasonableness to an essentially procedural issue (the refusal to stay proceedings) and held that unreasonableness is concerned with both the intelligibility of the justification a decision-maker has provided for a decision, as well as with the outcome of the decision. In *Li* itself, the decision to refuse a stay was found to be unreasonable due to the fact that the tribunal had given disproportionate weight to the interests of efficiency over fairness.[190] Allsop CJ has explained the new approach thus:

> [A]ny attempt to be comprehensive or exhaustive in defining when a decision will be sufficiently defective as to be legally unreasonable and display jurisdictional error is likely to be productive of complexity and confusion. One aspect of any such attempt can be seen in the over-categorisation of more general concepts and over-emphasis on the particular language of judicial expression of principle. Thus, it is unhelpful

[184] M Aronson, 'Some Australian Reflections on *Roncarelli v Duplessis*' (2010) 55 *McGill Law Journal* 615, 620, citing *Bofinger v Kingsway Group Ltd* (2009) 239 CLR 269, 300–01 [90]–[94] (Gummow, Hayne, Heydon, Kiefel and Bell JJ). Other examples include *Saeed v Minister for Immigration and Citizenship* (2010) 241 CLR 252 ('*Saeed*') and *Plaintiff S10/2011 v Minister for Immigration and Citizenship* (2012) 246 CLR 636.

[185] See J Goldsworthy, 'Australia: Devotion to Legalism' in J Goldsworthy (ed), *Interpreting Constitutions: A Comparative Study* (New York, Oxford University Press, 2006) 133, 153 ff; T Poole, 'Between the Devil and the Deep Blue Sea: Administrative Law in an Age of Rights' in L Pearson, C Harlow and M Taggart (eds), *Administrative Law in a Changing State: Essays in Honour of Mark Aronson* (Oxford, Hart Publishing, 2008) 15, 23 ff.

[186] O Dixon, Address on appointment as Chief Justice of the High Court of Australia (1952) 85 CLR xi, xiv.

[187] See D Heydon, 'Judicial Activism and the Death of the Rule of Law' (2004) 10 *Otago Law Review* 493.

[188] J Boughey (n 53) ch 5.

[189] *Li* (2013) 249 CLR 332.

[190] *Li* (2013) 249 CLR 332, 366 [74]. See also Edelman J's discussion of values in *Nathanson v Minister for Home Affairs* [2022] HCA 26, [89]–[91] (discussing the application of the new 'materiality' threshold for jurisdictional error).

to approach the task by seeking to draw categorised differences between words and phrases such as arbitrary, capricious, illogical, irrational, unjust, and lacking evident or intelligent justification, as if each contained a definable body of meaning separate from the other.[191]

## D. The Codification of Procedural Fairness in the Migration Act 1958 (Cth)

Over the last 30 years, the focus of codification efforts in Australian administrative law has been on the rules of procedural fairness. Specifically, the Commonwealth Parliament has made numerous attempts to '*replace* the uncodified principles of natural justice with clear and fixed procedures'.[192] These attempts began in 1992 with the Migration Reform Act 1992 (Cth) and have continued since, largely in response to courts interpreting the procedural codes more restrictively than the legislature would have liked.

There have been numerous iterations of the procedural codes in the Migration Act 1958 (Cth) and an evolution of the approach that the courts have taken to interpreting them over time. The fine details of both the legislation and case law have been examined by Grant Hooper in his doctoral thesis.[193] Space constraints do not permit a detailed analysis here. By way of a brief summary, the legislature has essentially sought to 'replace' the common law procedural requirements which give effect to natural justice with procedures set out in legislation in order to provide 'the certainty needed for effective administration of the migration program'.[194] However, these procedural codes cannot be separated from the legislature's attempts to limit judicial review. In combination, the ouster clauses and procedural codes were designed to do more than 'clarify' existing rules. They also sought to prevent courts from applying the expanded rules of natural justice in the migration context and from further expanding those rules, although this was not expressly stated in the explanatory material.[195]

Since the first iteration of the migration procedural code, courts have struggled to find a consistent and coherent approach to determining how the statutory procedures and ouster clauses affect and interact with the common law and the

[191] *Minister for Immigration and Border Protection v Stretton* (2016) 237 FCR 1, [2]. See further J Boughey (n 149). Another recent example is Edelman J's acknowledgment of the balancing of values at play in the recent development of the materiality threshold for jurisdictional error: *Nathanson v Minister for Home Affairs* [2022] HCA 26, [89]–[90].

[192] Explanatory Memorandum to the Migration Reform Bill 1992, [51], cited in *Re Minister for Immigration and Multicultural Affairs; Ex parte Miah* (2001) 206 CLR 57, note 66 (emphasis added).

[193] G Hooper, 'Parliament v The High Court? Natural justice, codification and the Australian Migration Act' (PhD Thesis, University of New South Wales, 2016) chs 6 f.

[194] Explanatory Memorandum, Migration Reform Bill 1992, Migration (Delated Visa Applications) Tax Bill 1992, 5.

[195] See generally G Hooper (n 193) ch 5.

Constitution,[196] as well as with other statutory provisions which suggest that the common law may still apply.[197] The uncertainty stems from two core legal principles which point in different directions.

The first is the principle that the legislature is free to determine the scope of statutory administrative power, subject to any constitutional limits on the legislature's own powers. This means that the legislature can, if it so chooses, oust common law principles, or interpretive presumptions, which ordinarily limit statutory executive power, including natural justice.[198] There is no clear constitutional basis in Australia for finding that executive power is limited by a duty to act fairly, or for finding that the legislature cannot oust any such common law or interpretive principle that ordinarily applies.[199]

On the other hand, if the legislature were to completely oust procedural fairness or limit it to the extent that it did not require decision-makers to in fact act fairly, it is often argued that the rule of law would be diminished, as decision-makers would be entitled to act arbitrarily.[200] In Australia, this argument also has a constitutional dimension because, as explained above, the High Court's judicial review jurisdiction is constitutionally entrenched. If Parliament can provide that a decision-maker is not required to act fairly, rationally or in accordance with the usual 'values'[201] commonly protected via judicial review, then the Court's jurisdiction to issue judicial review remedies would have no substance.[202]

The resolution that Australian courts have reached is to acknowledge Parliament's capacity to limit, and even oust, procedural fairness via statute, but to apply a (very) strong presumption that Parliament did not intend to do so.[203] Thus, procedural codes which offer less protection than the common law will usually be interpreted narrowly in their application. The result is that most fairness cases now come down to complex interpretive questions, requiring courts to determine the extent to which any residual common law principles are capable of applying.

Two recent High Court decisions highlight this complexity. *Minister for Immigration and Border Protection v SZMTA*[204] and *BVD17 v Minister for*

[196] See, eg, *Abebe v Commonwealth* (1999) 162 ALR 1, *Re Refugee Tribunal; Ex parte Aala* (2000) 204 CLR 82 (holding that the ouster and codes in place at the time only applied to review by the Federal Court, and not review under the Constitution); *Minister for Immigration and Multicultural Affairs; Ex parte Miah* (2001) 206 CLR 57 ('*Miah*') (holding that the procedural code applied generally to the exercise of power under the Act and not differentially to the Federal and High courts, but that it should be interpreted strictly, presuming that Parliament does not intend to restrict procedural fairness).

[197] See, eg, *Minister for Immigration & Multicultural & Indigenous Affairs v Eshetu* (1999) 197 CLR 611 (and decisions of courts below).

[198] *Twist v Randwick Municipal Council* (1976) 136 CLR 106, 109–10.

[199] Hayne J made this point in *Aala* (2000) 204 CLR 82, 142.

[200] See, eg, this suggestion of Gleeson CJ in *Plaintiff S157/2002 v Commonwealth* (2003) 211 CLR 476, 490–93.

[201] *Al-Kateb v Godwin* (2004) 219 CLR 562 (Gleeson CJ).

[202] This is explored in LB Crawford, 'The Entrenched Minimum Provision of Judicial Review and the Limits of "Law"' (2017) 45 *Federal Law Review* 569.

[203] *Miah* (2001) 206 CLR 57; *Saeed* (2010) 241 CLR 252.

[204] *Minister for Immigration and Border Protection v SZMTA* (2019) 264 CLR 421 ('*SZMTA*').

*Immigration and Border Protection*[205] both centred on the question of whether similar procedural codes in different parts of the Migration Act left any scope for common law fairness principles to apply. The provisions – sections 438 and 473GB of the Act respectively – essentially provide that the Department of Home Affairs can provide confidential information to the tribunal charged with reviewing a decision to refuse to issue a person with a visa. That information must be accompanied by a formal notification that the information is confidential. The relevant review tribunal is then granted discretion to have regard to the information, as well as discretion to disclose any of the information to the visa applicant. The provisions themselves are similar, but operate in different contexts. The context in issue in *SZMTA* is the ordinary tribunal review process. The context in which the provision in issue in *BVD17* operates is the 'fast-track' review process, which is designed to expedite decision-making and review of asylum applications by, for instance, preventing those subject to the fast-track process from adducing new evidence on review (absent exceptional circumstances) and making decisions on the papers alone.[206] The Migration Act 1958 (Cth) expressly states that each provision is part of a set of statutory procedures which is an exhaustive statement of the requirements of the natural justice hearing rule.[207]

The question in both cases was whether natural justice required the relevant tribunal to inform the applicant of the fact that it had received confidential information (although there was a discretion as to whether to disclose the information itself). In *SZMTA*, the High Court held that natural justice did require such notice after the Minister conceded this point (rightly, according to the Court).[208] This duty had not been clearly and expressly excluded by the Act. The joint judgment reasoned that the fact of notification 'alters the procedural context within which the Tribunal's duty of review is to be conducted'.[209] However, the Court went on to find that the failure to so notify the applicants in these cases had no material effect on the outcome of the cases and so would not be remedied.[210]

In *BVD17* the majority reached the opposite conclusion as to whether the statutory procedures displaced the common law requirement of notification. The reasons for doing so were primarily based on textual differences in the respective 'exhaustive statement' provisions. The provision in *SZMTA* provided that the procedural code was exhaustive 'in relation to the matters it deals with' whereas the provision in *BVD17* proclaimed that the procedures were exhaustive 'in relation to reviews conducted' by the review authority. According to the majority,

[205] *BVD17 v Minister for Immigration and Border Protection* (2019) 268 CLR 29 ('*BVD17*').

[206] See generally Andrew & Renata Kaldor Centre for International Refugee Law, *'Fast Track' Refugee Status Determination*, Research Brief, April 2019: www.kaldorcentre.unsw.edu.au/sites/default/files/Research%20Brief_Fast%20track_final.pdf.

[207] See Migration Act 1958 (Cth) ss 422B and 473DA respectively.

[208] *SZMTA* (2019) 264 CLR 421, 440 [27].

[209] *SZMTA* (2019) 264 CLR 421, 441 [30].

[210] The process of reasoning by which the majority and Nettle and Gordon JJ reached this conclusion differed, but the result was the same.

this difference evinced a legislative intention that the latter code completely replaced the common law principles in relation to reviews, whereas the former only replaced the common law in relation to the narrowly construed matters that the code actually addressed.[211]

Edelman J disagreed with the majority on this point, though not on the outcome. His Honour began his judgment by stating that 'Even with the benefit of omniscience, God still afforded Adam the benefit of the natural justice hearing rule' and explained that very clear language is required to displace the presumption that administrative decision-makers are expected to act in a fair manner.[212] Edelman J took a different interpretive approach to the majority, explaining that there are difficulties in attempting to delineate express requirements of procedural fairness and implied requirements which flow from express statutory procedures.[213] For example, where a provision states that a visa applicant may be given the particulars of confidential information at the tribunal's discretion, surely the manner in which those particulars are given must be fair. Thus, there is work for implications even where statutes purport to provide an exhaustive code. His Honour took the view that the linguistic differences between the provisions at issue in *SZMTA* and *BVD17* went to the 'range of matters that are the subject to the procedural fairness obligation', not to whether implications may be drawn from the express obligations.[214] Edelman J added that the presumption that Parliament does not intend to limit fundamental rights, including the right to a fair hearing, provides further support for his interpretation.[215]

The key point for these purposes that these cases and different judgments highlight is the complexity that procedural codes create for the relationship between statute and 'common law' interpretive presumptions.

Additionally, the High Court now takes the view that procedural fairness interacts with other principles and interpretive presumptions, including the requirement that decision-makers consider relevant material and, most importantly, the presumption of reasonableness. As noted above, in *Li*,[216] the High Court applied the standard of reasonableness to an essentially procedural decision. The Migration Review Tribunal had refused to issue a stay to give Ms Li the opportunity to seek a further review of the decision that she lacked the skill level required for the visa for which she had applied. The Tribunal had followed the procedures set out in the Migration Act 1958 (Cth) in exercising its powers, and those procedures were said to be an 'exhaustive statement of the requirements of the natural justice hearing rule'.[217] The High Court unanimously found that the Tribunal's decision to

[211] *BVD17* (2019) 268 CLR 29, 43 [31].
[212] *BVD17* (2019) 268 CLR 29, 46 [42].
[213] *BVD17* (2019) 268 CLR 29, 48–49 [48].
[214] *BVD17* (2019) 268 CLR 29, 49 [51].
[215] *BVD17* (2019) 268 CLR 29, 51 [55].
[216] *Li* (2013) 249 CLR 332.
[217] Migration Act 1958 (Cth) s 357A.

refuse the stay was legally unreasonable. The effect is that procedural discretions will be assessed against standards of fairness and reasonableness: in effect, unreasonableness now seems to offer an alternative basis to fairness for arguing that the decision-making process was so unjust as to take a decision-maker beyond power.[218] This avenue is particularly useful where the principles of fairness are set out in a strict and limited code.

Thus, the Commonwealth Parliament's efforts to codify the principles of procedural fairness have not achieved the stated objective of clarifying the rules of procedural fairness for decision-makers. Recent case law highlights that procedural codes have given rise to new, complex interpretive issues regarding how statutory procedural provisions interact with one another and with the common law. Nor have the procedural codes achieved the Commonwealth Parliament's unstated objective of restricting judicial intervention in cases where courts consider an administrative decision to have been made in an unjust manner. The scope of unreasonableness has now expanded so as to provide an additional or alternative basis for arguing that an unjust decision is unlawful.

## V. Conclusions

Australian legislatures have sought to 'codify' principles of administrative law largely in order to overcome problems associated with the technicality and complexity of the common law. More recently, they have also sought to define and limit common law principles of natural justice in the migration context with the stated objective of creating greater certainty for decision-makers. Codification has largely not had these desired effects. Instead, the dual systems of statutory and common law interpretive principles interact in ways which tend to create new technical problems for litigants, decision-makers and courts. This is true for both general judicial review statutes and for those which seek to codify natural justice.

The most significant objection to the codification of judicial review principles in Australia, both in the 1960s and subsequently, has been the fear that it will have the effect of stifling or ossifying the common law. There is some evidence that this may have occurred in Australia with respect to the codification of the 'grounds' of review in the ADJR Act as well as that Act's creation of a statutory right to reasons for administrative decisions. Each of these *may* have *contributed* to the High Court's refusal to develop and broaden Australian law in the same ways as has occurred in similar common law jurisdictions. However, the ADJR Act cannot be said to be the only or even the most significant force contributing to the High Court's reluctance to embrace doctrines of substantive legitimate expectations, proportionality and a wider common law right to reasons. For each, there

[218] A more recent case is *SZVFW* (2018) 264 CLR 541, discussed above in section III.A.iv. See further J Boughey (n 149) 130–35.

are strong constitutional reasons for the approach that the High Court has taken, in particular Australia's relatively strict separation of judicial power. Furthermore, recent developments in the administrative law principles of reasonableness and jurisdictional facts mean that Australian law now offers similar substantive protection to the law in Canada and the UK, albeit via different methods.

One apparent effect of the codification of administrative law principles in Australia has been in the methodology that litigants and courts use in judicial review cases. Compared with other common law jurisdictions, Australian administrative law remains relatively 'formalist' and 'legalist' in the way that it treats the statutory implications once said to be 'grounds' of review as a narrow set of rules. In contrast, courts in the UK and Canada seem to refer to broader values and principles in deciding judicial review applications. However, even this seems to be changing in Australia.

# 2

# Codification of Administrative Law in Austria

KONRAD LACHMAYER

## I. Introduction

In 2009, the Austrian Constitutional Court (ACC) was asked to pass judgment on whether an official warning of the Financial Market Authority represented a violation of a right.[1] The Austrian Banking Act[2] empowers the independent agency to inform the public if a certain bank or corporation is not allowed to carry out a certain form of bank business. As the Banking Act does not grant the possibility for legal protection, the legal issue at the ACC referred to the question of whether such an official warning is able to violate fundamental rights and, if so, what kind of legal protection would be necessary.

The reason for this constitutional question can be traced back to the gaps in codification of administrative law, which lead to deficits in effective legal protection against administrative action in Austria. Official warnings are not addressed as a form of administrative action by the Austrian Constitution;[3] moreover, the Austrian Constitution only offers legal protection if certain constitutionally recognised forms of administrative actions are involved. In the absence of a General Administrative Law Act (GALA), the ACC asked if the lack of specific legal protection provided by the Banking Act violates fundamental rights and the rule of law principle of the Austrian Constitution. The ACC came to the conclusion that legal protection must be provided, since an official warning can

[1] VfSlg (Collection of Cases at the ACC) 18.747/2009.

[2] Bundesgesetz über das Bankwesen enacted by BGBl 532/1993 as amended by BGBl I 141/2006; The Financial Market Authority is the Austrian federal supervisory authority for the banking, insurance, pension funds and securities sectors. It is established as an independent agency outside the hierarchical administration.

[3] The core document of Austrian constitutional law is the Federal Constitutional Act 1920, which was re-enacted by BGBl 1/1930 and last amended by BGBl 141/2022. Besides that, several other constitutional Acts and several hundred constitutional provisions exist.

interfere with the rights of the banking institution concerned.[4] As a consequence, the legislator amended the Banking Act to enable the bank concerned to obtain an administrative decision (after the official warning was publicly announced), which empowered the bank to gain an official procedure and thus legal and judicial protection.

This judgment can be viewed as an important step towards legal protection regarding both official warnings in particular and administrative action in general. The ACC was not in a position to create a new form of administrative action, but could claim – due to human rights and the rule of law – a constitutional necessity for legal protection to be provided in the case of an official warning, in particular in the case of banking law. In many instances, the case law of the ACC substitutes for the lack of a GALA in Austria. Although the Austrian Constitution authorises the legislator to define and determine forms of administrative action which lead to legal protection at administrative courts of first instance, Parliament has only implemented forms of administrative action as well as generalised statutory acts on administrative procedure to a limited extent.

The most famous codification of administrative procedure dates back to 1925, when Austria codified its administrative procedure of individual administrative decisions. After the enactment of the Federal Constitutional Act (FCA) in 1920, this was a crucial step for the new (much smaller) Austrian Republic. While this historic achievement might have been heroic, a broader codification of administrative law has not happened in the last 100 years. The FCA of 1920 and the General Administrative Procedural Act (GAPA) of 1925[5] remain the most important elements of codification of administrative law in Austria.[6]

However, the greatest impact on Austrian administrative law occurred with the accession to the European Union (EU) in 1995. The following 25 years led to a steady and substantial change in administrative organisation, tools and procedures. In 2022, Austria was part of a system of European multi-level governance, which has raised the question of the codification of EU administrative law. The scholarly ReNEUAL project[7] suggests – on an academic basis – the codification of administrative law in the EU, which would also dramatically change administrative law on a domestic level. An example of an implemented codification of a crucial part of administrative law exists by the enactment of the GDPR[8] in the context of the administrative processing of personal data.[9]

[4] The ACC named the right to freedom to carry on a business, the right to property and the right to data protection guaranteed by the Austrian Constitution as examples; VfSlg 18.747/2009.

[5] For the historical version, see Allgemeines Verwaltungsverfahrensgesetz enacted by BGBl 274/1925; the current version was enacted by BGBl 51/1991 and last amended by BGBl I 58/2018.

[6] See, regarding further elements, section IV below.

[7] For the ReNEUAL project, see: www.reneual.eu; for a presentation of the project's approach and findings in this book, see A Berger, 'Science Codification for the European Union: The ReNEUAL-Network', section II.

[8] Regulation 2016/679/EU of the European Parliament and of the Council of 27 April 2016 on the protection of natural persons with regard to the processing of personal data and on the free movement of such data, and repealing Directive 95/46/EC (General Data Protection Regulation) [2016] OJ L119/1.

[9] As long as none of the more than 100 opening clauses applies.

Beginning by answering the question of the Austrian understanding of administrative law (section II), this chapter focuses on the legal sources of administrative law (section III), as well as on the attempts, successes and failures of the codification of administrative law in Austria (section IV). The conclusion will discuss the limits of codifications (section V).

# II. The Definition and Delimitation of Administrative Law

## A. Defining Administrative Law in Austria

### *i. Distinguishing Administrative Law and Administration*

In Austria, administrative law is commonly understood as all legal rules referring to the administration (including government).[10] Administrative law therefore consists not only of acts of the administration, but also of constitutional and statutory law as well as of the case law of the judiciary. While this definition of the term 'administrative law' is undisputed, the understanding of what is part of the administration has been hotly debated over the last century. Two approaches can be distinguished: a positive and a negative approach towards the definition of administration.

### *ii. A Negative Understanding of Administration*

The dominant approach is a negative one. Administration is understood as all tasks of the state which are not legislation or jurisdiction.[11] The definition of legislation and jurisdiction seems easier and more precise; classic questions regarding this distinction remain (eg, parliamentary administration or judicial administration), but are essentially resolved. The establishment of the administrative courts of first instance (in 2014) created new challenges of classification. Not only are these administrative courts clearly assigned to the judiciary from an organisational perspective, but the function of these courts is also a judicial one. However, the power of the administrative courts to decide in administrative matters is remarkably high (which shows a clear shift from the administration to the judiciary). When it comes to the application of procedural law, the administrative courts also apply (at least in a subsidiary way) administrative (procedural) law. Although a clear formal distinction exists regarding administration and administrative courts, there are overlapping elements in the actual substance of administrative law.[12]

[10] See B Raschauer, *Allgemeines Verwaltungsrecht*, 5th edn (Vienna, Verlag Österreich, 2017) 7 ff; A Kahl and K Weber, *Allgemeines Verwaltungsrecht*, 7th edn (Vienna, Facultas, 2019) 27 ff.

[11] See W Antoniolli and F Koja, *Allgemeines Verwaltungsrecht*, 3rd edn (Vienna, Manz, 1996) 3 ff.

[12] See further section IV.D below.

Moreover, Austrian scholarship does not distinguish government from administration (when it comes to classification), but understands governmental tasks as part of the administration.[13] Finally, the negative definition of administration also has to deal with the delimitation between state functions and societal tasks (as administration is understood as all state functions except legislation and jurisdiction).[14]

### *iii. A Positive Understanding of Administration*

Different forms of positive definitions of administration also exist. A traditional approach refers to the hierarchical principle of administration in contrast to judicial independence.[15] Due to developments in EU law, more and more independent (regulatory) agencies have been established, which are not bound by governmental instructions. The hierarchical characteristic of the administration is therefore only of limited use in identifying administration nowadays. Other authors follow a typological approach and list the main authorities and functions of the administration.[16]

Besides the scholarly debate, constitutional and statutory law refer to the administration (as a legal term), which forms part of the interpretation by the courts. The concrete usage of the term 'administration' by constitutional and statutory law is interpreted in the context of the provision and therefore does not lead to a uniform understanding of the administration.[17]

Nowadays, questions regarding the definition of the administration are no longer debated by scholars. However, the underlying problems and challenges of the beginning of the twenty-first century are a core element of the scholarly debate.

## B. The Problems of Defining Administration and Administrative Law

First of all, the current challenges of a delimitation of administrative law are rooted in EU law, which has led both to the Europeanisation and judicialisation of administrative law in Austria as well as the transferal of significant rule-making powers to private actors. The aforementioned introduction of administrative courts of first instance has created a new organisational and functional concept of administrative law in Austria.[18] The Europeanisation of administrative law can also be observed in the establishment of independent agencies introduced and protected by EU law. The agency concept includes a European coordination of

[13] *cf* W Antoniolli and F Koja (n 11) 10 ff.
[14] *cf* A Kahl and K Weber (n 10) 29 ff.
[15] See W Antoniolli and F Koja (n 11) 341.
[16] *cf* A Kahl and K Weber (n 10) 34 ff.
[17] The term 'administrative law' differs in meaning depending on the source of law using it.
[18] See also section IV.D below.

administrative authorities as well as much more leeway for administrative authorities, including greater rule-making powers.[19] EU law has also led to a shift away from the state regulation of administrative law to private actors gaining incremental influence, including increasing certification processes, the relevance of soft law and technical standardisation. Private organisations create independent self-determining sets of rules, which are officially recognised by EU law and replace national regulatory approaches.[20]

The traditional understanding of the state and the administration cannot address these developments as administration or as administrative law. The Europeanisation and internationalisation of administrative law illustrate that an exact definition and categorisation is not possible in traditional categories of administrative law scholarship, which needs to open up towards more general governance studies at the interface between legal scholarship and political sciences.[21] The situation of administration and administrative law at the beginning of the twenty-first century in Austria can be characterised as complex, pluralistic and heterarchical, and it transcends the limits of law and legal acts.[22] However, looking back over the history of administration, the situation of administration before the second half of the nineteenth century was similar. Core differences in the twenty-first century relate to the digitalisation of law[23] (and society in general) as well as the quantity of (legal and non-legal) texts which have to be taken into consideration.

## C. The Approaches Towards General Administrative Law

While administrative law is clearly understood as a category of positive law, the Austrian understanding of general administrative law is first of all understood as a doctrinal approach to address general terminology, categories and concepts of administrative law.[24] The Austrian legal order does not contain one unified GALA. However, certain elements like administrative procedural law and basic

[19] Examples of independent agencies are the 'E-Control' (supervisory authority for the energy sector), the 'Schienen-Control' (supervisory authority for the railway sector) and the 'Datenschutzbehörde' (data protection authority under the GDPR); *cf* K Lachmayer, 'Regulatory Constitutional Law: The Implementation of European Regulatory Law in Austria in the Energy Sector' (2014) 2 *European Networks Law & Regulation Quarterly* 305.

[20] See I Eisenberger, 'Regelbildung durch Private' in C Fuchs et al (eds), *Staatliche Aufgaben, private Akteure I* (Vienna, Manz, 2015).

[21] *cf* P Zumbansen, 'Administrative Law's Global Dream: Navigating Regulatory Spaces between "National" and "International"' (2013) 11 *International Journal of Constitutional Law* 506.

[22] Examples in this regard are voluntary commitments connected with corporate social responsibility. The concept of 'consultation instead of penalties' has also become increasingly common in Austrian administrative law. See D Klose, '"Beraten statt strafen" – ein legistischer Schnellschuss?' (2019) 73 *Österreichische Juristenzeitung* 714.

[23] *cf* C Rupp, 'Status und Ziel von E-Government in Österreich' (2004) *Recht & Finanzen für Gemeinden* 100.

[24] See B Raschauer (n 10) 9 ff.

organisational structures, as well as administrative acts and other forms of administrative action, are determined generally by law. The Austrian Constitution is of great importance in shaping the administration in a 'general administrative law' approach.[25] Principles of administrative law are derived from constitutional law by the ACC.[26] Moreover, procedural statutory law, especially in the context of administrative decisions, serves a 'general administrative law' function.[27] The legal situation of 'general administrative law' in Austria could be described as constitutionalised on the one hand and semi-codified on the other.

# III. Legal Sources of Administrative Law

## A. The (Constitutional) Principles of Administrative Law

### *i. The Core Principles of Administrative Law*

The Austrian Constitution contains fundamental constitutional principles, which have been identified by the ACC and can be applied by the ACC to review constitutional law. One of these principles is the rule of law principle. As a meta-constitutional principle, it is also highly relevant to concretise and shape the principles of administrative law.

The principles of administrative law are laid down in Austrian constitutional law. These principles are not written down in a specific chapter of the Austrian Constitution, but are identified, concretised and developed by the case law of the ACC. The role of human rights law as well as EU law to unfold and shape these principles is significant. Although the case law creates a core of these principles, it cannot be argued that they are codified as a systematic and coherent catalogue of principles of administrative law. Nevertheless, these principles form as a whole the core principles of administrative law. Legal scholarship is able to bring the different principles together and to demonstrate the correlation between these principles.

The core principles of administrative law[28] are as follows:

- The principle of legality (Article 18 FCA) is the first and most prominent principle of administrative law. It states that the administration is bound to the acts of legislation; moreover, the legislation is bound to determine statutory law and not to delegate its function to the administration. It establishes

[25] Detailed provisions exist for administrative organisation as well as administrative acts. See A Kahl and K Weber (n 10) 82 ff.

[26] For the constitutional principles of administrative law, see section III.A below.

[27] While the prevailing literature on general administrative law does not currently include administrative procedural law, this has not always been the case. *cf* W Antoniolli and F Koja (n 11) 773 ff.

[28] Further principles could be identified, eg, the principle of efficiency. For the principle of efficiency, see A Kahl and K Weber (n 10) 127 ff.

a legal hierarchy, which determines the primacy of statutory law and forbids administrative acts from contradicting statutory law.[29]

- The principle of equality (Article 7 FCA) is a core principle with regard to the case law of the ACC. The Court derives several 'rule-of-law' principles from the principle of equality, including the principle of non-discrimination, the principle of reasonableness, the prohibition of arbitrariness and the principle of legitimate expectation. These principles bind not only the legislator, but also the administration (including the government).[30]
- The principle of proportionality is not explicitly formulated in constitutional law, but is an immanent part of human rights. Although it primarily addresses statutory law in the case law of the ACC, it also has its effects on administrative acts. First, administrative (statutory) law shapes the scope of administrative action; second, general ordinances of the administration are also bound by the principle of proportionality directly; and, third, statutory law – especially in the context of the encroachment of fundamental rights – regularly expresses the principle of proportionality as a compulsory specification for the administration.[31]
- The principle of effective legal protection was identified by the ACC as part of the constitutional 'rule of law' principle. Furthermore, the principle of legal protection was influenced by EU law, which requires effective legal protection in the enforcement of EU law, even when a domestic legal system would not provide a specific legal protection (the principle of equivalence).[32]
- The principle of (state) liability (Article 23 FCA) obliges the state to be liable for unlawful and culpable acts of administration. EU law extended the principle beyond the administration (and certain judgments of the judiciary) towards a general state liability, especially including the legislation and judgments of supreme courts.[33]

In addition to these constitutional principles, the GAPA also establishes and concretises procedural principles, like the principle of *ex officio* investigation, the fair trial principle (including the right to be heard), the principle of free appraisal of evidence, the principle of procedural efficiency and the principle of legal effect. Again, fundamental procedural principles are mentioned throughout the statutory Act and not summarised (eg, at the beginning of the Act). However, the GAPA must be understood as a codification of general administrative (procedural) law.[34]

[29] See B Raschauer (n 10) 222 ff.
[30] See M Pöschl, *Gleichheit vor dem Gesetz* (Vienna, Springer, 2008) 133 ff.
[31] See B Raschauer (n 10) 251.
[32] See U Giera and K Lachmayer, 'The Principle of Effective Legal Protection in Austrian Administrative Law' in Z Szente and K Lachmayer (eds), *The Principle of Effective Legal Protection in Administrative Law* (Abingdon, Routledge, 2017) 73 ff.
[33] See B Raschauer (n 10) 509 ff.
[34] See section IV.C below.

### *ii. The Missing Principles of Administrative Law*

Although various principles of administrative law exist in Austrian constitutional and statutory (procedural) law, certain principles are missing or play only a minor role in the Austrian legal system. The following four examples shall illustrate the potential of further relevant principles in Austrian administrative law: transparency, good administration, accountability and sustainability:

- Transparency: the Austrian Constitution is still based on the (monarchical) principle of official secrecy. Although a right to information exists, this right is very limited. While almost every country in Europe has established a Freedom of Information Act based on the transparency principle, Austria lags behind[35] when it comes to the constitutional and statutory implementation of transparency. In the last 10 years, various attempts to do this have failed (for political reasons that are unclear).
- Good administration: while Article 41 of the Charter of Fundamental Rights of the European Union[36] determines a right to good administration, the Austrian Constitution and procedural law only guarantee some individual elements of this right. The establishment of a comprehensive and coherent principle of good administration would foster the underlying idea of good administration. The Austrian ombudsman board is an organisational part of controlling good administration,[37] but has quite limited powers of enforcement.
- Accountability: although public liability for damages caused by state agents is guaranteed, the Austrian Constitution is lacking a broader general principle of accountability. While the government is legally (and politically) accountable, and the administrative authorities are accountable towards the government, accountability is still lacking in practice. The concept of legal protection still has structural deficits, and the government is still reluctant to create effective accountability, eg, regarding rights violations by police officers.
- Sustainability: although a constitutional objective of sustainability exists, the ACC did not activate it as a full constitutional principle. On the contrary, in a leading decision in 2016, the ACC demolished the legal importance of the sustainability principle from a constitutional point of view.[38] It will take a long time or a dramatic turnaround to establish the principle of sustainability as a general principle of administrative law in Austria. It still has statutory relevance in the field of environmental law in Austria.

[35] See www.rti-rating.org.

[36] Charter of Fundamental Rights of the European Union [2012] OJ C326/391.

[37] See W Berka, *Verfassungsrecht*, 7th edn (Vienna, Verlag Österreich, 2018) 295 ff.

[38] VfSlg. 20.185/2017. The decision concerned a permit for the construction of a third runway at Vienna International Airport. See also B Hollaus, 'Austrian Constitutional Court: Considering Climate Change as a Public Interest is Arbitrary – Refusal of Third Runway Permit Annulled' (2017) *ICL Journal* 467.

This brief analysis of principles of administrative law shows that there are many existing principles in place which can be derived from the Austrian Constitution as well as the general procedural acts. They are mainly concretised by the ACC and the case law of other courts. It would already be possible to strengthen them by formal codification. Moreover, the potential for further developments of principles of administrative law is still very high. However, the scholarly debate on the establishment and concretisation of these principles (except the transparency principle) is very poor.

## B. Constitutional Forms of Administrative Action

### *i. Defined Forms of Administrative Action*

The Austrian Constitution mentions different forms of administrative acts, which comprise the core of administrative action. Although they can be identified within the Constitution, they are not summarised and enumerated in one specific provision of the Constitution. Thus, already at a constitutional level, a strict codification does not exist. The judiciary and academic scholarship have determined and discussed these forms of administrative action. These standard forms include administrative ordinances, administrative decisions, administrative instructions and direct administrative law enforcement (eg, commands and force by the police).[39] The defined forms of administrative action are of particular importance regarding legal protection, which is bound to the specific form of administrative action.

Administrative ordinances are understood as general acts of administrative authorities (including the government), which address the population of the country or parts of it.[40] Ordinances include concretisations of statutory law (administrative law-making) as well as planning schemes or general orders (eg, concrete road traffic orders). A general administrative ordinance act is missing; certain procedural requirements can be derived from the Constitution, while other procedural provisions are part of the particular statutory law. A general procedural framework (besides the constitutional requirements) does not exist. Legal protection is provided by the ACC, which can review the legality of the administrative ordinance regarding statutory law.[41]

Administrative decisions refer to an individual act of an administrative authority (including the government), which addresses a concrete individual or a group of specified individuals.[42] Decisions include permits, administrative penalties or other administrative measures (eg, construction bans). The procedure of

[39] See A Kahl and K Weber (n 10) 226 ff.
[40] See J Aichlreiter, *Österreichisches Verordnungsrecht Band I* (Vienna, Springer, 1988) 29 ff.
[41] U Giera and K Lachmayer (n 32) 88.
[42] See B Raschauer (n 10) 320 ff.

administrative decisions is codified in the GAPA, but divergent provisions can be enacted in particular statutory law, if necessary. Legal protection is provided at the administrative court of first instance and finally at the ACC as well as at the Supreme Administrative Court.[43]

Administrative instructions are internal directives by the government or administrative authorities which address their own civil servants or other administrative authorities. These include internal decrees and edicts as well as individual instructions. From a legal perspective, they do not leave the internal domain of the state and do not address citizens externally. Although certain provisions in civil service law concretise administrative instructions, a codification of the procedure to instruct civil servants does not exist. Legal protection is limited, but instructions by non-competent authorities can be ignored.

Finally, direct administrative law enforcement refers to coercive measures of administrative authorities, especially law enforcement bodies (eg, police forces), which directly address individuals. They include commands as well as the physical exercise of violence (eg, stop and search or arrests). As law enforcement does not follow a specific procedure, only general constitutional requirements exist. Legal protection against law enforcement measures is provided by administrative courts of first instance and codified in the GAPA.[44]

### *ii. Further Forms of Administrative Action*

Besides these constitutional forms of administration, further administrative forms can be observed in Austrian administrative law. Although administrative contracts are not explicitly mentioned in the Constitution, specific statutory law (eg, the University Act)[45] uses the form of administrative contracts.[46] A general provision on administrative contracts in statutory law is missing.[47] The problem of legal protection is resolved by the ACC, since in the event of conflict, the government or the administrative authority has to issue an administrative decision. This decision can then be appealed at the administrative courts of first instance.

A specific form of administrative action is represented by the processing of personal data by the administration. While scholars acknowledge the existence of a specific form of an administrative processing of personal data,[48] the Austrian Constitution only refers to data processing in particular contexts of judicial data processing. The data protection authority has the power to ensure legal protection against administrative data processing. Substantive and procedural

[43] U Giera and K Lachmayer (n 32) 87 f.

[44] See B Raschauer (n 10) 370 ff.

[45] Universitätsgesetz 2002 enacted by BGBl I 120/2002, as amended by BGBl I 177/2021.

[46] See in this regard H Eberhard, *Der verwaltungsrechtliche Vertrag* (Vienna, Springer, 2005).

[47] However, administrative contracts require an explicit legal basis in order to be permissible; see H Eberhard, *Der verwaltungsrechtliche Vertrag* (Vienna, Springer, 2005) 300 ff.

[48] *cf* G Lienbacher, 'Datenschutzrecht und Staatsorganisation' in Österreichischer Juristentag (ed), *Verhandlungen des Österreichischen Juristentages 2012 I/2* (Vienna, Manz, 2013).

issues are mainly determined by the European GDPR.[49] The administrative decision of the data protection authority can be appealed against at the Federal Administrative Court.

Governmental or administrative information concerning the public does not represent a specific constitutional form of administrative action. However, the ACC has started to integrate forms of public information into the existing constitutional framework of administrative forms of action.[50] If informational measures can be related to administrative decisions or coercive measures by law enforcement bodies, the ACC accepts the claim of rights violation under the traditional forms of administrative action.

Since the establishment of administrative courts of first instance in particular, the Constitution empowers Parliament in a comprehensive approach to establish further forms of administrative action by statutory law, as well as to open up legal protection to other forms of administrative action.[51] In police and security law, a broader approach towards legal protection exists with regard to all kinds of informal and soft forms of administrative action, which can be complained about at the state administrative courts of first instance as long as a violation against statutory law or administrative ordinances is claimed.[52] However, so far, a general concept on a statutory level has not been introduced. Furthermore, public liability against all administrative action which was unlawful and culpable can be claimed as long as damage incurred.[53]

The Austrian Constitution also enables complaints against administrative non-action as long as an administrative decision is deemed necessary.[54] However, a general concept to file a complaint of administrative non-action regarding an administrative ordinance is missing. This has created various problems in the context of EU law, as the EU principle of equivalence also requires legal protection against non-action regarding administrative ordinances.[55]

Finally, different forms of administrative action exist in the government's private-sector administration activities. Typically, the traditional forms of private law (eg, contracts) will be used. Certain areas, like public procurement, which is mainly determined by EU law, follow specific forms and procedures, which lead to particular legal protection.[56]

[49] For an initial overview of the GDPR, see P Voigt and A von dem Bussche, *The EU General Data Protection Regulation (GDPR)* (Cham, Springer, 2017).

[50] See S Yaylagül, 'Staatliche Warnungen' (2020) 20 *juridikum* 498, 504 ff.

[51] This possibility also existed before, but was extended in art 130, para 2 FCA.

[52] Section 88, para 2 of the Security Police Act enacted by BGBl 566/1991, as amended by BGBl I 147/2022: 'In addition, the state administrative courts deal with complaints from people who claim that their rights have been violated in some other way by acts or actions by the security administration, unless this has been done in the form of an administrative decision.'

[53] See W Berka (n 37) 278 ff.

[54] For the complaint against non-action, see J Hengstschläger and D Leeb, *Verwaltungsverfahrensrecht*, 6th edn (Vienna, Facultas, 2018) 594 ff.

[55] See M Potacs, 'Säumnis des Verordnungsgebers' in M Holoubek and M Lang (eds), *Rechtsschutz gegen staatliche Untätigkeit* (Vienna, Linde, 2011) 233 ff.

[56] *cf* W Schwartz, 'The Development and Regulation of Public Procurement Law in Austria' (2003) 9 *European Public Law* 157.

## C. The Constitutional Organisation of the Administration

The federal government is organised into ministries, which are determined by the Federal Ministries Act.[57] This statutory Act can be understood as a form of organisational codification of the federal ministries. At a state level, particularities of state governments are limited by the constitutional framework.

From a classical perspective, the Austrian Constitution conceptualised the government and administration in a hierarchical way. Independent commissions and the transfer of power from the state to private organisations and individuals represented an exemption. In the last 30 years, the organisation of government and administration has significantly changed the whole structure. Different influences, in particular the accession to the EU, have led to the establishment of a variety of regulatory agencies and other independent administrative authorities. The Austrian Constitution has been amended and has integrated this new approach as an equivalent concept of administration. Nowadays, hierarchically organised administrative authorities constitute the administration along with independent agencies. The organisational structure of these independent agencies varies to a significant degree and a coherent approach is missing.

The other organisational shift away from the hierarchical structure of administrative authorities was the establishment of administrative courts of first instances in 2014. While subsequent stages of administrative proceedings existed in a hierarchical order, these kinds of administrative instances were abolished. An administrative decision can generally only be appealed at an administrative court (of first instance), but no longer at an administrative authority. This shift towards administrative adjudication also significantly changed the organisation of administration. The new organisation of administrative courts is also divergent as two federal courts and nine state courts have been established; however, the Austrian Constitution creates a certain coherent framework.

Austria is organised as a federal state and administration is mainly organised in cooperation between federal and state administration. Furthermore, local authorities exercise local issues in self-government and local autonomy. While this constitutionally established system did not change, the rise of independent agencies centralised administrative tasks. Moreover, the delegation of powers to private entities increased significantly in the last 25 years; however, most of them are owned by the federal state.

The rights and obligations of civil servants are determined by federal statutory law. A shift from the traditional civil servant as a federal official towards employed staff can be observed over the last 20 years. Moreover, the politicisation of the ministries is an ongoing process. While the number of traditional civil servants is

[57] Bundesministeriengesetz 1986 enacted by BGBl 76/1986, as amended by BGBl I 98/2022.

being systematically reduced, more and more policy-makers and political staff are being employed and increasingly integrated into the structure of federal ministries. This development is mostly lacking any statutory basis, but has been established within the internal organisational power of the government.

In conclusion, a major shift can be observed. Government ministries are being increasingly politicised, while independent agencies are taking over regulatory activities and administrative courts guarantee the rule of law in administrative decision-making. While the traditional model has been codified in the Austrian Constitution, newer developments are only partially included in the constitutional framework.

## D. The Constitutional Concept of Legal Protection in Administration Law

At a constitutional level, the possibilities of legal protection are mapped out. The Austrian judicial system includes three supreme courts. The ACC deals not only with questions of constitutional review (which also includes administrative ordinances), but also with rights violation of administrative action (especially by administrative decisions and coercive measures).[58] As the administrative courts of first instance will decide at first, the constitutional complaint must argue that with this decision a significant violation of the statutory acts or the procedural rules has occurred.[59] In any other case, the Supreme Administrative Court will review violations of substantive statutory law, procedural rules or administrative non-action.[60] However, the possibilities to file a complaint at the Supreme Administrative Court are limited to legal matters of fundamental importance. The third supreme court is the Supreme Court, which deals with highest instance civil and criminal matters (ordinary judiciary). Private actions of the administration as well as public liability will be dealt with by the ordinary courts and finally by the Supreme Court.[61]

The core level of legal protection will certainly be covered by the administrative courts of first instance: 11 different courts exist. Nine courts are state courts, but they will also deal with many federal issues, mainly in which state administration supports federal administration. Moreover, two federal courts have been established: one general Federal Administrative Court, which deals with selected federal matters (mainly concerned with cases of asylum and alien law, though many other subjects are also included), and a Federal Finance Court, which grants legal protection in tax matters.[62]

[58] *cf* K Lachmayer, 'The Austrian Constitutional Court' in A Jakab et al (eds), *Comparative Constitutional Reasoning* (Cambridge, Cambridge University Press, 2017) 82 f.

[59] See W Berka (n 37) 349 ff.

[60] See art 133 FCA.

[61] See B Raschauer (n 10) 501 ff.

[62] See art 129 FCA.

Administrative procedure is primarily codified in the GAPA and the Administrative Penalties Act (APA).[63] Furthermore, the Administrative Courts Procedural Act (ACPA)[64] determines the procedure at the administrative courts of first instance.[65] These statutory acts also grant procedural rights, which are partly guaranteed by the Constitution. Questions of administrative discretion are mentioned by the Constitution and the procedural acts,[66] but details are based on case law, especially by the Supreme Administrative Court.

## E. Interim Conclusions

When it comes to the codification of principles, acts, organisation and legal protection regarding the administration, a mixed picture can be observed. While the constitution serves to a certain extent as codification, procedural acts mainly exist regarding administrative decisions and court proceedings. Other parts, like administrative ordinances or other forms of administrative action, are far less codified. Furthermore, while some principles of administrative law exist in Austrian constitutional and statutory (procedural) law, other core principles are missing or play only a minor role in the Austrian legal system. EU law reshapes the whole system of Austrian administration, with the result that the domestic situation of administrative law is even more fragmented.

Therefore, general administrative law is first and foremost an academic discipline to bring together the European and constitutional frameworks, substantive statutes and procedural law and the case law of the supreme courts. The possibilities and potential for further codification are remarkably high.

# IV. The Codification of Administrative Law

## A. Codification(s)?

Codification understood as an act or process of arranging laws into a system[67] is confronted with different challenges, especially in administrative law. Three Austrian challenges for the codification of administrative law shall be addressed before analysing the details of Austrian codifications and non-codifications in

[63] Verwaltungsstrafgesetz 1991 enacted by BGBl 52/1991, as amended by BGBl I 58/2018; *cf* J Hengstschläger and D Leeb (n 54) 47 ff.

[64] Verwaltungsgerichtsverfahrensgesetz enacted by BGBl I 33/2013, as amended by BGBl I 109/2021.

[65] See W Berka (n 37) 310 ff.

[66] See art 130, para 3 FCA: 'Except in administrative criminal matters and in matters belonging to the jurisdiction of the federal administrative court of finance, there is no illegality if the law grants the administrative authority discretion and if this discretion has been exercised within the meaning of the law.'

[67] www.dictionary.cambridge.org/de/worterbuch/englisch/codification.

administrative law: the role of constitutional law (section IV.A.i); the role of the multi-level system (section IV.A.ii); and the relationship between general and special administrative law (section IV.A.iii). All three challenges are of crucial importance regarding the codification of administrative law in Austria.

### *i. Constitutional and Administrative Law*

The Austrian Constitution contains various details regarding administrative law. Thus, the Austrian Constitution forms the first codification of administrative law regarding administrative principles and the organisation of the administration, as well as the form of administrative action. On the one hand, the concepts are old and only partly adapted to the situation in the twenty-first century; on the other hand, it is important to acknowledge that amending the Austrian Constitution has mostly been relatively easy (for political reasons) and the Constitution grants a great deal of leeway to Parliament not only to concretise but also to codify administrative law questions of forms of action, procedure, organisation and legal protection.

While the Austrian Constitution is part of the Austrian concept of administrative law, it has also significantly influenced statutory administrative law. The rise of the constitutional principle of the rule of law (which has to be understood as a principle of administrative law) and the increasing importance of human rights (including procedural rights) in the case law of the ACC[68] have led to a 'constitutionalisation' of administrative law. However, the Austrian scholarship does not debate these developments from the perspective of constitutionalisation.

### *ii. Codification in a Multi-level System (Federal State/EU Law)*

The codification of administrative law (at a national level) is at odds with other levels of a multi-level system. Regarding the Austrian legal order, the role of the federal state and the accession to the EU have to be considered. The codification of administrative procedural rules at a federal level can serve as an example. A deviation by the legislation at a state level from these rules is only possible if necessary.[69] Codification thus implicitly creates a model of statutory centralisation. When it comes to the EU, Union law undermines domestic codification, as European ideas, principles and concepts do not fit into the Austrian system of administrative law. On the one hand, it is necessary to adapt fundamental legal,

[68] See K Lachmayer, 'Eine Sprache, zwei Rechtskulturen: deutsches und österreichisches Verfassungsrechtsdenken' in U Kischel (ed), *Der Einfluss des deutschen Verfassungsrechtsdenkens in der Welt: Bedeutung, Grenzen, Zukunftsperspektiven* (Tübingen, Mohr Siebeck, 2014) 78 ff; *cf* further H Eberhard, 'Judicial activism und judicial self restraint in der Judikatur des VfGH' in E Bernat et al (eds), *Festschrift Christian Kopetzki zum 65. Geburtstag* (Vienna, Manz, 2019) 141 ff.

[69] See art 11, para 2 FCA.

organisational and procedural structures to EU law;[70] on the other hand, this opens up the potential for new codification to implement European concepts in the domestic legal orders. Finally, the questions of European harmonisation and codifications lead to further (European) centralisation and make codifications of the Member States obsolete.

### *iii. The Relationship between General and Special Administrative Law*

Stronger approaches towards the increasing codification of administrative law have to be seen in the dynamic interrelation with special administrative law, which is in a constant state of development. General administrative law as codified principles, structures and procedures makes it more difficult to deviate in dynamic fields of administrative law or structural shifts in society (eg, environmental law or technology law). However, codification could also implement innovative elements to enable deviation and new developments, such as authorisation of living labs or regulatory sandboxes.[71] Moreover, general administrative law can open up functional, structural and procedural learning processes between different fields of special administrative law. The Austrian legal system has great potential to further develop general administrative law in order to strengthen the concept of administrative law for future challenges. The following section will not only trace the historical path of codification in Austrian administrative law, but will also address the potential of general administrative law for organisational, procedural and substantive changes.

## B. The Constitutional Codification of Administrative Law

As already mentioned, the Austrian Constitution can be understood as part of a codification of administrative law. When it comes to the aspect of creating a system, it is only organisational law which is codified in the Austrian Constitution. This organisational codification is twofold: on the one hand, the organisation of federal and state government[72] and the structures for authorities are regulated;[73] on the other hand, the organisation of the judiciary (including the possibilities of legal protection) is codified in the Constitution.[74]

Although the Austrian Constitution forms a legal framework for administrative principles and administrative action, as well as providing specifications for administrative procedures, it is not possible to talk of a codification regarding

[70] *cf* K Stöger, 'Gedanken zur institutionellen Autonomie der Mitgliedstaaten am Beispiel der neuen Energieregulierungsbehörden' (2010) 65 *Zeitschrift für Öffentliches Recht* 247.

[71] *cf* D Zetzsche et al, 'Regulating a Revolution: From Regulatory Sandboxes to Smart Regulation' (2017) *Fordham Journal of Corporate & Financial Law* 32, 64 ff; C Krönke, 'Regulatory Sandboxes aus der Perspektive des Allgemeinen Verwaltungsrechts' (2020) *Österreichische Zeitschrift für Wirtschaftsrecht* 108.

[72] See arts 69 and 101 FCA.

[73] *cf* arts 78a–78d FCA.

[74] See especially arts 129–36 FCA.

these elements of administrative law. The potential to develop these elements further and to create a more codified version of these elements definitely exists. Interestingly enough, an approach to amend the Constitution in this regard has not been part of the Austrian debate over the last few decades.[75]

As the Austrian Constitution is seen as easily amendable and does not form a codification on its own, it has been amended more than 100 times in the last 70 years[76] and includes more than 300 constitutional provisions in other statutory acts.[77] This situation has led to further fragmentation of the already incomplete codification which existed 100 years ago. Nevertheless, the possibilities to codify certain elements of administrative law in the core document (the FCA) still exist.

When it comes to the principles of administrative law, the case law of the ACC has had a significant impact on the development of the above-mentioned principles. A collection of principles in one article or one section of the Constitution is missing.[78] There has not even been a debate about it. However, the potential to clarify and to improve the general specifications for administrative law would be very great. An important step in reforming administrative principles in constitutional law would be the establishment of the transparency principle (instead of the principle of official secrecy) in the Constitution.

The same potential for codification can be seen regarding the different forms of administrative action. Most of them are mentioned in the Constitution in certain provisions, but not collected in one single provision; rather, they can be found in the context of constitutional rules of legal protection. A compilation of the forms of administrative action could integrate the case law of the ACC and create clarity on a constitutional level. Again, such a codification is not even debated, but its value would be significant.

In both cases (administrative principles as well as forms of administrative action), a codification in a GALA would also be possible. Codification at the level of statutory law exists regarding procedural law, but only concerning administrative decisions.

## C. The Codification of Administrative Procedural Law

The era of codification seemed to be the nineteenth century. The first and most important codification in Austria was the General Civil Code in 1812.[79]

[75] The agenda of the last constitutional reform project, the 'Österreich Konvent', did not include the question of constitutional administrative principles in its agenda. *Cf* the website of the 'Österreich Konvent' at www.konvent.gv.at/K/Willkommen_Portal.shtml; see also K Lachmayer (n 68) 65 ff.

[76] See W Berka (n 37) 24 f.

[77] eg, s 5, para 6 Federal Road Traffic Act (Straßenverkehrsordnung 1960) enacted by BGBl 159/1960, as amended by BGBl I Nr 122/2022; *cf* further H Eberhard and K Lachmayer, 'Constitutional Reform in Austria' (2008) 2 *ICL Journal* 112, 113 ff.

[78] However, *cf* arts 18–23 FCA.

[79] Allgemeines bürgerliches Gesetzbuch enacted by JGS 946/1811; for the development of the General Civil Code, see JM Rainer, 'Zur Entstehung des ABGB' in M Geistlinger et al (eds), *200 Jahre ABGB – Ausstrahlungen* (Vienna, Manz, 2011) 25 ff.

The enlightened approach was to bring all provisions for organising the life of the citizens into one code. This not only created legal certainty but also empowered citizens in relation to the state and society. Criminal codes have been enacted since the second half of the eighteenth century.[80] The second half of the nineteenth century saw the enactment of the first Austrian Constitution (1867) in five different acts.[81] It was not until after the First World War in 1920 that the Austrian Constitution was unified.[82] However, the formal concept of the Austrian Constitution meant that, besides the core document (the FCA 1920), several other constitutional acts and several hundred constitutional provisions exist.[83]

In the second half of the nineteenth century, the establishment of the Supreme Administrative Court (1875) led to an extensive case law with regard to administrative procedural law, which was not codified at that time. The Supreme Administrative Court established principles of administrative procedural law, which were understood as general principles of the rule of law.[84] At the exact same time, the Austrian Parliament, which was established with the Austrian Basic Laws in 1867, increased the intensity of statutory administrative law. The leeway of the monarchic administration was thus reduced step by step, by Parliament on the one hand and the Supreme Administrative Court on the other hand.

After the collapse of the Austro-Hungarian Empire and thus the monarchy in 1918 and the enactment of the FCA in 1920, the Republic of Austria was a democracy, a small federal state (instead of the huge monarchy it had been) in a major economic crisis. The financial pressures led to the necessary reform of the inefficient old monarchic administration, which also resulted in the codification of administrative procedure to increase efficiency of the administration. The enactment of the GAPA as well as the APA and the Administrative Enforcement Act[85] in 1925 created a solid basis for administrative procedural law in Austria, which codified the case law of the Supreme Administrative Court of the previous decades.[86] The establishment of the Constitutional Court in 1920 supplemented the Supreme Administrative Court in reviewing both administrative ordinances

[80] eg, the Constitutio Criminalis Theresiana of 1768.

[81] eg, Basic Law on the General Rights of Nationals (RGBl 142/1867); Basic Law on the Establishment of the Imperial Law Court (RGBl 143/1867); Basic Law on Judicial Power (RGBl 144/1867). See M Stelzer, *The Constitution of the Republic of Austria* (Oxford, Hart Publishing, 2011) 5 f.

[82] See A Gamper, 'The Centennial of the Austrian Federal Constitution', *Blog of the International Journal of Constitutional Law*, 1 October 2020, at: http://www.iconnectblog.com/2020/10/the-centennial-of-the-austrian-federal-constitution.

[83] H Eberhard and K Lachmayer (n 77) 113 ff.

[84] See T Olechowski, 'Die Entwicklung allgemeiner Grundsätze des Verwaltungsverfahrens' in M Holoubek and M Lang (eds), *Allgemeine Grundsätze des Verwaltungs- und Abgabenverfahrens* (Vienna, Linde, 2006) 21 ff; E Schulev-Steindl, *Verwaltungsverfahrensrecht*, 6th edn (Vienna, Verlag Österreich, 2018) 11 ff.

[85] For the historical version, see Verwaltungsvollstreckungsgesetz enacted by BGBl 276/1925; the current version was enacted by BGBl 53/1991 and was last amended by BGBl I 14/2022.

[86] *cf* T Olechowski (n 84) 38 ff.

and administrative decisions. The explicit establishment of the principle of legality in Article 18 FCA also fostered the overall importance of the rule of law.[87]

The codification of the administrative procedure in Austria proved to be a huge success. Further developments after the Second World War were integrated into the existing system, such as the legal protection against direct coercive measures.[88] At the end of the 1980s, due to the case law of the European Court of Human Rights, independent administrative tribunals were established.[89] The ACC started to intensify its human rights case law in the 1980s and expanded on its jurisdiction regarding the constitutional 'rule of law' principle in the 1990s.[90] The accession to the EU in 1995 led to a total revision of the Austrian Constitution, which also affected administrative procedural law.[91] Finally, all these developments resulted in the establishment of administrative courts of first instance in 2014.[92]

The codification of administrative procedural law did not have a negative impact on the development of administration procedures. However, further codifications were missing[93] (perhaps due to the lack of external and economic pressures). Legal protection regarding certain law enforcement Acts (concerning coercive measures by the police) have been integrated into the GAPA; other forms of administrative action still lack legal protection. An academic discussion as to what extent the codification of administrative procedure prohibited the extension of legal protection is missing. The establishment of the administrative courts of first instance required a new procedure for administrative courts, which can, however, serve as an example of 'bad' codification.

## D. The Administrative Courts Procedural Act as 'Bad' Codification

The dominance and importance of the GAPA in administrative procedure obviously proved to be an obstacle for a new codification – almost 90 years later – for the proceedings at the administrative court of first instance. Instead of establishing a fully fledged procedural Act for administrative court proceedings, the legislative

[87] See HP Rill, 'Art. 18 B-VG' in B Kneihs and G Lienbacher (eds), *Rill-Schäffer-Kommentar zum Bundesverfassungsrecht* (Vienna, Verlag Österreich, 2001) fn 1.

[88] Federal Constitutional Act Amendment 1975, Federal Law Gazette 302/1975; see also I Eisenberger et al, *Die Maßnahmenbeschwerde*, 2nd edn (Vienna, Verlag Österreich, 2016) 1 ff.

[89] See W Berka (n 37) 301.

[90] See M Hiesel, 'Die Rechtsstaatsjudikatur des Verfassungsgerichtshofes' (1999) 53 *Österreichische Juristenzeitung* 522, 522 ff.

[91] For the matter of the implementation of interim measures required under EU law, *cf*, eg, T Öhlinger and M Potacs, *EU-Recht und staatliches Recht*, 7th edn (Vienna, LexisNexis, 2020) 149 ff.

[92] See U Giera and K Lachmayer (n 32) 87 f; W Berka (n 37) 300 ff.

[93] See section IV.F below.

department in the federal chancellery (constitutional service) decided to establish a minimalist version. The ACPA only includes half of a codification.[94]

Section 17 ACPA determines that, in the administrative court proceedings, the GAPA will be correspondingly applied as long as the ACPA does not provide other specifications. Therefore, the ACPA does not regulate manifold questions of the court proceedings, which have to be applied by reading the GAPA in a corresponding manner.[95] This legislation strategy to make a normative reference to another procedure proves to be inadequate for many reasons.

First and foremost, while the GAPA determines an administrative procedure, the ACPA addresses court proceedings. The role of the administrative authority in administrative proceedings is to investigate and to decide. There are – in addition – multi-polar procedures (eg, including neighbours) and one-dimensional procedures, while the administrative court is always confronted with two opposite parties (the applicant and the administrative authorities).

Second, the provisions have to be applied in a 'corresponding' manner. This means that the administrative courts of first instance always have to adopt the administrative procedure regarding the objective and structure of the respective court's process. The normative application is therefore always different. It would have made much more sense to take on all provisions of the GAPA and to adopt them on a statutory level. The result would have been a different codification, which would have served the purposes of administrative court proceedings.[96]

The reason for the temptation for the legislator to take on the GAPA can be found in the function of the administrative courts of first instance, which not only review the administrative decision, but are empowered to decide the case themselves. However, the similarity of the power (to decide in the case)[97] did not justify the application of administrative procedural rules in court proceedings, though the constraint of a corresponding application did not improve the problematic reference.

In conclusion, the legislator missed an important opportunity to further develop procedural law in administrative matters. Although the application of the ACPA does not seem to create particular problems, a fully fledged codification would have improved legal certainty and clarity, especially for the applicants. It might be possible to argue that the old codification of the GAPA prohibited a new codification. However, the exact opposite case could also have been possible, since the old codification could have served as an inspiration for repeating the process of codification at the level of administrative courts of first instance.

[94] This is due to the ACPA referring broadly to the GAPA. See s 17 ACPA.

[95] See J Hengstschläger and D Leeb (n 54) 539 f.

[96] See for comparison the German 'Verwaltungsprozessrecht': K Pabel, 'Verwaltungsprozessrecht' (2007) 15 *Journal für Rechtspolitik* 287.

[97] The administrative courts of first instance as a rule decide on the merits of the case and remit only by way of exception. See s 28 ACPA.

## E. The GDPR as a Codification of the Digitalised Administration

A significant development of the last few decades is the increasing digitalisation of the administration. The processing of personal data by the government has created a new dimension of state interference into the rights of individuals. The Austrian approach towards data protection started in the late 1970s. The Austrian Data Protection Act was first enacted in 1978,[98] which established in Article 1 a fundamental right of data protection. The accession to the EU in the 1990s led to a substantive amendment in 2000 to implement the European data protection directive.[99] Finally, in 2018, the General Data Protection Regulation (GDPR) harmonised the concept of data protection in Europe.

The GDPR can be understood as a European codification of administrative action regarding the processing of personal data by the administration. Although the scope of the regulation is much broader,[100] it also creates substantive, procedural and organisational standards which have to be taken into account by all Member States. Nevertheless, the GDPR illustrates the possibilities and limits of codification of administrative law in a multi-level system. Thus, the Member States still have a certain amount of leeway due to various flexibility clauses of the GDPR.

The harmonising and thus also the codifying effect of the GDPR relates to the principles of data processing by the domestic administration, the rights of the data subjects, data security, the establishment and organisation of the national supervisory authority (including its powers), and the legal protection (including complaints lodged with the supervisory authority, effective judicial remedies and liability).[101]

While on the one hand the GDPR creates a certain harmonised level of data processing by domestic administration, the leeway is also significant. First of all, the scope of the GDPR excludes policing and public prosecution, as well as external affairs and policy fields outside the scope of the EU. Second, in certain areas, such as archiving or scientific and statistical purposes, the application of the GDPR is limited. Third, the rights of data subjects can be restricted due to the statutory law of the Member States (Article 23 GDPR). Fourthly, the legitimacy of data processing by the administration depends on the law of the Member States.

Remarkably, the Austrian legislator extended the application of the GDPR to all other areas (also in the sector of public administration), even if the scope of

[98] Federal Data Protection Act 1978, Federal Law Gazette 565/1978.

[99] Directive 95/46/EC of the European Parliament and of the Council of 24 October 1995 on the protection of individuals with regard to the processing of personal data and on the free movement of such data [1995] OJ L281/31; Federal Data Protection Act 2000, Federal Law Gazette I 165/1999.

[100] See Case C-272/19 *VQ v Land Hessen* ECLI:EU:C:2020:535.

[101] See P Voigt and A von dem Bussche (n 49).

the GDPR would exclude its application. Only in the field of policing and public prosecution does the Austrian Data Protection Act implement the particular EU Directive and a specific Research Organisation Act[102] determines data processing in the field of research.[103]

In conclusion, the GDPR illustrates that the codification of administrative law is no longer only a domestic issue. Another example relates to public procurement, which is also highly regulated at a European level, especially regarding its procedural elements.[104] When the EU starts to create legal frameworks in administrative law,[105] the possibility of codification at a national level might disappear, but a European harmonisation will enable a European codification, at least at a certain (more abstract) level. Particularities of the Member States will not vanish. Codification has to be understood differently, in a more complex concept of multi-level systems.

## F. Missing/Possible Codifications

The potential for further codification to improve the systematisation and stringency of administrative law is very great. The following examples will illustrate this.

### *i. Revisiting the Principles of Administrative Law*

The principles of administrative law are part of Austrian constitutional law. Most of the text dates back to 1920. While the state and society have changed, most of the principles remain the same. Articles 18–23 FCA contain most of these principles. A reformulation of these principles could create a new systematisation (eg, the principle of efficiency) and codification of the case law of the ACC (eg, effective legal protection), and important modifications and supplements (eg, the transparency principle).[106] The revision of the constitutional principles of administrative law is not very likely due to a lack of academic or political debate on this subject.

### *ii. General Ordinance Procedural Act*

Another example of a possible codification would be a General Ordinance Procedural Act. During the COVID-19 crisis, the lack of such an Act has become evident. The ACC requires justifications for certain rights-restrictive measures

[102] Forschungsorganisationsgesetz enacted by BGBl 341/1981, as amended by BGBl I Nr 116/2022.
[103] K Lachmayer, 'Die DSGVO im öffentlichen Bereich' (2018) 72 *Österreichische Juristenzeitung* 112, 113; K Lachmayer and E Souhrada-Kirchmayer, 'Datenschutzrecht in der wissenschaftlichen Forschung' (2018) 17 *zeitschrift für hochschulrecht, hochschulmanagement und hochschulpolitik* 153, 153 ff.
[104] *cf* W Schwartz (n 56) 157 ff.
[105] See in this context the ReNEUAL project (n 7).
[106] For the principles of administrative law, see section III.A above.

of the government, which have been enacted by ordinance.[107] However, the government could not provide the specific justifications due to deficits in the administrative procedure. Although the GAPA can only serve as a model to a limited extent, the possibility to create a similar (perhaps shorter) form of codification would determine the minimum requirements of a procedure to enact ordinances by the government or administrative authorities. Again, the political realisation of such a project is very unlikely, as there is neither an academic nor a political discussion about it.

### *iii. Freedom of Information Act*

In contrast to these two proposals, the enactment of a Freedom of Information Act is very likely. The efforts already made will enable the next step towards a codification of the freedom of information,[108] which will at least have the potential to change the culture of Austrian administration. While there are still voices in favour of prohibiting increased access to information concerning internal governmental activities, the importance of creating more effective access is steadily increasing as the politicisation of the ministries gains speed.

### *iv. A General Administrative Law Act?*

These examples illustrate singular examples of possible progress in the Austrian systematisation of administrative law. This leads to the final question regarding the possibility of a GALA. Again, a discussion is not taking place, which reduces the likelihood of such a step in Austrian administrative law. However, the substantive potential of a GALA is quite clear. A GALA could close the gaps regarding the missing codification of forms of administrative action. The Act could serve not only to enumerate and define different administrative forms, but could also link them with legal protection at the administrative courts of first instance. This statutory law would finally remove the still existing deficits in legal protection in administrative law in Austria. Moreover, the case law of the ACC and the Supreme Administrative Court regarding the implementation of administrative Acts shaped by the EU could be codified.

## V. Conclusion

Austrian administrative law is partly codified and has the potential for further codification. But is codification still a concept which seems attractive in the twenty-first century?

[107] See ACC 1 October 2020, G 271/2020-16, V 463-467/2020-16.
[108] *cf* in this context M Bertel, 'Informationsfreiheit statt Amtsgeheimnis?' (2014) 22 *Journal für Rechtspolitik* 203.

In the nineteenth century, codifications seemed to promise a new organisation of society with codified law playing an important role. The codifications promised legal security, clarity and even legal protection. The climax of these rule-of-law developments was the codification of constitutional law, which re-created the legal system. The codification of administrative law served the specific purpose of empowering the individual to enforce its rights against the state.

In the twenty-first century, we are living in a post-codification era. Old codifications are perforated with European and international law as well as weakened by the transferal of significant rule-making powers onto private actors. The power of codifications is decreasing. Hybrid legal pluralism triggered by internationalisation and involvement of private actors has created fragmentations in international law, constitutional law and administrative law. The network society is mirrored in legal multi-level networks, which enact new law in increasingly shorter time periods. Codification seems to be a relic from times long gone.

Paradoxically, the potential of codification still exists today. Austrian administrative law can serve as an example. Structural dynamics have not been addressed or even discussed in a systematic way. But this is what codifications have to offer. The answer provided by codifications is to build a systematic approach in times of confusion. A political debate concerning a codification of administrative law (which has not taken place so far) would enable legal scholarship as well as political bodies to question the traditional and confused legal structures. The situation has not changed since the beginning of the twentieth century, when the case law of the Supreme Administrative Court had to compensate for the structural deficits of administrative procedural law in Austria. At the beginning of the twenty-first century, the benefits of the codification of administrative law would be still the same as 100 years ago: legal certainty, efficient administration and effective legal protection.

# 3

# Codification of Belgian Administrative Law

## *'Nothing is Written'**

STÉPHANIE DE SOMER AND INGRID OPDEBEEK

## I. The Definition and Delimitation of Belgian Administrative Law

There is no consensus in Belgian legal doctrine on an overall definition of (general) administrative law. A well-known textbook, which has now reached its 22nd edition, describes administrative law as 'the law that applies itself to regulating the state's task after one has left out the legislative and judicial task'.[1] Hence, administrative law is deemed to regulate *one* of the powers of the *trias politica*: the executive. This definition is still a good starting point, but (like all definitions) has its flaws.

First, it presupposes that it is evident to define and demarcate 'the executive' as a separate state power in the Belgian legal order. An outsider who read the Belgian Constitution would have to conclude that the federal executive power rests (exclusively) with the King and his ministers (Article 37 of the Constitution). In reality, executive power is scattered and resides with various state, semi-state and non-state actors. The same is true at the level of the regions and communities (Belgium's federated entities).[2] Debates continue as to the extent to which some of these bodies (government-owned enterprises, autonomous public bodies with a private law form etc) fall within the scope of certain rules or principles of administrative law.

* Quote from *Lawrence of Arabia*.

[1] A Mast, J Dujardin, M Van Damme and J Vande Lanotte, *Overzicht van het Belgisch Administratief Recht* (Mechelen, Kluwer, 2021) 3. All translations in the chapter have been done by the authors.

[2] For a glimpse into the complexity of Belgian administrative organisation, see S de Somer (ed), *Bestuursorganisatierecht* (Bruges, die Keure, 2020).

Second, while it is true that administrative law has not been developed to regulate the activities of the legislature or the judiciary, it may do so in specific circumstances, ie, when these institutions exercise *administrative* power. If a parliamentary assembly, for instance, takes a decision relating to its administrative staff or to public procurement, that decision is subject to judicial review by the Council of State, ie, the general administrative court[3] and to the statutory legislation on the duty to give reasons[4]. Moreover, all the courts, including the civil courts, have the power to set aside (disapply) these administrative acts if they are unlawful (Article 159 of the Constitution), in the same way as they do for administrative acts issued by executive bodies.

Third, state actors that pertain to the executive power from an institutional point of view may sometimes contribute to the legislative or judicial function. In those cases, typical rules or principles of administrative law may not apply to them. According to the Council of State, for instance, the Minister of Justice does not act as a so-called 'administrative authority' (ie, a concept central to the definition of the Council of State's jurisdiction) when (s)he contributes directly to the execution of criminal judgments. This is, for instance, the case if (s)he decides to transfer a person, who does not consent, to a foreign prison following a sentence of life imprisonment imposed by a criminal court.[5] Moreover, it is important to acknowledge that executive or administrative bodies, even if they do not act as 'auxiliaries' of the legislature or the judiciary, assume a wide variety of tasks, which cover a much broader range of actions than merely 'executing' statutory law. The normative powers of executive bodies, for instance, have extended in the last few decades. Certainly, many normative acts still intend to execute legislation, but many others rely on an explicit delegation by the legislature to enact rules that would have otherwise been made by that legislature itself. Parts of this normative dimension of the executive power are regulated by constitutional law; many of the principles of 'good law-making' that apply to statutory legislation will, for instance, also apply to subordinate legislation. However, administrative law plays an important role too. For instance, Belgium's general administrative court, the Council of State, has the power to suspend and quash subordinate legislation (not only administrative decisions with an individual scope) and will apply the principles of 'good administration' (eg, the prohibition of bias) to these acts as far as is relevant.

[3] Article 14, § 1, first indention, 2° Gecoördineerde wetten op de Raad van State.

[4] Wet 29 juli 1991 betreffende de uitdrukkelijke motivering van bestuurshandelingen, BS 12 September 1991, as interpreted by the Constitutional Court in Arbitragehof 29 January 2004, n° 17/2004.

[5] eg, CoS 25 October 2016, n° 236.252, Klepadlo.

Administrative authorities are also increasingly involved in law enforcement (ie, the field of 'administrative enforcement') and take up quasi-judicial tasks such as conflict resolution. This is, for instance, the case for the independent regulatory bodies in the network industries, whose status and missions are today to a large extent determined by EU law.[6] Considering the increasing importance of administrative enforcement, a whole new area within general administrative law has started to develop, where scholars are seeking general rules and principles that govern this aspect of the executive's actions specifically.[7]

On the cover of our textbook on Belgian general administrative law[8] (see Figure 3.1 below), we use the image of a tree to visualise what administrative law is and what role it fulfils. The tree's *roots* are what we call the 'meta values' of administrative law: its underlying constitutional values (democratic governance, separation of powers and the rule of law) and the principles of good governance (eg, accountability, effectiveness/efficiency, integrity, participation and transparency), which inspire many of the recent developments in administrative law. The *treetop*, with numerous branches and leaves, represents the specific branches of administrative law (planning law, environmental law, asylum law, educational law etc). Between the two is the *trunk*, which grows from the roots and feeds the treetop. The idea that we want to convey is that general administrative law covers those concepts, theories, principles and rules that are either common to all specific areas of administrative law or serve as a 'safety net' if the often technical and detailed rules in those specific areas do not offer a solution to a certain problem. Figure 3.1 shows a picture of the tree. The words in the trunk (in Dutch) refer to key topics of general administrative law, such as the principles of good administration and the concept of an 'administrative act'.

The following topics are typically discussed in textbooks on general administrative law: its sources and instruments, the powers and prerogatives of the administration, the status of its staff (especially tenured civil servants, but also employees working under contracts) and property (goods), administrative organisation, the various guarantees with a preventive purpose offered to citizens and other administrations faced with administrative action (eg, the principles of good administration, freedom of information and the duty to give reasons) and the various forms of appeal and judicial review against administrative action.

[6] See S De Somer, *Autonomous public bodies and the law: a European perspective* (Cheltenham, Edward Elgar, 2017); S De Somer, 'The powers of national regulatory authorities as agents of EU law' (2018) *ERA Forum* 581.

[7] For a first attempt to identify some of these rules and principles, see I Opdebeek and S De Somer (eds), *Bestuurlijke handhaving in vogelvlucht* (Bruges, die Keure, 2018).

[8] I Opdebeek and S De Somer, *Algemeen bestuursrecht – Grondslagen en beginselen* (Antwerp, Intersentia, 2019).

**Figure 3.1** Picture of the tree on the authors' textbook on general administrative law (reproduced with the kind permission of Intersentia)

# II. Legal Sources of Belgian Administrative Law

## A. Introduction

'Who is still able to find their way in the labyrinth that is Belgian administrative law?' This question opens the abstract on the cover of our textbook, which was introduced above. Whereas many other areas of the law in Belgium are governed by a single or a limited number of dominant legislative act(s) (the Civil Code, the Criminal Code, the Code on Economic Law, the Code of Companies and Associations etc), those who study administrative law do not have that luxury. Administrative law is a mishmash of legislation (often only aimed at tackling a single problem) and principles or theories developed in the case law (unwritten law). Administrative law indeed often seems an impenetrable labyrinth. It is a puzzle for which the player himself/herself has to locate all the pieces in the first place before (s)he can start fitting them together. 'Law finding' in this area of the law is therefore particularly challenging.

## B. Forms of Action (ie, Instruments)

Central to administrative action is the principle of legality in its formal meaning, ie, the basic premise that all executive power is conferred power. Apart from the powers that the Constitution itself has entrusted to the executive, it possesses only those powers that the legislature has explicitly provided it with. This principle is expressed in Article 105 of the Constitution for the federal executive and Article 78 of the Special Act on the Reform of the Institutions[9] (SARI) for the regions and communities (the federated entities). These provisions only speak of the King (ie, the federal Government) and the governments at the level of the federated entities (ie, central government institutions). However, the principle of conferred powers applies to decentralised authorities too. The legislature who wishes to entrust them with decision-making powers, has to enshrine these powers in that legislative Act and the decentralised body only possesses those specific statutory powers. For the federated entities, this is explicitly mentioned in Article 9 of the SARI; for the federal level, the Constitution is silent. However, legal doctrine assumes that Article 105 of the Constitution expresses a more general legal principle of conferred powers (with constitutional value), which also applies to decentralised entities.[10]

[9] The SARI is a statutory Act with special weight governing the organisation, competences and powers of the federated entities.

[10] See, eg, I Mathy, 'Être ou ne pas être une personne juridique distincte de l'État, la Communauté ou la Région? L'autonomie avec ou sans personnalité juridique' in P Jadoul, B Lombaert and F Tulkens (eds), *Le paraétatisme. Nouveaux regards sur la décentralisation fonctionnelle en Belgique et dans les institutions européennes* (Brussels, la Charte, 2010) 31, 49 ff and 77 ff.

The principle of conferred powers refers both to the substantive competences of the executive body (which goals can/should it pursue with its actions?; which responsibilities have been entrusted to it?) and to the unilateral decision-making powers that these bodies possess to fulfil their missions. Decision-making powers implying that the administration can unilaterally determine the legal position of an individual indeed always require an explicit basis in the legislation.[11] This is, for instance, the case for the power to grant or refuse a permit (eg, to build or to exercise a certain profession) or the power to impose administrative sanctions.

Rule-making by the administration is considered a special form of *unilateral decision-making*. Hence, the same principle of conferred powers applies. The King (federal Government) derives some of his rule-making powers directly from the Constitution, such as the power to enact subordinate legislation that does nothing more than execute federal statutory acts (Article 108 of the Constitution). A similar power follows from Article 20 of the SARI for the federated entities. However, the decentralised entities and other autonomous public bodies can only enact rules if and to the extent that statutory legislation grants them this power.

The power to take unilateral decisions is often considered one of the key characteristics of administrative authorities; it is their prerogative and distinguishes them from private actors. However, administrative authorities also fulfil their missions, making use of private law instruments such as *contracts*. No written source of Belgian law enshrines general rules on if, when or under what circumstances the administration can conclude contracts. Yet, it is generally accepted that the 'contractual route' is open to the administration, based on the so-called 'tweewegenleer' ('theory of the two routes'), for which Belgian (mostly Flemish) legal doctrine has sought inspiration from Dutch law. It is assumed that the rule enshrined in Article 5.40 of the Civil Code, according to which everyone can conclude a contract if they have not been declared incapable by the law, applies to the administration too and that the principle of conferred powers, which requires an explicit statutory basis in every individual case, does not apply to contracts.[12] However, some limits have been recognised by legal doctrine in this respect, again mostly copied from Dutch law.[13] In recent years the courts have started to contribute to this debate as well. In two landmark judgments, for instance, the Council of State has clarified that an administrative authority entering into a contract violates the prohibition of bias (a principle of good administration) if, in that contract, it commits itself to exercising the (discretionary) powers entrusted

[11] See, eg, K Leus, 'Overeenkomsten met de overheid en overheidsovereenkomsten: bijzondere overeenkomsten en algemeen belang. De "gemene", de "gemengde" of de "zuivere" rechtsleer?' in *Bijzondere overeenkomsten, XXXIVe Postuniversitaire cyclus W. Delva 2007–2008* (Mechelen, Kluwer, 2008) 405, 409.

[12] eg, D D'Hooghe, 'Overeenkomsten met de overheid' in *De overeenkomst, vandaag en morgen, XVIe Postuniversitaire cyclus W. Delva* (Antwerp, Kluwer, 1990) 129, 134 ff. Not all legal doctrine agrees on this line of reasoning, however. See, eg, K Leus (n 11) 405, 409 and 411 ff.

[13] See the summary in I Opdebeek and S De Somer (n 8) 140.

to it by statutory law in a certain way.[14] The administration cannot, for instance, declare that it will, in the future, grant planning permission for a specific project; it will have to assess the application after it has been submitted, respecting the substantive and procedural rules then in place and making use of its power and duty to take into account all the specifics of the case.

Belgian legislation, case law or legal doctrine does not genuinely acknowledge the difference between 'contrats administratifs' (administrative contracts) and 'contrats de l'administration' (private law contracts), as is the case in the French tradition. However, some contracts are specific to the administration, since one of the parties will always be an administrative authority. Specific rules may apply to these contracts and these can follow from legislation, case law, legal doctrine or a combination of these sources. Public procurement, for instance, is governed by extensive and detailed (federal) legislation, which implements EU directives. The same is true for concessions for works and services. Concessions of so-called 'public domain goods', which grant an exclusive right of use on, for instance, a part of the beach or a park, are in principle subject to the rules of private law (the general law on contracts). Yet, often, specific legislation applies to specific types of concessions (eg, concessions for graves). Moreover, both the case law (the Council of State and civil courts) and legal doctrine have put forward a number of 'corrections' on private law that are deemed necessary for reasons of public interest, eg, to ensure the continued use of the good in question in the public interest.[15] It is assumed, for instance, in much of the case law and legal doctrine that the administration can put an end to the contract unilaterally if this is in the general interest.[16]

Another important instrument is *soft law*. Specific legislation may allow or oblige the administration to issue policy rules, circulars etc on a specific matter. Neither the Constitution nor any legislative Act regulates the power of the administration to issue soft law if a specific statutory basis is lacking. It is in the case law of the Council of State and legal doctrine that we find the acknowledgement of a principle that administrative authorities can subject their own discretionary powers (and those of the entities under their hierarchical authority) to 'directives' or 'rules of conduct' to ensure consistency.[17] In the Council of State's case law, rules and principles have been developed governing the legal status of these instruments.

[14] CoS 28 May 2014, n° 227.578, Provincie Vlaams-Brabant et al; CoS 7 July 2016, n° 235.392, Orye. This and subsequent case law concerning similar cases provoked a lot of questions and caused uncertainty for local authorities. See, eg, S De Somer, 'De invloed van beleidsovereenkomsten op de onpartijdigheid van het bestuur: "partij = partijdig?"' (2020) *Tijdschrift voor Gemeenterecht* 209; S Verbeyst, 'Voorafgaande contractuele afspraken nekken RUP Vijverhof. Welk lot is deze overeenkomsten nog beschoren?' (2019) *Tijdschrift voor Ruimtelijke Ordening, Omgeving en Stedenbouw* 229.

[15] See, eg, S Van Garsse, *De concessie in het raam van de publiek-private samenwerking* (Bruges, die Keure, 2007).

[16] See, eg, Court of Appeal Antwerp, 4 September 2014, n° 2012/AR/1256.

[17] See, eg, the references in K Leus, *Pseudo-wetgeving* (Antwerp, Maklu, 1992) 140; D D'Hooghe, 'Bestuurlijke vrijheid geklemd tussen de beginselen inzake rechtszekerheid, wettigheid en veranderlijkheid', (1993–94) *Rechtskundig Weekblad* 1091, 1095.

The power to impose *administrative sanctions* was mentioned previously as an example of a unilateral decision-making power, which thus requires an explicit legislative basis. In Flanders, a recent statutory Act (decree) discussed further under section 3 of this report[18] offers an autonomous basis for Flemish administrative authorities to impose administrative fines, but only as an alternative to criminal sanctions enshrined in the applicable sectorial legislation (implying that the public prosecutor decides not to pursue the case before the criminal courts).[19] However, sanctions are not the only instruments of administrative enforcement. Enforcement requires supervisory powers, which often restrict fundamental rights. Under Belgian constitutional law, this means that they require a basis in statutory law. As a reaction to an (impending) infringement, administrative authorities may also have powers to impose preventive or reparatory measures, which are not sanctions, since they do not aim to punish, but which may have equally far-reaching consequences (eg, the closure of a company for safety reasons). Like sanctions, these powers will be anchored in statutory law.

In conclusion, identifying the instruments that the administration can use to complete its missions requires studying a variety of sources. As far as the power to enter into contracts and to issue soft law are concerned, the courts and legal doctrine have in reality offered justifications for practices that were already widespread, but were not (and are still not) as such acknowledged by the Constitution.

The administration's *powers and duties to impart information* to citizens are spread over a variety of legislative acts. Article 32 of the Constitution qualifies freedom of information, ie, right of access to public documents, as a fundamental right. The various legislatures (both at the federal level and the level of the federated entities) have issued legislative acts giving further content to this right, anchoring the procedure to obtain access, the exceptions that apply etc. This legislation also lays down certain obligations for administrative bodies to provide the public with information *on their own initiative*.[20] The duty of care, a principle of good administration (see section II.C below), can sometimes also function as a source of a duty for the administration to inform citizens.

## C. Principles of Action

Neither at the federal level nor at the level of the federated entities (which, within certain limits, have the competence to legislate on issues of general administrative law for the administrations under their responsibility) has the legislature issued

[18] Kaderdecreet Bestuurlijke Handhaving. This decree does not have automatic supplementary force: see below, section III.B.

[19] See art 51. See below: there are plans to replace the decree by a new one. The available texts reveal, however, that a similar provision to article 51 of the current decree would be included in that new instrument.

[20] eg, arts II.1 ff of the Flemish Bestuursdecreet.

a general legislative framework on administrative procedure, comparable to, for instance, the German Verwaltungsverfahrensgesetz. Such a general legislative framework could regulate the following questions:

- What are the time limits within which the administration has to take a decision, especially after an application/question to do so by a citizen?
- What happens if the administration does not respect that time limit?
- Which acts of the administration are subject to a duty to give reasons?
- Under what circumstances is the administration obliged to hear persons affected by its intended decision?
- Under what circumstances is the administration obliged to organise a consultation of another form of participation?
- Can administrative acts be revoked?

The answers to these questions are found in different sources of law. Some aspects of administrative procedure are regulated by statutory acts. This is, for instance, the case for the duty to give reasons: an important federal statutory Act of 1991 (which also applies to the federated entities) contains general rules; however, specific legislation can enshrine more specific or stricter rules. For other aspects, there is no legislative framework and the principles of good administration, developed in the case law (see below), fill the gaps when the specific legislation enshrining a decision-making power is silent. This is the case for the duty to hear persons affected by administrative decisions: if the legislation conferring the power on the administration is silent, the case law of the Council of State on the *audi alteram partem* principle determines under which conditions and how a hearing has to be organised. The same applies to timely decision-making: in the absence of normative provisions, the reasonable time requirement applies, ie, another principle of good administration.

The principles of good administration have primarily been developed in the case law of the Council of State.[21] Both French and Dutch administrative law served as an inspiration.[22] Moreover, some principles of administration have a direct link with the Belgian Constitution or with fundamental rights enshrined in the European Convention on Human Rights (ECHR). The principle of equality is, for example, a derivative of Articles 10 and 11 of the Constitution. The case

[21] See I Opdebeek and M Van Damme (eds), *Beginselen van behoorlijk bestuur* (Bruges, die Keure, 2006); SB Messaoud and F Viseur (eds), *Les principes généraux de droit administratif – Actualités et Applications Pratiques* (Brussels, Larcier, 2017).

[22] See the references in P Popelier, 'Beginselen van behoorlijk bestuur: begrip en plaats in de hiërarchie van de normen' in I Opdebeek and M Van Damme (eds), *Beginselen van behoorlijk bestuur* (Bruges, die Keure, 2006) 3, 4. Popelier refers to the legal scholar Suetens, whose research played a substantial role in the introduction of the Dutch principles of good administration in the Belgian case law. See L-P Suetens, 'Algemene rechtsbeginselen en algemene beginselen van behoorlijk bestuur in het Belgisch administratief recht' (1970) *Tijdschrift voor Bestuurswetenschappen en Publiekrecht* 379.

law on the reasonable time requirement has, for instance, been influenced by Article 6 ECHR and the European Court of Human Rights' case law.[23]

We have no obvious evidence that private law concepts and principles, such as good faith, have also influenced the development of principles of good administration in the Council of State's case law. Nevertheless, it seems obvious that the principles of good administration are in essence concretisations of the general duty of care to which all legal subjects – citizens and the administration – are subject.[24] In civil law, this duty is mostly associated with Articles 1382 ff of the (old) Belgian Civil Code, ie, Belgian tort law. Moreover, there are an increasing number of judgments issued by the civil courts that interpret private law concepts, such as 'good faith', in the light of principles of good administration when they apply these concepts to the actions of public actors.[25]

There is no exact consensus on a list of principles of good administration, but there is an agreement that the following principles qualify as such: the principle of due care, *audi alteram partem* (duty to hear), the principle of impartiality (prohibition of bias), the duty to have (adequate, proper, reasonable) reasons (*not* the duty to give reasons – see above), the principle of reasonableness, the principle of proportionality, the principle of equality and non-discrimination, the principle of legal certainty (including the prohibition of retroactivity), the duty to respect legitimate expectations and the reasonable time requirement. Whereas some of these principles have no *direct* impact on the contents of the administrative decision (eg, the duty to hear or the reasonable time requirement) and are hence more procedural than substantive in nature, they naturally all aim to force administrations to take proper, well-informed decisions. Even though we have no exact figures to substantiate this claim, it is obvious that the administrative courts are more reluctant to grant relief due to a substantive illegality than they are for procedural deficiencies. Annulments for a violation of legitimate expectations or the principle of reasonableness are therefore rare. However, in the past decade, (some chambers of) the Council of State have let go of the requirement that only 'obvious' unreasonable behaviour can be sanctioned, which came down to a marginal scrutiny.[26] It remains to be seen whether this will in reality signify a change in the intensity of review.[27]

Whereas the principles of good administration typically entail *guarantees* for citizens, as a counterweight for the often exorbitant powers of the administration,

[23] See, eg, CoS, 21 November 2016, n° 236.468, Van Mieghem.

[24] I Opdebeek, *Rechtsbescherming tegen het stilzitten van het bestuur* (Bruges, die Keure, 1992) 31.

[25] See I Opdebeek and S De Somer, 'De polsstokwerking van de beginselen van behoorlijk bestuur: export en reflexwerking?' in S Lierman and L Wiggers-Rust (eds), *Platform voor publiek- en privaatrecht in dialoog* (Nijmegen, Wolf Publishers, 2021) 83.

[26] See, eg, CoS, 10 July 2012, nos 220.242 and 220.243, Universiteit Gent.

[27] On the standard and intensity of review applied by the courts with respect to administrative acts, see P-J van de Weyer, *De rechterlijke toetsing van bestuursrechtelijke handelingen. De invloed van de vereiste van volle rechtsmacht in de zin van artikel 6 EVRM* (Antwerp, Intersentia, 2021).

another set of principles primarily intend to *reinforce* those powers: the so-called 'lois du service public' (laws of public service).[28] These include the principle of continuity, the principle of change and the principle of equal utilisation. The principle of continuity, for instance, allows the members of administrative bodies whose mandate has expired to lawfully continue to take decisions until the competent entity has appointed new members. The principle of change allows administrative bodies to change the place of employment of (tenured) civil servants if this is necessary to ensure the continued provision of a public service. These principles, which were transposed from French law, have been recognised by both the administrative and civil courts as general principles of administrative law.

As far as administrative law principles are concerned, Belgian law is still evolving. Scarcely more than a decade ago, for instance, the highest courts in Belgium began to recognise a new general principle: the so-called principle of 'equality of citizens vis-à-vis public burdens'. In a nutshell, this principle grants citizens a right to compensation for the damage resulting from legitimate public action (in the public interest) when certain conditions (thresholds) have been fulfilled.[29] According to the Supreme Court (Court of Cassation) and the Constitutional Court, this principle finds its origins in a number of articles of the Constitution (Articles 10, 11 and 16, ie, the principle of equality and non-discrimination and the protection of property rights vis-à-vis public actors).[30] However, it seems that inspiration was also drawn from France and the Netherlands, where this principle is also known.

EU law also has an impact in this respect. Increasingly, Belgian principles of good administration have to be interpreted in the light of their European counterparts, which may offer more guarantees to citizens. For instance, the 'duty of transparency' that public actors have to respect whenever they grant so-called 'scarce rights' flows directly from the case law of the Court of Justice of the European Union (based on Articles 49 and 56 of the Treaty on the Functioning of the European Union) of and/or the Services Directives, and has found its way to the case law of the Belgian Council of State.[31]

## D. Administrative Organisation

The Constitution and the SARI contain very few provisions on administrative organisation. It is assumed that the King (the federal Government), as head of the

[28] See H Dumont et al (eds), *Le service public 2. Les 'lois' du service public* (Bruges, die Keure, 2009); S Ben Messaoud and F Viseur (n 21).

[29] See S De Winter, 'Property Restrictions in the Public Interest in Light of the Equality of Citizens before Public Burdens' in J Robbie and B Akkermans (eds), *Property Law Perspectives VII* (The Hague, Eleven International Publishing, 2021) 87.

[30] See, eg, Court of Cassation, 24 June 2010, n° AR C.06.0415; Constitutional Court, 19 April 2012, n° 55/2012.

[31] eg, CoS, 23 December 2015, n° 233.355, nv Kinepolis Mega.

federal executive power (Article 37 of the Constitution), decides on the organisation of the central administrations (the ministries and agencies without legal personality). The same applies to the regional and communal governments as far as their central administrations are concerned (Article 87 of the SARI). Central administration at the federal level and that of the federated entities is organised according to the principle of hierarchy: the civil servants working in these services are subject to the hierarchical authority of the competent minister(s). This principle as such is not enshrined in the Constitution or in the SARI. It is derived from the fact that the executive is accountable to Parliament, which means that it has to possess the power to intervene in individual cases by giving orders, by revoking decisions or via substitution.

The Constitution *does* dedicate substantial attention to the so-called 'territorially decentralised bodies', ie, the provinces and municipalities (Articles 41 and 162). It enshrines their existence and autonomy to decide on matters of provincial/local interest as well as a number of basic rules from which the competent legislature cannot deviate, such as the principle that their councils are elected bodies. Pursuant to Article 6, VIII of the SARI, the regions are competent to legislate on the organisation and functioning of the provinces and municipalities. Hence, all the regions have enacted their own legislation in this respect (eg, the Provinciedecreet and the Decreet Lokaal Bestuur in Flanders).

By nature, provisions in (quasi-)constitutional documents evolve slowly and tend to lag behind reality. As has been the case in most European states, Belgian public administration has seen a proliferation of autonomous or independent agencies in the past few decades. Often, these agencies have their own legal personality and are thus not part of central administrative organisation. According to a general legal principle, legal personality can only be granted by or pursuant to a legislative act. Hence, the creation of so-called 'decentralised' administrative bodies requires an intervention by the legislature. As far as the federated entities are concerned, Article 9 of the SARI offers an explicit basis for this principle and specifies that the legislature at the level of the federated entities not only has to create these separate legal persons, but also has to legislate on their composition, the competences that they enjoy, the way in which they function (make decisions) and the forms of oversight to which they are subject. The Constitution does not provide anything similar for the federal level; in fact, it does not contain a single provision on autonomous public bodies (independent or executive agencies). The principles that apply to their creation and institutional design have been developed mainly in the case law of the Constitutional Court, in the advisory practice of the Council of State (Legislative Section) and in legal doctrine. The emergence of independent agencies that are insulated from any form of political influence or oversight, ie, the so-called *autorités administratives indépendantes*,[32] has given rise to fierce constitutional debates.[33] Clear provisions

[32] These include mainly regulatory bodies in the network industries and the data protection authority.

[33] See, eg, S De Somer, 'The Political Independence of National Regulatory Authorities: EU Impulse versus National Restraint' (2015) *Revue du droit des industries de réseau* 193.

in the Constitution and the SARI on the possibility of entrusting such bodies with executive power are lacking. EU law increasingly obliges Member States to create these types of bodies and to entrust them with far-reaching (rule-making, adjudicatory and quasi-judicial) powers. The Belgian Constitutional Court has mainly referred to these obligations of supranational law to legitimise delegation to these bodies.[34]

For some types of autonomous public bodies, the legislature has enacted framework legislation. However, the contents of this legislation vary. At the federal level, the most important examples are an Act of 1954 containing provisions on the forms of administrative and financial oversight that apply to (a large number of) decentralised agencies and an Act of 1991 governing the legal position of the federal economic government-owned enterprises. At the Flemish level, the Kaderdecreet Bestuurlijk Beleid used to offer a good example of framework legislation governing the creation, institutional design and forms of control applicable to autonomous public bodies (Flemish agencies). At present, most of the provisions in the Kaderdecreet have been abolished and included in the Bestuursdecreet (see below), but the latter is less ambitious and no longer anchors any provisions on the motives/valid reasons for agencification.

Increasingly, the provision of public services is outsourced to private entities as well. Various constitutional rules and general legal principles influence the extent to which this is possible and the conditions that have to be respected, but neither the Constitution nor the SARI contains any explicit provisions in this respect.[35] The same is true of the delegation of rule-making powers to private entities.[36]

Agencification in the form of decentralisation typically involves the creation of a legal person *sui generis*. The legislature is not bound by private company and association law. Increasingly, however, legislatures do make use of private law forms, such as by authorising the executive to establish an agency in the form of a private foundation. There are no specific constitutional or legal provisions prescribing the possibilities and limits that exist in this respect either. Again, legal doctrine has deduced these from a series of constitutional and quasi-constitutional provisions and principles.[37]

Belgium does not know a single set of legal provisions governing the status of all government staff. Tenured civil servants[38] are typically subject to a set of specific rules, governing their selection and appointment, deontology (professional ethics)

[34] See, eg, Constitutional Court, 18 November 2010, n° 130/2010.

[35] M De Groot, *Overheidstoezicht op private rechtspersonen belast met taken van openbare dienst* (Bruges, die Keure, 2018).

[36] C Jenart, *Outsourcing rulemaking powers: constitutional limits and national safeguards* (Oxford, Oxford University Press, 2022).

[37] See, eg, F Vandendriessche, *Publieke en private rechtspersonen: naar een graduele, meerduidige en evolutieve benadering van het onderscheid in de wetgeving en de rechtspraak* (Bruges, die Keure, 2004).

[38] Government staff employed via contract are subject to the rules of general employment law, even though specific rules may apply to them too, as far as these are compatible with general employment law.

and discipline, the way in which they are evaluated, the various ways in which their employment can come to an end etc. These rules vary at the various political and administrative levels. At the federal level, for instance, the King has the (exclusive) competence to enact rules for the civil servants in central government services (eg, working in ministries) via royal decrees. This competence is derived from Articles 37 and 107, second indention of the Constitution. The various governments of the federated entities have a similar competence for their central level administrations (Article 87, §4 of the SARI). However, the federal legislature is competent to legislate on pensions, including those of the government staff at the level of the federated entities. As mentioned earlier, the regions are competent to legislate on the organisation and functioning of the provinces and municipalities. The Flemish legislature has enacted a number of general rules on provincial and municipal government staff, which were complemented by subordinate legislation issued by the Flemish Government. Nevertheless, the provinces and municipalities themselves enjoy considerable autonomy in this respect and have their own by-laws anchoring specific rules for their staff. For some specific functions, such as police personnel (Article 184, first indention of the Constitution), the Constitution requires statutory law to define (at least) the essential aspects of the rules applicable to civil servants.

Even though all this statutory and subordinate legislation often contains quite detailed provisions on the legal position of civil servants, the role played by the unwritten principles of good administration, developed in the case law, should not be underestimated. They offer important guarantees to civil servants, concerning, for example, equal access to the public service (the principle of equality), the right to be heard in a number of cases (eg, in case of a negative evaluation) and the right to a decision by an impartial administration (eg, in disciplinary cases). Since many rules governing the status of civil servants are not anchored in statutory law but in subordinate legislation, and since subordinate legislation has to comply with the principles of good administration,[39] the Council's case law has an important unifying effect in this area of general administrative law.

## E. Preventive Legal Protection (During the Administrative Procedure), Appeal and Judicial Review

As mentioned earlier, there is no legislative Act (either at the federal level or at the level of the sub-state entities) containing general or default rules on administrative procedure. The legislation entrusting the administration with a specific decision-making power will typically contain rules on the procedure to be followed. The gaps in the legislation are filled by the principles of good administration

[39] There is an ongoing debate in Belgian legal doctrine on the question of whether the principles of good administration have constitutional value, which would mean that statutory law would have to comply with them/respect them as well.

(see section II.C above), such as the *audi alteram partem* principle, and by other general theories developed in the case law (eg, on the withdrawal of administrative acts).

Up until today, there is no general principle of good administration obliging administrative authorities to organise consultations or other forms of public participation for specific decisions. They are only obliged to do so if the applicable norm says as much. At the local level in particular, participation plays an increasingly important role, as it does in the fields of planning and environmental law.[40] However, there are no general rules on how participatory procedures, such as public inquiries, have to be organised. Again, the case law and legal doctrine have played an important role in developing principles in this respect, which complete the specific legislative provisions that may apply.[41] The same is true for obligations to consult experts or advisory bodies.[42]

Preceding a procedure before the (administrative) courts, citizens who want to challenge an administrative act may have to pass the stage of administrative appeal. This is only obliged if the applicable legislation provides for an administrative appeal procedure. As is so often the case for Belgian administrative law, the principles that govern these administrative appeals have been developed in the case law and in legal doctrine.[43]

The Constitution contains a number of articles relating to the judicial protection of citizens against the executive or administration. First of all, it offers all courts (the regular – ie, civil and criminal – and administrative courts) a mandate (and even obliges them) to set aside (disapply) administrative acts (both with a normative and an individual scope) that are unlawful (Article 159 of the Constitution). Second, it recognises the existence of the Council of State (ie, the highest and general administrative court in Belgium) and anchors the possibility for the federal legislature to establish other administrative courts (Articles 160–61 of the Constitution). Third, it contains the basic rules on the jurisdiction of the 'normal' (civil and criminal) courts vis-à-vis the administrative courts (Articles 144–46 of the Constitution) and appoints the Supreme Court (Court of Cassation) as the arbitrator for conflicts on that division of jurisdiction (Article 158 of the Constitution). However, as is often the case, these constitutional provisions are broad and open-ended. For instance, the demarcation of the division of the civil and criminal courts' jurisdiction vis-à-vis that of the administrative courts is the topic of a long-standing debate in the case law and in legal doctrine.[44] The lack of

[40] See, eg, the various references in the Flemish Code on Spatial Planning (Vlaamse Codex Ruimtelijke Ordening) to the organisation of public inquiries.

[41] See E Lancksweerdt, *Handboek Burgerparticipatie* (Bruges, die Keure, 2009).

[42] See S Denys, *Advisering het bestuursrecht door publiekrechtelijke organen* (Bruges, die Keure, 2008).

[43] See J Goris, *Georganiseerde bestuurlijke beroepen* (Bruges, die Keure, 2012).

[44] See, eg, C Berx, *Rechtsbescherming van de burger tegen de overheid: een analyse van het systeem van administratieve rechtspraak in België* (Antwerp, Intersentia, 2000); J Goossens, 'De vervaagde grens tussen burgerlijke en administratieve rechter' (2014) *Tijdschrift voor Bestuurswetenschappen en Publiekrecht* 275.

clarity offered by the Constitution in this respect is problematic, since the rule of law requires that citizens know to which court they can turn for legal protection against the administration.

The Council of State is the general administrative court for judicial review of administrative acts of the Belgian administrative authorities. The Coordinated Acts on the Council of State – ie, a federal legislative Act that is regularly amended[45] and that is complemented by a number of executive decisions – is the general legislative framework regulating:

- the Council of State's competences *ratione personae* (which authorities are subject to its jurisdiction?);
- its competences *ratione materiae* (which types of acts can be challenged?);
- its powers (the type of judicial relief that it can offer);
- the procedure that applies.

Despite the existence of this already quite detailed normative framework (or perhaps because of it?), the case law plays an important role in this respect as well. Especially in recent years, the Council's General Assembly has pronounced a series of landmark judgments on the Council's competences and powers.

Neither the Constitution nor the SARI grants the federated entities (the regions and communities) the power to establish administrative courts. However, the Flemish region in particular has successfully invoked Article 10 of the SARI, recognising the existence of so-called 'implied powers', to create a number of Flemish administrative courts, removing important areas of Flemish administrative law from the Council of State's jurisdiction (eg, judicial review of decisions on planning permission or environmental permits).[46] Most of these courts have been brought together under the umbrella of the so-called 'Dienst van de Bestuursrechtscolleges' or 'DBRC', which translates as the 'Service of the Administrative Courts'. This is not a unified administrative court, but a service meant to increase cooperation and coordination between the three Flemish courts concerned. Its creation has gone hand in hand with the enactment of a single Flemish decree governing the organisation and functioning of these courts. A number of provisions in the 'DBRC-Decreet' apply to all these administrative courts, while others are specific to one or more of them.

The civil courts also play an increasingly important role in the legal protection of citizens against the administration. Most[47] tort cases against the administration are brought before the civil courts, with Article 1382 of the (old) Civil Code as their legal basis. As mentioned previously, Article 159 of the Constitution gives

[45] The last important innovations to this Act were introduced in 2014, when the Council, for example, obtained a power to grant compensation under specific conditions.

[46] See, eg, J Vanpraet, *Vlaamse bestuursrechtscolleges in een grondwettelijk perspectief. Grenzen en mogelijkheden van een Vlaamse Justitie* (Bruges, die Keure, 2015).

[47] Recently, the legislature also granted specific powers to the Council of State in this respect (art 11*bis* of the Coordinated Acts on the Council of State).

the civil courts a mandate and even obliges the courts to disapply unlawful administrative acts. Increasingly, however, the civil courts also use this provision to give injunctions to the administration if citizens are able to invoke so-called 'subjective rights' (ie, a highly debated notion in Belgian administrative law).[48]

Apart from administrative appeals and judicial review, citizens also enjoy rights of complaint, either with the administrations themselves or with ombudsmen. Neither the Constitution, nor the SARI contains general provisions in this respect, but specific legislative acts have introduced various complaint mechanisms at various political and administrative levels. However, a general legislative framework is lacking.

### F. Conclusion on Legal Sources of Administrative Law

The Constitution and the SARI are important starting points for many aspects of general administrative law in Belgium, but their provisions are naturally broad and open-ended; they require further legislative intervention and judicial interpretation. The number of legislative acts enshrining general rules of administrative law is low. On the other hand, the Council of State's contribution to the development of administrative law as a separate, stand-alone branch of public law, independent of constitutional law, has been considerable. Belgian general administrative law is still to a large extent judge-made law, which makes it different from most areas of private law. Moreover, both the judge-made law and the legislation that govern administrative law are increasingly influenced by EU law, as is the case in all EU Member States.[49]

## III. The Codification of Belgian Administrative Law

### A. Introduction

'Codification' can have various meanings. In a narrow sense, it can only refer to harmonisation or to bringing judge-made law (case law) together into a coherent text. Here, we start from a broad concept of codification, covering every initiative to lay down the rules and principles of administrative law in (binding) *written* law.

As sections I and II of this chapter have shown, Belgium does not have general statutory legislation on administrative procedure or general administrative law more broadly, either at the federal or at the sub-state level. Thus, the codification

[48] See I Cooreman (ed), *De wettigheidstoets van artikel 159 van de Grondwet* (Bruges, die Keure, 2010) 364; J Theunis, *De exceptie van onwettigheid: onderzoek naar de rol en de grenzen van artikel 159 van de Grondwet in de Belgische rechtsstaat* (Bruges, die Keure, 2011) 777.

[49] See, eg, in this book R Caranta, 'Administrative Proceedings in Italy' who also regularly refers to the impact of EU law.

of administrative law is partial and the degree to which administrative law is codified also differs at the various political levels. In the remainder of this chapter, we will focus on the federal level and the Flemish region/community.

## B. Development and Dynamics of the Sources

One of the most important recent developments with respect to the sources of administrative law is the Flemish legislature's urge to legislate in the area of general administrative law and, hence, to create its own 'home-grown' set of rules. The closest thing to a general Act on administrative law that Flanders has is the Bestuursdecreet, which was published in the Official Gazette on 19 December 2018. First, this decree compiled a number of existing Flemish decrees in the area of general administrative law, such as the Decree on Freedom of Information and the Complaints Decree. Second, however, it introduced a number of *new* provisions concerning, amongst other things, communication between citizens and the government, the exchange of messages, experimental legislation and zones subject to a decreased level of rules. A second example of Flemish legislation in the area of general administrative law concerns enforcement. In 2019, the first part of the Kaderdecreet Bestuurlijke Handhaving, ie, a framework decree on administrative enforcement, was enacted. This first part concerned supervision and administrative sanctions. The second part, which would have been enacted later on, would have covered preventive or reparatory measures. However, it never came to that, mostly because the enthusiasm among enforcement bodies to 'accede' to the decree turned out to be low. In the summer of 2022, the Flemish Government launched a first draft of a new initiative: the Kaderdecreet voor de Handhaving van de Vlaamse Regelgeving (Framework Decree for the Enforcement of Flemish Legislation). At the time of writing, no draft had yet been submitted to the Flemish Parliament. However, the documents published by the Flemish Government to initiate consultations of advisory bodies revealed that the initial Kaderdecreet was deemed too complex and elaborate. Moreover, a few of the more substantive choices made had turned out not to be desirable in the eyes of the enforcement bodies that the Government had hoped would accede to the Kaderdecreet. The draft also immediately includes provisions on preventive or reparatory measures.[50] As is the case with the current Kaderdecreet, the provisions in the decree would be of a supplementary nature: sectorial decrees can deviate from them. Moreover, sectorial legislation has to contain an explicit declaration that the Kaderdecreet applies before its provisions have legal force in that specific domain; only some provisions will apply to all Flemish legislation automatically.

[50] See the Flemish Minister of Justice and Enforcement's note to the Flemish Government, available at: beslissingenvlaamseregering.vlaanderen.be/?search=handhaving%20van%20de%20vlaamse%20regelgeving.

Another recent development is the increasing importance of the case law of the General Assembly of the Council of State, Administrative Litigation Section, which has a special role in guarding the uniformity in the Council's case law. Recent judgments have often concerned questions related to the procedure before the Council of State itself (the Coordinated Acts on the Council of State). Many of the debates underlying these judgments have originated from unclear legislation. Examples are a series of judgments on the recently introduced competence of the Council of State to grant compensation after it has decided that an administrative act is unlawful (Article 11*bis* of the Coordinated Acts on the Council of State).[51]

There are only a few examples of legislation codifying existing case law. The best examples can probably be found in the Coordinated Acts on the Council of State. In 2014, for instance, the legislature introduced the requirement that claimants should have an interest in the grievances that they invoke in their petition (Article 14, § 1, second indention), which was a principle that had already been recognised and applied by the Council.

## C. The Relationship between the Codified and Uncodified Parts of Administrative Law

An ongoing debate in Belgian legal doctrine concerns the relationship of the principles of good administration (and general principles of administrative law in a more general sense) to written, statutory law. For a long time, the dominant opinion in legal doctrine has been that general principles of law can *supplement* or *complete* statutory law, but cannot be applied *contra legem*. The legislature would always have a possibility to deviate from a general principle of law and to declare it inapplicable.[52] With respect to some general principles of good administration, such as the principle of equality and that of legal certainty, it is now quite generally accepted that they have constitutional value, meaning that the legislature should also respect them. Moreover, some have defended that all principles of good administration have constitutional value,[53] finding evidence for their claim in the case law of the Constitutional Court. However, the Council of State[54] and the Supreme Court[55] do not follow this thesis. A similar debate exists with

[51] CoS, general assembly, 21 June 2018, n° 241.865, Lenglez; CoS, general assembly, 21 June, n° 241.866, Gemeente Sint-Gillis; CoS, general assembly, 22 March 2019, n° 244.015, Moors.

[52] eg, J De Staercke, 'Beginselen van behoorlijk bestuur en hiërarchie van de normen' (2004) *Nieuw Juridisch Weekblad* 1406.

[53] Most notaby Popelier, in, eg, P Popelier (n 22) 3.

[54] See, eg, CoS, 28 November 2017, n° 239.955, Purnode, stating that general principles of law occupy, in the hierarchy of norms, an inferior position to that of statutory law; CoS, 16 January 2018, n° 240.430, Duwijn, stating that the principles of good administration do not prevail over clear statutory provisions.

[55] See, eg, Cass, 13 February 2013, AFT 2013, 50, with a case note by Patricia Popelier, where the court states that the principle of legitimate expectations does not apply when this would be contrary to statutory law.

respect to the previously mentioned 'laws of public service', even though one does find some (mostly indirect) indications in the case law of the Council of State and the Supreme Court of a recognition of constitutional value as far as they are concerned.[56]

## D. Reasons for Codification

The reasons for legislative intervention[57] in the field of general administrative law vary. We have been able to detect the following, which are not mutually exclusive, meaning that a single codification initiative may be prompted by multiple considerations. The reasons given in sections III.D.i–III.D.iii all represent *obligations* for the legislature to codify, while the reasons given in sections III.D.iv–III.D.ix result from the legislature's *own initiative*.

### *i. The Constitution or Statutory Laws with Special Value Make a Legislative Intervention Mandatory*

In some cases, the Constitution or a statutory law with a special value provides that certain rules have to be adopted by statutory law (a federal act, a regional or communal decree or ordinance). Typically, these are rules for which the intervention of a democratically elected parliament is deemed necessary. A first example is the previously mentioned statutory legislation at the regional level laying down the rules on the organisation and functioning of the provinces and local authorities, pursuant to Article 162 of the Constitution. Another example is the federal statutory act and those of the federated entities on freedom of information. Article 32 of the Constitution provides that statutory law lays down the exceptions and conditions to which the right to consult 'administrative documents' and to receive a copy is subject. Yet another example is the statutory legislation on expropriation. Article 16 of the Constitution provides that both the cases in which a person can be expropriated and the way in which this is done (the procedure) should be anchored in statutory law.[58] In the same way, Article 160 of the Constitution charges the federal legislature with the task of making rules on the composition, powers and functioning of the Council of State. These are found in the Coordinated

[56] See, eg, V Vuylsteke and S De Somer, 'Le principe de continuité du service public. The Show Must Go on …' in S Ben Messaoud and F Viseur (eds), *Les principes généraux de droit administratif – Actualités et Applications Pratiques* (Brussels, Larcier, 2017) 229. Contra, eg, P-O De Broux, 'La continuité du service public: l'étonnante destinée d'un principe élémentaire' (2014) *Chroniques de Droit Public – Publiekrechtelijke Kronieken* 640.

[57] We focus on codification by the legislature here, which has the residual competence to make rules. As explained, in some areas (eg, civil servant law), rule-making is to a large extent entrusted to the executive.

[58] Both the federal legislature and those of the federated entities have competences in this respect, resulting in various statutory laws. See arts 6*quater* and 79 SARI.

Acts on the Council of State. The organisation and powers of the integrated policy service and the essential elements of its staff's legal status have to be governed by (federal) legislation as well (Article 184 of the Constitution).

### *ii. EU Law Makes a Legislative Intervention Mandatory*

According to the Court of Justice of the European Union (CJEU), Member States must implement directives in a manner which fully meets the requirement of legal certainty and must consequently transpose their terms into national law as *binding provisions*.[59] Transposing EU legislation into national law will often require an intervention by the legislature. EU legislation, however, is typically sectorial (it covers, for example, environmental law, food safety law or network regulation) and usually does not have any direct influence on *general* administrative law. To a much greater extent, the case law of the CJEU has influenced general administrative law in the Member States (and is still doing so, for example, with respect to the definition of principles of good administration). However, public procurement law, which could be considered a part of general administrative law, *is* subject to detailed European legislation with lengthy, complex and technical national legislation as a consequence. The procurement directives have evolved over time, often codifying important case law of the CJEU.

In the area of economic public law, the EU Services Directive contains general rules on authorisations (permits) for service providers (eg, on the criteria on the basis of which an application for an authorisation will be assessed, on the duration of the authorisation and on the administrative procedure). The Belgian legislature has implemented these rules via a statutory Act of 26 March 2010, the provisions of which were later integrated into the Belgian Code on Economic Law. One could debate whether these rules are part of *general* administrative law, but they do apply to a fairly broad range of authorisations and constitute the 'default' in this respect: they fill the gaps in specific legislation on authorisations for the provisions of services.[60] Depending on how one wishes to delineate 'general administrative law', this could be considered a rare example of codified general administrative law being the direct result of EU legislation.

### *iii. A Ruling by the Constitutional Court Makes a Legislative Intervention Mandatory*

In some cases, new legislative provisions in the field of administrative law are the result of case law of the Constitutional Court. This is typically the case when the

[59] See, eg, Case 239/85 *Commission v Kingdom of Belgium* ECLI:EU:C:1986:457, [1986] ECR 3645.

[60] According to the explanatory statement, see MvT ontwerp van dienstenwet, ParlSt Kamer 2009-10, n° 2338/1, 16.

Constitutional Court rules that legislation contains gaps that create a discriminatory treatment. An example is found in a number of judgments of the Constitutional Court that have obliged the federal legislature to extend the Council of State's jurisdiction to certain decisions (of an administrative nature) taken by legislative and judicial bodies.[61]

A recent example are the Constitutional Court's judgments with respect to the lack of statutory legislation on the duty to have proper reasons and the duty to communicate these reasons for the dismissal of administrative staff employed via contract. Whereas employees in the private sector (via a collective labour agreement) and tenured civil servants (via the legislation on the duty to give reasons) do enjoy guarantees in this respect, the administration's contractual staff remain devoid of a similar protection. The Court's message that the legislature should without further delay enact such rules dates back to 2016 and it repeated this again in 2018.[62] However, no statutory law has been issued yet.

### *iv. The Legislature Wishes to Introduce New Rights or Guarantees for Citizens that have not Yet been Recognised by the Case Law*

In some cases, the legislature takes the initiative to legislate in the field of general administrative law without being obliged to do so because by higher laws or because of a judgment of the Constitutional Court. An example is the federal Act of 29 July 1991 on the duty to give reasons. This statutory legislation enshrines a general duty (subject to only a few exceptions) for administrative authorities to give explicit reasons for their written decisions with an individual scope and to include these in the decision itself. A non-binding resolution adopted by the Committee of Ministers of the Council of Europe as well as legislation adopted in other European countries may have put pressure on the Belgian legislature to provide such a guarantee,[63] but there were no compelling constitutional arguments to do so. Before the enactment of this legislation, the Council of State did not recognise a general duty to give reasons (this was only guaranteed under specific conditions).

In some cases the case law may not yet have had an opportunity to develop, because it was outpaced by reality requiring an urgent change in the law. For instance, the COVID-19 crisis has given rise to temporary legislation in the field of general administrative law at various political levels in Belgium, such as with respect to (the suspension of) deadlines (for administrative procedures, appeals and even judicial review) and the possibility for administrations to decide via

[61] Constitutional Court, 15 May 1996, n° 31/96; Constitutional Court, 1 July 2010, n° 79/2010; Constitutional Court, 10 March 2011, n° 36/2011; Constitutional Court, 20 October 2011, n° 161/2011.

[62] Constitutional Court, 30 June 2016, n° 101/2016; Constitutional Court, 5 July 2018, n° 84/2018.

[63] See I Opdebeek and A Coolsaet, 'De Wet Motivering Bestuurshandelingen: een korte, maar revolutionaire wet' in I Opdebeek and A Coolsaet (eds), *Formele motivering van bestuurshandelingen* (Bruges, die Keure, 2013) 3, 6.

electronic procedures.[64] It remains to be seen whether and to what extent some of these new written rules will survive the crisis and will become part of the legislative framework permanently.

### *v. The Legislature Wishes to Confirm (Constant) Case Law*

Examples of the codification of constant case law in Belgian general administrative law are scarce. However, one clear example is found in Article 14, § 1, second indention of the Coordinated Acts on the Council of State. This provision essentially requires a claimant before the Council of State to demonstrate an interest in the grounds for review that (s)he raises. This requirement was already well established in the Council of State's case law before being enshrined in the legislation in 2014. Another example is found in Article 3, § 3 of the Flemish Expropriation Decree (Vlaams Onteigeningsdecreet), which, apart from the four conditions enshrined in Article 16 of the Constitution, enshrines an additional condition, ie, that of the 'onteigeningsnoodzaak' (the need to expropriate). The existence of this condition had already been recognised before in the case law of the Supreme Court (Court of Cassation) and the lower courts.[65]

### *vi. The Legislature Wishes to Go against Constant Case Law*

It may happen that the legislature is dissatisfied with certain developments in the case law and thus enacts legislation that would make it impossible for the courts to continue on that path. No obvious examples come to mind in the field of *general* administrative law. An example in the field of planning law that caused some controversy was the Flemish legislature's attempt to enlarge the possibilities to build constructions in so-called 'landschappelijk waardevol agrarisch gebied' (agricultural zones with scenic value).[66] This legislative intervention was explicitly motivated by the restrictive case law of the Council of State and the 'Raad voor Vergunningsbetwistingen' (Flemish Council for Disputes Regarding Permits), which made it very difficult for applicants to obtain a building permit in these areas.[67] However, the Constitutional Court annulled this provision, since it was deemed contrary to Article 23 of the Constitution, guaranteeing the right to a dignified life, which includes the right to a healthy environment. The Court derives

[64] See S De Somer, 'Over corona en continuïteit: bestuursrecht in tijden van quarantaine' (2020) *Rechtskundig Weekblad* 1445.

[65] Cass, 3 February 2000, AR C.96.0380.N, ArrCass 2000, 288; Cass, 11 September 2003, AR C.01.0114.N, ArrCass 2003, 1634, Pas 2003, 1380; Rb Leuven, 26 February 2014, TBO 2014, 271. The recognition of this condition in the case law was in turn inspired by art 1 of the First Additional Protocol to the European Convention on Human Rights.

[66] For this purpose, art 5.7.1 of the Flemish Code on Spatial Planning (Vlaamse Codex Ruimtelijke Ordening) was adapted.

[67] MvT Ontwerp van decreet houdende wijziging van diverse bepalingen inzake ruimtelijke ordening, milieu en omgeving, ParlSt 2016–17, nr 1149/1, 19.

a 'standstill requirement' from this constitutional provision, signifying that the legislature should refrain from significantly lowering the existing level of protection. In this case, the Court indeed found such a significant decline in the level of protection. For that reason, the Court deemed it problematic that the introduction of this provision had not been preceded by a public inquiry, since – under normal circumstances – zoning provisions are enacted via zoning plans and not via legislation. The former are preceded by an obligatory public inquiry on a draft, whereas enacting legislation is not. Hence, the Court found that Article 23 of the Constitution as well as Articles 10 and 11 (enshrining the principle of equality and the prohibition to discriminate) had been violated.[68]

In the past, there have been occasions where the legislature intervened when the Council of State annulled an administrative act or was about to do so with the aim of 'validating' the act and thus preventing or undoing the annulment. This technique is highly controversial and its compatibility with the Constitution is subject to conditions.[69]

### *vii. The Legislature Wishes to Compensate for Lacunas in Specific Legislation*

In Flanders, the previously mentioned Kaderdecreet Bestuurlijke Handhaving intended to provide general, supplementary rules on administrative enforcement for the areas that fall within the Flemish legislature's competence. The explanatory statement to the Act that introduced the first part of the decree explicitly stated that it did not aimed to bring uniformity, but merely aimed to streamline Flemish law on administrative enforcement.[70] The new initiative to enact a Kaderdecreet voor de handhaving van de Vlaamse regelgeving (see above) seems to have the same goal.[71]

### *viii. The Legislature Wishes to Compile/Coordinate Legislation*

Again at the Flemish level, the recently enacted and previously mentioned Bestuursdecreet, even though it also contains a number of new rules, is largely a compilation of (provisions in) decrees that already existed before, but that have now been brought together into a single legislative text. The previously mentioned Flemish Expropriation Decree, integrating the rules on both the administrative

[68] Constitutional Court, 17 October 2019, n° 145/2019.

[69] See, eg, F Judo and M Daelemans, 'Wetgevende validatie en de Raad van State. Een belemmering voor of (soms) een weg naar rechtsherstel?' in I Cooreman, D Lindemans and L Peeters (eds), *De tenuitvoerlegging van arresten van de Raad van State* (Bruges, die Keure, 2012) 195 ff.

[70] MvT voorontwerp van kaderdecreet betreffende de bestuurlijke handhaving, ParlSt VlParl 2018–19, n° 1825/1, 8.

[71] See the Flemish Minister of Justice and Enforement's note to the Flemish Government, available at: beslissingenvlaamseregering.vlaanderen.be/?search=handhaving%20van%20de%20vlaamse%20regelgeving, 3.

and judicial procedure for expropriation, is another example.[72] A recent (joint) decree and ordinance regarding freedom of information[73] integrates a number of separate legislative texts into a single text applicable to a large number of administrative bodies operating in the Brussels-Capital Region.[74]

### *ix. The Legislature Wishes to Enact a General Framework for its Own Future Intervention*

The legislature may also intend to limit its own discretionary power in future statutory acts by enacting general rules of administrative law. In other words, it makes its own future decisions in the field of administrative law subject to conditions. An important example were the provisions in the Kaderdecreet Bestuurlijk Beleid on the valid reasons behind the creation of and delegation of executive tasks to Flemish agencies with legal personality. The Kaderdecreet has now largely been abolished and its provisions integrated into the Bestuursdecreet, but the new decree did not retain the provisions on the motives behind agencification. The explanatory statement to the Bestuursdecreet justifies this change referring to the fact that provisions of this type are not binding to the legislature, since it can always deviate from them in specific legislation.[75] The question arises as to whether this argument is entirely correct. Some have suggested that the principle of equality, which has constitutional value, could have played a role in the legal enforceability of the rules of the Kaderdecreet. This principle would require the equal treatment of all agencies, under the condition that they are sufficiently comparable and if there is no objective or reasonable justification for differentiation.[76] Moreover, according to the Belgian constitutionalist Popelier, the legislature is under a duty to give reasons for any deviation of a general statutory Act in a more specific statutory Act by means of reasonable arguments, which are objectively justifiable.[77] In case of an irreconcilability that has not been motivated, the general rule would have priority.[78] In her argumentation, Popelier refers to the importance of coherence. A different conclusion would, according to the author, be 'little conducive

[72] S Verbist and C Bimbenet, 'Het Vlaams Onteigeningsdecreet. Vloek of zegen voor de lokale besturen?' (2018) *Tijdschrift voor Gemeenterecht* 18, 19 and 38.

[73] Gezamenlijk decreet en ordonnantie van 16 mei 2019 van het Brussels Hoofdstedelijk Gewest, de Gemeenschappelijke Gemeenschapscommissie en de Franse Gemeenschapscommissie van 16 mei 2019 betreffende de openbaarheid van bestuur bij de Brusselse instellingen, BS 7 mei 2019.

[74] F Schram, 'Nieuwe openbaarheidsregels op het grondgebied van het Brussels Hoofdstedelijk Gewest' (2019) *Tijdschrift voor Bestuurswetenschappen en Publiekrecht* 567.

[75] MvT ontwerp van bestuursdecreet, ParlSt VlParl 2017-18, n° 1656/1, 119–20 and 127.

[76] K Verhoest, F Vandendriessche and J Rommel, 'Verzelfstandiging in Vlaanderen: theorie en praktijk' in P Jadoul, B Lombaert and F Tulkens (eds), *Le paraétatisme. Nouveaux régards sur la décentralisation fonctionnelle en Belgique et dans les institutions européennes* (Brussels, la Charte, 2010) 369, 392.

[77] P Popelier, *De wet juridisch bekeken* (Bruges, die Keure, 2004) 348, with reference to P Popelier, *Rechtszekerheid als beginsel voor behoorlijke regelgeving* (Antwerp, Intersentia, 1997) 559.

[78] P Popelier, *Rechtszekerheid als beginsel voor behoorlijke regelgeving* (n 77) 559.

for the accessibility of legislation, which precisely depends on the coherence that is based on the general framework that serves as an interpretative framework for more precise rules'.[79]

## E. Reasons for Further Codification in the Future

In the past, two legislative initiatives (one in 2000 and one in 2003)[80] have been launched in the federal Parliament[81] to enact a General Act on Administrative Law, following the Dutch example.[82] In the end, these initiatives did not result in actual legislation. This is probably due to the fact that they were drafted by members of the opposition and were not deemed important or urgent enough by the majority parties. An article analysing the proposals and their use for Belgian administrative law distinguishes two main reasons why general legislation would be beneficial: it would provide a remedy for gaps in legislation in specific fields of administrative law and it would reduce the need for specific legislation, and hence lead to more uniformity.[83] As such, these are reasons to have a system of 'general administrative law' in the first place, irrespective of whether its rules and principles are partly, mostly or entirely codified in written, statutory legislation. However, there seem to be two main reasons to strive for a more complete codification of rules and principles of general administrative law.

### *i. Increasing Knowledge of General Administrative Law*

General administrative law differs from many areas of private law in that it mainly regulates the behaviour and decision-making of the administration by giving that administration powers on the one hand, and giving those who undergo those powers (citizens and other administrations) a number of guarantees with respect to how those powers are exercised on the other hand. General administrative law rarely imposes obligations on citizens, although there is a growing body of

[79] ibid.

[80] The 2003 draft started from the same text as the 2000 draft, but took into account (most of) the remarks made by the Council of State, Legislation Section on the 2000 draft (eg, with respect to the competences of the federal state).

[81] For Flanders, there have been reflections on the possibility of a general decree on administrative law in legal doctrine. See J De Staercke and J Van Steelandt (eds), *Een Algemeen Decreet Bestuursrecht in Vlaanderen?* (Antwerp, Intersentia, 2004).

[82] The 2000 initiative explicitly refers to the Netherlands and Germany, where such legislation existed already at the time: ParlSt Kamer 1999–2000, nr 679/001, 3. The Council of State, Legislation Section, also noted that many provisions in the draft law had been literally copied from the Dutch Algemene wet bestuursrecht (ParlSt Kamer 2002–03, nr 679/002, 9).

[83] E Van de Velde, 'De zin of onzin van een algemene wet bestuursrecht rechtsvergelijkend doorgelicht' (2003–04) *Rechtskundig Weekblad* 1321. On the harmonisation of Belgian administrative law, see also G Debersaques (with the cooperation of S De Clercq), *Bestuursrecht harmoniseren? Preadvies Vereniging voor de Vergelijkende Studie van het Recht van België en Nederland* (Deventer, Kluwer, 2004) 79.

case law of the Council of State on the so-called 'principles of good citizenship' (ie, duties of loyal cooperation with the administration and the administrative courts).[84] For that reason, it may be argued that traditional arguments of legal certainty apply less to administrative law than to private law. Yet, guarantees are only effective if citizens know of their existence and are effectively able to invoke them. Moreover, codification can increase knowledge of the law, since legislation is usually better known to administrative authorities than principles that flow from the case law of the courts.[85] Hence, it has the potential of leading to better, lawful decision-making and less litigation or at least fewer annulments of administrative acts.

An additional argument in this respect is the rise of specialised administrative courts. In most cases, their judgments are subject to appeal (on points of law only) to the Council of State. Hence, the Council of State oversees the uniform application of general administrative law. Nevertheless, the Council's ability to give guidance to the specialised administrative courts depends on the initiative of the parties. A codification of the basic theories, rules and principles of administrative law would increase the knowledge of general administrative law of courts that often deal with technical issues, but that need knowledge of general administrative law to fill the gaps in the legislation. The civil courts, whose interpretation and application of the law can ultimately be controlled by the Court of Cassation but not by the Council of State, would a fortiori benefit from codification.

### *ii. Increasing the Democratic Legitimacy of General Administrative Law*

The question also arises as to whether some choices with respect to the concepts, rules and principles of general administrative law should not be made by the legislature rather than by the courts. There is, for instance, an ongoing debate on the delineation of the concept 'administratieve overheid/autorité administrative' (administrative authority), which is crucial for the demarcation of the Council of State's power of judicial review and of a series of legislative acts in the area of general administrative law, such as the previously mentioned federal Act of 29 July 1991 on the duty to give reasons. This debate is not value-free: its results determine which authorities are and which authorities are not subject to important guarantees that general administrative law offers. Yet, it has been left entirely to the courts (the Council of State and the Supreme Court) to define criteria for demarcation.[86]

[84] See, eg, S Lierman and M Meulebrouck, 'Krijtlijnen voor de versterking van behoorlijk burgerschap' in R Leysen, K Muylle, J Theunis and W Verrijdt (eds), *Semper perseverans. Liber amicorum André Alen* (Antwerp, Intersentia, 2020) 465 ff.

[85] In that sense, see J De Staercke, 'Naar een Algemene wet bestuursrecht in België?' (2006) *Nederlands Tijdschrift voor Bestuursrecht* 3.

[86] See I Opdebeek and S De Somer (n 8) 314 ff.

## F. Pitfalls of Codification/Points of Attention for the Future

Finally, Belgium's limited experiences with codification in the field of general administrative law have inspired us to formulate the following caveats, which we believe should be points of attention for legislatures in the future.

### *i. The Trend of Codifying Rules without Normative Content*

According to a substantive principle of good legislation, legislative texts should contain provisions with a normative scope only. Recommendations, mere guidelines for administrations (eg, good or best practices), declarations of intent etc do not belong in legislative texts.[87] Only recently, in its advisory opinion concerning a so-called 'Klimaatwet' (Climate Act), the Council of State, Legislation Section warned the legislature against its intention to enshrine what it called 'applicable general principles of environmental policy', which were too vague to be operable in a legal context.[88]

Yet, in practice, we find an increasing number of these types of provisions in statutory legislation. An example is found in Article II.2 of the Flemish Bestuursdecreet, which states that the authorities that fall within their scope have to 'actively provide information, at their own initiative, on their policies, regulations and service provision, every time that this is useful, important or necessary'. They also have to ensure that 'this information reaches as many persons, associations and organisations in the target group as possible. They choose adequate strategies of communication for topics concerning target groups that are difficult to reach'.

This is a vague provision, which seems difficult to enforce. Another example is found in Article 4 of the Flemish Kaderdecreet Bestuurlijke Handhaving, ie, the Framework Decree on Administrative Enforcement, stating that administrative enforcement should be 'selective, decisive, independent, transparent, professional, on the basis of cooperation and in accordance with the principle of proportionality'. Whereas the latter is a principle of good administration, most of the adjectives used in the rest of this provision have no direct legal or normative significance.

### *ii. Codified General Administrative Law as a 'Pull Factor' for Judicial Review*

One of the primary goals behind the introduction of a general duty to give reasons via a federal statutory act[89] was to inform those confronted with administrative

[87] H Coremans, M van Damme, J Dujardin, B Seutin and G Vermeylen, *Beginselen van wetgevingstechniek en behoorlijke regelgeving* (Bruges, die Keure, 2016) 141.

[88] AdvRvS nr 65.404/AV bij het voorstel van bijzondere wet over de coördinatie van het beleid van de federale overheid, de Gemeenschappen en de Gewesten met betrekking tot klimaatverandering en het vaststellen van algemene langetermijn doelstellingen, ParlSt Kamer 2018–19, nr 3517/4, 18.

[89] Wet 29 juli 1991 betreffende de uitdrukkelijke motivering van de bestuurshandelingen, BS 12 september 1991 as interpreted by the Constitutional Court in Arbitragehof 29 januari 2004, n° 17/2004.

decisions affecting them on the reasons behind those decisions, so that they would be able to make an informed choice whether or not to use the available appeal mechanisms and/or ask for judicial review. The legislature wanted to avoid so-called 'blind' recourse to appeal bodies or courts. The expectation was that the number of appeals or requests for judicial review would fall, as in many cases citizens would realise that the decisions were well founded and seeking redress would be of little use.[90] However, in practice, the very opposite happened: citizens started challenging administrative acts *because* the duty to give reasons had not been (sufficiently) respected. Since then, most petitions for judicial review submitted to the Council of State contain a grievance related to the duty to give reasons.[91]

Our point here is not that anchoring the duty to give reasons in statutory law was an error; quite the opposite in fact. However, it seems likely that anchoring general duties for administrative authorities in written law (legislation) makes citizens (and their legal representatives) more confident to enforce these duties than they would be if these would follow from general principles developed in the case law. This is merely a hypothesis, for which we do not have empirical evidence. Yet, if this is true, it seems important that legislatures are aware of this. Surely, administrative law has a legitimising and protecting function, but it has to take into account administrative efficiency too and avoid pointless delays due to judicial proceedings. In its case law, the Council of State has often ruled that even though the rules of the statutory legislation on the duty to give reasons had not been respected, the *goals* behind the legislation had been reached because the claimant had learnt about the motives behind the decision in some other way.[92] It would perhaps have been advisable for the legislature to include a provision in this respect in the Act itself,[93] in order to discourage claimants from seeking an annulment for merely formal reasons and thus creating perverse effects.

### *iii. Codification does not Necessarily Reduce the Importance of Case Law as a Source of Law*

Codification of general administrative law may raise the expectation of making this area of the law less reliant on judicial law-making, but this is not necessarily true.[94] Again, Belgium's statutory legislation on the duty to give reasons offers a fine example of this. The Act dates back to 1991 and contains only seven (short) articles, but it has given rise to an impressive body of case law of the Council of State and the specialised administrative courts that gives further content to the

[90] On this 'preventive' role of the Act, see I Opdebeek and A Coolsaet (n 63) 3, 7.
[91] ibid 7.
[92] See I Opdebeek and A Coolsaet, 'Sancties bij schending van de wet motivering bestuurshandelingen' in I Opdebeek and A Coolsaet (eds) (n 63) 183, 189 ff.
[93] Since 2014, a general provision in this sense is included in art 14, § 1, second indention of the Coordinated Acts on the Council of State.
[94] See also G Debersaques (n 83) 48 ff.

statutory provisions. The main monograph on the duty to give reasons in Belgian law contains over 500 pages and mainly relies on the case law to identify principles on the interpretation and application of the mostly open-ended provisions in the act.[95]

### *iv. There's No Rest for the Wicked: Codification Requires Follow-up and Evaluation*

Codification may sometimes seem to be the culmination or end of a process, but it is also the beginning of a new one, as it entails new work for legislators. Once a rule or principle has been entrenched in written law, it will be there until the responsible law-maker decides to change it. Its purpose or meaning may evolve with interpretation, but only insofar as the rules for interpreting written law allow for this to take place. In Belgian law, for instance, the adage 'in claris non fit interpretatio', meaning that things that are clear cannot be subject to interpretation, will restrict judicial creativity in, for instance, giving an evolutive interpretation to norms. Hence, the responsibility to remove or alter obsolete or simply 'bad' norms rests with the legislator, which should be expeditious and evaluate their work at a regular basis.

In Flanders, plans to introduce the second part of the Kaderdecreet Bestuurlijke Handhaving went hand in hand with an evaluation of the first part, resulting in a number of adaptations only a very short time after the rules had entered into force (May 2019). Experts from various institutions (the administration, the courts, universities etc) were involved in its evaluation, via a workshop launched by SERV,[96] which resulted in a detailed report.[97] Perhaps this evaluation came (too) early, since experience working with the actual provisions in the decree was lacking at the time.[98] On the other hand, a substantial part of the criticism expressed by experts when the decree was launched related to conceptual and systemic problems (eg, a lack of clarity regarding the decree's relationship to legislation in other areas of the law, such as criminal law). Hence, the team responsible for drafting the decree did well in responding quickly and wanting to rectify these issues. Eventually, as explained earlier in this text, the Flemish Government chose not to submit a draft for the second part to the Flemish Parliament, but came with a new legislative initiative, which takes into account many of the concerns expressed on the initial (first part of) the Kaderdecreet Bestuurlijke Handhaving. It remains to be seen how the Flemish Parliament will further deal with this.

[95] I Opdebeek and A Coolsaet (eds) (n 63).

[96] The Social and Economic Council of Flanders (SERV), ie, the main advisory body to the Flemish Government on Flemish socio-economic policy.

[97] Verslag SERV-Rondetafel evaluatie decreet bestuurlijke handhaving 17 February 2020, www.serv.be/serv/evenement/rondetafel-bestuurlijke-handhaving.

[98] See above, section II.A.

Sometimes, awareness that a certain topic is subject to strong differences in opinion among lawyers that are still ongoing may precisely be a reason for the legislature to *refrain* from adopting new written rules. A recent example is found in the new book on 'Goods' of the Belgian Civil Code, which entered into force on 1 September 2021. On the topic of 'public domain goods', the legislature decided to adopt a 'neutral position' on a number of fiercely debated questions in this respect in the case law and legal doctrine. It explicitly referred to the role of the latter in making the text evolve 'in the direction that seems most desirable'.[99] In our opinion, such an approach is desirable when the relevant (socio-economic) facts or conditions evolve quickly or are uncertain at the time of legislating, but not when (as is the case for the topic of public domain goods) debates in case law and legal doctrine have been ongoing for years (or even decades) and are of a more principled nature. In those cases, it is up to the legislature to make a decision on what the law should be, instead of letting courts and legal doctrine continue to quarrel.

# IV. Conclusion

In terms of codifying general administrative law, Belgium is probably not the ideal legal system for those looking for widespread experience from which to draw inspiration. Indeed, very little of general administrative law is written law. However, in Flanders, this is slowly changing, and the developments regarding the framework legislation on enforcement reveal that those involved in drafting and adjusting the decree are taking its legislative quality seriously. The COVID-19 crisis has also revealed that some of the current rules and principles of administrative law, as developed in the case law, are not always adjusted to emergencies. Perhaps this will give rise to more permanent legislative frameworks (at the various political and legislative levels) for administrative procedure in a state of emergency or even – more generally – to an Administrative Procedure Act.

However, as for the future of codification in Belgian administrative law, nothing is written. We have discussed a number of possible reasons for further codification in this chapter, as well as pitfalls to be avoided and points to be kept in mind. Yet, even more than other areas of the law, administrative law will often require a difficult balancing exercise, since both the general interest and individuals' interests are at stake. This often makes it particularly challenging to adopt written legislation: a single rule may hold the promise of clarity, but it may not offer an adequate solution for every case and may thus even lead to injustice. Unwritten principles may therefore often be preferable, as long as there is a coherent judicial interpretative practice and a tradition of legal doctrine critically analysing that case law.

[99] MvT wetsvoorstel houdende invoeging van boek 3 'Goederen' in het nieuw Burgerlijk Wetboek, ParlSt Kamer 2019, n°173/1, 111.

In another chapter in this book on Austria, Konrad Lachmayer suggests that codification would enable legal scholars and politicians to 'question the traditional and confused legal structures'.[100] Perhaps this is the best argument for Belgium to embark on a new attempt to make a General Act on Administrative Law. This exercise, which would have to be based on wide consultations, would force all those involved to face inconsistencies in the prevailing law and to update and simplify the body of rules and principles where this is possible. The challenges originating from the fast-evolving possibilities offered by automated decision-making that all administrations face seem to require at least an evaluation of prevailing law. As Ariane Berger's chapter in this volume reminds us, this is currently also a major concern for the EU law-makers and one of the 'hot topics' of scholarly research on EU administrative law.[101] It is clear that legislatures carry a responsibility to assess if prevailing administrative law still offers sufficient protection to citizens when administrations and civil servants share decision-making power with computers. A thorough revision of the whole of (general) administrative law seems preferable to the hurried introduction of a set of specific rules only governing the use of artificial intelligence in administrative decision-making.

[100] See in this book K Lachmayer, 'Codification of Administrative Law in Austria', section V.

[101] See in this book A Berger, 'Science Codification for the European Union – The ReNEUAL Network: On the Limits of Legal Control of Innovation and Technology'.

# 4

# A Persistent Taste for Diversity

## *Codification of Administrative Law in Canada*

PIERRE ISSALYS

Any discussion of administrative law in Canada runs the risk of misunderstandings about what is meant by 'administrative law' in that country. For a number of reasons, Canadian jurists approach and define this branch of the law in different ways. Some appreciation of these differences is therefore necessary as a preliminary step, which is taken in section I of this chapter. While such disparity of views does not affect the listing of sources of administrative law, it does modify to some extent the relationships between sources, as will be seen in section II. Section III will then attempt, while keeping in mind the different approaches to administrative law, a brief survey of the chequered pattern of codification in this branch of Canadian legal systems.

Different understandings of the subject, variations in the arrangement of sources, disparate results – these features of administrative law in Canada all point towards a basic, ingrained inclination to diversity. Therefore, attempts at codifying this branch of the law have to adjust to a somewhat uncongenial environment.

## I. Defining and Mapping Administrative Law

The phrases 'administrative law' and 'droit administratif' both appeared in Canada in the late nineteenth century to describe the case law produced by superior courts through the exercise of their supervisory authority over actions by public and private bodies and organisations, mainly local government authorities.[1] However, from the 1960s onwards, 'droit administratif' acquired a different, much broader

[1] JA Corry, 'Administrative Law and the Interpretation of Statutes' (1935–36) 1 *University of Toronto Law Journal* 286, 286; RCB Risk, 'Lawyers, Courts, and the Rise of the Regulatory State' (1984) 9 *Dalhousie Law Journal* 31, 35 f.

meaning, nowadays only partially acknowledged in relation to the English phrase 'administrative law'.[2]

Current dictionaries of Canadian legal terminology in English and in French point at this *difference in usage*. Thus, the *Dictionary of Canadian Law* offers two meanings for the phrase 'administrative law'.[3] One of these is rather vague: 'The law relating to public administration.' The other, on the contrary, is replete with technical and specific words: 'The law which relates to the organisation, duties and quasi-judicial powers of the executive, to proceedings before tribunals and to the making of subordinate legislation.' This is readily intelligible for someone familiar with the field, but requires ordinary readers to look up other entries in the dictionary.

By contrast, the *Dictionnaire de droit québécois et canadien* provides a single definition that combines a systemic view and ordinary language: 'Branche du droit public qui régit l'organisation et le fonctionnement de l'administration publique ainsi que ses relations avec les citoyens.'[4] While 'droit public' is a term of art, 'public' provides the common reader with a rough understanding of what is involved.

What is implicit in this contrast of course goes much deeper than the encounter between two languages or between two types of reasoning – inductive and deductive. It points at the very structure of the legal system and the essentials of legal thinking. On the one hand, reference is made to 'the law' as a unitary whole; on the other hand, 'le droit' is viewed as fundamentally divided between public law and private law. In the English-language definition, readers can feel an immediate concern with real-life occurrences ('powers', 'proceedings', 'making of') and technical concepts ('quasi-judicial', 'tribunal', 'subordinate legislation'), as well as an apparent lack of concern with paradox ('judicial powers of the executive'). In the French-language definition, what seems to matter most is ordering the legal universe on the basis of broad and simple dichotomies: the concept of 'le droit', being first structured implicitly by the basic public/private dichotomy, is further structured by the internal/external dichotomy: 'organisation et fonctionnement'/'relations avec les citoyens'.

At another level, divergent views about the meaning of 'administrative law' and 'droit administratif' reflect different outlooks on the state.[5] The adoption of a broad meaning for the French phrase has coincided with the sudden, powerful and lasting development of state activity in Quebec – a development that, in English Canada, happened earlier and more gradually, and focused mainly on the federal government.

[2] For early occurrences of this broader meaning, see PB Mignault, *Manuel de droit parlementaire* (Montreal, Périard, 1889) 252; MA Bernard, *Manuel de droit constitutionnel et administratif* (Montreal, Théorêt, 1901).

[3] D Dukelow, *Dictionary of Canadian Law*, 4th edn (Toronto, Thomson Carswell, 2011).

[4] H Reid, *Dictionnaire de droit québécois et canadien*, 5th edn (Montreal, Wilson & Lafleur, 2015).

[5] R Leckey, 'Territoriality in Canadian Administrative Law' (2004) 54 *University of Toronto Law Journal* 327, 328, 331 ff; D Lemieux, 'The Codification of Administrative Law in Québec' in G Huscroft and M Taggart (eds), *Inside and Outside Administrative Law: Essays in Honour of David Mullan* (Toronto, University of Toronto Press, 2006) 240 f.

This duality of approaches to administrative law is of course only one aspect of the peculiarly and increasingly complex legal structure of Canada. Leaving aside, for the purposes at hand, many issues contributing to that complexity, three basic facts stand out as determinants of the scope and contents of the rubric 'administrative law'. First, at least in terms of antecedence, is the mixed character of the legal system of Quebec, within which the relationship between the common law and civil law components has been gradually and subtly changing in favour of the latter.[6] Second is the strong version of federalism practised in Canada, which implies the co-existence of complete and distinct state apparatuses at both the federal level and in each of the provinces.[7] The third element is the bijural character of the federal legal system, superimposed as it were on top of the 10 provincial legal systems.[8] Cutting across all three phenomena, linguistic duality further thickens the rich legal-institutional fabric of the country. All of this is relevant in some way to a discussion of sources and of codification, as will be seen later on in this chapter.

To return now to matters of definition and delineation, Canadian *textbooks* on administrative law develop an outlook on the discipline that generally reflects the position of their author within that complex legal culture. Indeed, the word 'textbook' itself is used here as mere shorthand: it overlooks significant differences, both formal and substantive, between learned ('doctrinal') legal writing by Anglophones and *la doctrine* produced by Quebec Francophone authors.[9] Even as they describe their subject matter, administrative law textbooks display notable differences in emphasis.

Thus, Robert Reid's *Administrative Law and Practice* (1971) took its title as self-explanatory and abruptly began the first of its 22 chapters, entitled 'The Right to Be Heard', with the statement that this right is of 'fundamental importance to administrative law'.[10] Thirty years later, by contrast, David Mullan's *Administrative Law* grappled with the difficulty of defining its subject.[11] Administrative law 'at its most general' was described by him as 'statutes, principles and rules that govern the operations of government', embracing both 'the relationships that exist among branches of government and the relationship between government agencies and

[6] D Lemieux, 'Le rôle du Code civil du Québec en droit administratif' (2005) 18 *Canadian Journal of Administrative Law and Practice* 119.

[7] H Brun, G Tremblay and E Brouillet, *Droit constitutionnel*, 6th edn (Cowansville, QC, Éditions Yvon Blais, 2014) 90 ff, 413 ff; P Hogg, *Constitutional Law of Canada*, 5th edn (Scarborough, ON, Thomson Carswell, 2009) 121 ff.

[8] On the implications of this third factor, see JF Gaudreault-DesBiens, *Les solitudes du bijuridisme au Canada. Essai sur les rapports de pouvoir entre les traditions juridiques et la résilience des atavismes identitaires* (Montreal, Thémis, 2007).

[9] R Macdonald, 'La nature, le rôle et l'influence de la doctrine universitaire en droit administratif québécois' (1985) 26 *Cahiers de droit* 1071.

[10] R Reid, *Administrative Law and Practice* (Toronto, Butterworths, 1971) 1 f. A later statement that this approach was the prevailing one is likely to be still valid, at least in English Canada: Canada, Law Reform Commission, *Towards a Modern Federal Administrative Law* (Ottawa, Law Reform Commission, 1987) 1 ff.

[11] D Mullan, *Administrative Law* (Toronto, Irwin Law, 2001) 3 f.

the constituencies with which they deal'. But Mullan then went on to present it, in a 'negative guise', as the 'legal parameters by which the courts supervise the exercise of powers that exist by virtue of statute or royal prerogative'. In the end, giving up the attempt at definition, the author made it clear that his book would deal essentially with the judicial review of decision-making by the public authorities. In 2001 too, Lisa Braverman saw the subject of her book, *Administrative Tribunals*, as an expansive category, which was as difficult to define as administrative law itself; the latter she described as having three components: subordinate legislation, the actions of administrative tribunals and remedies against unlawful administrative action.[12]

More recent English-language textbooks position themselves variously on the ground mapped out by Mullan's alternative definitions. David Jones and Anne de Villars (2014) emphasise that administrative law deals with the limitations on the actions of officials and with the remedies against unlawful action, while pointing out that 'the mere fact that the government is the government does not give it particular rights or powers'.[13] The textbook authored by a group of professors that includes David Mullan (2015) takes a broader view, describing administrative law as 'a branch of public law [that, like constitutional law,] concerns the legal structuring and regulation of sovereign authority, both in the state's relations with individuals and in the allocation of authority among various institutions' and observing that much of it is 'the law governing the implementation of public programs, particularly at their point of delivery'.[14] Guy Régimbald (2015) acknowledges that 'any attempt to define administrative law may prove under-inclusive', since the subject 'includes not only governmental activity but the structure of government'; he then describes the discipline in terms of its 'responsibility to control government powers' and its 'duty to ensure that decision-makers stay within the boundaries of their competence'.[15] John Swaigen (2016) tries to combine approaches by focusing on procedure, that is, 'rules and principles that regulate how … government departments and agencies … and other bodies created or given powers by statute must behave when carrying out their functions', but also on 'the authority of the superior courts to supervise how these departments and agencies carry out their powers'.[16] Other writers, such as Sara Blake (2017) or Lorne Sossin and Emily Lawrence (2018), keep a more concentrated focus on 'how decisions are made in individual cases', 'complaint procedures and remedies', 'public decisions that affect a person or a group of people', the last-mentioned authors indeed stating

[12] L Braverman, *Administrative Tribunals: A Legal Handbook* (Aurora, ON, Canada Law Book, 2001) 19 ff.

[13] DP Jones and A de Villars, *Principles of Administrative Law*, 6th edn (Toronto, Carswell, 2014) 3.

[14] G van Harten, G Heckman, D Mullan and J Promislow, *Administrative Law: Cases, Texts and Materials*, 7th edn (Toronto, Emond Montgomery, 2015) 3 f.

[15] G Régimbald, *Canadian Administrative Law*, 2nd edn (Markham, ON, LexisNexis, 2015) 1.

[16] J Swaigen, *Administrative Law. Principles and Advocacy* (Toronto, Emond Montgomery, 2016) 16 f, 21, 54.

that most of administrative law 'arises from' such public decisions – a statement that perfectly suits the common law worldview.[17]

Over the same period, most textbooks on administrative law by Francophone authors from Quebec have consistently put forward a broad view of the legal framework of public administration, based on three major themes: organisation, action and control. The influence of French law was initially made explicit in Michel Rambourg's proposed definition (1969).[18] However, references to national and British sources predominate in René Dussault's *Traité de droit administratif canadien et québécois* (1974),[19] Patrice Garant's *Droit administratif* (since 1981),[20] René Dussault and Louis Borgeat's much-enlarged *Traité de droit administratif* (1984),[21] and Pierre Issalys and Denis Lemieux's *L'action gouvernementale* (since 1997).[22] All these works lend support, at least implicitly, to the view expressed in the 1984 *Traité* that limiting the scope of administrative law to its controlling function underestimates the importance – including from the citizen's perspective – of legal rules regarding the structure and action of public administration.[23] This consensus among Francophone scholars writing in Quebec extends to works dealing with the judicial review of administrative activity; most authors of such works make it clear that their subject corresponds to only a part of the broader discipline.[24]

While textbooks do not provide conclusive evidence of terminological usage, they do reflect and influence the most current understanding of legal terms and categories. In the case of 'administrative law', clearly the dominant usage in English Canada suggests a 'defensive', 'red-light' approach to the subject, emphasising the protection of individual rights and a degree of diffidence in the face of government intervention. By contrast, the dominant French usage in Quebec suggests sensitivity to the need for government intervention on behalf of the public interest and therefore a 'positive', 'green-light' approach to 'le droit administratif' that includes confidence in the ability of rules to prevent abuse or misfeasance by power-holders.[25]

[17] S Blake, *Administrative Law in Canada*, 6th edn (Toronto, LexisNexis, 2017) 4; L Sossin and E Lawrence, *Administrative Law in Practice* (Toronto, Emond Montgomery, 2018) 4.

[18] M Rambourg, 'Notions générales sur le droit administratif canadien et québécois' in R Barbe (ed), *Droit administratif canadien et québécois* (Ottawa, Éditions de l'Université d'Ottawa, 1969) 11.

[19] R Dussault, *Traité de droit administratif canadien et québécois* (Quebec City, Presses de l'Université Laval, 1974).

[20] P Garant, *Droit administratif*, 7th edn (Montréal, Éditions Yvon Blais, 2017) 7 f.

[21] R Dussault and L Borgeat, *Traité de droit administratif*, 3 vols (Quebec City, Presses de l'Université Laval, 1984–89) vol I, 18; see also the preface to the English-language version of parts of this work: *Administrative Law: A Treatise*, 5 vols (Toronto, Carswell, 1985–90) vol 1, vii. Further references to this work are to the original French version.

[22] P Issalys and D Lemieux, *L'action gouvernementale*, 4th edn (Montreal, Éditions Yvon Blais, 2020) 13.

[23] R Dussault and L Borgeat (n 21) vol I, 38; L Borgeat, 'Les enjeux méconnus de l'autre droit administratif' (1994) 73 *Revue du Barreau canadien* 319.

[24] G Pepin and Y Ouellette, *Principes de contentieux administratif*, 2nd edn (Cowansville, QC, Éditions Yvon Blais, 1982) 1 ff, 35 f; however, see P Lemieux, *Droit administratif*, 6th edn (Sherbrooke, QC, Éditions de la Revue de droit de l'Université de Sherbrooke, 2014).

[25] The 'red light'/'green light' metaphor is of course borrowed from C Harlow and R Rawlings, *Law and Administration*, 3rd edn (Cambridge, Cambridge University Press, 2009) ch 1.

Each of these *contrasting approaches* leads to greater emphasis being placed on some parts of the law than on others. The dominant view of administrative law in Anglophone Canada, having as its core concern the protection of the rights and interests of citizens in the context of individualised decision-making by the public authorities, gives priority to matters of administrative procedure and, from that angle, attaches some importance to the distinction between different forms of executive action. By contrast, the distinction between 'general' and 'special' administrative law has little relevance where one approaches the whole field through a discussion of judicial review as its key general feature.[26] Such an approach tends to downplay the role of administrative law as regards the substantive contents of public action and therefore shows reluctance in laying down principles of executive action. These principles, and even more so matters of administrative organisation, are largely viewed as questions better kept within the realm of policy, with the partial exception of matters of public finance.

The dominant view of 'le droit administratif' in Quebec, being more systemic, sees all four areas as legitimate objects for legal ordering. Thus, administrative organisation is dealt with in some detail, principles of executive action tend to be spelled out with increasing explicitness, different forms of executive action are subjected to distinct and fairly elaborate statutory regimes, and the approach to administrative procedure, including its attendant preoccupation with citizens' rights and interests, is systematic rather than context-sensitive. However, the contrast with Anglophone Canada should not be overemphasised; after all, the most basic, foundational elements in both approaches are the same, as will be seen from a survey of the sources of administrative law. While some textbooks refer to the 'general'/'special' distinction for expositive purposes, this is not reflected in the explicit structure of legislative sources. Some features of Quebec administrative law also appear in certain other provinces of Canada. Overall, however, the flavour of this area of the law certainly forms part of what makes Quebec a 'distinct society', having 'distinct legal traditions and social values'.[27] The subject of codification illustrates this, as will be seen from a consideration of the sources from which administrative law is derived in Canada.[28]

## II. Sources of Administrative Law

The current situation as regards the sources of administrative law in Canada may only be described having recourse to *history*. When the French settler colonies

[26] This approach and its relevance for Canada come out vividly in the Australian chapter in this book by J Boughey, 'The "Codification" of Administrative Law in Australia', sections I and IV.

[27] *Reference Re Supreme Court Act* 2014 SCC 21 para 49. Canadian cases and legislation, both federal and provincial, are available online at www.canlii.org.

[28] On the linguistic and territorial divide in administrative law scholarship, see R Leckey, 'Prescribed by Law/Une règle de droit' (2007) 45 *Osgoode Hall Law Journal* 571.

of Acadia and New France were ceded to Great Britain in 1713 and 1763, the public law of England was introduced in the territories now forming the eastern and central parts of Canada. The effect of British conquest on the private law of New France was initially in doubt. The issue was resolved by an Act of the British Parliament in 1774, confirming French law, as it had been applied in New France, as the authoritative source in matters of 'property and civil rights' over a large territory corresponding roughly to present-day Quebec and Ontario.[29] Leaving aside a number of exceptions and niceties, this implied that the 'great divide' in sources of the law was to run between private law and public law.

The public law of England was based at the time, as it still is to a significant extent, on accumulated case law – the common law – as well as a few constitutional documents such as Magna Carta, the Petition of Right 1628, the Bill of Rights 1689 and the Act of Settlement 1701.[30] Its actual working depended, as it still does, on a body of conventional institutions and practices such as parliamentary procedure, the Cabinet or the Prime Minister. The vast body of legislation associated, in Britain as elsewhere, with the growth of the modern state had not yet appeared at the end of the eighteenth century. 'Administrative law' was an unknown and meaningless phrase in a system where the common law ruled indiscriminately over public authorities and private persons. However, the Act of 1774, in pointing imprecisely at 'property and civil rights' as a distinct area of law, implied some departure from that basic unity of the law in the case of the territory then known as the 'Province of Quebec'.

A complex series of occurrences since 1774 has altered the fundamental structure of the sources of law in Canada. Two events stand out as particularly significant. In 1866, the legislature of what had become the 'Province of Canada' adopted the Civil Code of Lower Canada, codifying the body of French law still applicable in the territory corresponding to modern-day Quebec, along with other sources.[31] The following year, the British Parliament enacted the British North America Act 1867 (BNA Act 1867), uniting a group of colonies under a federal system of government.[32] Two features of that Act are directly relevant in

[29] An Act for making more effectual Provision for the Government of the Province of Quebec in North America, 14 Geo III c 83 (UK), now Quebec Act, 1774, RSC (1985) app II no 2, s viii. This enactment, and others of constitutional significance referred to in this chapter, are available online at www.canadiana.ca.

[30] On the previous history of the common law, see in this book EL Rubin, 'The United States: Systematic But Incomplete Codification', section II. From a Canadian perspective, see M Rowe and M Collins, 'The History of Administrative Law' (2021) 34 *Canadian Journal of Administrative Law and Practice* 87.

[31] On the genesis of that code, see: JEC Brierley, 'Quebec's Civil Law Codification: Viewed and Reviewed' (1968) 14 *McGill Law Journal* 521; S Normand, 'La codification de 1866 : contexte et impact' in P Glenn (ed), *Droit québécois et droit français: communauté, autonomie, concordance* (Cowansville, QC, Éditions Yvon Blais, 1993) 43; M Morin, 'Portalis c. Bentham? Les objectifs assignés à la codification du droit civil et du droit pénal en France, en Angleterre et au Canada' in RA Macdonald (ed), *Perspectives on Legislation* (Ottawa, Law Commission of Canada, 1999) 141; EH Reiter, 'Imported Books, Imported Ideas: Reading European Jurisprudence in Mid-nineteenth Century Quebec' (2004) 22 *Law and History Review* 445.

[32] 30–31 Vict c 3 (UK), now the Constitution Act, 1867, RSC (1985) app II no 5.

connection with the sources of the law. First, the preamble to the Act describes the constitutional arrangements set out in its provisions as 'similar in principle to [the Constitution] of the United Kingdom'. This suggests the continued existence of unwritten constitutional principles that are able to complement the actual contents of that Act and to inform its overall architecture.[33] Second, the phrase 'property and civil rights' re-appears, this time to describe one of the classes of matters coming exclusively under the legislative authority of each of the federated provinces (section 92(13)).[34] This ensured that the predominantly French-speaking Province of Quebec would keep control over the existence and evolution of its newly adopted Civil Code.

What does this mean in relation to the sources of administrative law in Canada today? Clearly, there are *constitutional norms* among these sources. However, only a fraction of these appear as textual provisions. For instance, the BNA Act 1867 (now called the Constitution Act, 1867) devotes only a few provisions to the 'Executive Power', several of them being today of mere historical interest (sections 9–16 and 58–68). A few more provisions deal with public revenues, debts, assets and taxation (sections 102–26). Apart from passing references to public 'offices' or 'officers', there is no mention of public administration as an object of legislation among the matters assigned respectively to the federal Parliament and the provincial legislatures. Perhaps the most significant provision is that 'the Executive Government and Authority of and over Canada is … declared to continue and be vested in the Queen' (section 9). This confirms that Canadian administrative law incorporates the common law concept of the Crown, with its attendant prerogatives and special rules, obviously subject to the constraining provisions of the Bill of Rights 1689 and the Act of Settlement 1701.[35] Of course, the Crown, as well as other 'dignified parts' of the Constitution made partially explicit in the Constitution Act, 1867, such as the Privy Council, blend into the institutional apparatus and underlying 'principles' that evolved out of British constitutional history until 1867.[36]

This massive reliance on the common law and on the conventional framework of executive authority, operating beyond the terms of the Constitution Act, 1867,

[33] *Reference re Remuneration of Judges of the Provincial Court of Prince Edward Island* [1997] 3 SCR 3. An open-ended list of further unwritten constitutional principles was spelled out in the *Reference re Secession of Quebec* [1998] 2 SCR 217 (federalism, democracy, constitutionalism and the rule of law, protection of minorities).

[34] *Citizens' Insurance Co v Parsons* (1881) 7 AC 96 (PC); *Secretary of Prince Edward Island v Egan* [1941] SCR 396.

[35] M Firmini and J Smith, 'The Crown in Canada' in PC Oliver, P Macklem and N DesRosiers (eds), *Oxford Handbook of the Canadian Constitution* (Oxford, Oxford University Press, 2017) 129; D Smith, *The Invisible Crown: The First Principle of Canadian Government* (Toronto, University of Toronto Press, 1995).

[36] The phrase 'dignified parts' was coined in the 1867 work by W Bagehot, *The English Constitution* (London, Oxford University Press, 1968) 4. The House of Lords is also one of those parts that was adapted to suit Canadian conditions: *Reference re Senate Reform* 2014 SCC 32.

applies equally at the federal level and the provincial level. Indeed, no province has to this day enacted a single document that could stand as a full constitution, though all have made use of their constitutional authority to 'make laws amending the constitution of the province'.[37] Such action has taken the form of ordinary statutes dealing, inter alia, with the organs and structure of the province's executive. Some such statutes having constitutional significance will be referred to later on in this chapter.

A further point about the constitutional norms governing administrative law in Canada is relevant for the present purposes. While key institutions of administrative law, such as the Prime Minister, the budget or judicial review, remain to this day conspicuously absent from constitutional texts, some pre-existing principles, institutions or conventions did receive formal recognition in the Constitution Act, 1867. For instance, British parliamentary practice about the presentation of bills involving the expense of public money was 'codified' (in the peculiar sense that will be developed later on in this chapter) in section 54.[38] So was the Crown's immunity from taxation in section 125.[39] Indeed, section 53 implicitly relied on a cardinal principle of English public law, which requires parliamentary consent to taxation; to that extent, this principle was also thereby 'codified'.[40]

Thus, most of what is relevant to administrative law in the Constitution Act, 1867 takes its meaning in the light of the traditional relation of statute law to common law in the English legal system. The original BNA Act 1867 was, after all, an ordinary British statute.

The Constitution Act, 1982 has added new elements to the constitutional framework of administrative law.[41] Apart from effecting the 'patriation' of the constitutional order, it introduced a Canadian Charter of Rights and Freedoms that expressly applies to the 'government' of Canada and of each province.[42] Interpreting the word 'government' in this new context has sometimes proved difficult; interestingly, this issue received much the same solution as the older problem of identifying 'agents of the Crown'.[43] As regards the sources of administrative law, the key point of the Constitution Act, 1982 is that the latter ranks the 'Constitution of Canada' as the 'supreme law of Canada', having primacy over 'any law'

[37] BNA Act 1867 (n 32) s 92(1), now replaced by s 45 of the Constitution Act, 1982, RSC (1985) app II no 44. British Columbia does have a formal Constitution Act, RSBC 1996 c 66; however, this statute is a rather unsystematic collection of provisions dealing mainly with the Legislative Assembly and, to a lesser extent, with the executive. In British Columbia as in other provinces, the substantive Constitution would include a number of statutes regulating the major institutions of government and spelling out fundamental rights and liberties.

[38] *Eurig Estate (Re)* [1998] 2 SCR 565, 581 f.

[39] *Re Exported Natural Gas* [1982] 1 SCR 1004, 1067.

[40] *Confédération des syndicats nationaux v A-G Canada* 2008 SCC 68, paras 81 ff.

[41] Constitution Act, 1982 (n 37) app II no 44. The political legitimacy of that constitutional reform remains questionable, the National Assembly of Quebec having to this day denied its consent thereto.

[42] Part I, especially s 32.

[43] *McKinney v University of Guelph* [1993] 3 SCR 229; *cf Westeel-Rosco v Board of Governors of South Saskatchewan Hospital Centre* [1977] 2 SCR 238.

('toute règle de droit').[44] Again, interpreting the word 'law' has proved troublesome: the Civil Code of Lower Canada and its successor the Civil Code of Québec of 1994 clearly qualify as 'a law', but what about the common law?[45]

Therefore, constitutional enactments have little to say about executive action by the Crown. They direct their readers to look instead at common law rules and conventional arrangements. However, both of these may be modified, supplemented, confirmed or ruled out by legislation. While legislation may thus supplant the common law, it operates against a background of common law rules and institutions. Among the latter are the Crown's prerogative powers. Yet, in the case of Quebec, legislation includes the Civil Code, parts of which expressly apply to the state (ie, the Crown); indeed, the Code as a whole forms the *jus commune* of Quebec, thus confining the common law to a residual role in matters of Quebec public law.[46]

Given such a constitutional and systemic context, one could only expect that executive action in Canada would be shaped essentially through *legislation*. Under the federal system introduced by the Constitution Act, 1867, the legislative and executive branches of government both have a compound nature. There are 11 legislative authorities, each exercising sovereign law-making powers on matters allocated to it by the Constitution Act, 1867, subject only to the Canadian Charter of Rights and Freedoms.[47] Similarly, there are 11 distinct executives, each enjoying the prerogative powers of the Crown and operating within the broad framework of constitutional enactments, conventions of the Constitution, and specific enactments adopted by the relevant legislative authority – federal or provincial as the case may be.[48] Provincial legislatures and governments operate with a keen concern for their autonomy. While there are many instances of cooperation and frequent borrowing of ideas and practices between them, this is less true in matters of public

[44] 30–31 Vict c 3 (UK), now the Constitution Act, 1867, RSC (1985) app II no 5 s 52; *Re Manitoba Language Rights* [1985] 1 SCR 721.

[45] On this issue, see H Brun, G Tremblay and E Brouillet (n 7) 977 f.

[46] Civil Code of Québec, CQLR c CCQ-1991 preliminary provision (Code as *jus commune*) and art 300 (Code applies as a suppletive source to legal persons established in the public interest, ie, 'personnes morales de droit public') and 1376 (rules on obligations apply to the state, its bodies and all other legal persons established in the public interest). The Civil Code, as well as Quebec legislation generally, can be accessed online at: www.legisquebec.gouv.qc.ca. See: *Prud'homme v Prud'homme* 2002 SCC 85; *Finney v Barreau du Québec* 2004 SCC 36; P Garant, 'Code civil du Québec, Code de procédure civile et société distincte' (1996) 37 *Cahiers de droit* 1141; D Lemieux (n 6); F Allard, 'La disposition préliminaire du Code civil du Québec, l'idée de droit commun et le rôle du Code en droit fédéral' (2009) 88 *Revue du Barreau canadien* 275. *cf* the role of the civil law with respect to public administration in the Netherlands in this book: Y Schuurmans, T Barkhuysen and W den Ouden, 'Codification of Administrative Law in the Netherlands', section I.

[47] PW Hogg (n 7) para 12.1(a); H Brun, G Tremblay and E Brouillet (n 7) 412 ff.

[48] J Fournier and A Binette, 'La Couronne : vecteur du fédéralisme canadien' (2017) 58 *Cahiers de droit* 625. The regulation of the securities market illustrates the complexity of achieving co-operation on the basis of 'watertight' jurisdictions: *Reference re Securities Act* 2011 SCC 66; *Reference re Pan-Canadian Securities Regulation* 2018 SCC 48. In this respect, federalism operates rather differently in Canada and Germany: see in this book M Heintzen, 'Codification of Administrative Law in Germany and the European Union', section I.A.iii and A Berger, 'Science Codification for the European Union: The ReNEUAL Network', section III.A.iii.

law.[49] Thus, the Uniform Law Conference of Canada, an intergovernmental body with recommendatory powers, rarely deals with administrative law subjects.[50] All legislative authorities have been making creative use of their law-making powers in matters relating to the executive, ie, in the field of administrative law.[51]

This is clearly visible in the area of administrative organisation. In all 11 Canadian jurisdictions, executive authorities belong to two major types: departments and agencies. Departments (or ministries) come under the immediate authority of a minister. Ministers being in theory close advisors to the Queen ('privy councillors'), the Crown's prerogative powers extend to the creation of departments. Nowadays, the legislatures of all the provinces (but not the federal Parliament) have 'codified' this prerogative authority.[52] Such general provisions, based on section 63 of the Constitution Act, 1867 and analogous enactments, clearly stand on a constitutional level.[53] However, a department may also be set up by a specific statute. This is standard practice at the federal level, in Ontario and in Quebec; British Columbia and Manitoba use both methods.[54] In all provinces (but again, not at the federal level), a general statute dealing with the organisation of the executive lays down some basic elements of the structure and activity of departments (eg, delegation of authority within a department).[55] Throughout Canada, the departmental form of organisation usually follows a pattern established in the mid-nineteenth century.[56] This basic stability stands in sharp contrast to

[49] But see: JI Gow, *Learning from Others: Administrative Innovations among Governments* (Toronto, Institute of Public Administration of Canada, 1994); A Lawlor and JP Lewis, 'Evolving Structure of Governments: Portfolio Adoption across the Canadian Provinces from 1867 to 2012' (2014) 57 *Canadian Public Administration* 589. On broader interprovincial dynamics, see: K Banting, 'Canada: Nation-Building in a Federal Welfare State' in H Obinger et al (eds), *Federalism and the Welfare State: New World and European Experiences* (Cambridge, Cambridge University Press, 2005) 89; G Charland, 'Le Québec comparé et les finances publiques au Canada, 1992–2002' in J Crête (ed), *Politiques publiques : le Québec comparé* (Quebec City, Presses de l'Université Laval, 2006) 71.

[50] The Conference drafted uniform Acts on regulations (1983), regulatory offences procedure (1992) and public inquiries (2004), as well as a Model Administrative Procedure Code (1991). None of these appears to have exerted much influence over provincial legislators. Together, and with a few additional proposals on public law subjects, they represent only a small proportion of the Conference's total achievements. See the Conference's website: www.ulcc.ca.

[51] *cf* the autonomy of Swiss cantons in this respect in this book F Uhlmann, 'Codification of Administrative Law in Switzerland', section I.B.

[52] eg, Manitoba: Executive Government Organization Act, CCSM c E170, s 8.

[53] Section 63 of the Constitution Act, 1867 (n 32) provides that in Ontario and Quebec, ministers are to be appointed by the Lieutenant Governor (ie, the Queen's representative); similar provisions applied in 1867 to ministers in Nova Scotia and New Brunswick (s 88) or were made in respect of other provinces in the various enactments through which they were brought into the federation.

[54] eg, Canada: Department of Transport Act, RSC (1985) c T-18; Ontario: Ministry of Health and Long-Term Care Act, RSO 1990 c M.26; British Columbia: School Act, RSBC 1996 c 412, pt 9; by contrast, there is no specific statutory basis for British Columbia's Ministry of Indigenous Relations and Reconciliation.

[55] eg, Alberta: Government Organization Act, RSA 2000 c G-10.

[56] JE Hodgetts, *Pioneer Public Service: An Administrative History of the United Canadas, 1841–1867* (Toronto, University of Toronto Press, 1955) ch VI, especially 25 ff, 91 ff; S Wilson, *Canadian Public Policy and Administration: Theory and Environment* (Toronto, McGraw-Hill Ryerson, 1981) chs 10 and 11; OP Dwivedi and JI Gow, *From Bureaucracy to Public Management: The Administrative Culture of the Government of Canada* (Peterborough, ON, Broadview Press, 1999) chs 3 and 6.

contemporary political and administrative practice, which favours frequent redistribution of tasks among departments to keep in step with social needs and policy priorities. The legal framework of departmental organisation is therefore kept to a minimum.[57] Pragmatism – a key word to understand all things Canadian – clearly takes precedence over explicit legislative ordering.

Agencies – ie, non-departmental components of the executive – come in large numbers and with a great variety in terms of function, size and form.[58] One thing they have in common is that a statute must explicitly provide for their existence. This is because, unlike departments, they do not come under the direct and constant supervision of a minister who would take responsibility before Parliament for any mistake, maladministration or misfeasance. Rather, Parliament grants some autonomy to agencies. Agencies require autonomy because of the nature of their activity – which may consist in providing independent advice,[59] managerial expertise,[60] adjudicative skills,[61] regulatory capabilities,[62] business acumen[63] or capacity for large-scale service delivery.[64] However, such autonomy has to be limited: Parliament, as it sets up agencies, therefore provides for specific channels of accountability and responsiveness on their part. All of this generates a vast body of necessarily specific legislation dealing with agencies' purposes, organisation, powers, financing, expenditures and supervision. Here again, pragmatism is the key word, with the added justification that agencies differ from one another, from the standpoint of their activity, much more than departments do. At the very most, Parliament will depart from an agency-specific approach by providing a uniform statutory framework for a category of agencies (eg, child and youth protection centres or administrative tribunals); yet, in several cases, such categories will be based on ad hoc purposes rather than on institutional logic (eg, 'departmental corporations').[65]

[57] This is particularly true of federal departments: eg, Department of Citizenship and Immigration Act, SC 1994 c 31.

[58] JE Hodgetts, *The Canadian Public Service: A Physiology of Government 1867–1970* (Toronto, University of Toronto Press, 1973) ch 7; Canada, Law Reform Commission, *Independent Administrative Agencies*, Working Paper 25 (Ottawa, Law Reform Commission, 1980); A Gélinas, *L'intervention et le retrait de l'État : l'impact sur l'organisation gouvernementale* (Quebec City, Presses de l'Université Laval, 2002); R Dussault and L Borgeat (n 21) vol I, 132 ff.

[59] eg, Ontario: Greenbelt Act, SO 2005 c 1 (Greenbelt Council).

[60] eg, Newfoundland and Labrador: Public Procurement Act, RSNL c P-41.001 (Public Procurement Agency).

[61] eg, British Columbia: Employment and Assistance Act, SBC 2002 c 42 (Employment and Assistance Appeal Tribunal).

[62] eg, Canadian Radio-Television and Telecommunications Commission Act, RSC (1985) c C-22.

[63] eg, Manitoba Hydro Act, CCSM c. H190.

[64] eg, Quebec: Act respecting health services and social services, CQLR c S-4.2 pt II (health and social services institutions).

[65] ibid, where provisions specific to child and youth protection centres add to or derogate from the basic regime of social services institutions. The Administrative Tribunals Act, SBC 2004 c 45, establishes a common regime for tribunals in British Columbia. The federal Financial Administration Act, RSC (1985) c F-11 s 2 and sched II provides for the Governor in Council to classify agencies as 'departmental corporations', thereby bringing them under specific provisions of the Act.

Legislation also plays a significant role in specifying various forms of executive action. In typical common law fashion, legislatures gradually adopted classifications of government actions first developed in the case law in order to carve out of the broad category of 'public power' types of power made subject to specific rules. Such is the case nowadays with several forms of executive action: investigative action in the form of a public inquiry, regulatory action in the form of regulation-making and patrimonial action in the form of procurement contracts. Each of these is subject to a legislative regime in federal law[66] and in the law of all provinces.[67] The case of individualised decision-making powers is different. Only the four larger provinces have subjected them to unified legislative treatment;[68] under federal law and in the other provinces, such powers remain governed by the common law and by sectoral legislative provisions. However, some of these sectoral regimes may be quite extensive and significant: individualised decision-making in matters of taxation is a case in point.[69] Another area where sectoral regimes have been spreading rapidly in recent years is the matter of administrative money penalties.[70] Whether general or sectoral in scope, all such legislative regimes essentially deal with administrative procedure.

However, it should be emphasised that in most cases, the process of regime-building has not been deductive, ie, the contents of a given regime did not develop logically from a clearly defined concept of the type of executive action to which it would apply. Instead, regime-building has proceeded inductively, starting from desired outcomes in terms of government action, from existing piecemeal statutory provisions and from constraints imposed by the then current state of the common law, and moving to a choice about which rules could conveniently be imposed on which set of actions – hence, a context-sensitive, unsystematic approach to the design of rules and a largely pragmatic definition of their range of application. To some extent, Quebec legislative regimes depart from this inductive approach, insofar as they are grounded in doctrinal definitions of the different types of executive action rather than on ad hoc definitions making implicit reference to the common law.[71]

[66] Inquiries Act, RSC (1985) c I-11; Statutory Instruments Act, RSC (1985) c S-22; Financial Administration Act (n 65) pt III.1.

[67] eg, Quebec: Act respecting public inquiry commissions, CQLR c C-37; Regulations Act, CQLR c R-18.1; Act respecting contracting by public bodies, CQLR c C-65.1.

[68] Ontario: Statutory Powers Procedure Act, RSO 1990 c S-22; Quebec: Act respecting administrative justice, CQLR c J-3; British Columbia: Administrative Tribunals Act (n 65); Alberta: Administrative Procedure and Jurisdiction Act, RSA 2000 c A-3. The last two statutes apply only to a limited number of agencies. The Ontario statute applies whenever a hearing is required by law prior to a decision. The Quebec statute applies, albeit differently, to a broad range of individualised decisions by departments and agencies; see below n 119 and corresponding text.

[69] eg, Newfoundland and Labrador: Revenue Administration Act, SNL 2009 c R-15.01, pts I and II.

[70] eg, Canada: Agriculture and Agri-Food Administrative Money Penalties Act, SC 1995 c 40; Quebec: Environment Quality Act, CQLR c Q-2, ss 115.13–115.28; British Columbia: Safety Standards Act, SBC 2003 c 39, ss 40–41.

[71] This might be a reflection of the greater familiarity of Quebec jurists with the concept of 'administrative act': D Mockle, 'De quelques influences croisées dans l'élaboration de la théorie des actes administratifs' in S Lavallée and P Issalys (eds), *Vastes mondes. Études en l'honneur du professeur Denis Lemieux* (Montreal, Éditions Yvon Blais, 2018) 245.

Quebec legislation also occasionally stands apart from federal and most other provincial legislation in terms of being less averse to laying down principles of executive action. Yet, even in Quebec administrative law, the expression of such principles is far less elaborate than in, say, Swedish, Italian, Portuguese, Spanish or South African legislation – let alone the statements to be found in the constitutions of those countries.[72] Such wide-ranging principles do exist in the Canadian legal order; they mostly derive from the common law. Essentially, they boil down to a pair of key concepts. One is the rule of law, requiring that executive action be grounded in, and limited by, the law of the land as applied by an independent judiciary.[73] The other is parliamentary sovereignty, requiring that executive action be conducted in the public interest, as defined by Parliament mainly in the form of statutes. However, very few Canadian statutes have attempted to formulate the public interest in the quality of administrative action in terms of values such as impartiality, economy, timeliness, efficiency, good faith, accessibility and accountability. Again, this apparent disinterest in the expression of abstract principles reflects the essentially pragmatic – rather than programmatic – approach of Canadian legislators to administrative law.

This, of course, does not mean that legislatures lack interest in administrative law in the broad sense of that phrase. Very extensive legislation, both federal and provincial, deals with 'special' branches of administrative law, such as public finance, the public service, or lands, resources and other public property. While recent legislation on such topics has tended to go beyond its rather technical contents to formulate guiding principles,[74] older statutes have left to judicial interpretation the task of distilling principles from disparate, specific and mundane provisions.[75]

The reliance on legislation for the development of administrative law, especially since the 1960s, has entailed a pervasive presence of *regulations* as a source of law in this field. This reflects two features of Canadian public law. First, regulation-making authority can only derive from explicit legislation; Crown prerogative no longer serves as a significant basis for laying down rules of general application. Second, most statutes do confer regulation-making powers on some part of the executive. In a number of cases, the need to exercise such powers never arises.

[72] *cf* in this book J Reichel and M Ribbing, 'Codification of Administrative Law in Sweden', section II.B; also in this book R Caranta, 'Administrative Proceedings in Italy', sections II and IV.B; Constitution of the Portuguese Republic 1976, art 266 and Código do Procedimento Administrativo, DL 4/2015, arts 3–19; Spanish Constitution 1978, art 103.1 and Ley de Régimen jurídico del Sector público, 40/2015, art 3; Constitution of the Republic of South Africa 1996, art 168 and Public Administration Management Act, Act 11 of 2014, s 4.

[73] The preamble to the Constitution Act, 1982 (n 37) somewhat obliquely refers to the rule of law ('la primauté du droit') as being 'recognized by' the principles upon which Canada is founded. It shares this status with 'the supremacy of God'. Already before 1982, the rule of law and parliamentary sovereignty were implicitly included among the principles of the Constitution of the UK, referred to in the preamble to the Constitution Act, 1867 (n 32).

[74] eg, Ontario: Crown Forest Sustainability Act, SO 1994 c 25, ss 1–2.

[75] eg, Canada: Fisheries Act, RSC (1985) c F-14; *Comeau's Sea Foods v R* [1997] 1 SCR 12; *Saulnier v Royal Bank of Canada* 2008 SCC 58.

In other areas, by contrast, the legislation is very sketchy and most of the legal ordering has to be developed through regulations. In the typical situation, the statute, while substantial, calls for complementary rules in the form of regulations, which operate with the same binding force as the statute itself.

Federal and provincial governments have had to respond, over the last four decades, to the concerns loudly voiced by business interests about the constraints and burdens flowing from the regulation of economic activity – in particular those associated with regulations. Following, or even anticipating, the lead given by the Organisation for Economic Co-operation and Development (OECD), Canadian governments have thus adopted policies to contain the growth of regulatory law and alleviate its effects on businesses.[76] Interestingly, changes in parts of the regulation-making process (eg, regulatory impact analysis, or public consultation on draft regulations) have been introduced mostly via political and administrative guidance rather than through amendments to the legal framework of regulation-making powers. A breach was thus opened in the classical model of law-making: the production of a certain type of legal norms (regulations) is no longer entirely governed and sanctioned by other legal norms, but instead incorporates 'mandatory' phases devoid of legal sanction.[77]

All three types of positive norms – constitutional enactments, statutes and regulations – operate against the background and upon the foundations provided by the *common law*. This phrase, of course, is shorthand to describe the body of rules formulated over the centuries by English, then British, courts and then by the courts in the various territories brought together in 1867–73 and 1949 to form present-day Canada. This body of rules still forms a residual source of administrative law, insofar as it is not superseded by local legislation.[78] This last reservation is particularly significant in Quebec, where, as was mentioned above, the Civil Code has direct relevance for the legal regime of executive action.

Being a residual source does not confine the common law to insignificance, even in Quebec.[79] On the contrary, the accumulated case law is frequently relied upon in matters of administrative procedure,[80] or for the characterisation of forms of executive action,[81] or even for upholding the basic principles

[76] eg, Canada, Treasury Board Secretariat, Cabinet Directive on Regulation, 2018 (available online at: www.tbs-sct.gc.ca); Ontario, Ministry of Government and Consumer Services, Ontario Regulatory Policy, 2014 (available online at: www.ontariocanada.com); Quebec, Décret concernant l'organisation et le fonctionnement du Conseil exécutif, D. 166-2017, [2018] 150 GOQ II 31, app A (Politique gouvernementale sur l'allégement réglementaire et administratif) (available online at: www.mce.gouv.qc.ca).

[77] *Conseil du patronat du Québec c PG Québec* [2003] RJQ 3154 (CS); *Amalorpavanathan v Minister of Health* 2013 ONSC 5415; *Canadian Union of Public Employees v A-G Canada* 2018 FC 518.

[78] Of course, in all Canadian jurisdictions as in Britain (see in this book S Nason, 'Codification of Administrative Law in the United Kingdom: Beyond the Common Law', s IV), statute law, if only by its sheer volume, has come to overshadow the common law in most fields of executive action.

[79] *2747-3174 Québec Inc v Régie des permis d'alcool* [1996] 3 SCR 919, paras 82–109.

[80] eg, *Baker v Canada (Minister of Citizenship and Immigration)* [1999] 2 SCR 817 on the duty to give reasons.

[81] eg, *Bell Canada v Canadian Telephone Employees Association* 2003 SCC 36 on the characterisation of an order as a regulation.

of executive action.[82] The most significant part of that case law is generated through the judicial review of the legality of executive action.[83] This power of review, vested in the superior courts, is itself an element of the common law. Characteristically, Quebec has for a long time chosen to set out in a legislative provision the inherent judicial review powers of its superior court.[84] This enactment tellingly illustrates the other way in which the common law part of administrative law remains significant: it provides the material from which legislatures derive legislative norms – a form of 'codification' to which this chapter will presently return.

Last, but certainly not the least significant, in this survey of the sources of Canadian administrative law come *administrative norms*. The role of these non-legal standards of conduct in the deployment of legal ordering was pointed out above in relation to policy documents governing the regulation-making process. Indeed, albeit to a more limited extent, the making of statutes is itself coming to be governed not only by constitutional requirements or parliamentary procedure, but also by administrative norms of this type (eg, by the policy requirement in Quebec that a legislative impact analysis be published as soon as a bill is laid before Parliament).[85]

Among legally relevant administrative norms, the canonical form is the departmental or agency manual or set of guidelines governing the interpretation, application and enforcement of a statute or regulation. It is commonly felt that one cannot fully understand and predict the operation of statutory and regulatory schemes without taking into account such administrative instruments.[86] Quite apart from the issue of their recognition as a form of 'law', the design and formulation of administrative norms often strongly resemble those of proper legal norms.[87] Their status and location within the conventional hierarchy of legal norms remain problematic; yet, legal norms themselves sometimes refer to the existence of administrative norms, thus conferring upon them at least some legally binding force.[88] Statutes occasionally provide expressly for the making

[82] eg, *Roncarelli v Duplessis* [1959] SCR 121 on the duty to exercise discretionary powers for proper purposes.

[83] 'Significance' here should not be confused with volume: the number of judicial review cases represents only a very small fraction of the vast body of case law generated by adjudicative, regulatory or other agencies in the exercise of their respective jurisdiction. Where this jurisdiction extends to a broad range of subjects – as is the case, for example, with the Administrative Tribunal of Québec or the Nova Scotia Utility and Review Board – that case law may become quite significant and acquire some precedential value, even though such bodies remain subject to judicial review by the relevant superior court.

[84] Code of Civil Procedure, CQLR c C-25.01 s 34.

[85] Quebec, Décret concernant l'organisation et le fonctionnement du Conseil exécutif (n 76) app A s 19.

[86] Publication of such documents is normally made mandatory; eg, Quebec: Regulation respecting the distribution of information and the protection of personal information, CQLR c A-2.1, r 2 s 4.

[87] *Greater Vancouver Transportation Authority v Canadian Federation of Students* 2009 SCC 31.

[88] *Friends of the Oldman River Society v Canada (Minister of Transport)* [1992] 1 SCR 3.

and effect of such documents.[89] Indeed, since acceptance grows with familiarity, administrative norms may be acquiring legitimacy as a standard phase in a sort of graduated *cursus*: from case-by-case decision to administrative norm to regulation to legislation – and then perhaps to code?[90]

However that may come to be, administrative norms already proliferate in all areas. They may deal with administrative organisation (eg, instructions about the delegation of decision-making authority); they may state principles of executive action (eg, interpretative statements of policy about the meaning of the 'public interest' in a particular legislative context); they often structure administrative procedures (eg, guidelines on the granting of a paper, electronic or *in vivo* hearing); or they may discipline forms of executive action (eg, guidance on the choice among a range of instruments). Administrative norms also occur in many special areas, such as financial administration (eg, rules on travel expenses by civil servants on official business). In spite of the hugely significant part played by administrative norms in executive action, their making and form remain largely unregulated.

## III. Codification and Administrative Law

In Canadian usage, both English and French, the word 'codification' may convey *several meanings*. First, in both languages, it may refer to the action of formulating in a single, orderly, systematic and coherent enactment all the essential rules forming a fairly extensive branch of the legal system.[91] This first meaning obviously describes the defining feature of so-called 'civilian' legal systems. Codes elaborated in this way form part of legislation, though they usually enjoy some logical pre-eminence among other laws by reason of their scope and foundational character.

A second Canadian usage refers to the action of formulating in a legislative enactment some rule or set of rules previously recognised in the common law.[92] A codification in this second sense has occurred with respect to judicial review.

[89] eg, Canadian Air Transport Security Authority Act, SC 2002 c 9 s 4; Farming and Food Production Protection Act, SO 1998 c 1 s 9. Such a statutory basis is required for laying down guidelines directed by Cabinet or a minister to a non-departmental agency, whereas guidelines directed at departmental officials are viewed as an instance of a minister's authority to instruct his subordinates, as is the case, for instance, in Belgium: see in this book S de Somer and I Opdebeek, 'Codification of Belgian Administrative Law: "Nothing is Written"', section II.B.

[90] *Capital Cities Communications v Canadian Radio-Television Commission* [1978] 2 SCR 141.

[91] J Vanderlinden, 'Qu'est-ce qu'un code?' (2005) 46 *Cahiers de droit* 29; D Walker, *The Oxford Companion to Law* (Oxford, Clarendon Press, 1980) 237; K Sojka-Zielinska, 'Codification' in AJ Arnaud (ed), *Dictionnaire encyclopédique de théorie et de sociologie du droit* (Paris/Brussels, LGDJ/Story Scientia, 1988); AF Bisson, 'Effet de codification et interprétation' (1986) 17 *Revue générale de droit* 359; D Baranger, *Penser la loi* (Paris, Gallimard, 2018) 281 ff.

[92] R Sullivan, *Sullivan on the Construction of Statutes*, 6th edn (Markham, ON, LexisNexis, 2014) 545 ff, 744 f; PA Côté and M Devinat, *Interprétation des lois*, 5th edn (Montreal, Éditions Thémis, 2021) 61 ff; A Grenon, 'Codes et codifications : dialogue avec la common law?' (2005) 46 *Cahiers de droit* 53.

As mentioned above, the inherent supervisory jurisdiction of the superior court was placed on a statutory basis in Quebec in 1897,[93] while the remedies flowing from that jurisdiction benefited from successive statutory simplifications at various points in time in federal law[94] and in the law of Quebec, Ontario and British Columbia.[95] This practice illustrates the relationship between common law and statute law in a system based on English law – as is public law in Canada. This form of 'codification' raises a host of baffling issues (eg, what happens when a statute attempts to reformulate a common law rule about the management of the common law/statute law relationship?).[96] Codification in this sense is therefore often viewed with either apprehension or scepticism by common lawyers, depending on whether they foresee that codification will inhibit further development of the common law, or that greater certainty of the law through codification will prove more apparent than real.

Examples of 'codification' in the first sense easily come to mind. Predictably, they belong to the Quebec system of private law: the Civil Code of Québec and the Code of Civil Procedure.[97] Some other instances from Quebec relate to other branches of the law, though their scope is more limited (the Code of Penal Procedure, the Highway Safety Code or the Professional Code)[98] or their contents fall short of being exhaustive (the Labour Code or the Municipal Code).[99] The preliminary provision in both the Civil Code and the Code of Civil Procedure confers on these two enactments a foundational role in respect of the whole Quebec legal system and states that they are to operate 'in harmony' with the general principles of law and with the Charter of Human Rights and Freedoms, a quasi-constitutional statute.[100] The other codes, by contrast, are the same rank as any other statute. In Quebec legislative usage, the word 'code' is also closely associated with the notion of a standard of conduct or practice – hence the existence of a code of ethics for parliamentarians, in the form of a statute[101] and of a host of regulations bearing the word 'code' in their title.[102]

[93] *Code of Civil Procedure*, 60 Vict c 48 art 50; see R Dussault and L Borgeat (n 21) vol III, 51 ff and *Reference re Code of Civil Procedure (Que)*, art 35 2021 SCC 27, paras 42–51, 63 and 68.

[94] Federal Court Act SC 1970-71-72 c 1 s 18; now Federal Courts Act RSC (1985) c F-7 s 18–18.1.

[95] Code of Civil Procedure (n 84) art 529; Judicial Review Procedure Act, RSO 1990 c J.1; Judicial Review Procedure Act, RSBC 1996 c 241. *cf* the recent British and Australian debates on the merits and perils of codifying judicial review powers and grounds for their exercise: see in this book S Nason (n 78) section IV.B and J Boughey (n 26) section IV.

[96] On the rule about the Crown's position in relation to the binding effect of statutes, see: *Alberta Government Telephones v Canada (Canadian Radio-Television and Telecommunications Commission)* [1989] 2 SCR 225; R Sullivan (n 92) 857 ff; PA Côté and M Devinat (n 92) 246 ff.

[97] Above nn 46 and 84.

[98] CQLR cc C-25.1, C-24.2 and C-26 respectively.

[99] CQLR cc C-27 and C-27.1 respectively.

[100] CQLR c C-12. See: AF Bisson, 'La Disposition préliminaire du Code civil' (1999) 44 *Revue de droit de McGill* 539; C Piché, 'La disposition préliminaire du Code de procédure civile' (2014) 73 *Revue du Barreau* 135.

[101] Code of Ethics and Conduct of the Members of the National Assembly, CQLR c C-23.1.

[102] eg, Code of ethics applicable to the members of the Administrative Tribunal of Québec, CQLR c J-3 r 1; Code of Conduct for Lobbyists, CQLR c T-11.011 r 2; Pesticide Management Code, CQLR c

Among the statutory codes, the Professional Code deserves special mention. Its adoption in 1973 marked the 'publicisation' of the law of organised professions; these had developed since the mid-nineteenth century as purely private associations. The Code refashioned these professional groupings according to a uniform basic regime, which could be extended in the future to emerging professions. It also assigned to all 'professional orders' an overarching purpose of protecting the public. Finally, it brought the orders under supervision and regulation exercised jointly by a public agency and the council of ministers. Under the Code come two dozen complementary statutes, each dealing specifically with one of the professional orders; the latter, in turn, are charged with developing regulations on matters such as admission, practice, and ethics.[103] If only because of the systemic character it has imparted on the law of professions, the Professional Code rightly deserves its name. From the standpoint of the present chapter, it is also noticeable as an adaptation of codal technique to public law purposes.

One is hard-pressed to find examples of 'codification' in the first sense in federal law or in the legal systems of the common law provinces. The only clear instance would be the Canadian Criminal Code, which brought together, in 1892, in a fairly systematic arrangement rules previously scattered among a number of statutes and in the common law.[104] The Canada Labour Code, which has some public law aspects, also displays some characteristics of a true code.[105] Apart from these two federal codes, various provincial enactments bear a title containing the word 'code', despite having often a very narrow or mundane object or a very modest rank in the legal system. Thus, some provinces have a Human Rights Code that may contain a Bill of Rights, but usually concentrates on prohibiting discrimination in employment or in the provision of goods, services or accommodation.[106] A few provincial statutes, or even regulations, also appear as 'codes' in the area of labour law, even though nothing distinguishes them from ordinary enactments.[107] Further away from the 'general part' of administrative law, the word 'code' is sometimes used in mere regulations of a highly technical nature (on building practices, safety features or professional standards) which may incorporate normative instruments produced in the private sector.[108] Overall, then, in common law Canada,

P-9.3 r 1; Construction Code, CQLR c B-1.1 r 2. Local councils are required to adopt codes of ethics and conduct for municipal officers and employees: Municipal Ethics and Good Conduct Act, CQLR c E-15.1.0.1.

[103] eg, Architects Act, CQLR c A-21. Over 20 professional orders have no specific enabling statute and stand regulated by the Code alone.

[104] Criminal Code, RSC (1985) c C-46.

[105] Canada Labour Code, RSC (1985) c L-2.

[106] Manitoba: Human Rights Code, CCSM c H175 and Saskatchewan Human Rights Code, 2018, SS 2018 c S-24.2. Similar statutes in other provinces bear the title 'Human Rights Act'. The Quebec statute on basic human rights and liberties (above n 100) expresses its broader scope and quasi-constitutional nature through being titled a Charter; see P Bosset and M Coutu, 'Acte fondateur ou loi ordinaire? Le statut de la Charte des droits et libertés de la personne dans l'ordre juridique québécois' (2015) *Revue québécoise de droit international* (n° spéc.) 37.

[107] eg, Alberta: Labour Relations Code, RSA 2000 c L-1.

[108] eg, Nova Scotia: Electrical Code Regulations, NS Reg. 95/99; Ontario: X-ray Safety Code, RRO 1990 Reg. 543; New Brunswick: Code of Conduct, NB Reg. 2018-64, made under the Local Governance Act.

the concept of code is used infrequently and suggests ideas of exhaustiveness and technicality in relation to a carefully defined subject – that is, the quintessential qualities of a statute in a common law system!

Just as there are would-be codes that cannot be differentiated from ordinary statutes, or indeed from regulations, there are ordinary statutes that in fact play the role of a code and take on some of its formal features. For that reason, in English-Canadian usage, such statutes are frequently described as 'complete codes' or 'exhaustive codes' in relation to their subject matter.[109] Such statutes may deal with some part of the common law, and may then express an intention to replace common law rules with entirely new ones.[110] Alternatively, they may appear in areas of the law unknown to classical common law, such as social security, public health or environmental protection. Apart from their occasional borrowing of common law concepts, such legislative schemes stand as it were on their own, may therefore be interpreted on their own terms and may thus avoid the constraints of the traditional common law/statute law relationship. It is through the existence of this type of statutes that one may discern some degree of codification in Canadian administrative law. The legal system of Quebec is not in this respect markedly different from the other Canadian legal systems; it simply makes use more readily of this type of legislation, which in modern days sits in a comfortable relationship with the Civil Code.[111]

The following brief survey of this type of semi-codal statutes (or perhaps they might be termed 'proto-codal') elaborates on our earlier remarks about the objects dealt with in statutes falling under the rubric of administrative law. Given the number of such statutes in the 11 Canadian legal systems, the variety of subjects they cover and the differences in the treatment of those subjects, it is only possible here to present an overview based on a sample of illustrations. None of these should be taken as necessarily representative. Several of them being of quite recent vintage, they just might be pointing at future developments in administrative law. Their 'codal' quality will be assessed mainly by reference to three features: the scope of the Act, the presence of overarching principles, and the degree of exhaustiveness in the treatment of their subject matter.

Returning to legislation on *administrative organisation*, the statute that comes nearest to a code is the Alberta Public Agencies Governance Act of 2009.[112]

[109] See: *Gifford v Canada* 2004 SCC 15; *Gladstone v Canada* 2005 SCC 21; *Re Canada 3000 Inc* 2006 SCC 24; *Thibodeau v Air Canada* 2014 SCC 67. On such 'complete codes', see P Forget and M Devinat, 'La rhétorique du code complet : unir pour exclure' in N Lambert (ed), *At the Forefront of Duality/À l'avant-garde de la dualité* (Cowansville, QC, Éditions Yvon Blais, 2011) 251.

[110] On the relationship of this type of statute with the common law, see R Sullivan (n 92) 537 ff.

[111] Though difficult border issues may still arise: *Doré v Verdun (City of)* [1997] 2 SCR 862; *Perron-Malenfant v Malenfant (Trustee of)* [1999] 3 SCR 375; *Isidore Garon Ltée v Tremblay* [2006] 1 SCR 27.

[112] SA 2009 c A-31.5. For a discussion of this Act, see P Noreau, F Houle, M Valois and P Issalys, *La justice administrative: entre indépendance et responsabilité* (Cowansville, QC, Éditions Yvon Blais, 2014) 213 ff.

Without parallel elsewhere in Canada, this Act brings all non-departmental entities (ie, agencies) of the Alberta government under a common regime. Yet, the Act seeks a balance between uniformity and the specific needs associated with a given agency's particular function. To this end, some categories of agencies – agencies carrying out adjudicative functions, as well as advisory agencies – attract particular provisions that reflect their need for more independence from their responsible minister. While the guiding principles of the Act appear only in its preamble, one could easily derive them from the wording and effect of actual provisions. Overall, these deal in a fairly exhaustive way with the most crucial and sensitive issue raised by the creation of independent agencies in a Westminster-type parliamentary system: the relationship between agencies and central government.

The most that has been achieved so far by some of the other Canadian systems in addressing this issue in a systemic fashion rather than on a case-by-case basis is the enactment of a common regime for some category of agencies. Examples of such 'limited codes' might be the regime of 'Crown corporations' under the federal Financial Administration Act[113] or that of Ontario 'adjudicative tribunals' under the Adjudicative Tribunals Accountability, Governance and Appointments Act.[114] The first of these two enactments scores high in terms of exhaustiveness, but lacks explicit and specific principles; the second does spell out key notions of accountability, transparency, efficiency and independence, but applies much more narrowly than the Alberta statute on public agencies.

Among statutes dealing with *forms of executive action*, there is much common ground between all 11 Canadian regimes. Out of a general concept of executive decision-making have been carved, through the case law and legislation, two broad types of activity – rule-making in the form of regulations, as well as investigative work in the form of public inquiries – leaving individualised decision-making as the residual and canonical form of executive action.[115] As was pointed out above, some provincial systems have subjected the latter to 'basic codes'.[116] These largely amount to a partial codification of common law rules of administrative procedure.[117] Executive action in the form of contract stands apart, if only because it remains, to a very variable extent, regulated by the general law of contracts.

[113] Above n 65, pt X.

[114] SO 2009 c 33 sched 5; see P Noreau, F Houle, M Valois and P Issalys (n 112) 229 ff.

[115] The same point is made by Felix Uhlmann with respect to Switzerland; see in this book F Uhlmann (n 51) sections II.B and III. In Canada as well, individual decision-making under a myriad of different statutory regimes represents the key instrument of policy implementation and the main focus of administrative law.

[116] Above n 68 and corresponding text.

[117] Such a codification had been advocated for a long time; see: JA Corry, *The Growth of Government Activities since Confederation* (Ottawa, King's Printer, 1939) 17; J Beetz, 'Uniformité de la procédure administrative' (1965) 25 *Revue du Barreau* 244; S Comtois, 'On the Opportunity of Codifying Administrative Procedure' (1987–88) 1 *Canadian Journal of Administrative Law and Practice* 119; *contra*: J Willis, 'The McRuer Report: Lawyers' Values and Civil Servants' Values' (1968) 18 *University of Toronto Law Journal* 351. Particularly influential was the code proposed by Y Ouellette and D Paradis, *Règles de procédure des tribunaux administratifs du Québec* (Cowansville, QC, Éditions Yvon Blais, 1985), on which the Uniform Law Conference of Canada largely based its own Model Administrative Procedure Code of 1991 (above n 50).

An early example of codification of rules governing individualised decision-making is Ontario's Statutory Powers Procedure Act of 1971.[118] This restatement of basic rules of procedure has been since developed and updated to cover practices such as electronic hearings. It applies whenever an administrative decision-maker is required by law (ie, by statute or at common law) to hold some form of hearing prior to his decision. The Act expressly states as its objective the just, cost-effective and expeditious determination of issues on their merits. It allows decision-making authorities a substantial margin for development and adaptation of the statutory requirements through the making of their own complementary rules of procedure. Though the Act shows the strong gravitational pull exercised by the model of judicial decision-making, it does attempt to adjust that model to the requirements of large-scale decision-making by executive bodies.

The Quebec legislature attempted the same 25 years later, from a different approach and with the benefit of a substantial evolution in Canadian common law, in the Act respecting administrative justice of 1996.[119] The Act aims broadly at all individualised decision-making by departments and most agencies. Since the Act refers to 'decisions', it reaches informal administrative action only insofar as the latter is connected to some formal decision.[120] It divides the field between two types of decisions: first-line decision-making (the 'exercise of an administrative function') and decision-making by an appellate authority upon a challenge raised by an aggrieved citizen against that initial decision (the 'exercise of an adjudicative function').

The Act lays down different basic rules of procedure to apply respectively to each type of decision-making. Both sets of rules derive from the undefined concept of 'administrative justice' and take account of its specific character, presumably in relation to 'court justice'.[121] Both aim at ensuring quality, promptness and accessibility in that form of justice, while safeguarding fundamental rights.[122]

[118] Above n 68. For a discussion and assessment of this Act, see: J Maciura and R Steinecke, *The Annotated Statutory Powers Procedure Act* (Aurora, ON, Canada Law Book, 1998); D Mullan, '*Willis v McRuer*: A Long-Overdue Replay with the Possibility of a Penalty Shoot-out' (2005) 55 *University of Toronto Law Journal* 535; K Wileman, R Ivri, L Nastasia and D Pressman, *Tribunal Practice and Procedure* (Toronto, Emond Montgomery, 2018) ch 1.

[119] Above n 68. The Supreme Court of Canada decision in *Nicholson v Haldimand-Norfolk Regional Board of Commissioners of Police* [1979] 1 SCR 311 had turned away from the sharp contrast between 'administrative' and 'judicial' or 'quasi-judicial' proceedings in favour of a broad-range 'duty to act fairly'. This enabled the development of a flexible, across-the-board approach to administrative justice.

[120] *cf* the scope of the American federal Administrative Procedure Act, discussed in this book in EL Rubin (n 30) section IV.

[121] The concept of administrative justice developed in this Quebec statute is therefore much wider than the subject matter of the French Code de justice administrative, which applies to the various levels of administrative courts (see in this book D Costa, 'Codification of Administrative Law: A French Oxymoron', section III). Such a broader view implies that executive authorities making individual decisions 'pursuant to norms and standards prescribed by law' are thereby involved, together with courts or court-like adjudicative bodies, in the achievement of a just social order.

[122] Interestingly, the new Code of Civil Procedure of 2014 (n 84) sets out, in its preliminary provision, exactly the same objectives of quality, promptness and accessibility for civil justice; the specific character of administrative justice must therefore lie elsewhere, ie, in the fact that it is delivered not only by court-like bodies, but also by public officials engaged in the daily implementation of statutes.

They repeatedly emphasise concern for the quality of communications between the citizen and the administrative authority. Other legislation or regulations may complement the rules set out in the Act.[123]

Rules applying to 'administrative functions' are of a broad and basic nature, though they specify variants in the case of decisions involving either permits and licences or indemnities and benefits. Some rules confer subjective rights on citizens (eg, the right to reasons for an unfavourable decision), while others contain broad duties for administrative authorities (eg, the requirement that proceedings be conducted without formality). The overarching requirement in that first-line context is the 'duty to act fairly', a direct borrowing from contemporary common law.

Rules that apply to 'adjudicative functions', on the other hand, are based on the notion of 'fair process' and the 'duty to act impartially', both of which are also derived from the common law. They therefore focus on public hearings, though they emphasise flexibility and allow for an active role on the part of the decision-maker. The concept of 'adjudicative function' indirectly gives shape to a category of agencies: 'bodies of the administrative branch charged with settling disputes between a citizen and an administrative authority'; the bulk of the Act is indeed devoted to setting up the main agency in that category, the Administrative Tribunal of Québec. Through this organisational component, as well as through the broad scope of its procedural parts, the Act respecting administrative justice exerts a systemic influence over administrative law in Quebec and therefore to some extent plays the role of a code.[124] Topics that could conceivably be brought under this 'quasi-code' include the imposition of administrative money penalties and the use of digital technology in individual decision-making.[125] As it now stands, this piece of Quebec legislation fits well into the long series of statutes extending from the Austrian Act of 1925 to the French Code of 2016.[126] Given the

[123] eg, Tax Administration Act, CQLR c A-6.002.

[124] On the Act respecting administrative justice, see: G Pepin, 'La loi québécoise sur la justice administrative' (1997) 57 *Revue du Barreau* 633; MJ Longtin, 'La réforme de la justice administrative: genèse, fondements et réalités' in *Actes de la XIIIe Conférence des juristes de l'État* (Cowansville, QC, Éditions Yvon Blais, 1998) 65; D Lemieux, *Justice administrative. Loi commentée*, 3rd edn (Brossard, QC, Publications CCH, 2009); F Houle, 'A Brief Historical Account of the Reforms to the Administrative Justice System in the Province of Quebec' (2009) 22 *Canadian Journal of Administrative Law and Practice* 47; J Forgues, N Béliveau and K Fournier, *Loi sur la justice administrative annotée* (Cowansville, QC, Éditions Yvon Blais, 2014); P Garant, *La justice invisible ou méconnue* (Montreal, Éditions Yvon Blais, 2014) ch 2.

[125] P Issalys, 'Physionomie de l'administration sanctionnatrice' in S Lavallée and P Issalys (eds), *Vastes mondes. Études en l'honneur du professeur Denis Lemieux* (Montreal, Éditions Yvon Blais, 2018) 145; D Mockle, 'La question du droit dans la transformation numérique des administrations publiques' (2019) 49 *Revue de droit de l'Université de Sherbrooke* 223. Developments concerning administrative penalties in Canada since 2000 closely resemble those in Norway described in this book by JC Fløysvik Nordrum, 'Codification of Norwegian Administrative Law', section IV.

[126] See in this book K Lachmayer, 'Codification of Administrative Law in Austria', section IV.C and also D Costa (n 121) section II.

explicitness and generality of its principles, as well as its relatively non-technical wording, it seems particularly akin to its Swedish counterpart, though its treatment of first-line decision-making is 'minimalist' to an even higher degree.[127]

Code-making has occurred much more widely in respect of executive action taking the form of regulations. Nearly all Canadian legal systems, following the lead given by the federal Regulations Act of 1950, feature a statute governing the process by which regulations are made, published and come into force.[128] Several of them, like the recent Saskatchewan Legislation Act, include regulations along with statutes in a broader concept of legislation, to which are attached general rules of interpretation.[129] The current federal statute also includes regulations in a broader category of 'statutory instruments' that share some aspects of the regulation-making process, but do not generally acquire the legally binding force of regulations.[130] The Quebec 'code' on regulation-making broke new ground in 1985 by requiring public notice and comment of draft regulations; Manitoba recently followed suit, though only in the case of some draft regulations.[131]

Public inquiries are a form of action extensively used by the executive in all Canadian systems since the late nineteenth century. Commissions of inquiry have assisted in the development of public policy in several major areas. Federal and provincial legislation indeed provides, in very similar terms, for inquiries into maladministration or any other matter of public concern.[132] Provisions govern the mandate, appointment, powers and immunities of commissions, as well as evidence and procedure before them. Even though the contents of such statutes reflect in part the common law on administrative decision-making and do not include statements of principle, they can be viewed as self-contained 'codes' on the subject of inquiries, especially since some other statutes refer to the set of investigative powers conferred on commissions in order to attribute such powers to other administrative entities.[133]

All Canadian legal systems basically rely, for the ordering of executive action in the form of contracts, on the general law of contracts, as well as on the international legal framework of government procurement. However, they vary in

[127] See in this book J Reichel and M Ribbing (n 72) section III.A.

[128] eg, British Columbia: Regulations Act, RSBC 1996 c 402. For an overview based on all Canadian systems, see: JM Keyes, *Executive Legislation*, 3rd edn (Markham, ON, LexisNexis, 2021) chs 7 ff.

[129] Legislation Act, SS 2019 c L-10.2.

[130] Statutory Instruments Act (n 66).

[131] Quebec: Regulations Act (n 67) ss 8–14 and 25; Manitoba: Statutes and Regulations Act, CCSM c S207, pt 6.1. At least some draft regulations are published in the federal and Ontario systems, but only as a matter of regulatory policy; failure to publish the draft does not invalidate the regulation.

[132] eg, Saskatchewan: Public Inquiries Act, SS 2013 c P-38.01; New Brunswick: Inquiries Act RSNB 2011 c 273. See: E Ratushny, *The Conduct of Public Inquiries: Law, Policy, and Practice* (Toronto, Irwin Law, 2009); S Ruel, *The Law of Public Inquiries in Canada* (Toronto, Carswell, 2010); R Bessner and S Lightstone (eds), *Public Inquiries in Canada: Law and Practice* (Toronto, Thomson Reuters, 2017).

[133] eg, Financial and Consumer Affairs Authority of Saskatchewan Act, SS 2012 c F-13.5; New Brunswick: Maritime Provinces Harness Racing Commission Act, RSNB 2014 c 119.

terms of the extent of the public law ordering that they superimpose on these general rules.[134] Part of this additional ordering is not strictly legal in nature; much of it takes the form of policies, guidelines, standard forms, good practice documents and the like. In some provinces, such as Ontario, the statutory framework for government contracts is minimal.[135] At the federal level, Parliament has merely spelled out basic principles and rules in a few provisions of the Financial Administration Act[136] and the associated Government Contracts Regulations.[137] However, most provinces have adopted fairly extensive legislation on public sector contracts, some of them differentiating construction contracts from contracts for goods and services.[138] In the case of Quebec, Nova Scotia, and Newfoundland and Labrador, recent legislation on government contracts displays 'codal' qualities: it applies to all types of contracts, expresses principles and values, and provides exhaustive treatment of the subject while making appropriate reference to other sources of the total 'framework' – regulations, policy documents, and international and intergovernmental agreements.[139]

As regards the *principles of executive action*, the common law foundations of Canadian public law – the rule of law and parliamentary sovereignty – leave ample room for legislatures to develop and supplement them. However, until recently, the formulation of broad principles was largely absent from legislative practice. Whoever was concerned with principles assumed they could be extracted through analysis from specific, matter-of-fact, detailed and often technical provisions.[140] Even in modern Quebec, reconciled with strong and bold state action and familiarised with the broad language of a Civil Code, few statements of principle found their way into the statute book. Nowadays, however, a statement of objects, purposes and general principles has come to appear in many statutes.[141] In this way, general principles of executive action may be progressively taking shape in several of the Canadian legal systems.

[134] On public procurement contracts generally, see: P Giroux, D Lemieux and N Jobidon, *Contrats des organismes publics. Loi commentée*, 2nd edn (Brossard. QC, Wolters Kluwer CCH, 2013); P Garant (n 20) ch V; P Emanuelli, *Government Procurement*, 4th edn (Markham, ON, LexisNexis, 2017); D Lemieux, 'La "civilisation" des contrats administratifs au Québec' in G Clamour and M Ubaud-Bergeron (eds), *Contrats publics. Mélanges en l'honneur du professeur Michel Guibal* (Montpellier, Presses de la Faculté de droit de Montpellier, 2006) 433.

[135] Ministry of Government Services Act, RSO 1990 c M.25; as in other Canadian systems, directives and guidelines are relied on to develop the statutory framework: Broader Public Sector Accountability Act, SO 2010 c 25 pt V (procurement standards).

[136] Financial Administration Act (n 65) pt III.1.

[137] SOR/87-402.

[138] eg, Prince Edward Island: Crown Building Corporation Act, RSPEI 1988 c C-31 and Public Purchasing Act, RSPEI 1988 c P-32; British Columbia: Procurement Services Act, SBC 2003 c 22.

[139] Quebec: Act respecting contracting by public bodies (n 67); Nova Scotia: Public Procurement Act, SNS 2011 c 12; Newfoundland and Labrador: Public Procurement Act (n 60).

[140] R Sullivan (n 92) 274 ff; PA Côté and M Devinat (n 92) 442 ff.

[141] eg, Canada: Prisons and Reformatories Act, RSC (1985) c. P-20, ss 7 (purpose) and 7.1 (principles); Broadcasting Act, SC 1991 c 11, ss 3 (broadcasting policy) and 5 (regulatory policy); Manitoba: Mines and Minerals Act, CCSM c M162, s 2 (purpose and principles); Nova Scotia: Environment Act, SNS 1994–1995 c 1, s 2 (purpose, goals and principles); New Brunswick: Maritime Economic

Indeed, the advent of the concept of public governance has encouraged the move towards explicitly principled legislation in administrative law.[142] Though the concept remains, in itself, fuzzy and generally implicit, it has taken root in contemporary public law through a number of principles originally derived from the governance of business firms: principles such as effectiveness, efficiency, quality and accountability.[143] The latter, in particular, has achieved high legislative visibility on its own. Accountability has been associated with a whole range of matters: budget management, ethical requirements for public officials, regulation of economic activity, fiscal transparency, results-based management, relationships within departments and agencies as well as between them etc.[144] Further development of the concept of governance also introduced among the principles of executive action notions such as transparency, information, 'stakeholder' participation in decision-making or even social acceptability. The explicit reference to principles of governance in a number of statutes seems to elevate them to the level of more classical – and yet generally implicit – principles usually associated with the rule of law, such as legality, fairness, legal certainty, rule-based enforcement and responsibility.[145]

The spread of explicitly principled legislation as an appropriate basis for executive action might have also benefited from the emergence of sustainable development as a guiding concept. However, principles derived from that concept only found legislative expression in Manitoba in 1997, then in Quebec in 2006, and more recently at the federal level and in some of the other provinces.[146] So far, the

Cooperation Act, RSNB 2014 c.118, ss 1 (purpose) and 3 (principles); Quebec: Act to affirm the collective nature of water resources and to promote better governance of water and associated environments, CQLR c C-6.2, ss 4–7 (principles); Act to ensure the occupancy and vitality of territories, CQLR c O-1.3, s 5 (principles). On this evolution in drafting practices, see: J Lagacé, 'Les éléments introductifs de la loi et les définitions' in R Tremblay (ed), *Éléments de légistique* (Cowansville, QC, Éditions Yvon Blais, 2010) 541, 545 f, 559 ff; R Sullivan (n 92) 454 ff.

[142] R Caranta describes a similar development in Italian administrative law: R Caranta (n 72) section IV.D.

[143] D Mockle, 'Les principes de la nouvelle gouvernance publique' in G Guglielmi and É Zoller (eds), *Transparence, démocratie et gouvernance citoyenne* (Paris, Université Panthéon-Assas, 2014) 89; R Heintzman and L Juillet, 'Searching for New Instruments of Accountability: New Political Governance and the Dialectic of Democratic Accountability' in H Bakvis and M Jarvis (eds), *From New Public Management to New Political Governance* (Montreal/Kingston, McGill/Queen's University Press, 2012) 342.

[144] Canada: Federal Accountability Act, SC 2006 c 9; British Columbia: Budget Transparency and Accountability Act, SBC 2000 c 23; Alberta: Alberta Accountability Act, SA 2014 c 9; Manitoba: Regulatory Accountability Act, CCSM c R65; Ontario: Adjudicative Tribunals Accountability, Governance and Appointments Act (n 114); Quebec: Public Administration Act, CQLR c A-6.01; Nova Scotia: Regulatory Accountability and Reporting Act, SNS 2015 c 35.

[145] Indeed, it has been argued that such principles of governance should receive formal constitutional recognition: N DesRosiers, 'Pour une charte de bonne gouvernance publique' (2015) *Revue québécoise de droit international* (n° spéc.) 171.

[146] Quebec: Sustainable Development Act, CQLR c D-8.1.1; Canada: Sustainable Development Act, SC 2008 c 33; Manitoba: Climate and Green Plan Implementation Act, CCSM c C134; Nova Scotia: Sustainable Development Goals Act, SNS 2019 c 26.

concept of sustainable development has had a very limited impact on the overall structure of legislation – which, sadly, may well reflect its impact on the actual conduct of executive action.

Even though principles related to public governance, and in a much smaller measure to sustainable development, have the potential to shape executive action, the Canadian systems of legislation do not currently reflect this potential.[147] Since these new concepts began to emerge in legal consciousness over the last two decades of the twentieth century, so far they have had only a limited and fragmented impact on these systems. In the case of sustainable development, once principles of action had been stated in legislation, things went on as if the law generally, and legislation in particular, had little more to say or do to mould executive action according to these principles. As for the numerous principles derived from the concept of public governance, some of them at least received specific applications in the statute book. However, such applications remain scattered among a variety of contexts, unrelated to each other and – this is certainly the case with the principle of accountability – so diverse as to render unintelligible the core meaning of the principle. All of this suggests that, however fruitful or useful these concepts and principles may be from the standpoint of management techniques, they have so far proved too malleable to anchor definite institutions of administrative law or even to operate as organising themes for legislation about executive action. It would appear that a 'Code of Public Accountability' or a 'Sustainable Development Code' still lie some way off in the distance …

# IV. Conclusion

Large-scale codification cannot be said to characterise administrative law in Canada. This finding is valid whichever way one defines administrative law. In the narrow sense that equals administrative law with judicial review of administrative action, whatever codification exists takes the form of a restatement – albeit with welcome simplifications – of the common law about the remedies available to challenge the legality of some executive action. This has indeed taken place at the federal level and in several provinces. If one looks instead at administrative law in the broader sense adopted in this chapter, a brief survey such as this suggests that codification has only occurred in a fragmented way, producing small-scale codes – something of an oxymoron. This state of affairs is, after all, unsurprising, given that public law in Canada is founded on the common law tradition. The fact that administrative law in Quebec is not markedly different in this respect is only a reminder that, as far as public law is concerned, Quebec does also belong to the

[147] Unlike what is being said of the principles of good administration as they operate in European legal systems (see in this book A Berger (n 48) section II.B.i.b), developments from the concepts of governance or sustainable development in Canadian law mostly amount to a 'bundle of rules' rather than a 'coherent whole'.

common law world. While this certainly provides a plausible explanation for the limited scope of codification in Canadian administrative law, it is not a complete explanation. Other factors, in our view, come into play. Some of them have already been pointed out in this chapter. It now seems appropriate to return to them and add some additional possible explanations.

There is no denying that legal culture and the structure of legal knowledge determine the interest or disinterest in codified law. In a legal culture centred on judge-made law, and in a legal science defining administrative law usually in terms of judicial review over the exercise of public authority, the question of whether such authority is based on a 'code' rather than on an ordinary statute, or on some other source of legal power, is almost indifferent. In the tradition of the English common law, the fact that Parliament has authorised executive action through a 'complete code' on a given subject may modify the extent to which earlier precedents may be taken into account, but it does not fundamentally alter the position of the court reviewing the legality of that action. Codification, and the degree to which it relates to common law, are options left open for Parliament. From the point of view of the common lawyer, who stands at the receiving end, codification is nothing more than a (slightly) different way of (occasionally) drafting statutory law – hence the disinterest in codification.

Another explanatory factor, which is certainly not peculiar to Canada, is the multiplicity of sources from which contemporary administrative law is derived. Materials with which to build a code in this branch of the law come in many different shapes or forms. The main ones, in the case of Canada, have been described above; to that survey should be added a mention of the impact of international law, and especially the law of international trade, on internal administrative law. The task of codifying such a composite set of norms, standards and legally significant practices is made all the more daunting. True, the same may be said nowadays of many other areas of the law. Yet, administrative law may offer the most topical example to illustrate a broader question: is codification sensible and possible given the composite and fragmented nature of what counts as law in the contemporary world?

A third explanatory factor, again not specific to Canada but certainly much in evidence in that country, is the transformation undergone by institutions of administrative law.[148] By this is meant the gradual 'deconstruction' of canonical forms of executive action, giving birth and currency to new and startling phrases describing new forms of that action: 'negotiated rule-making', 'contractual standard-setting', 'partnerships' of various types between public and private actors, 'guidelines', 'active tolerance', 'regulatory self-management', 'compliance agreements' and many

[148] As a Belgian writer perceptively observed 70 years ago, codification cannot be carried out successfully in an area of the law that is in a state of crisis due to its accelerated growth or transformation: J Lespès, 'La codification des principes généraux du droit administratif' (1950) 16(1) *Revue internationale des sciences administratives* 36. This begs the question whether codification makes any sense in this 'Age of Acceleration'; for a positive answer, see C Kessedjian, 'Le temps du droit au XXIe siècle – Compatibilité avec la codification?' (2005) 46 *Cahiers de droit* 547.

other hybrids between classical instruments of administrative law.[149] Yet, on the contrary, codes evoke fixed, stable and typified institutions under which the diversity of actual instances may be exhaustively subsumed. In the face of constantly emerging innovations, which remain 'unrecognisable' on the basis of canonical types, codification – certainly if conducted on a large scale – may prove to be a futile attempt at devising sustainable new categories.

Worldwide phenomena such as the two just described only tend to consolidate the belief in pragmatism. Pragmatism has already been referred to as a defining feature of Canadian administrative law, indeed of anything in Canada having to do with the management of public affairs. Under that philosophy – which pretends not to rely on any set philosophy in the sense of systematic worldview – what matters is what works. What is necessary is strictly what is needed to 'make things work' acceptably. Codification will rarely meet such a test of necessity, except perhaps codification in its limited form as a restatement, simplification or improvement of a segment of the common law. Even the Canadian Criminal Code of 1892 could at least in part be justified in such a limited way. For its part, the Civil Code of Québec of 1994, as the culmination of 40 years of preparatory work, clearly responded to the need to 'make things work' in contemporary Quebec society, in view of the enormous socio-political changes over the preceding decades, as well as to reassert the juridical component of Quebec national identity.[150] But absent such pressing demands, if not from society then at least from the legal professions and the public authorities, codification of administrative law, on a large scale at least, is unlikely to appear as a pragmatic necessity.[151]

Another relevant factor is also distinctly Canadian: the federal character of the political and legal regime. As pointed out earlier in this chapter, the Constitution Act, 1867 has been interpreted so as to vest in each province, as well as in the federal institutions, all the internal attributes of a state, including the full legal capacity of the Crown as the head of each executive. This has left each legislature with a free hand in matters of administrative law and has encouraged the development of different 'styles' of legislation in this field. While basic common law concepts and rules, as well as the legacy of British constitutional history, preserve a significant degree of uniformity, all 11 systems developed autonomously in ways that show some originality. The room left for the operation of common law rules, Crown discretion, or ad hoc arrangements therefore varies from one system to

[149] See: P Issalys, 'Choosing among Forms of Public Action: A Question of Legitimacy' in P Eliadis, M Hill and M Howlett (eds), *Designing Government. From Instruments to Governance* (Montreal/Kingston, McGill/Queen's University Press, 2005) 154; D Mockle, *La gouvernance, le droit et l'État* (Brussels, Bruylant, 2007) 22 ff.

[150] On the link between codification and national identity, in the case of Wales, see in this book S Nason (n 78) section V.B.

[151] As Heintzen remarks in the German case (M Heintzen (n 48) section I.C), proposals and pleas from academic writers, or from the Bar, carry less weight than political impulses and, above all, preferences within public administration. In the Canadian case, this state of affairs interacts in a mutually reinforcing way with the notion, entertained by many common lawyers, that much of what is included in 'le droit administratif' is not really 'law' at all.

the other. The above survey gave indications of this concerning administrative organisation, administrative procedure and principles of executive action. To put it succinctly, Canadian federalism has led to the development of different political cultures, and political culture exerts a strong influence on the development of administrative law. From this viewpoint, the case of the Canadian federal state is suggestive. For instance, federal political culture generally favours (powerful) inducement, rather than regimentation, to achieve federal policy goals through (or in spite of) provincial measures. In this light, it may be revealing that the two instances of federal statutes bearing the name 'Code' deal with two areas where federal jurisdiction had been clearly established: criminal law, and a few important but limited sectors of the workforce. Outside such areas, flexibility, indetermination, 'nudges', ad hoc arrangements and a measure of accommodation will generally be the methods for advancing federal policy goals – hardly a promising climate for grand codification designs.[152]

The Canadian variant of federalism has another side effect that works against the hopes of would-be codifiers. Preparing codifications consumes time, expertise and other resources. The disparity among provinces in terms of population and economic structure is such that only the larger provinces, as well as the federal government, could afford to develop and implement large-scale codifications. Codification proposals at the federal level face an additional hurdle: all federal legislation has to harmonise with both common law and civil law concepts, each of them expressed in both official languages. Even codification in the narrow sense, ie, reformulating common law rules, may prove costly. A way to reduce the problem of costs would be cooperation. This is what the Uniform Law Conference has been achieving with some success in areas of private law, but in matters of public law, this has not proved practicable, in part because of the strength of distinct political cultures. Lately, provincial governments have sought to harmonise the scope and substance of norms regulating economic activity; intergovernmental agreements and 'mirror legislation' have occurred in this field, but are still a far cry from what could be considered as uniform 'codification'.[153]

Taken together, the factors mentioned so far may be pointing at an underlying consideration that explains the limited appeal of codification within Canadian legal systems. In the last analysis, codification evokes the concept of unity. It materialises as a single text. It concentrates in its provisions all essential elements of a whole branch of a legal system, if not of that entire system, thereby

[152] The Canada Health Act, RSC (1985) c C-6, stands as the classic instance of 'codifying' sector-specific principles for executive action, and indeed for legislation, made effective through a mixture of coercion and co-operation.

[153] Canadian Free Trade Agreement (on line: www.cfta-alec.ca); Trade and Cooperation Agreement between Ontario and Québec (www.ontario.ca); New West Partnership Agreement (www.newwest-partnershiptrade); Maritime Economic Cooperation Act, SNS 1992 c 7 and its mirror Acts in the three other Atlantic provinces.

emphasising the unity of that branch or system. Where previously dispersion of norms prevailed, between separate statutes, throughout a body of case law, or among a variety of more or less authoritative sources, a single text brings order, hierarchy, internal logic, uniformity and consistency. One might say, then, that codification is intrinsically centripetal: a code is the centre of some legal universe. However, Canada is a centrifugal country. History and geography have made it so. The very existence of 11 Canadian legal systems testifies to the persistence, over 250 years, of unresolvable tensions between the 'centre' and the 'peripheries' – not to mention uncertainty about the location of the 'centre'. In such a context, 'code', with its strong connotations of unity, is a loaded word. Its limited use in Canadian legal systems may indicate that legislators are quite conscious of its strategic possibilities and limitations. Thus, the Canadian Criminal Code of 1892 was an early statement about federal (impliedly 'central') state identity, as well as about social values uniting all Canadians. For their part, the Quebec Civil Codes of 1866 and 1994, especially the latter, were statements about the unity, specific character and modernity of a 'distinct society' centred on a different language, a different approach to legal ordering and (in the case of the older Code) a different view of the role of religion in society. The federal code was a strategic centripetal move, while the Quebec codes were strategic centrifugal moves to establish a centre away from the centre. In both cases, the codal form sought to convey a concept of unity around a centre – a concept that, in the Canadian context, remains open to many interpretations, qualifications and perspectives.

Codifying administrative law is therefore no simple business, at least in Canada, if only because the concept of diversity is coming to be integral to Canadian identity – and, increasingly, to Quebec identity as well. Reflections on the Canadian case might indeed lead one to wonder whether codifying that branch of the law can be treated as a relatively simple, technical operation in any country. After all, the very concept of a code seems to imply in its makers ambitions (political and social, as well as properly legal) of a higher level than those associated with drafting just another law, however complex, about just any topic. Administrative law, as it happens, is no ordinary topic: it is at once too closely connected to the everyday working of vital parts of the state apparatus, and too directly relevant to the role of government in the everyday life of individuals and society. Considering all that is involved in codification and in codifying administrative law, perhaps Canadians are not alone in viewing it as a pretty formidable task.

# 5

# Codification of Administrative Law

## *A French Oxymoron*

DELPHINE COSTA

## I. The Definition and Delimitation of Administrative Law

In French law, administrative law is very widely understood. Because French organisation is highly centralised, French administrative law is traditionally the expression of the authority of the state and its administration.[1] Obviously, French administrative law was considered as a true legal discipline towards the end of the nineteenth century, with the advent of the Third Republic (1875–1940); this construction is based on myths that are precisely the foundation of French administrative law.[2] Even if this legal discipline is linked to the French institutional and political history, it has more or less inspired many other legal systems.[3]

[1] B Plessix, *Droit administratif général*, 3rd edn (Paris, LexisNexis, 2020) 240: 'le droit administratif français … est indissolublement lié, jadis à la construction, aujourd'hui à la pérennité de la forme étatique. Au commencement du droit administratif, il faut donc d'abord repartir de cette fameuse création intellectuelle, de ce pur concept juridique, qui sert de support institutionnalisé, rationalisé et sécularisé à l'exercice du pouvoir politique à l'égard d'une population et d'un territoire, que l'on appelait jadis République, Gouvernement ou Couronne, et que l'on nomme État depuis le XVII$^{e}$ siècle' ('French administrative law … is indissolubly linked, once to the construction, now to the sustainability of the state form. At the beginning of administrative law, we must therefore start from this famous intellectual creation, from this pure legal concept, which serves as an institutionalised support, rationalised and secularised to the exercise of political power over a population and territory, formerly known as the Republic, Government or Crown, and known as the State since the seventeenth century') (all citations are translated by the author).

[2] G Bigot, *Ce droit qu'on dit administratif … Études d'histoire du droit public* (Paris, La mémoire du droit, 2015) ; M Touzeil-Divina, *Dix mythes du droit public* (Paris, LGDJ, 2019).

[3] S Cassese, *La construction du droit administratif, France et Royaume-Uni, trad. de l'italien par J Morvillez-Maigret* (Montchrestien, Clefs Politique, 2000); L Neville Brown, JS Bell, with J-M Galabert, *French Administrative Law*, 5th edn (Oxford, Clarendon Press, 1998) 3: 'the developed system of *droit administratif*, centred upon the Conseil d'Etat, forms the basis of many continental systems, and has influenced such international institutions as the Administrative Tribunals of the United Nations Organization and, more importantly, the Court of Justice of the European Communities'.

Moreover, despite of special administrative law in a number of matters, such as urbanism, public procurement and contracts, sustainable development, security, civil service and so on, there is, in fact, a general administrative law.

## A. The Definition Criteria of General Administrative Law

There is a set of rules applicable to all persons – public or even private – involved in administrative action. These persons can be in charge of national or local government or even special missions.[4] They can be tasked with a public service or, at least, with a mission of general interest. When private persons are involved with such a mission, there are under control of a public person.[5] General administrative law can be thus defined by an organic criterion, but it can also be defined by the intended purpose of the action, when it is a public service or a mission of general interest (purposive criterion). It can further be defined by a material criterion, because those persons in charge of administrative action have elements of public authority such as taxing power, enforcement authority, public policy or unilateral action.[6] The scope of general administrative law is very wide in the French legal system.[7]

## B. The Rules of General Administrative Law

French general administrative law imposes a lot of rules. Some principles regard administrative action: goal of general interest, lawfulness, equality, neutrality and secularism, transparency and impartiality, prohibition of retroactivity, and proportionality (see below, section II).

Further, administrative law applies to both administrative decisions and public contracts, to police activities, to administrative rule-making and regulation,

[4] At a national level, there is the President of the Republic, the Prime Minister, the ministers and other independent public/administrative authorities; at a local level, there are regional, departmental and communal councils and presidents ('mayors' in communes); at both a national and local level, those persons who have some special missions are qualified as 'public establishments'.

[5] CE, sect, 22 February 2007, *Association du personnel relevant des établissements pour inadaptés*, *Rec CE* 92, concl C Verot; F Lenica and J Boucher, 'Chronique de jurisprudence administrative' (2007) *Actualité juridique – Droit administratif* 793. *cf* the German and EU chapter in this book on the distinction between direct and indirect public administration: M Heintzen, 'Codification of Administrative Law in Germany and the European Union', section I.B.iv.

[6] TC, 29 December 2004, *Epoux Blanckeman c Voies navigables de France*, n° C3416; TC, 12 December 2005, *EURL Croisières de Lorraine La Bergamote c Voies navigables de France*, n° C3455: 'activités qui, telles la réglementation, la police ou le contrôle, ressortissent par leur nature de prérogatives de puissance publique' ('activities which, such as regulation, police or control, by their nature fall within the prerogatives of public authority').

[7] It can be compared to Swedish administrative law, as is pointed out in the Swedish chapter in this book: J Reichel and M Ribbing, 'Codification of Administrative Law in Sweden', section II.A.

to administrative punitive power, to public property and to the responsibility (liability) of public persons:[8] the variety of its application is extraordinarily wide.[9]

As already noted, administrative law concerns both public and private persons: public such as the state, local authorities (territorial communities: communes, departments and regions), public establishments, enterprises and entities, independent administrative authorities; and private such as civil servants, associations and enterprises. It defines relationships between those persons: decentralisation, delegation and devolution.[10]

Finally, many principles of administrative procedure are fixed by general administrative law like the right to be heard, the right to participate, the right to fairness … These principles concern the procedure not only before administrative authorities but also before administrative jurisdictions, even if they are more extensive in the latter option (see below section II).

## II. Legal Sources of Administrative Law

Legal sources of general administrative law are the Constitution, laws and codes, secondary legislation,[11] and mostly court practice because of the central role of the French Council of State in the delimitation and definition of legal principles of administrative law for more than two centuries.[12] Thus, it is relevant to group legal principles of general administrative law by sources,[13] distinguishing different questions.

### A. The French Constitution

The actual French Constitution was adopted 4 October 1958 and established the Fifth French Republic. The formal text of this Constitution does not set out any

[8] As Heintzen points out in the both German and EU chapter in this book, 'state liability [is] a codificatory "no go"' (M Heintzen (n 5) section III).

[9] The fight against the COVID-19 pandemic illustrates the broad scope of administrative law, which has been present in numerous forms of legislation and regulations since March 2020 (see: www.vie-publique.fr/sites/default/files/basic_page/pdf/Textes-Covid-19.pdf).

[10] Specifically: Law n° 82-213, 2 March 1982, relative aux droits et libertés des communes, des départements et des régions; Orientation Law n° 92-125, 6 February 1992, relative à l'administration territoriale de la République. See below, section II.

[11] The structure of French law is inspired by the legal categories from Roman law and is based upon legislation, which is the expression of sovereignty since the French Revolution: C Jauffret-Spinosi, 'La structure du droit français' (2002) *Revue internationale de droit compare* 265, esp at 265.

[12] B Pacteau, *Le Conseil d'État et la fondation de la justice administrative au XIXe siècle* (Paris, Presses universitaires de France, 2003) 264; C Jauffret-Spinosi (n 11) 268; G Braibant, 'Le rôle du Conseil d'État dans l'élaboration du droit' in G Teboul, D Pouyaud and J Ziller (eds), *Mélanges René Chapus, Droit administratif* (Paris, Montchrestien, 1992) 91 ff.

[13] P Gonod and O Jouanjan, 'À propos des sources du droit administratif. Brèves notations sur de récentes remarques' (2005) *Actualité juridique – Droit administratif* 992.

human rights or fundamental liberties, because it was adopted during a political crisis.[14] Therefore, it refers to other constitutional sources, such as the French Declaration of Human and Civil Rights of 26 August 1789 and the Preamble to the Constitution of 27 October 1946, both of which state two different kind of human rights – first political and second social and economic.[15] In the French constitutional sources, there is no precise reference to the public administration. However, some legal constitutional principles of public law relate to administration:[16]

- *Principles of administrative action*: only secularism and equality are stated in the constitutional sources. Article 1 of the French Constitution of the Fifth Republic reads as follows: 'France shall be an indivisible, secular, democratic and social Republic … It shall respect all beliefs.' And equality is one of the most significant principles in the text of 1958, even in Article 1: 'It shall ensure the equality of all citizens before the law, without distinction of origin, race or religion.' Equality is also present in the French Declaration of 1789 (Articles 1 and 6).[17]
- *Forms of action*: no constitutional principle regards administrative forms of action. Some articles concern only the division of powers between the two major administrative authorities – the President of the Republic and the Prime Minister – for the exercise of general regulatory power by decree.[18]
- *Administrative organisation*: since 2003, decentralisation has been stated in Article 1 of the French Constitution: 'France … shall be organised on a decentralised basis.' Many details are described in the formal text of the Constitution as relationships between the state and territorial communities, some being rather autonomous and others very independent[19] (for example, New Caledonia).[20] However, in the Preamble to the Constitution of 1946,

[14] Comité national chargé de la publication des travaux préparatoires des institutions de la Ve République, *Documents pour servir à l'histoire de l'élaboration de la Constitution du 4 octobre 1958* (Paris, La Documentation française, 4 vols, 1987, 1988, 1991, 2001).

[15] The French Constitution has been supplemented by the 2004 Environmental Charter, which proclaims the main principles relating to the preservation of biodiversity and the rights and duties towards future generations (the precautionary principle, sustainable development): constitutional law n° 2005-205, 1 March 2005, relative à la Charte de l'environnement, *Journal official*, 2 March 2005.

[16] *cf* the Austrian chapter in this book on the codification of the administrative law by the Constitution: K Lachmayer, 'Codification of Administrative Law in Austria', sections III.A and IV.A.i.

[17] Article 1: 'Men are born and remain free and equal in rights. Social distinctions may be based only on considerations of the common good.' Article 6: 'The Law is the expression of the general will. All citizens have the right to take part, personally or through their representatives, in its making. It must be the same for all, whether it protects or punishes. All citizens, being equal in its eyes, shall be equally eligible to all high offices, public positions and employments, according to their ability, and without other distinction than that of their virtues and talents.'

[18] Article 13: 'The President of the Republic shall sign the Ordinances and Decrees deliberated upon in the Council of Ministers. He shall make appointments to the civil and military posts of the State.' Article 21: 'The Prime Minister shall direct the actions of the Government … Subject to article 13, he shall have power to make regulations and shall make appointments to civil and military posts.'

[19] Title XII: 'Of Territorial Communities', arts 72 to 75-1.

[20] Title XIII: 'Transitional provisions pertaining to New Caledonia'.

'nationalisation of public services'[21] is planned, but these days, it is privatisation rather than nationalisation that is allowed by statutes.[22] 'Nationalisation' then becomes an obsolete principle of administrative organisation.

- *Administrative procedure*: there is no constitutional principle concerning administrative protection. Some general principles only relate to the judicial authority[23] and not the administrative authorities.

## B. General Legislation and Codes

General legislation and codes[24] were not frequently used in French administrative law, which was more concerned by sectorial and limited laws.[25] Yet, since the 1970s, some general legislation concerns public administration and sets out a number of principles of general administrative law. These general legislation are now continued by a new general code that groups together many of these principles:

- *Principles of action*: since 2016, legality (lawfulness) is affirmed in a new general code, the Code of relations between the public and the administration, at its beginning.[26] Impartiality, equality, neutrality and securalism are also mentioned in this code,[27] but these principles are not defined precisely.[28]
- *Forms of action*: no general legislation relates to forms of action. The new 2016 code only distinguishes three sorts of administrative acts: regulatory, individual,

[21] Paragraph 9: 'All property and all enterprises that have or that may acquire the character of a public service or de facto monopoly shall become the property of society.'

[22] For example, about 'Aéroports de Paris' and 'La Française des jeux': Law n° 2019-486, 22 May 2019, relative à la croissance et à la transformation des entreprises (loi PACTE), arts 130 and 137.

[23] Title VIII: 'Of Judicial Authority', art 66: 'No one shall be arbitrarily detained. / The Judicial Authority, guardian of the freedom of the individual, shall ensure compliance with this principle in the conditions laid down by statute'; art 66-1: 'No one shall be sentenced to death.' In the Declaration of 1789, some principles concern criminal procedure (prohibition of arbitrary detention, lawfulness of offences and penalties, presumption of innocence: arts 7, 8 and 9).

[24] On the structuration of the French legislation even by the codification, see C Jauffret-Spinosi (n 11) 266.

[25] M Touzeil-Divina, 'De Gérando et l'enseignement du droit administratif' (2013) *Revue d'histoire des facultés de droit et de la science juridique* 395.

[26] Code des relations entre le public et l'administration, CRPA (Code of relations between the public and the administration), art L. 100-2: 'L'administration agit dans l'intérêt général et respecte le principe de légalité. Elle est tenue à l'obligation de neutralité et au respect du principe de laïcité. Elle se conforme au principe d'égalité et garantit à chacun un traitement impartial' ('Administration acts in the general interest and respects the principle of legality. It is bound by the obligation of neutrality and respect for the principle of secularism. It complies with the principle of equality and guarantees everyone impartial treatment').

[27] P Terneyre and J Gourdou, 'L'originalité du processus d'élaboration du code : le point de vue d'universitaires membres du "cercle des experts" et de la Commission supérieure de la codification' (2016) *Revue française de droit administratif* 9.

[28] C Vautrot-Schwarz, 'Codifier et définir. L'exemple des définitions dans le Code des relations entre le public et l'administration' (2016) 8 *Droit administratif* 23; D Costa, 'Nullus codex sine definitione' (2014) *Actualité juridique – Droit administratif* 185.

and not regulatory and not individual.[29] These distinctions have some important consequences for the legal regime of these acts, especially in relation to their coming into force, or amending or deleting them.[30]

- *Administrative organisation*: some general legislation defines principles of administrative organisation, especially decentralisation.[31] There is a special code that governs this matter.[32] But there is no legislation about principles of administrative organisation such as hierarchy or delegation. Since 2017, there has been general legislation on public and independent administrative authorities.[33] However, some other forms of general legislation have related to rights and obligations of public servants since 1983–84, albeit subject to numerous modifications (the last of which was in August 2019).[34] A new general code dedicated to civil service was finally adopted in 2021.[35]
- *Administrative protection*: since 2016 and the adoption of the Code of relations between the public and the administration, few principles are stated in this code, such as the right to be heard[36] and the right to fairness.[37] These

[29] CRPA (Code of relations between the public and the administration) art L. 200-1: 'Pour l'application du présent livre, on entend par actes les actes administratifs unilatéraux décisoires et non décisoires. / Les actes administratifs unilatéraux décisoires comprennent les actes réglementaires, les actes individuels et les autres actes décisoires non réglementaires. Ils peuvent être également désignés sous le terme de décisions, ou selon le cas, sous les expressions de décisions réglementaires, de décisions individuelles et de décisions ni réglementaires ni individuelles' (For the purposes of this section, unilateral administrative acts are decisory and non-decisory administrative acts. / Unilateral administrative acts include regulatory acts, individual acts and other non-regulatory decisory acts. They may also be referred to as decisions or, as the case may be, as regulatory decisions, individual decisions and decisions that are neither regulatory nor individual).

[30] CRPA (Code of relations between the public and the administration), arts L. 240-1 ff; see above, section III.D.i.

[31] Law n° 82-213, 2 March 1982, relative aux droits et libertés des communes, des départements et des régions; Law n° 2015-991, 7 August 2015, portant nouvelle organisation territoriale de la République ('loi NOTRe'); Law n° 2022-217, 21 February 2022, relative à la différenciation, la décentralisation, la déconcentration et portant diverses mesures de simplification de l'action publique locale.

[32] Code général des collectivités territoriales, CGCT (General Code of Local Authorities): Law n° 96-142, 21 February 1996, relative à la partie législative du Code général des collectivités territoriales; Decree n° 2000-318, 7 April 2000, relative à la partie réglementaire du Code général des collectivités territoriales.

[33] Organic Law n° 2017-54, 20 January 2017, relative aux autorités administratives indépendantes et autorités publiques indépendantes; Law n° 2017-55, 20 January 2017, portant statut général des autorités administratives indépendantes et des autorités publiques indépendantes.

[34] Law n° 83-634, July 13th 1983, portant droits et obligations des fonctionnaires; Law n° 84-16, 11 January 1984, portant dispositions statutaires relatives à la fonction publique de l'État; Law n° 84-53, 26 January 1984, portant dispositions statutaires relatives à la fonction publique territoriale; Law n° 86-33, 9 January 1986, portant dispositions statutaires relatives à la fonction publique hospitalière; Law n° 2019-828, 6 August 2019, de transformation de la fonction publique.

[35] Code général de la fonction publique, CGFP (Civil Service General Code): Ordinance (delegated legislation) n° 2021-1574, 24 November 2021, portant partie législative du code général de la fonction publique, *Journal officiel*, 5 December 2021; C de Salins, B Chavanat and J Michel, 'Le code général de la fonction publique, enfin!' (2022) *Actualité juridique – Droit administratif* 287; F Melleray, 'Le code général de la fonction publique : une arlésienne?' (2019) *Actualité juridique – Fonction publique* 309.

[36] CRPA (Code of relations between the public and the administration), arts L. 121-1 ff.

[37] ibid art L. 100-2 (see above n 26).

principles were first stated in some general laws adopted in the 1970s[38] and updated in 2000.[39]

## C. Secondary Legislation and Sectorial Codes

Secondary legislation and sectorial codes concern more special administrative law[40] than general administrative law:

- *Principles of action*: no secondary legislation concerns these principles. It is logical because precisely principles of action belong to general and not special administrative law.
- *Forms of action*: many sectorial codes relate to some forms of action, such as local authorities (code général des collectivités territoriales),[41] public contracts (code de la commande publique),[42] public property (code général de la propriété des personnes publiques)[43] or police activities (code de la sécurité intérieure).[44]
- *Administrative organisation*: as previously noted, there is a sectorial code for relationships between the state and the territorial communities. In addition, many special laws delegate some missions of general interest to private

[38] Law n° 78-753, 17 July 1978, portant diverses mesures d'amélioration des relations entre l'administration et le public; Law n° 79-587, 11 July 1979, relative à la motivation des actes administratifs et à l'amélioration des relations entre l'administration et le public.

[39] Law n° 2000-321, 12 April 2000, relative aux droits des citoyens dans leurs relations avec les administrations; P Ferrari, 'Les droits des citoyens dans leurs relations avec les administrations; commentaire général de la loi n° 2000-321 du 12 avril 2000' (2000) *Actualité juridique - Droit administratif* 471.

[40] In the Italian chapter in this book, R Caranta explains the same about sectoral codification (R Caranta, 'Administrative Proceedings in Italy', section II).

[41] G Braibant, 'Le code général des collectivités territoriales' (1996) *Revue française de droit administratif* 177; see before n 32.

[42] Code de la commande publique (CCP; Public Procurement Code), see below n 65; H Hoepffner and P Terneyre, 'La place des principes dans le code de la commande publique' (2019) *Revue française de droit administratif* 206; C Maugüé and S Roussel, 'La codification de la jurisprudence dans le code de la commande publique : jusqu'où?' (2019) *Revue française de droit administratif* 213; F Melleray and R Noguellou, 'La codification de règles jurisprudentielles' (2019) *Actualité juridique - Droit administratif* 381; P Bourdon, 'Le code de la commande publique: une codification à droit quasi-constant' (2020) *Actualité juridique - Droit administratif* 149.

[43] Code général de la propriété des personnes publiques (CGPPP; Public Property General Code): Ordinance n° 2006-460, 21 April 2006, relative à la partie législative du code général de la propriété des personnes publiques; Decree n° 2011-1612, 22 November 2011, relatif aux première, deuxième, troisième et quatrième parties réglementaires du code général de la propriété des personnes publiques; P Yolka, 'Naissance d'un code: la réforme du droit des propriétés publiques' (2006) 24 *La semaine juridique - édition entreprise act* 269; C Maugüé, G Bachelier, 'Genèse et présentation du code général de la propriété des personnes publiques' (2006) *Actualité juridique - Droit administratif* 1073.

[44] Code de la sécurité intérieure (CSI; Internal Security Code): Ordinance n° 2012-351, 12 March 2012, relative à la partie législative du code de la sécurité intérieure; Decree n° 2013-1112, 4 December 2013, relatif à la partie réglementaire du code de la sécurité intérieure; Decree n° 2013-1113, 4 December 2013, relatif aux dispositions des livres Ier, II, IV et V de la partie réglementaire du code de la sécurité intérieure.

entities, in the cultural, social or sporting field. For example, the Sport Code allows some 'federations' – under powers delegated by the minister of sports – to exercise missions of public service such as the organisation of national or international competitions.[45]

- *Administrative protection*: no specific secondary legislation concerns this protection, except the Administrative Justice Code, which has existed since 2001, but especially dedicated to administrative jurisdictions, not to administrative authorities. This code concerns administrative tribunals, administrative courts of appeal and the Council of State, and outlines, at its beginning, the main principles of judicial protection and processual organisation.[46]

## D. Court Practice

Court practice is very important in French administrative law; often, it precedes legislation or codes.[47] As one great French jurist said, 'administrative law is fundamentally jurisprudential'.[48] Despite the fact that in France there is a three-tiered system of administrative courts (as previously exposed, administrative tribunals, administrative courts of appeal and the Council of State),[49] the main producer of general administrative law is the French Council of State itself, which has existed since 1799, despite its dual function as advisor and judge. It is the source of many principles of general administrative law.[50] Created under the 'Consulate' (1799–1804)[51] headed by Napoleon Bonaparte, this institution is still the nerve centre of administrative law and beyond in French law, both because of its dual function and the influence of its members, inside and outside of the

[45] Code du sport (Sport Code), arts L. 131-1 ff, L. 131-14 and 15; Ordinance n° 2006-596, 23 May 2006, relative à la partie legislative du code du sport; Decrees n° 2007-1132 and 2007-1133, 24 July 2007.

[46] Administrative Justice Code, arts L. 1 to L. 11; F Lombard, 'L'utilité contentieuse du Titre préliminaire du Code de justice administrative' (2009) *Actualité juridique – Droit administratif* 1755; see above section III.D.ii.

[47] As S De Somer and I Opdebeek point out in their chapter in this book, French general administrative law, like Belgian general administrative law, 'is still to a large extent judge-made law' (S De Somer and I Opdebeek, 'Codification of Belgian Administrative Law: "Nothing is Written"', section II.F.

[48] R Chapus, *Droit administratif général*, 15th edn, vol 1 (Paris, Montchrestien, 2001) 6, fn 11; G Vedel, 'Le droit administratif peut-il être indéfiniment jurisprudentiel?' (1979) 31 *Études et documents du Conseil d'État* 31.

[49] It is the same in the Swedish system, as is pointed out in the Swedish chapter in this book: J Reichel and M Ribbing (n 7) section III.B. The same remark can be noted in France as in Sweden: 'the administrative courts were still considered to constitute a form of 'superior authorities' and to fall within the administrative structure rather than the judiciary' (section III.B).

[50] M Long, P Weil, G Braibant, P Delvolvé and B Genevois, *Les grands arrêts de la jurisprudence administrative*, 23rd edn (Paris, Dalloz, 2021) 1160 (hereinafter *GAJA*); see also J-C Bonichot, P Cassia and B Poujade, *Les grands arrêts du contentieux administratif*, 8th edn (Paris, Dalloz, 2022) 1592 (hereinafter *GACA*).

[51] The contemporeanous Council of State was established by the Constitution of the Consulate in 13 December 1799 (22 Frimaire an VIII).

Council of State (government, public establishments, private companies, Superior Codification Commission[52]).[53] The Council of State was, at its creation, contemporary with the 'Civil Code', another Napoleonic achievement, but was built 'against' the latter, unrivalled in administrative field, and 'against' the Court of Cassation – the supreme court in private law – in order not only to create French administrative law but also to justify its own existence.[54]

- *Principles of action*: the principle of legality was first established by case law before being enshrined by statute law with the 2016 Code.[55] The same is true for principles of equality,[56] neutrality,[57] secularism[58] and impartiality.[59] But some other principles are still only jurisprudential, such as proportionality[60] and the prohibition of retroactivity.[61]
- *Forms of action*: many rules are specified by case law. The French Council of State defined the categories of regulatory acts[62] and individual decisions, as well as that of public contracts,[63] because legislation was often silent on these matters. However, the Code of relations between the public and the administration and the Public Procurement Code have codified – and have been tempted to simplify – the previous case law,[64] although in relation to contracts, EU law has challenged its influence on French case law.[65]

[52] See below n 78.

[53] G Bigot (n 2) 31 ff; D Lochak, *Le rôle politique du juge administratif français* (Paris, LGDJ, 1972); B Latour, *La fabrique du droit, Une ethnographie au Conseil d'État* (Paris, La Découverte, 2002); B Pacteau, *Le Conseil d'État et la fondation de la justice administrative au XIXe siècle* (Paris, PUF, 2003); A Hachemi, *Le juge administrative et la loi (1789–1889)* (Paris, LGDJ, 2020).

[54] F Burdeau, *Histoire du droit administratif* (Paris, PUF, 1995); G Bigot, *L'autorité judiciaire et le contentieux de l'administration : vicissitudes d'une ambition (1800–1872)* (Paris, LGDJ, 1999); S Gilbert, *Le juge judiciaire, gardien de la propriété privée immobilière, étude de droit administratif* (Paris, Mare et Martin, 2011).

[55] CE, ass, 17 February 1950, *Min Agriculture c Dame Lamotte, Rec CE* 110, *GAJA* (n 50) n° 56, 383.

[56] CE, ass, 7 February 1958, *Syndicat des propriétaires de forêts de chênes-lièges d'Algérie, Rec CE* 74.

[57] CE, ass, 28 May 1954, *Barel et autres, Rec CE* 308, *GAJA* (n 50) n° 63, 444.

[58] CE, ass, 2 November 1998, *Kherouaa et autres, Rec CE* 389.

[59] CE, sect, 2 March 1973, *Dlle Arbousset, Rec CE* 190.

[60] CE, 19 May 1933, *Benjamin, Rec CE* 541, *GAJA* (n 50) n° 42, 280. As Heintzen points out in the German and EU chapter in this book, this principle 'owes its establishment to the case law of the Prussian Higher Administrative Court' (M Heintzen (n 5) section I.A.ii).

[61] CE, ass, 25 June 1948, *Société du Journal « l'Aurore », Rec CE* 289, *GAJA* (n 50) n° 55, 375.

[62] CE, 6 December 1907, *Compagnie des chemins de fer de l'Est et autres, Rec CE* 913, concl J Tardieu, *GAJA* (n 50) n° 17, p 106.

[63] CE, 6 February 1903, *Terrier, Rec CE* 94, concl J Romieu, *GAJA* (n 50) n° 11, p 71; CE, 4 March 1910, *Thérond, Rec CE* 193, concl G Pichat, *GAJA* (n 50) n° 19, p 121; CE, 31 July 1912, *Sté des granits porphyroïdes des Vosges, Rec CE* 909, concl L Blum, *GAJA* (n 50) n° 23, 148.

[64] See above, nn 26 and 42.

[65] Directives 2014/24/UE and 2014/25/UE, 26 February 2014, *JOUE L* 28 March 2014; decree n° 206-360 and 361, 25 March 2016, relatifs aux marches publics et aux marches de défense et de sécurité; directive 2014/23/UE, 26 February 2014, JOUE L 28 March 2014; decree n° 2016-65, 1 February 2016, relatif aux contrats de concession; ordinance n° 2018-1074, 26 November 2018, portant partie législative du code de la commande publique; decree n° 2018-1075, 3 December 2018, portant partie réglementaire du code de la commande publique.

- *Administrative organisation*: judge-made law outlines some principles of administrative organisation, such as relationships between the state and the territorial communities[66] or even between the main administrative authorities such as the President of the Republic and the Prime Minister.[67]
- *Administrative protection*: all principles of administrative protection originated, first, in judge-made law. Moreover, the theory of 'general principles of administrative law' has been born in many famous cases, for example on the right to be heard.[68]

Lastly, one further remark can be made: some questions of general administrative law are influenced by the European Convention on Human Rights, especially principles of action and administrative protection and procedure. Judge-made law by the European Court of Human Rights is very important and can thus be a main source of French administrative law. A similar comment can be made about the Court of Justice of the European Union in relation to both special administrative law (public procurement) and principles of good administration in the EU Charter of Fundamental Rights.[69]

## III. The Codification of Administrative Law

The codification of administrative law presents some peculiarities in French law and has both benefits and disadvantages. But first the consequences of the legal sources of administrative law must be mentioned.

### A. The Consequences of the Legal Sources of Administrative Law

Differences between sources of administrative law have some consequences: when an administrative action or act is controlled by the administrative judge, the control depends on which source is the foundation of this action or decision.[70] This control, in relation to the French law on which the administrative act or action is based, is dissymmetrical: the control of constitutionality is indirect – through the Constitutional Council – while the control of conventionality is direct.

[66] CE, sect, 18 April 1902, *Commune de Néris-les-Bains*, *Rec* CE 275, *GAJA* (n 50) n° 9, 61.
[67] CE, 27 April 1962, *Sicard*, *Rec CE* 279; CE, ass, 10 September 1992, *Meyet*, *Rec CE* 327, concl D Kessler.
[68] CE, sect, 5 May 1944, *Dame Trompier-Gravier*, *Rec CE* 133, *GAJA* (n 50) n° 50, 338; CE, ass, 26 October 1945, *Aramu*, *Rec CE* 213.
[69] Charter of Fundamental Rights of the European Union [2012] OJ C326/391.
[70] *cf* the Italian chapter in this book, R Caranta (n 40) section IV.D.

- *If the source is constitutional*, the administrative judge cannot control by himself the legality of the administrative action or the administrative decision. He can only, if certain conditions are fulfilled, ask the constitutional judge to control the constitutionality of the national law which is the basis of the administrative action or decision.[71]
- *If the source is international* – for example, EU law or European Convention on Human Rights law – the administrative judge can control the compatibility between international law (primary and secondary) and administrative actions or decisions directly or indirectly by controlling, if necessary, the internal law which is the basis of these actions or decisions.[72]
- On the contrary, when the source of administrative action or decision is *general or sectorial legislation or codes*, the control of the administrative judge is direct and extensive: he can control the action or the decision directly against the legislation or the codes.
- The control of the administrative judge is even deeper when the source of the administrative law is *judge-made law* because he has full discretion to modify its own jurisprudence. Incidentally, the French Council of State does not hesitate to interpret laws and codes, or even to amend them.[73]

Because of these differences, codification seems to be a good solution to provide the administrative judge with a large degree of control over both administrative acts and actions.

## B. Peculiarities of the Codification of French Administrative Law

In French law, the legislative codification is defined as the process to bring together and classify in thematic codes all the laws in force on the date of the adoption of these codes.[74] As Issalys points out in his chapter in this volume, in law, and especially in administrative law, codification refers 'to the action of formulating in a single, orderly, systematic and coherent enactment all the essential rules forming

[71] Article 61-1 of Constitution of 4 October 1958: 'If, during proceedings in progress before a court of law, it is claimed that a legislative provision infringes the rights and freedoms guaranteed by the Constitution, the matter may be referred by the Conseil d'État or by the Cour de Cassation to the Constitutional Council which shall rule within a determined period.'

[72] CE, ass, 20 October 1989, *Nicolo, Rec CE* 190, concl P Frydman, *GAJA* (n 50) n° 82, p 612; CE, ass, 19 April 1991, *Belgacem & Mme Babas, Rec CE* 152 and 162.

[73] CE, ass, 17 February 1950, *Min Agriculture c Dame Lamotte* (n 55); see also CE, ass, 13 July 2016, *Czabaj* (see n 126).

[74] Article 3, Law n° 2000-321, 12 April 2000 (n 39): 'La codification législative rassemble et classe dans des codes thématiques l'ensemble des lois en vigueur à la date d'adoption de ces codes.'

a fairly extensive branch of the legal system';[75] such an enactment is thus called a 'code'. In French law, it is composed of two parts: a legislative one, adopted by the Parliament or, more frequently, by governmental delegated legislation; and a regulatory one, directly adopted by the government.

In 2016, the codification of general administrative law especially concerns general administrative actions and acts: it provides principles and forms of administrative action.[76] Thus, it is both procedural and substantive.[77] The process of the codification of the relationship between administrative authorities and citizens has taken a long time because of peculiarities of the French codification system.

The French Council of State is both the supreme administrative judge and the government's advisor. Further, the influence of its members on the state apparatus is very significant, because they are present in the highest echelons of the state. Legally, it is the Prime Minister who presides the Superior Codification Commission, but its vice-president – who is involved in the day-to-day codification process – is a member of the Council of State.[78] That is the reason why the codification of administrative law was so time-consuming: unofficially, it is because the Council of State did not trust the transformation of judge-made law (ie, administrative law made by itself) into codified law.[79] Its fears were exaggerated because, since 2016, the Council of State interprets the Code of relations between the public and the administration[80]

[75] See in this book P Issalys, 'A Persistent Taste for Diversity: Codification of Administrative Law in Canada', section III.

[76] Article 3, Law n° 2013-1005, 12 November 2013, habilitant le gouvernement à simplifier les relations entre l'administration et les citoyens: 'Ce code regroupe et organise les règles générales relatives aux procédures administratives non contentieuses régissant les relations entre le public et les administrations de l'État et des collectivités territoriales, les établissements publics et les organismes chargés d'une mission de service public. Il détermine celles de ces règles qui sont applicables aux relations entre ces administrations et entre ces administrations et leurs agents. Il rassemble les règles générales relatives au régime des actes administratifs' (This code brings together and organises the general rules relating to non-contentious administrative procedures governing relations between the public and the administrations of the state and the local authorities, public institutions and bodies entrusted with a public service mission. It shall determine those rules which are applicable to relations between these administrations and between these administrations and their servants. It brings together the general rules on the system of administrative acts); T Boussarie, *La codification de la procédure administrative : Études autour du code des relations entre le public et l'administration* (Paris, Mare & Martin, 2021) 698; A Zaradny, 'Le Code des relations entre le public et l'administration est-il la *lex generalis* des relations entre l'Administration et le public ?' (2016) 8 *Droit administratif* 33; A Zaradny, 'Codification et État de droit' (thesis, Paris, Université Paris II, 2011) 896.

[77] It is different from the APA (Administrative Procedure Act, 1946) in US administrative law: *cf* the US chapter in this book: EL Rubin, 'The United States: Systematic But Incomplete Codification', section V and also section III on the presentation of the APA, which 'divides administrative action into two categories: rule-making and adjudication'.

[78] Decree n° 89-647, 12 September 1989, relatif à la composition et au fonctionnement de la Commission supérieure de codification; Code of relations between the public and the administration, art L. 351-1; see below, section III.C.

[79] P Gonod, 'La fin de "l'exception française"?' (2014) *Actualité juridique – Droit administratif* 395.

[80] Code des relations entre le public et l'administration, CRPA (Code of relations between the public and the administration) – see above, n 26.

in the way it thinks necessary. Thus, there is neither petrification nor ossification[81] of the general administrative law, since it had been codified. Actually, when the case law is codified, the Superior Codification Commission distinguishes the petrifying codification from the reforming codification: the former does not modify the codified principle or rule, unlike the latter.[82] In administrative matters, the latter way has been preferred.

The codification of the relations between the public and the administration was specific: it was 'experimental' for the Superior Codification Commission, for many reasons.[83] First, it was elaborated with the collaboration of a 'circle of experts'.[84] Second, there has been a derogation from the 'codistic' techniques of numbering the articles of the code: legislative and reglementary articles are not separated into two parts of the code, but interspersed throughout the sub-parts of the code.[85] Third, it was not a 'general' code (understood in the sense of being 'total' or 'global'), but it intended to bring together all 'general rules' concerning the relations between citizens and public administration.[86] Lastly, the codification has obviously brought together existing principles and rules, whether they were legislative, regulatory or jurisprudential, but it has also innovated by creating new rules.[87] The case law has then been greatly simplified – and amended – by the codification, but this has not prevented the administrative judge from again interpreting the code base on advances in case law.

One example is typical: in the Code, there are three types of administrative acts: regulatory, individual, and not regulatory and not individual. The Code also adds that these acts are administrative decisions,[88] ie, which changes the legal order; thereby those acts and decisions can be controlled by the administrative judge. However, in March 2016, the Council of State held, in an important judgment, that some administrative acts are not decisions, but can still be controlled

[81] *cf* the Norwegian chapter in this book: JC Fløysvik Nordrum, 'Codification of Norwegian Administrative Law', section VII.B; *cf* also the Australian chapter in this book: J Boughey, 'The "Codification" of Administrative Law in Australia', sections IV.C and IV.C.iii on 'ossifying the common law'.

[82] On the Public Property General Code (n 43), see Superior Codification Commission, *Rapport annuel 2015* (Paris, Les éditions des Journaux Officiels, 2016) 14.

[83] Superior Codification Commission (n 82) 8 ff; Superior Codification Commission, *Rapport annuel 2014* (Paris, Les éditions des Journaux Officiels, 2015) 21 ff: avis sur le projet de code des relations entre le public et les administrations (advice on the draft code on relations between the public and the administrations), 28 March 2014.

[84] Superior Codification Commission (n 83) 21; see P Terneyre and J Gourdou (n 27) on the participation of scholars to this circle and thus the elaboration of this code.

[85] Superior Codification Commission (n 83) 22; Superior Codification Commission (n 82) 8, 68 (Conseil d'État, avis de l'assemblée générale (advice of the general assembly), 8 October 2015).

[86] Superior Codification Commission (n 83), p 21.

[87] Article 3, Law n° 2013-1005, 12 November 2013 (n 76).

[88] *cf* the Swiss chapter in this book: F Uhlmann, 'Codification of Administrative Law in Switzerland', section II.B.

by the administrative judge.[89] The court practice is against the Code, but prevails over it.[90] Moreover, the Code did not change following this new interpretation, which nevertheless prevails. This would not be possible without the central role played by the French Council of State in the process of the creation of both legislation (and codes) and judge-made law, especially in the administrative field.[91]

In addition, when the process of codification was successfully undertaken, it was led by two persons at the head of the 'circle of experts', one member of the Council of State, one another member of a subordinated administrative court, who in turn became a member of the Council of State. They proceeded by codifying the administrative case-law, especially from the Council of State.[92] Actually, the process of codification is unusual not only in administrative law, but also in the entire legal system.

## C. The Process of Codification in the French Legal System

In the legal French system, there were three major periods of codification (1804, 1948 and 1989) and nowadays codification is an integral part of a bigger process – the simplification of law – the objectives of which are both the accessibility and intelligibility of law required by constitutional law.[93] It has a pedagogical aim, which distinguishes it from the ordinary legislative writing.[94] Even if 'codification is a cooperation tool between the legislative and the executive',[95] it has become a governmental matter, and only partially parliamentary,[96] with some exceptions.

[89] CE, ass, 21 March 2016, *Fairvesta International GmbH*, req n° 368082, *Rec CE* 77, concl S von Coester; CE, ass, 21 March 2016, *Société NC Numericable*, n° 390023, *Rec CE* 89, concl V Daumas; both *GAJA* (n 50) n° 113, 955.

[90] It seems the same in England and Wales, as Nason points out in her chapter in this book: S Nason, 'Codification of Administrative Law in the United Kingdom: Beyond the Common Law', section IV.1.

[91] See above, nn 53 and 54.

[92] M Vialettes and C Barrois de Sarigny, 'Le projet d'un code des relations entre le public et les administrations' (2014) *Actualité juridique – Droit administratif* 402; M Vialettes and C Barrois de Sarigny, 'La fabrique d'un code' (2016) *Revue française de droit administratif* 4.

[93] J-E Schoettl, note sous CC, décision n° 99-421 DC, 16 December 1999, *Codification par ordonnances*, (2000) *Actualité juridique – droit administratif* 31; S Lamouroux, 'La codification ou la démocratisation du droit' (2001) *Revue française de droit constitutionnel* 801; C Cerda-Guzman, 'Codification et constitutionnalisation', thesis (Bordeaux, Université Bordeaux IV, 2010).

[94] Superior Codification Commission, *Rapport annuel 2017* (Paris, Les éditions des Journaux Officiels, 2018) 6; Superior Codification Commission, *Rapport annuel 2018* (Paris, Les éditions des Journaux Officiels, 2019) 7: 'A la différence de la loi ordinaire qui doit ne comporter que des dispositions de portée normative, la spécificité d'un code est de pouvoir comprendre, dans la mesure du strict nécessaire, des dispositions de nature exclusivement pédagogique afin d'éclairer et de guider les usagers, pour un meilleur accès au droit' (Unlike the ordinary law which must include only provisions of normative scope, the specificity of a code is to be able to understand, to the extent strictly necessary, provisions of an exclusively pedagogical nature in order to enlighten and guide users, for better access to the law).

[95] Article 1.3, Circular, 30 May 1996, relative à la codification des textes législatifs et réglementaires, NOR: PRMX9601534C.

[96] *cf* Y Robineau, 'Droit administratif et codification' (1995) *Actualité juridique – Droit administratif* NS 110, 111: 'le Parlement devient acteur de la codification' (the Parliament becomes actor of the

- It is only when some *social issues* are involved that codes are amended directly by the Parliament, which discusses the draft codification, as was the modification of the 'Civil Code',[97] on homosexual marriage[98] or medical assistance for procreation.[99]
- These exceptions aside, for most codes, the Parliament is only consulted by the government, which obtains the power to adopt some delegated legislation by 'ordinance'.[100] The whole process is coordinated by the Superior Codification Commission, which is composed of senior officials, including magistrates, parliamentarians (deputies and senators) and scholars, in close contact with the government's General Secretariat.[101] Often, the process is facilitated by working groups:[102] some are ministerial or interministerial, while others are composed by members of the Council of State; less frequently, some scholars can participate to those working groups.[103] The Superior Codification Commission shall draw up an annual report on its activities, which details the codification process in the past year.[104]
- Methods of codification have been thoroughly experienced since the existence of the Commission (1989), even though they have been criticised:[105] more than 65 codes exist in the French legal system, almost all based on a similar plan of formal distribution of the articles in two separated parts: the legislative one and the regulatory one.[106] These methods use software tools, especially 'Magicode', which was developed by both a private company and the Superior Codification Commission in 1991 and has been constantly upgraded

codification) and 114: 'il y a un temps pour codifier et un temps pour réformer' (there is a time to codify and a time to reform); G Braibant, 'Problèmes actuels de la codification' (1994) *Revue française de droit administratif* 663, 664: 'On est passé de la codification "administrative" … à une codification partiellement législative' (We have moved from an 'administrative' codification … to a partially legislative codification).

[97] Civil Code, promulgated on 21 March 1804 and amended many times subsequently.

[98] Law n° 2013-404, 17 May 2013, ouvrant le mariage aux couples de personnes de même sexe.

[99] Law n° 2021-1017, 2 August 2021, relative à la bioéthique: arts 6 and 7 amend the Civil Code, while arts 1–5 amend the Public Health Code.

[100] P Gonod, 'La simplification du droit par ordonnance' (2003) *Actualité juridique – Droit administratif* 1652. In the Italian chapter in this book, Caranta explains the same in Italy (R Caranta (n 40) s VI).

[101] G Braibant, 'Codifier pour mieux réformer: entretien avec O Dufour', (1997) 140 *Les petites affiches* 5; G Braibant, 'Codifier: Pourquoi? Comment?' (1995) 73 *Revue française d'administration publique* 127. Article 2, Decree n° 89-647, 12 September 1989, relatif à la composition et au fonctionnement de la Commission supérieure de codification, amended since 1989.

[102] Article 1.1.4, Circular (n 95).

[103] This was the case for the codification of the Code of relations between the public and the administration; see above, n 84.

[104] See www.legifrance.gouv.fr/contenu/menu/autour-de-la-loi/codification/rapports-annuels-de-la-commission-superieure-de-codification.

[105] H Moysan, 'La codification à droit constant ne résiste pas à l'épreuve de la consolidation' (2002) 4 *Droit administratif* 6. *cf contra* R Schwartz, 'Éloge de la codification' (2002) 12 *Droit administratif* 11.

[106] M Guyomar, 'Les perspectives de la codification contemporaine' (2014) *Actualité juridique – Droit administratif* 400.

and improved.[107] Actually, these methods have fostered the emergence of a new discipline, alongside 'legistic':[108] 'codistic'.[109] Thanks to these methods, the codification can operate in different ways:[110] without any change of positive law, by simple reorganisation or by depth consolidation.[111] The first possibility is the default methodology, which admits the other two as exceptions, when it is necessary but rare to rewrite principles and rules.[112] Codifying existing laws makes it possible to separate two successive steps of legal evolution: 'the recasting of the law on the one hand and its reform on the other'.[113] When codification is innovative, it recasts and reforms at the same time, as the Superior Codification Commission did with the Code of relations between the public and the administration (see above, section III.B).[114]

## D. Advantages and Disadvantages of Codification

### i. *Advantages of the Codification of Administrative Law*

When it is codified, administrative law offers the advantage of being reliable. The chapter on the Netherlands in this volume points out in relation to the Dutch General Administrative Law Act (GALA) that the codification allows certainty,

[107] Annex 24, 'Un outil informatique pour la codification: Magicode' in Superior Codification Commission (ed), *Rapport annuel 2007* (Paris, Les éditions des Journaux Officiels, 2008) 78 ff.

[108] Premier ministre (Secrétariat Général du Gouvernement), Conseil d'État, *Guide de légistique*, 3rd edn (Paris, La documentation française, 2017) 109 ff (1.4.2. Codification).

[109] See above, n 94.

[110] As Caranta points out in the Italian chapter in this book, 'testi unici' can be 'compilativi' or 'innovativi' (R Caranta (n 40) s VI).

[111] M Guyomar, 'Y compris à droit constant, la codification revêt une dimension non seulement formelle mais aussi substantielle. Entretien avec Mattias Guyomar' (2015) 48 *La semaine juridique édition générale* 1271.

[112] Article 3, para 2, Law n° 2000-321 (n 39): 'Cette codification se fait à droit constant, sous réserve des modifications nécessaires pour améliorer la cohérence rédactionnelle des textes rassemblés, assurer le respect de la hiérarchie des normes et harmoniser l'état du droit' (Such codification shall be carried out with existing laws, subject to such modifications as may be necessary to improve the consistency of the texts collected, to ensure compliance with the hierarchy of norms and to harmonize the state of the law); art 2.1.1, Circular (n 95): 'la discussion devant le Parlement peut conduire à ajouter à la codification à droit constant quelques amendments de fond tendant à améliorer la legislation.' (the discussion before Parliament may lead to the addition to the codification of the existing laws of some substantive amendments aimed at improving legislation).

[113] Superior Codification Commission (n 82) 12: 'L'avantage de la codification à "droit constant" est de permettre de clairement distinguer deux opérations de nature différente et qui doivent, en principe, être successives: la refonte du droit, d'une part, puis sa réforme, de l'autre' ('The advantage of codification under "existing law" is that it is possible to distinguish clearly between two operations of a different nature which must, in principle, be successive: the recasting of the law, on the one hand, and its reform, on the other').

[114] See above n 87.

accessibility, and uniformity of the legal rules applicable to the administration.[115] That is the reason why the French general administrative law was codified: to be more easily understood by both administration and citizens and to be most likely applied, especially by the administrative authorities:[116]

- For example, the withdrawal of an administrative act (ie, revocation with retroactivity) was submitted to very unclear judge-made law. Schematically, the Council of State decided in 2001 and 2009 that both past and future revocation and even only future revocation was subject to two main conditions: one attached to a time limit of four months after the elaboration of the administrative act and the other attached to the unlawfulness of the act.[117] Other conditions affected the discretion of the administrative authority to revoke the act, whether optionally or obligatorily, retroactively or not. In this peculiarly tricky field, codification simplifies matters. It is considered to be a codification of the judge-made law.
- Another example results from the codification of the rule which states that the silence of an administrative authority, following a citizen's request, becomes a positive answer. Until a 2013 Law,[118] which was codified in 2016,[119] an opposite rule was applicable (the administrative silence became a negative decision). Nowadays, since 2013, without any modification in 2016: 'The two-month silence of the administration on a request is a decision on acceptance.' Because this new rule contained mainly exceptions, the 2016 Code is clear and more applicable than the 2013 Law. However, it refers to a governmental website: it is possible to find some tables which describes the exceptions, but some of them only have an information value, not a legal value. Thus, the Code does not cover all administrative law.

[115] See the Dutch chapter in this book: Y Schuurmans, T Barkhuysen and W den Ouden, 'Codification of Administrative Law in the Netherlands', sections III.C and V. See also the British chapter in this book: S Nason (n 90) section IV.C.

[116] M Vialettes and C Barrois de Sarigny, 'Questions autour d'une codification' (2015) *Actualité juridique – Droit administratif* 2421. *cf* the Belgian chapter in this book: S De Somer and I Opdebeek (n 47) section III.E.

[117] CE, ass, 26 October 2001, *Ternon, Rec CE* 497, concl F Seners; CE, sect, 6 March 2009, *Coulibaly*; Code of relations between the public and the administration, arts L 240-1 ff; G Éveillard, 'La codification du retrait et de l'abrogation des actes administratifs unilatéraux' (2015) *Actualité juridique – Droit administratif* 2474; Superior Codification Commission (n 82) 45 ff, avis portant sur le projet de code des relations entre le public et l'administration (advice on the draft code on relations between the public and the administration), séance du 10 février 2015: this advice refers specifically to the judgments of the Council of State of 2001 and 2009. *cf* the German chapter in this book: M Heintzen (n 5) section I.B.ii.

[118] Law n° 2013-1005, 12 November 2013, habilitant le Gouvernement à simplifier les relations entre l'administration et les citoyens.

[119] Code of relations between the public and the administration, arts 231-1 ff.

### *ii. Disadvantages of the Codification of Administrative Law*

The French codification of administrative law has some disadvantages. Like any other source, the code can be interpreted or even transformed by the administrative supreme judge.[120] Some examples are very surprising in this respect:

- There is a French code specifically dedicated to the judicial rules of the administrative trial, which came into force in 2001: it is the Administrative Justice Code.[121] As usual with French codification, its elaboration was supervised by the Superior Codification Commission and prepared by a working group, composed mainly of members of the Council of State, who were especially interested in this codification insofar it concerns the procedure before administrative jurisdictions (the Council of State, administrative courts of appeal and administrative tribunals).[122] Some estimate that this Code has been elaborated only by the members of the Council of State, but the working group set up to prepare this Code included one very famous Parisian Full Professor of Administrative Law, René Chapus.[123] Yet, once again, the Council of State plays as key role to codify some rules that were mostly old and needed to be amended and reordered; most of these rules concern precisely the Council of State and the other administrative ordinary courts, which is not in the least bit surprising.[124]
- In the Administrative Justice Code, there was a rule favourable to citizens: when an administrative decision did not mention in the written notification the time limit and the competent judge, the recipient could contest this decision forever. In the Code, the rule was very clear: 'Time limits for appeals against an administrative decision may be invoked only on condition that they have been mentioned, together with the means of appeal, in the notification of

[120] As De Somer and Opdebeek explain in the Belgian chapter in this book, 'Codification does not necessarily reduce the importance of case law as a source of law' (S De Somer and I Opdebeek (n 47) s III.6.3.

[121] J Arrighi de Casanova, 'Commentaire de l'ordonnance n° 2000-387 du 4 mai 2000 *relative à la partie Législative du Code de justice administrative*; Commentaire des décrets n° 2000-388 et 2000-389 du 4 mai 2000 *relatifs à la partie Réglementaire du Code de justice administrative*' (2000) *Actualité juridique – Droit administratif* 639; R Chapus, 'La justice administrative: évolution et codification. Lecture du code de justice administrative' (2000) *Revue française de droit administratif* 929.

[122] The French Council of State can be the judge of first instance, for important requests, such as actions against governmental Acts, rarely the appeal judge and frequently the judge of Cassation (ie, last instance).

[123] J-M Sauvé, 'L'apport de René Chapus au contentieux administratif' in B Plessix (ed), *Hommage à René Chapus* (Paris, Éditions Panthéon-Assas, 2020); arrêté du vice-président du Conseil d'État, 27 December 1987, instituant la 'Commission spéciale pour l'examen des textes intéressant le contentieux administratif'; R Denoix de Saint Marc, 'Le Conseil d'État, acteur déterminant de l'élaboration des lois et règlements' (2006) 10–11 *La Semaine Juridique* 118.

[124] J Arrighi de Casanova, 'Le Code de justice administrative' (2000) *Actualité juridique – Droit administratif* 639; R Chapus, 'Lecture du Code de justice administrative' (2000) *Revue française de droit administratif* 929; S Deygas, 'La création du Code de justice administrative' (2000) 7 *Procédures* 3.

the decision.'[125] The redaction of this rule did not change in the Code, despite a very important judgment of the Council of State, which in July 2016 decided that this rule could apply only for a reasonable time, bearing in mind that for the Council of State, one year was considered reasonable.[126] Thus, the article of the Code which imposes no time limit for recipients is outdated. It must be understood in the light of the 2016 judgment. The question is: why was the Code not modified by the government? Why does the judgment of the Council of State prevail despite any regulatory change? Perhaps because precisely a regulatory change is operated by an administrative act of the Prime Minister, which can be contested before the administrative judge, that is, for Prime Ministers' acts, the Council of State. Even if the new rule is justified by the principle of legal certainty, which is an important non-codified underpinning of administrative action, and even if a regulatory act of the Prime Minister can be considered as legal by the administrative judge, it is easier not to change the Code.

## IV. Summary and Conclusion

In this context, there is no major difference between codified and uncodified general administrative law. There is no difference for the administrative judge, who interprets all administrative rules as he thinks necessary. The difference is for the administrative authorities and for citizens who should have some clear and reliable rules when codified.

The clearness of codes comes from the sequencing of norms: all general principles – when they exist – and specific rules conform to a precise and mostly complete schedule. This means that, without prior consolidation, most of the time, codification is not effective, but, conversely, codification does not prevent reform.

In addition, when rules result from EU law (as for public contracts)[127] or are involved in new areas (for example, sustainability),[128] it is easier to codify them. No doubt the influence of the Council of State is less significant in those areas than for defining principles of administrative action. In the future, perhaps codification may be of interest to some specific areas of administrative action.

[125] Article R. 421-5, Administrative Justice Code: 'Les délais de recours contre une décision administrative ne sont opposables qu'à la condition d'avoir été mentionnés, ainsi que les voies de recours, dans la notification de la décision.'

[126] CE, ass, 13 July 2016, *Czabaj, Rec CE* 340, concl O Henrard.

[127] Code de la commande publique (Public Procurement Code) about procurement contracts and concessions – see above, n 65.

[128] Code de l'environnement (Environmental Code): Ordinance n° 2000-914, 18 September 2000, and Decree n° 2005-935, 2 August 2005.

In conclusion, in a country which imagines that it is the birthplace of codification,[129] the codification of administrative law can be improved. It is necessary to remember the following sentence by Portalis, one of the writers of the Civil Code in the Napoleonic period (1804): 'laws are made for humans, not humans for laws'.[130]

[129] M Guyomar (n 111) 1271: 'La codification est une des caractéristiques du génie juridique français' (Codification is one of the characteristics of French legal genius).

[130] J-E M Portalis, *Discours préliminaire sur le projet de Code civil présenté le 1er pluviôse an IX par la Commission nommée par le gouvernement consulaire, in Discours, rapports et travaux inédits sur le Code civil publiés par le Vicomte de Portalis* (1844) 5: 'les lois sont faites pour les hommes, et non les hommes pour les lois'.

# 6

# Codification of Administrative Law in Germany and the European Union

MARKUS HEINTZEN

This chapter addresses the question of the codification in general administrative law by two different legal systems: the federal legal system of the Federal Republic of Germany and the legal system of the European Union (EU). As with all the chapters in this volume, the basis for this is a questionnaire, which distinguishes five main thematic components of general administrative law for comparative purposes and requests that these five main components be assigned to legal sources, in particular constitutional and statutory law, but also case law.

Because there is no special relationship between German and European administrative law, both areas are separated. German administrative law is examined first. EU law follows because it was only created on the basis of the law of the Member States, including Germany, from the outset and because the legal power of the EU for codification is limited due to the principle of conferral (Article 5(1) of the Treaty on European Union (TEU))[1] and the procedural autonomy of the Member States (Article 291(1) of the Treaty on the Functioning of the European Union (TFEU)).[2] The codification process in Germany was and is not inspired by Europe. German general administrative law had already found its present form before the legislative activity of the EU had reached the volume necessary for a codification claim in the early 1990s. Despite the fact that Germany is open to EU law and to integration,[3] there is a fear that important institutions of general administrative law in Germany, namely subjective public rights,[4] will be questioned by Europe.

[1] Consolidated Version of the Treaty on European Union [2012] OJ C326/13.

[2] Consolidated Version of the Treaty on the Functioning of the European Union [2012] OJ C326/47.

[3] However, on EU law and the European Court of Justice, see BVerfG, judgment 5 May 2020, 2 BvR 859/15, paras 102 ff, 116 ff, BVerfGE 154, 17, esp 94 (an English translation is available on the website of the court – https://www.bundesverfassungsgericht.de/e/rs20200505_2bvr085915en.html – where the court, in the context of an ultra vires review, criticises the European Court of Justice (quite understandably) due to its argumentation being 'simply no longer comprehensible'. On the consideration of the guarantees of the European Convention of Human Rights and the decisions of the European Court of Human Rights in German law, still fundamental BVerfGE 111, 307 (317 ff, Görgölü).

[4] See below, section II.A.

# I. Administrative Law in Germany

## A. Definitions and Delimitations of Administrative Law

### *i. Administration and General Administrative Law*

The first question to be answered is: what is meant by administrative law? This question catches a German scholar of administrative law on the wrong foot, because in Germany the first question that is usually asked in textbooks is: what is meant by administration? The answer is: administration is something complex, which cannot be defined, but only circumscribed,[5] whereby this circumscription involves considerable references to private law. Very common are negative definitions in the sense of administration being the activity and organisation of the state, which are not legislation, government, military and jurisdiction.[6]

On the question of what administration describes in a positive sense, there is a wide range of definitions[7] and paraphrases, some more blurry than others, which can be found in the textbooks on general administrative law, of which there are about 15 that have been published since 2010 in Germany.[8] The following are viewed as essential features: the enforcement of public law in individual cases and the social shaping in the context of the law, especially by subordinate public authorities. It is common to divide them into intervention or regulatory administration, service administration, infrastructure administration and ensuring the provision of private services.

Against this backdrop, administrative law has been well established as a subfield with its own identity and yet clear internal structures since the end of the so-called 'Policey- und Staatswissenschaft' in the nineteenth century. 'Policeywissenschaft' stands for expediency in an authoritarian sense and 'Staatswissenschaft' stands for an empirical description of state activity, which perhaps identifies particular branches of administration, but does not provide any legal systematisation.

[5] E Forsthoff, *Lehrbuch des Verwaltungsrechts*, vol 1, *Allgemeiner Teil*, 10th edn (Munich, CH Beck, 1973) p 1.

[6] The situation is similar in Austria; see in this book K Lachmayer, 'Codification of Administrative Law in Austria', sections II.A.ii and II.A.iii.

[7] A well-known attempt at defining the term is given in HJ Wolff and O Bachof, *Verwaltungsrecht*, vol 1, 9th edn (Munich, CH Beck, 1974) s 2 III: 'Public administration in the material sense is hence the manifold, conditional or only purpose-built, thus insofar heteronomous, only partly planning, participatingly decisively executing and creating fulfilment of matters of the community and its members as such by the therefore appointed trustees of the community.'

[8] See H Maurer and C Waldhoff, *Allgemeines Verwaltungsrecht*, 20th edn (Munich, CH Beck, 2020) p xxxvii. In 2014 even a jubilee publication with the title *Allgemeines Verwaltungsrecht* (ie, general administrative law) appeared in honour of Professor Ulrich Battis. Arguably, the first textbook with the title *Allgemeines Verwaltungsrecht* was written by the Austrian Adolf Merkl and published in 1927. See further C Kremer (ed), *Die Verwaltungsrechtswissenschaft in der frühen Bundesrepublik (1949–1977)* (Tübingen, Mohr Siebeck, 2017). H Maurer and C Waldhoff do not list books from Austria and Switzerland, which can be added to the total of 15; eg, U Häfelin, G Müller and F Uhlmann, *Allgemeines Verwaltungsrecht*, 8th edn (Zurich, Dike, 2020).

Administrative law covers the lawfulness of the administration, priority and reservation of the law, and the rule of state.

In the Roman law tradition, the German legal system is characterised by the dualism of private and public law. In public law, a further distinction is made between state law, which at its core is constitutional law, and administrative law. 'State law' is typically German; it is difficult to find a good translation making clear the (small) difference between constitutional and state law, which is continued in the different terms 'constitutional court' and 'state court'. In administrative law, the classification of a general part, in contrast to special administrative law (with its specialist disciplines), has become commonplace.

The indefinability of administration and the established status of general administrative law are not contradictory; rather, they complement each other. General administrative law has a coordinating and regulatory function, which is intended to make it easier for the practitioner of law to find his way around the complex, confusing world of special administrative law, which is not free of contingency and coincidence.

## *ii. Historical Development*

This development was not started by a legislator, and certainly not a legislator of a centralised state. At the beginning there was the case law of individual administrative courts, first in Baden (1863) and especially in Prussia, Bavaria and Saxony, and also textbooks written by university professors. It should be pointed out, for example, that the principle of proportionality, with its sub-elements of suitability, necessity and adequacy, owes its establishment to the case law of the Prussian Higher Administrative Court;[9] the Federal Constitutional Court was able to build on this when it adopted this principle in its jurisdiction on fundamental rights in the 1950s.

Regarding the textbooks, two should be emphasised: the *Institutionen des deutschen Verwaltungsrechts* (*Institutions of German Administrative Law*) by Fritz Fleiner (1st edn 1911, 8th edn 1928) and *German Administrative Law* (*Deutsches Verwaltungsrecht*) by Otto Mayer (1st edn 1895/96, 3rd edn 1924). The title 'Institutions' was chosen by Fleiner in conscious connection with the 'institutiones' of Roman law (Gaius and Justinian). Mayer's textbook was written during his time as a professor at the University of Strasbourg; this city belonged to the German Reich from 1871 to 1918 and this university acted as a bridge between France and Germany, for which Mayer is a very good example. Fleiner was also a crossing borders; having grown up academically in Zurich, he was a professor in Germany from 1906 to 1915 and then continued his work in Switzerland.[10]

[9] See B Remmert, *Verfassungs- und verwaltungsrechtsgeschichtliche Grundlagen des Übermaßverbots* (Heidelberg, CF Müller, 1995).

[10] With regard to Fleiner, *cf* the Swiss chapter in this book: F Uhlmann, 'Codification of Administrative Law in Switzerland', section I.A.

The sequence of court decisions, textbooks and laws raises the general question of what is meant by codification. The archetype of a codification, the Corpus Juris Civilis of the East Roman Emperor Justinian (created 528–34 CE), includes all these elements.[11] Here, it can only be pointed towards the difference between a codex and a codification as well as towards the existence of codification research,[12] which mainly deals with traditional codes of civil and criminal law. In principle, a distinction can be made between the most complete possible summary of already-existing law, which is intended to change little or nothing about this law, but only to present it more clearly, and the reorganisation of a larger area of law, which is committed to conceptual and substantive guiding principles. In order to be suitable for codification, an area of law must have its own identity, a minimum volume that is admittedly hardly quantifiable and potential for abstraction. The latter applies to general administrative law *per definitionem*. It and its main areas are also sufficiently complex.

### *iii. The Threefold Division of Contemporary General Administrative Law in Germany*

Coming back to Germany and to general administrative law: to be precise, there are three general sections of administrative law in Germany today. In addition to the general section of administrative law in itself, there is general tax law and general social security law. Accordingly, there are three general procedural laws concerning the magisterial procedure (the Verwaltungsverfahrensgesetz (Administrative Procedure Act, VwVfG of 1977),[13] the Abgabenordnung (Fiscal Code, AO)[14] and the Sozialgesetzbuch Teil X (Tenth Book of the Social Security Code, SGB X)),[15] three procedural laws concerning the judicial procedure (the Verwaltungsgerichtsordnung (Code of Administrative Court Procedure, VwGO),[16] the Finanzgerichtsordnung (Code of Fiscal Court Procedure, FGO)[17] and the

[11] See C Möller, 'In unam reducere consonantiam – Justinians Verhältnis zur Überlieferung des römischen Rechts' (2019) 74 *Juristen-Zeitung* 1084.

[12] From a public law perspective, see, eg, A Voßkuhle, 'Kodifikation als Prozess' in H Schlosser (ed), *Bürgerliches Gesetzbuch 1896–1996* (Heidelberg, Augsburger Rechtsstudien 27, 1997) 77 ff.

[13] Verwaltungsverfahrensgesetz in der Fassung der Bekanntmachung vom 23. Januar 2003 (BGBl I, 102), zuletzt geändert durch Artikel 24 Absatz 3 des Gesetzes vom 25. Juni 2021 (BGBl I, 2154).

[14] Abgabenordnung in der Fassung der Bekanntmachung vom 1. Oktober 2002 (BGBl I, 3866; 2003 I, 61), zuletzt geändert durch Artikel 33 des Gesetzes vom 5. Oktober 2021 (BGBl I, 4607). An English translation of the Fiscal Code, but not the Administrative Procedure Code, is available at www.gesetze-im-internet.de/translations, a website operated by the Federal Ministry of Justice.

[15] Das Zehnte Buch Sozialgesetzbuch – Sozialverwaltungsverfahren und Sozialdatenschutz – in der Fassung der Bekanntmachung vom 18. Januar 2001 (BGBl I, 130), zuletzt geändert durch Artikel 45 des Gesetzes vom 20. August 2021 (BGBl I, 3932).

[16] Verwaltungsgerichtsordnung in der Fassung der Bekanntmachung vom 19. März 1991 (BGBl I, 686), zuletzt geändert durch Artikel 2 des Gesetzes vom 8. Oktober 2021 (BGBl I, 4650).

[17] Finanzgerichtsordnung in der Fassung der Bekanntmachung vom 28. März 2001 (BGBl I, 442, 2262; 2002 I, 679), zuletzt geändert durch Artikel 19 des Gesetzes vom 5. Oktober 2021 (BGBl I, 4607).

Sozialgerichtsgesetz (Social Court Act, SGG))[18] and three jurisdictions with three supreme federal courts at their apex (the Bundesverwaltungsgericht (Federal Administrative Court, BVerwG, located in Leipzig), the Bundessozialgericht BSG (Federal Social Court, located in Kassel) and the Bundesfinanzhof BFH (Federal Fiscal Court, located in Munich)).

The oldest of these is the fiscal jurisdiction; the Reichsfinanzhof (Fiscal Court of the German Reich) was created in 1918, in line with the general upturn of tax law after the First World War and the enormous financial needs of the state. The Federal Social Court and the Federal Administrative Court were created in the early days of the Federal Republic of Germany in 1953. Before 1933 – ie, before the Nazi regime – legal protection was granted in general administrative matters, in accordance with the federal tradition of Germany, by the courts of the Länder, in particular by the Prussian Higher Administrative Court in Berlin and the Bavarian Administrative Court in Munich. These traditions still linger subliminally. In the southern German Länder, the administrative courts of second instance are not called Oberverwaltungsgerichte (which would be in keeping with Prussian tradition), but Verwaltungsgerichtshöfe (section 184 VwGO).

In social security law, legal protection was provided not by the courts, but by administrative authorities, in particular by the Reichsversicherungsamt (Insurance Office of the German Reich). This distinction between administrative authorities and courts is similar to the distinction between courts and tribunals in the Anglo-American world. Social law has now been codified in the Social Code for social policy reasons. The Social Code comprises 12 books, three of which contain general social administration law, a total of about 2,400 sections, but according to section 68 no 1 SGB I[19] still not all of the social security law; for example, the law of educational support for students or the social security court system are excluded. Currently, a new book of the social code has been discussed, which is supposed to aggregate the social right of compensation. This book would be the thirteenth book, but the number 13 bodes mischief. Therefore – and this is not a joke[20] – the German legislature is considering skipping 13 and putting into effect the SGB XIV[21] after the SGB XII.[22]

Comparable codification efforts in environmental law have failed.[23] The subject matter has proven to be too complex – EU law, federal law, state law, parliamentary

[18] Sozialgerichtsgesetz in der Fassung der Bekanntmachung vom 23. September 1975 (BGBl I, 2535), zuletzt geändert durch Artikel 13 des Gesetzes vom 5. Oktober 2021 (BGBl I, 4607).

[19] Das Erste Buch Sozialgesetzbuch – Allgemeiner Teil – (Artikel I des Gesetzes vom 11. Dezember 1975, BGBl I, 3015), zuletzt geändert durch Artikel 32 des Gesetzes vom 20. August 2021 (BGBl I, 3932).

[20] The 14th Book of the Social Code came into force at the end of 2019: Law of 12 December 2019 (BGBl I, 2652).

[21] Sozialgesetzbuch Vierzehntes Buch – Soziale Entschädigung – vom 12. Dezember 2019 (BGBl I, 2652), zuletzt geändert durch Artikel 49 des Gesetzes vom 20. August 2021 (BGBl I, 3932).

[22] Das Zwölfte Buch Sozialgesetzbuch – Sozialhilfe – (Artikel 1 des Gesetzes vom 27. Dezember 2003, BGBl I, 3022, 3023), zuletzt geändert durch Artikel 3 des Gesetzes vom 23. Mai 2022 (BGBl I, 760).

[23] M Kloepfer, *Umweltrecht*, 4th edn (Munich, CH Beck, 2016) paras 152 ff, with a reference to European framework directives at the end.

laws, ordinances and technical regulations – and, furthermore, the enormous need for change is in tension with the fact that codifications are created for consistency.

Of these three pillars, the tax law pillar is the oldest. However, in the 1970s it came under the influence of general administrative law to such an extent that the AO was revised in 1977 and adapted to the VwVfG. As a result, differences remained modest – sometimes differences in detail, which can be surprising, such as the correction of obvious mistakes.[24] In recent times there have been opposing trends. Especially in terms of dealing with the phenomenon of the digitisation of administration, social security and tax law have been more innovative.

While legislation, including procedural legislation, is federal legislation in social security and tax law, the federal structure of the Federal Republic of Germany is clearly noticeable in general administrative law. In accordance with Article 83 of the Grundgesetz (German Constitution, GG)[25] the Länder shall execute federal laws in their own right. Even though legislation is predominantly a matter for the federal government under Germany's federal separation of powers, its administration is primarily a matter for the Länder and the municipalities which are part of the Länder.

It follows that in addition to the federal Administrative Procedure Act, there are also corresponding laws of the Länder; in part, these laws are literally in accordance with federal law and some of them contain dynamic references to the federal law. In addition, it should be noted that there is an exception – that appeals to the Federal Administrative Court can be based on a provision of the administrative procedure Act of a Land, insofar as this provision corresponds to the wording of the Federal Administrative Procedure Act (section 137 subsection 1 no 2 VwGO); otherwise state law is not revisable, ie, it is not subject to the cognition of the BVerwG.

Moreover, due to the federal distribution of legislative competences in Germany, a comprehensive codification of general administrative law is practically impossible. This applies especially to administrative organisation and public service law.

Consequently, it is also difficult in some areas of administrative law to achieve a uniform solution at the federal level, because the Länder have a right of approval in the Federal Council (Bundesrat) and can block federal legislation. A good example of this is the state liability law. Its main pillar is section 839 BGB (Civil Law Code),[26] which stipulates a personal liability of civil servants, which is then

[24] See A Musil, 'Die Berichtigung von Verwaltungsakten wegen offenbarer Unrichtigkeiten' (2001) *Die Öffentliche Verwaltung* 947.

[25] Grundgesetz für die Bundesrepublik Deutschland in der im Bundesgesetzblatt Teil III, Gliederungsnummer 100–1, veröffentlichten bereinigten Fassung, zuletzt geändert durch Artikel 1 u. 2 Satz 2 des Gesetzes vom 29. September 2020 (BGBl I, 2048).

[26] Bürgerliches Gesetzbuch in der Fassung der Bekanntmachung vom 2. Januar 2002 (BGBl I, 42, 2909; 2003 I, 738), zuletzt geändert durch Artikel 2 des Gesetzes vom 21. Dezember 2021 (BGBl I, 5252).

transferred to the state by Article 34 GG. In addition – and unusually for a civil law country – there exists quite of lot of case law, especially from the Federal Court of Justice. The attempt in October 1982 to establish a federal regulation for the first time failed before the Federal Constitutional Court because of a lack of legislative competence on the part of the federation. Twelve years later, the federation was given this competence by constitutional amendment, but with the proviso that a corresponding federal law requires the approval of the Federal Council. This legislative competence has now been lying dormant for 25 years and is expected to remain dormant, because the Länder, with which most of the administrative activity and therefore a much greater liability risk lies, fear that the federal government wants to leave their track with the citizens and voters through generous liability rules at the expense of the Länder.

## B. Legal Sources of General Administrative Law

The main task of this chapter is to assign the most important thematic building blocks of general administrative law, on the one hand, to the various sources of law, on the other hand.

According to the questionnaire on which this chapter is based, the main building blocks should be: principles of action, forms of action, administrative organisation and administrative protection. This list seems very familiar to a German observer, as it contains the main bullet points of German administrative law textbooks. It could certainly be refined and configured slightly differently, but hardly supplemented. Important refinements which may be mentioned and that go beyond the keywords already mentioned are:

- concerning the principles: commitment to the constitution and constitutionalisation;
- concerning the principles of protection: the doctrine of subjective public rights;
- concerning the forms of action: the consequences of errors and, in addition to contracts, obligations in general; and
- concerning protection: the state liability law.

In Germany the point of discretion would be subsumed under principles and split up into discretion regarding legal consequences, and discretion regarding undetermined legal terms and planning considerations. Furthermore, since it is the subject of the most important law in general administrative law, the procedure would be an independent main point. Furthermore, procedural law not only serves to protect the citizen, but also establishes duties and obligations for them in the interests of an objectively correct and legal administrative decision. This argues in favour of making it an independent fifth point.

From the German point of view, a conceivable addition would be the right of public property and facilities and their use by the general public. Conversely, public service law, tax and duties law[27] and procurement (public contracts, expropriations) are regarded as matters of special administrative law.

### *i. Principles of Action*

German administrative law is oriented towards principles. The main principles are: the lawfulness of the administration, the prohibition of arbitrary action, the requirement of a fair trial, the definiteness, clarity and publicity of norms and individual decisions, the protection of legitimate expectations, the proportionality principle, the right to be heard and effective legal protection.[28] Not all of these principles are explicitly enshrined in the Constitution. However, this does not prevent German administrative lawyers from assigning them constitutional status. In the absence of explicit regulation, they are understood as part of the principle of rule of law,[29] which, in addition to the democratic, social and federal state principles, is a fundamental norm of the German legal order, which even constitution-changing law must not infringe; only a modification for a special situation according to its nature for evidently appropriate reasons is admissible.[30] The 'Rechtsstaatsprinzip' (principle of the rule of law) is the guiding principle, similar to the 'Rechtsgleichheit' (principle of legal equality) that served as basis for further rights in Switzerland before the Constitution of 1999. Other principles (such as protection of legitimate expectations or proportionality) are deduced from it. This does not change the fact that the principle of the rule of law is only casually mentioned in the GG (Article 23, paragraph 1, sentence 1 and Article 28, paragraph 1, sentence 1, but not Article 20, the basic provision) and that the protection of legitimate expectations and proportionality are not explicitly mentioned at all. Principle means a legal norm, not soft law – a legal norm that can be enforced by constitutional and administrative courts. Principle also means that the legislator can allow exceptions, but these must be legally justified before the principle.

As early as 1959, the then President of the Federal Administrative Court, Fritz Werner, qualified administrative law as concrete constitutional law.[31] This formula has often been cited, and today constitutionalisation, along with digitisation and Europeanisation, is a megatrend of administrative law in Germany.

After these remarks on the Constitution as a legal source, a brief reference to the legislature is given: principles evade its grasp. If section 85, sentence 1 of the

[27] Concerning tax law, see above, section I.A.

[28] For this listing, see HD Jarass and B Pieroth, *Grundgesetz Kommentar*, 16th edn (Munich, CH Beck, 2020) art 20, paras 37 ff.

[29] For a critical stance on the interpretation of the rule of law as a general clause, see P Kunig, *Das Rechtsstaatsprinzip* (Tübingen, Mohr Siebeck, 1986).

[30] See, comparably worded, BVerfGE 30, 1 (24), where the Federal Constitutional Court had to deal with the concealment of surveillance by intelligence services of written correspondence and telecommunications, and the consequential impossibility of judicial protection.

[31] F Werner, 'Verwaltungsrecht als konkretisiertes Verfassungsrecht' (1959) *Deutsches Verwaltungsblatt* 527.

German Fiscal Code states that '[t]he tax authorities have to set and raise the taxes in accordance with the laws evenly', then only what is stated in the Constitution is repeated: lawfulness and uniformity of the administration.

### *ii. Forms of Action*

Concerning the forms of action of the administration, little is to be found in German constitutional law. Since the forms of action concern the daily contact of the administration with the citizen, the law adopted by the Parliament suggests itself as a level of regulation.

The main topic of the federal Administrative Procedure Act is, in addition to the inquisitorial principle as the guiding principle of the administrative procedure, the administrative act as the typical form of administrative action. It is comprehensively regulated in sections 35–53 of this Act (textbook definition, delimitation to executive norm-setting, incidental provisions, form (also electronic), definiteness and explanation, discretion, announcement, effectiveness, in particular incontestability, illegality and their consequences, repeal, including protection of legitimate expectations).

The protection of legitimate expectations in the case of the repeal of favourable administrative acts helps to demonstrate how the legislator was able to take up the preparatory work of the administrative courts. For a long time, it was considered to be undisputed that an unlawful administrative act may be revoked in accordance with the principle of legality of administration, even if the addressee trusts in its existence. It was alleged that trust in illegal state action does not merit legal protection. This has been disputed by administrative courts, evoking the principle of the rule of law. The first relevant decisions in the 1950s[32] were spectacular. They restricted the possibility of withdrawing unlawful administrative acts on the grounds of legitimate expectations. This position subsequently prevailed and was adopted by the federal legislator in 1977 in section 48, paragraphs 2–4 of the Administrative Procedure Act (VwVfG).

Until the 1970s, it was disputed in Germany as to what extent the administration was allowed to face the citizen not only as an addressee of a one-sided regulation but also as a contractual partner. This question was answered by the Administrative Procedure Act in a positive way, although the nine provisions that have been made so far still leave some questions. Areas of special administrative law, which are 'contract-friendly', are public building law, while civil service law and tax law are 'contract-hostile'.

Less distinct is the generalisation concerning the instruments of the planning administration. The federal building code[33] of 1986 is a discipline-specific

[32] OVG Berlin, *Deutsches Verwaltungsblatt* 1957, 503; Bundesverwaltungsgericht, Amtliche Entscheidungssammlung (BVerwGE) vol 5, 312, vol 8, 261, vol 9, 251.

[33] On the remaining legislative powers of the Länder, ruling out a regulation by the Bund, see the so-called 'advisory opinion on building law' of the Federal Constitutional Court of 1954 (BVerfGE 3, 407).

codification, which regulates the structure of the process of planning and the balancing requirement as the central legal criterion, even regulating a requirement of the conservation of plans, limiting the consequences of errors.[34] Special planning decisions (eg, in the field of road or air traffic law, the law of energy supply or waste management) are the topic of individual special planning laws. The general declarations of sections 72–78 of the Administrative Procedure Act often cannot be applied, when there are *leges speciales* which have precedence.

Executive legislation, which can be understood as the fourth form of administrative action in the list presented here, affects the separation of powers through competition with parliamentary legislation and therefore has to be constitutionally regulated. A distinction must be made between legislative decrees, statutes and administrative regulations. The GG and the Constitutions of the Länder agree that decrees – ie, provisions of the ministerial administration that are concretions of parliamentary laws – require parliamentary authorisation, which is sufficiently definite in terms of its content, purpose and extent. Materially, the same applies to statutes issued by the executive, that is to say regulations issued by independent administrative bodies executing their right to self-government. Administrative regulations – ie, executive instructions and guidelines to the subordinate authorities on how to interpret laws or how to exercise their discretion dutifully and evenly – are to be distinguished from decrees and statutes by the executive. They are autonomous laws of the administration, which in principle only deploy legal effects within the administration. A fourth form of executive regulations can be mentioned here; these are technical regulations prepared by the administration, often in cooperation with experts or other private partners.

'Sanction' in the general sense of inflicting a disadvantage with the aim of enforcing the law is not a specific form of action in German administrative law. Here, a distinction is made between enforcement as a preventive measure aimed at bending the will and punishment as a repressive measure, which does not exclude using detention as an alternative means of enforcement.[35] Administrative enforcement is regulated in federal and state administrative enforcement laws, which are added to the administrative procedure laws as part of general administrative law. In principle, the authority that issued the administrative act to be enforced is responsible for its enforcement. Coercive measures are normally qualified as administrative acts to which the general rules apply (with exceptions – for example, no suspensive effect of remedies and no prior legal hearing if this would jeopardise the success of the measure). There are further laws for the application of direct coercion, which is due to the explosive nature of these means under the rule of law.

[34] Sections 1 VI/VII, 2–4c, 214–16 BauGB. See further J Kersten, 'Baurecht' in F Schoch (ed), *Besonderes Verwaltungsrecht* (Munich, CH Beck, 2018) ch 3, paras 5 ff.

[35] On this, see C Waldhoff, 'Vollstreckung und Sanktionen' in W Hoffmann-Riem, E Schmidt-Aßmann and A Voßkuhle (eds), *Grundlagen des Verwaltungsrechts*, vol 3, 2nd edn (Munich, CH Beck, 2013) s 46, paras 104 ff on the administrative enforcement; see also paras 192 ff on sanctions and paras 213 ff on the reshaping through EU law. The postdoctoral thesis by C Waldhoff on this topic has not yet been published.

In the case of repressive measures, a distinction must be made between criminal penalties, administrative offences, and disciplinary and professional law. Criminal penalties contain a socio-ethical expression of condemnation and may only be imposed by the courts. There are links between criminal law and special administrative law (keyword: administrative accessoriness of environmental criminal law). Administrative offences are legal violations of minor importance, but they justify a reminder of duties, which is usually issued in the form of a fine notice, ie, an administrative act. Judicial protection against this is governed by the Administrative Offences Act; the ordinary courts, which are also responsible for criminal cases, are competent in this matter, not the administrative courts. The distinction between 'criminal' criminal law and administrative offence law is difficult, challenging and in a constant state of change, particularly as a result of so-called decriminalisation. Disciplinary law is concerned with breaches of duty by civil servants, judges and soldiers, while the law of professional conduct is concerned with breaches of obligations by members of the independent professions such as doctors or lawyers. The responsibility for the latter lies with the organisations under the public law of these professions.

### *iii. Administrative Procedure*

For the reasons given above, procedure is here considered as a separate point and detached from protection. Procedure, unlike the right to good administration within the meaning of Article 41 of the European Charter of Fundamental Rights,[36] not only includes the protection of the citizen, but also his duties and obligations of cooperation. This is briefly touched upon using the example of tax law, for two reasons. First, in tax law, the taxpayer's duties of cooperation are particularly distinct, because without the cooperation of the taxpayer, the tax authorities are hardly able to ascertain the tax bases. If a taxpayer does not fulfil this obligation to cooperate, the tax authorities may, under the laws of all Western states, estimate the tax bases and have the power to prevent the estimation from being too low by using security surcharges. Second, in tax law, there is a new type of non-legal rules for administrative action, something outside the usual legal sources: computer programs, algorithms and artificial intelligence. Section 88, paragraph 5 of the Fiscal Code should be cited here, which deals with the review of the documents submitted by the taxpayer using officially prescribed data sets. It states that:

> Revenue authorities may use automated systems (risk management systems) to gauge whether further investigations and reviews are necessary [sentence 1] … At a minimum, risk management systems must ensure that: 1. a sufficient number of cases are selected, on the basis of random selection, for comprehensive review by officials, 2. officials review those cases sorted out as requiring review, 3. officials are able to select cases for comprehensive review, 4. regular reviews are conducted to determine whether

[36] Charter of Fundamental Rights of the European Union [2012] OJ C326/391.

> risk management systems are fulfilling their objectives. The details of risk management systems must not be made public if doing so could jeopardise the consistency and lawfulness of taxation [sentences 3 and 4].

This regulation has been valid since 1 January 2017. In this respect, Germany is following the practice of other EU Member States, which was pioneered by the Netherlands.

There is nothing surprising in German law about the *procedural rights* of the citizen or, more technically speaking, of the parties involved in the administrative procedure. The Administrative Procedures Act cited above guarantees the following rights:

- a right to electronic communication (section 3a), which can, however, also turn into an obligation to use electronic communication;
- a right to a procedure that is in principle non-formal, simple, expeditious and expedient (section 10);
- a right to assistance or representation by an authorised representative or counsel (section 14);
- a right to be heard on the relevant facts before an onerous administrative decision is taken (section 28, including the exceptions in paragraphs 2 and 3);
- a right to inspection of files (section 29);
- a right to confidentiality of personal data (section 30);
- a right to a statement of reasons for the administrative decision (section 39).

The legal provisions listed here are concretisations of the constitutional principle of the rule of law.[37] The legislature may therefore formulate and restrict them, but not abolish them.

### *iv. Administrative Organisation*

In Germany, administrative organisation law is 'constitutional law' to a surprising extent. Both the GG (Articles 83–91 and 91a–91e) and the constitutions of the Länder (regarding Berlin: Articles 66–77 of the Constitution of Berlin)[38] contain sections on the administration, mainly dealing with questions of administrative organisation. Constitutionally prescribed or permitted are as follows:

- The distinction between federal administration and administration by the Länder, the general prohibition of a mixed administration by the Federation and the Länder, and the admissibility of administrative cooperation between the Länder.

[37] On the theoretical distinction between rules and principles in the German-language area, see especially R Alexy, *Theorie der Grundrechte* (Suhrkamp, Berlin, 1984).

[38] Verfassung von Berlin vom 23. November 1995 (GVBl 1995, 779), zuletzt geändert durch Gesetz vom 17.05.2021 (GVBl 502).

- The distinction between direct and indirect public administration. Administration by the federation or a Land is direct; legal entities are the Federation or the Länder; and the acting body is assigned to one of these legal entities. Administration by an independent legal entity under public law, which is subject to legal supervision by the Federation or the Länder only, is indirect. Among these independent legal entities under public law, the municipalities, towns and districts are particularly noteworthy. In all constitutions one finds guarantees of municipal self-government, as well as in the GG, the German Federal Constitution, which is surprising because the municipalities in Germany are not considered to be a third level of the state, but part of the Länder.
- The division of the (direct) administration according to the 'department principle', whereby only the existence of a few ministries, especially the Ministry of Finance and, at the federal level, the Foreign Office and the Ministry of Defence, are constitutionally prescribed.
- The structure of the direct administration, which is divided into the supreme, upper, middle and lower authorities. Supreme authorities are typically ministries, ie, the political level of the administration. Lower authorities are the working level of the administration, which are often municipal, but also directly public authorities. Middle authorities are connecting links between the political and working levels, which have supervisory and coordinative functions, like the government presidiums as mid-level authorities with essentially comprehensive competence in the Länder. Upper authorities are responsible for specialised administrative tasks that can be carried out centrally without further administrative substructures – for example, the Federal Central Tax Office, which is responsible for administrative cooperation with foreign countries.[39]
- The specification of three types of indirect public administration: bodies organised on a membership basis, function-oriented institutions (Anstalten) and foundations managing assets, such as the Prussian Cultural Heritage Foundation.
- The distinction between mere legal supervision (concerning the indirect public administration and the relationship of the federation to the countries) and technical supervision (within the direct public administration) (Fachaufsicht).
- The need for justification of independent, non-instruction-dependent administrative bodies in the face of the principle of democracy.

[39] Higher authorities, a traditional type of authority in Germany, and agencies, a new type of authority at European level, are similar. Independently of this, changes in the concepts of higher and intermediate authorities should be considered; however, this is a German issue.

- An institutional constitutional requirement of the specific enactment of a statute for the creation of new authorities and for fundamental changes in the structure of the authorities.

In order to give an impression of how specifically questions of the administrative organisation are constitutionally regulated in Germany, Article 90, paragraph 2 GG, amended in July 2017, may be quoted:

> The administration of the federal motorways shall be a matter for the federal administrative authorities. The Federation may make use of a company under private law to discharge its responsibilities. This company shall be in the inalienable ownership of the Federation. Third parties shall have no direct or indirect holding in the company and its subsidiaries. Third parties shall have no holdings in the framework of public-private partnerships in road networks comprising the entire federal motorway network or the entire network of other federal trunk roads in a Land or significant parts of these networks. Details shall be regulated by a federal law'

If, following the hierarchy of the legal system, one steps from the constitutional to the level of subconstitutional laws, one will find only a few statements concerning general administrative law at the federal level. For good reasons of federal separation of powers, the federal legislator is denied full access to the administrative organisation, especially to the municipal administration. There are exceptions for parts of the administration, such as the Financial Administration Act, including administrative regulations concretising this law, such as the principles of the reorganisation of the tax offices and the reorganisation of the taxation procedure, which unitarily regulate the organisational and working structures of the tax offices (which are authorities of the Länder).[40] A different situation is to be found in the Länder. Here, the legislature has complete access on the authorities (including the municipal authorities), which can assume the proportions of a codification. Most Länder have general administrative organisation laws. Regarding Berlin, which, as a city state, has a special role, the Allgemeines Zuständigkeitsgesetz (General Competence Act)[41] can be mentioned.[42] The model for this is the General Administrative Law of the State of Schleswig-Holstein of April 1967, which aims to codify the organisational and procedural law of the administration and thus is also a testament to the innovative strength of federal systems; this law was a signpost for the Federal Administrative Procedure Act, which came into force 10 years

[40] *cf* K von Lewinski, 'Kodifikation des Verwaltungsorganisationsrechts' in C Franzius, S Lejeune, K von Lewinski, K Meßerschmidt, G Michael, M Rossi, T Schilling and P Wysk (eds), *Beharren. Bewegen. Festschrift für Michael Kloepfer zum 70. Geburtstag* (Berlin, Duncker & Humblot, 2013) 793 (805 f). A draft of such a codification can be found in R Loeser, *Das Bundes-Organisationsgesetz* (Baden-Baden, Nomos, 1988).

[41] Gesetz über die Zuständigkeiten in der Allgemeinen Berliner Verwaltung (Allgemeines Zuständigkeitsgesetz – AZG) in der Fassung vom 22. Juli 1996 (GVBl 1996, 302, 472), zuletzt geändert durch Gesetz vom 12.05.2022 (GVBl 191).

[42] In the announcement of 22 July 1996, Gesetz- und Verordnungsblatt Berlin 1996, 302 ff.

later. Containing about 340 regulations, it comes closest to what one imagines to be a codification of general administrative law in Germany.[43]

After constitution and subconstitutional law, a third and obvious level of regulation for matters of administrative organisation is administrative provisions, as a consequence of the so-called organisational power of the government. Individual examples of such regulations, which exist at the national level and the Länder level, are omitted here.

## *v. Administrative Protection*

According to Article 92, 1st half-sentence GG, the judicial power is entrusted to the judges. Administrative control in the broader sense continues to take place as self-regulation by the administration and by the public.[44]

Legal protection against public authority is a fundamental right in Germany, for the enforcement of which the constitutional complaint to the Federal Constitutional Court is available in most cases. Article 19, paragraph 4 GG states: 'Should any person's rights be violated by public authority, he may have recourse to the courts. If no other jurisdiction has been established, recourse shall be to the ordinary courts.' This regulation was celebrated in 1949 as the 'capstone in the vault of the rule of law'.[45] It corresponds to a general clause of the administrative courts, which provides legal protection in all public law disputes, regardless of the form of the action chosen.

As a consequence, restrictions on legal protection, such as those on the suspensive effect of legal remedies, must have a constitutional basis. This explains why, for example, questions of interim legal protection in the administrative process found their way into the fundamental right to asylum in Article 16a GG. Thus, Article 16a, paragraph 2, sentence 3 reads as follows: 'In the cases specified in the first sentence of this paragraph [entry from an EU Member State or another safe third country], measures to terminate an applicant's stay may be without regard to any legal challenge that may have been instituted against them.' In this way, it is intended to prevent the suspensive effect of legal remedies against measures to terminate an applicant's stay, combined with the long duration of appeals procedures, from leading to a de facto right of residence, which might become increasingly established over time.

Returning from this exception to the principle of the guarantee of effective legal protection – with suspensive effect – it should be noted that legal protection is granted against any administrative measure rather than only against

[43] In the announcement of 2 June 1992, Gesetz- und Verordnungsblatt Schleswig-Holstein 1992, 243. For a summary of this law, see K von Lewinski (n 40) 793 ff.

[44] See W Kahl, 'Kontrolle: Begriff, Funktionen und Konzepte' in W Hoffmann-Riem, E Schmidt-Aßmann and A Voßkuhle (n 35) 459 ff.

[45] QR Thoma, 'Über die Grundrechte im Grundgesetz für die Bundesrepublik Deutschland' in H Wandersleb and E Traumann (eds), *Recht – Staat – Wirtschaft III* (Dusseldorf, Schwann, 1951) 9.

formal administrative acts, provided that there is a possibility that this measure may infringe individual rights. The scope of individual rights is broad: freedom, equality and personality are fully protected by fundamental rights. Legal protection is essentially granted by independent administrative courts and comprises up to three instances. In many cases, this is preceded by preliminary proceedings conducted within the administration, which, in addition to providing legal protection for the citizen, serves to ensure self-regulation by the administration and to relieve the burden on the courts, and in which not only the legality but also the reasonableness of administrative actions is examined.

From the point of view that looks at legal sources, German state liability law is particularly interesting. Earlier in this chapter, some remarks on this were made from a federal point of view. Now, the 'cocktail' of legal sources that is revealed shall be unfolded in all its glory. It consists of a codification of civil law, one constitutional article, a bold analogy by the Federal Court of Justice (ie, case law), the failed attempt of establishing a federal law and the proclamation of customary law. In order to make things understandable, an observer should approach this in chronological order. In the beginning, there was the idea that the unlawful culpable behaviour of its employees, which causes damage to the citizen, does not have to be attributed to the state; the public servant was liable just like a private person, and the liability was therefore regulated in section 839 BGB. This was the situation in 1900, which was quickly perceived as unfair, because a public servant is a bad debtor. The liability according to section 839 BGB was therefore transferred to the state through constitutional articles (Article 34 GG today, which has been the case since 1949), but it remained a fault-dependent liability based on civil tort law. The requirement of culpability was also perceived as unfair; the Federal Court of Justice (BGH) therefore ruled that if the state already owed compensation for lawful expropriations, it would a fortiori be liable for unlawful damage to property, without culpability of any kind (1952). Nearly 30 years later, the federal legislator adopted this in a State Liability Act (1981).[46] However, two beats of the drum by the Federal Constitutional Court immediately followed. In 1981, the Court stated that, for budgetary reasons, it could not be right to base monetary claims against the state on a fortiori conclusions and other case law;[47] rather, a statutory law basis was to be demanded (which, in the meantime, had come into existence with the State Liability Act). However, in 1982, the Court annulled the State Liability Act because it held that the federal government lacked the legislative competence for the regulation of the liability of the Länder and the municipalities.[48] This second decision of the BVerfG raised the question of whether or not the former case law of the Federal Court of Justice – liability for unlawful interference with property, without regard to culpability – could be upheld despite the first decision of the

[46] Staatshaftungsgesetz vom 26. Juni 1981 (BGBl I, 553).
[47] BVerfGE 58, 300.
[48] BVerfGE 61, 149.

Federal Constitutional Court. The Federal Court of Justice stated that its construction of liability had a legal basis and was not mere case law. Although there was no law passed by a parliament, its case law had grown to become customary law over the previous 30 years. The situation has remained like that ever since. A law of responsibility, as exists at the federal level in Switzerland,[49] currently does not exist in Germany. A state liability law had been in place in the German Democratic Republic (GDR) since 1969, which provided a liability without a culpability criterion and sounded modern to a Western reader, but remained ineffective in the hands of socialist legal practitioners. This changed when the GDR law continued to be applicable after the reunification of Germany as a law of the Länder and fell into the hands of the West German courts. These courts briefly developed a regime of liability that was pleasingly effective from the point of view of affected citizens, but was abolished or weakened by the legislators of the East German states. This may suffice for now on the issue of liability. The EU law section of this chapter will return to the subject (non-contractual liability of the EU under Article 340(2) TFEU and Article 41(3) of the European Charter of Fundamental Rights).

The figure of an ombudsman is much less well received in Germany than in other European countries. The approximately 5,000-page work *Grundlagen des Verwaltungsrechts* (*Basics of Administrative Law*), edited by Hoffmann-Riem, Schmidt-Aßmann and Voßkuhle, devotes only about half a page to this topic. On the other hand, commissioners who deal with special issues using mainly informal means are widespread, such as data protection or women's commissioners.

## C. Codification

Codifications demand great political and legal efforts. The energies by which they are fed are not academic in nature. It is never really about what might motivate professors, namely perfecting the legal system. The motives are partly of a sectoral political nature and partly of a general political nature.[50]

Motivated by sectoral political considerations, the project of a Social Security Code was started in the 1970s under a social-liberal federal government and claims to regulate all rights and obligations in social service areas by law (section 31 SGB I). As a result, which is unusual for a codification, about one-third of one of the books – sections 228–319 SGB VI[51] (pension insurance) – consists of special and transitional regulations. Overall, it is a socio-politically motivated regulatory approach.

[49] F Uhlmann, *Schweizerisches Staatshaftungsrecht* (Zurich, Dike, 2017).

[50] See G-C von Unruh, 'Kodifiziertes Verwaltungsrecht' (1988) *Neue Zeitschrift für Verwaltungsrecht* 690.

[51] Das Sechste Buch Sozialgesetzbuch – Gesetzliche Rentenversicherung – in der Fassung der Bekanntmachung vom 19. Februar 2002 (BGBl I, 754, 1404, 3384), zuletzt geändert durch Artikel 6a des Gesetzes vom 22. November 2021 (BGBl I, 4906).

A generally politically motivated project in Germany was the Reichsjustizgesetze (Judiciary Laws of the German Reich) after the unification of the state in 1867. These laws related to civil and criminal law. Regarding public law, only the Gewerbeordnung (Trade, Commerce and Industry Regulation Act),[52] which ensured trade freedom from 1869, will be mentioned here.

A codification of general administrative law could be assigned to the sectoral political concern of the improvement of the rule of law. But it could also be viewed in a general political way as an attempt by a central authority to gain influence, if not dominance, over decentralised administrations. If this central authority is the EU Commission, the 'octopus of competences', it can be certain of resistance from Germany.

In conclusion, it should be noted that in Germany, there is some codification of general administrative law, especially the Administrative Procedure Act. However, much is not codified, or even regulated by legislation, but by case law, constitutional principle or customary law. Furthermore, in Germany, as far as general administrative law is concerned, codification fatigue can be observed, both politically and scientifically.[53] More recent laws, which do not simply take the form of a law but of a code of law, often fail to meet the expectations of a codification.[54] An ever-increasing refinement of constitutional principles and the particular emphasis of individual legal protection against administrative action are regarded as too one-sided, however justified these concerns are. Instead, the so-called 'Neue Verwaltungswissenschaft' (new science of administrative law) is increasingly interested in the actual effects of administrative action, with interdisciplinary borrowings (the control theory approach).[55]

# II. Administrative Law in the EU

## A. The Procedural Autonomy of Member States and Counteractive Tendencies

This section will deal with the administrative law of the EU. A contextual transition is hardly possible, because the contrast is sharp. The idea of codification conflicts

[52] Gewerbeordnung in der Fassung der Bekanntmachung vom 22. Februar 1999 (BGBl I, 202), zuletzt geändert durch Artikel 1 des Gesetzes vom 19. Juni 2022 (BGBl I, 918).

[53] Similarly, see M Kloepfer, *Verfassungsrecht I* (Munich, CH Beck, 2011) s 21, para 18; O Lepsius, 'Gesetzesstruktur im Wandel' (2019) *Juristische Schulung* 14, 17. This was different 30 years ago – see, eg, F Hufen, 'Gesetzesgestaltung und Gesetzesanwendung im Leistungsrecht' in *Veröffentlichungen der Vereinigung der Deutschen Staatsrechtslehrer (VVDStRL)*, vol 47 (Berlin, Walter de Gruyter, 1989) 142 (153 f).

[54] As an example: the Lebensmittel- und Futtermittelgesetzbuch (Food and Animal Feed Code) of 1 September 2005 (LFGB) in the announcement of 3 June 2013 (BGBl I, 1426).

[55] See W Hoffmann-Riem, E Schmidt-Aßmann and A Voßkuhle (eds), *Grundlagen des Verwaltungsrechts*, vol 3, 2nd edn (Munich, CH Beck, 2013).

with a guiding principle of the legislative activity of the EU, the principle of conferral of powers (Article 5(1) TEU). A general administrative law of the EU does not exist; the Union has no legislative powers in that regard.[56] While, as noted above, there are about 15 recent textbooks on German general administrative law, there is not one German-language textbook specifically dedicated to European general administrative law. The work *Europäisches Verwaltungsrecht* by the ECJ Judge and university professor von Danwitz comes closest;[57] it was published in 2008 and has not gone into a new edition yet. In this book, a distinction between the textbook-like and case law foundations of European administrative law, the EU's own administrative law, the collective administrative law, ie, the execution of EU law (regulations and directives) by the Member States, and a cooperation law for administrative bodies in Europe[58] is made.

The textbook-like and case law foundations are suitable for 'general administrative law', while the EU's own administrative law is probably too narrow as a basis.[59] However, as in the case of the more specific provisions of collective administrative law, the principle of procedural autonomy of the Member States, which was probably first proclaimed in the *Milchkontor* decision of the ECJ[60] and has meanwhile been regulated in Article 291(1) TFEU, is paramount. According to this, apart from the few cases of the EU's own administration, the implementation of EU law is a matter for the Member States, enforcement is governed by the law of the Member States, and the Member States have procedural autonomy, with two limitations: the implementation of EU law must not be worse than the implementation of the law of the Member States; and the implementation of EU law must be effective.[61]

[56] T von Danwitz, *Europäisches Verwaltungsrecht* (Heidelberg, Springer, 2008) 609 ff.

[57] See n 56. *cf* further E Schmidt-Aßmann and B Schöndorf-Haubold (eds), *Europäischer Verwaltungsverbund. Formen und Verfahren der Verwaltungszusammenarbeit in Europa*, (Tübingen, Mohr Siebeck, 2005); JP Terhechte (ed), *Verwaltungsrecht der Europäischen Union* (Baden-Baden, Nomos, 2011); W Kahl, 'Dogmatik im EU-Recht' (2019) *Archiv des öffentlichen Rechts* 144, 159 (193 ff); W Kahl, 'Die Europäisierung als Herausforderung an Systembildung und Kodifikation' (2010) *Die Verwaltung, Supplement* 10, 39 (56 f).

[58] A good example for this is the structured automatic exchange of financial data between EU tax authorities; *cf* S Schurowski, *Der automatische Austausch von Finanzkonteninformationen in Steuersachen. Eine einfachgesetzliche, verfassungsrechtliche und europarechtliche Untersuchung* (Berlin, Duncker & Humblot, 2020).

[59] *cf* L Hartmann, *Die Kodifikation des Europäischen Verwaltungsrechts* (Tübingen, Mohr Siebeck, 2020), who points out that 34 EU regulations establish a decentralised agency and have potential for a standardisation in terms of legal status and organisational structure, administrative board, executive director and complaints committee (ch 9), and that the same applies to 27 EU regulations which contain procedural and substantive rules on decisions directed at the citizens (ch 10).

[60] Joined Cases 205–215/82 *Deutsche Milchkontor GmbH and Others v Federal Republic of Germany* ECLI:EU:C:1983:233, [1983] ECR 2633.

[61] On these limiting principles, see R Streinz, 'Grundsätze des indirekten Vollzugs und der Verfahrensautonomie' and D-U Galetta, 'Grundsätze der Äquivalenz und der Effektivität', both in W Kahl and M Ludwigs (eds), *Handbuch des Verwaltungsrechts*, vol 2 (CF Müller, Heidelberg, 2021) ss 45 and 46.

Procedural autonomy and its two limitations, unlike general administrative law, do not affect the relationship between the administration and the citizen, but the relationship between the administration of the Member States and law-makers at the EU level. The distinction between citizen-related and EU-related principles should not be exaggerated. This can be demonstrated by the *Alcan* case, a *cause célèbre* of European administrative law from the German point of view, in which the European Court of Justice, the German Federal Administrative Court and the Federal Constitutional Court were involved.[62] It was about a subsidy to a (as it turned out) non-competitive German aluminium smelter, which was granted to rescue jobs. The subsidy contradicted the state aid law of the EU; therefore, the EU Commission demanded its repayment. This claim was difficult to convey legally in Germany because it contradicted the requirement to protect the legitimate expectations of the beneficiary when unlawful but favourable administrative acts are repealed. Why should an achievement of the German rule of law be sacrificed on the altar of EU subsidy law? The EU prevailed in this conflict. The Canadian parent company of the now-insolvent German aluminium smelter had to repay the subsidy to the German Land Rhineland-Palatinate. The repercussions for general administrative law are as follows: national rules that the legitimate expectations in the protection of subsidy grants are worthy of protection and that such decisions may not subsequently be withdrawn are subject to limitations by EU law.[63]

As another example of the influence of EU law on a key term of German general administrative law, in which individual protection and EU integration policy intermingle, the subjective public right may be mentioned. According to the German legal tradition, such a subjective right can only be derived from a norm of objective law if the creator of the norm *aims* at granting individual protection. In contrast to the German concept, the European understanding goes further. Here it is enough if a norm *in fact* benefits an individual. In particular, this broad understanding has integration-political reasons, since a side effect of subjectivising norms of WU law is that the individual is empowered to assert them before the courts, and legal protection serves not only the interests of the individual, but also those of the EU in terms of the respect for the law and its enforcement in the Member States.[64]

The EU's powers of limitation and extension are not based on legislative powers – which are bounded – but on jurisdictional competences that can be exercised on the basis of indefinite, flexible provisions of primary law using considerable *effet utile* and can penetrate deeply into established national administrative structures.

[62] For comprehensive references, see H Maurer and C Waldhoff, *Allgemeines Verwaltungsrecht*, 20th edn (Munich, CH Beck, 2020) s 11, para 57.

[63] Evidence of the court decisions handed down in this 'judicial thriller' can be found in H Maurer and C Waldhoff, *Allgemeines Verwaltungsrecht*, 20th edn (Munich, CH Beck, 2020) s 11, para 57.

[64] See J Masing, *Die Mobilisierung des Bürgers für die Durchsetzung des Rechts* (Berlin, Duncker & Humblot, 1997).

A third example of the same effect after the protection of legitimate expectations (*Alcan*) and subjective public rights are, with regard to Germany, rulings of the European Court of Justice (ECJ) on the question of whether Germany can implement EU Directives into national law through administrative regulations. Administrative regulations are a legal source of German administrative law whose special feature is that they are only binding for the administration, not for citizens or courts, so they do not need to be based on a parliamentary law and can be changed flexibly.[65] The latter was seen as an advantage in Germany concerning environmental standards, such as the requirements for discharging wastewater into bodies of water. In this regard, it was insofar as being spoken of administrative regulations. The ECJ has objected to this legal disposition, which, for that matter, is by no means uncontested in Germany as well.[66] EU Directives would have to be transposed into generally binding national law.[67]

## B. Periodisation of the Development in the EU

While trying to describe the stages of this developmental process,[68] one should mention the following points: (1) the Treaty of Paris and the Treaties of Rome, which were the contractual beginnings of the EU; (2) the case law of the ECJ, which has gained a general administrative profile from the beginning of the 1980s; (3) the contributions of jurisprudence that can be compared to Fleiner's institutions of German administrative law; (4) a concentration of the secondary law on basic regulations and framework directives; and (5) the constitutionalisation of primary law in 2009.

The EEC Treaty of 1958 already contained important statements on general administrative law. Mention should be made of Articles 230, 288 and 340(2) TFEU. The catalogue of forms of action in Article 177 of the EEC Treaty (now Article 288 TFEU) was, at a time when the European Parliament was still called the European Assembly and had far fewer powers than it has today, a catalogue of administrative forms of action. Today's Article 340(2) TFEU assumes that there are general principles of law in the legal systems of Member States, including the field of non-contractual liability. The former Article 173 of the EEC Treaty (today Article 230 TFEU) contains in paragraph 2 the basic structure of a doctrine of error and failure. A provision such as section 46 of the German Administrative Procedure Act does not fit into this regime. According to this provision, the annulment of an

[65] See above, section I.B.ii.

[66] *cf* BVerfGE 78, 214 (227); 80, 257 (265).

[67] ECJ, 28 February 1991, ECR I-825 (867). See M Kloepfer, *Umweltrecht*, 4th edn (Munich, CH Beck, 2016) s 3, paras 127 ff.

[68] Partly it is being spoken of a 'consolidation phase'; *cf* P Axer, B Grzeszick, W Kahl, U Mager and E Reimer, 'Das Europäische Verwaltungsrecht in der Konsolidierungsphase' (2010) *Die Verwaltung*, supplement 10.

administrative act cannot be claimed for the sole reason that the Act came into being through the infringement of regulations governing procedure, form or local competence, where it is evident that the infringement has not influenced the decision on the matter. This is an expression of the idea prevalent in Germany, but not in Europe, that procedural law is only *serving law*.

General administrative law at the EU level owes further advances in terms of its development to case law of the ECH, such as the *Milchkontor* decision of 1983. An indication of greater interventionism[69] by the Court is the decision in *Rewe-Zentralfinanz*,[70] which is seven years older and in which it dealt with competences and procedure for the assertion of citizen's rights which accrued from the direct effects of Community law.

A first standard work of jurisprudence on 'European administrative law' from the German perspective is the two-volume work of Jürgen Schwarze, which was published in 1988.[71] This presents the substance structured according to principles: lawfulness and freedom of choice, the principles of equality and of non-discrimination, proportionality, the protection of legitimate expectations and the principles of the rule of law.

While primary law, general principles of law and ECJ case law are top-down approaches that do not require an authorisation by primary law to regulate general administrative law,[72] the concentration of EU secondary legislation is a bottom-up approach. For some 20 years, there have been *framework* directives, such as the Water Framework Directive 2000/60/EG,[73] or *basic* regulations. Although these regulations, insofar as they are of an administrative nature, remain special administrative law, they have a generalising effect. Here a middle level of generalisation is reached.[74] The generalisation effect has a price: exemptions. For example, the EU's General Data Protection Regulation contains 60 exemptions.[75]

The Lisbon Treaty includes further contributions to general administrative law: the regulations on executive legislation in Articles 290 and 291 TFEU and general administrative requirements in Article 41 of the Charter of Fundamental Rights and Article 298 TFEU. Article 298(2) TFEU is the basis for the now

[69] This wording is to be found in U Haltern, *Europarecht*, vol 2, 3rd edn (Tübingen, Mohr Siebeck, 2017) 357 ff.

[70] Case 33/76 *Rewe-Zentralfinanz eG and Rewe-Zentral AG v Landwirtschaftskammer für das Saarland* ECLI:EU:C:1976:188, [1976] ECR 1989.

[71] J Schwarze, *Europäisches Verwaltungsrecht* (Baden-Baden, Nomos, 1988), English translation: J Schwarze, *European Administrative Law* (London, Sweet & Maxwell, 2006).

[72] On their lesser importance, see C Möllers, 'Allgemeines Verwaltungsrecht in einer doppelt gegliederten Rechtsordnung' in PF Bultmann (ed), *Allgemeines Verwaltungsrecht. Festschrift für Ulrich Battis zum 70. Geburtstag* (Munich, CH Beck, 2014) 101 (114).

[73] Directive 2000/60/EC [2000] OJ L327/1.

[74] On the middle level, see J Kersten and S-C Lenski, 'Die Entwicklungsfunktion des Allgemeinen Verwaltungsrechts' (2009) *Die Verwaltung* 42, 501 (524 ff).

[75] J Kühling and J Raab, 'Einführung' in J Kühling and B Buchner (eds), *DS-GVO, BDSG Kommentar*, 2nd edn (Munich, CH Beck, 2020) paras 98 ff, especially 101; J Taeger and B Schmidt, 'Einführung'

numerous regulatory and executive agencies of the EU.[76] What is surprising about these agencies from the perspective of German administrative organisation law is that they have the status of legal entities. This contradicts the basic idea that legal entities have organs and authorities, but that organs and authorities are not legal entities, and leads to a follow-up question which can only be hinted at here: is there a common European understanding of the concept of a legal entity under public law?[77]

The ReNEUAL[78] draft of 2014 is a model for an administrative procedure law, with an emphasis on the rights rather than the obligations of citizens. However, beyond the circles of those directly involved and specialists, it has not received much attention in Germany.[79] Nevertheless, the ReNEUAL work went on and expanded to cover digitalisation.[80]

## III. Conclusion

In Germany, the 'codification' of (general) administrative law is not a topic that is currently being discussed. Administrative procedure law concerning the magisterial and judicial procedures is codified; innovations caused by the development of computer technology can be integrated into the existing general works of regulation (eg, section 35a of the Administrative Procedure Code or section 88, paragraph 5 and section 155, paragraph 4 of the Fiscal Code).[81] A codification of

in J Taeger and D Gabel (eds), *DGSVO, BDSG Kommentar*, 3rd edn (Frankfurt am Main, Deutscher Fachverlag, 2019) paras 50 ff (especially 60).

[76] Listed in: M Ruffert in C Calliess and M Ruffert (eds), *EUV, AEUV Kommentar*, 6th edn (Munich, CH Beck, 2022) art 298, paras 9 and 11. See also L Hartmann (n 59). Agencies have similarities with the German type of higher authority mentioned above in section I.B.iv.

[77] See also, with further proof, M Ruffert (n 76).

[78] ReNEUAL stands for Research Network on European Union Administrative Law.

[79] *cf* www.reneuval.eu; P Craig, H Hofmann, J-S Schneider and J Ziller (eds), *ReNEUAL Model Rules on Administrative Procedure* (Oxford, Oxford University Press, 2017). From the German-language literature, see: W Abromeit, 'Der ReNEUAL-Musterentwurf für ein Europäisches Verwaltungsverfahrensrecht' (2016) *Die Öffentliche Verwaltung* 345; J-P Schneider, HCH Hofmann and J Ziller, 'Die ReNEUAL Model Rules 2014: Ein Verwaltungsverfahrensrecht für Europa' (2015) *Juristenzeitung* 265; W Kahl, 'Kodifizierung des Verwaltungsverfahrensrechts in Deutschland und in der EU' (2018) *Juristische Schulung* 1025; S Lenz, 'Der ReNEUAL-Musterentwurf für ein Europäisches Verwaltungsverfahrensrecht in der Diskussion' (2016) *Neue Zeitschrift für Verwaltungsrecht* 38; B Stüer, 'ReNEUAL-Musterentwurf für ein EU-Verwaltungsverfahrensrecht' (2016) *Deutsches Verwaltungsblatt* 100; F Schoch 'Einleitung' in F Schoch and J-P Schneider (eds), *Verwaltungsverfahrensgesetz VwVfG* (Munich, CH Beck, 2021) para 724. With a focus on the right to inspect files, see J Ritter, *Die Akteneinsicht im Eigenverwaltungsverfahrensrecht der Europäischen Union* (Berlin, Duncker & Humblot, 2020) 319 ff.

[80] On ReNEUAL 2.0, see in this book A Berger, Science Codification for the European Union – The ReNEUAL Network: On the Limits of Legal Control of Innovation and Technology', section II.B.

[81] On the relationship between the federal Act to promote electronic government (25 July 2013, BGBl I, 2479) and the more general administrative procedure code, see T Siegel, 'E-Government und das Verwaltungsverfahrensgesetz' (2020) *Deutsches Verwaltungsblatt* 552, 552 ff.

administrative organisation law is not possible for federal reasons. Concerning the principles, a reduction of rule-of-law exaggerations is instead indicated.

At the European level, things look different. On the one hand, federal doubts about codification are even more serious. On the other hand, there are general political motives here: codification is a nice term for a further shift of competences towards the EU. The fact that European codification efforts, such as the ReNEUAL project, start with the rights of the citizen in the administrative procedure, might be tactically motivated. Citizens' procedural rights are standard in many EU Member States and do not cost a lot (as opposed to state liability, which is a codificatory 'no-go' area). It will be difficult to find severe deficiencies concerning the rule of law in Germany that justify European regulations with regard to administrative procedures, with the exception of the topic of excessively long administrative procedures. On the other hand, politically, strengthening citizens' rights is always easy to sell. The *Akerberg-Fransson* decision of the ECJ is a good example of this dichotomy and has been justifiably criticised by the German Federal Constitutional Court for being a ultra vires decision.[82]

This leads to the final question about the sense and the value of a discussion on a general administrative law in Europe. There are EU Member States without a national constitution and without national regulations on the individual rights of citizens in administrative proceedings and on their judicial enforcement. In such situations, a scientific, comparative law discussion can provide indications for improvements. The same applies to the legal regulation of the administrative activity of the EU itself, which is currently being developed, even if this administrative activity must be kept within limits for reasons of competence. It is still very much a matter of self-assurance and highlighting the differences that nevertheless exist at a high level in relation to the rule of law. Pioneering achievements like those of Fritz Fleiner or Otto Mayer[83] are no longer possible. Points that especially struck me when writing this chapter are the traditional nature of administrative organisation and, in jurisdictions other than Germany, a stronger emphasis on procedures and procedural rights, which have become somewhat self-evident in Germany.

[82] BVerfG, judgment 24April 2013, 1 BvR 1215/07, BVerfGE 133, 277 (316 para 91), *contra* ECJ, Case C-617/10 *Åklagaren v Hans Åkerberg Fransson* ECLI:EU:C:2013:105. On the lines of conflict between the BVerfG and the ECJ, which the BVerfG describes using the terms 'identity control', 'constitutional control' and, in particular, 'fundamental rights control' and 'ultra vires control', see above n 3.

[83] See above, section I.A.ii.

# 7

# Administrative Proceedings in Italy

ROBERTO CARANTA

## I. The Definition and Delimitation of Administrative Law

Italy, and the Kingdom of Sardinia before the unification of the country (1861), very much followed France in giving shape to the state and its organisation. This example resulted in a highly centralised state, with a central government organised along line ministries.[1] Deconcentrated local offices were hierarchically subordinated to the ministries. Municipalities enjoyed limited degrees of autonomy and their decisions were submitted to *ex ante* control by prefects, the deconcentrated ministerial officials of the Ministry of the Interior.[2] The Consiglio di Stato, already created in the Kingdom of Sardinia in 1831,[3] was tasked with advising the government on legal issues, including on last instance administrative appeals. Later in the nineteenth century, it also assumed jurisdictional functions. Its role in shaping Italian administrative law could hardly be overestimated.[4]

The French influence was already manifest in the names for high-ranking public officials and for the corresponding offices. The names of numerous – and the most relevant – institutions were direct translation from the French, as was the case with both the 'Conseil d'Etat' and the 'préfets'. Even the officials heading the deconcentrated offices of the Ministry of Finance had their titles translated from the all-powerful 'intendants des finances' of the *Ancien Régime*. One exception was the 'province' (provinces), as the functional equivalent of the 'départements', for which a name recalling Roman glories was preferred.

[1] A Sandulli and G Vesperini 'L'organizzazione dello Stato unitario' (2011) *Rivista Trimestrale di Diritto Pubblico* 47, 47 ff; see also G Iudica, 'L'unificazione attraverso l'organizzazione' and AM Chiariello, 'L'organizzazione centrale dello stato e il modello ministeriale' both in R Cavallo Perin, A Police and F Saitta (eds), *L'organizzazione delle pubbliche amministrazione tra Stato nazionale e integrazione europea* (Florence, Firenze University Press, 2016) 107 ff and 223 ff respectively.

[2] G Grüner, 'Il prefetto e l'organizzazione amministrativa periferica dello Stato' in R Cavallo Perin, A Police and F Saitta (n 1) 343 f.

[3] GS Pene Vidari, 'Il Consiglio di Stato Albertino: istituzione e realizzazione' in *Atti del convegno celebrativo del 150° anniversario della istituzione del Consiglio di Stato* (Milan, Giuffrè, 1983) 21 ff.

[4] S Cassese, 'Il contributo dei giudici allo sviluppo del diritto amministrativo' (2020) *Giornale di Diritto Amministrativo* 341, 341 ff.

Closely following the French model, which in turn arguably perfected the much older Roman and canonical law traditions, Italian administrative law foresees a highly formalised and stylised type of administrative action. Decisions are taken in writing. In the preamble to the decisions or administrative acts, reference is made to the relevant legal sources. Hierarchy portends a form of administrative procedure since decisions by local authorities and inferior officials can be challenged in front of higher officials.

In this context, administrative law was – and is – understood as the bodies of rules of primary and secondary law regulating the activities of state officials. From a 'law in the books' perspective at least, Italy conformed and still conforms to Max Weber's stereotype of a legal-rational administrative state. Additionally, administrative activities were also – and are – regulated by a few provisions in the Criminal Code (typically having some rules on corruption etc).

Judicial review mostly falls under the jurisdiction of administrative courts (first instance courts and the Consiglio di Stato). It focuses on the legality of the decision taken. Apart from the marginal hypothesis of nullity making the decision totally void and devoid of any effect, three grounds of illegality have been enshrined in Italian legislation since 1889 and are now 'codified' in Article 21 *octies* l. 7 agosto 1990, n 241 Nuove norme in materia di procedimento amministrativo e di diritto di accesso ai documenti amministrativi (hereinafter APA). They are: (a) breach of law (any legal source being included, from the Constitution down to secondary sources such as regulations (*regolamenti*)); (b) lack of competence; and (c) misuse of power (*eccesso di potere*). The same triad is spelt out in Article 29 of Dlgs 2 luglio 2010, n 104, Attuazione dell'articolo 44 della legge 18 giugno 2009, n 69, recante delega al governo per il riordino del processo amministrativo, which is actually the judicial administrative procedure code (hereinafter CPA). Breaches of the procedural rules may affect the legality of the final decision taken and may thus fall under (a) (see section III below).

*Eccesso di potere* initially took inspiration from the French *détournement de pouvoir*, but throughout the years has come to cover a wide range of possible misuses of discretionary powers. Consequently, misuse of powers in Italy is a much wider category than the ground under the same label in Article 262(2) of the Treaty on the Functioning of the European Union (TFEU),[5] including, for instance, manifest errors of assessment. However, courts cannot go into the merits of a decision taken by the administration and substitute it with one of their own. There exists a dangerously thin line between misuse of power and merits, and, besides obiter dicta, administrative courts appear to prefer proceeding on a case-by-case basis or possibly adhering to discreet standards applied in different sectors of administrative litigation.[6]

[5] Consolidated Version of the Treaty on the Functioning of the European Union [2012] OJ C326/47.

[6] Going beyond speculations and ad hoc analysis of individual cases would require much detailed case law analysis, which is not much practised in Italian academia and is made difficult by the sparse factual details found in most judgments. A small sample research revealed a disconnect between

A good instance is provided by the case law concerning the appointment to the highest judicial functions in Italy. For members of 'ordinary' (ie, civil and criminal) courts, the decision belongs to the 'Consiglio Superiore della Magistratura' (CSM), an institution established by the Constitution to uphold the independence of the judges and chiefly composed by judges elected by their peers. Still, appointment decisions are administrative acts and, as such, their review falls under the jurisdiction of administrative courts. A recent judgment concerned the appointment of the second highest-ranking 'ordinary' judge, the adjunct president of the Court of Cassation.[7] The runner-up challenged the decision, arguing that he possessed stronger titles and merits, and therefore deserved to be chosen. The Consiglio di Stato started by avowing that the CSM – an organ specifically set up by the Constitution with an exclusive competence concerning the career of ordinary judges – enjoys a wide level of discretion. The decisions of the CSM may be reviewed only for unreasonableness, factual errors, or lacking or insufficient motivation. Hence, the administrative court could not be allowed to substitute its views as to the merits of the candidates for those entertained by the CSM.[8] This apparent self-restraint did not stop the Consiglio di Stato from finding that the CSM had breached its own internal rules as to which indicator of merit was relevant for the promotion by preferring a candidate that on the face of these indicators looked like the weaker option.[9] On the basis of these rules, it held that specific experience relevant to the office sought was most important and found the decision to be unlawful, in that it did not explain why experiences outside the Court of Cassation (ie, working at the Ministry of Justice as chief advisor on matters of legislation) were instead preferred.[10]

In another recent instance, the economic operator ranked second in an award procedure for the building of a large new hospital challenged the application of complex award criteria to its tender and to the winning tender.[11] The Consiglio di Stato first recalled that *eccesso di potere* is integrated when a decision is manifestly unreasonable, the facts have been wrongly assessed or it is contradictory.[12] Concerning the matter of complex factual assessments, the Consiglio di Stato indicated that only abnormal decisions will be considered illegal,[13] meaning decisions which are clearly wrong.[14] Simply debatable conclusions will not lead

the actual decision and the dicta used to uphold it: R Caranta and B Marchetti, 'Judicial Review of Regulatory Decisions in Italy; Changing the Formula and Keeping the Substance?' in O Essens, A Gerbrandy and S Lavrijssen (eds), *National Courts and the Standard of Review in Competition Law and Economic Regulation* (Groningen, Europa Law Publishing, 2009) 145 ff.

[7] Cons Stato, Sez V, 15 July 2020, n 4584.

[8] ibid para 9.

[9] ibid para 10.

[10] ibid para 10.1.3.

[11] Cons Stato, Sez III, 2 September 2019, n 6058.

[12] ibid para 4.3.

[13] ibid para 5.2.

[14] ibid para 5.3 (*palese inattendibilità* and *evidente insostenibilità*, which might be loosely translated as assessments being clearly unbelievable and that plainly cannot be argued for).

to a finding of illegality as they would pertain to the merits of the decision.[15] That being said, the judgment continued at great length (more than 30 pages) disproving one by one the many grounds raised by the appellant, at times pointing out that it misread the documents of the procedures,[16] at other times noting that the winning tender was indeed articulated and substantiated enough,[17] and at yet other times again turning the tables on the appellant, stating that it did not show that the challenged assessment was wrong.[18]

As will be further illustrated in the following section, the review by the Consiglio di Stato in its capacity as the top administrative court in the country is very much built around the scattered original materials made up of ad hoc legislative texts and scant provisions on remedies to develop rules and principles regarding elements necessary for the legality of administrative decisions and the subsequent procedure to be followed in adopting them.

Section II will illustrate the sources relevant for administrative law. Conforming to the traditional Italian approach, the administrative organisation will then be briefly discussed in section III. Section IV will contain a more substantial exploration of the principles and rules regulating administrative action. The forms of action, including appeals, will be touched upon thereafter in section V, followed by a presentation of codification of administrative law in section VI and conclusions in section VII.

## II. Legal Sources of Administrative Law

To date, international law and, to a much greater extent, EU law hold much relevance for many administrative law activities in Italy.

Concerning international law, the Aarhus Convention on Access to Information, Public Participation in Decision-Making and Access to Justice in Environmental Matters is particularly relevant for what is a major area in administrative law.[19]

Because of the principle of attributed competencies or conferral (Articles 4 and 5 of the Treaty on European Union (TEU)),[20] EU institutions do not have the power to enact general administrative law rules that are applicable to the Member States. This a fortiori concerns the internal organisation of the Member States, given their residual institutional competence. It is worth remarking that

[15] ibid.

[16] eg, ibid para 11.5.

[17] eg, ibid paras 12.1.9 and 14.2.*d*).

[18] eg, ibid paras 13.5 and 14.2.*b*).

[19] A Comino, 'The Application of the Aarhus Convention in Italy' in R Caranta, A Gerbrandy and B Müller (eds), *The Making of a New European Legal Culture: The Aarhus Convention* (Groningen, European Law Publishing, 2018) 155 ff.

[20] Consolidated Version of the Treaty on European Union [2012] OJ C326/13.

administrative law as applied to the EU institutions and agencies themselves is still far from being codified.[21] However, Articles 41 and 42 of the Charter of Fundamental Rights (CFR)[22] on the right to good administration and on the right of access respectively do apply horizontally to all EU institutions, bodies, offices and agencies, and the case law of the European Court of Justice has developed a number of general principles pertaining specifically to administrative law.[23]

Within these limits, EU – and to a lesser extent European Convention on Human Rights (ECHR) – law have become a major force for change in Italian administrative law. This is specifically true concerning many areas of substantive law, such as regulated economic activities (eg, many professions) competition and state aid, services of general economic interest (SGEIs), public contracts (procurement contracts and concessions) and, in some instances, environmental protection.

Possibly of even greater importance, EU law has also dented the traditional corporatist ethos of Italy that informed administrative law, which was heavily geared towards the protection of vested interests. EU law has brought about an entirely new approach to market regulation based on competition rules and the prohibition of state aid. The EU approach brings to the fore the rights of market participants in many areas, including the provision of services. This fresh approach has significantly changed the rules about many professions, licensing and authorisations, to name just a few, introducing public tendering procedures where once cronyism flourished.[24]

It should be emphasised that the EU increasingly limits the Member States' residual procedural autonomy and enacts rules concerning remedies, as is the case again with public contracts.[25]

Outside the area of judicial protection, including reference to undue delays in issuing final judgments[26] and sanctions,[27] the European Convention on Human Rights (ECHR) is much less often referred to in the case law and literature concerning administrative law.[28] However, it was instrumental in forcing the

[21] P Craig, H Hofmann, J-P Schneider and J Ziller (eds), *ReNEUAL Model Rules on EU Administrative Procedure* (Oxford, Oxford University Press, 2017); see in this book the analysis by A Berger, 'Science Codification for the European Union – The ReNEUAL-Network: On the Limits of Legal Control of Innovation and Technology'.

[22] Charter of Fundamental Rights of the European Union [2012] OJ C326/391.

[23] J Schwarze, *European Administrative Law* (Brussels, Office for Official Publications of the European Communities, 2006).

[24] A good instance of the change is provided by the actions brought by the incumbent to fight the *mise en concurrence* of lakeside concessions which were brought to the Court of Justice of the European Union: Joined Cases C-458/14 and C-67/15 *Promoimpresa and Others* EU:C:2016:558.

[25] For an overview, see M Eliantonio and E Muir, 'The Interplay between Legislative Provisions and Fundamental Rights in Ensuring Effective Judicial Protection and the Effectiveness of EU Law' (2020) Special issue of the *Review of European Administrative Law* 1.

[26] See S Mirate, 'La Convenzione Europea dei diritti dell'uomo e i giudici nazionali. Corte di cassazione e Consiglio di Stato a confronto' in G Rolla (ed), *Il sistema europeo di protezione dei diritti fondamentali e i rapporti tra le giurisdizioni* (Milan, Giuffrè, 2010) 337.

[27] See Cons Stato, Sez VI, 26 March 2015, n 1595, discussed below, section III.

[28] B Biancardi, 'Comment to Article 79, Section IV, Protocollo 16 CEDU' in G Falcon, F Cortese and B Marchetti (eds), *Commentario breve al codice del processo amministrativo* (Milan, CEDAM, 2021).

law-makers, who could count on the benevolence of the Constitutional Court, to change the rules providing very low levels of compensation even in the event of procedurally unlawful expropriation.[29] Yet, more often than not, attempts to rely on the ECHR to challenge domestic provisions have floundered in Italian courts. Article 1 of Protocol 1 of the ECHR has been referred to in order to upheld legislative rules excluding those found to be linked to organised crime from participating to public award procedures by the decentralised police authority (Questore).[30] The same provision was considered to allow a rule giving municipalities the power to take buildings constructed without a legal authorisation.[31] Finally, Article 1 of Protocol 1 was again referred to the Constitutional Court challenging the legality under many aspects of emergency legislation following the 2008 financial crisis that provided the transformation of the larger 'people's bank' into companies limited by shares.[32] However, the Court considered the provision to be in line with the ECHR and with the Italian Constitution.[33]

The 1948 Constitution[34] has the highest rank among the Italian sources. Article 117(1) – as recast in 2001 – provides that legislative power is to be exercised in compliance with the Constitution and respecting the constraints deriving from EU law and international obligations. The Constitution has very few provisions concerning the administration of the state, its subdivision and their activities. In essence, these provisions recall the legality principle in shaping the state organisation and some specific activities (see below, section IV). Moreover, Article 97 of the Constitution spells out the principles of impartiality and *buon andamento*. Impartiality specifies the more general equality or non-discrimination principle enshrined in Article 3 of the Constitution. *Buon andamento* reflects early nineteenth-century terminology which in turn derives from the medieval idea of *buon governo*.[35] As such, it seems to have a different focus from and to be a less precise principle than the right to good administration as protected by Article 41 CFR. Indeed, *buon andamento* is not traditionally seen as providing a right to users of public administration services and might more be correctly translated into the

[29] See the analysis and full references in S Mirate, 'The ECrtHR Case Law as a Tool for Harmonization of Domestic Administrative Laws in Europe' (2012) 2 *Review of European Administrative Law* 50, 50 ff; more recently, see Cons Stato (Ad Plen), 9 February 2016, n 2, commented upon in P Urbani, 'L'A.P. del CDS alla ricerca della tutela della proprietà privata nelle vicende espropriative "anomale"' (2016) 5 *Giurisprudenza Italiana* 1212, 1212 ff.

[30] Cons Stato, Sez III, 9 October 2018, n 5784.

[31] Cons Stato, Sez VI, 7 February 2018, n 775.

[32] Cons Stato, Sez VI, Ord, 15 December 2016, n 5277.

[33] Corte cost, 15 May 2018, n 99, commented upon by G Scianscia 'La Corte costituzionale sulla riforma delle "popolari"' (2018) 5 *Giornale Diritto Amministrativo* 597, 597 ff and by L Boggio, 'Proprietà azionaria e diritto societario speciale bancario: limiti al rimborso' (2018) 11 *Giurisprudenza Italiana* 2395, 2395 ff. A parallel case, which did not raise issues with reference to the ECHR, was referred to the Court of Justice: Case C-686/18 *OC and Others* ECLI:EU:C:2020:567.

[34] Costituzione della Repubblica Italiana.

[35] See R Caranta, 'Good Administration in the Age of Governance' in P Heritier and P Silvestri (eds), *Good Government, Governance, Human Complexity* (Florence, Olschki, 2012) 143.

more modern terms of efficiency and effectiveness. As such, perceived breaches of *buon andamento* could not be challenged in the courts. Article 98 on the duties of public servants and Article 28 on their responsibilities buttress the principles in Article 97 of the Constitution.[36]

More recent case law is seeing the principles in Article 97 – at times together with the equality principle – as underpinning review for *eccesso di potere*. A good instance of this is provided by a case concerning the composition of local committees competent to manage hunting in some areas in Lombardy. Members of the committee had to be named based on the proposal from the most representative farmers' associations. The regional government defined representativeness based on the number of associates resident in the municipalities concerned. Both the general act setting the criterion for representativeness and the actual decision were challenged by one of the largest national farmers' associations. The association claimed that relying on residence was unlawful as this premise favoured an association including not only active farmers, but also retired ones, family members of farmers and other professionals in the agriculture sector not actually tilling the land. The Consiglio di Stato overturned the first instance judgment and found the appeal to be well founded.[37] It read in the applicable legislation a requirement that the members of the committees represent those really engaged in farming, so that relying on residence alone is manifestly illogical and unreasonable.[38] Rebutting the defendant regional government's assumption that it enjoyed a wide level of discretion in setting the criteria for representativeness, the Consiglio di Stato held that the ground of *eccesso di potere* allows the administrative courts to check that even discretionary decisions correspond to the constitutional 'canons' of non-discrimination, *buon andamento* and impartiality.[39]

The legality principle was at the basis of Italian administrative law well before the Constitution and has survived the perils of Fascism. However, administrative rules were traditionally scattered across hundreds of sectoral rules and legal texts. A good example of this is provided by the founding legal text of Italian administrative law, the l. 20 marzo 1865, n 2248 per l'unificazione amministrativa del Regno d'Italia (laws of administrative unification). Adopted after most of the unification of Italy had been achieved, but at a time when the Pope still held Rome and the region around it, the 1865 law had six annexes. Annex A concerned local government (provinces and municipalities). Annex B was dedicated to public security and gave rules on many activities, including theatres, hotel, restaurants and pubs (*osterie*), the press, prostitution and so on. Its provisions included administrative

[36] F Cortese, 'The Liability of Public Administration: A Special Regime between Formal Requirements and Substantial Goals' in G della Cananea and R Caranta (eds), *The Tort Liability of Public Authorities in European Laws* (Oxford, Oxford University Press, 2020) 61 ff.

[37] Cons Stato, Sez III, 19 June 2019, n 4183.

[38] ibid para 7.4.

[39] ibid para 7.8.

fines and jail terms. Annex C concerned public health. Annex D extended the jurisdiction of the Consiglio di Stato to the whole Kingdom, while Annex E outlined remedies against administrative actions. Annex F was dedicated to public works, but also covered inland water regimes, railways concessions etc. A few months later, the l. 25 giugno 1865, n 2359, espropriazioni per causa pubblica, regulating expropriation was also approved.[40]

The burden to develop general principles from these utterly chaotic legislative materials fell squarely upon the case law of the Consiglio di Stato. For instance, from the duty to give reasons in the law on expropriation, the Consiglio di Stato deduced a general duty to give reasons for all decisions detrimentally affecting the addressee's rights and interests.[41] However, the Consiglio di Stato did not go as far as laying down a duty to give reasons for all administrative decisions, including those beneficial to the addressee but potentially harmful for third parties. Under Article 3 of Annex E to l. 20 marzo 1865, n 2248, such a duty was laid down for decisions rendered on appeal by a higher hierarchical authority, but the provision was never taken as a basis for a wider duty.

The Consiglio di Stato went well beyond developing general principles from punctual legislative provision. It was ready to fill in the gaps in the system providing remedies where those were lacking. Italy had borrowed from France the rule of the *recours préalable* following which the Consiglio di Stato could be seised only after all administrative appeals had been exhausted. Too often administrative authorities short-circuited the system by simply failing to decide on the appeals. In the well-known *Longo* case, the Consiglio di Stato equated this omission, or rather the silence kept on the appeal notwithstanding a request to act, to a negative decision which could be challenged before it.[42]

Currently, the pointillist approach to administrative law of Italian law-makers is to some extent remedied: (a) by a partial codification enacted through the APA, which originally laid down general rules on administrative proceedings and the right of access to documents, but since the amendments in 2005 has codified the regime of administrative acts and decisions; and (b) by sectoral codification in areas such as urban planning and expropriation, environmental protection, cultural heritage and public contracts. The extent to which this is successful is conditioned by a strong tendency to make and remake rules according to the political expediency of the moment (see below, section VI).

[40] See A Romano, 'La legislazione del 1865' in R Cavallo Perin, A Police and F Saitta (eds), *L'organizzazione delle pubbliche amministrazione tra Stato nazionale e integrazione europea* (Florence, Firenze University Press, 2016) xxxi.

[41] Cons Stato, Sez IV, 17 May 1907, n 178 (1907) *Foro Italiano* III, 161, concerning the refusal by the ministry to allow the raise of ship tickets for emigrants. See also Cons Stato, Ad Gen, 3 febbraio 1908, commented upon by F Cammeo, 'Gli atti amministrativi e l'obbligo di motivazione' (1908) III *Giurisprudenza Italiana* 253, 253 ff, concerning the denied approval of a contract; it is worth noting that the annotator, a most prominent scholar of that time, criticised the decision that highlighted the wide discretion enjoyed by the decision-maker.

[42] Cons Stato, Sez IV, 22 August 1902 n 429; see V Parisio, 'The Italian Administrative Procedure Act and Public Authorities' Silence' (2013) 36 *Hamline Law Review* 3, 3 ff.

## III. Organisation

As already noted, Article 97 of the Constitution lays down the principle of legality with reference to the organisation of the state. The Constitution also somewhat enhanced the autonomy of local government (provinces and municipalities), but state deconcentrated organs mostly remained in place. Constitutional provisions introducing regions as an intermediate government level between the state and local government with competence for a range of subject matters were finally implemented in 1970.[43]

In 2001, a constitutional reform did away with the state *ex ante* control on decisions taken by local government and purportedly enhanced the competences of the regions. Concerning specifically administrative functions, the new Article 118 of the Constitution enacts the subsidiarity principle, including in its horizontal dimension favouring the involvement of civil society and its organisations. Measures taken to combat the financial crises and a strongly centralist-biased case law of the Constitutional Court, coupled with the non-implementation of the financial provisions in the Constitution (Article 119), have undone any progress towards empowering the regional level of government.[44]

Moreover, key subconstitutional level legislation still pre-dates the 2001 constitutional reform, so consequently implementation has lagged behind. A case in point is Dlgs 18 Agosto 2000, n 267, Testo unico delle leggi sull'ordinamento degli enti locali (hereinafter TUEL), concerning local government legislation – an early instance of sectoral codification that was only amended rather than being replaced after the constitutional reform.

The most relevant changes seen in the past few decades reflect the changes in the role of the state in economic management activities. The state has changed its position from one of a monopolist or market participant to serving as a market regulator. Under the influence of EU law, utilities were largely liberalised, and financial constraints coupled with the application of EU state aid law by the European Commission have led to the sale/privatisation of many state-owned enterprises (SOEs) focusing on traditional manufacturing activities. Still, even today, SOEs are an important feature in Italy at the central, regional and local levels. More specifically, the state retains shares in a number of previously monopolist companies, as is the case in the transport (trains and Alitalia/ITA), energy and gas sectors. Local services such as transport and waste collection and treatment are also often managed by companies owned by the relevant municipalities, at times according

[43] B Caravita, 'Italy: Between the Hybrid State and Europe's Federalizing Process' in J Loughlin, J Kincaid and W Swenden (eds), *Routledge Handbook of Regionalism & Federalism* (New York, Routledge, 2013) 287.

[44] For an assessment, see R Toniatti, 'Le prospettive di revisione costituzionale e l'ipoteca neo-centralista sulla riforma dell'ordinamento regionale', available at www.rivistaaic.it/it/rivista/ultimi-contributi-pubblicati/roberto-toniatti/le-prospettive-di-revisione-costituzionale-e-l-ipoteca-neo-centralista-sulla-riforma-dell-ordinamento-regionale.

to the in-house rules now codified in Article 12 of Directive 2014/24/EU in public procurement.[45]

From the point of view of state organisation, over the course of more than 30 years, these developments have transpired into ad hoc legislation, thus creating a number of independent administrative authorities charged with regulating the market or sectors thereof.[46] Possibly the most important of these authorities is the Autorità garante della concorrenza e del mercato', also known as the Antitrust Authority, which is called upon not only to enforce competition rules but also to aid in the transition from a state-dominated market to a competitive model.[47]

Independent administrative authorities have also been introduced for purposes that go beyond market regulation in an effort to depoliticise given decisions. This has been the case with strikes in essential services of general economic interest, telecommunications, privacy and, more recently, the fight against corruption.[48]

The pressing need to make Italy more competitive on international markets has led to other innovations in the organisation of the state. Such innovations have been very much inspired by New Public Management reforms. One example is the single contact point for entrepreneurs wanting to start some economic activity ('sportello unico') by Dlgs 31 marzo 1998, n 112 Conferimento di funzioni e compiti amministrativi dello Stato alle regioni ed agli enti locali, in attuazione del capo I della legge 15 marzo 1997, n 59 (re-allocation of state administrative powers to the regions and to local authorities).[49]

Finally, as will be further explored in the next section, some of the general procedural rules on administrative procedures brought about by the APA might also be considered 'organisational' in a wide sense.

## IV. Administrative Procedures between General Principles, General Rules and Specific Legislation

### A. General Principles

As previously discussed, the Constitution itself recalls the legality principle with reference to a number of detrimental administrative decisions (taxation, military

[45] Directive 2014/24/EU of the European Parliament and of the Council of 26 February 2014 on public procurement and repealing Directive 2004/18/EC [2014] OJ L94/ 65; N Belhocine and LF Jirasavetakul, 'Lessons from Two Public Sector Reforms in Italy', *IMF Working Paper* WP/20/40, 1, at 4 ff, available at www.imf.org/en/Publications/WP/Issues/2020/02/21/Lessons-from-Two-Public-Sector-Reforms-in-Italy-49034.

[46] See R Caranta, 'Independent Administrative Authorities in Italy' in R Caranta, M Andenas and D Fairgrieve (eds), *Independent Administrative Authorities* (London, BIICL, 2004) 93 ff.

[47] D Kerwer, *Regulatory Reforms in Italy: A Case Study in Europeanisation* (London, Routledge, 2001) especially 89 ff.

[48] R Caranta (n 46).

[49] For some reason, the derivation of many reforms from New Public Management is not acknowledged by the law specialists, while it is commonly referred to by political scientists: see, eg, S Cavatorto and A La Spina, *The Politics of Administrative Reform in Italy* (London, Palgrave Macmillan, 2020) 44.

draft, mandatory medical treatments and expropriations) and spells out the principles of impartiality and *buon andamento*.

According to the case law of the Constitutional Court, the principle of due process has no underpinning in the Constitution.[50] This stance, which is occasionally softened with reference to the APA,[51] has been recently affirmed by the plenary session of the Court of Cassation in a taxation case.[52] The Court specifically held that a general principle of prior hearing going beyond specific legal provisions to this effect cannot be deduced from Article 97 of the Constitution.[53] The Court went so far as to prepare itself to concede that EU law, insofar as it is relevant for tax law, indeed foresees such a right to a fair hearing. It should be noted here that according to the Court, this does not change the domestic legal situation outside the areas in which EU tax rules apply.[54] The ECHR was not referred to in these cases.[55]

As will be further investigated in this chapter, Article 1 APA has a list of general principles of administrative law. Due process is not listed therein, but Article 7 provides a general right for all those potentially affected by a decision being considered by the public administration to have access to documents and to make their views known before the decision is taken. However, under Article 13(2) APA, these provisions do not apply in tax proceedings (as was the case in the judgments under discussion).

An articulate judgment by the Consiglio di Stato following a challenge brought against a sanctioning decision of CONSOB – the financial markets regulator – sheds much light on how due process is also understood in the context of the ECHR.[56] The addressees of one of such sanctions claimed that it was unlawful because it was based on the regulation issued by CONSOB laying detailed procedural rules that

[50] The leading case is Corte cost 2 March 1962, n 13 (1962) *Giurisprudenza Italiana* I, 1, 920 ff; see critically E Palici di Suni, 'Inerzia della Pubblica Amministrazione e giusto procedimento' (1992) *Giurisprudenza italiana* I, 13 ff.

[51] Corte cost, 23 March 2007, n 103, commented upon by A Massera, 'Il difficile rapporto tra politica ed amministrazione: la Corte costituzionale alla ricerca di un punto di equilibrio' (2007) 12 *Giornale Diritto Amministrativo* 1307, 1307 ff – the Court quashed a law providing for the automatic termination of all contracts with directors (*dirigenti*) in all branches of state administration 60 days after the new elections. Relying on art 98 of the Constitution, which provides that all public servants serve the nation and thus implicitly not the ruling party or coalition, the Constitutional Court found that these contracts could only be terminated with cause, following an administrative proceeding to give the concerned director the possibility to exonerate himself or herself. For good measure, the Court added that, especially after the entry into force of the l. 7 Agosto 1990, n 241, such a proceeding is also essential to ensure the compliance with the principles of due process (*giusto procedimento*).

[52] Cass civ, Sez Un, 9 December 2015, n 24823; this stance was implicitly approved by Corte cost, Ord, 24 November 2017, n 243.

[53] Cass civ, Sez Un, 9 December 2015, n 24823, para 4.

[54] ibid para 5; see critically G Vanz, 'Problemi aperti in tema di contraddittorio nei procedimenti di accertamento tributario nella prospettiva dei rapporti tra ordinamento nazionale e ordinamento europeo' (2019) 4 *DPCE Online* 2619 ff, especially 2631 ff, available at www.dpceonline.it/index.php/dpceonline/article/view/848.

[55] As for the possible relevance of the ECHR in these cases, see G Vanz (n 54) 2632 fn 49.

[56] Cons Stato, Sez VI, 26 March 2015, n 1595, commented upon by B Raganelli, 'Sanzioni CONSOB e tutela del contraddittorio procedimentale' (2015) 4 *Giornale Diritto Amministrativo* 511, 511 ff.

was itself unlawful, inter alia because of the breach of Article 6 ECHR. Assuming that the sanction was criminal in nature, the applicants argued that the objective independence of the 'judge' was lacking, given that both the office preparing the file containing the evidence concerning the alleged breach and the board deciding on the fine are part of the same structure. Based on a detailed analysis of the case law of the Strasbourg Court, the Consiglio di Stato initially concluded that the sanctions at issue are criminal only *lato sensu*, meaning that the full panoply of procedural judicial guarantees does not need to apply during the administrative procedure, provided that, as this is the case, they are fully operational when and if the administrative decision is subject to judicial review.[57] In other words, according to the Consiglio di Stato, a full metamorphosis of the administrative procedure still placing the decision-maker on a different level from the accused into a fully fledged criminal trial based on the equality of arms between the parties is not required under Article 6 ECHR.[58] Still, the Consiglio di Stato held that the specific Italian legislation concerning sanctioning proceedings under the competence of market regulators requires that the private parties are informed of each decision taken, including in the investigation phase. These parties must also be given the opportunity to comment on each decision taken, rather than just being given the right of access to documents and the right to send briefs at the opening of proceedings, as is generally foreseen under Article 7 APA. Since this was not the case, the sanction was quashed.[59]

## B. General Rules Embodying General Principles

Article 1(1) APA opens with a salvo of principles. After being amended in 2005, it mentions attention to costs ('economicità'), efficacy, impartiality, openness and transparency, and the principles of Community law.

The reference to 'principles of Community law' – now EU law – is normally understood as covering proportionality and legitimate expectations. The former was already known in Italy at least with reference to fines and administrative sanctions generally.[60] The latter was alien to the local administrative tradition with the exception of salary levels and other benefits of public servants. Today the provisions in Articles 21 *quinquies* and 21-*nonies* APA, as added in 2005, concerning respectively withdrawal for public interest reasons and annulment by the

[57] Cons Stato, Sez VI, 26 March 2015, n 1595, paras 13 ff.

[58] ibid para 18.

[59] ibid paras 27 ff. What was specifically criticised was that the conclusions of the office charged with proposing a draft decision were not communicated to the addressees of the final decision so that they could make their views known before that decision was taken.

[60] A Sandulli, 'Eccesso di potere e controllo di proporzionalità: Profili comparati' (1995) *Rivista trimestrale di diritto pubblico* 329ú329 ff.

decision-makers, are cast along the lines of the protection of legitimate expectation, even if the precise concept is not openly referred to.

The protection of legitimate expectations in Italy also covers what (albeit limited) non-retroactivity is acknowledged in administrative law. For instance, the retroactive setting, during the course of the year, of the prices for diagnostics paid by the National Health Service (NHS) to private service providers was considered unlawful, since the prices were set at a lower level than in previous years in order to reduce the costs to the public purse without taking account of the legitimate expectation of those providers.[61] Legitimate expectations were also successfully invoked to justify the proactive-only effect of changes to the interpretation of administrative procedural rules which created a preclusion on judicial review.[62] The principle is not always sufficient to avoid a retroactive effect of an administrative decision. For instance, a recent judgment held that legitimate expectations could not help an economic operator to defeat the final determination of a grant at a lower level than had been earlier indicated by the administration. The Consiglio di Stato considered that a professional should know that such discrepancies may occur and that only the final determination could be relied upon.[63]

It is of the utmost important to stress that EU administrative law principles are made into general principles of Italian administrative law; therefore, they apply in the country quite independently of whether or not EU law is being given effect, and following a 2005 decision made by the national law-makers.

Moreover, Article 1(2) APA enacts the rule that only in exceptional and duly motivated cases may the public administration impose procedural requirements not foreseen by the applicable law. This is considered to be the basis for a general principle forbidding procedural overkill (*non aggravamento*). This does not dispense from duly applying each and every crazily detailed rule, of which Italian administrative legislation is already overburdened.[64] However, at least such a principle makes it difficult for public administrations to impose additional extra-legal requirements. One area where this was used was in relation to authorisation proceedings for the installation of telecommunication antennas. While the government had simplified the rules for authorisation procedures, some municipalities, fearful of electrosmog, still tried to block those installations requiring additional documents etc, but these attempts were defeated in court.[65]

[61] Cons Stato, Sez III, 6 March 2015, n 1149.

[62] Cons Stato, Sez VI, 3 December 2018, n 6858.

[63] Cons Stato, Sez III, 17 January 2020, n 412.

[64] For instance, the case law is set in terms of holding that the principle in question does not excuse applicants from lodging documents etc that the competent authority might already have because of other proceedings: eg, Cons Stato, Sez IV, 27 October 2009, n 6591 – the assumption is that efficacy requires not burdening the decision-makers with the task of searching their files.

[65] Cons Stato, Sez III, 9 July 2018, n 4189; see also Cons Stato, Sez V, 9 October 2013, n 4698. In that case, the municipality superseded deciding on a request for a building permission, citing no further substantiated need for additional investigations.

## C. Principles in Sectoral Legislation

Lists of principles may also be found in sectoral legislation and codifications. The most egregious example of this was the 2006 Public Contracts Code enacted by Dlgs 12 aprile 2006, n 163 Codice dei contratti pubblici relativi a lavori, servizi e forniture in attuazione delle direttive 2004/17/CE e 2004/18/CE. This contained not one but three lists of principles: (a) 'principles' in Article 2; (b) 'principles for contracts not covered under the Code' in Article 27; and (c) the principles of the EC Treaty for the choice of the concessionnaire of services in Article 30(2). The same principles, without any additional specification, were also recalled for the choice of the contractor for sponsorship contracts in Article 26(1).[66] Moreover, the principles of the APA were also recalled in Article 4 of the 2006 Public Contracts Code with reference to proceedings within the competence of the then public procurement oversight authority.[67] Finally, the 'principles of impartiality and *non aggravamento*' were spelt out in Article 231. The problem was that the various lists and specific provisions noted above included different principles. Apparently, the reasons for this overkill of principles was that different experts were charged with drafting different blocks of the Code, and the different parts were never coordinated. While an aesthetic disgrace, these discrepancies among the lists did not lead to problems in the interpretation and application of the Code. This apparent paradox is explained by the different 'nature' of different principles of administrative law, which will be examined later on in this chapter.

Sectoral legislation and codifications often embody ad hoc principles. For instance, the Environmental Code, enacted with Dlgs 3 aprile 2006, n 152 norme in materia ambientale, after being amended in 2008, spells out a number of principles specific to that fields. Article 3 *ter*, concerning the 'principle of environmental action', recalls the precautionary principle and the polluter pays principle (referring specifically to the then Article 174 TCE).[68] Article 3 *quater* is dedicated to the 'principle of sustainable development' and provides that every activity relevant under the Code must conform to the principle of sustainable development to ensure that satisfying today's needs is not done to the detriment of future generations. The second indent of the latter provision specifies the principle of sustainable development, which provides that administrative action must aim at implementing this principle so that, when weighing up competing public and private interests in the

[66] M Mattalia, 'Il contratto di sponsorizzazione' in TS Musumeci (ed), *La Cultura ai privati* (Padua, CEDAM, 2012) 51.

[67] See also art 10, para 9 recalling the general principles of the law in binding contracting entities that are different from contracting authorities in naming an organisation unit as responsible for the contracting procedure.

[68] See Cass civ, Sez Un, 31 October 2019, n 28094, which considered to be illegal a positive EIA adopted notwithstanding the fact that the scientific opinion given by the regional environmental agency was negative.

exercise of its discretion, the protection of the environment and of the cultural heritage is given greater weight. Finally, Article 3 *quinquies* specifies the subsidiarity principle and that of loyal cooperation between the different territorial levels with reference to environmental matters.

Considerations pertaining to sustainability that have formed part of legislation have not always been granted the rank of principles. Article 2(2) of the 2006 Public Contracts Code indicated that the principle of attention to costs could be bent, if so provided under specific provisions of the same Code, to social and environmental criteria. Article 4(1) of the new (2016) Public Contracts Code (Dlgs 18 aprile 2016, n 50 Attuazione delle direttive 2014/23/UE, 2014/24/UE e 2014/25/UE sull'aggiudicazione dei contratti di concessione, sugli appalti pubblici e sulle procedure d'appalto degli enti erogatori nei settori dell'acqua, dell'energia, dei trasporti e dei servizi postali, nonché per il riordino della disciplina vigente in materia di contratti pubblici relativi a lavori, servizi e forniture) implementing the 2014 procurement and concessions directives has instead raised 'environmental protection and energy efficiency' among the general principles for the award of contracts not covered or not fully covered by the Code. In line with the worst tradition of messy legislation, for the contracts covered under the Code, Article 30(1) has instead used the more restrained approach previously found in Article 2(2) of the old Code, simply adding to the list that now includes 'social needs, health considerations, protection of the environment and of the cultural heritage, and promotion of sustainable development also including energy efficiency'. Why sustainability should amount to a principle for the award of contracts not covered or not fully covered under the Code, while being simply a derogation from the principle of attention to costs allowed in specific circumstances for the award of contracts covered could only be explained with very poor legislative drafting. So far, this incongruous state of the legislation has not led to any litigation.

## D. Principles Having Different Values?

A big question concerns the real legal value of this large panoply of principles. It might sound like old positivist thinking, but it is submitted that there is a significant difference between, on the one hand, principles which are relevant for the judicial review of the legality of specific administrative decisions and, on the other hand, principles which are more policy-oriented or whose use is instead confined to the assessment of the output efficiency of services of the state or other public law entity.

Among the long list of principles in Article 1 APA, only impartiality (and openness/transparency), proportionality and the protection of legitimate expectations are clearly justiciable in the sense that within the limits described above for the latter principle, they can be directly referred to in order to challenge the legality of an administrative decision. Concerning, for instance, impartiality, the Consiglio di Stato held that this principle spelt out in Article 97 of the Constitution is applicable even when sector-specific legislation does not refer to it.[69] In that case, a *carabiniere* had been sanctioned by the commander of his unit for having written a libellous letter to the Ministry of Defence against the same commander. The Consiglio di Stato affirmed the first instance judgment holding that even if under military rules sanctions fall under the competence of the unit commander, in this case impartiality required the commander to recuse himself from the proceeding.[70]

*Buon andamento* and, even more so, cost-consciousness, efficacy and efficiency deserve to be classed among the policy-oriented principles. As noted above, together with impartiality, *buon andamento* is today considered as grounding the judicial review of *eccesso di potere*. The rest of the principles just recalled clearly borrow from 'New Public Management' parlance.[71] As these principles pertain to overall administrative action and operations in a fairly wide sense rather than to individual or specific decisions, these 'principles' are not used per se and alone to ground challenges to the legality of specific administrative decisions.

Still, the practice is less tidy and even the 'soft' principles may be referred to in judgments – and are often referred to – to reinforce – or to embellish – the reasons for quashing or more rarely upholding a given administrative decision.[72] In a recent e-procurement case, following a malfunctioning of the operative program that did not allow tenders to be uploaded before the deadline, the contracting authority decided to extend the deadline for two days and put a notice to this effect on the dedicated website created for the contract documentation.[73] A company that had complained about the malfunctioning challenged the award, arguing that: (a) it was not given any information about the extension of the deadline; and (b) the extension was too short for it to be aware of the new opportunity and upload all documents to the website. The first ground did not raise any question of principle as it turned on the interpretation of a specific provision in the 2016 Public Procurement Code, which provided that news of the extension was to be given on the dedicated website and in any other way the contracting authority thought fit. The Consiglio di Stato held that the contracting authority could choose whether additional publicity was needed and by what means. This choice could only be reviewed under the principles of loyal cooperation and proportionality, which could be translated in the criteria of good faith and fairness, which are in turn part of the 'concept' of *buon andamento*.[74] However, on the facts of the case it would

[69] Cons Stato, Sez II, 9 March 2020, n 1654.

[70] ibid para 3, in which the principle of impartiality is recalled three times (once along *buon andamento*).

[71] S Kuhlmann, 'New Public Management in Continental Europe: Local Government Modernization in Germany, France and Italy from a Comparative Perspective' (2010) 88 *Public administration* 1166, 1116 ff, especially at 1122 ff.

[72] See also Cons Stato, Sez V, 15 July 2020, n 4584, para 9.2, referring to *buon andamento* and impartiality as the bases for the duty to give reasons; reasonableness is referred together with *buon andamento* at para 10.1.3 to stress that merit requirements for a given position depend on the office whose attribution is sought.

[73] Cons Stato, Sez III, 29 July 2020, n 4811.

[74] ibid para 3.3.

not be proportional to require the company to constantly check the website, so the choice made was not consistent with the principles of fairness, loyal cooperation and good faith.[75] The same reasons led it to find that the two-day extension was not sufficient, given that it had not been announced to the individual participants.[76]

This case is interesting in that it both shed some light on the extent to which Italian administrative courts are ready to review discretionary decision and because it shows how both hard and soft principles (or *buon andamento* at least) together can be combined to justify a judgment. However, the actual outcome of each individual case very much depends on the court's appreciation of the facts.

## V. Forms of Action

The President of the Republic at the request of the Prime Minister and the ministers may enact implementing rules (regulations). Regions and municipalities may enact similarly named rules and also enjoy relevant planning powers. The power to enact non-legislative rules is today acknowledged, and in any case frequently used, by independent administrative authorities.

However, unlike the German Verwaltungsverfahrensgesetz,[77] the APA does not cover, and instead expressly excludes from its coverage regulations, planning decisions and acts of general application (Article 13). Rules specific to each of these measures apply and are normally based on representative democracy institutions. This goes very much against the general idea behind the 1990 reform, which was to enhance public participation in the decision-making process.[78]

However, the case law of the Consiglio di Stato has imposed notice and comment procedures to rule-making by independent administrative authorities. The reasoning has been that the lack of democratic legitimacy of decisions taken by those authorities must be compensated by participatory rights bestowed on those concerned by their rules.[79]

Unilateral and binding *provvedimenti* (administrative decisions) are the instrument of choice for public authorities. They go by many and different names,

[75] ibid para 3.5.

[76] ibid para 4.

[77] Verwaltungsverfahrensgesetz in der Fassung der Bekanntmachung vom 23. Januar 2003 (BGBl I, 102), zuletzt geändert durch Artikel 24 Absatz 3 des Gesetzes vom 25. Juni 2021 (BGBl I, 2154).

[78] BG Mattarella, 'Participation to Rulemaking in Italy' and R Caranta, 'Participation into Administrative Procedures: Achievements and Problems', both in (2010) 2 *Italian Journal of Public Law* 339 and 311, 339 ff and 311 ff respectively, available at www.ijpl.eu/assets/files/pdf/2010_volume_2/IJPL%20volume%202_2010.pdf.

[79] The leading case is Cons Stato, Sez VI, 27 December 2006, n 7972, commented upon by M Poto, 'Autorità amministrative indipendenti e garanzie partecipative' (2007) *Responsabilità civile* 1143, 1143 ff; see now R Titomanlio, 'Riflessioni sul potere normativo delle Autorità amministrative indipendenti fra legalità "sostanziale", legalità "procedurale" e funzione di regolazione' (2017) 1 *NOMOS* 1, 1 ff, available at www.nomos-leattualitaneldiritto.it/wp-content/uploads/2017/05/Titomanlio.pdf.

such as authorisations, licences and permits. The amendments to the APA introduced in 2005 have very much codified the scholarly and jurisprudential learning concerning *provvedimenti*.

Increasing pressure to make administrative procedures leaner and faster coupled with apparatchiks' suspicion towards outward liberalisation has led to the incremental increase over the past 30 years of situations in which a positive decision is assumed to be granted if the decision-maker fails to act within a given deadline (the so-called *silenzio assenso*). The default deadline is 30 days from the day the concerned party requested a favourable decision, but specific and longer deadlines may be set by the public administration concerned, although ordinarily not exceeding 90 days (Article 2, paragraphs 2 and 3 read together with Article 20 APA).[80]

In some circumstances, laid down in general by Article 19 APA, the party interested in pursuing an economic activity may start it immediately after notifying the competent authority of his or her intent to do so (segnalazione certificata di inizio attività (SCIA)).[81]

Specific deadlines are given to the competent authority both in the case of *silenzio* and in case of SCIA to check whether the party concerned does indeed fulfil the legal requirements for the type of activity concerned.

Articles 11 and 15 APA respectively introduced and codified *accordi* (agreements) in the pursuit of the public interest with private parties and among public administrations. These are public contracts in name only, Italian scholars having been historically prudish in terms of accepting that the public interest might be the object of negotiations.[82]

The state and other public law entities may be parties to contracts, including procurement and concessions (under the EU definition).[83] Within some limits, they can hold shares and be partners in companies.

In the nineteenth century, Italy followed the French rule of *recours préalable* that made the prior exhaustion of administrative remedies a condition precedent to judicial review. As noted above, the rule was used too often to delay access to justice. Consequently, it was abandoned in 1971 when the first instance regional administrative courts were created. The demise of the appeal system was not much

[80] See V Parisio (n 42).

[81] See G Corso, 'The Evolution of Italian Administrative Procedures, 1990–2009' (2011) 34 *International Journal of Public Administration* 87, 87 ff, at 94 f; R Caranta, 'The Quest for Quality and Speed in Italian Administrative Law: Or the Tale of Some Elusive Targets' in C Backes, M Eliantonio and S Jansen (eds), *Quality and Speed in Administrative Decision-Making: Tension or Balance?* (Cambridge, Intersentia, 2016) 26 ff.

[82] G Greco, *Accordi e amministrativi tra provvedimento e contratto* (Turin, Giappichelli, 2003); the case law increasingly treats them as unilateral decisions. See critically M Ramajoli, 'Gli accordi tra amministrazione e privati ovvero della costruzione di una disciplina tipizzata' (2019) 4 *Diritto Amministrativo* 674, 674 ff.

[83] See K Bonsignore and ME Comba, 'PPPs and Concessions in Italy: Lots of Good Intentions Hindered by a Highly Complicated Regulation' in P Bogdanowicz, R Caranta and P Telles (eds), *Public-Private Partnerships and Concessions in the EU* (Cheltenham, Edward Elgar, 2020) 89 ff.

lamented and this creates an unfavourable environment for alternative dispute resolution (ADR) in Italian administrative law.[84]

Concerning instead judicial protection, a general principle of effective judicial protection is enacted in Article 24 of the Constitution. The legality review of administrative measures, including regulations and individual decisions and any measure in between, in principle falls under the review of administrative courts (regional administrative tribunals (TAR) at first instance and the Consiglio di Stato on appeal). However, ordinary civil and criminal courts have the power to set aside illegal administrative measures to which they should otherwise give effect in a judgment pending before them. Moreover, the Court of Cassation is tasked with patrolling the judicial competence boundaries, including between administrative and ordinary courts, so that judgments of the Consiglio di Stato may be challenged before it, but only concerning grounds of competence.[85]

As already noted, courts' review is limited to legality issues and courts cannot revisit the merits of the administrative decisions, which does not mean that their oversight might not be very probing (see above, sections I and IV.D).

## VI. The Codification of Administrative Law

Attempts at making administrative law clearer by gathering together sectoral provisions spread across dozens of different texts, typically spanning decades, is not a new practice in Italy. Yet, the problem arises that these provisions were not called 'codes' until fairly recently. These restatements of sectoral administrative law were instead called *testi unici*, meaning the one and only legal text regulating a given sector.

One early example of this which remains partially in force to date is a collection of public security rules in R.D. 18 giugno 1931, n 773, Testo Unico delle leggi di pubblica sicurezza (TULPS). Once its powers were consolidated, the Fascist regime took no chances and recast and hardened domestic security rules, some of them dating to Annex B of l. 20 marzo 1865, n 2248 per l'unificazione amministrativa del Regno d'Italia.[86]

Historically speaking there are two kinds of *testi unici*: those simply collecting existing rules (*testi unici compilativi*) and those – which make up the bulk of *testi*

[84] R Caranta and M Comba, 'Administrative Appeals in Italy: On the Brink of Extinction or Might They Be Saved (and are They Worth Saving)?' in DC Dragos and B Neamtu (eds), *Alternative Dispute Resolution in European Administrative Law* (Berlin, Springer, 2014) 113.

[85] *Randstad Italia SpA* (*Pending*) and the opinion of AG Hogan in Case C-497/20 *Randstad Italia SpA v Umana SpA Azienda USL Valle d'Aosta, IN VA SpA, Synergie Italia agenzia per il lavoro SpA* ECLI:EU:C:2021:725.

[86] For the historical context, see L Lacchè, 'The Shadow of the Law: The Special Tribunal for the Defence of the State between Justice and Politics in the Italian Fascist Period' in S Skinner (ed), *Fascism and Criminal Law: History, Theory, Continuity* (Oxford, Hart Publishing, 2015), especially 23 ff.

*unici* adopted over the past two decades – completely recasting the existing legislation, including by adopting new rules (*testi unici innovativi*). The latter type is very much akin to codification, while the former more closely resembles a compilation exercise to bring together rules previously scattered throughout numerous texts from different times.

*Testi unici* take the form of delegated legislation enacted by the President of the Republic based on a proposal from the government, which in turn acts on the basis of directives given through an enabling law passed by Parliament. Delegated legislation has the same rank among the Italian sources of law as Acts of Parliament, and so it can change pre-existing primary law rule. Delegated legislation is the standard route to enact complex legislation, for which lengthy debates in both Houses of Parliament are ill-suited.

A relevant modern case of 'codifying' *testi unici* is the TUEL, which, as already noted, was amended but was not totally recast after the 2001 constitutional reform.

A special case among *testi unici* is represented by DPR 6 giugno 2001, n 380, a *testo unico*, which, following the French model, amalgamates both legislative and secondary rules concerning urban planning and building activities. The unique nature of this *testo unico* lies in its design, which leaves to each rule its original rank in the source of law.

Codes are also enacted through delegated legislation. It should be noted that from the formal and procedural point of view, codes are thus undistinguishable from *testi unici* or any otherwise named piece of delegated legislation. As such, they have the same rank among the sources of law as any piece of legislation enacted by Parliament.[87]

A fine example of this can be found in what is presently called the Public Contracts Code (Codice dei contratti pubblici). Originally Dlgs 18 aprile 2016, n 50 referred to the three 2014 EU procurement and concessions directives it was implementing and was entitled: 'Attuazione delle direttive 2014/23/UE, 2014/24/UE e 2014/25/UE sull'aggiudicazione dei contratti di concessione, sugli appalti pubblici e sulle procedure d'appalto degli enti erogatori nei settori dell'acqua, dell'energia, dei trasporti e dei servizi postali, nonché per il riordino della disciplina vigente in materia di contratti pubblici relativi a lavori, servizi e forniture.'

It was branded with its brash new title following its significant amendment in 2017 by Article 1, Dlgs 19 aprile 2017, n 56. Besides the title, the modifications enacted in 2017 indeed cemented the Public Contract Code as a veritable repository of the rules applicable to all public contracts, thus going well beyond procurement and works and services concessions covered under the EU Directives.[88] Notably, even contracts from which the public administration earns some revenues, such

[87] V Onida et al, *Constitutional Law in Italy*, 2nd edn (Alphen aan den Rijn, Wolter Kluwers, 2020) 56 f.

[88] Concerning sale and lease contracts, see Cons Stato, Sez comm spec, 10 May 2018, n 1241, commented upon by A Meale, 'I contratti attivi e passivi di acquisto o di locazione di immobili della P.A.' (2018) *Giurisprudenza Italiana* 1979, 1979 ff; see also Cons Stato, Sez V, 29 January 2020, n 720.

as public domain concessions, are now brought under the general principles laid down in Article 4 of the Code.[89]

A possibly definitive witness to the interchangeability of names between codes and *testi unici* is provided by Dlgs 3 aprile 2006, n 152. It is officially and soberly named as Norme in materia ambientale (Rules in environmental matters), but it is variously referred to as the Testo unico in materia ambientale (TUA) or as the Codice dell'ambiente (Environmental Code).[90]

Another perplexing facet of present-day codification *à l'italienne* is that whatever their names, codes are in a constant state of flux.[91] Because these complex pieces of delegated legislation often contain unclear provisions or show gaps as soon as their application starts, enabling legislation typically gives the government the power to enact additional delegated rules within one year after the first legal text is enacted. For instance, Dlgs 3 aprile 2006, n 152, the Environmental Code was corrected and completed after a few months by Dlgs 8 novembre 2006, n 284 Disposizioni correttive e integrative del decreto legislativo 3 aprile 2006, n 152, recante norme in materia ambientale (basically, provisions to amend and integrate the provisions on the environment).

The 2016 Public Contracts Code bears another disreputable badge of distinction. A second enactment was necessary after just a few months after the Code entered into force in order to correct hundreds of clerical mistakes. The text's carelessness was due to the haste in which it was drafted, after the government suddenly decided it was a matter of national pride to implement the 2014 Public Procurements and Concessions Directives within the deadline.[92]

However, changes never stop. Mario Chiti roughly calculated that more than half of the provisions in the 2016 Public Contracts Code were modified in the space of merely three years.[93] The rather shocking number of times that provisions of the Environmental Code have been changed is now nearing 30. The TUEL has been amended several times, including by urgent measures intended to jump start economic growth. These measures are approved by the government (formally by the President of the Republic) and then sanctioned, and often modified in the process, by Parliament. For instance, the TUEL has recently been modified by DL 14 dicembre 2018, n 135 Disposizioni urgenti in materia di sostegno e semplificazione per le imprese e per la pubblica amministrazione (urgent measures for helping firms and simplifying administrative processes), sanctioned by L 11 febbraio 2019, n 12 conversione in legge, con modificazioni, del decreto-legge

[89] eg, TAR Campania, Salerno, Sez I, 19 March 2019, n 413.

[90] eg, S Nespor and AL de Cesaris, *Codice dell'ambiente* (Milan, Giuffrè, 2009).

[91] See S Cassese, 'Codici e codificazioni: Italia e Francia a confronto' (2005) *Giornale diritto amministrativo* 95, 95 ff; BG Mattarella, 'Codificazione', in S Cassese (ed), *Dizionario di diritto pubblico*, vol II (Milan, Giuffrè, 2006) 937 ff.

[92] See MP Chiti, 'Il decreto "sblocca cantieri": ambizioni e limiti' (2019) *Giornale di Diritto Amministrativo Amministrativo* 720, 720 ff (the deadline was missed by only one day, but the entry into force of the Code the day after its publication in the *Official Journal* had a chilling effect on the number of contracts awarded that lasted a number of months).

[93] ibid.

14 dicembre 2018, n 135, recante disposizioni urgenti in materia di sostegno e semplificazione per le imprese e per la pubblica amministrazione (the law sanctioning the above-mentioned urgent measures).

Finally, it should be noted that administrative law is not the only area affected by sectoral codification. One instance of this is provided by Dlgs 3 luglio 2017, n 117, Codice del Terzo settore (Code for the non-profit sector). This specific piece of legislation is of interest here since it contains a title regulating the relations between public law entities and the non-profit sector, allowing the former to entrust NGOs with the provision of (normally social) services of general interest (Title VII; Articles 55 ff).[94]

## VII. Conclusions

Codification is very much a necessity in all main areas of administrative law where super-abundant legislation flourishes unchecked. The legality principle is very much at the root of Italian administrative law, but dealing with hundreds of provisions scattered among many uncoordinated legal texts flies in the face of this principle.

The problem is the constant changes to 'codes' that can be seen in Italy. A recommendation from a recent International Monetary Fund (IMF) working paper reads 'Do not backtrack on or weaken reform objectives'. While inevitably there is learning by doing and the need to adapt policies and procedures to new issues or obstacles that may arise, care needs to be taken not to weaken the overall reform objectives. Consideration could be given to reviewing experience and contemplating changes on a periodic basis, say every five years, rather than during the budget or other legislative discussions.[95]

This is easier said than done. Legislative changes variably depend on the whims of the ministry of the moment (usually lasting no more than a couple of years in office), on the power of lobbies helping special interests to escape from the generally applicable rules,[96] on the undeniable need to try and right the shaky economic boat that is Italy, and finally on the necessity to periodically (but basically every year or so) feed foreign investors with 'reforms'. None of these factors is going to go away any time soon, and in fact COVID-19 has brought about new wide-ranging changes to the legislation concerning public procurements, the environment and beyond.[97]

[94] See S Poledrini, *Le social entreprise in Italia: modelli a confronto* (Milan, Franco Angeli, 2019), especially 33 ff.

[95] N Belhocine and LF Jirasavetakul (n 45) 12 with reference for the reform of SOEs; see also at 25 with reference to public procurement reform: 'backtracking should be avoided, while periodic reviews (say every 5 years) could be considered as an oversight instrument to assess progress and make changes as needed'.

[96] See MP Chiti (n 92).

[97] Dl 16 luglio 2020, n 76, sanctioned with widespread changes by l. 11 settembre 2020, n 120 'Misure urgenti per la semplificazione e l'innovazione digitale'.

# 8

# Codification of Administrative Law in the Netherlands

YMRE E SCHUURMANS, TOM BARKHUYSEN AND WILLEMIEN DEN OUDEN*

## I. The Definition and Delimitation of Administrative Law

The Netherlands has one of the most comprehensive codifications of general administrative law worldwide, in an Act that contains over 500 provisions. That is the Algemene wet bestuursrecht (Awb) (General Administrative Law Act (GALA)), which is partly available in English.[1] On the one hand, this results in a detailed codification of administrative duties and procedures; on the other hand, the limited scope of the Act still leaves large parts of administrative action uncodified. In this chapter we will describe the major topics of this book, but will emphasise the impact a comprehensive codification has on the development of administrative law. One of the effects of the extensiveness of the codification is that 'administrative law' and 'GALA' as concepts seem to coincide. For administrative law practitioners and scholars, it can be hard to see that there may be themes, public law values and legal solutions outside this codification. The GALA is administrative law and administrative law tends to be the GALA.[2]

* Parts of this chapter have been previously published in T Barkhuysen, W den Ouden and YE Schuurmans, 'The Law on Administrative Procedures in the Netherlands' (2012) *Netherlands Administrative Law Library*, DOI 10.5553/NALL/.000005 and in J-B Auby, *Droit Administratif* (Brussels, Bruylant, 2013) 253 ff.

[1] The English version of the Constitution of the Kingdom of the Netherlands can be found at www.rijksoverheid.nl. The GALA (translation in English) can be found on the websites of various public authorities with a partly international audience, such as the tax authorities (www.belastingdienst.nl). The version in English holds all stages, but is not totally up to date. All Dutch legislation and regulations can be found on the governmental website: wetten.overheid.nl. All parliamentary papers on the codification of the GALA be can accessed at: www.pgawb.nl.

[2] In this chapter we chose not to include detailed source references, because more detailed information is almost only available in Dutch-language publications. For general information on Dutch administrative law, we would like to refer to some renowned handbooks. Standard textbooks on Dutch administrative law and the law of administrative procedure include the following: HD van Wijk,

## A. Administrative Law

Administrative law can be described as the law of, for and against the government in its relation to citizens. It derives from the law-making powers of democratic institutions, gives public bodies the instruments to shape and interfere in legal relationships, and gives those governed legal protection against these actions. Conceptually we define three functions of administrative law: a legitimising, an instrumental and a protective function. Besides this framing of the essence of administrative law, in the Netherlands there is not a strong dogmatic view or debate on what administrative law is. If a topic falls within the scope of the GALA, this topic will certainly receive full attention from administrative law scholars, practitioners and courts. Moreover, as we will describe later on, civil law is thought to be the general law to be applied; administrative law only applies if a statute so regulates. Administrative law is what the legislator wishes it to be, namely when it deems it necessary to attribute a public law power to the administration.

There are three key definitions in the GALA that denote the fundamental orientation of the Act: administrative authority, interested party and order. Article 1:1 GALA contains a definition of an administrative authority; subsequently, the GALA provides for general rules governing acts performed by administrative authorities. Most rules in the GALA relate to specific acts, namely *besluiten* (orders). Article 1:3 GALA includes a definition of an order: a written decision of an administrative authority constituting a public law juridical act. This provision determines to a great extent the scope of the rules of the GALA and the scope of Dutch administrative law in general. An appeal to the administrative law court lies only against orders of administrative authorities (Article 8:1 GALA). Appeals can be exclusively filed by 'interested parties', a concept defined in Article 1:2 GALA. Prior to the GALA, the right of appeal of interested parties was often restricted to *beschikkingen* (individual decisions). It was the legislator's intention that the GALA should broaden the scope of administrative law and that orders

W Konijnenbelt and RM van Male, *Hoofdstukken van bestuursrecht*, 16th edn (The Hague, Elsevier Juridisch, 2014); M Schreuder-Vlasblom, *Rechtsbescherming en bestuurlijke voorprocedure*, 6th edn (Deventer, Kluwer, 2017); RJN Schlössels and SE Zijlstra, *Bestuursrecht in de sociale rechtsstaat*, 6th edn (Deventer, Kluwer, 2010); AT Marseille and HD Tolsma et al, *Bestuursrecht: Dl. 2, Rechtsbescherming tegen de overheid, bestuursprocesrecht*, 7th edn (The Hague, Boom Legal Publishers, 2019); T Barkhuysen et al, *Bestuursrecht in het Awb-tijdperk*, 8th edn (Deventer, Kluwer, 2018); LJA Damen, *Bestuursrecht: Dl. 1, Systeem, bevoegdheid, bevoegdheidsuitoefening, handhaving*, 4th edn (The Hague, Boom Legal Publishers, 2013).

As for English-language and French-language literature, reference is made to the following works: PC Adriaanse, T Barkhuysen, W den Ouden and YE Schuurmans, 'Faciliter la mise en oeuvre de droit communautaire : l'exemple de droit administratif néerlandais' (2009) 129 *Revue Française d'Administration Publique* 131; LJ van den Herik, EH Hondius and WJM Voermans (eds), *Introduction to Dutch Law*, 6th edn (Alphen aan den Rijn, Kluwer Law International, 2022); JG Brouwer and AE Schilder, *A Survey of Dutch Administrative Law* (Nijmegen, Ars Aequi Libri, 1998).

Case law research can be conducted on www.rechtspraak.nl and www.raadvanstate.nl (public databases of the judiciary). Other helpful websites include www.verenigingbestuursrecht.nl (association for administrative law).

(including regulations, policy rules and plans) should be the central concept of administrative law. The Act provided that after five years, the exclusion of the right to appeal against rules would be abolished. However, after several years, the legislator feared mass litigation if such an appeal against rules existed and a distortion of the constitutional equilibrium, and maintained the exclusion (Article 8:3 GALA).[3] As a consequence, Dutch administrative law still focuses on the legal protection against individual decisions, like permits, benefits, administrative fines and revoking decisions. Executive action in general is a much broader concept and falls mostly outside the scope of the Act, and cannot be appealed in administrative law courts;[4] those who wish to litigate against these actions need to approach the civil courts and fall back on tort law.

## B. Constitutional Law

While in various chapters in this volume, one can read that administrative law is concrete constitutional law,[5] this is not the case in the Netherlands. Even insofar as constitutional norms do underpin certain sections of the GALA, these cannot be invoked directly to ground a cause of action – in the Dutch context, judicial review of the constitutionality of legislation and treaties is prohibited.[6] This design of the legal system has resulted in a scholarly study of administrative law and constitutional law as two rather separated disciplines. Consequently, there are quite a few themes that might be considered part of administrative law in other legal systems, but that are regarded primarily as being of a constitutional nature in the Netherlands. These include the rules governing the election and appointment of specific officials and the organisation of referenda. In general, the rules concerning the structure and operation of administrative authorities are part of constitutional law, such as the voting system used within administrative authorities of municipalities, provinces and regional water authorities.

As the GALA relates mainly to orders, there is a clear difference between *constitutionally regulated* decision-making processes at the central government level, which result in primary legislation, 'general administrative orders' (comparable to 'orders in council' in the UK and 'executive orders' in the US) and ministerial regulations on the one hand, and *administrative* procedures on the other hand, which usually result in *beschikkingen* (personal decisions). The same difference

[3] Previously this exclusion was laid down in art 8:2 GALA.

[4] Just like the APA in the US, see in this book EL Rubin, 'The United States: Systematic But Incomplete Codification', section IV; only ch 2 and art 3:1(2) GALA do apply to executive action, but the impact of these general provisions is limited (and hardly litigated in costly civil law court procedures).

[5] See, eg, in this book M Heintzen, 'Codification of Administrative Law in Germany and the European Union', section I.B.i; and F Uhlmann, 'Codification of Administrative Law in Switzerland', section IV.B.

[6] Article 120 of the Dutch Constitution.

exists at the decentralised level, when it comes to the preparation of generally binding regulations by municipal and provincial councils, inter alia. The 'constitutional decision-making' is hardly governed by the GALA at all. For example, under Article 1:1(2)(a) GALA, the primary legislator is not regarded as an administrative authority and hence does not fall within the scope of the GALA. Under Article 8:3 GALA, no appeal lies to the administrative law court against rules and policy. The Dutch legal system is not familiar with a concept like the notice-and-comment rule-making procedure or with other modes of formal participation rights of citizens in rule-making. This might be a consequence of the pluralistic political party system and the traditional 'polder model' in the Netherlands.[7] The political system is based on consensus, which may be very hard to reach within coalitions and should not be too easily overturned by courts. That said, interested parties may appeal against their individual implementing decision and then claim that the decision is based on unlawful rules.

## C. Civil Law

In addition, there are subjects that are associated with civil law rather than administrative law. Contrary to many other legal systems in the Netherlands, civil law is generally applied in contractual relationships involving public authorities. According to the most commonly accepted 'general doctrine', civil law is the 'general law'. Administrative law only governs relations between the government and citizens on a subsidiary basis, that is, if this is explicitly regulated by law. This 'general doctrine' also means that a public body is allowed to use private law instruments insofar as this does not interfere with its public powers.[8] Law on agreements, including rules on the formation and execution of contracts, is laid down in the Burgerlijk Wetboek (BW) (Civil Code). This code does not contain separate provisions on contracts with the government. However, the civil court may flesh out the open standards defined in the general rules by applying administrative law standards, such as the general principles of sound administration.

In general, the civil law courts fulfil a role as residual courts in disputes with the government. As long as a plaintiff puts forward a civil law-based claim, the civil courts accept competence to rule on the claim made. However, when an appeal within administrative courts has been open to the plaintiff, his or her claim will be

[7] eg, B van Klink and NT Arnoldussen, 'Dutch Legal Culture: Limits to the Soft Approach' in LJ van den Herik, EH Hondius and WJM Voermans (n 2) 13 ff.

[8] eg, L van den Berge, 'Rethinking the Public-Private Law Debate in the Age of Governmentality and Network Governance: An Analyses of French, English and Dutch Administrative Law' (2018) 5(2) *European Journal of Comparative Law and Governance* 119, 119 ff; FJ van Ommeren, 'Governance and the Public-Private Law Divide in the Netherlands' in ALB Colombi Ciacchi et al (eds), *Law and Governance: Beyond the Public-Private Law Divide?* (The Hague, Boom Legal Publishers, 2013).

deemed inadmissible within the civil law courts. As a result, civil law courts can rule on torts, on disputes about contracts and about regulations, and on disputes concerning deeds of fact.

# II. Sources of Administrative Law in the Netherlands

## A. The GALA

*The* source of administrative law is definitely the GALA, as it lays down a broad range of general rules, from the different forms of action, to the principles to be applied, to the forms of legal protection that can be obtained. It regulates both the decision-making within the administration and the appeals procedure within courts (or, to frame it in a German comparison: the GALA is both a Verwaltungsverfahrensgesetz as a Verwaltungsgerichtsordnung). Comparatively it is supposed to be one of the most extensive administrative law codifications. It consists of 11 chapters, encompassing over 500 sections at the time of writing. Many provisions are rather technical in nature with numerous procedural aspects, while the codification of general administrative law principles is rather sober, which is described below in section III.D. For example, the principle of equality and the legal protection of expectations have not been codified.

Besides the GALA, there are hundreds if not thousands of statutory provisions that grant administrative authorities the power to act for the purpose of performing a public service and that regulate such action in a detailed way. This includes specific rules in numerous branches of law, such as social security law, immigration law and environmental law. In any given case, there is a strong interaction between these sector-specific rules and the GALA: administrative powers are created within the specific laws (eg, to grant a subsidy or permit, or to fine an offender); the GALA itself provides hardly any powers. Whenever a special law empowers any administrative authority to issue an order, it is required, when exercising such powers, to comply with the GALA rules.

## B. The Relationship between the GALA and Specific Legislation

The relationship between general and special rules is more precisely defined by the GALA. In this context, four kinds of general rules can be distinguished. First, the GALA contains mandatory provisions. These are rules that are applicable, without any exceptions, to all administrative law interactions – for example, the rule that administrative powers may not be used for a purpose other than for which they were conferred (Article 3:3 GALA). Secondary legislators cannot make any exceptions to this. Apart from mandatory law, the GALA includes rules that are considered the 'best regulation' for normal cases, but that can be departed from in special cases, as well as by secondary legislators. This holds true, for example, of the provision that an application for an individual decision must be submitted in writing (Article 4:1 GALA): sometimes it should also be possible to do so orally, because the standard rule includes the phrase 'unless otherwise provided by law'. In addition, there are situations where it is hard to define a generally applicable rule, but where it is desirable to create a 'residual provision' in case the drafters of special legislation fail to include a provision. An example of this can be found in Article 4:13 GALA. The time limit for an individual decision depends on the type of decision applied for and that is why this time limit had better be laid down in a special law. However, in the absence of a special time limit, the general (and waivable) GALA provision applies, which states that the decision must be rendered within 'a reasonable period', which cannot exceed eight weeks in that case. Finally, the GALA contains provisions that may well be called 'optional'. The GALA contains an extended preparatory procedure for orders that involve many interested parties or have a significant impact on the surroundings. This uniform preparatory public procedure of Division 3.4 is applicable if it is so provided by the special legislator or by the relevant administrative authority making the order. Especially in the field of environmental law, this preparatory procedure is prescribed.

Consequently, the GALA provides for an inherently flexible regulatory framework for Dutch administrative procedures, leaving the drafters of special laws and administrative authorities with wide scope for discretion in some respects. In addition, it should be borne in mind that the GALA does not have a special status as an Act of Parliament. This means that special laws of the same status (other statutes) may permit departures from the GALA. Even so, the 'Aanwijzingen voor de regelgeving' (Drafting Instructions for Legislation)[9] provide that departures from the GALA should be permitted only where these are necessary and that the reason for the departures must be stated in the explanatory memorandum to the special statute. Important specific statutes containing departures from the GALA include the Vreemdelingenwet 2000 (Aliens Act 2000) and the Algemene wet inzake Rijksbelastingen (General Act on Government Taxes).

## C. Policy Rules

In legal practice, administrative policy rules form an important source of detailed administrative law. Once an administrative power has been vested upon an administrative authority, this power implies the competence to establish policy rules. Article 4:81 GALA explicitly states that an administrative authority may establish policy rules in respect of a power conferred to it, which is exercised under

[9] A circular of the Prime Minister of 18 November 1992 (see wetten.overheid.nl), used at government ministries.

its responsibility or which has been delegated by it. These policy rules lay down a general rule for weighing interests, determining facts or interpreting statutes (Article 1:3(4) GALA). Citizens can invoke the application of policy rules on the basis of the principle of legal certainty. However, the rules are not formally binding in the way that regulations are. The administrative authority shall act in accordance with the policy rule unless, due to special circumstances, the consequences for one or more interested parties would be out of proportion with the purposes of the policy rule (Article 4:84 GALA).

Where in some legal systems there can be a debate as to whether administrative authorities have the competence to draft policy rules (because that may interfere with the legislator's competence), in the Dutch legal order the discussion is rather if an authority is obliged to draft policy rules to ensure legal certainty, consistency and equality. Within government, administrative efficiency is highly valued, which leads to the practice of very detailed policy rules, from which public authorities hardly deviate in practice. Currently it is under debate as to whether the possibility to deviate under Article 4:84 GALA should be transformed into a *legal duty* to deviate if the proportionality principle so requests. This is part of a broader debate on how to transform a rather technical, bureaucratic administrative law into a more responsive legal order and a more principle-based administration (see below, section IV.B).[10]

## D. Additional Sources of General Administrative Law

Though the GALA itself is broad in terms of regulated topics, it does not cover all topics that one might expect to find in a general codification. Most notably, the access to public information is left out of the Act; it is codified in the Wet openbaarheid van bestuur (Access to Information Act). This is quite striking, because it had been the plan from the outset to incorporate this piece of legislation within the GALA, as it uses the same general concepts and definitions like 'order' and 'administrative authorities'. Over the years, the incorporation plans were delayed and eventually abandoned, with the argument being that in essence access to information is a constitutional right linked to the proper functioning of democracies. The legislator considered it to be 'inappropriate' to adopt these democratic rights within a general Act on administrative law, which may illustrate a distorted relationship between administrative and constitutional law.

There have also been topics that were not that relevant, or too controversial, or not fully formed at the time of enactment of the GALA. As will be described below in section III.C, one of the main goals of the GALA was to systematise and codify existing case law. Topics like data-handling and the protection of personal

[10] See, eg: www.prettigcontactmetdeoverheid.nl; and YE Schuurmans, AEM Leijten and JE Esser, *Bestuursrecht op maat* (Leiden, Leiden University, 2020).

information is an example of a field of law that was not fully formed to codify at that moment. The legislator also considered some general legal principles to be underdeveloped in case law, so that they could not be codified in the 1990s. For example, the principle of equality, the principle of legal certainty and the principle of legitimate expectations were left out of the GALA not because the legislator denied their importance, but because the criteria and conditions to invoke these principles were not yet crystallised. This illustrates that for a long time, legal principles, especially those granting rights to citizens, were not that well developed in the legal system. Dutch administrative law traditionally grants public powers to public authorities, and states instructional norms and procedures with which the administration needs to comply. The notion that citizens could pose subjective rights against the state was for a long time commonly rejected and, consequently, more substantive legal principles have only materialised more recently in case law. The codification of administrative law principles within the GALA is not meant to be exhaustive. People may still invoke unwritten legal principles that are developed in case law. As a consequence, unwritten general administrative law is still relevant, especially in the field of principles of action.

There is one specific statute that makes general exceptions to the rules of the GALA. During the financial crisis that started in 2007/2008, the government wished to accelerate the realisation of major infrastructural projects to stimulate the economy. It had the impression that the GALA contained too many burdensome administrative procedural rules that caused delays in large building projects. In order to reduce these burdens, it experimented with variations from the GALA in the Crisis- en herstelwet (Crisis and Recovery Act). For example, in procedures (on environmental law projects) that fall within the scope of the Crisis and Recovery Act, local public authorities are denied legal standing and the time limits for raising grounds of appeal are far more strict than under the GALA. The government highly valued this system of 'efficient procedures', and it eventually decided to convert the temporarily Act into a permanent law and to transfer some provisions (like the introduction of a *Schutznorm* for plaintiffs) to the GALA (see Article 8:69a GALA).

## E. The Constitution

The importance of the Grondwet (Constitution) as a source of administrative law is rather limited in the Netherlands. The Constitution defines the organisational structure of government, from municipal to provincial and nationwide authorities, and confers powers upon the various branches of government. But, as stated above in section I, this tends to be framed solely as a part of constitutional law and not of an administrative law nature. To understand this perception, it should be noted that the Netherlands does not have a constitutional court and nor does it grants courts with the power to undertake a review on constitutionality. Article 120 of the Constitution explicitly states that the constitutionality of Acts of Parliament and treaties shall not be reviewed by the courts. Consequently, the constitutional provisions hardly form an integral aspect of administrative law. However, the political climate is changing after various scandals over harsh legislation and the current government plans to draft a bill to change Article 120 of the Constitution. Courts have neither jurisdiction to review whether the formal procedures for making statutes have been properly followed, nor the power to review statutes on their compliance with legal principles[11] Finally, within the Constitution, provisions on the administration are scarce. Article 107 of the Constitution holds that the general rules of administrative law shall be laid down in an Act of Parliament, but it does not lay down any individual right to a good administration or administrative justice.[12]

## F. European and International Law

The above-mentioned specific feature of the Dutch Constitution partly explains why the influence of international and EU law on the Dutch administrative law system can hardly be overstressed. In particular, the European Convention on Human Rights (ECHR), the Treaty on European Union and the Charter of Fundamental Rights of the European Union[13] have partly taken over the function of the national Constitution. These can be seen as important sources for Dutch administrative law, especially in terms of the regulation of legal principles and administrative law protection.[14] This impact is greatly increased due to Article 93 and 94 of the Dutch Constitution, which give direct effect to international law within the Dutch legal system. Individuals can invoke self-executing treaty provisions in court, and in the event of any conflict, these will prevail over national law.

A codification of European administrative law in the future will likely have an effect on the GALA. In 2021 a scholarly committee composed of eminent administrative law professors published a report on this subject. In this report they foresee, amongst other things, the introduction of various new principles of good administration and more attention for citizens' rights, a section on the withdrawal and rectification of decisions and a section on international administrative assistance.[15] In general, the orientation towards European administrative law in

[11] HR 27 Januari 1961, ECLI:NL:PHR:1961:AG2059 (*Prof Van den Berg*); HR 14 April 1989, ECLI:NL:HR:1989:AD5725 (Harmonisatiewet).

[12] See generally:H Corder, 'A Right to Administrative Justice: "New" or Just Repacking the Old?' in A von Arnauld, K von der Decken and M Susi (eds), *The Cambridge Handbook of New Human Rights* (Cambridge, Cambridge University Press, 2020).

[13] Charter of Fundamental Rights of the European Union [2012] OJ C326/391.

[14] Recently the ECJ ruling of 14 January 2021, Case C-826/18 (*Varkens in Nood*) on art 9 of the Convention on access to information, public participation in decision-making and access to justice in environmental matters (Aarhus) had a huge impact on the system of administrative adjudication, as members of the public could no longer be forced to participate in the uniform preparatory public procedure before they had access to the courts.

[15] Commissie Europeanisering algemeen bestuursrecht, *Europa en het algemeen bestuursrecht* (The Hague, Boom Juridisch, 2021), with a summary in English.

Dutch scholarship is quite positive. Although the committee opposes a mandatory applicability of a European GALA, it favours a voluntary adoption of many rules, concepts and principles by the Dutch legislator or courts, with the ambition of achieving a harmonised general administrative law.

## G. Conclusion

In general, one can say that the GALA is *the* source of administrative law, combined with sector-specific legislation, regulations and policy rules. Principles of action are partly codified in the GALA (eg, the duty to state reasons and the duty of due care), are derived from the ECHR and EU law, and still form an important part of unwritten law. So, if an administrative law topic is not regulated in either the GALA or sector-specific legislation, the courts may find a basis of administrative law in unwritten legal principles or international and European law. Though, as will be described below in section III.B, Dutch administrative law has a tradition of judicial deference to administrative decision-making. Consequently, if an administrative law topic falls outside a regulation, courts regularly decide that it is up to the discretion of the administration on how to deal with that topic (eg, how to withdraw certain decisions).

When it comes to forms of administrative action and administrative organisation, the GALA provides less guidance. Some forms of action, such as rule-making, policy-making and contracts, are not considered to be part of Dutch administrative law. Also, the organisation of the administration mainly falls outside the scope of administrative law. The Constitution lays down the basic rules for the organisation of the state, but as there is no constitutional review within courts, these constitutional provisions are non-appealable norms. However, administrative protection is extensively regulated in the GALA. The ECHR and EU law form an important additional source of administrative law.

# III. The Codification of Administrative Law

## A. Historical Development: Before the GALA

The development of the Dutch GALA should be viewed in relation to the nature and extent of government action in the Netherlands. Until the second half of the nineteenth century, such government action primarily comprised, apart from legislation, the regulation and maintenance of public order. The major expansion of government action did not take place until the second half of the nineteenth century as a result of the democratisation of society and the adoption of general suffrage, first for men (in 1917) and, soon afterwards, for women (1922). The subsequent socialisation of society meant that the government adopted many measures in such fields as working conditions, public housing and public health. Due to the economic crisis of the 1930s and the emergency measures the government took to deal with this crisis, government regulation of economic matters became common. After the Second World War, the reconstruction of the Netherlands required government action in a variety of fields in society. The nation's rapidly growing prosperity soon prompted the government to create an extensive social security system, bringing the scale of government action and the underlying legislation in the Netherlands to a climax.

In that time of sharp increase in government action, the technique of 'gelede normstelling' (delegated rule-making power) reached its full potential in the Netherlands. This technique means that specific rules are not just laid down in statutes, but that, quite frequently, rule-making powers are delegated to subordinate legislators. Besides, such legislation often confers discretionary administrative powers on public authorities on a large scale. Due to the enormous size and diversity of administrative law and the phenomenon of delegated rule-making powers, administrative law became a complex branch of law.

Accordingly, calls for systematisation and simplification through codification were to be expected. Already in 1905 there had been an attempt to create administrative justice by means of a first draft of a Code on administrative actions, drawn up by Secretary JA Loeff. This draft tried to expand the competence of civil law courts to administrative law disputes. After a fierce scholarly debate, specifically with Professor AAH Struycken, the bill was withdrawn, because judicial review (at that time with many noblemen on the courts) was seen as a danger to modern democracy. Administrative decision-making primarily asked for expertise and policy considerations, and was thought to be hardly limited by legal norms. For a long time, this event set the stage for the political and scholarly debate on the system of legal protection in the Netherlands.

Consequently, legal protection was mainly organised within the administrative system. Administrative powers were regulated in separate statutes, which also frequently created special legal procedures. This has given rise to a highly fragmented system of administrative procedures, somewhat like the British tribunal system.[16] It would take until 1976 (*Wet* administratieve rechtspraak overheidsbeschikkingen, Wet Arob) before the Netherlands would have a general procedure for judicial review, but many specialised tribunals and courts remained in place until the enactment of the GALA.

[16] See in this book S Nason, 'Codification of Administrative Law in the United Kingdom: Beyond the Common Law', section IV.B. Nowadays, there is a clear-cut divide between administrative and judicial bodies in the Netherlands, but this has not always been the case. The Dutch supreme administrative law court (the Administrative Jurisdiction Division of the Council of State) has developed out of an administrative body and for a long time, appeal lay mainly to this administrative body ('the Crown'). Article 6 ECHR prompted the replacement of this kind of legal protection by a final appeal to a 'real' court, ECtHR 23 October 1985, App No 8848/80 (*Benthem v The Netherlands*).

In 1983, it was laid down in Article 107 of the Dutch Constitution that the general rules of administrative law had to be adopted by an Act of Parliament. It is not without reason that this constitutional provision refers to 'general rules of administrative law'; it was expressly not the legislator's intention to come to a comprehensive, exhaustive administrative code.

## B. The Role of Doctrine and Dutch Legal Culture

Mainly because of this long absence of general administrative law courts and the patchwork of relevant statutes and regulations, administrative law as a scholarly discipline emerged rather late. The first handbook on administrative law was published in 1932.[17] The majority of the subsequent scholarly work was invested in systematising this new field of law, in the creation of a common vocabulary and in trying to derive common notions and principles to map an administrative law system. The Association for Administrative Law (VAR)[18] was of paramount importance in terms of the development of legal doctrine in this field of law. From 1939 onwards, it published *Preadviezen* annually, in which eminent law professors, judges and attorneys conceptualised many themes of administrative law. It also created special committees or working groups on major themes such as administrative law principles, the future of the administrative justice system and the EU influence on national administrative law.

Doctrine did look to other countries to see how an administrative law system could be shaped and what kind of general administrative law principles were developed in countries with a more mature administrative law system. For a long time, the French and German legal systems have been the ones that Dutch law professors mainly studied and looked to for inspiration.[19] Although the impact on the courts system (mainly a French blueprint) was evident and legal theory was clearly inspired by German (and Austrian) scholarship,[20] it is hard to say whether the Dutch system is orientated towards one of these systems. The strong German focus on the *Rechtsstaat* and a full jurisdiction of the administrative law courts does not relate to Dutch legal culture, where the emphasis is instead on democracy and the sovereignty of Parliament (and a constitutional prohibition on courts from reviewing the constitutionality of parliamentary acts). The French legal system

[17] CW van der Pot et al (eds), *Nederlandsch bestuursrecht,* (Alphen aan den Rijn, Samsom, 1932).

[18] www.verenigingbestuursrecht.nl.

[19] JP de Jong, *Bestuursrecht van vreemde herkomst: een onderzoek naar de bronnen en grondslagen van een drietal centrale elementen van de Nederlandse bestuursrechtstheorie* (Zwolle, WEJ Tjeenk Willink, 1988).

[20] In particular, Professor Buijs studied Austrian and Prussian administrative law extensively as a form of inspiration to Dutch law: see JT Buijs, 'De administratieve rechtspraak in Duitschland', *Bijdragen tot de kennis van het staats-, provinciaal en gemeentebestuur in Nederland*, Deel 21 (1877), pp 1 ff (Deel I), pp 145 ff (Deel II).

did not fit smoothly, with a broad jurisdiction for administrative law courts (while the Netherlands favours the general doctrine of civil law as the general law to be applied). Also the procedural law of the Conseil d'État met with opposition in Parliament because it was considered far too complex and costly for adoption within the Netherlands.[21] From a constitutional and separation of powers perspective, the Dutch system instead has parallels with the British system: both have a strong focus on the role of Parliament, grant wide discretionary powers to the administration and have a legal tradition in which courts show deference to administrative decision-making.

Moreover, the interplay between academia and legal practice is strong within the Netherlands. Many law professors also function as deputy judges in courts. For a long time, there has existed a publication culture in which academics write extensive case notes on important court rulings. There are numerous legal journals that exclusively publish case law and case notes.[22] Consequently, a lively academic debate exists, which is strongly fuelled by case law, that legal scholars recognise in common law scholarship. Many study whether the GALA has been properly applied in these cases, whether the interpretation of the law is coherent compared to similar cases, and whether a more dynamic interpretation is needed due to developments in, for example, society, technique or European and international law.

## C. The Codification of the GALA

The preparation of the GALA took a long time. As early as 1982, the government set up an initial working party led by the then State Secretary of Justice, Michiel Scheltema, which was assigned the job of drafting general rules of administrative law. In addition to legislative staffers, administrative law academics invariably sat on this commission. The Scheltema Commission stated that the most important objective of the codification of general rules of administrative law was the promotion of uniformity of administrative legislation. Further, administrative legislation had to be systematised and, where possible, simplified, and significant administrative case law developments could be codified. Finally, the Commission considered the possibility of adopting general rules for administrative law subjects that, by their nature, are not suitable for specific statutes. In the end, the preliminary drafts drawn up by the Scheltema Commission evolved into the GALA.

[21] KAWM de Jong, *Snel eenvoudig en onkostbaar: Over continuïteit en verandering in de aard en de inrichting van het bestuursprocesrecht in 1815 tot 2015* (The Hague, Boom Juridische uitgevers, 2015) pp 26 ff.

[22] Administratieve Beschikkingen (AB, published by Kluwer) and Jurisprudentie Bestuursrecht (JB, published by Sdu) are the most commonly read. Landmark cases of Dutch administrative law are collected in T Barkhuysen et al (eds), *AB Klassiek* (Deventer, Kluwer, 2016).

The GALA is a piece of legislation that continues to evolve. By design, it is a 'modular Act', as it is called, which means that it is enacted in stages. The first two major stages of the Act entered into force on 1 January 1994. These laid a solid foundation of an Act designed to provide a regulatory framework for administrative authorities that issue orders and to grant interested parties the ability to undertake judicial review. In 1998 a third stage was enacted (mainly on supervision over administrative authorities) and 2009 saw the enactment of a fourth stage (mainly on rules of enforcement, including administrative fines). In addition, minor and major legislative proposals designed to supplement the GALA are instituted quite regularly, which means it is an ongoing legislative process. More recent adaptations include a revision of Chapter 8 of the GALA to make court procedures more efficient[23] and adaptations relating to the digitalisation of government, which result in possibilities to communicate and litigate electronically.[24]

## *i. The Nature of the GALA*

Given the objective of making administrative law uniform, the legislator had to make some fundamental choices. In the explanatory memorandum[25] to the first stage, the legislator mentions themes that may show a 'fundamental orientation'. In quite a detailed fashion, it deals with the general approach of the legal relationship between administrative authorities and citizens. It argues that this relationship has developed into a 'mutual relationship' between the administration and individuals. The legislator advanced a larger responsibility for individuals, resulting in procedural duties such as the duty to state the grounds of appeal and to adduce evidence. Many scholars objected to this view because of the unilateral law-making power of the administration. Many years later, we have to conclude that although the procedural obligations of individuals have increased significantly, the concept of a mutual relationship did not take root.

It was judicial procedure law in particular that prompted the legislator to present fundamental considerations about the nature of administrative law and the duties of the court. An important development is that the legislator gave priority to legal protection over the principle of legality. This means that if any order conflicts with specific rules but the interested party has not objected to these illegalities, the order does not have to be annulled. In doing so, the legislator has opted to develop procedural law in the direction of a 'recours subjectif', trend that has indeed become stronger over time. The conditions for having standing have

[23] Wet aanpassing bestuursprocesrecht of 2013 (Parliamentary papers 32450, *Stb* 2012, 682).

[24] Vereenvoudiging en digitalisering procesrecht of 2016 (KEI; Parliamentary papers 34059, *Stb* 2016, 288) and a proposal to transform the possibility of electronical communication into a right of digital access to the administration, Wet modernisering elektronisch bestuurlijk verkeer, (Parliamentary papers 35261).

[25] All parliamentary papers on the GALA, including the explanatory memoranda, can be found at: www.pgawb.nl.

been specified and individualised, a *Schutznorm* has been added and the possibilities to settle disputes definitely have been extended.[26] The legislator attaches great significance to judicial efficiency; procedural law should be both effective and efficient. In addition, there should be a low threshold for administrative proceedings. Individuals should be able to go to court without incurring high costs, with few formalities and without an attorney-at-law. The court is active and may, if necessary, counterbalance the inequality between the individual and the administrative authority.

Apart from the above, the GALA – and, indeed, Dutch administrative law in general – is not defined by dogmas to a great extent; the Act is of quite a practical, detailed and procedural nature. There are multiple rules on modes of communication, hearings, fact-finding possibilities and publication duties, to name but a few. General legal principles are more scarce (those present are noted in the text below), and those of a more substantive nature are almost entirely absent. If we combine these features with a culture of wide discretionary administrative powers and judicial deference, it may be clear that procedural law is very well developed, but the system scores less on substantive values and principles governing public administration.[27]

### *ii. The Structure of the GALA*

After the key definitions in the Chapter 1, Chapter 2 of the GALA continues with general rules about the relationship between citizens and administrative authorities. These rules apply to all dealings between individuals and administrative authorities, and are of a general nature, like the language that can be used to communicate.[28] There are some relatively new provisions about electronic communication between administrative authorities and interested parties, which are already proposed to be revised in order to grant citizens a right of digital access to the administration.[29]

Chapter 3 contains general provisions on 'orders' (called decisions in most other systems), such as provisions concerning the preparation and notification of orders, and the duty to state reasons for them. This chapter places important quality requirements on the decision-making practice. For example, orders must be prepared with due care (Article 3:2 GALA), powers may not be used for any purpose other than that for which they were conferred by the legislator

[26] KJ de Graaf and AT Marseille, 'On Administrative Adjudication, Administrative Justice and Public Trust: Analyzing Developments of on Access to Justice in Dutch Administrative Law and its Application in Practice' in S Comtois and KJ de Graaf (eds), *On Lawmaking and Public Trust* (The Hague, Eleven International Publishing, 2016) 103 ff.

[27] *cf* the Netherlands Opinion on the Legal Protections of Citizens of the Venice Commission, Opinion No 1031/2021.

[28] Communication in another language is allowed if it is more effective and does not harm the interests of third persons (art 2:6 GALA); communication in English is generally accepted.

[29] Articles 2:13–2:17 GALA; see above n 24.

(Article 3:3 GALA) and the interests concerned must be weighed in a proportionate manner (Article 3:4 GALA).

Next, Chapter 4 of the GALA includes provisions on specific types of orders, such as individual decisions and, particularly, on orders granting subsidies and orders relating to money debts arising from administrative law. For example, there are provisions allowing interested parties to express their views and to participate, on the time limit for orders and on what an interested party can do if the administrative authority fails to meet this time limit for decision-making.

Chapter 5 of the GALA relates to the enforcement of regulation by administrative authorities. It provides for general rules for inspections and for administrative sanctions that are important in practice, including the 'last onder bestuursdwang' (administrative enforcement order) (ie, an administrative measure for the restoration of a legal situation) and the administrative fine.

Chapters 6, 7 and 8 contain rules for legal protection under administrative law. Review within the administration is still a key feature of the system of legal protection. Interested parties can only ask for judicial review if they previously lodged an appeal within the administration.[30] The benefits of administrative review are still highly valued: it is an informal procedure, in which errors of the administration can be easily corrected and many disputes get resolved. It functions as an important funnel; about 90 per cent of all objectives get resolved, which lowers the burden on the administrative law courts. In most cases, rulings of administrative courts are open to appeal to the Administrative Jurisdiction Division of the Council of State.[31] Chapter 9 of the GALA deals with complaint handling by administrative authorities (like the National Ombudsman) and Chapter 10 contains provisions on the conferral of powers and the delegation of the power to make orders, and on the supervision of administrative authorities. The final provisions of the Act, which include the duty to draw up evaluation reports, are laid down in Chapter 11.

As a result, the GALA has become a 'layered' act, structured from general towards ever more specific provisions. For example, where an administrative authority makes an order to pay an advance in anticipation of a sum of money to be paid later (Article 4:95 GALA, included in Division 4.4 GALA), the rules of Chapter 2 concerning dealings between individuals and administrative authorities are applicable to this order, as are the provisions on orders laid down in Chapter 3. Further, the specific provisions relating to individual decisions of Division 4.1 of the GALA are applicable.

### *iii. Towards Uniformity in Administrative Law*

All in all, the enactment of the first four stages of the GALA and some smaller legislative proposals formed a legislative operation that cannot be easily surpassed,

[30] Articles 8:1 juncto 7:1 and 6:13 GALA.

[31] The Dutch appeal system is fragmented. In some cases, appeal lies to other appellate courts, such as the Central Appeals Tribunal, the Trade and Industry Appeals Tribunal, and the Tax Courts.

in terms of its scope and speed, in the Netherlands. The operation not only introduced a general Act with a broad scope of application, but also triggered a huge operation to amend other legislation. The legislation needed to amend special laws, so as to bring them into line with the provisions of the GALA, comprises thousands of amendments spread across hundreds of statutes. The impact of this Act on Dutch administrative law has therefore been great; some have even called it a cultural revolution in the field of administrative law. The GALA has triggered a process leading towards greater uniformity. This huge codification project was broadly supported by political factions, as a paramount incentive of the operation was to increase the accessibility of administrative law, to simplify it and hence to contribute to effective administration.

# IV. Dynamics and Debates

## A. The Effects of Codification

Over the last 25 years, the administrative law community has periodically celebrated through conferences and publications the fact that the GALA has been in force for 5, 10, 15 or 25 years.[32] Praise for the GALA seems primarily related to the clear systematisation of a previous dispersed field of law. This systematisation with uniform rules has various benefits. Administrative law as a field of law has become far more accessible, in which legal rules are better known. General codification fuels deliberation. The full attention of the legislator and parliamentary and scholarly debates results in a higher quality of law. Now that all legal actors share the same vocabulary, they have the language to discuss the objectives of legal norms and the desirability of their application. In general, it is thought that the GALA has formed a true accelerator for legal development, both within the administration and the courts.[33]

It is hard to say more exactly what the effect of a general codification is. In a study into the effect of the codification of the fourth stage, it appeared that the topic codified and the primary objective for codification were of relevance.[34] If the main objective is the codification of an already-existing practice, the effect of the codification seems limited and hardly steering the direction of legal development.

[32] FAM Stroink et al (eds), *Vijf jaar JB en Awb* (The Hague, Sdu, 1999); FAM Stroink et al (eds), *Tien jaar JB en Awb* (The Hague, Sdu, 2004); T Barkhuysen, W den Ouden and JEM Polak (eds), *Bestuursrecht harmoniseren: 15 jaar Awb* (The Hague, Boom Legal Publishers, 2010); T Barkhuysen et al, *25 jaar Awb. In eenheid en verscheidenheid* (Deventer, Kluwer, 2019).

[33] M Scheltema, 'Codificatie van het bestuursrecht' (1996) *Nederland Tijdschrift voor bestuursrecht* 2, 2 ff; BJ Schueler, 'De Awb en de bijzondere delen van het bestuursrecht' in T Barkhuysen, W den Ouden and JEM Polak (eds), *Bestuursrecht harmoniseren: 15 jaar Awb* (The Hague, Boom Legal Publishers, 2010) pp 173 ff.

[34] R Ortlep, W den Ouden, YE Schuurmans et al, 'Nut en noodzaak van een algemene codificatie van bestuursrecht' (2014) *Netherlands Administrative Law Library*, DOI: 10.5553/NALL/.000020.

If, on the other hand, the codification strives to harmonise a highly dispersed legal topic, the codification seems to be able to truly direct legal development, as was the case for subsidies and inspections in the Netherlands. Another factor that is in play concerns the burdensomeness of the rules for the administration. If the codification facilitates the decision-making process or grants broader powers to administrative authorities, one can expect a willingness within the administration to apply the new rules. The GALA, for example, broadened the fact-finding possibilities for administrative authorities during inspections, which were highly welcomed in practice. If, on the contrary, the rules raise administrative duties, one sometimes sees the reflex that public authorities draw up 'new' uncodified legal instruments so as to evade administrative duties. In financial law, administrative authorities created new financial instruments that supposedly purposely did not fit in the definition of subsidies within the GALA and consequently had less clear rules to comply with.[35]

Codification does not inherently lead to uniform law in practice. As described above in section II, the GALA has no special status as a statute; deviations can be made by the legislator and sometimes even by the administration itself. Relatively little is known of how often these deviations appear in practice. The Ministries of Finance and of Education in particular are notorious for their desire to draw up their own specific rules. The general rules of the GALA would leave insufficient room for carefully shaping the decision-making with due regard for the special characteristics of the branch of law concerned. In an evaluation of the rules on money debts in administrative law (Title 4.4 GALA), researchers found that in practice, sector-specific rules were far more often applied than the 'general' rules of the GALA.[36] A rule does not become inherently 'general' in practice if it makes it to a general rule in the GALA.

There might also be the effects of non-codification of certain themes. As systematisation improves the accessibility of law, non-codification may leave certain themes underdeveloped. Naturally, case law can fill that gap, but scholarly and professional attention for these dispersed themes seems more scarce. When it comes to the GALA, many scholars are of the opinion that the ratio between procedural and substantive norms is off-balance. In particular, the lack of more substantive legal principles, granting citizens subjective rights, has been criticised. Sometimes the impression arises that the GALA legislator sticks to provisions of a more procedural and technical nature to avoid the need to make difficult material choices. Given its general nature, the GALA contains mostly procedural rules and, as a result, decision-making practice – and legal scholarship – shows a strong focus on procedure.

This supposedly leads to a 'juridification' of the relationship between citizens and the administration, which is reinforced by the jurisdiction provisions in

[35] R Ortlep, W den Ouden, YE Schuurmans et al (n 34).

[36] W den Ouden, CNJ Kortmann et al, *De bestuursrechtelijke geldschuldenregeling. Titel 4.4 Awb geëvalueerd* (The Hague, WODC, 2013).

the GALA. Individuals cannot submit their entire 'relationship' with the administration to the court, but only the issues that arise from orders that have been issued. Consequently, a multitude of fragmented procedures may arise. This strong orientation of the GALA on the 'order' concept is increasingly being criticised, but it is doubtful whether this fundamental orientation will soon be discarded.

That said, the legislator is willing to experiment with general administrative law. A recent phenomenon is that legal concepts which differ from the GALA rules are put to the test in special laws, also for the purpose of ascertaining whether they could eventually be incorporated into the GALA. Various provisions to improve the efficiency of legal procedures were firstly introduced in the Crisis and Recovery Act (see above, section II.D) and later on were adopted in the GALA. Currently the government plans to experiment with a broader concept of jurisdiction, making it possible for administrative law courts to review the legal relationship integrally in a specific field of social welfare.

## B. Debates on Future Developments

Finally, it is debated whether the pursuit of generally applicable administrative law has gone too far or whether provisions have become too detailed. Many experts have come to regret the absence of a comprehensive view on the legislative project of the GALA. Over the years, it seemed that the legislator paid particular attention to sub-topics, which were put on the political agenda more or less randomly. Even now, it is often pointed out that the present GALA fails to deal with obvious topics, such as provisions on the withdrawal of decisions, data-handling and a right to information, as well as provisions on administrative contracts. But political interest in the GALA has been poor in recent years[37] and little capacity to improve the GALA has been left within the Ministries of Justice and Internal Affairs. As a result, the expectations for a new stage for the GALA are low.

Undeniably, the GALA has contributed to the positive development of administrative law in the Netherlands, but the question arises as to whether there should be more room for variability, less attention paid to technicalities and a stronger focus on legal principles. Possibly, legal principles and principles of good administration bring more coherence and logic to a system than an extensive codification does. Former State Secretary of Justice Scheltema stated that if he were to work again on the GALA from scratch, he would define the objectives of the codification differently. Back then, the objectives fitted within the bureaucratic administrative state, focusing on systems, internal logic and legal certainty. However, nowadays he would aim for more reflection on the concept of the rule of law and how the GALA helps citizens to perceive they truly live in a *Rechtsstaat*. In recent years,

[37] For this political notion, see also in this book M Heintzen (n 5) section I.C.

he has made it his mission to transform administrative law so as to fit into a more responsive legal order.[38] Now that we have so much more knowledge and awareness of the (sometimes limited) capacities of citizens and the complexity of many specialised administrative fields of law, we need to reconsider if the GALA really adds to administrative justice. The instrumental and procedural nature of the GALA sometimes seems to strengthen the position of the administration rather than that of citizens.

As is the case in the UK, it has been debated whether proportionality should be recognised as a general principle of domestic administrative law and a ground for review, meaning that all administrative decisions must be proportionate to the aims they seek to achieve.[39] Should the GALA be adjusted so as to force public authorities to always consider the proportionality of their decisions, even if statutes leave little room for such a proportionality review?[40] Many scholars see the need for a more principle-based orientation within the administration and a more rigorous review of administrative action, especially when fundamental rights are in play. This general opinion is not only influenced by notions of legitimacy and a more responsive government, but also by a desire for a better alignment with European law. In a legal opinion of the Advocates-General of 2021, it is recommended to develop a proportionality test in line with the three-step test of the European Court of Justice, a recommendation which has been adopted by the highest administrative law court.[41] Increasingly, the idea that Dutch administrative law should develop towards stronger subjective citizens' rights and a broader spectrum of legal principles is taking root. 'The GALA is a general administrative law Act that, according to Dutch tradition, does not build a strong bridge between constitutional guarantees and the requirements of good governance. This can and must be (gradually) changed under the influence of EU Law.'[42] The Act should be written less from the perspective of lawyers and more from that of citizens. Consequently, legal principles should be formulated less as administrative rules of conduct and more as general citizens' rights. For instance, a duty of due care can be transformed into a right to transparent administration, a right to have a participative and responsive administration, and a right to understandable an accessible information.

[38] M Scheltema, 'Bureaucratische rechtsstaat of responsieve rechtsstaat' (2015) 37 *Nederlands Tijdschrift voor Bestuursrecht* 287, 287 ff; M Scheltema, 'De responsieve rechtsstaat: het burgerperspectief' (2019) 24 *Nederlands Tijdschrift voor Bestuursrecht* 246, 246 ff.

[39] *cf* S Nason (n 16) section II.

[40] eg, JCA de Poorter, 'A Future Perspective on Judicial Review of Generally Binding Regulations in the Netherlands: Towards a Substantive Three-Step Proportionality Test' in J de Poorter, E Hirsch Ballin and S Lavrijssen (eds), *Judicial Review of Administrative Discretion in the Administrative State* (The Hague, TMC Asser Press/Springer, 2019) 83 ff.

[41] Opinion of Advocates-General Widdershoven and Wattel 7 June 2021, ECLI:NL:RVS:2021:1468; ABRvS 2 February 2022, ECLI:NL:2022:285.

[42] Commissie Europeanisering algemeen bestuursrecht, *Europa en het algemeen bestuursrecht* (The Hague, Boom Juridisch, 2021) p 82 (citation originally in Dutch).

In the extension of this development, more attention is paid to insights into procedural justice.[43] Administrative authorities should focus less on the legal side of objections and more on the importance and nature of the objection lodged by individuals. Within academia and Parliament, discussion has occurred on whether a legal obligation for the administration to investigate the possibility to meet the objections of citizens should be incorporated into the GALA, even if the objections do not relate to the unlawfulness of the decisions. Although no major stages are expected, the GALA is still adjusted on a regular basis so as to steer administrative law development in a certain direction.

## V. Conclusion

The GALA has been a milestone for Dutch administrative law and is definitely the main legal source. With the introduction of this Act on general rules of administrative law, more uniformity and systematisation has been achieved, and hence the clarity and accessibility of administrative law has been improved. Through this standardisation, the GALA has raised administrative law as a field of study to a higher level. Administrative authorities, courts and legal scholars use the same vocabulary to explain the rules and principles.

Even so, this extensive codification also has its drawbacks. The GALA tends to be a system on its own with its focus on systematisation. Its detailed rules may overshadow the general principles and public law values that are behind these detailed provisions. The procedural nature of many general rules is thought to have led to an imbalance in scholarly and practical attention for substantive versus procedural administrative law topics. Critical comments on this do not fall on deaf ears and lead to various plans to adjust the GALA in order to make it contribute to a more responsive administrative legal order.

[43] This development is also promoted by the Ministry of the Interior and Kingdom Relations; see K van den Bos, L van der Velden and EA Lind, 'On the Role of Perceived Procedural Justice in Citizens' Reactions to Government Decisions and the Handling of Conflicts' (2014) 10(4) *Utrecht Law Review* 1, 1 ff.

# 9

# Codification of Norwegian Administrative Law

JON CHRISTIAN FLØYSVIK NORDRUM

## I. The Definition and Delimitation of Administrative Law

### A. Introduction

In this chapter I give an overview of Norwegian administrative law with an emphasis on the sources of administrative law and its codification. By 'codification', I mean rules given in laws passed by Parliament. The core of the concept is when Parliament issues a statutory law that reflects a rule that already applies, but from another source of law, being the Constitution, administrative regulations or unwritten rules of any kind. It does not need to be an exact reflection – the law may be clarified or changed – but it replaces rules that are in place but not in statutory law. Outside my concept of codification is, for instance, when the administration writes down administrative practice in guidelines or administrative regulations.

### B. General and Special Administrative Law

Commonly *forvaltningsrett* (administrative law) refers to the body of legal rules that governs the relationship between the government and the citizens, the administration internally and the activities of governmental bodies, and judicial review of such activities. It is common to distinguish between *allmenn forvaltningsrett* (general administrative law) and *spesiell forvaltningsrett* (special administrative law). The former refers to rules that apply to the administration in general, while the latter refers to rules that apply only to a specific sector. It is also common to distinguish between *prosessuell* (procedural) and *materiell* (substantive) administrative law.[1]

[1] See in general HP Graver, *Alminnelig forvaltningsrett*, 5th edn (Oslo, Universitetsforlaget, 2019); T Eckhoff and E Smith, *Forvaltningsrett*, 12th edn (Oslo, Universitetsforlaget, 2022).

# II. Legal Sources of Administrative Law

## A. Introduction

Roughly described, procedural administrative law is codified, whereas substantive administrative law traditionally followed from case law. A significant recent development is the work and proposal by the Law Commission on the Public Administration Act (the PAA Commission), which was appointed by Royal Decree of 23 October 2015 to conduct a comprehensive review of the current Public Administration Act (PAA) and related non-statutory administrative law.[2] The PAA Commission has proposed codifying some elements of substantive administrative law.[3]

## B. Constitutional Basis

The constitutional reform of 2014 introduced a new chapter in the Constitution called *menneskerettigheter* ('Human Rights'). Several provisions have bearings on administrative law. Until then, very few constitutional paragraphs were directly relevant for administrative law. Some of the paragraphs are almost replicas of the European Convention on Human Rights (ECHR),[4] and the committee preparing the constitutional amendments explicitly referred to the ECHR.[5] Examples are access to court and fair trial (§ 95 of the Constitution),[6] the right to equal treatment before the law and the prohibition on disproportionate differential treatment (§ 98), the right to respect for privacy and family life (§ 102), children's rights (§ 104) and the right to education (§ 109).

The committee preparing the amendments stated that the proposal was in line with *gjeldende rett* (current law). However, these provisions, *in tandem* with the ECHR, have provided separate grounds for the Supreme Court to further develop administrative law (see below, section VII.C).

[2] The PAA Commission issued a comprehensive report in 2019. The report has been published in the Norwegian Official Reports (NOU) series as NOU 2019: 5 Ny forvaltningslov. An English summary is included in the report (at 52–64).

[3] The proposal would replace lov 10. februar 1967 om behandlingsmåten i forvaltningssaker (forvaltningsloven). The official translation reads: Act 10 February 1967 relating to procedure in cases concerning the public administration (Public Administration Act).

[4] Convention for the Protection of Human Rights and Fundamental Freedoms (Rome, 4 November 1950).

[5] Dokument 16 (2011–2012), Rapport til Stortingets presidentskap fra Menneskerettighetsutvalget om menneskerettigheter i Grunnloven.

[6] Kongeriket Norges Grunnlov 17. mai 1814 (Grunnloven).

## C. Legislation

The most important statutes of a *general* administrative nature are the PAA (1967), the Freedom of Information Act (2006),[7] the Archives Act (1992)[8] and the Civil Service Act (2017).[9] It is also worth mentioning the Instructions for official studies (2016),[10] which are an executive order with requirements on, inter alia, regulatory impact assessments, public hearings and the evaluation of statutes and regulations.

In addition, several Acts have general relevance for the administration. Two examples are the statutes incorporating the main part of the EEA agreement[11] (EEA Act 1992),[12] facilitating the incorporation of EEA-relevant EU directives and regulations, and the Human Rights Act 1999,[13] which incorporates several human rights conventions, most importantly the ECHR. In addition, there are broad statutes – for example, the Act on Services (2009)[14] – regulating the establishment of service providers within the scope of the EEA agreement, which in effect makes the administrative principles of EU law applicable to a wide range of sectors.[15]

Some statutory legislation has limited scope, but contains *general provisions* with a broader scope. An example is the Nature Diversity Act 2009,[16] which in §§ 7–12 contains principles for all decision-making in the public sector that may affect the environment, and which also makes it mandatory to consider the precautionary principle prior to any action of the public administration that may affect the environment. Another example is Chapter 14 of the Planning and Building Act 2008,[17] which makes regulatory impact assessment mandatory for all public actions and planning regardless of whether the Act itself applies. This Act with regulations on impact assessment implements, inter alia, the EU

[7] Lov 19. mai 2006 nr 16 om rett til innsyn i offentleg verksemd (offentleglova). The Freedom of Information Act (2006) replaced the Freedom of Information Act (1970). The 2006 Act strengthened access to information in line with the constitutional amendments in 2004 that included a principle of freedom of information.

[8] Lov 4. desember 1992 nr 126 om arkiv (arkivloven).

[9] Lov 16. juni 2017 nr 67 om statens ansatte mv (statsansatteloven).

[10] Instruks om utredning av statlige tiltak (utredningsinstruksen), fastsatt ved kgl res 19. februar 2016.

[11] Avtale om Det europeiske økonomiske samarbeidsområde (EØS), undertegnet i Oporto 2. mai 1992.

[12] Lov 27. november 1992 nr 109 om gjennomføring i norsk rett av hoveddelen i avtale om Det europeiske økonomiske samarbeidsområde (EØS) mv (EØS-loven).

[13] Lov 21. mai 1999 nr 30 om styrking av menneskerettighetenes stilling i norsk rett (menneskerettsloven).

[14] Lov 19. juni 2009 nr 103 om tjenestevirksomhet (tjenesteloven). The statute implements Directive 2006/123/EC of the European Parliament and of the Council of 12 December 2006 on services in the internal market [2006] OJ L376/36.

[15] On the relationship between and influence of EU administrative law on Norwegian administrative law, see CC Eriksen and HH Fredriksen, *Norges europeiske forvaltningsrett, EØS-avtalens krav til norske forvaltningsorganers organisering og saksbehandling* (Oslo, Universitetsforlaget, 2019).

[16] Lov 19. juni 2009 nr 100 om forvaltning av naturens mangfold (naturmangfoldloven).

[17] Lov 27. juni 2008 nr 71 om planlegging og byggesaksbehandling (plan- og bygningsloven).

Directives on Strategic Environmental Assessment (SEA).[18] In some areas there are specific comprehensive Acts governing administrative procedure, such as the Tax Administration Act 2016,[19] while in other areas some specific procedural rules are given that deviate from the general rules in the PAA.

There are several bodies with important tasks in the administrative system, which are governed by separate Acts. Examples are the Parliamentary Ombud Act 2021[20] and the National Insurance Court Act 1966.[21]

## D. Preparatory Works

In general, and particularly in administrative law, *preparatory works* are an important source of law.[22] This Norwegian and to a large extent also *Nordic* tradition of relying on preparatory works must be seen in the light of how Acts are prepared in the Norwegian system. Often the process starts with an ad hoc legislative commission issuing an extensive report (an *NOU*),[23] forming what is described by political scientists as a *policy advisory system*.[24] Interpretative guidelines in the preparatory works also play an important role due to the Norwegian legislative technique of short statutes with extensive delegation and the regular use of vague and broad terms.

The courts give considerable weight to preparatory works and the intention of the legislator in general. This has consequences for codification processes because the preparatory works fill the gaps in legislation and often give restatements of unwritten law, in a sense importing unwritten law as an underlying premise for legislation.[25]

## E. Administrative Practice

In several areas, administrative practices are, at least in practical terms, important sources of law. There is a doctrinal debate as to whether it is appropriate to view

[18] Directive 2001/42/EC of the European Parliament and of the Council of 27 June 2001 on the assessment of the effects of certain plans and programmes on the environment (the SEA directive) [2004] OJ L197/30.

[19] Lov 27. mai 2016 nr 14 om skatteforvaltning (skatteforvaltningsloven).

[20] Lov 18. juni 2021 nr 121 om Stortingets ombud for kontroll med forvaltningen (sivilombudsloven).

[21] Lov 16. desember 1966 nr 9 om anke til Trygderetten (trygderettsloven).

[22] See JCF Nordrum, *Bedre regulering – årsak-virkningsanalyser i norsk reguleringsprosess* (Oslo, Gyldendal, 2019) 485 ff.

[23] Reports from Norwegian law commissions are published in an official publication series entitled Norges offentlige utredninger (NOU). It is common to refer to these reports simply as an 'NOU'.

[24] J Christensen and C Holst, 'Advisory Commissions, Academic Expertise and Democratic Legitimacy: The Case of Norway' (2017) 44(6) *Science and Public Policy* 821.

[25] On the use of preparatory works in Nordic countries, see A Peczenik, *On Law and Reason*, 2nd edn (Dordrecht, Springer, 2009) ch 6.6.

such practice as *a source of law*. Still, partly as a consequence of the obligation to treat similar cases similarly, administrative practice is to a large extent binding on the administration itself. Due to the lack of administrative courts and the passive role of the courts in a wide range of areas, the significance of administrative practice should not be underestimated.

In some areas, administrative practice is routinely systematised and published in special publications. One example is the *Skatte ABC* (Tax ABC),[26] which was published for the first time in 1979 and is revised annually; it provides a summary practice, individual cases and interpretative statements, making it an instruction for the administration as well as it provides guidance for the general public. Studies have shown that such publications are used frequently and, in some areas, are the only source consulted by civil servants in practice.[27]

These types of publication are also quite often referred to in relevant preparatory works, and thereby facilitate codification. Examples of this are the codification of administrative practice and regulations in an Act relating to Social Services (1991) and the comprehensive General Social Insurance Act (1997).[28] The Supreme Court routinely refers to such publications as evidence of administrative practice.[29]

Sectors where court intervention is rare may experience self-enforcing loops: the administration issues guidelines where it refers to the administrative practice and its interpretation of other legal sources, which again forms the basis for administrative practice. One important example here is welfare authorities, where such loops are criticised in legal doctrine for easily being biased and decoupled from their statutory basis.[30]

# III. Principles of Action

## A. The Principle of Legality

The core principle of Norwegian administrative law is the *legalitetsprinsippet* (principle of legality), which has been considered a principle of unwritten constitutional

[26] Skatte-ABC 2022, www.skatteetaten.no/rettskilder/type/handboker/skatte-abc/gjeldende.

[27] T Eckhoff and HP Graver, *Regelstyring av lokale forvaltningsvedtak – Praktisering av bygningsloven* (Oslo, Tano, 1991).

[28] Lov 13. desember 1991 nr 81 om sosiale tjenester mv (sosialtjenesteloven); Lov 28. februar 1997 nr 19 om folketrygd (folketrygdloven). The law commissions preparing these acts explicitly described their proposals as mainly a codification of, inter alia, administrative practice. See NOU 1985: 18 Lov om sosiale tjenester mv; NOU NOU 1990: 20 Forenklet folketrygdlov. In the latter report the Commission formulated as an overarching objective 'to prepare a codified and consolidated statute, not a reform' (at 76) and 'important rules that now only are available in guidance from the welfare authorities should be codified' (at 80).

[29] See in general T Eckhoff and J Helgesen, *Rettskildelære*, 4th edn (Oslo, Tano, 1997) 223 ff.

[30] I Ikdahl, 'Hvilken vekt skal man legge på Trygderettens praksis? – Argumenter fra en empirisk studie av rettsutvikling i trygderettsforvaltningen' in R Førde, M Kjelland and U Stridbeck (eds), *Cand. mag., cand.med., cand.jur, cand.alt – Festskrift til Aslak Syse* (Oslo, Gyldendal Norsk Forlag, 2016).

law for a long time.[31] It was explicitly included in the Constitution as part of a larger constitutional modernisation that took place in 2014.

§ 113 of the Constitution states that: 'Infringement of the authorities against the individual must be founded on the law.'[32] Closely related to the administrative principle of legality is the prohibition on retroactive legislation (see § 97 of the Constitution, with its corollary for regulations in § 37 PAA) and the penal principle of legality (see § 96 of the Constitution). The latter has also been invoked in administrative proceedings concerning administrative sanctions and control as an argument for a stricter requirement of legality due to the penal character of the sanctions.[33] The principle of legality has been fleshed out primarily through case law.

An important formulation of how clear and definite the legislation must be was given in a Supreme Court decision from 1995:

> [T]he requirements of clear legal grounds must be considered in light of, inter alia, the area concerned, the nature of the intervention, how it affects and how burdensome it is to the party. Other sources than the law itself must also be considered taken in consideration the particularities of the case.[34]

This is sometimes referred to as the as *relativeness* of the principle of legality. The main question is how intrusive an administrative action or decision is. Consequently, decisions to use force in mental health care or in child welfare must be based on a precise and definite legislative formulation, whereas the requirement is more lenient for, eg, the regulation of business activities for the common good. A Supreme Court decision from 2010 illustrates the latter, the Court stated that the legislator chose the open wording 'den ansvarlige' (the accountable) deliberately to ensure that the administration, in the particular case, could decide who was to pay for the environmental impact assessment.[35]

There is currently a debate in Norway as to whether *the legislative techniques* give sufficiently precise and definite legislative text. The Parliamentary Ombudsman and the Norwegian National Human Rights Institution have criticised the wording in recent bills (see, eg, proposals on revisions to the Child Welfare Act 1992[36] and a new general Act on the Use of Force in Care)[37] for not being sufficiently precise. However, the Ministry of Justice criticised the same texts for being *too precise*, arguing that the text gave too little leeway for professional discretion and secondary legislation.[38]

[31] See generally T Eckhoff and E Smith (n 1) 353 ff; HP Graver (n 1) 79 ff.

[32] This is the translation given by the Storting (the Norwegian Parliament).

[33] See, eg, Rt 2002 p 1298 (Polarlaks). 'Rt' refers 'Norsk Retstidende' – the official Norwegian bulletin until 2015 for decisions from the Høyesterett (the Norwegian Supreme Court).

[34] Rt 1995 p 530 (*Fjordlaks*).

[35] Rt 2010 p 306 (*Hempel*).

[36] Lov 17. juli 1992 nr 100 om barneverntjenester (barnevernloven).

[37] NOU 2016: 16 Ny barnevernslov – Sikring av barnets rett til omsorg og beskyttelse; NOU 2019: 14 Tvangsbegrensningsloven – Forslag til felles regler om tvang og inngrep uten samtykke i helse- og omsorgstjenesten.

[38] Prop 169 L (2016–2017) Endringer i barnevernloven mv (bedre rettssikkerhet for barn og foreldre).

The general principles that administrative decision-making must be based on rational and relevant reasons, and cannot be arbitrary and capricious are not codified, but are developed in case law and in the doctrine, and are often referred to in preparatory works.[39] There is an ongoing debate in Norway as to whether to codify these principles, and the PAA Commission proposes codifying the main content of the abuse principle (*misbrukslæren*, rules on ultra vires).[40] One reason why, so far, few have argued that there is an acute need to put these principles into legislation might be that the Supreme Court seems to treat all these questions *en bloc* when considering whether the *written reasons* for administrative decisions are sufficient, and does not leave any doubt as to whether all the relevant considerations has been taken in to account.[41]

## B. The Principle of Proportionality

There is no explicit general constitutional or legislative formulation of a principle of proportionality in Norwegian administrative law. Some requirements of proportionality enjoy a constitutional basis, eg, § 98 of the Constitution, which states: 'No human being must be subject to unfair or disproportionate differential treatment.'

It is debated whether a *general* unwritten principle of proportionality actually exists in Norwegian administrative law.[42] However, the case law makes it clear that administrative decisions cannot be *grossly* disproportionate and that there are some decisions that can be construed to apply a principle of proportionality.[43] In addition, in all fields that are within the scope of the ECHR (eg, health law and child welfare legislation) or within the scope of the EEA agreement, it follows from the relevant European sources that actions must be proportionate. While the Supreme Court has refrained from formulating an explicit general principle of proportionality, it has tended to conclude that the written reasons given are not sufficient when presented with seemingly disproportionate administrative actions.[44]

Further, a number of specific Acts codify a principle of proportionality (eg, in health and welfare legislation) often formulated as a *prinsippet om mildeste inngrep* (least intrusive means) and often in regulatory law where administrative actions are typically deemed 'necessary'. Often these legislative formulations are legislative

[39] See generally, T Eckhoff and E Smith (n 1).

[40] NOU 2019: 5 Ny forvaltningslov p 548.

[41] See in general OH Moen, *Forvaltningsskjønn og domstolskontroll* (Oslo, Gyldendal, 2019).

[42] See ibid; M Stub, *Tilsynsforvaltningens kontrollvirksomhet* (Oslo, Universitetsforlaget, 2011).

[43] See, inter alia, Rt 1973 p 460 (*Fjærkre*), which concerned an administrative order to slaughter poultry due to potential contamination and health hazards. The court found that the order was 'unnecessary'.

[44] See, eg, Rt 1981 p 745 (*Isene*) and Rt 2000 p 1066. See in general OH Moen (n 41) ch 5.5.5.

requirements that have been formulated and claimed to be a codification of a general principle of proportionality.[45]

## C. The Principle of Minimum Standards or Responsibility

Closely related to principles of proportionality is the principle of a *minimumsstandard* (minimum standard). The origins of this doctrine can be traced back to Supreme Court cases from the 1960 and 1970s, where the educational authorities were held liable for damages caused by malpractice concerning pupil's educational needs. The principle was then applied in health law in a landmark case from the Supreme Court in 1990, in which the Court held that a decision on healthcare given to a disabled woman did not meet a minimum standard.[46]

In several areas, the existence of this standard is now recognised explicitly by the legislator through codification, often phrased as a *forsvarlighetsprinsipp* (principle of responsibility) – examples are § 4–1 of the Health and Care Service Act and § 1–4 of the Child Protection Act.[47] Even though the wording differs, it is clear from at least some of the preparatory works that the intention is to codify the court-made principle of minimum standards. The Education Law Commission proposing a new Education Act has proposed codifying the principle in § 1–3 of the Education Act.[48] This proposal also relied on the constitutional right to education, included in § 104 of the Constitution in 2014, which makes it explicit that educational services must meet a minimum threshold.[49]

## D. The Principle of Good Faith and Legitimate Expectations

There is no explicitly formulated principle of *good faith* or *legitimate expectation* in Norwegian administrative law. However, it is of legal relevance in many contexts whether actions are taken in good faith, and likewise foreseeability and legitimate expectations are core values often referred to as arguments. When considering whether administrative decisions giving rights to citizens are invalid, due to, for example, procedural faults, a major consideration is whether the citizen in good faith has exercised the right and has legitimate expectations to continue doing so.

[45] See, eg, Ot prp nr 100 (2002–2003) Om lov om matproduksjon og mattrygghet mv (matloven) p 157 (preparatory works to the law on food production and food safety).

[46] Rt 1990 p 874 (*Fusa*); in education law the Court found that special education provided did not meet the minimum requirements in Rt 1993 p 811 (*Malvik*).

[47] Lov om 24. juni 2011 nr 30 kommunale helse- og omsorgstjenester m.m. (helse- og omsorgstjenesteloven); Lov 17. juli 1992 nr 100 om barneverntjenester (barnevernloven).

[48] The codification of the principle is discussed in NOU 2019: 23 Ny opplæringslov pp 191 ff.

[49] The Human Rights Committee preparing the amendements explicitly referred to a minimum standard, Dokument 16 (2011–2012) Rapport til Stortingets presidentskap fra Menneskerettighetsutvalget om menneskerettigheter i Grunnloven p 222.

## E. Administrative Liability

The administration can be liable for losses caused by administrative activity or passivity. The Act on Damage Compensation 1969[50] codified – in very brief terms – general court-made principles of tort law as they apply to administrative actions. These general rules are mainly developed through the interplay between legal doctrine and case law. However, there are examples of extensive codification of rules on public liability in specific areas; one example is the Patient Harm Act, which codifies with some modifications the tort principles for health services.[51] The Patient Harm Act is also an example that courts may be hesitant to establish or expand legal responsibility where the unwritten law is unclear or does not substantiate the claim.[52]

# IV. Forms of Actions

The most important source of administrative law is the PAA, which entered into force on 1 January 1970.[53] This was the first general Norwegian administrative procedure Act, although there had been several statutes with extensive regulations of administrative proceedings in specific areas. The statute regulates the conduct of administrative bodies in general. In addition, there are specific rules concerning *forskrifter* (administrative rule-making), *enkeltvedtak* (individual administrative decisions) and *forvaltningssanksjoner* (administrative sanctions).[54]

Administrative rule-making is an important feature of the Norwegian administrative state. In several sectors, the statutes primarily serve as a legal basis for administrative rule-making and individual decision-making. Comparatively, Norwegian administrative statutes are very short.[55]

There is a distinction between *sentrale forskrifter* (central secondary legislation) and *lokale forskrifter* (local secondary legislation).[56] Local secondary legislation applies to a limited geographical area and is often enacted by municipalities.

*Instrukser* (instructions) are legally binding directives within the administration. There is no general statutory legislative basis for the use of such instruments, and the rules are unwritten, but can be seen as a function of § 3 the Constitution, which states that the executive power is vested in the King.[57] In certain areas, the

[50] Lov 13. juni 1969 nr 26 om skadeerstatning (skadeerstatningsloven).

[51] Lov 15. juni 2001 nr 53 om erstatning ved pasientskader mv (pasientskadeloven). See generally N Nygaard, *Skade og ansvar* (Oslo, Universitetsforlaget, 2007) 470 ff.

[52] Rt 1978 s 482 ('It is a task for the legislator to consider whether there should be strict liability' (at 487)).

[53] Lov 10. februar 1967 om behandlingsmåten i forvaltningssaker (forvaltningsloven).

[54] The latter was enacted 1 July 2017.

[55] See JCF Nordrum (n 22) 254 ff.

[56] The latter corresponds roughly to the English term *by-laws*. In Norwegian context the same term is used (*forskrifter*) and both categories are covered by Chapter 7 in the PAA.

[57] See generally T Eckhoff and E Smith (n 1) 532; HP Graver (n 1) 163 ff.

authority to issue instructions is given an explicit statutory basis. And sometimes *forskrifter* (secondary legislation) is, misleadingly, denoted 'instruks' (instructions). One example of this is the Prosecution Instructions.[58]

In several areas, the administration uses broad agreements with business organisations to regulate entire sectors. One example is the NOx Agreement 2018–25,[59] which is an agreement between 15 business organisations and the Ministry of Climate and Environment, with the aim to facilitate concrete reductions in nitrogen oxide emissions. This instrument is hybrid in character, involving several different mechanisms. There is no general legislative basis for the use of such instruments, and for some issues, the legal status is unresolved. The legislator has recognised the existence of such an agreement through granting exemptions from environmental fees for those that are parties to the agreements.[60]

A significant part of administrative law is given as *soft law*, eg, *veiledninger* (guidelines) and *tolkningsuttalelser* (interpretative statements). In some areas, such sources have great practical significance. Therefore, there has been a debate as to whether the use of such instruments should be regulated and subjected to procedural rules (eg, in the PAA).[61] The PAA Law Commission discussed whether to codify principles for the use of such instruments and proposed not doing so.[62]

For many questions concerning individual permits, there are unwritten principles of administrative law. One example is that *conditions* laid down in permits, granted on a discretionary basis, must be relevant and proportionate to the end they serve.[63] Another example is questions of how far the administration can standardise the execution of statutory discretion.[64] One type of individual decisions, *konsesjoner* (administrative concessions), deserves to be mentioned separately. In several sectors, administrative concessions are the most important steering tool and are regulated in ways that make it reasonable to talk of different *concession systems*. Some of these systems rely on elaborate statutory provisions. In some systems, concessions are transferable. The terminology differs; sometimes such instruments are referred to as tradeable permits or tradeable quotas. This is an important form of action in resource management (eg, the Act on Maritime Resources[65] establishing a system of fish quotas) and pollution control (eg, the Climate Quota Act).[66]

[58] Forskrift 28. juni 1985 nr 1679 om ordningen av påtalemyndigheten (Påtaleinstruksen).

[59] Miljøavtale om reduksjon av NOx-utslipp for perioden 2018–2025, 24. mai 2017.

[60] Forskrift 11. desember 2001 nr 1451 § 3-19-12.

[61] See, eg, FA Innjord, 'Almene råd og vejledninger – styring og skøn' (2009) *Forhandlingerne på Det 38. nordiske juristmøte i København 2008* 207.

[62] NOU 2019: 5 Ny forvaltningslov 505 ff.

[63] The PAA Committee proposes codifying these principles for 'pedagogical reasons' – NOU 2019: 5 Ny forvaltningslov p 548.

[64] See generally OH Moen (n 41)) 399 ff.

[65] Lov 6. juni 2008 nr 37 om forvaltning av viltlevande marine ressursar (havressurslova).

[66] Lov 17. desember 2004 nr 99 om kvoteplikt og handel med kvoter for utslipp av klimagasser (klimakvoteloven).

The Law Commission on the Use of Administrative Sanctions published a seminal report in 2001 proposing a major reform aiming at the systematic use of administrative sanctions and reactions as an alternative to criminal proceedings.[67] Since then, Norway has radically shifted from criminal enforcement of administrative law to administrative enforcement, in large and important sectors, such as the maritime sector, aquaculture, fisheries, energy, labour, building law and environmental law. Norway has been a frontrunner in this respect in the Nordic countries.[68] Currently, around 100 statutes confer this power upon the administration, and in 2017 the PAA was extended with two new chapters with general rules on administrative sanctions and on coercive fines. Administrative sanctions are defined as a 'negative reaction that may be applied by an administrative agency in response to an actual breach of a statute, regulation or individual decision, and which is deemed to be a criminal sanction pursuant to the European Convention on Human Rights' (see § 43 PAA). The reference to the ECHR is included to ensure that the use of negative reactions does not violate the requirements of a fair trial (Article 6 ECHR) and the prohibition on double jeopardy (*ne bis in idem*) (Article 4 of Protocol 7). The PAA has specific provisions on the use of *overtredelsesgebyr* (administrative fines: § 44), *administrativt rettighetstap* (administrative deprivation of rights: § 45) and *foretakssanksjon* (administrative corporate sanctions: § 46). There are other sector-specific administrative sanctions in specialised Acts. One example is *tilleggsskatt* (surtaxes) in § 14–3 of the Tax Administration Act, which is an important tool in tax administration. If the purpose of the action is to prevent possible future breaches rather than to punish committed breaches, and thereby falls outside the definition of an administrative sanction, the action is considered an *forvaltningsreaksjon* (administrative reaction). The most important administrative reaction is coercive fines (§ 51 PAA).

The administration may act on the same footing as a private entity and conclude *private contracts*, and regularly does so. However, in specific areas there are rules regulating the administration's use of private contracts, eg, for government procurement and employment contracts for public servants. In other areas, there are different hybrid instruments in use, which are often referred to as *forvaltningsavtaler* (administrative contracts). The common denominator is that public action is related to or is an integral part of the contract. There is no general statute regulating the use of such contracts. There is a substantial case law concerning the legal boundary between administrative contracts and administrative decisions. In some sectors there are statutory rules governing the use of contracts. One example is Chapter 17 of the Planning and Building Act on *utbyggingsavtaler* (land development contracts).[69] The limits on the use of such contracts have been developed

[67] NOU 2003:15 Fra bot til bedring – Et mer nyansert og effektivt sanksjonssystem med mindre bruk av straff.

[68] L Halila, V Lankinen and A Nilsson, *Administrativa sanktionsavgifter – en nordisk komparativ studie* (Copenhagen, Nordisk ministerråd, 2018) 295 ff.

[69] Act of 27 June 2008 No 71 Relating to Planning and the Processing of Building Applications.

through interplay between codification by the legislator and developments in case law.

## V. Administrative Organisation

The Norwegian administration is arranged hierarchically. The executive power is vested in the 'King', which in reality is the King-in-Council, which consists of the cabinet and the King. The ministries are rather small and primarily prepare legislation, issue some regulations and give interpretations on questions of law (in addition to general policy-making and budget preparations). Executive powers may be delegated within the boundaries set by § 28 of the Constitution, which states that 'matters of importance shall be presented in the Council of State … and such matters shall be dealt with by them in accordance with the decision adopted in the Council of State'. In practice, this is understood to set few limits on delegation. Sometimes the legislator explicitly limits the possibility to delegate executive powers in the statute itself.

In practice, the *agencies* serve very important functions in most fields.[70] Even though the agency model has a long tradition in Norway, agencification has been intensified in the last few decades and has to a greater extent been organised through agencies than was the case before. Only fragments of the doctrine on delegation are codified, and primarily with a negative approach; unless it is clearly stated otherwise in the statute, the unwritten rules on delegation determine to what extent authority can be delegated. As a rule, the ministries can instruct agencies, but in some fields, statutory provisions block instructions and thereby create independent or partly independent agencies.

The classical hierarchical structure at the state and local levels has been fragmented, and the public administration is now organised in various ways. There are different forms of organising cooperation between different municipalities, and several different forms of public companies rely on specific statutory basis – examples are *state enterprise* regulated by the Act on State-Owned Enterprises[71] and *municipal undertakings* regulated by Chapter 9 in the Local Government Act.[72] In addition, in several fields, public administration is organised through limited companies. This development poses new challenges to administrative law.

Private organisations may be delegated rule-making and decision-making authority. In some areas (eg, fishery management), private entities play an important role in the regulatory system, and in several fields, such as health and child welfare, services are provided by private entities, which at the same time are given some administrative authority, such as to execute individual decisions.

[70] In Norwegian, there are several different terms used to describe a directorate: *direktorat, tilsyn, verk, vesen* etc.

[71] Lov 30. august 1991 nr 71 om statsforetak.

[72] Lov 22. juni 2018 nr 83 om kommuner og fylkeskommuner (kommuneloven).

The standing of *civil servants* is regulated in the legislation. § 22 of the Constitution provides special protection to *embetsmenn* (senior civil servants appointed by the King-in-Council). These groups include high-ranking officials, for example, secretary generals (*departementsråd*), director generals (*ekspedisjonssjef*) and deputy director generals (*avdelingsdirektør*) in the ministries and heads of agencies, but also some special advisors, such as the Legal Advisors in the Legislation Department in the Ministry of Justice, are appointed as *embetsmenn*. The standing of *embetsmenn* (senior civil servants) and *statsansatt* (other civil servants) are regulated by the Act Relating to Civil Servants.[73] Local civil servants are regulated by general labour law.

The administration has the right within statutory limitations to instruct civil servants. In several areas the status of civil servants is codified. There are examples of specific codified rules governing civil servants in different parts of the administration. One example is Chapter IV of the Police Act, which gives specific rules for civil servants in the police.[74] The rules are specified in the General Instructions on Police Service.[75] Another example is the Health Personnel Act.[76] Another important soft law instrument is the Ethical Guidelines for the Public Service that apply to all civil servants at the state level.[77]

# VI. Administrative Protection

## A. Introduction

In the Norwegian system, the most important general safeguards are the general procedural rules, the administrative complaint mechanism and judicial review by the courts. In addition, several different ombudsmen mechanisms are worth mentioning.

A 'party' to an administrative proceeding which may end in an individual decision is given a set of rights in Chapters IV–VI PAA. A party is 'a person to whom a decision is directed or whom the case otherwise directly concerns'. The threshold is a consideration of how strongly the individual is affected.

## B. Administrative Procedure

Since Norway does not have a system of administrative courts, the administrative complaint mechanism is de facto the most important safeguard for citizens and

[73] Lov 16. juni 2017 nr 67 om statens ansatte mv.
[74] Lov 8. april 1995 nr 53 om politiet (politiloven).
[75] Instruks 22. juni 1990 nr 3963 alminnelig tjenesteinstruks for politiet (politinstruksen).
[76] Lov 2. juli 1999 nr 64 om helsepersonell mv (helsepersonellloven).
[77] Etiske retningslinjer for statstjenesten, 2017, Kommunal- og moderniseringsdepartementet.

companies. There is a general right to appeal individual decisions in § 28 PAA. There are two grounds for standing: first, *parties* to the case and second others who have *rettslig klageinteresse* ('legal interest') in appealing the case, eg the case affects them to the degree that is reasonable to give standing (see § 28 PAA). The wording 'legal interest' corresponds to the required legal standing for court. Case law and the preparatory works to the PAA clarify that the threshold for an administrative complaint must be lower than the threshold for bringing a legal action to a court (locus standi).

Case law clearly establishes that organisations can have the required 'legal interest' to complain. This was first established by the Supreme Court in a series of cases, first (and prominently) in the field of environmental law, where environmental organisations were granted standing in *courts* and, as a consequence, standing to also appeal administrative decisions.[78] The Dispute Act of 2008 explicitly gives organisations the right to bring action in their own name.[79] The Commission proposing a new PAA recommends codifying similar rules in the PAA.[80] This is an example of a typical interplay between courts interpreting legislative concepts dynamically, and the legislator thereafter codifying the new interpretation explicitly.

The appellate instance is the immediate superior administrative body to the administrative agency that made the administrative decision. Special statutes sometimes deviate from these general rules, for example by establishing special complaint mechanisms or (rarely) precluding the possibility to complain.

The administrative appellate instance tries the case anew (*de novo review*). However, if the appellate instance is a state body, it shall give 'great weight to the interest of local self-government when trying discretionary issues' (see § 34 PAA). These rules are a consequence of the requirement of § 49 of the Constitution to maintain local government.

There are several rights in the PAA that are meant to enable the parties to a case to represent their interests. § 16 PAA requires that the administration notify the parties of any possible decision and gives the party a right to be heard. § 17 PAA requires the administration to analyse the case thoroughly, including actively informing the parties on issues of particular relevance to them, as well as seeking the opinions of underage parties. The right of children to be heard is mentioned explicitly in the provision, but also follows from § 104 of the Constitution and the Human Rights Act, which incorporates the Convention on the Rights of Children.

[78] Rt 1980 p 569 (*Alta*), Rt 1992 p 1618 (*Fremtiden i våre hender*) og Rt 2003 p 833 (*Stopp Regionfelt Østlandet*).

[79] Lov 17. juni 2005 nr 90 om mekling og rettergang i sivile tvister (tvisteloven).

[80] NOU 2019: 5 Ny forvaltningslov.

## C. Court Protection

Review of administrative decisions relies on a constitutional basis. § 89 of the Constitution stipulates that:

> In cases for the courts, the courts have the right and duty to review whether if it violates the Grunnlov to apply a statutory provision, or if it violates the Grunnlov or any statutory provision to apply any other decisions using public authority.

This paragraph was included in the Constitution through amendments in 2014 (review of statutes) and 2020 (review of administrative decisions), codifying a long-standing unwritten constitutional rule. There is a debate as to whether the codification of these rules in the constitution may have changed the content of the law; the intent of the Storting is not clear from the preparatory works.[81] This codification process has sparked a debate on whether the procedure of constitutional amendments needs to be revised, the argument being that strict and formal procedures often lead to unwanted and non-democratic results.[82]

There is no system of administrative courts in Norway.[83] Norwegian courts have, with a few exceptions, *general jurisdiction*. However, courts review relatively few administrative cases (there are other review mechanisms; see section VI.D below). The Domstolskommisjonen (the Norwegian Court Commission), a commission evaluating the organisation and independence of Norwegian courts, found that that court review of administrative decisions in Norway are relatively sparse compared to other European countries and the Commission warns that:

> Overall, there is a danger that the threshold for court review of cases where the administration is a party is so high that it weakens the possibility of changing the administrations practice where there should be a need to turn around. Ultimately, this means that the courts do not fulfil their role as guarantor for citizens against injustice.[84]

Administrative cases in courts are handled by the general rules for civil proceedings in the Dispute Act 2005.[85]

In some areas, there are special court-like administrative bodies, which handle administrative questions in particular areas. Examples of such court-like bodies are the Fylkesnemnda for barnevern og sosiale saker (County Social Welfare Board) and the Trygderetten (National Insurance Court). The special procedures for these bodies are codified and can be described as a mix between civil procedure and administrative procedure. Still, the Høyesterett (Norwegian Supreme Court) 'pronounces judgment in the final instance' (see § 88 of the Constitution).

[81] E Smith, 'Er Høyesterett en konstitusjonsdomstol?' (2017) *Jussens Venner* 98.
[82] See E Holmøyvik, 'Stortingets upresise presisering av Grunnlova § 89' (2020) *Juridika*, juridika.no/innsikt/stortingets-upresise-presisering-av-grunnlova-89.
[83] The Norwegian system is similar to the Danish and the Icelandic systems (west Nordic systems) and different from the Swedish and Finnish system of administrative courts (east Nordic systems).
[84] NOU 2020: 11 Den tredje statsmakt – Domstolene i endring p 67.
[85] Lov 17. juni 2005 nr 90 om mekling og rettergang i sivile tvister (tvisteloven).

The Dispute Act does not contain any general rules on standards of review on administrative decisions; the rules on court review are mainly developed through an interplay between legal doctrine, case law and legislation. The role of the courts is to control administrative decisions, not to examine the case anew. How closely the courts will review administrative decisions depends on the interpretation of the relevant statutory text as well as the preparatory works. If there is clear guidance, for instance, that the statute explicitly confers discretionary authority on the administration to decide the course of action, then the court will only review whether the procedure is in accordance with law, whether the facts of the case are correct and whether the decision is arbitrary or capricious.

If there is no clear guidance in the statutory text or in the preparatory works, typically when the wording consists of vague descriptive terms (eg, 'vulnerable') or normative terms (eg, 'reasonable'), the courts will examine the basis for the specification of the terms. If the basis is professional, localised or political considerations, the courts will hesitate to review the considerations, but not if the considerations are more moral or legal in nature.[86]

The legislator has in some statutes explicitly regulated, or discussed in the preparatory works, what the court can or cannot review. For 'administrative decisions on coercive measures in the health and social services', the Dispute Act prescribes a special type of procedure in Chapter 36. The special procedure gives the court, inter alia, the authority to try cases *de novo*, including jurisdiction to take into consideration new facts as they are presented to the court and to give a final decision. Another example is court review of administrative sanctions (see § 50 PAA).

The result of the court review is normally to declare the decision valid or invalid. In some fields, the legislator has given the court jurisdiction to decide on the substance and thereby end the case, eg, for administrative coercive actions reviewed in accordance with Chapter 36 of the Dispute Act.

## D. Other Forms of Protection: Ombudsmen and Administrative Audit

An important mechanism in the Norwegian administrative system is the *ombudsman*. Most important is the Sivilombudet (Parliamentary Ombudsman for Public Administration). The Parliamentary Ombudsman has a constitutional basis. The Constitution explicitly states in § 75 litra l that the Parliament can appoint an ombudsman to control the administration to ensure that citizens do not experience injustice.

The Parliamentary Ombud for Public Administration was established by the Parliamentary Ombudsmans Act in 1962[87] and is now regulated by the

[86] See, eg, Rt 2007 p 257 (*Trallfa*).
[87] Lov 22. juni 1962 nr 8 om Stortingets ombudsmann for forvaltningen (sivilombudsmannsloven).

Parliamentary Ombud Act 2021.[88] The Ombud might consider cases on its own initiative or in response to a complaint (see § 5 Parliamentary Ombud Act). In several fields, the Ombud, especially for those types of cases that are seldom taken to court, is instrumental in developing administrative law. There are several examples where the Ombud has given rights to individuals without a basis in statutory legislation or case law and thereby in reality has developed administrative law. One example is a statement from 2018 where the Ombud concluded that even though a teacher perhaps was not a 'party' to the case in issue, and therefore did not have rights after PAA, she was affected by the case to such an extent that she was entitled to see the documents of the case. The Ombud based this right on 'unwritten requirements of good administration'.[89]

There are also several other ombudsmen with different jurisdictions; examples are the Norwegian Parliamentary Ombud for the Armed Forces; the Ombud for Children; the Equality and Anti-Discrimination Ombud; and, at the county level, eg, the Health and Social Services Ombud.[90] These ombudsmen are all established by statutory legislation, serve a supervisory role and give advice in individual cases. Commonly, the administration will respect statements given by the Ombud.

The Office of the Auditor General monitors the public sector and has a constitutional basis in § 75 litra k of the Constitution, and is regulated by the Act on the Auditor General.[91] One form of audit is *administrative audit* (*forvaltningsrevisjon*), which is a systematic review of whether parliamentary decisions and intentions have been fulfilled (§ 9). The Norwegian National Human Rights Institution is established by a separate Act[92] and is mandated to contribute to the enforcement of human rights in Norway on a systemic level. It seems as though the reports from the institution have had impact in the legislative process on areas where administrative law has a human rights dimension.

# VII. The Reasons for and Consequences of Codification of Administrative Law

## A. Introduction

First, a brief comment should be made to clarify the concept of 'codification'. Often the term is used colloquially to refer to the passing of any legislation. By 'codification', I refer to the passing of primary and secondary legislation which mirrors,

[88] Lov 18. juni 2021 nr 121 om Stortingets ombud for kontroll med forvaltningen (sivilombudsloven).

[89] Sivilombudsmannens uttalelse 29. juni 2018 (sak 2018/496).

[90] Lov 18. juni 2021 nr 115 om Stortingets ombudsnemnd for forsvaret; Lov 6. mars nr 5 om barneombud; Lov 2. juli 1999 nr 63 om pasient og brukerrettigheter ch 8.

[91] Lov 7. mai 2004 nr 21 om Riksrevisjonen.

[92] Lov 22. mai 2015 nr 33 om Norges nasjonale institusjon for menneskerettigheter.

adjusts or alters an unwritten rule or a rule that followed from legal text lower down in the hierarchy (eg, administrative practice) but also elaboration in statutes based on the constitution or international law. It is quite common in Norway that the legislator acknowledges the existence of unwritten law and restates the law in preparatory works or refers to the existence in the legislative text, often with reference to general administrative rules.[93] This strategy does not fit squarely into common notions of codification, but has similarities with codification.

Between 1950 and 1970, there was an intense codification process. The process can be seen as a response to the extensive delegation of legislative power to the administration, as well as delegation of executive power within the administration. Sparked by this development and a lack of procedural guarantees, the Forvaltningslovkomiteen (Law Commission on a Public Administration Act) was established. The Commission issued a seminal report in 1958,[94] discussing fundamental control mechanisms and procedural administrative law. Prior to this codification, rules were scattered around in a few statutes, regulations and guidelines, and often deduced from vague unwritten principles. The proposal systematised and strengthened administrative procedural law through systematic codification, which in the end resulted in three major Acts: the Ombudsman Act (1962), the PAA (1967) and the Freedom of Information Act (1970).[95] The Commission's work was carried out between 1951 and 1958.

Between 1970 and 2000, the modern regulatory state developed through special statutory legislation in different fields. For example, there was intensive legislative activity in areas such as product control, protection of the environment, and energy, oil and gas regulation, educational law and welfare legislation. Some of these processes had the character of codification – one example is the Petroleum Act 1985, which codified rules and principles already established in administrative practice and contracts.[96]

After 1990, administrative laws and principles have in many cases been codified, often as a result of reception of international law, most notably EU law through the EEA agreement (EEA/EU law), but also as a result of the profound impact of the ECHR. During this period, law commissions have revised several of the early general and specific Acts on administrative laws. A key question in these legislative processes seems to be whether to codify administrative practice or unwritten principles.

[93] One example is the provision regulating when the administration can change an administrative decision in §35 PAA, where it is stated that the limitations in the provisions do not apply if the decision can be changed with referral to 'general administrative law', which is meant to be a reference to unwritten rules.

[94] NUT 1958:3 Innstilling fra Komiteen til å utrede spørsmålet om mer betryggende former for den offentlige forvaltning, Spørsmålet om mer betryggende former for den offentlige forvaltning.

[95] The Freedom of Information Act (2008) replaced the Freedom of Information Act (1970), strengthening access to information in municipalities and publicly controlled private entities.

[96] See Ot prp nr 72 (1982–83) Lov om petroleumsvirksomhet p 35.

## B. Codified Rights Originally Established by the Supreme Court

In several fields, the Supreme Court has recognised rights, either by referring to unwritten principles or by referring to human rights or other superior grounds. It has also expanded rights already conferred in statutory legislation by reference to human rights or constitutional law. One example is the landmark case in 1977, where the Supreme Court decided that patients had the right to access their own medical records.[97] Patients could not invoke the general right to access documents in the PAA or the Freedom of Information Act because these documents probably fell under the exemptions for internal documents. The Supreme Court stated that, regardless of exemptions in the general Acts, patients had a specific right to see medical records and that the right was based on 'general principles'. This decision was in turn codified, specified and expanded, resulting in the current rules on access to medical journals in Chapter 5 of the Patient Rights Act.[98] Another example is the decision in a landmark case in the Supreme Court in 1990,[99] in which it found that a decision on healthcare given to a disabled woman did not meet the required minimum standard. This minimum standard has later been codified in several areas. The development of this principle started as a fragment of a principle in tort law cases in education law, which was referred to in preparatory works, gradually developing into a fully fledged principle, which in turn ended up being codified (see above, sections III.B and III.C).

## C. The Constitutionalisation of Administrative Law

Traditionally, constitutional sources have had a limited influence on administrative law. However, several constitutional amendments enacted in the last generation have significance for administrative law; the right to a clean environment (1992, § 112); the freedom of information principle (2004, § 100); a comprehensive catalogue of fundamental rights (2014, Chapter E); local democracy (2014, § 49); and court review of administrative acts (2020, § 89).

The commission preparing the catalogue of fundamental rights included in the Constitution in 2014 explicitly stated that the amendments were only a codification and were not meant to change the law. However, there are clear indications in the case law of the Supreme Court that the constitutionalisation of at least some of these rules has facilitated constitutional review. As the then Supreme Court judge Arnfinn Bårdsen described it:

> [T]he Supreme Court's mandate as a guardian of fundamental rights and freedoms and the rule of law has been consolidated, clarified, and democratically anchored.

[97] Rt 1977 p 1035 (*Sykejournal*).
[98] Lov 2. juli 1999 nr 63 om pasient og brukerrettigheter (pasient- og brukerrettighetsloven).
[99] Rt 1990 s 874 (*Fusa*).

> Expanding the Constitution's catalogue of protected rights and freedoms – ranking them as lex superior – has inevitably, substantially broadened the Supreme Court's constitutional repertoire.[100]

The case law of the Supreme Court seems to back this assessment. Arguably, this may be a general mechanism of codifying administrative law principles in the Constitution.

## D. International Law as a Ground for Legislation and Codification (1990–2020)

The ECHR and the EEA agreement have had a profound impact on Norwegian legislation, and has led to codification in lieu of interpretative guidelines in the preparatory works or administrative practice.

One example of this is how the Supreme Court has drawn on the ECHR when reviewing cases involving fundamental rights, initially most prominently in criminal procedure and thereafter in administrative procedure. This case law prompted the legislator to establish the Menneskerettighetslovutvalget (Human Rights Law Commission, 1989–93) to review the need to codify human rights.[101] The Commission proposed a bill that led to the Human Rights Act (1999), incorporating, inter alia, the ECHR.

The Human Rights Act gave the Supreme Court a basis for actively developing administrative law in the light of the ECHR.[102] One example is the codification and clarification of citizens' rights in cases concerning administrative sanctioning. A series of judgments by the Supreme Court paved the way for legislative reforms, codifying the interpretation of ECHR rights by the Supreme Court in several cases.[103]

The EEA agreement is a major cause for legislation. The Commission evaluating the implications of the agreement described the legislation and regulations enacted to implement EU law in 1992–2011 as 'the greatest reception of foreign law ever in Norwegian legal history' and continued: 'In twenty years EU-law has become an integrated and major part of the Norwegian law.' The EEA/EU in

[100] Arnfinn Bårdsen, 'The Norwegian Supreme Court as the Guardian of Constitutional Rights and Freedoms', joint seminar between the Constitutional Court of Austria and the Supreme Court of Norway, Vienna, 29–30 October 2015, www.venice.coe.int/CoCentre/Bardsen_Arnfinn_The_Nordic_Supreme_Courts_as_CCs.pdf.

[101] NOU 1993: 18 Lovgivning om menneskerettigheter, Ot prp nr 3 (1998–99) Om lov om styrking av menneskerettighetenes stilling i norsk rett (menneskerettsloven).

[102] JE Skoghøy, 'Forvaltningssanksjoner, EMK og Grunnloven' (2014) *Jussens venner* 297.

[103] NOU 2003: 15 Fra bot til bedring – Et mer nyansert og effektivt sanksjonssystem med mindre bruk av straff.

tandem with the ECHR is considered by the Commission as a 'dual order of law with traits of federal system, where national legal system persists, but subverted to a common European legal framework'.[104]

The EEA/EU has prompted codification of administrative law developed in case law and administrative practice to be codified.[105] In some areas the EEA/EU has been among the reasons given for codifying Norwegian administrative practice, while in other areas European case law has been codified. A recent example of the former is the proposal to codify the principles of cost recovery for the administrative processing of applications in § 18 PAA.[106] Currently, these rules are derived from administrative orders and some specific statutory provisions. The proposal to codify is partly to explicitly conform to EEA/EU legislation. An example of the latter is the codification of in the Act on Public Procurement in § 4, which means that the administration, when procuring, must follow the general principles of EEA/EU law developed in case law, such as proportionality.[107]

## E. Codification as a Result of International Policy Benchmarking

Although it is not yet an important factor in codification processes, it is worth mentioning the ongoing discussion on whether to codify administrative practice to conform to ideas of good regulation, prompted by assessments of the Norwegian regulatory systems in country reports by the World Bank and the Organisation for Economic Co-operation and Development (OECD).[108] Several recommendations build on the presumption that statutory rules are better than secondary legislation, administrative practice or private standards. In order to *score* better on this assessment, a viable strategy is simply to codify.[109]

[104] NOU 2012: 2 Utenfor og innenfor – Norges avtaler med EU.

[105] The significance of EEA/EU law for Norwegian administrative law is covered in a discussion paper included in the report proposing a new administrative Act: NOU 2019:5 Ny forvaltningslov vedlegg 5, Christoffer C Eriksen og Halvard H Fredriksen, EØS-rettslige rammer for ny forvaltningslov. An extended version was published as Christoffer C Eriksen and Halvard H Fredriksen, *Norges europeiske forvaltningsrett – EØS-avtalens krav til norske forvaltningsorganers organisering og saksbehandling* (Oslo, Universitetsforlaget, 2019).

[106] NOU 2019: 5 Ny forvaltningslov p 750. The proposal builds on a similar provision in the Act on Services (2009), which implements Directive 2006/123/EC of the European Parliament and of the Council of 12 December 2006 on services in the internal market [2006] OJ L376/36.

[107] The preparatory works Prop 51 L (2015–2016) Lov om offentlige anskaffelser (anskaffelsesloven) p 81 clarify that the intention was to codify principles that are part of EEA/EU law, but also partly follows from Norwegian unwritten procurement principles.

[108] Norway – Preparing for the Future Now, OECD Reviews of Regulatory Reform, OECD 2003, Regulatory Indicators Survey results, OECD 2014, Measuring Regulatory Quality and Efficiency – Economy Profile 2016 (Norway), Doing Business, landrapport, Verdensbanken, 2016.

[109] See in general JCF Nordrum (n 22).

## F. Codification of Unwritten Customary Law as a Continuous, Gradual Process

Over the last few decades, the legislator has codified the legal grounds for the use of administrative authority in several areas, such as the grounds for using force. One example is the general authority of the police to use force to establish and maintain order developed in case law and administrative practice, and described in several preparatory works as well as the legal doctrine. Still, the legislator chose to codify the general authority in § 7 of the Police Act, arguing that legislation gave better guidance and served to clarify matters.[110]

Another example is the authority of teachers and headteachers to take action to maintain order in schools and classrooms. Traditionally, this authority has relied on customary law, but gradually the legislator has codified this general authority in several provisions in the Education Act (eg, § 9 A-11).[111] Lately, there has been a discussion as to whether to codify all forms of use of force in the Education Act and the Kindergarten Act.[112] In these areas, so far authorities have relied on a customary right of caretakers to use some force in the absence of the parents. Similar codification processes can be observed in several fields, such as health law, welfare law and military law.

## G. Codification Processes Caused by Policy Initiatives to Increase Accessibility and to Facilitate Good Legislative Structure

General initiatives to improve accessibility to the law have been another reason for consolidating and codifying unwritten rules. One important example is the General Social Insurance Act 1997, which was a result of a systematic gathering and codification of rules given in regulations, guidelines and administrative practice.[113] Another example is the proposals of the PAA Law Commission to codify, inter alia, rules on delegation, abuse of discretion and further codification of the rules on invalid decisions, the argument being that it makes the statute easier to understand for laypersons.[114] A foundational work was the Commission

[110] Ot prp nr 22 (1994–95) Om lov om politiet (politiloven).

[111] Lov 17. juli 1998 nr 61 om grunnskolen og den videregåande opplæringa (opplæringslova).

[112] Lov 17. juni 2005 nr 64 om barnehager (barnehageloven).

[113] Lov 28. februar 1997 nr 19 om folketrygd (folketrygdloven). A less ambitious codification was the National Insurance Act of 1967. The act is built on the proposal in NOU 1990: 20 Forenklet folketrygdlov. The process of consolidation started with the Social Insurance Act (1966) and the intention to, on a later stage, to codify were expressed in the preparatory works, Ot prp nr 17 (1965–66).

[114] See, eg, NOU 2019: 5 Ny forvaltningslov p 58, 156, 546, 558, 620.

on the Structuration of Laws and Regulation (1992).[115] The Committee made several proposals to codify case law to improve accessibility, but also with a view to facilitate a good legislative structure.[116]

## H. Codifications as a Method for Reviewing and Clarifying Unwritten Rules

Codification processes are often combined with attempts to *clarify* administrative law. This process serves as a means of evaluating the current administrative law. Codification processes are part of the interplay between the legislator and the executive, where the former can critically assess rules developed by the latter. In several administrative sectors, the courts play a marginal role in the development of law. This may also cause continued legal uncertainty because there is a lack of authoritative legal clarification. In some of these fields, administrative practice becomes, in practice, an important source of law. Codification can be a method to review the principles developed through administrative practice, and codification in turn facilitates the review of administrative practice from courts as well as other control mechanisms, such as those performed by the Auditor General and the County Governors.

## I. Codification as Part of the Legislative Cycle

In the last few years, there have been more bills in general and important specialised administrative areas than ever before. Examples of Acts that are either recently proposed by law commissions or have been recently enacted are the Public Administration Act, the Archive Act, the Education Act, the General Act on the Use of Force in Health and Welfare, the Statistics Act and the Municipality Act.[117] It is worth noting that in all these reports the discussion of whether to codify case law, administrative practice or unwritten rules has been central. Codification seems to be a part of a continuous legislative cycle: when law commissions evaluate current legislation and propose changes, codification is often a question that

[115] NOU 1992: 32 Bedre struktur i lovverket.

[116] That codification would contribute to good structure was also an argument for the proposal to codify rules on delegation by the PAA Commission; see NOU 2019: 5 Ny forvaltningslov p 58.

[117] NOU 2019: 5 Ny forvaltningslov; NOU 2019: 9 Fra kalveskinn til datasjø – Ny lov om samfunnsdokumentasjon og arkiver; NOU 2019: 23 Ny opplæringslov; NOU 2019: 14 Tvangsbegrensningsloven – Forslag til felles regler om tvang og inngrep uten samtykke i helse- og omsorgstjenesten; NOU 2018: 7 Ny lov om offisiell statistikk og Statistisk sentralbyrå; NOU 2016: 4 Ny kommunelov.

the commission will consider, and in central fields there is a tendency to codify case law, administrative practice and unwritten law.

## J. Codification has Provided a Coherent System of Procedural Administrative Law

Major codification processes, such as the PAA, have served to systematise and make fragmented law coherent, with unified concepts, terminology and rules. There is a clear tendency for codification processes to have served to structure administrative law and to frame general legal questions. This systematisation has clearly eased access to, and knowledge of, administrative law. The codification of general administrative law has provided fertile ground for general textbooks on administrative law.[118]

## K. Codification has not Led to Ossification

It is hard to find indications that codification has led to *ossification*. There are probably two reasons for this. First, Norwegian legislative language is typically concise and leaves interpretative room and room for discretion, and there is in general a pragmatic approach to law, where the intention of the legislator is given considerable weight. This open-ended, pragmatic legislative style, combined with a liberal interpretative style, may serve as an antidote against ossification. Codification of administrative law seems to provide an *anchor* for case law rather than fully replacing it as a source of law. The interplay between interpretation by courts, administrative practice and the legislation is key to understanding the development of administrative law.

## L. The System of Law Commissions Facilitates Codification Processes

It is relatively easy to initiate legislative processes in the Norwegian system. Law commissions are regularly appointed to review and propose legislation.[119] In the Norwegian system, there is both a capacity and a will to initiate large legislative processes, and codification is often considered a viable option.

[118] The most prominent general textbooks are T Eckhoff and E Smith (n 1) and HP Graver (n 1).

[119] IL Backer, *Loven – hvordan blir den til?*, 2nd edn (Oslo, Universitetsforlaget, 2022) 42 ff; JCF Nordrum (n 22) 485 ff.

## VIII. A Brief Conclusion

Norwegian administrative law is largely codified, with some notable exceptions, most prominently substantive administrative law. Codification of administrative law is a continuous process in Norway; fewer and fewer areas are based solely on other sources of law, such as case law. Codification is seen as a natural part of any process legislating administrative law.

# 10

# Codification of Administrative Law in Sweden

JANE REICHEL AND MICHAELA RIBBING*

## I. Introduction

In this chapter, the codification of administrative law in Sweden is presented. As will be shown, Swedish administrative law has a long history and is well developed in terms of codification. It may be stated already at this point that the Swedish administrative model differs from those in other countries dealt with in this volume. The differences are most significant in relation to the Anglo-Saxon countries, although some common, central administrative law principles can be found, such as the principles of legality, legal certainty and equality or objectivity.[1] From a European perspective, European Union (EU) law has had a major impact, meaning that several principles of good administration, which are seen in the contributions from other European countries, are also included in Swedish law.[2] Principles of good administration emanating from the European Convention on Human Rights (ECHR),[3] as interpreted by the European Court of Human Rights, as well as other documents from the Council of Europe, have also affected the national administrative orders.[4] The European Court of Human Rights draws inspiration from legal

* The authors wish to express their gratitude to Professor Felix Uhlmann and the participants in the Codification of Administrative Law workshop in Zurich in January 2020 for lively and enriching discussions, and to Professor Henrik Wenander, Lund, and doctoral student Andreas Knutsson, Stockholm, for their insightful comments on earlier drafts. Thanks also to doctoral student Sandra Thobaben, Stockholm, for help with editing the footnotes.

[1] See in this book the chapters on Australia, Canada, the UK and the US.

[2] See in this book the chapters on Austria, Belgium, France, Germany, Italy, the Netherlands and the EU. Though Norway and Switzerland are not members of the EU, other European commitments influence the application of general principles of administrative law.

[3] The Convention for the Protection of Human Rights and Fundamental Freedoms (Den europeiska konventionen angående skydd för de mänskliga rättigheterna och grundläggande friheterna), Rome 4 November 1950.

[4] U Stelkens and A Andrijauskaitė, 'Sources of Pan-European General Principles of Good Administration' in U Stelkens and A Andrijauskaitė (eds), *Pan-European General Principles of Good Administration* (Oxford, Oxford University Press, 2020) 19 ff. Regarding Sweden, see J Reichel and H Wenander, *Europeisk förvaltningsrätt i Sverige* (Stockholm, Norstedt, 2021).

orders beyond Europe, both international law and domestic law, which also trickle down into the legal orders of the Member States.[5] In this context, it can be noted that Sweden belongs to the East Nordic public law system together with Finland, including Åland. This system differs from that in West Nordic legislation seen in Denmark, including the Faroe Islands, and Greenland, Iceland and Norway.[6]

# II. The Definition and Delimitation of Administrative Law in Sweden

## A. General Administrative Law

In Swedish law, public law typically includes administrative law and constitutional law.[7] Administrative law regulates the public administration, which according to Chapter 1, section 8 of the Instrument of Government[8] is exercised by state and municipal administrative authorities.[9] Administrative law is divided into two areas: general administrative law, including administrative procedural law at the level of authorities, administrative court procedural law, general municipal law and transparency and secrecy law; and sector-specific administrative law.[10]

Sector-specific administrative law encompasses rules regarding social welfare and public order regulations for various branches of the administration, such as police forces, public rescue services, legal authorities, environmental authorities, road traffic, culture, food and businesses, and migration.[11] It may be noted that some areas such as healthcare, which in many other countries are dominated by private enterprises, fall within the public sector in Sweden and, as such, are generally subject to administrative law. It is interesting to note that substantive

[5] See, for example, the influential case *Zolotukhin v Russia*, App No 14939/03 (ECtHR, 19 February 2009).

[6] H Wenander, 'Full Judicial Review or Administrative Discretion? A Swedish Perspective on Deference to the Administration', in G Zhu (ed), *Deference to the Administration in Judicial Review: Comparative Perspectives* (Cham, Springer Nature, 2019); H Wenander, 'Europeanisation of the Proportionality Principle in Denmark, Finland and Sweden' (2020) 13 *REALaw* 133, 134 ff.

[7] For a discussion on public law in a Swedish context, see, for example, H Wenander, 'Varför offentlig rätt?' (2019) 1 *Förvaltningsrättslig tidskrift* 97; I Cameron, 'What's in a Name?' (2019) 3 *Förvaltningsrättslig tidskrift* 317.

[8] Regeringsformen (1974:152).

[9] It should be noted that Instrument of Government is the most central of Sweden's four constitutional Acts. The others three are the successionsordningen (1810:0926) (Act on Succession), tryckfrihetsförordningen (1949:105) (Freedom of the Press Act) and yttrandefrihetsgrundlagen (1991:1469) (Fundamental Law on Freedom of Expression).

[10] Administrative contracts are usually not dealt with in general legal doctrine on administrative law, apart from in relation to public procurement. These contracts will not be addressed here.

[11] H Ragnemalm, *Förvaltningsprocessrättens grunder*, 10th edn (Stockholm, Jure, 2014) 19 ff; H Strömberg and B Lundell, *Allmän förvaltningsrätt*, 27th edn (Stockholm, Liber, 2018) 16; H Strömberg and B Lundell, *Speciell förvaltningsrätt*, 20th edn (Stockholm, Liber, 2019); L Lerwall (ed), *Makt, myndighet, människa*, 4th edn (Uppsala, Iustus, 2020); U von Essen, A Bohlin and W Warnling Conradson, *Förvaltningsrättens grunder*, 3rd edn (Stockholm, Norstedts juridik, 2020) 51.

administrative law has been identified as the fastest-developing legal area in Sweden, at a pace determined mainly by the development within the EU.[12]

Administrative law includes rules on the organisation and forms of operation of the administrative authorities and rules on public administration, whether exercised by administrative authorities or by other bodies. In addition, administrative law includes rules on the relationships between individual and state bodies, whether the rules are handled by administrative authorities, administrative courts or general courts.[13]

The main statutory Act within administrative law in Sweden is the Administrative Procedures Act (APA).[14] According to section 1 APA, as a general rule, the law applies to all authorities when processing matters. Thus, the procedure rules in the APA apply to the entire administration.[15] For municipalities, the Local Government Act also applies.[16] This Act includes procedural rules and according to section 2 APA, the Local Government Act shall be applied instead of the APA in certain situations. Sector-specific administrative law deals with substantive and procedural rules for specific administrative areas. It should be noted that the sector-specific administrative law for some areas encompasses many procedural rules.[17]

Control over the administrative decisions carried out by the administrative courts is regulated by the Administrative Court Procedure Act (ACPA).[18],[19] The procedures laid down in the ACPA apply to court procedures for all types of administrative decisions. It should be noted that there are sections in the ACPA that contain references to rules in the Code of Judicial Procedure, ie, the Act applicable to procedures in general courts. These relate only to certain demarcated procedural situations.[20] In addition, administrative courts have to apply the Administrative Court Act,[21] which regulates organisational issues, competence/quorum and voting rules.

The regulation of the entire administrative procedure – ie, the processing of matters at a decision-making authority and their review in an administrative court – is thus spread over multiple laws and approximately 240 sections. Although it seems at first glance that the administrative procedure is largely regulated, it

[12] R Lavin, 'Administrative Law in Swedish Legal System' in Michael Bogdan (ed) *Swedish Legal System* (Stockholm, Norstedts juridik, 2010) 66 f.

[13] H Strömberg and B Lundell (n 11) 15.

[14] Förvaltningslagen (2017:900).

[15] Prop 2016/17:180, 25–27.

[16] Kommunallagen (2017:725).

[17] See further below, section II.A.

[18] Förvaltningsprocesslagen (1971:291).

[19] In this context, it can be noted that there are special land and environmental courts, which hear cases that concern, for example, environmental and water issues, property registration, and planning and building matters. Organisationally, these courts are treated as one of the general courts rather than one of the administrative courts.

[20] This applies, for example, to situations of oral proceedings, handling of evidence and impartiality; see further M Ribbing, *Förvaltningsprocessen och rättegångsbalken* (Stockholm, Jure, 2018) 103 ff.

[21] Lagen (1971:289) om allmänna förvaltningsdomstolar.

should be noted that the regulation is not detailed. The reason is a desire to meet the needs of authorities and courts for flexibility in the processing of matters and cases, respectively.[22] The discussion here focuses on the procedure under the APA.

## B. The Central Principles of Swedish Public Law

According to Chapter 1, section 1 of the Instrument of Government, the Swedish democracy is based on the principle of sovereignty of the people – all public power 'proceeds' from the people. Furthermore, according to the same section, Swedish democracy is founded on the free formation of opinion and on universal and equal suffrage. The Parliament (Riksdagen) is the foremost representative of the Swedish people.[23] While there is no formal division of powers expressed in the Constitution, there is a functional division between state bodies. According to the basic principles of the Constitution, the main division is between the democratically elected Parliament and regional and municipal councils on the one hand and the Government (Regeringen), courts and public administration on the other. Courts are thus defined as a specific type of authorities, but not administrative authorities.[24] It can also be mentioned that Sweden is a so-called constitutional monarchy.[25]

Alongside the principle of democracy, Chapter 1, section 1 of the Instrument of Government declares the principle of legality as a foundational principle for the Swedish state. All public power is to be exercised under the law. The public administration has no inherent right to use public powers and, accordingly, all acts must have a legal basis. In addition, Chapter 1, section 9 of the Instrument of Government states that courts, administrative authorities and other entities performing public administration functions are to uphold the principles of objectivity when doing so. The principle of proportionality is also of central importance. This principle is not explicitly mentioned in the Instrument of Government, but is a foundational principle in Swedish law with constitutional status.[26] According to

[22] Prop 2016/17:180 91 and 186; M Ribbing (n 20) 71 ff.

[23] Chapter 1, s 1 and ch 1, s 4 of the Instrument of Government.

[24] See further W Warnling Conradson, H Bernitz, L Sandström and K Åhman, *Statsrättens grunder*, 6th edn (Stockholm, Norstedts juridik, 2018) 44 ff.

[25] Chapter 1, s 5 and ch 5, s 1 of the Instrument of Government; successionsordningen (Act on Succession); W Warnling Conradson, H Bernitz, L Sandström and K Åhman (n 24) 110. Belgium, Norway and the UK are also monarchies; see the chapters on these countries in this book.

[26] Compare ch 2, s 15 of the Instrument of Government, which includes a proportionality test for limitations on fundamental rights, and ch 14, s 3 of the Instrument of Government, under which a proportionality test is to be applied when regulating municipal self-government. See further H Wenander, 'Europeanisation of the Proportionality Principle in Denmark, Finland and Sweden' (n 6) 133 ff. In relation to principles of public law, see L Marcusson (ed), *Offentligrättsliga principer*, 4th edn (Uppsala, Iustus 2020); see also below, section III.C.

the principle of independence, found in Chapter 12, section 2 of the Instrument of Government, courts and administrative authorities are both expected to fulfil their obligations independently under the law.[27] Human rights and fundamental freedoms are to be respected.[28]

Chapter 1, section 2 of the Instrument of Government stipulates certain values that state bodies must strive to realise. The provision sets out objectives for the democratic aspirations of society. Public power must be exercised so that the equal value, freedom and dignity of all citizens are respected. Public power must also strive for the welfare of the individual and the protection of social rights, a sound environment, democracy, and the private and family life of the individual, as well as participation and equality, and support for minorities.[29]

In Swedish constitutional tradition, the freedom of the press and the public access to official documents play an important part in guaranteeing the influence and involvement of the public in government affairs and in the development of civil rights. The right of access to documents goes back to 1766 and is prescribed in one of the four constitutional documents, the Freedom of the Press Act.[30,31]

Lastly, in order to promote a sound administrative culture, the Government commissioned a survey on the aforementioned central principles of Swedish public law, which was published in the form of a report in 2013.[32] The report identified six principles describing behaviours and attitudes that should characterise all government employees: democracy, legality, objectivity, freedom of opinion, respect and efficiency, and service. The Statskontoret (the Swedish Agency for Public Management) has been tasked with implementing and communicating the principles, thus contributing to and co-ordinating the state authorities' work towards a sound administrative culture.[33]

[27] See further below, section IV.A.i.

[28] Chapter 2 of the Instrument of Government includes a list of fundamental rights and freedoms that the legislator must uphold. Further, the ECHR is awarded a special status in ch 2, s 19 of the Instrument of Government; J Reichel, 'The Pan-European General Principles of Good Administration in Sweden – Undeniable But Partial Vehicles of Change' in U Stelkens and A Andrijauskaitė (eds), *Good Administration and the Council of Europe: Law, Principles and Effectiveness* (Oxford, Oxford University Press, 2020) 257 ff.

[29] Prop 1973:90, 194, 236; prop 1975/76:209, 127–31, 137; prop 2001/02:72 15–24; prop 2009/10:80, 186–91, 246.

[30] Tryckfrihetsförordningen (1949:105).

[31] B Wenngren, H-G Axberger, J Hirschfeldt and K Örtenhed (eds), *Press Freedom 250 Years. Freedom of the Press and Public Access to Official Documents in Sweden and Finland – A Living Heritage from 1766* (Stockholm, Sveriges riksdag, 2017); see further A Bohlin, *Offentlighetsprincipen*, 9th edn (Stockholm, Norstedts juridik, 2015); B Lundell and H Strömberg, *Handlingsoffentlighet och sekretess*, 13th edn (Lund, Studentlitteratur, 2019).

[32] Den gemensamma värdegrunden för de statsanställda (2013) *Värdegrundsdelegationen*.

[33] Den statliga värdegrunden – gemensamma principer för en god förvaltning (2019) *Statskontoret*.

## III. Legal Sources of Administrative Law in Sweden

### A. The APA

Neither the Swedish administration nor the administrative courts had an Act on procedures until the early 1970s, when the APA and the ACPA were enacted.[34] This can be compared with the procedural code for general courts, which was enacted in 1734. The APA has been thoroughly amended twice, in 1986 and 2017, while the 1971 ACPA is still in force.[35] Earlier administrative procedural rules were to a large extent developed in case law inspired by general procedural law, codified in an unmethodical, disorganised manner and spread across a range of special statutory laws and regulations.[36] A key aim for the 1971 APA was to draft an Act that was short, simple and easy to understand in order to facilitate its application by officials who were not lawyers.[37] These ideals still apply today and in the preparatory works to the 2017 APA, it was stated that this intention was to be maintained.[38] In terms of content, the APA thus reflects the traditional Swedish understanding of the role of public authorities in the Swedish administrative model. The partially independent authorities are to use the public powers bestowed on them to guide and assist the public and the individuals whose matters are being processed.[39] In legal doctrine, it has been emphasised that the administrative authorities shall take the individual by the hand and guide them.[40] Beyond these service-oriented traits of the Swedish APA, the interest in legal certainty for individuals has become greater.[41]

As with the previous APAs, the contents of the 2017 APA have been designed to be as pedagogical and easily accessible as possible for both officials and the public. This is seen in the extensive use of headings, among other things.[42] The introductory provisions of the law, sections 1–8 APA, concern its scope and the principles of good administration. These are followed by provisions on several general requirements for the processing of matters, for instance in relation to

[34] The reform was called *förvaltningsrättsreformen* (the administrative law reform); see prop 1971:30; bet 1971:KU36; rskr 1971:222.

[35] 1986 APA (1986:223), see preparatory works: prop 1985/86:80; bet 1985/86:KU21; rskr 1985/86:202; 2017 APA (2017:900), see preparatory works: prop 2016/17:180; bet 2017/18:KU2; rskr 2017/18:2.

[36] Prop 1971:30 Del 1 239–241; see also F Sterzel, 'Lagstiftning om förvaltningsförfarandet' (1984) 4–6 *Förvaltningsrättslig tidskrift* 322, 328, 331.

[37] Prop 1971:30 Del 1 286–289; see also F Sterzel (n 36) 402 and 409.

[38] Prop 2016/17:180 65.

[39] L Marcusson and F Sterzel, 'Introduktion till den nya förvaltningslagen – En långdragen process med start på 1940-talet' (2018) 3 *Förvaltningsrättslig tidskrift* 399, 402, 408.

[40] T Hellners and B Malmqvist, *Förvaltningslagen med kommentarer* (Stockholm, Norstedts juridik, 2007) 11. In later editions of this textbook, the importance of the duty to provide services to individuals is described in neutral terms.

[41] The strengthening of legal certainty for individuals has been identified as a core reason for the 2017 reform of the APA; see prop 2016/17:180 1.

[42] Prop 2016/17:180 20, 21 and 23.

access to files and conflicts of interest (sections 9–18 APA). Thereafter, the Act follows the progress of an individual matter, from initiation, preparation and decision to correction, amendment and appeals. To start with, provisions which concern how a matter is initiated and measures taken when documents are submitted are found in sections 19–22 APA. These are followed by provisions on the preparation of matters – mention may be made in particular of the investigative responsibility and documentation of information (sections 23–27 APA). Next comes a set of provisions concerning decision-making procedures, and requirements on giving reasons for decisions made and when decisions may be enforced (sections 28–35 APA). An important issue is under what circumstances a decision-making authority can correct or change decisions. Provisions on this can be found in sections 36–39 APA. The final provisions of the APA concern appeals, such as provisions on the entities to which decisions may be appealed and who may appeal decisions (sections 40–49 APA).

According to section 1 APA, the core part of the Swedish APA is applicable only to the processing of matters at an administrative authority. In administrative legal doctrine, the area falling outside the processing of a matter is defined as *faktiskt handlande* (administrative factual conduct). As already mentioned, the introductory provisions of the APA relate to the scope of the law (sections 1–4) and the basis for good administration (sections 5–8), including the principles of legality, objectivity and proportionality as well as service to the public, accessibility and co-operation between public authorities. The provisions on good administration apply not only to the processing of administrative matters, but also to other administration, ie, administrative factual conduct. The requirements on service, accessibility and co-operation seldom come under the review of the administrative courts, but are monitored by the Parliamentary Ombudsmen (Justitieombudsmännen (JO)), whose decisions are generally considered to carry persuasive authority.[43]

A specific feature of the Swedish APA that is relevant to address in this context is that it is subsidiary to other Acts enacted by the Parliament and governmental ordinances. Section 4 of the APA reads as follows: 'If another act or an ordinance contains a provision that differs from this Act, that provision is applied.' The 1971 and 1986 APAs contained corresponding sections, giving precedence to other acts and ordinances in case of inconsistent rules. The Government may thus enact an ordinance with rules deviating from the APA, a fact that has been criticised in the legal doctrine.[44] Many such acts and ordinances exist, creating specific rules for social services, social insurance, building and planning etc.[45] An example may be

[43] JO 2019/20 s. 440; JO dnr. 2991-2006, decision 2007-10-03. See further below, section III.C; and L Enqvist, *En myndighet i samverkan: Försäkringskassans rättsliga förutsättningar att samverka med Arbetsförmedlingen samt hälso-och sjukvården* (Umeå, Umeå universitet, 2019).

[44] L Marcusson and F Sterzel (n 39) 399 ff.

[45] eg, socialförsäkringsbalken (2010:110) (Social Insurance Code); utlänningslagen (2005:716) (Aliens Act).

given from the area of higher education. According to sections 25 and 32 APA, individuals have a right to be heard in administrative matters and a right to reasoned decisions. However, Chapter 1, section 4a of the Ordinance on Higher Education[46] holds that these sections are not applicable in matters concerning admission to or grading within higher education. If an individual requires it, reasons for grading decisions should be given afterwards, if possible and if it is necessary for the individual to exercise their rights.

Preparatory works are generally considered to have a high degree of legal authority in the Swedish legal system.[47] The two main documents are Statens Offentliga Utredningar (SOU) (Swedish Government Official Reports) and *propositioner (prop)* (legislative bills), where the latter carry greater authority. Further, *betänkanden (bet)* (committee reports) from parliamentary committees can occasionally include additional information. The Government Official Reports are organised in the form of a public authority and are led by special inquirers or, in the case of larger reports, by representatives of the Parliament. In both cases, the actual report is usually drafted by a former or sitting judge, together with a group of qualified lawyers and adjunct experts. The report normally includes qualified assessments of the law as it stands, a description of previous legislative works, comparative studies on legal solutions from other countries (usually the Nordic ones), as well as reasoned proposals for changes.[48] As mentioned above, the first Swedish APA from 1971 was preceded by an exceptionally long period of legislative work, which produced several Government Official Reports[49] and a legislative bill.[50] The two reforms of the APA were also preceded by thorough investigations.[51] It should be noted that the inquiry on the current APA was led by the former Swedish judge in the Court of Justice of the European Union and Justice of the Supreme Administrative Court, Hans Ragnemalm.[52] The report contained about 800 pages. The reasoning behind the process of codification of Swedish general administrative law is thus well documented.

After legislation, the second most important source of general administrative law is case law, which is dealt with in the following section.

[46] Högskoleförordningen (1993:100).

[47] L Carlson, *The Fundamentals of Swedish Law*, 3rd edn (Lund, Studentlitteratur, 2019) 45; PO Ekelöf, 'Teleological Construction of Statutes' in A Peczenik, L Lindahl and GC van Roermund (eds), *Theory of Legal Science* (Dordrecht, Springer, 2011) 75, 93; A Peczenik, 'Principer i det svenska statsskicket' in N Berggren, N Karlson and J Nergelius (eds), *Makt utan motvikt: Om demokrati och konstitutionalism* (Stockholm, Stockholm City University Press, 1999) 123.

[48] M Zamboni, 'Methods of Ex-ante Evaluation in Legislation: The Swedish Model' in K-H Kim (ed), *Goals and Methods of Ex-Ante Evaluation of Legislation, Proceedings of the 2019 KLRI International Conference of Legislative Evaluation in Seoul* (Seoul, Korea Legislation Research Institute, 2019) 9; I Cameron, 'Några reflektioner över lagberedning ur ett jämförande perspektiv' (2020) 1 *Svensk Juristtidning* 14, 20; L Marcusson, 'Utredare i staten' (2020) 1 *Svensk Juristtidning* 44, 46.

[49] SOU 1946:69; SOU 1955:19; SOU 1964:27; SOU 1968:27.

[50] Prop 1971:30 med förslag till lag om allmänna förvaltningsdomstolar.

[51] The 1986 APA: SOU 1981:46; SOU 1983:73; prop 1985/86:80; the 2017 APA: SOU 2010:29; prop 2016/17:180.

[52] See further below, section III.D.

## B. Case Law

Sweden has a three-tier system of administrative courts, with the Supreme Administrative Court at the top.[53] In an international comparison, the role of courts in Swedish constitutional system has for a long time been rather modest.[54] Due to an allocation of tasks, rather than a division of power, within the Swedish administrative model, the Swedish administration has been allocated functions similar to those of courts: independent decision-making, requirements on objectivity and a mandate to ignore provisions that are in conflict with any rule in fundamental law or other superior statutes.[55] Further, since medieval times, the tradition has been to appeal decisions within the administrative structure, initially to the sovereign and later to a superior authority, with the Government as the final instance.[56] At the beginning of the 1970s, the administrative courts were still considered to constitute a form of 'superior authorities' and to fall within the administrative structure rather than the judiciary one.[57] Even though the role and function of the Swedish administrative courts have gradually shifted towards those seen in more traditional courts, some 'authority-like' features remain, as will be discussed below.[58]

The administrative courts' main task under the general form of review – administrative judicial appeal – is to ensure the legal protection of the individual and that the decision on appeal is substantively correct.[59] Like the administrative authorities, the courts thus have an independent mandate to investigate cases and may, to a certain degree, consider new circumstances and evidence in a case.[60] Courts have the same mandate as authorities to reconsider a decision and may replace the decision of an authority with their own.[61]

[53] The administrative courts consist of the Administrative Court (12 courts), the Administrative Court of Appeal (four courts) and the Supreme Administrative Court. The migration courts are part of the administrative courts.

[54] M Zamboni, 'The Positioning of the Supreme Courts in Sweden: A Democratic Oddity?' (2019) 4 *European Constitutional Law Review* 668, 672; J Nergelius, *Konstitutionellt rättighetsskydd: svensk rätt i ett komparativt perspektiv* (Stockholm, Norstedts juridik, 1996) 660; W Warnling-Nerep, *Rättsmedel – om- & överprövning av förvaltningsbeslut* (Stockholm, Jure, 2015) 27.

[55] Chapter 1, s 9 and ch 12, ss 2 and 10 of the Instrument of Government; see further M Kumlien, *Professorspolitik och samhällsförändring. En rättshistorisk undersökning av den svenska förvaltningsrättens uppkomst* (Stockholm, Institutet för rättshistorisk forskning, 2019) 215; M Zamboni (n 54) 672.

[56] W Warnling-Nerep (n 54) 17; L-G Malmborg, 'Sweden' in J-B Auby (ed), *Codification of Administrative Procedure* (Brussels, Brulyant, 2014) 362.

[57] R Lavin, *Domstolar och administrativ myndighet* (Stockholm, Norstedts, 1972) 7 ff.

[58] G Wahlgren, 'Några provokativa funderingar kring förvaltningsförfarandet' (1995) 5–6 *Förvaltningsrättslig tidskrift* 203; see further below, section IV.C.iv.

[59] M Ribbing (n 20) 45; see further below, section IV.C.iv.

[60] Section 8 ACPA.

[61] Section 29 ACPA; see further H Ragnemalm, *Administrative Justice in Sweden* (Stockholm, Juristförlaget, 1991) 210.

## C. Decisions from the Parliamentary Ombudsmen and Guidance Documents

Due to the aforementioned features in relation to case law, the main focus of administrative courts has traditionally been the substantive parts of sector-specific administrative law rather than general administrative law issues, such as administrative procedures at the authority level. The court may hear pleas connected to transgressions of individuals' right to be heard, insufficient investigations on the part of an administrative authority etc, but the task of reviewing general procedural matters has traditionally been allocated to the JO.[62] Though the decisions of the Ombudsmen are not legally binding, not even for those at which the decisions are directed, they are considered to carry a high level of persuasive authority and are generally observed by administrative authorities and courts.[63]

Lastly, guidance documents enacted by public authorities, so-called *allmänna råd* (General recommendations), and other types of guidelines play an important role in practice.[64] General recommendations are non-binding rules, but have an official status. According to the Ordinance on Official Gazettes,[65] the term 'General recommendations' refers to general recommendations on the application of a statute, act of law or delegated legislation, which state how an entity may or ought to act in a certain regard.[66] As discussed by Henrik Wenander, guidance documents played an instrumental role in the Swedish Government's and the Swedish Public Health Authority's strategies to maintain social distancing and prevent the spread of the coronavirus during the COVID-19 pandemic.[67]

## D. Legal Doctrine

Legal doctrine has played an important role in the development of general administrative law. When administrative law was established as a legal subject in its own right at the end of the nineteenth century, Swedish legal scholars were highly influenced by French and, in particular, German scholars.[68] Swedish courts quote legal doctrine to a certain extent, though general courts do so more than administrative courts.

[62] J Reichel, *God förvaltning i EU och i Sverige* (Stockholm, Jure, 2006) 332. In this context, it should be mentioned that there are four Parliamentary Ombudsmen who are appointed directly by the Parliament.

[63] M Ribbing (n 20) 17.

[64] L Bejstam, 'Kan allmänna råd ändras när och hur som helst?' (2000) 1 *Förvaltningsrättslig tidskrift* 23, 24.

[65] Författningssamlingsförordningen (1976:725).

[66] Section 1 of the Ordinance on Official Gazettes; see further H Wenander, 'Sweden: Non-binding Rules against the Pandemic – Formalism, Pragmatism and Some Legal Realism' (2021) 12 *European Journal of Risk Regulation* 127.

[67] H Wenander (n 66) 134 ff.

[68] M Kumlien (n 55) 145.

In administrative law and elsewhere, it seems to be common among Swedish scholars that professors are active in other legal arenas. At the beginning of the last century, several professors in administrative law were also active as politicians.[69] Several professors have also functioned as judges in the Supreme Administrative Court or as Parliamentary Ombudsmen. Hans Ragnemalm is a prominent example, having served as a professor in public law, Parliamentary Ombudsman, Justice and later President of the Supreme Administrative Court, and the first Swedish judge in the Court of Justice of the European Union. He also led the work of the governmental inquiry that drafted the 2017 APA.[70] There are several other examples, but it will suffice to mention Rune Lavin, a professor in administrative law, Parliamentary Ombudsman, Judge at the Supreme Social Insurance Court, and Justice and later President of the Supreme Administrative Court,[71] and Elisabeth Rynning, a professor of medical law, who held a position as Judge in the Supreme Administrative Court and Chief Parliamentary Ombudsman. Legal doctrine has thus influenced administrative law in different ways, both directly and indirectly.

There is one area in which differences of opinion within Swedish administrative law scholarship are particularly apparent, namely the terminology used for describing procedural rules in the APA and the ACPA, respectively. Hans Ragnemalm refers to both as administrative procedure rules,[72] while Rune Lavin and other authors use this term exclusively for rules and principles that apply in administrative courts.[73] The differences in views can be explained by the closeness in the relationship between the administrative authority and the administrative courts.[74] The courts' reviews of administrative authorities' decisions are thus closely related to the administrative authorities' procedures.[75] Hans Ragnemalm therefore uses the same terminology for both, whereas other authors distinguish between the two. Since Ragnemalm led the work of drafting the 2017 APA, it may be assumed that his view has influenced the design of that Act. Rune Lavin has recently criticised the existence in the APA of rules on issues relating to administrative courts, for example, those relating to appeal. In his view, these belong in the ACPA.[76]

In the following section, the Swedish administrative organisation, important administrative principles and the foundations for the administrative procedure will be described and discussed.

[69] ibid 259 ff.

[70] SOU 2010:29.

[71] R Lavin, *Femtiofem år av offentligrättslig forskning* (Lund, Juristförlaget i Lund, 2020).

[72] H Ragnemalm (n 11) 32.

[73] R Lavin, *Förvaltningsprocessrätt*, 4th edn (Stockholm, Norstedts juridik, 2020) 15 ff. See also M Ribbing (n 20) 31.

[74] See further above, sections II.B and IV.C.iv.

[75] M Ribbing (n 20) 32.

[76] R Lavin, 'Förvaltningsdomstolarna och förvaltningslagen' (2019) 3 *Förvaltningsrättslig tidskrift* 361.

# IV. Organisation, Principles and Administrative Procedure in Sweden

## A. Administrative Organisation

### *i. The Swedish Administrative Model*

The Swedish state is organised into three political and administrative levels: a national level which is divided into 21 regions (regional level) and 290 municipalities (municipal level). Each level is governed by a democratically elected body: the Parliament, and regional and municipal councils. It should be mentioned that the municipalities operate under the constitutionally protected principle of local self-government in accordance with Chapter 14 of the Instrument of Government. The regions and municipalities are responsible for the implementation of vast policy areas, for example, healthcare, local public transport, social services, housing and education.

In the Swedish administrative model, the executive branch is organised in a dualistic manner. Administrative bodies are organisationally and legally separate from the Government, and regional and municipal councils, respectively, and enjoy partial independence from the Government in accordance with the principle of independence.[77] The Government Offices are comparatively small, whereas central administrative authorities are large and well staffed. Much of the expertise in sector-specific areas is allocated to the level of authorities rather than to the Government Offices. The administrative authorities are clearly part of the executive branch, falling under the command and control of the Government, as stipulated in Chapter 12, section 1 of the Instrument of Government, but enjoy a certain level of independence.

Constitutionally, the administrative model rests on two pillars. The first is relevant primarily for the state level: the state administrative authorities may only be commanded and controlled by the Government as a whole, not by any individual minister.[78] Second, all authorities, both state and municipal, are granted a constitutionally protected sphere of independent decision-making. According to the principle of independence in Chapter 12, section 2 of the Instrument of Government, no public authority, including the Parliament or the decision-making body of any local authority, may determine how an administrative authority shall decide in a particular matter relating to the exercise of public authority vis-a-vis an individual or a local authority, or relating to the application of law. A decision by

[77] U von Essen, A Bohlin and W Warnling Conradson (n 11) 115; P Hall, 'The Swedish Administrative Model' in J Pierre (ed), *The Oxford Handbook of Swedish Politics* (Oxford, Oxford University Press, 2015).

[78] Chapter 7, s 3 and ch 12, s 1 of the Instrument of Government. The administrative bodies of the municipalities are more closely integrated into the political structures of the municipal councils; see ch 6 of the Local Government Act.

the JO can be mentioned here, in which the JO criticised the head of a municipal board for having intervened regarding a decision on the refusal of alcohol licensing at a popular local restaurant and for having demanded renewed – and perhaps more lenient – inspections.[79]

Ministerial interference is thus prohibited. The administration is to be governed by law, not by political decrees in individual matters. As discussed above, Swedish administrative courts have been characterised as being similar to administrative authorities.[80] It should therefore be underlined that Swedish authorities can also be characterised as court-like. To put it differently: the Swedish constitutional tradition has not upheld a strict division between courts and public authorities.[81] Another trait worth mentioning is that Chapter 12, section 10 of the Instrument of Government allows all public authorities, in addition to the courts, to perform reviews of whether laws and other statutes are in compliance with higher-ranking law. This has long been controversial and is not of any real practical importance.[82]

### *ii. Rules Applicable to the Role of Officials in Sweden*

As seen above, the Swedish administrative model entails certain restrictions on political interference in order to keep political considerations out of administrative decision-making. The focus of the Instrument of Government is instead on the importance of objectivity for courts and administrative authorities alike: Chapter 1, section 9 of the Instrument of Government holds that: 'Courts of law, administrative authorities and others performing public administration functions shall pay regard in their work to the equality of all before the law and shall observe objectivity and impartiality.'[83]

The principle of objectivity is also reiterated in section 5 APA, together with the principle of legality and the principle of proportionality, under the heading 'The basis of good administration', which will be discussed further below.[84] The Swedish JO is instructed to pay special attention to the requirements of objectivity and impartiality in its investigations, and has often delivered detailed decisions on their significance.[85]

[79] JO 2009/10 s 384.

[80] Section 12, para 2 of the Instrument of Government. See above, section III.B.

[81] T Bull and F Sterzel, *Regeringsformen: en kommentar*, 4th edn (Lund, Studentlitteratur, 2019) 259, 275; H Wenander, 'Varför en rätt till domstolsprövning av förvaltningsbeslut? Utvecklingslinjer i svensk och finsk rätt mot bakgrund av Europakonventionen' in R Arvidsson, P Leviner, J Reichel, M Zamboni and K Åhman (eds), *Festskrift till Wiweka Warnling Conradson* (Stockholm, Jure, 2019) 437.

[82] H Wenander, 'Förvaltningens lagprövning' (2015) 3 *Förvaltningsrättslig tidskrift* 455.

[83] J Reichel, 'What is it the Public Has a Right to Know? The Right to Privacy for Officials and the Right Access to Official Documents – European and Swedish Perspectives' in A Koltay and P Wragg (eds), *Research Handbook on Comparative Privacy and Defamation Law* (Cheltenham, Edgar Elgar, 2020).

[84] See below, section V.C.

[85] Section 3 lagen (1986:765) med instruktion för Riksdagens ombudsmän (Act with Instructions for the Parliamentary Ombudsmen); see, for example, JO decision on 22 October 2018, matter no 753-2017, JO 2015/16 s 412 and JO 2005/06 s 351.

The requirements of objectivity and integrity that follow with employment at a state body are further regulated in the APA and the Public Employment Act.[86] In order for the principle of objectivity to have an impact in the public administration, sections 16–18 APA stipulate, in brief, that a person may be considered disqualified from processing a matter if it concerns someone closely associated with them. Anyone who knows of any circumstance that could constitute a ground for disqualification is obliged to disclose it. Further, section 7 of the Public Employment Act holds that officials may not have any employment or assignment or perform any activity that may jeopardise their impartiality at work or which may damage the authority's reputation.

### *iii. The Delegation of Tasks to Private Entities*

The functional division of powers and tasks laid out in Chapter 1, section 8 of the Instrument of Government holds that public administration is to be carried out by the state and municipal authorities. Legal entities under private law fall outside the scope of the Instrument of Government and therefore cannot, as a general rule, carry out administrative tasks.[87] However, this organisational division has not been systematically maintained. Under both the Instrument of Government and the Local Government Act, the delegation of tasks or services entailing the exercise of authority requires a legal basis in a statutory Act enacted by the Parliament.[88]

Private entities have always been present in Swedish administration, but a marked increase can be noted during the 1980s. Today, private entities carry out a large part of public administration, especially at the municipal level. Questions regarding access to documents, administrative protection within processing of matters and access to courts have largely been resolved on a case-by-case basis, based on sector-specific legislation combined with minimalistic general legislation.[89] The Supreme Administrative Court found that a decision on allocation of public funding made by the Riksidrottsförbundet (National Sports Federation) was to be appealable to administrative courts, since the decision was consider to fall within the concept of a civil right according to Article 6 ECHR.[90]

## B. Forms of Action

### *i. Administrative Rule-Making*

The competence of state entities to enact binding general norms is regulated in Chapter 8 of the Instrument of Government. The point of departure is that

[86] Lagen (1994:260) om offentlig anställning.
[87] Å Örnberg, *Kommunal verksamhet genom privaträttsliga subjekt* (Stockholm, Jure, 2014) 363.
[88] Chapter 12, s 4 of the Instrument of Government; ch 3, s 12 of the Local Government Act.
[89] Lagen (1986:1142) om överklagande av beslut av enskilda organ med offentliga förvaltningsuppgifter (the Act on Appeal of Decisions Made by Private Entities with Public Administrative Tasks).
[90] HFD 2019 ref 43.

central legal areas are to be regulated by means of legal Acts enacted by the Parliament.[91] In many areas, the Parliament can delegate the power of regulation to the Government via ordinances (*cf* Chapter 8, sections 3–5 of the Instrument of Government). The Government also has a direct competence to enact provisions relating to the implementation of laws as well as provisions which do not require adoption by the Parliament under the Instrument of Government, mainly regarding favourable, voluntary or neutral public law.

If the Parliament delegates regulation power to the Government, it may allow the Government to subdelegate to administrative authorities or municipalities, in accordance with Chapter 8, section 10 of the Instrument of Government. This is often done via a framework act, supplemented by a government ordinance and rule-making by administrative authorities. The Government may also delegate its own competence to enact ordinances to administrative authorities or municipalities – see Chapter 8, section 11 of the Instrument of Government. In practice, the administrative authorities have a wide level of competence to enact binding rules. Fredrik Sterzel has compared the situation to an iceberg, where only the tip is regulated by the Parliament, whereas the vast majority of rules are enacted under the surface by the administrative authorities.[92] For example, most EU Directives are implemented via administrative rule-making.[93]

### *ii. Administrative Decisions*

The most central form of action in Swedish administrative law is the administrative decision, the result of an administrative case. However, it is not easy to give a clear and comprehensive definition of what constitutes an administrative decision in Swedish law. A general starting point in legal doctrine is that a decision is to include a statement through which an authority wants to influence the actions of individuals or other authorities.[94] With regard to the ultimate effect of decisions, decisions can be classified into that contain 'direct' or 'indirect' patterns of action. Direct patterns have a close relationship with legal guarantees for realisation, such as ordering a property owner to demolish a building or issuing a ban on using a building or instating a directive to a ministry to grant compensation. Decisions that have indirect patterns of action often refer to preliminary notices, such as pre-tax notices. Thus, such decisions do not have any immediate effect; however, they may later serve as patterns of action.[95]

[91] It should be noted that the Constitution can only be amended after very careful consideration in a special procedure described in ch 8, s 14 of the Instrument of Government. Constitutional laws are enacted by means of two identical decisions of the Parliament. These decisions must be separated by a general election.

[92] F Sterzel, *Författning i utveckling: tjugo studier kring Sveriges författning* (Uppsala, Iustus, 2009) 19.

[93] D Mattsson, 'Implementering av europarätten i Sverige – några reflektioner om utvecklingen' (2009) 3 *Europarättslig tidskrift* 418.

[94] H Ragnemalm (n 11) 21, 23.

[95] ibid 24 ff.

In addition, subdivisions can be made as follows, though it should be noted that this division is not absolute. A distinction can be made between informal and formal decisions. This is related to how closely the decision-making process is regulated and whether the decision is documented in writing (even electronically).[96] A distinction can also be made between decisions that are internal to the public authority and external decisions. External decisions may constitute general decisions, norm decisions, decisions directed towards the public at large, or individual decisions directed at specific addressees, either other public bodies or one or more individuals, organisations, companies or natural persons. The content of a decision can also be considered. If a decision is favourable to an individual, it concerns a benefit of some kind. Decisions can also be onerous and require an individual to either act or refrain from action.[97]

Lastly, a distinction can be made based on the part of the procedure in which a decision is made. Preparatory decisions refer to decisions that are intended only to provide the basis for a later, final decision. Final decisions mean that the authority terminates its processing of the matter by settling the subject at hand. Decisions in the latter category are also referred to as 'main decisions'. Decisions that do not include any position from the authority on the substantive matter may include 'rejection of an application', 'dismissal' or 'referral' to another authority.[98]

## C. Administrative Protection

### *i. General Requirements for the Processing of Matters*

The starting points for the procedure are laid down as general requirements for the processing of matters in the APA, focusing on individual administrative decisions in their final form – ie, main decisions. The first part of the APA includes general requirements: all matters should be processed as simply, quickly and inexpensively as possible without compromising legal certainty for individuals and the procedure is, as a general rule, in writing (section 9), provisions on access to files (section 10), failure to act (sections 11 and 12), interpretation and translation (section 13), representation (sections 14 and 15), and rules on impartiality (sections 16–18). A little clarification should be provided here regarding some of the principles mentioned in these sections in the APA.

A basic characteristic of the Swedish administration is stipulated in section 9, namely the ideal of efficient, yet foreseeable and secure procedures. This means that efficiency interests must be balanced against the interest of legal certainty for the individual concerned, considering impartiality, investigation, participation and reasoning for decisions, as well as the interest of a decision being founded

[96] See s 31 and compare s 33, last paragraphs of the APA.
[97] See, for example, H Strömberg and B Lundell (n 11) 60 ff.
[98] See, for example, H Ragnemalm (n 11) 22.

on adequate or correct grounds.[99] However, as with the German rules on administrative procedure, the Swedish APA not only encompasses protection of the citizen, but also duties and obligations of co-operation.[100] For example, according to section 20, an authority may order an individual to remedy a deficiency in their petition to the authority, informing the individual that non-compliance may result in the petition not being considered.

The principle of access to files, stipulated in section 10, is of central importance for achieving legal certainty. The Supreme Administrative Court has considered the principle of access to files to be so central that it constitutes a general legal principle, which applies regardless of specific legal basis in the applicable law.[101]

Lengthy processing has long been a real problem in Swedish administration.[102] This was considered to be unsatisfactory. Therefore, provisions were introduced in the APA to strengthen the individual's chances to getting an effective examination and a final decision in any matter that has been processed for an unreasonable length of time. The right to remedies and judicial review within a reasonable time under Article 6(1) and (13) ECHR and Article 47 of the EU Charter of Fundamental Rights is also of importance.[103] Two provisions on measures against slow processing have been introduced in the 2017 APA: one concerns notification of delay (section 11) and the other concerns measures for processing that is delayed (section 12). The effects of the introduction of these sections can be seen, for example, in several decisions from the Parliamentary Ombudsmen concerning slow processing.[104]

The subsequent sections of the APA reflect the course of a matter and the four phases into which processing of matters can be divided: the initial, preparation, decision-making and enforcement phases. The following subsections of this text focus on the preparation of matters, administrative decisions and their reassessment and appeal of decisions. These aspects have been highlighted because important principles that have been developed in practice were codified in the APA 2017 or given a broader scope in order to strengthen legal certainty for individuals.

### *ii. The Preparation of Matters*

After a matter has been initiated at an authority, the decision-making authority's investigation into the matter begins. The preparatory works of the APA emphasise

[99] Prop 2016/17:180 74 and 75.

[100] See in this book M Heintzen, 'Codification of Administrative Law in Germany and the European Union', section I.B.iii.

[101] RÅ 1994 ref 79; RÅ 2001 ref 27.

[102] Between 2006 and 2008, the JO each year received approximately 500–600 complaints regarding lengthy processing; see SOU 2010:29 291–294.

[103] Charter of Fundamental Rights of the European Union [2012] OJ C326/391; prop 2016/17:180 107.

[104] See, for example, JO decision on 27 October 2020, matter no 221-2019 and 10 December 2021, matter no 6744-2020.

that the primary responsibility for the correct processing of the matter falls upon the first instance, the administrative authority, in order that the number of appeals may be restricted.[105] The authority's investigation of a matter involves a range of measures that are central for the individual from a legal certainty point of view, such as the responsibility to investigate (section 23), when a party may provide information orally (section 24), communication (section 25), referral (section 26) and documentation of data (section 27). Some of these measures will be described in greater detail below.

The authority should, according to section 23, ensure that a matter is investigated to the extent required by its nature. The authority has the ultimate responsibility for ensuring that the decision support in a matter is such that it results in a materially correct decision. The provision was included in the 2017 APA, but has previously been applied under the so-called *officialprincipen* (general principle of the duty to investigate). The provision is a codification of practice in the area and is a clearer delineation of Sweden's commitments under EU law and the so-called principle of care. As there are many matters of various kinds, the provision has been given a general form.[106]

Another important measure is the obligation to allow the individuals concerned a right to be heard (section 25 APA). The principle states that no one should have their affairs assessed unheard. The main rule applies to all types of matters that can arise during proceedings, whether a matter is beneficial to or burdensome for the parties concerned.[107] The provision thus entails a strong right to participate in the proceedings, and deficits in upholding this right have been severely criticised by the JO on several occasions.[108]

Further, an authority that receives information in some other way than through a document must, according to section 27, record that information as soon as possible if it is deemed to be of significance for a decision in the matter. The provision is intended to ensure the individual's right to full access to files, to ensure that the authority can fulfil its obligation to give parties the opportunity to be heard and to ensure effective judicial review.[109]

### iii. The Reassessment of Decisions

The Swedish APA and the general principles contain two mechanisms for changing an administrative decision after the decision has become final: 'correction' and 'reconsideration'.[110] Previously, only case law and legal doctrine expressed the

[105] Prop 2016/17:180 148.
[106] Prop 2016/17:180 149.
[107] Prop 2016/17:180 154–57.
[108] See, for example, JO decision on 4 December 2018, matter no 6539-2017.
[109] See further, for example, JO decision on 19 September 2018, matter no 3969-2017; J Reichel, 'Openness and Transparency' in P Cane, H Hofmann, E Ip and P Lindseth (eds), *The Oxford Handbook of Comparative Administrative Law* (Oxford, Oxford University Press, 2020) 935 ff, 938, 941.
[110] For the sake of completeness, it should be mentioned that in s 39 there is a so-called litispendence rule which creates a limited scope to change decisions that have been appealed.

principles in their entirety, whereas the 1971 and 1986 APA merely included some main rules. The first attempts to transpose the principles into legislation failed.[111] However, in the 2017 APA, explicit rules with defined exceptions were introduced, which were designed to give both authorities and individuals clear information regarding when authorities may and should change their own decisions. The risk that authorities would erroneously refrain from changing decisions was considered too great to leave this outside legislation. In addition, individuals might feel compelled to appeal a decision to bring about a change, instead of expecting the authority to correct the decision. The purpose of introducing provisions was to strengthen the legal certainty for individuals and reduce the risk of unnecessary appeals. The design of the regulations is intended to be as comprehensive and clarifying as possible. Still, it is almost impossible to have complete legislation in this area. The idea is that case law will complement and clarify the rules.[112]

The prerequisite for correction is found in section 36 APA. A decision that contains an obvious error due to a typo, a calculation mistake or other similar minor flaw may be corrected by the authority that enacted the decision. The idea is to make it possible to rectify such errors in a simple and formless manner, without having to appeal the decision in court. Section 36 APA does not impose any restrictions on the type of decision that can be changed in this way; thus, decisions that are favourable to the individual can also be changed. It is important to emphasise that there is no requirement for the authority to change a decision in such cases as these, but that the authority 'may' do so.[113]

The second category, reconsideration, is regulated in sections 37 and 38 APA. In this case, the substance of a decision can also be changed under certain circumstances. Section 37 APA focuses on the situation where reconsideration is optional for an authority and states that an authority may change a decision which it has enacted as the first instance if it finds that the decision is erroneous due to new circumstances or for some other reason. In the second paragraph, it is clarified that this does not apply to decisions that are favourable to the affected party. However, there are three exceptions to this rule, which were first developed in case law and have been codified in the 2017 APA. The exceptions are if it is stated, in the decision itself or in the statutory law upon which the decision is based, that the decision may be revoked under certain conditions, if there are compelling security reasons requiring that the decision be changed immediately, or if the error is due to the affected party providing incorrect or misleading information. It should be noted that there was a fourth exception prior to the introduction of the 2017 APA.[114] However, the Supreme Administrative Court has ruled that since the introduction of the 2017 APA, favourable decisions can only be changed in the cases specified

[111] SOU 2010:29 571–79.

[112] Prop 2016/17:180 221 and 222; SOU 2010:29 579 f.

[113] Prop 2016/17:180 223–27.

[114] In RÅ 2000 ref 16, the Supreme Administrative Court found that a favourable decision for continuous social benefits could be reconsidered if the circumstances changed and it was no longer reasonable that the benefits remained in place.

in section 37 APA.[115] This case is an example of the interplay between practice and codification.

Section 38 APA deals with the situation where an authority must reconsider a decision, which is the case if it finds that the decision is manifestly inaccurate in any substantive respect because new circumstances have arisen or for any other reason, and the decision can be changed quickly, easily and without detriment to any individual party.

### iv. *Appeal of Administrative Decisions*

There are two main ways to appeal administrative decisions in Swedish law: administrative judicial appeal and municipal appeal. Further, there is a more limited procedure, under the Act on Legal Review of Certain Governmental Decisions,[116] for decisions enacted by the Government which cannot be appealed otherwise. The latter procedure will not be discussed here.

Administrative judicial appeal is regulated in the ACPA and the APA. Provisions on appeal in the APA are found in sections 42–48, such as the criteria under which parties may appeal a decision. The right to appeal has undergone fundamental changes in Swedish law since the mid-1980s – from a right to appeal within the administrative organisation, with the Government as the final instance, to a general right of access to court. Initially, the development was motivated chiefly by the wish to reduce the burden on the Government, but the interest of fulfilling the requirements of the ECHR and EU law eventually became the prime reason for reform.[117] Today, a decision that may be assumed to affect someone's situation in a not insignificant way can be appealed by the person concerned by the decision if the decision affects them adversely.[118] As in Austria, the increased importance awarded to the individual right of access to courts has affected Swedish public law in a pervasive manner and means that politically sensitive matters may be settled within the judiciary rather than within the political arena.[119]

Due to these historical reasons, as also briefly discussed above, the mandate of administrative courts is to some degree 'authority-like' and includes an independent duty to ensure that a matter is investigated to the extent that the nature of the matter requires. Further, the administrative courts have the same decision-making competence as the deciding administrative authority and may carry out all-round assessments of any appealed decision, including both legality and suitability or reasonableness.[120] Thus, the scope of the review is wide and the court may, instead

[115] HFD 2021 ref 12.
[116] Lagen (2006:304) om rättsprövning av vissa regeringsbeslut.
[117] W Warnling-Nerep (n 54) 30.
[118] Sections 41 and 42 APA.
[119] See in this book K Lachmayer, 'Codification of Administrative Law in Austria', section III.A; J Reichel and K Åhman, 'Tjugofem år av Europarätt i Sverige' (2020) 5 *Sieps* 1, 56, 59; M Zamboni (n 54) 683 ff. See further below, section V.B.
[120] H Wenander, 'Full Judicial Review or Administrative Discretion?' (n 6) 409.

of quashing a decision, change it in substance or replace it with its own.[121] Since the mid-1990s, there has been a two-party procedure in administrative courts, where the administrative authority that enacted the decision in the first instance becomes the counterparty of the person appealing the decision.[122]

Decisions taken by municipal organs which do not concern matters specially regulated may be appealed by a special remedy called *laglighetsprövning* (legality review) under the Local Government Act. A legality review differs from the administrative judicial review in several important aspects. First, the right to appeal a decision is granted to all members of a municipality, whether or not they are personally affected by the decision.[123] Second, the procedure is a strict legality review, where the court will assess the decision on four grounds: if it has been made in due order; if it refers to a matter outside the competence of the municipality; if the deciding body has exceeded its powers; or if the decision otherwise is contrary to an act of law or other statutory provision.[124] Third, the administrative court may not consider any circumstances other than those that the appellate referred to before the end of the appeals period.[125] Even if there are grounds for allegations of illegality, they cannot be tried if they were made after the end of the complaint or only in a higher instance.[126] Fourth, the administrative court may, unlike in administrative law appeals, only quash the decision, not substitute it.[127] As held by Henrik Wenander, the judicial review under municipal appeal allows some discretionary action at the municipal level, which may be linked to the constitutional principle of local self-government.[128]

# V. The Process of Codification in Swedish Administrative Law

## A. The Legal Consequences of Sources

Scandinavian legal realism has been quite influential in Swedish legal thinking during most of the twentieth century, and the theory has also influenced how legal

[121] Sections 29 and 30 ACPA; H Wenander, 'Full Judicial Review or Administrative Discretion?' (n 6) 410.

[122] Section 7a ACPA; for more on the definition of a party in the administrative procedure, see R Lavin (n 73) 61 ff.

[123] Chapter 1, s 5 and ch 13, s 1 of the Local Government Act; compare, regarding administrative appeals, s 42 APA and s 33 ACPA.

[124] Chapter 13, s 8 of the Local Government Act; compare, regarding administrative appeals, ss 29 and 30 ACPA.

[125] Chapter 13, s 11 of the Local Government Act and s 37, para 2d ACPA; compare, regarding administrative appeals, ss 4, 5 and 29 ACPA.

[126] RÅ 1975 ref 63.

[127] Chapter 13, s 8, para 3d of the Local Government Act. However, according to ch 13, s 9, the decision need not be set aside if an error has no significance for the outcome of the case. The same applies if the decision has come to lose its meaning because of later occurrences.

[128] H Wenander, 'Full Judicial Review or Administrative Discretion?' (n 6) 412.

sources are perceived.[129] The core of Scandinavian legal realism is its objective of a 'scientific' approach to the law. In essence, this means that the law should be understood as separate from metaphysical elements.[130] Legal concepts and categories are per se conceived as being detached from any system of moral, religious or political values.[131] Alf Ross held that legal concepts, such as ownership, are in reality meaningless words (like 'tû-tû'), without any semantic reference, serving solely as tools for representation.[132] In order to be able to gain any knowledge on the contents of a legal concept, lawyers must search in the legal sources that make up part of the law in force. The doctrine of legal sources is thus normative, not merely descriptive.[133] Law-defining actors, such as courts and judges, play a central part in Scandinavian realism, since their task is to define the contents of the law by reference to valid legal sources.[134] In Sweden, the centrality of the Parliament in the law-making process, together with the comparatively weak position held by the courts, has placed a focus on legislation.[135] Further, the interpretation of the legal text in light of the legislative preparatory works has held a very strong position in the Swedish hierarchy of legal sources.[136] Also, the understanding of legal concepts as empty vessels has led to the denial of the existence of legal rights per se.

In constitutional law, it may be noted that the 1809 Instrument of Government became obsolete when parliamentarism and democratic elections were introduced in around 1920. Still, a new Instrument of Government was not enacted until 1974. This *interim* period has in legal doctrine been referred to as the 'constitution-less half century'.[137] Kumlien has held that constitutional arguments were rare in the legal debate during this period and were generally not considered serious.[138] This further contributed to a sceptical view of constitutional or higher-ranking legal rights. To this day, the Instrument of Government identifies the principle of the sovereignty of the people as the governing principle for the organisation of the state, with the Parliament being the people's foremost representative.[139]

[129] However, not many scholars refer to the theory in practice; see J Samuelsson, 'Bulleri buller bock. Hur många horn står opp? Kommentar till J Strangs "Two Generations of Scandinavian Legal Realism"' (2009) 1 *Retfaerd* 83, 87.

[130] J Reichel, 'European Legal Method from a Swedish Perspective: Rights, Compensation and the Role of the Courts' in R Nielsen, U Neergaard and L Roseberry (eds), *Towards a European Legal Method: Synthesis or Fragmentation*? (Copenhagen, Djøf Publishing, 2011) 247.

[131] M Zamboni, *Law and Politics: A Dilemma for Contemporary Legal Theory* (Berlin, Springer, 2008) 96.

[132] A Ross, 'Tû-tû' (1957) 70 *Harvard Law Review* 812, 820; V Lundstedt, *Legal Thinking Revised: My Views on Law* (Stockholm, Almqvist and Wiksell, 1956) 301; see further R Nielsen, 'Scandinavian Legal Realism and EU Law' in U Neergaard, R Nielsen and L Roseberry (eds), *The Role of Courts in Developing a European Social Model: Theoretical and Methodological Perspectives* (Copenhagen, Djøf Publishing, 2010) 240.

[133] A Ross, *On Law and Justice* (London, Stevens, 1958) 29, 104.

[134] Ross especially emphasised the predictive nature of the work of lawyers; see ibid 42; and also R Nielsen (n 132) 237.

[135] J Nergelius (n 54) 611; M Zamboni (n 131) 106; see also above s II.1.

[136] PO Ekelöf (n 47) 93; A Peczenik (n 47) 123.

[137] F Sterzel (n 92) 19.

[138] M Kumlien (n 55) 167.

[139] Chapter 1, s 1 and ch 1, s 4 of the Instrument of Government.

This majoritarian understanding of democracy has traditionally prevailed in Sweden and the other Nordic states.[140] The Nordic states have thus historically allocated the task of choosing what role individual rights should play in their domestic legal systems to the Parliament instead of to the courts.[141] As will be discussed below, the process of Europeanisation of Swedish law in general and of Swedish public law in particular has led to what has been referred to as a 'rights revolution'.[142]

The theoretical and methodological approaches in general administrative law deviate from this perspective to a certain extent. As seen above in section II.A, the first APA was enacted in 1971 and was a minimum regulation designed to be filled out by other legal sources. The great need for a flexible procedure and a space for issuing regulations specific to a certain part of the administration has justified that the APA remains designed to ensure only a minimum level of legal certainty for individuals.[143] Further, due to the specific position of the administrative courts, JOs have played an influential role in developing general administrative law. The JO review is less formal than that of courts. The Ombudsmen have repeatedly held that an administrative authority cannot merely follow the letter of the law, but can also be obliged to uphold the principles behind the law in a wider field.[144] An example can be given from 2016, before the entry into force of the present APA, in a case regarding the question of whether the police was obliged to address the legal representative of a woman when executing a decision on extradition. Since the actions undertaken by the police were administrative factual conduct, not processing of a matter, the core parts of the APA, including the right to representation, were not applicable. The JO found that the police should uphold the right anyway:[145]

> However, the fact that a provision in the Administrative Procedure Act is not directly applicable to a situation does not exclude that there may still be grounds for applying the provision. The purpose behind the Act, including the interest in achieving good administration and a secure procedure, often justifies their application in these situations as well.

The 2017 APA has not changed these provisions, so it can be assumed that the Parliamentary Ombudsmen would reach the same conclusion today. General principles of law have thus played a greater role in general administrative law than in other areas of Swedish law.

[140] A Ross, *Varför demokrati?* (Stockholm, Santérus Förlag, 2003) 89; H Tingsten, *Demokratins problem* (Stockholm, Norstedt, 1945) 102; J Nergelius (n 54) 133; M Wind, D Sindbjerg Martinsen and G Pons Rotger, 'The Uneven Legal Push for Europe: Questioning Variation When National Courts Go to Europe' (2009) 10 *European Union Politics* 63, 71.

[141] R Nielsen (n 132) 229 ff, 261; T Ojanen, 'From Constitutional Periphery toward the Center: Transformation of Judicial Review in Finland' (2009) *Nordisk tidsskrift for menneskerettigheter* 194, 197.

[142] T Bull, 'Rättighetsskyddet i Högsta förvaltningsdomstolen' (2017) 3 *Svensk juristtidning* 216, 216.

[143] Prop 2016/17:180 s. 39.

[144] See, for example, JO 1996/97 s 179; JO 1997/98 s 306 on the obligation to apply rules on hearing parties and reasons for decisions outside the sphere of application of the 1986 APA.

[145] JO decision on 6 September 2016, matter no 7291-2014.

## B. European Influences: From the Eighteenth Century to the Twentieth Century

General codifications of law were previously carried out in Sweden from the Middle Ages onwards, with the last major code being enacted in 1734. As noted by Claes Peterson, even though the code has been referred to as 'the first modern Code of Enlightenment', it did not constitute a break with previous legal traditions. Law was still understood as a metaphysical element rather than a political tool, where the goal was to come as close as possible to a legal order given by God.[146] The 1734 code contained nine parts (*balkar*) on marriage, inheritance, real property, agriculture, trade, criminal behaviour, criminal sentencing, recovery proceedings and general court procedures. The different parts have been reformed one by one over the years. Though no general code has been enacted since 1734, several central legal Acts still retain their original names. Examples include *äktenskapsbalken* (the Marriage Code)[147] and *jordabalken* (the Land Code).[148] Some more recent statutory acts that have also been named codes are *miljöbalken* (the Environmental Code)[149] enacted in 1998 and *socialförsäkringsbalken* (the Social Insurance Code) from 2010.[150]

Today, the title *balk* does not entail a specific legal status relative to other statutory law, beyond signalling that the Act in question is a central and comprehensive piece of legislation in a specific area of law. General administrative law has not been encompassed by these codifications, either in the earlier acts or in more recent years. However, the *socialförsäkringsbalken* does include several chapters on administrative procedure rules applicable to that area of law.[151]

A more recent form of Europeanisation, which has gradually become included in Swedish statutory law, emanates from the Council of Europe and the EU. In this case, it is not a question of a general or even a co-ordinated and coherent legislative strategy. The development has been neither linear nor without friction. However, it is evident that the ECHR and the EU have had a fundamental impact on the Swedish legal order as a whole, perhaps most obviously on constitutional and administrative law.[152] The influence on Swedish law has been substantial in relation to both substantive law and the use of applicable legal sources, where case

[146] C Peterson, '1734 års lag – en medeltida lagbok eller en upplysningskodifikation? Till frågan om synen på lagändring i det förliberala samhället' in R Sandberg (ed), *Studier i den äldre historien tillägnade Herman Schuck* (Stockholm, Minab/Gotab, 1985) 276, 299.

[147] Äktenskapsbalken (1987:230).

[148] Jordabalken (1970:994).

[149] Miljöbalken (1998:808).

[150] Socialförsäkringsbalken (2010:110).

[151] See, for example, ch 108 (recovery and interest rates), ch 110 (handling of cases), ch 111 (self-service services via the internet), ch 112 (decisions) and ch 113 (correction, reconsideration and appeal of decisions) in the socialförsäkringsbalken (Social Insurance Code).

[152] J Reichel and H Wenander (n 4) 241; J Reichel, 'Europeiska principer för god förvaltning och 2017 års förvaltningslag' (2018) 3 *Förvaltningsrättslig tidskrift* 423.

law and general principles of law have increased in importance.[153] Perhaps the most important change relates to the understanding of individual rights in the Swedish legal order. Justice Thomas Bull, previously a professor of constitutional law, recently stated that the protection of rights in Swedish law has undergone a revolution, as Swedish courts are more frequently and with greater confidence upholding fundamental rights based on the Swedish Constitution, the ECHR or EU law.[154] Some areas have undergone radical changes, with one example being the inclusion in the 2017 APA of a general right to appeal administrative decisions to court (sections 41 and 42 APA), which was developed in case law.[155] It can be noted that after the provisions were introduced, the Supreme Administrative Court has in several decisions further clarified what constitutes an appealable decision.[156] Thus, the long-standing tradition of appealing administrative decisions within the administrative structure has been abandoned. Some other areas have remained more or less intact, such as the partially independent status of administrative authorities and the focus on service as a central part of good administration.

Focusing on the 2017 APA more specifically, it is clear that the ECHR and EU law have influenced the drafting of that Act in several ways. When Sweden joined the EU in 1995, the Government stated in the preparatory works for the Accession Act that the 1986 APA complied with the requirements of EU law and that no changes were required.[157] This may have been accurate at the time, but the process of Europeanisation has both deepened and widened subsequently. In the preparatory works for the 2017 APA, the ECHR and EU law were referred to on several occasions to justify changes and the introduction of new rules, in particular the introduction of the principle of proportionality as part of good administration, the procedure on failure to act and the aforementioned right of access to court.[158]

In the following section, limiting principles on the exercise of power that have been codified are discussed.

## C. Codification of Principles of Action

One of the novelties in the 2017 APA is the introduction of the concept of good administration. The concept is included in the heading 'the basis of good administration' before an introductory part of the APA, laying down provisions on the principles of legality, objectivity and proportionality (section 5), on service (section 6), on accessibility (section 7) and on co-operation between authorities

[153] J Reichel and K Åhman, 'Tjugofem år av Europarätt i Sverige' (2020) 5 *Sieps* 1, 57, 59.
[154] T Bull (n 142).
[155] eg, the basis for a procedure regarding whether a decision can be considered appealable was laid out in RÅ 2004 ref 8.
[156] See, for example, HFD 2019 ref 21, 2019 ref 43, 2020 ref 12 and 2020 ref 14.
[157] Prop 1994/95:19 531.
[158] Prop 2016/17:180, 60–62, 101–09, 244–50 and 260–63.

(section 8). As mentioned above, the principles of legality and objectivity are governed by the Instrument of Government. To strengthen the rule of law at the national level, and as a consequence of processes of Europeanisation, these principles are now also included in section 5 of the 2017 APA.[159]

The principle of legality requires that all onerous public law – ie, interventions against individuals – must have clear constitutional support in sources that make up the legal order.[160] Objectivity entails an obligation to act objectively and impartially. This includes a prohibition on irrelevant considerations and considerations other than those which, according to the applicable law, are to be applied when examining a matter.[161] It also means creating consistency in decision-making. The administration is also characterised by the fact that a balance should be upheld between general and individual interests. Simply put, the principle of proportionality means that every intervention measure must be capable of satisfying the intended purpose, must be necessary to achieve this purpose and must bring benefits that are proportional to the damage caused by the measure; in other words, the authorities should 'not shoot mosquitoes with guns'.[162] It is clear from the case law that the principle of proportionality is well established in Swedish administrative law. The requirements of proportionality are particularly high in relation to interventions that can be compared to trading prohibitions.[163]

A central part of the Swedish understanding of good administration lies in the obligation of the authorities to provide good services to the public. The authorities are to assist the public in various ways. The provision in section 6 APA stipulates the level of service that an individual can expect when dealing with the authorities. An authority shall ensure that contacts with individuals are smooth and simple. The service duty is understood as an expression of professionalism.[164]

Another aspect of the principle of good administration is that the authorities, under section 7, should be as available to the public as possible. This applies not only to visits and telephone calls from individuals, but also to authorities being available by email or through a website.[165] An authority must, according to section 8 APA, co-operate with other authorities in its area of activity. The obligation is general, but not unlimited. The forms of collaboration vary depending on the purpose – for example, providing archive documents or responding to a referral request.[166] In contrast to the rest of the APA, the part of the Act which stipulates the basis of good administration is applicable to administrative factual conduct, as well as to processing of matters (section 1).

[159] Prop 2016/17:180, 57–61.

[160] See, for example, JO 2012/13 32. On the principle of legality, see further C Lebeck, *Legalitetsprincipen i förvaltningsrätten* (Stockholm, Norstedts juridik, 2018).

[161] Prop 2016/17:180 59, 60; see, eg, JO 2006/07 s 362.

[162] Prop 2016/17:180, 60–64; see further H Wenander, 'Proportionalitetsprincipen i 2017 års förvaltningslag' (2018) 3 *Förvaltningsrättslig tidskrift* 443.

[163] See, for example, HFD 2017 ref 5.

[164] Prop 2016/17:180, 66–68.

[165] Prop 2016/17:180, 68–70.

[166] Prop 2016/17:180, 70–73.

One central issue that may arise during the processing of a matter is the question of the temporal application of a provision when an Act has been enacted or redrafted and transitional provisions are missing. It should be noted that the ban on retroactivity under Chapter 2, section 10 of the Instrument of Government only concerns retroactive penal and tax law. Since there is no general provision in the APA or the ACPA regarding the law that is to be applied when transitional provisions are lacking, the issue has largely been left to the administrative courts to resolve. The Supreme Administrative Court has considered this matter in some cases and has established a starting point, but has also stated that there are several exceptions to this principle.[167] It ruled that which administrative law provisions are to be applied in a case is generally governed by the regulations in effect at the time of the hearing. In subsequent case law, further aspects have been presented and special emphasis has been placed on the nature of the provision and the effects that could arise if the new wording of a rule were applied before a legislative change came into force.[168]

## D. Has the Codification of the Administrative Law Finally Materialised?

As discussed above, administrative procedural law for both administrative authorities and courts was uncodified in Swedish law until 1971, while procedural law for general courts was codified as early as 1734. When a new procedural code for the general courts was enacted in the 1940s, an initiative was taken to regulate administrative procedures for both administrative authorities and administrative courts. The legislative work was lengthy and the two Acts (the APA and the ACPA) were not enacted until 1971. The reform also resulted in a new organisation for general administrative courts, whereby a three-tier administrative court system was introduced.[169]

One of the questions thoroughly investigated within the legislative work from the 1940s onwards was whether the APA ought to be comprehensive and detailed or provide minimum rules of a general nature.[170] Initially, a comprehensive code was drafted, but in the end the legislature chose a minimalistic option. As mentioned above, a key aim was to draft an Act that was short, simple and easy to understand so as to facilitate its application by officials who were not lawyers.[171] The first

[167] See mainly HFD 2021 ref 21; RÅ 1988 ref 132; RÅ 1996 ref 57.

[168] See, eg, HFD 2021 ref 12; RÅ 2003 ref 88; RÅ 2004 ref 82.

[169] The Administrative Court of Appeal was established in 1799 and the Supreme Administrative Court in 1909. In the 1970s, a first instance was added: the Administrative Court. The mandate of these courts was also expanded at this time and has been gradually widened subsequently. See further SOU 1994:117 33; W Warnling-Nerep, *Rätten till domstolsprövning & rättsprövning*, 3rd edn (Stockholm, Jure, 2008) 34.

[170] L Marcusson and F Sterzel (n 39) 402.

[171] ibid 402, 409; see also above, section II.A.

APA of 1971 contained 20 sections, which was expanded to 33 in a redrafted Act in 1986. When the third APA was enacted in 2017, the aim was – for the first time – to provide a comprehensive set of rules for processing administrative matters.[172] Thus, the 2017 APA contains provisions which codify rules developed and clarified based on case law and the practice of the Parliamentary Ombudsmen. One example is seen in the aforementioned rules on the duty to investigate (section 23), whereas other principles have been more comprehensively regulated, such as correction and reconsideration of administrative decisions (sections 36–38) and rules on access to courts (sections 40–44). A litispendence rule has also been included (section 39), which states that the authority can no longer reconsider its decision once the files have been handed over to a court for appeal. The position of the Act as a central law for the administrative authorities has thus been strengthened. Fredrik Sterzel and Lena Marcusson have remarked that it is only with the 2017 APA that the ideas of the initial 1940 legislative work have been realised.[173]

In addition to serving as a comprehensive Act, the 2017 APA aims at strengthening legal certainty for the individuals concerned.[174] As discussed above, the Swedish administrative model means that authorities are independent, well staffed and somewhat court-like.[175] The organisational structure is in itself considered to guarantee an objective and qualified processing of matters, where the authorities are tasked with providing the individual concerned with all the administrative services that the law stipulates. The authorities have thus played an essential role in the development of the Swedish welfare state. The other side of the coin is that the role of the Swedish administration can be described as paternalistic or majoritarian, where the state – rather than private entities, civil societies, non-governmental organisations (NGOs) etc – is responsible for ensuring the rights of the people.[176] After joining the EU in 1995, this understanding of the role of the administration has been challenged.[177] A clear example is seen in the effects that the Aarhus Convention – implemented in Sweden via EU law – has had on the rights of environmental NGOs to challenge administrative activities.[178] In controversial matters, such as the hunting of wolves, environmental NGOs has used the platform provided by the Aarhus rights of information, participation and access to courts to influence the political debate on biological diversity in Sweden.[179]

[172] Prop 2016/17:180, 1.

[173] L Marcusson and F Sterzel (n 39) 400, 404, 407.

[174] Prop 2016/17:180, 1.

[175] See above, section IV.A.i.

[176] On the role of the Swedish Consumer Ombudsman, see A Bakardjieva Engelbrekt, 'Institutional Theories, EU Law and the Role of Courts for Developing a European Social Model' in U Neergaard, R Nielsen and L Roseberry (eds), *The Role of Courts in Developing a European Social Model: Theoretical and Methodological Perspectives* (Copenhagen, Djøf Publishing, 2010) 259 ff, 339.

[177] J Reichel (n 62) 574.

[178] J Reichel, 'Judicial Control in a Globalised Legal Order: A One Way Track? An Analysis of the Case C-263/08 *Djurgården-Lilla Värtan*' (2010) 3(2) *REALaw* 69, 80.

[179] J Darpö and Y Epstein, 'Thrown to the Wolves: Sweden Once Again Flouts EU Standards on Species Protection and Access to Justice' (2015) 1 *Nordisk miljörättslig tidskrift* 7.

In the 2017 APA, the procedural protection of individuals was strengthened in several ways. First, central aspects of the APA were previously applicable only to matters that involved the exercise of public authority, leaving out matters where the authority was, for example, a party in a commercial contract, including in public procurement.[180] Today, the right to be heard, the right of access to files and the right to a reasoned decision apply to almost all administrative matters. Further, these central procedural rules have been given a wider area of application, with fewer exceptions available.[181]

The comprehensive approach may also entail a 'one-size-fits-all' view that does not benefit individual interests in all cases. The new litispendence rule in section 39 APA may thus be interpreted as prohibiting an authority from changing a decision on social benefits in an informal and timely manner if the prerequisites for reconsideration are at hand, as was the practice before the entry into force of the 2017 APA.[182] The need for a more customised administrative procedure can be realised via sector-specific legislation, since the APA is subsidiary to other legislative Acts and ordinances.[183] On the other hand, an extensive use of sector-specific legislation may undermine the position of the APA as the central Act for authorities.[184]

An important limitation remains, namely that the main part of the APA is only applicable when processing administrative matters, and not in administrative factual conduct. As seen by the decision of the JO, the interest of good administration may 'often require' authorities to apply the rules also in such situations.[185] Even though the 2017 APA is more comprehensive than its predecessors, the non-traditional use of general principles as a source of law in Sweden may be presumed to continue in general administrative law.

## VI. Conclusions

In this chapter, the Swedish system for codification of administrative law has been presented. In summary, the Swedish definition and delimitation of administrative law mainly encompasses rules on the organisation and forms of operation of authorities, rules on public administration and rules on the relationship between individual and state bodies. In legal doctrine, the focus has traditionally been on processing of individual matters, whereas administrative factual conduct is dealt with to a lesser extent and other areas, such as administrative contracts, have

[180] Sections 14–17, 20–21 1986 APA.

[181] V Persson, 'Obehövlig kommunikation och beslutsmotivering' (2018) 3 *Förvaltningsrättslig tidskrift* 499.

[182] L Hjorth Warlenius, 'Omprövning efter att beslutet överklagats – En granskning av nya förvaltningslagens litispendensreglering' (2020) 1 *Förvaltningsrättslig tidskrift* 35.

[183] Section 1 APA; see also above, section II.A.

[184] L Hjorth Warlenius (n 182) 35 ff.

[185] See eg, JO decision on 6 September 2016, matter no 7291-2014.

largely been neglected. Further, administrative law can be viewed as having several subdivisions: general administrative law, including procedural law at the level of authorities, administrative court procedural law, general municipal law, sector-specific administrative law, and transparency and secrecy law.

The first APA (1971) was a minimum regulation to be filled out by other legal sources. This means that administrative authorities cannot only observe the letter of the law. Instead, an administrative authority can be obliged to uphold the principles underlying the law in a wider field, with the procedural protection of individuals naturally being of central importance. One could say that general principles play a larger role in administrative law than in other areas of Swedish law. However, it should be noted that the APA has, through legal reforms in 1986 and 2017, become more comprehensive, mainly as a result of principles developed in practice having been codified. It is also clear that the ECHR and EU law influenced the drafting of the 2017 APA in several ways. The position of the APA as a central law for the administrative authorities has thereby been strengthened. It has been remarked that with the APA 2017, the ideas underlying the initial legislative work have finally been realised. Even so, it may be presumed that general administrative principles will remain an important cornerstone of general administrative law.

# 11

# Codification of Administrative Law in Switzerland

FELIX UHLMANN

## I. The Notion of (General) Administrative Law in Switzerland

### A. Background and Function

One may start with a clarification: there is no such thing as a 'general administrative law' in Switzerland in the sense of a legal Act of Parliament encompassing general rules in the context of administrative law. Such general laws do exist in other areas of the law. The general rules on contracts have been codified in the first division of the Code of Obligations.[1] The first book of the Penal Code[2] is dedicated to the 'general provisions', as the unofficial English translation reads, dealing with the territorial and personal scope of the law, general terms such as intention and negligence, omission and commission, attempts, participation (incitement, complicity), errors of fact and of law, defences such as legitimate self-defence or necessity etc. There exists no comparable legal basis for administrative law or, at least, only in specific areas, such as subsidies (see below, section II.C).[3]

[1] Bundesgesetz betreffend die Ergänzung des Schweizerischen Zivilgesetzbuches (Fünfter Teil: Obligationenrecht) vom 30. März 1911 (SR 220) (Federal Act on the Amendment of the Swiss Civil Code (Part Five: The Code of Obligations)).

[2] Schweizerisches Strafgesetzbuch vom 21. Dezember 1937 (SR 311.0) (Swiss Criminal Code).

[3] Some doctrine argues that because of the differences in administrative law, no general part can be created as in private or criminal law. See P Karlen, 'Abschied vom Allgemeinen Verwaltungsrecht? Gedanken zu einer Neuorientierung der Verwaltungsrechtslehre' in M Rüssli, J Hänni and R Häggi Furrer (eds), *Staats- und Verwaltungsrecht auf vier Ebenen, Festschrift für Tobias Jaag* (Zurich, Schulthess, 2012) 21 f; P Tschannen, *Systeme des Allgemeinen Verwaltungsrechts* (Bern, Stämpfli, 2008) fn 366 f. Another part of the doctrine considers a codification of a general part of administrative law to be beneficial and possible. See A Griffel, *Allgemeines Verwaltungsrecht im Spiegel der Rechtsprechung* (Zurich, Schulthess, 2017) fn 18; A Griffel, 'Dynamik und Stillstand im Verwaltungsrecht' in M Rüssli, J Hänni and R Häggi Furrer (eds), *Staats- und Verwaltungsrecht auf vier Ebenen, Festschrift für Tobias Jaag* (Zurich, Schulthess, 2012) 14; R Suhr, *Möglichkeiten und Grenzen der Kodifizierung des allgemeinen Teils des schweizerischen Verwaltungsrechts* (Basel, G Krebs AG, 1975) 105 f.

General administrative law (or administrative law) may more aptly be characterised as a *method or discipline*. Indeed, the term goes rather back to dogmatic origins than to legislative sources.[4] It was introduced by the scholar Fritz Fleiner in his book entitled *Institutionen des Deutschen Verwaltungsrechts* (1911).[5] The word 'Institutionen' (institutions) makes it clear that the source of administrative law does not come from the legislator.[6] Later books on (general) administrative law focus on court decisions.[7] Modern books deal with 'administrative law' or 'general administrative law', whereas the term 'general' itself is not without critique.[8] In the French-speaking part of Switzerland, following the French tradition, one typically speaks only of 'droit administratif' (administrative law).[9]

This dogmatic origin suggests that general administrative law in Switzerland must be understood less by its sources than by its *functions*. There is a broad consensus that some general rules apply to more or less any field of administrative law.[10] Some scholars critically remark that general administrative law should not consist only in generalisations.[11] Nevertheless, the legislator of specific legislation will typically rely on these general rules. This reliance may come in form of terms: an administrative decision is a *terminus technicus* that will have the same meaning throughout administrative law and the legislator will expect that the authorities will understand that the specific law refers to this cornerstone of administrative action. However, it should also be noted that the harmonisation

[4] G Biaggini, 'Was ist das "Allgemeine" des "Allgemeinen Verwaltungsrechts"?' (2016) *Schweizerisches Zentralblatt für Staats- und Verwaltungsrecht* 333, 333 f; U Häfelin, G Müller and F Uhlmann, *Allgemeines Verwaltungsrecht* (Zurich, Dike, 2020) fn 6.

[5] F Fleiner, *Institutionen des Deutschen Verwaltungsrechts* (Tübingen, Mohr Siebeck, 1911). Despite the dogmatic origin, it is important to note that Fleiner pursued an inductive method. In his work, he tried to extract the common concepts and institutes of general administrative law from the laws. See A Kley, *Geschichte des öffentlichen Rechts der Schweiz*, 2nd edn (Zurich, Dike, 2015) 70.

[6] See also in this book M Heintzen, 'Codification of Administrative Law in Germany and the European Union', section I.A.ii.

[7] M Imboden, *Schweizerische Verwaltungsrechtsprechung, Die Rechtsgrundsätze der Verwaltungspraxis, erläutert an Entscheiden der Verwaltungsbehörden und Gerichte* (Basel, Helbing Lichtenhahn, 1960).

[8] G Biaggini (n 4) 333 f; see also P Karlen (n 3) 23.

[9] *cf* the titles of the following textbooks: P Moor, A Flückiger and V Martenet, *Droit administratif, Les fondements*, vol 1, 3rd edn (Bern, Stämpfli, 2012); T Tanquerel, *Manuel de droit administrative*, 2nd edn (Geneva, Schulthess, 2018). For an exception, *cf* J Dubey and J Zufferey, *Droit administratif général* (Basel, Helbing Lichtenhahn, 2014).

[10] A Griffel, *Allgemeines Verwaltungsrecht* (n 3) fns 8, 11; B Waldmann and R Wiederkehr, *Allgemeines Verwaltungsrecht* (Zurich, Schulthess, 2019) ch 1, fn 8. Wiederin points out for Austria that the consensus on the goal of administrative law (abstraction, identification of commonalities, elaboration of ideas for order and presentation of basic lines) is only superficial. In fact, three different concerns (unification and codification, simplification and organisation, and sub-area integration and clustering) are pursued under this goal (E Wiederin, 'Allgemeines Verwaltungsrecht Auf der Suche nach dem Sinn' in D Ennöckl, N Raschauer, E Schulev-Steindl and W Wessely (eds), *Über Struktur und Vielfalt im Öffentlichen Recht, Festgabe für Bernhard Raschauer* (Vienna, Springer, 2008) 289 ff). In my opinion, this probably also holds true for Switzerland.

[11] P Karlen (n 3) 21 ff; B Schindler, '100 Jahre Verwaltungsrecht in der Schweiz' (2011) *Zeitschrift für schweizerisches Recht* 331, 416 f; see also P Tschannen (n 3) fn 380. It is argued that the doctrine should also focus in future on the differences and compare the different laws.

and homogenisation function of the general terms may be undermined by the legislator by using the same terms differently in numerous special Acts or by using different terms for the same thing. This will be discussed below in sections II.B and II.C. Despite the great importance that the terms and definitions have for general administrative law, it consists of more than just them. It may serve as a basis for governmental action. Many specific laws define the sanctions an authority may apply in order to implement the law, but even in the absence of any provisions on sanctions, there exist some instruments commonly accepted by doctrine or courts such as *Ersatzvornahmen* (substitute performances). The legal basis for such instruments is the duty of the authority to fulfil a certain task. Some sanctions are implicitly 'included' in this duty.[12]

General administrative law will also restrict governmental action. The principle of proportionality is a requirement for any lawful administrative act. The legislator will rarely use this term, or only as a 'reminder' to the authority, sometimes giving this idea a more precise meaning in a certain legal context.[13] It should be added that the legislator is not necessarily above the rules of general administrative law: the principle of legality addresses both the legislator and the authorities, meaning that not only must administrative authorities adhere to the law, but also that the law itself needs a certain legal quality such as a minimal density and rank.[14] Other principles are at the disposition of the legislator (eg, a statute of limitations)[15] and others are in a complex interplay between being a binding rule to the legislator, but by the same token a rule to be concretised or modified by the legislator, such as the aforementioned principle of proportionality.[16] It goes without saying that the *marge de manoeuvre* of the legislator to design administrative law will depend on the legal (constitutional) basis of the general administrative law, one of the key questions that will be discussed in this chapter.

[12] A Griffel, *Allgemeines Verwaltungsrecht* (n 3) fn 571; U Häfelin, G Müller and F Uhlmann (n 4) fn 1472; P Tschannen, U Zimmerli and M Müller, *Allgemeines Verwaltungsrecht*, 4th edn (Bern, Stämpfli, 2012) § 32, fn 23; B Waldmann and R Wiederkehr (n 10) ch 6, fn 20. By considering the duty to be implicitly included, the doctrine reconciles the substitute performances with the principle of legality.

[13] G Müller and F Uhlmann, *Elemente einer Rechtssetzungslehre*, 3rd edn (Zurich, Schulthess, 2013) fns 308 ff; F Uhlmann and J Bukovac, 'Das Verhältnismässigkeitsprinzip aus dem Blickwinkel der Rechtsetzungslehre' in Zentrum für Rechtsetzungslehre and F Uhlmann (eds), *Verhältnismässigkeit als Grundsatz der Rechtsetzung und Rechtsanwendung, 17. Jahrestagung des Zentrums für Rechtsetzungslehre* (Zurich, Dike, 2019) 36 ff.

[14] F Uhlmann, 'Legalitäsprinzip' in O Diggelmann, M Hertig Randall and B Schindler (eds) *Verfassungsrecht der Schweiz*, vol 2 (Zurich, Schulthess, 2020) fns 20 ff; F Uhlmann, 'Administrative Law' in M Thommen (ed), *Introduction to Swiss Law* (Berlin, Carl Grossmann, 2018) 193 ff; F Uhlmann and F Fleischmann, 'Das Legalitätsprinzip – Überlegungen aus dem Blickwinkel der Wissenschaft' in Zentrum für Rechtsetzungslehre and F Uhlmann (eds), *Das Legalitätsprinzip in Verwaltungsrecht und Rechtsetzungslehre, 15. Jahrestagung des Zentrums für Rechtsetzungslehre* (Zurich, Dike, 2017) 13 ff.

[15] According to doctrine, the statute of limitations is an unwritten general principle of law, which is at the disposal at the legislator. *cf* U Häfelin, G Müller and F Uhlmann (n 4) fns 147, 153 ff; P Tschannen, U Zimmerli and M Müller (n 12) § 16, fn 9; B Waldmann and R Wiederkehr (n 10) ch 1, fn 25.

[16] F Uhlmann and J Bukovac (n 13) 34 ff.

The function of administrative law explains its attraction to the legislator in specific areas of administrative law: it is convenient that the legislator may rely on general rules. It makes the specific legislation 'lighter' in the sense that it does not need to be burdened with self-evident, generally accepted rules of administrative law.[17] Furthermore, still from the standpoint of specific legislation, one may also contend that general administrative law offers a welcome flexibility to the legal text: if specific legislation relies on general administrative law, it will also adapt accordingly if general administrative law develops. If all the rules were to be laid down in specific legislation, the legislator must constantly observe whether amendments should be made in order to 'keep up' with developments of general administrative law. Hence, general administrative law offers *convenience* and *flexibility* to specific legislation.[18]

From a wider perspective, general administrative law offers *coherence* to the administrative law systems. It ensures that the general ideas of administrative law are applied similarly in all territories of administrative law.[19] It has been sometimes claimed that due to the strong specialisation, too little attention is paid to general administrative law. Indeed, if lawyers and courts in banking law consult only banking law cases, it may well be possible that different approaches to the same basis questions of administrative law develop.[20] Such has been the case in the area of dealing with formal errors before lower courts; different chambers of the Swiss Supreme Court have developed stricter and more lenient views on this subject, which was clearly undesirable.[21] This shows that general administrative law not only offers advantages from the viewpoint of specific legislation, but also that the legal order as a whole may benefit from general administrative law.

[17] From the point of view of legislative theory, a general part, legal definitions and references fulfil a comparable function, which is to avoid repetition (*cf* G Müller and F Uhlmann (n 13) fns 196 ff, 355, 362). From this perspective, general administrative law assumes a similar function.

[18] A comparable idea underlies dynamic references (*cf* ibid, fns 368 ff).

[19] G Biaggini (n 4) 334; A Griffel, *Allgemeines Verwaltungsrecht* (n 3) fn 10; U Häfelin, G Müller and F Uhlmann (n 4) fn 5; B Schindler (n 11) 419; P Tschannen, U Zimmerli and M Müller (n 12) § 1, fn 34; B Waldmann and R Wiederkehr (n 10) ch 1, fn 8. Tschannen points out that (general administrative) law can hardly get beyond subsystems, since an overall system is artificial, confusing and rigid. Therefore, it is important to ensure that the elements of one subsystem can be linked to those of another (P Tschannen (n 3) fn 380).

[20] F Uhlmann, 'Entwicklungen im Verwaltungsrecht' (2018) *Schweizerische Juristen-Zeitung* 424, 424; for remarks on the loss of importance of general administrative law through special administrative law, see also A Griffel, 'Dynamik und Stillstand' (n 3) 14; on the same from the Austrian point of view, see E Wiederin (n 10) 286 f.

[21] For the different court practices and the tendential preference for the more lenient practice, see M Albertini, *Der verfassungsmässige Anspruch auf rechtliches Gehör im Verwaltungsverfahren des modernen Staates, Eine Untersuchung über Sinn und Gehalt der Garantie unter besonderer Berücksichtigung der bundesgerichtlichen Rechtsprechung* (Bern, Stämpfli, 2000) 462, 467 f; L Kneubühler, 'Gehörsverletzung und Heilung, Eine Untersuchung über die Rechtsfolgen von Verstössen gegen den Gehörsanspruch, insbesondere die Problematik der sogenannten "Heilung"' (1998) *Schweizerisches Zentralblatt für Staats- und Verwaltungsrecht* 97, 103 ff, 112, 116; R Wiederkehr, 'Die Begründungspflicht nach Art. 29 Abs. 2 BV und die Heilung bei Verletzung' (2010) *Schweizerisches Zentralblatt für Staats- und Verwaltungsrecht* 481, 499 ff.

## B. Typical Areas

If one looks at the question of what is understood by general administrative law, one may well turn to textbooks and treatises in this area. There are of course noticeable differences in terms of the subjects dealt with in these books – some include procedure, some not – but the core subjects are not in dispute. Typical topics include the following:

- *Principles of action*: legality, proportionality, rationality, good faith and legitimate expectations, prohibition of retroactivity etc.
- *Forms of action*: administrative decisions, administrative contracts, private law contracts, administrative rule-making and regulation, information to the public, administrative sanctions etc.
- *Administrative organisation*: the principle of hierarchy, centralisation and decentralisation, delegation of tasks, delegation of tasks to private entities, establishing of decentralised agencies and enterprises, rights and obligations of civil servants etc.
- *Administrative protection*: administrative procedure, including the right to be heard and other principles of fairness, court protection, including administrative discretion etc.

Books differ in terms of what subjects they treat as 'general' or 'special': this may be said for monopolies and concessions, subsidies, police action, zoning and expropriation, public fees etc. Although these topics are more special than the basic principles such as proportionality, which are actually sometimes derived from the very general ideas of administrative law, these topics are also general in the sense that they apply to a variety of specific laws, and hence are in line with the function of general administrative law as described above (see above, section I.A).[22]

A final point should be made about federalism in Switzerland: the notion of Swiss administrative law is misleading in the sense that there is not just one general administrative law but a federal administrative law and 26 cantonal (state) administrative laws.[23] Still, books on Swiss administrative law usually pass over this nuance, at least in their title.[24] From a legal standpoint, in principle, cantonal and federal administrative law need not to be congruent as the cantons are free in terms of their organisation, which includes administrative law. As far as the

[22] A Griffel, *Allgemeines Verwaltungsrecht* (n 3) fns 7 ff; P Tschannen (n 3) fn 368 f; P Tschannen, U Zimmerli and M Müller (n 12) § 1, fns 36 ff; B Waldmann and R Wiederkehr (n 10) ch 1, fn 8.

[23] *cf* the autonomy of the Canadian provinces; see in this book P Issalys, 'A Persistent Taste for Diversity: Codification of Administrative Law in Canada', section II.

[24] For this reason, it has already been criticised that general administrative law suffers from a 'Föderalismusblindheit' (blindness to federalism) (*cf* G Biaggini, *Theorie und Praxis des Verwaltungsrechts im Bundesstaat, Rechtsfragen der 'vollzugsföderalistischen' Gesetzesverwirklichung am Beispiel des schweizerischen Bundesstaates unter vergleichender Berücksichtigung der Rechtsverwirklichungsstrukturen in der Europäischen Gemeinschaft* (Basel, Helbing Lichtenhahn, 1996) 308 ff; B Schindler (n 11) 381, 416).

Constitution requires a minimum standard in some areas (eg, the right to be heard), this must be respected. However, practically speaking, many questions of administrative law are treated alike in the Confederation and the cantons. The federal rules also serve as an example and are tacitly integrated into the cantonal system.[25] This could also be explained by the three-layered structure of general administrative law (federal authorities applying federal law, cantonal authorities applying cantonal law and cantonal authorities enforcing federal law), because cantonal authorities must apply federal law in the last case anyway.[26] This is not to say that there are no noticeable differences. For example, the problem of missing legal protection against harmful real acts has been solved quite differently by the cantons.[27] Still, for the purposes of this chapter, one may speak of general administrative law as the distillate of federal and cantonal rules.

# II. Sources of General Administrative Law in Switzerland

## A. The Constitution

'Verwaltungsrecht ist konkretisiertes Verfassungsrecht' ('Administrative law is concretised constitutional law').[28] This is also true in the opposite direction.[29] This quote is roughly 60 years old, but certainly still relevant and true.[30] The Swiss Supreme Court has in a long and creative court practice carved out a set of rules that build the cornerstone of fair proceedings. The equal protection clause served as the constitutional basis – not an obvious choice, but there were few anchorages in the Swiss Constitution of 1874. The Swiss Supreme Court considered unfair

[25] For example, the federal definition of administrative decision is implicitly used by the cantons. See for the definition art 5 of the Bundesgesetz über das Verwaltungsverfahren (Verwaltungsverfahrensgesetz, VwVG) vom 20. Dezember 1968 (SR 172.021) (Federal Act on Administrative Procedure (Administrative Procedure Act, APA)); see also U Häfelin, G Müller and F Uhlmann (n 4) fn 852; B Waldmann and R Wiederkehr (n 10) ch 4, fn 13.

[26] See for the three-layer-structure G Biaggini (n 24) 319 ff.

[27] A Griffel, *Allgemeines Verwaltungsrecht* (n 3) fn 64; U Häfelin, G Müller and F Uhlmann (n 4) fn 1436; P Tschannen, U Zimmerli and M Müller (n 12) § 38, fn 23; B Waldmann and R Wiederkehr (n 10) ch 4, fns 191, 197 f.

[28] F Werner, 'Verwaltungsrecht als konkretisiertes Verfassungsrecht' (1959) *Deutsches Verwaltungsblatt* 527. See also M Heintzen (n 6) section I.B.i.

[29] M Müller, *Verwaltungsrecht, Eigenheiten und Herkunft* (Bern, Stämpfli, 2006) 17 ff.

[30] In this context, it is worth noting that there is a dispute as to whether only self-executing administrative regulations in the Constitution are sources of administrative law. Some scholars argue that in all other cases, the Constitution acts only as a basis, directive or barrier, but not as a source and that these must be observed by all authorities rather than only administrative authorities (P Tschannen, U Zimmerli and M Müller (n 12) § 17, fns 3 ff; B Waldmann and R Wiederkehr (n 10) ch 1, fns 15 f; *contra* U Häfelin, G Müller and F Uhlmann (n 4) fns 52 ff). The dispute is without consequence, because there is agreement on the matter.

proceedings as a denial of justice – more precisely, as a denial of a specific right resulting in inequality if this right was granted to others.[31] The Swiss Supreme Court also intervened against arbitrariness, often against cantonal Acts where the Court had to apply only lenient scrutiny, but was willing to maintain some basic legal standards both in procedure and in the outcome.[32] As there were only limited grounds for appeal to bring a cantonal case before the Swiss Supreme Court, namely the violation of fundamental rights such as the equal protection clause encompassing the prohibition of arbitrariness and of denial of justice, the cantonal administrative law was strongly shaped by constitutional principles. Still, it was not always clear whether the Swiss Supreme Court quashed a cantonal decision because it violated constitutional standards or whether the cantonal decision just was arbitrary because it grossly violated cantonal practice in other cases. So, in other words, the constitutional core of administrative law was evident in some areas, nebulous in others.

The constitutional dimension became more transparent with the enactment of the Swiss Constitution of 1999. Here, the constituent had to decide which aspects of administrative law were to be transposed into constitutional terms. The task is remarkable because, for purely political reasons, the constitutional reform was designed as a 'Nachführung' (mere update), meaning that it was a reform in form only, but not in substance. In this context the doctrine distinguishes between the Constitution in the formal sense and the Constitution in the material sense. 'Constitution' in the formal sense is understood to mean all norms that came into being in the constitution-making process. By contrast, 'Constitution' in the material sense is understood to mean all norms that enjoy constitutional status due to their importance. In particular, unwritten fundamental rights are also included here. The aim of the constitutional reform was to include all norms of the Constitution in the material sense in the Constitution in the formal sense so that they are congruent.[33] Hence, at least in theory, the Swiss Constitution should identify what part of general administrative law is constitutional in nature (or was in 1999).

Indeed, some aspects of administrative law are now clearly rooted in the Constitution. This holds true for procedural safeguards and guarantees (Articles 29, 29a and 30 of the Constitution) which was undisputed in the making.[34] It is also

[31] G Bachmann, *Anspruch auf Verfahren und Entscheid, Der Zugang zum Verwaltungsverfahren und zur Verwaltungsrechtspflege unter besonderer Berücksichtigung der verfassungsrechtlichen Verfahrensgarantien* (Bern, Stämpfli, 2019) 157 ff.

[32] F Uhlmann, *Das Willkürverbot (Art. 9 BV)* (Bern, Stämpfli, 2005) fns 24 ff.

[33] G Biaggini, 'Grundfragen der Verfassungsstaatlichkeit' in G Biaggini, T Gächter and R Kiener (eds), *Staatsrecht*, 2nd edn (Zurich, Dike, 2015) fns 2 ff; for the 'update', see generally Botschaft über eine neue Bundesverfassung (BBl 1997 I 1) 28 ff, 34 f, 36 ff; H Koller, 'Die Nachführung der Bundesverfassung' in Y Hangartner and B Ehrenzeller (eds), *Reform der Bundesverfassung, Beiträge zum Verfassungsentwurf vom 19. Juni 1995* (St Gallen, Dike, 1995) 50 ff; G Müller, 'Zur Bedeutung der Nachführung im Rahmen der Reform der Bundesverfassung' (1997) *Zeitschrift für Schweizerisches Recht* 21, 21 ff.

[34] Botschaft über eine neue Bundesverfassung (BBl 1997 I 1), 181, 183, 502 ff, 523 f.

noteworthy that the Swiss Constitution, under its general provisions, stipulates 'Grundsätze rechtsstaatlichen Handelns' (fundamental principles of the rule of law, unofficially translated by the federal chancellery as 'rule of law'), encompassing that all activities of the state must be based on and are limited by law (the principle of legality) and that state activities must be conducted in the public interest and be proportionate to the ends sought (the principle of public interest and the principle of proportionality). This triad of lawful action was generally accepted when fundamental rights were restricted; as a constitutional principle it has a more recent history[35] (although the Swiss Supreme Court made it clear two decades earlier that the principle of legality also applies to state services and not only restrictions).[36] Furthermore, the powerful doctrine of legitimate expectations received a solid footing in constitutional law (Article 9 of the Constitution).[37] Other principles remain rather homeless: the principle of non-retroactivity is a likely candidate for a constitutional basis, but it remains rather unclear whether it should be understood as a consequence of the principle of legality, of the principle of good faith, or both, and to what extent its main ideas are protected by the Constitution.[38] The same holds true for the principle that fees for state services should not exceed the costs in the respective domain of administrative law ('Kostendeckungsprinzip' (cost recovery principle)); in my opinion, it has little or no constitutional footing, but that is not uncontroversial[39] (whereas the twin principle of equivalence according to which state services should result in a reasonable fee is derived from the principle of proportionality and hence is constitutional).[40]

It comes to no surprise that the Constitution is strongest in administrative law when it restricts governmental action. Its principles are protective in nature and often have the status of fundamental rights. This is obvious for procedural

[35] For the prinicple of legality, *cf* R Hertach, *Das Legalitätsprinzip in der Leistungsverwaltung* (Zurich, Schulthess, 2012) 1, 6 ff; for the principle of proportionality, *cf* Hofstetter, *Das Verhältnismässigkeitsprinzip als Grundsatz rechtsstaatlichen Handelns (Art. 5 Abs. 2 BV), Ausgewählte Aspekte* (Zurich, Schulthess, 2012) fns 13 ff.

[36] BGE 103 Ia 369, consideration 5 f, 380 ff.

[37] See generally A Griffel, *Allgemeines Verwaltungsrecht* (n 3) fns 170 ff; U Häfelin, G Müller and F Uhlmann (n 4) fns 624 ff; P Tschannen, U Zimmerli and M Müller (n 12) § 22, fns 1 ff; F Uhlmann, 'Administrative Law' (n 14) 194 ff; B Waldmann and R Wiederkehr (n 10) ch 5, fns 111 ff.

[38] A Griffel, *Allgemeines Verwaltungsrecht* (n 3) fn 306; U Häfelin, G Müller and F Uhlmann (n 4) fns 266 f; G Müller, 'Zulässigkeit der begünstigenden Rückwirkung, Zugleich ein Beispiel für die Wirkungen ungenauen Zitierens' (2017) *Schweizerisches Zentralblatt für Staats- und Verwaltungsrecht* 268, 269; F Uhlmann, 'Administrative Law' (n 14) 199; B Waldmann and R Wiederkehr (n 10) ch 1, fn 52. Sometimes the requirement of legal equality (art, 8 para 1 of the Constitution) is also mentioned as a basis for the principle of non-retroactivity (A Griffel, *Allgemeines Verwaltungsrecht* (n 3) fn 307; G Müller (n 38) 269). In the ECHR, the prohibition of retroactivity is explicitly laid down in art 7(1) ECHR, but only for criminal proceedings.

[39] U Häfelin, G Müller and F Uhlmann (n 4) fn 2778; *contra* P Karlen, *Schweizerisches Verwaltungsrecht, Gesamtdarstellung unter Einbezug des europäischen Kontexts* (Zurich, Schulthess, 2018) 430; P Tschannen, U Zimmerli and M Müller (n 12) § 58, fn 10; B Waldmann and R Wiederkehr (n 10) ch 8, fn 37.

[40] A Griffel, *Allgemeines Verwaltungsrecht* (n 3) fn 488; U Häfelin, G Müller and F Uhlmann (n 4) fn 2785; P Tschannen, U Zimmerli and M Müller (n 12) § 58, fn 19; B Waldmann and R Wiederkehr (n 10) ch 8, fn 32.

guarantees, but less so for principles attributed to the rule of law. In sum, such principles form the guard rails of general administrative law in Switzerland.[41]

## B. General Legislation and Codes (on Administrative Procedure)

As described above in section I.A, there is no general administrative law code in Switzerland. Still, laws play an important role in shaping general administrative law.

Some sort of codification can be found in administrative and court procedure Acts, as is the case in many countries.

The impulse for the codification of administrative procedure in Switzerland came from the doctrine. Two lectures[42] given at the Swiss Jurists' Day led the Swiss Jurists' Association in 1950 to adopt a resolution[43] calling for constitutional and administrative jurisdiction. The concern finally found its way into Parliament, which commissioned Imboden to draw up a preliminary draft of the law. In addition to expanding administrative jurisdiction, Imboden also proposed regulating non-contentious and internal administrative proceedings.[44] Eventually, the Mirage affair in 1964, which shook confidence in the Federal Council and the Federal Administration, increased the pressure to develop and regulate administrative jurisdiction. Finally, the Federal Act on Administrative Procedure (Administrative Procedure Act (APA))[45] was adopted on 20 December 1968.[46] At that time, some cantons already had laws going back to the nineteenth century, while others had no laws[47] at all until 2000.[48] But overall, it can be said that the

[41] U Häfelin, G Müller and F Uhlmann (n 4) fn 54 f; P Karlen (n 39) 88; P Tschannen, U Zimmerli and M Müller (n 12) § 17, fns 3, 6 f; T Tanquerel proposes ideas for aiming at 'good administration', notably a right to coherence of the administration or a principle of good faith extended (T Tanquerel 'Les grands principes : origine, état des lieux et perspectives' in F Bellanger, F Bernard (eds), *Les grands principes du droit administratif* (Schulthess Éditions romandes, 2022), 24 ff.

[42] M Imboden, 'Erfahrungen auf dem Gebiet der Verwaltungsrechtsprechung in den Kantonen und im Bund' (1947) *Zeitschrift für schweizerisches Recht* 1a; H Zwahlen, 'Le fonctionnement de la justice administrative en droit fédéral et dans les cantons' (1947) *Zeitschrift für schweizerisches Recht* 95a; see also Botschaft des Bundesrates an die Bundesversammlung über das Verwaltungsverfahren (BBl 1965 II 1348) 1357 f; B Schindler, 'Die Kodifikation des Verwaltungsverfahrens in der Schweiz' (2013) *Zeitschrift für neuere Rechtsgeschichte* 33, 37. This is not to say that there were no previous discussions in the doctrine (see for references B Schindler (n 11) 361).

[43] Schweizerische Juristenverein, 'Résolutions/Resolutionsentwurf' (1950) *Zeitschrift für schweizerisches Recht* 442a, 442a ff.

[44] Botschaft des Bundesrates an die Bundesversammlung über das Verwaltungsverfahren (BBl 1965 II 1348) 1357 f; B Schindler (n 42) 37.

[45] Bundesgesetz über das Verwaltungsverfahren (Verwaltungsverfahrensgesetz, VwVG) vom 20. Dezember 1968 (SR 172.021) (Federal Act on Administrative Procedure (Administrative Procedure Act, APA)).

[46] B Schindler (n 42) 37 f.

[47] *cf* Verwaltungsverfahrensgesetz des Kantons Appenzell Innerrhoden vom 30. April 2000 (GS 172.600).

[48] B Schindler (n 11) 406; B Schindler (n 42) 34; see generally R Schweizer, 'Auf dem Weg zu einem schweizerischen Verwaltungsverfahrens- und Verwaltungsprozessrecht (Nach einem Vortrag vom 28.

codification development began similarly to that at the federal level from 1950 onwards.[49] The reason for the codification of administrative law in the APA was the fragmentation and incompleteness of the former administrative procedural law. It has been argued that codification can solve these problems and achieve legal certainty, more legal protection and relieve the Federal Supreme Court.[50]

In the canton of Zurich, the reason for codification was the realisation that democratic instruments alone do not guarantee legal administration and that the Federal Supreme Court does not provide sufficient legal protection.[51] There were different authorities, private organisations and the Zurich law association which were pushing for codification. But the enactment of an Administrative Procedure Act failed in Zurich in 1933 due to a referendum, as the Government Council was critical of the law and argued that the activity of an administrative court could become an obstacle to government activity.[52] It was not until 1958 that the Administrative Procedure Act was passed in Zurich, but it achieved a large majority in a renewed referendum.[53]

Swiss administrative procedure is built around the idea of an administrative act, the *administrative decision* (or administrative ruling in the translation from the federal chancellery). In short, administrative acts are decisions of the authorities in individual cases that are based on public law and establish, amend or withdraw the rights or obligations of private parties. They are the key instrument to implement administrative law and are the predominant form of (formal) action by the authorities. Legal protection goes hand in hand with the existence of an administrative decision, and legal protection against informal ('real') acts was introduced only a decade ago.[54]

The enactment of secondary legislation and administrative rules follows a more political logic and offers little or no protection under a due process clause.[55] The existence of administrative contracts is implicitly accepted, but usually not regulated.[56] The same holds true for private law contracts (with the exception of

November 1989 an der Juristischen Abteilung der Hochschule St Gallen)' (1990) *Schweizerisches Zentralblatt für Staats- und Verwaltungsrecht* 193.

[49] B Schindler (n 11) 406.

[50] Botschaft des Bundesrates an die Bundesversammlung über das Verwaltungsverfahren (BBl 1965 II 1348) 1349 ff; M Imboden (n 42) 45a ff, 81a ff; B Schindler (n 42) 34 ff.

[51] A Griffel, commentary on Einleitung, in A Griffel (ed), *Kommentar zum Verwaltungsrechtspflegegesetz des Kantons Zürich (VRG)* (Zurich, Schulthess, 2014) Einleitung, fn 6.

[52] A Griffel (n 51) Einleitung, fn 8.

[53] Gesetz über den Rechtsschutz in Verwaltungssachen des Kantons Zürich (Verwaltungsrechtspflegegesetz) vom 24. Mai 1959 (OS 40, 546).

[54] See generally A Griffel, *Allgemeines Verwaltungsrecht* (n 3) fns 23 ff; U Häfelin, G Müller and F Uhlmann (n 4) fns 849 ff; P Tschannen, U Zimmerli and M Müller (n 12) § 28, fns 1 ff; F Uhlmann, 'Administrative Law' (n 14) 202 ff; B Waldmann and R Wiederkehr (n 10) ch 4, fns 12 ff.

[55] U Häfelin, W Haller, H Keller and D Thurnherr, *Schweizerisches Bundesstaatsrecht*, 10th edn (Zurich, Schulthess, 2020) fn 845a; R Kiener, W Kälin and J Wyttenbach, *Grundrechte*, 3rd edn (Bern, Stämpfli, 2018) § 40, fn 17; R Kiener, B Rütsche and M Kuhn, *Öffentliches Verfahrensrecht*, 2nd edn (Zurich, Dike, 2015) fn 189.

[56] B Waldmann and R Wiederkehr (n 10) ch 4, fns 135 ff.

public procurement, where legislation is in abundance since the translation of the Government Procurement Agreement (GPA) into national law).[57]

The brief overview shows that legislation in administrative procedure is by no means a complete codification in the sense that it covers all the questions that are typically raised as far as forms of actions are concerned. It concentrates on administrative decisions and their procedure before authorities and courts, relying on the fact that other questions are covered by general administrative law. It is no coincidence that the emergence of such laws in the cantons spans many decades, as it was perfectly legitimate to rely for such questions on general administrative law consisting of administrative and court practice and doctrine. Administrative and court practice in particular ensured legal certainty by becoming customary law or creating unwritten constitutional rights.[58] Still, there was pressure (also political) to regulate the basic questions of Swiss administrative procedure by law. In substance, cantonal procedures vary, eg, regulating administrative contracts or the revocation of administrative decisions instead of leaving this to general administrative law.[59]

The differences in administrative procedure highlight the complementary, flexible nature of general administrative law – which would not be the case if its existence could be explained by constitutional law only. In the area of administrative procedure, the Swiss Supreme Court meticulously differentiates between the constitutional minimal standard and cantonal law that may grant more procedural rights than the Constitution. The Court reiterates that the canton can do so and starts the legal analysis with the question whether the cantonal rights go further than the Constitution (which is rarely the case).[60] This technique is less strictly applied when it comes to other areas of general administrative law.

Another example of a successful codification is the Federal Act on the General Part of Social Insurance Law.[61] Before the enactment the Swiss social insurance law followed many different systems,[62] which were far from

[57] The main sources of national law adopted under the GPA are: Bundesgesetz über das öffentliche Beschaffungswesen (BöB) vom 21. Juni 2019 (SR 172.056.1) (Federal Act on Public Procurement (PPA)); Verordnung über das öffentliche Beschaffungswesen (VöB) vom 12. Februar 2020 (SR 172.056.11) (Ordinance on Public Procurement (PPO)); and Interkantonale Vereinbarung über das öffentliche Beschaffungswesen (IvöB) vom 15. November 2019 (available at SAR 150.960). See generally Botschaft zur Totalrevision des Bundesgesetzes über das öffentliche Beschaffungswesen (BBl 2017 1851), 1858 ff; G Biaggini, A Lienhard, M Schott and F Uhlmann, *Wirtschaftsverwaltungsrecht des Bundes,* 6th edn (Basel, Helbing Lichtenhahn, 2016) 81 ff.

[58] Botschaft des Bundesrates an die Bundesversammlung über das Verwaltungsverfahren (BBl 1965 II 1348) 1351 f; B Schindler (n 42) 36 f.

[59] The administrative contract is, for example, regulated in arts 123 ff of the Gesetz über die Verwaltungsrechtspflege des Kantons Glarus (Verwaltungsrechtspflegegesetz, VRPG) vom 4. Mai 1986 (GS III G/1). The revocation of administrative decisions is, for example, regulated in art 28 of the Gesetz über die Verwaltungsrechtspflege des Kantons St Gallen (VRP) vom 16. Mai 1965 (sGS 951.1).

[60] eg, Federal Supreme Court decision 1P.34/2003 of 20 March 2003, consideration 2.3.

[61] Bundesgesetz über den Allgemeinen Teil des Sozialversicherungsrechts (ATSG) vom 6. Oktober 2000 (SR 830.1).

[62] The Swiss social insurance system is made up of the following schemes: health insurance, accident insurance, military insurance, unemployment insurance, family benefits in agriculture, income

an overall concept.[63] For example, elementary terms such as 'employee' were defined differently in the different systems. Also, the rules for the reduction or denial of a benefit varied from system to system, and the legal protection was also designed differently in the systems.[64] Although the legislator paid attention to compatibility when enacting new laws and the former Federal Insurance Court also promoted unification by laying down general principles, the differences nevertheless affected the coherence of social insurance law. For this reason, there was an undisputed need for codification.[65] In this case, an important step towards codification was taken by the Schweizerische Gesellschaft für Versicherungssecht (Swiss Society of Insurance Law) when one of its working groups prepared a draft of an Act on the general part of social insurance law. The Federal Act on the general part of social insurance law was finally drafted and adopted on this basis.[66] It should be mentioned at this point that the law was drafted by Parliament as part of a parliamentary initiative and not, as is usually the case, by the Federal Administration.

## C. Specific Legislation

One can debate whether the Federal Act on Subsidies[67] qualifies as specific legislation or whether it is part of general administrative law (see above, section I.B). It is certainly noteworthy that the enactment of this Act (and with comparable Acts at the cantonal level) was indeed linked to the idea of codification in the sense that the legal situation should be streamlined and made coherent within the many special laws providing for subsidies.[68] These goals were undisputed, as

replacement for members of the armed forces and civil defence, old-age and survivors' insurance, disability insurance, supplementary benefits to old-age, survivors' and disability insurance, and occupational old-age, survivors' and disability provision. The 10 systems still exist, but they have been made coherent by the Federal Act on the general part of social insurance law.

[63] Parlamentarische Initiative Sozialversicherungsrecht Stellungnahme des Bandesrates vom 17. April 1991 (BBl 1991 II 910) 911; G Frésard-Fellay, 'Commentary on Einführung and Art 23 ATSG' in G Frésard-Fellay, B Klett and S Leuzinger (eds), *Basler Kommentar, Allgemeiner Teil des Sozialversicherungsrechts* (Basel, Helbing Lichtenhahn, 2020) Einführung, fns 1 ff.

[64] Parlamentarische Initiative Allgemeiner Teil Sozialversicherung, Bericht der Kommission des Ständerates vom 27. September 1990 (BBl 1991 II 185) 236.

[65] Parlamentarische Initiative Sozialversicherungsrecht Stellungnahme des Bandesrates vom 17. April 1991 (BBl 1991 II 910) 911; G Frésard-Fellay (n 63) Einführung, fn 5; U Kieser, commentary on Vorbemerkungen in *Schulthess Kommentar, Kommentar zum Bundesgesetz über den Allgemeinen Teil des Sozialversicherungsrechts ATSG*, 4th edn (Zurich, Schulthess, 2020) Vorbemerkungen, fns 24 ff. Interestingly, Nordum mentions the Norwegian General Social Insurance Act 1997 as an example of an important codification to increase accessibility in Norway (see in this book JC Fløysvik Nordrum, 'Codification of Norwegian Administrative Law', section VII.G).

[66] Parlamentarische Initiative Sozialversicherungsrecht Stellungnahme des Bandesrates vom 17. April 1991 (BBl 1991 II 910) 910 f; G Frésard-Fellay (n 63) Einführung, fns 77; U Kieser (n 65) Vorbemerkungen, fns 31 ff.

[67] Bundesgesetz über Finanzhilfen und Abgeltungen (Subventionsgesetz, SuG) vom 5. Oktober 1990 (SR 616.1).

[68] Botschaft zu einem Bundesgesetz über Finanzhilfen und Abgeltungen (BBl 1987 I 369), 373 f; A Griffel, *Allgemeines Verwaltungsrecht* (n 3) fn 517; U Häfelin, G Müller and F Uhlmann (n 4) fn 2529.

the former federal subsidy system was characterised as a jungle due to the plurality of its terms, legal institutions, legal levels and the density of regulation. Some of the differences were justified by the specificities of the individual funding areas, but many differences were not factually justified and were based on coincidences or a lack of consideration by the legislator.[69] The Federal Supreme Court also came to this conclusion in a decision and further criticised the legislator and the administration for apparently not paying special attention to the determination of time limits and their proper standardisation.[70] Despite the undisputed goal, there were also critical voices, which argued that a general subsidy Act could not be adapted to the specificities of the individual subsidy areas. The Federal Council countered that the differences undoubtedly had to be taken into account, but that this did not exclude the formulation of general principles and procedural rules, and the standardisation of legal institutions.[71] Finally, the Federal Act on Subsidies was enacted in 1990 and consequently defines in Article 1, paragraph 2 the following as its objective: '[The Act] lays down principles for lawmaking and formulates general provisions on [subsidies].' This comes quite close to what has been defined as the function of general administrative law, ie, formulating general provisions.[72]

The Swiss Act on Subsidies and its cantonal siblings are specific pieces of legislation in the sense that they apply, as the titles suggest, to subsidies only. Still, they raise questions that are typically discussed in general administrative law. To name but a few: subsidies are usually granted by way of an administrative decision, but an administrative contract can be concluded if the competent authority has considerable administrative discretion or if it should be excluded that the recipient unilaterally waives the task (Article 16, paragraphs 1 and 2). This comes quite close to what is proposed in general administrative law. So should the scope of Article 16, as a general rule, be extended to all legal relationships in administrative law?[73]

A similar question is raised by the Federal Act on Public Procurement[74] and its predecessors: before the conclusion of a private law contract, the process of

[69] Botschaft zu einem Bundesgesetz über Finanzhilfen und Abgeltungen (BBl 1987 I 369) 371 f.

[70] BGE 98 Ib 351 consideration 2b, 357.

[71] Botschaft zu einem Bundesgesetz über Finanzhilfen und Abgeltungen (BBl 1987 I 369) 376.

[72] Griffel argues that the subsidy system is more likely to be classified as special administrative law due to the legal regulation (A Griffel, 'Dynamik und Stillstand' (n 3) 14).

[73] One could also ask if art 30, para 1 PPA, which generally states that benefits which have been wrongfully granted in violation of legal provisions or on the basis of incorrect or incomplete facts can in principle be revoked, and art 30, para 2, which states that revocation is waived if this would result in unreasonable financial losses, if the infringement was not easily recognisable to the recipient or if the incorrect or incomplete determination of the facts is not due to culpable action on the part of the recipient, could not be generalised. This is probably not the case, as the rule in general administrative law is that an order can only be revoked if there are grounds similar to a revision (*cf* B Waldmann and R Wiederkehr (n 10) ch 4, fn 94).

[74] Bundesgesetz über das öffentliche Beschaffungswesen (BöB) vom 21. Juni 2019 (SR 172.056.1) (Federal Act on Public Procurement (PPA)).

decision-making with the administrative authority is governed by public law and offers legal protection for applicants under public law, commonly labelled as 'Zweistufentheorie' (theory of the two steps).[75] May one contend that the logic of the PPA is applicable to all private law contracts rightfully concluded by the government? Some scholars are at least not averse to this, specifically on the grounds that legal protection is otherwise inadequately guaranteed.[76] On the other hand, there is a strong opinion in the doctrine, which vehemently denies the application in other areas on the grounds that the theory has its origin in a very specific historically context, so it should not be transferred, and that the application would violate the principle of legality.[77]

Back to the Federal Act on Subsidies: the question of a 'model solution' may not only be raised in connection with general administrative law, but also if a more specific regulation is contrasted to a more general legislative rule. The APA requires that administrative decisions must be clearly marked as thus and must come with reasons and an instruction on how to appeal. For subsidies, there are some facilitations: an administrative decision is required to reject applications, but benefits to a large number of recipients can be granted informally (Article 16, paragraphs 4 and 5 of the Federal Act on Subsidies). Should this (plausible) rule be extended to all forms of governmental benefits, leaving the stricter scope of subsidies? The question remains unsolved.[78] It highlights the power of specific rules that can be extended by analogy to other areas of administrative. However, no overreaching strategy has been brought forward to deal with these questions.

## D. Private Law

Private law has long been the source of general administrative law and it still is. Private law is much older than administrative law and has been, as in many civil law countries, extensively codified in Switzerland in the Code of Obligations from 1881 and the Swiss Civil Code of 1907. Both sources have been influential on general administrative law.

[75] A Abegg, *Der Verwaltungsvertrag zwischen Staatsverwaltung und Privaten, Grundzüge einer historisch und theoretisch angeleiteten Dogmatik öffentlichrechtlicher und privatrechtlicher Verwaltungsverträge* (Zurich, Schulthess, 2009) 93 f; A Griffel, *Allgemeines Verwaltungsrecht* (n 3) fn 91; U Häfelin, G Müller and F Uhlmann (n 4) fns 1392 ff; P Tschannen, U Zimmerli and M Müller (n 12) § 34, fn 6; B Waldmann and R Wiederkehr (n 10) ch 4, fn 167.

[76] P Moor and E Poltier, *Droit administratif, Les actes administratifs et leur contrôle*, vol 2, 3rd edn (Bern, Stämpfli, 2011) 450; P Tschannen, U Zimmerli and M Müller (n 12) § 34, fn 6.

[77] A Abegg, 'Funktion und Rechtsnatur des Vergabeverhältnisses in Deutschland und in der Schweiz' (2008) *Baurecht* 147, 150 f; I Häner, 'Der verwaltungsrechtliche Vertrag – Verfahrensfragen' in I Häner and B Waldmann (eds), *Der verwaltungsrechtliche Vertrag in der Praxis* (Zurich, Schulthess, 2007) 46; C Pappa and D Jaggi, 'Rechtsschutz Dritter beim Abschluss von verwaltungsrechtlichen Verträgen' (2012) *Aktuelle Juristische Praxis* 800, 801 ff.

[78] It is at least worth noting that in practice the authorities sometimes grant benefits (which are no subsidies), eg, 'Bürgernutzen' (citizen benefits) informally, but without reference to art 16, paras 4 and 5 SuG.

General administrative law has borrowed many ideas from private law. This is especially true when it comes to administrative rights and obligations, where the civil law influence is still quite prominent. Historically, attempts have been made to follow civil law dogma by introducing 'subjective rights' in administrative law.[79] The discussion in legal protection has shifted from subjective rights to administrative decisions defining rights and obligations.

Still, as specific legislation is often silent on these questions, representation, assignment, interests, waiver, unjustified enrichment, statute of limitations etc concerning administrative rights still refer to the highly developed civil law tradition.[80] Nowadays, courts will typically first turn to other administrative law sources to find an equitable solution that can be introduced by analogy to a specific area. If there is no obvious analogy, civil law solutions often seem fitting.[81]

It is also quite common that administrative law implicitly or explicitly refers to civil law.[82] State liability is based on specific Acts from the confederation and the cantons. These Acts use terms like 'damage', 'causality'[83] or 'self-negligence', relying on the fact that these terms will be understood and interpreted in line with the civil law tradition.[84] However, it is important to note that not every term common in civil law has to have the same meaning in administrative law.[85] Acts regulating civil service declare the Code of Obligations applicable in the case of gaps in the Act.[86] Sometimes Acts are more cautious, referring to civil law only *sinngemäss* (analogously), hereby stipulating that civil law shall be used only when fitting in a particular case.[87]

[79] For the historical common ground but also the differences between private and public subjective rights, see T Gächter, *Rechtsmissbrauch im öffentlichen Recht, Unter besonderer Berücksichtigung des Bundessozialversicherungssrechts, Ein Beitrag zu Treu und Glauben, Methodik und Gesetzeskorrektur im öffentlichen Recht* (Zurich, Schulthess, 2005) 296 ff; A Kölz, 'Die Legitimation zur staatsrechtlichen Beschwerde und das subjektive öffentliche Recht' in J Aubert and P Bois (eds), *Mélanges André Grisel, Recueil de travaux offert à M. André Grisel* (Neuchâtel, Ides et Calendes, 1983) 745 ff; against the abandonment of the methodological figure of subjective law, see M Kaufmanm, *Der öffentlichrechtliche Anspruch, unter besonderer Berücksichtigung seiner Rolle im Prozessrecht* (Zurich, Schulthess, 2015) 179 ff, 355 ff.

[80] U Häfelin, G Müller and F Uhlmann (n 4) fn 252; B Waldmann and R Wiederkehr (n 10) ch 1, fn 35.

[81] BGE 140 II 384, consideration 4.2, 396.

[82] U Häfelin, G Müller and F Uhlmann (n 4) fns 245 ff; P Tschannen, U Zimmerli and M Müller (n 12) § 18, fns 8 f; B Waldmann and R Wiederkehr (n 10) ch 1, fns 33 ff.

[83] Please note that the requirement of causality is derived from the word 'zugefügt' (causes) in both civil and administrative law.

[84] A Griffel, *Allgemeines Verwaltungsrecht* (n 3) fns 543 f, 546 ff, 554; U Häfelin, G Müller and F Uhlmann (n 4) fns 2101, 2127, 2129; P Tschannen, U Zimmerli and M Müller (n 12) § 60, fns 11 ff, § 61, fn 13, § 62, fns 12 ff; B Waldmann and R Wiederkehr (n 10) ch 9, fns 25 f, 34 ff.

[85] U Häfelin, G Müller and F Uhlmann (n 4) fn 246; P Tschannen, U Zimmerli and M Müller (n 12) § 18, fn 8; B Waldmann and R Wiederkehr (n 10) ch 1, fn 33.

[86] eg, art 105, para 1 of the Personalgesetz des Kantons Bern (PG) vom 16. September 2004 (BSG 153.01); art 4 para 1 of the Gesetz über das Arbeitsverhältnis der Mitarbeitenden des Kantons Graubünden (Personalgesetz, PG) vom 14. Juni 2006 (BR 170.400).

[87] eg, art 6, para 2 of the Bundespersonalgesetz (BPG) vom 24. März 2000 (SR 172.220.1).

The main influence of civil law on general administrative law is demonstrated where rights and obligations are concerned and in areas with some resemblance to civil law (eg, state liability, civil servants).[88] Still, civil law may become quasi-constitutional in the sense that it becomes accepted as *allgemeine Rechtsgrundsätze* (general principles of law), rules so evident (to lawyers) that they are valid across the entire legal order. For example, the duty to pay interest in case of default is so generally accepted that it must be observed even in the absence of any rooting in specific legislation. Also, administrative rights must cease to exist by lapse of time.[89] Certainly, the legislator may overcome such general principles of law by explicit regulation, but it may fall into the trap of arbitrariness if the deviation may not be convincingly justified.[90] However, this statement must be qualified in that, according to Article 190 of the Constitution, unconstitutional federal laws must also be applied by the courts. This means that the restriction of arbitrariness cannot be enforced in court against federal laws.[91]

Another principle from private law was even more prominent in administrative law. The Swiss Civil Code (CC) requires from everyone that he or she acts in good faith: 'Every person must act in good faith in the exercise of his or her rights and in the performance of his or her obligations and the manifest abuse of a right is not protected by law' (Article 2).[92] This rule was applied in all areas of law. It has served not only to require fairness in any procedure before the authorities (and vice versa), eg, restricting excessive formalism, but has also laid the groundwork for the protection of legitimate expectations, namely in case of erroneous governmental information. It was not explicitly mentioned in the Swiss Constitution of 1874, but was understood by the Federal Supreme Court first as a 'general principle of law' and later as a constitutional principle. Thus, it could prevent the correct application of the law in certain situations. Acting in good faith received its baptism in the Constitution of 1999: it was included in the basic principles creating the rule of law in Article 5 of the Constitution. Article 2 CC continues to exist, but it is technically superseded by the Constitution.[93]

## E. Doctrine, Courts and Administrative Practice

As described above, administrative law has a relatively long tradition in manuals and textbooks. Courts have been creative in terms of developing standards of

[88] U Häfelin, G Müller and F Uhlmann (n 4) fn 248.

[89] For the 'general principles of law', see generally A Griffel, *Allgemeines Verwaltungsrecht* (n 3) fns 136 ff; U Häfelin, G Müller and F Uhlmann (n 4) fns 145 ff; P Tschannen, U Zimmerli and M Müller (n 12) § 16, fns 9 ff; B Waldmann and R Wiederkehr (n 10) ch 1, fn 25.

[90] F Uhlmann (n 32) fn 28.

[91] M Looser, *Verfassungsgerichtliche Rechtskontrolle gegenüber schweizerischen Bundesgesetzen, Eine Bestandesaufnahme unter Berücksichtigung der amerikanischen und deutschen Verfassungsgerichtsbarkeit, der Geschichte der schweizerischen Verfassungsgerichtsbarkeit sowie der heutigen bundesgerichtlichen Praxis* (Zurich, Dike, 2011) § 13, fn 75.

[92] Schweizerisches Zivilgesetzbuch vom 10. Dezember 1907 (SR 210) (Swiss Civil Code).

[93] See generally BGE 94 I 513 consideration 4a, 520 ff; T Gächter (n 79) 4 f.

good administration, relying on the Constitution, specific legislation and private law, but also on doctrine. There are some examples where general administrative law has been practically created *ex nihilo*. The origins of the doctrine of non-retroactivity are unclear to say the least, court and doctrine quoting each other with no obvious starting point or explanation – somehow it became generally accepted.[94]

Similarly, administrative law was imported from foreign countries, mostly Germany and France. There are still traces where doctrinal lines vary in the German and French-speaking parts of Switzerland as a result from importing different ideas into Swiss administrative law. For example, this is the case for the understanding of public property, although the doctrines are converging.[95] The influence is still felt by the sheer amount of legal literature produced, especially in Germany. The doctrinal points are often more refined and can be referred to if the main ideas are the same in both countries and the question has not been addressed in Switzerland.[96]

The interplay between courts and doctrine is quite strong.[97] The Swiss Supreme Court extensively quotes legal literature, and decisions of the Swiss Supreme Court are closely followed by the doctrine. There are some areas where one can observe noticeable differences, as in the case of the question whether a state-owned enterprise is fully bound to fundamental rights,[98] but standpoints tend to weaken over time. Taken together, courts and doctrine strongly shape the understanding of Swiss administrative law, of course typically referring to the legal sources that have been analysed before (the Constitution, codes, special legislation and private law).

[94] F Uhlmann and R Trümpler, '"Das Rückwirkungsverbot ist im Bereich der Amtshilfe nicht von Bedeutung" – Überlegungen zum Urteil des Bundesverwaltungsgerichts vom 15. Juli 2010 betreffend den UBS-Staatsvertrag' (2011) 1 *Zeitschrift für schweizerisches Recht* 139, 142 f, 153, 155; see also A Griffel, 'Intertemporales Recht aus dem Blickwinkel des Verwaltungsrechts' in Zentrum für Rechtsetzungslehre and F Uhlmann (eds), *Intertemporales Recht aus dem Blickwinkel der Rechtsetzungslehre und des Verwaltungsrechts, 13. Jahrestagung des Zentrums für Rechtsetzungslehre* (Zurich, Dike, 2014) 16 f; *cf* with critical references to misquotations and methodological deficits G Müller (n 38) 272, 276.

[95] The monistic theory of public property from France used to be important in some of the French-speaking cantons of Switzerland. Today, the dualistic theory of public property originating from Germany has prevailed throughout Switzerland. *cf* J Dubey and J Zufferey (n 9) fns 1493 ff; A Griffel, *Allgemeines Verwaltungsrecht* (n 3) fn 398; U Häfelin, G Müller and F Uhlmann (n 4) fns 2245 ff; B Hürlimann-Kaup and F Nyffeler, 'Die grundbuchliche Behandlung der nicht im Privateigentum stehenden und der dem öffentlichen Gebrauch dienenden Grundstücke nach Art. 944 ZGB, Gleichzeitig ein Beitrag zu den herrenlosen und den öffentlichen Sachen gemäss Art. 664 ZGB' (2016) *Schweizerische Zeitschrift für Beurkundungs- und Grundbuchrecht* 81, 98 f (with further references); B Moor, F Bellanger and T Tanquerel, *Droit administratif, L'organisation des activités administratives, Les biens de l'Etat*, vol 3, 2nd edn (Bern, Stämpfli, 2018) 642 ff; T Tanquerel (n 9) fns 179 f; P Tschannen, U Zimmerli and M Müller (n 12) § 47, fns 3 ff.

[96] See generally for 'foreign' influences M Müller (n 29) 82 ff, 99 ff, 108, 112 f; B Schindler (n 11) 388 ff.

[97] M Müller (n 29) 108 f.

[98] G Müller, 'Zur Grundrechtsbindung der öffentlichen Unternehmen der Elektrizitätswirtschaft in der Schweiz' in I Appel, G Hermes and CH Schönberger (eds) *Öffentliches Recht im offenen Staat, Festschrift für Rainer Wahl zum 70. Geburtstag* (Bern, Stämpfli, 2012) 353 ff.

This corresponds to the methodological principle according to which the court shall follow established doctrine and case law.[99]

Administrative authorities usually rely on court decisions and doctrine when giving reasons for an administrative decision. There are no extensive handbooks on administrative law from the Confederation and the cantons – interestingly in stark contrast to legislative theory and drafting guides,[100] where the administrative authorities have long been dominant. This is not to say that administrative authorities had no say over general administrative law. The expert opinion of the Federal Office of Justice and decisions of the Federal Council have been published in their own law review,[101] a tradition which can also be found in the cantons, albeit to a lesser extent. These opinions and decisions were regularly quoted by doctrine and courts. However, their influence is diminishing as the executive branch was continuously relieved from administrative appeals and superseded by courts. In many cantons, the government still handles administrative appeals, but for most matters the last say in the canton is by the administrative courts, a requirement stipulated by federal law.[102] In sum, administrative practice cannot be considered the third main creator of general administrative law it once was.

## F. Human Rights

Human rights, here understood as fundamental rights granted by international treaties, play a relatively minor role in shaping administrative law. This may be explained by the simple fact that the Swiss Supreme Court had a long tradition of granting unwritten fundamental rights, with the result that the legal landscape of Switzerland was usually quite in line with an international treaty when it adhered to it. This is not to say that these treaties did not have an effect on the Swiss Constitution; the European Convention on Human Rights (ECHR)[103] in particular has repeatedly been a challenge, although less so in administrative law.

There are notable exceptions to confirm this rule: as described above, administrative appeal often went to the cantonal executive and then directly to the Swiss

[99] This principle is stated in art 1, para 3 CC, which directly addresses only civil courts, but the methodical principles are binding throughout the entire legal system. *cf* S Emmenegger and A Tschentscher, *Schweizerisches Zivilgesetzbuch, Band I Einleitung und Personenrecht, 1. Abteilung Einleitung Artikel 1–9 ZGB* (Bern, Stämpfli, 2012) art 1, fn 484.

[100] Federal Office of Justice, *Gesetzgebungsleitfanden, Leitfaden für die Ausarbeitung von Erlassen des Bundes* (Bern, Federal Office of Justice, 2019).

[101] Verwaltungspraxis der Bundesbehörden (VPB).

[102] For the extension of judicial control, see: A Misic and N Töpperwien, *Constituional Law in Switzerland*, 2nd edn (Alphen aan den Rijn, Kluwer, 2018) fns 240 ff; F Uhlmann, 'Administrative Procedure' in M Thommen (ed), *Introduction to Swiss Law* (Berlin, Carl Grossmann, 2018) 221 f. For an overview of the current institutional framework, see F Uhlmann (n 102) 232 ff.

[103] Konvention zum Schutze der Menschenrechte und Grundfreiheiten (Europäische Menschenrechtskonvention) vom 4. November 1950 (SR 0.101).

Supreme Court, which had only limited grounds for review. The European Court of Human Rights considered this system insufficient for civil rights according to Article 6 ECHR, a term understood as broadly encompassing some typical areas of Swiss administrative law.[104]

A more recent example is the right to reply in administrative proceedings. The Swiss Supreme Court had to bring its stricter practice into line with the more extensive rights under the ECHR.[105]

## G. EU Law

Switzerland is not a member of the European Union (EU). Although there is a substantial amount of EU law that is relevant in Switzerland, either by reference through bilateral agreements[106] or through 'autonomer Nachvollzug' (autonomous adaptation),[107] there is hardly any trace of EU law when it comes to general administrative law.[108] This may change over time as EU law may become even more relevant, but at present one can exclude EU law as a source of general administrative law.

# III. Assessment and Tendencies in Switzerland

To date, the idea of a codification of administrative law has never been seriously discussed by the authorities in Switzerland.[109] Interestingly, an Austrian scholar points out a similar finding for Austria.[110] One may take from this fact that no need was felt to streamline general administrative law and that the solutions offered by court decisions and doctrine were considered satisfactory. On a more critical note,

[104] A Misic and N Töpperwien (n 102) fns 241, 243; F Uhlmann (n 102) 221 f; from a historical perspective, see generally A Kley-Struller, 'Der Anspruch auf richterliche Beurteilung "zivilrechtlicher" Streitigkeiten im Bereich des Verwaltungsrechts sowie von Disziplinar- und Verwaltungsstrafen gemäss Art. 6 EMRK' (1994) *Aktuelle Juristische Praxis* 23, 28 ff.

[105] See generally BGE 133 I 100 considerations 4.2 ff, 102 ff; P Goldschmid, 'Auf dem Weg zum endlosen Schriftenwechsel? Zum jüngsten die Schweiz betreffenden Urteil des Europäischen Gerichtshofs für Menschenrechte zum Thema Gewährung des rechtlichen Gehörs Beschwerde Nr. 33499/96 vom 21. Februar 2002' (2002) *Zeitschrift des bernischen Juristenvereins* 281, 281 ff; see also H Aemisegger, 'Die Bedeutung der Rechtsprechung des Bundesgerichts zur EMRK für die Kantone' in S Besson and EM Belser (eds), *Die Europäische Menschenrechtskonvention und die Kantone, BENEFRI-Tagung im Europarecht des Instituts für Europarecht* (Zurich, Schulthess, 2014) 127 f.

[106] U Häfelin, G Müller and F Uhlmann (n 4) fns 129 ff; P Karlen (n 39) 105 f; P Tschannen, U Zimmerli and M Müller (n 12) § 17, fns 21 f.

[107] U Häfelin, G Müller and F Uhlmann (n 4) fn 199; P Karlen (n 39) 96; P Tschannen, U Zimmerli and M Müller (n 12) § 17, fns 19 f; B Waldmann and R Wiederkehr (n 10) ch 19, fn 13.

[108] P Tschannen, U Zimmerli and M Müller (n 12) § 17, fn 18.

[109] A Griffel, *Allgemeines Verwaltungsrecht* (n 3) fn 18; A Griffel, 'Dynamik und Stillstand' (n 3) 14.

[110] E Wiederin (n 10) 291.

one might contend that administrative law was 'always there' and nobody really cared about the weaknesses.[111] There is no empirical data to assess how satisfied Swiss citizens and lawyers are with the current system. At least, anecdotal wisdom tells us that law students typically struggle with administrative law (and only later, if they persevere, appreciate its intricacies), which may be a sign that the system is not entirely satisfactory.

The doctrinal statements show a mixed picture. Some consider a codification of general administrative law to be impossible. They argue that general administrative law does not consist of a common structure and only limitedly follows general rules.[112] Further reasons given for the legislative reluctance to codify general administrative law are misjudgement of the need for regulation, negligence, political enforceability and, from a federal perspective, competence concerns.[113] The lack of codification has been described as a characteristic of Swiss administrative law.[114] Some scholars consider general administrative law to be only marginally amenable to codification, but support such codification in this limited area (procedural law, basic provisions).[115] On the other hand, some scholars are in favour of a codification of general administrative law. It is argued that a codification of general administrative law would strengthen its control and harmonisation function, that this would counteract a creeping loss of importance of general administrative law, that general administrative law could be cleansed of problems and inconsistencies, and that the subject matter would become more accessible.[116] In this context, one scholar points out that the process of the digitalisation of administration can and should be used to initiate a codification of administrative law.[117] It is also noteworthy that according to one scholar, doctrine and practice suffer from a legitimacy problem as a basis of administrative law.[118] This could probably best be solved with a codification. Despite these voices, it should be noted, as already mentioned, that the discussion on the codification of general administrative law in Switzerland is not particularly intense.

[111] eg, A Griffel critically describes large parts of general administrative law as a 'Rumpelkammer' (junk room) because terms and methodical figures from different epochs lie crosswise in confusion (A Griffel, *Allgemeines Verwaltungsrecht* (n 3) fn 17).

[112] P Karlen (n 3) 21; see also G Biaggini (n 24) 237.

[113] G Biaggini (n 24) 237; for the administrative procedure and basic provisions, see also A Kölz and P Kottusch, 'Bundesrecht und kantonales Verwaltungsverfahrensrecht, Eine Problemübersicht' (1978) *Schweizerisches Zentralblatt für Staats- und Verwaltungsrecht* 421, 437, 458.

[114] B Schindler (n 42) 33.

[115] G Biaggini (n 24) 237.

[116] A Griffel, *Allgemeines Verwaltungsrecht* (n 3) fn 18; A Griffel, 'Dynamik und Stillstand' (n 3) 14; see also Glaser, 'Einflüsse der Digitalisierung auf das schweizerische Verwaltungsrecht' (2018) *Schweizerische Juristen-Zeitung* 181, 190.

[117] A Glaser (n 116) 181, 190.

[118] P Tschannen (n 3) fn 368. Tschannen argues that courts tend to follow a singular pragmatism more than a generalised system, and that they sometimes quote the doctrine and sometimes they do not, with no clear rule behind this disparity. Further, he claims that it is quite difficult for monographs to get considered in a textbook and that textbooks in general are the work of individuals who hardly interact with each other. Finally, he claims that the prevailing doctrine is also subjectively shaped.

It should also be noted that the legal landscape has changed considerably since the advent of general administrative law. At the time of its emergence, many core topics of general administrative law were not regulated at all or only selectively, which is why dogma could metaphorically develop in a 'greenfield'.[119] Since then, an immense number of special laws have been enacted, some of which, as mentioned above, are poorly co-ordinated with each other or with the general principles. As unwritten general administrative law, except for unwritten constitutional law, is derogated by laws,[120] it cannot fulfil its harmonisation and homogenisation function in these cases. This was the reason for some of the codifications and explains how a codification could counteract the creeping loss of importance and strengthen the harmonisation and homogenisation function.[121]

The fact that the legislature has so far refrained from codifying general administrative law despite the advantages of doing so could also have political reasons in addition to the above-mentioned arguments of the opponents of codification. The political hurdles in Switzerland's democratic system can be vividly illustrated by the example of the total revision of the Federal Constitution. The massive opposition to a preliminary draft of a Constitution, which also envisaged drastic substantial changes, showed that such a project would hardly find the necessary majorities. For this reason, recourse had to be made to the above-mentioned (see section II.A) 'mere update' concept.[122] Since in Switzerland both federal and cantonal laws are subject to referendum, it could make sense to also follow this path for a codification of general administrative law in order to achieve the necessary majorities. The concept of the 'mere update' has made the total revision of the Constitution capable of gaining majority support, but it also carries with it the danger that such a modest revision approach can mobilise only a few politicians because of its rather low 'political attractiveness' and therefore also risks falling behind in favour of more urgent business.[123] The former can be countered by selective reforms of the content of non-controversial issues, the latter by a time limit, which, according to a scholar and former Federal Council member, is of fundamental importance in large legislative projects.[124] In Parliament it was also argued against the 'mere update' that this would equate to cementing the conditions of the time.[125] The Federal Council contradicted this with the argument that the Constitution can be partially revised at any time following a popular

[119] B Schindler (n 11) 406.

[120] U Häfelin, G Müller and F Uhlmann (n 4) fns 147, 169 f, 173; P Tschannen, U Zimmerli and M Müller (n 12) § 16, fns 4, 7, 9; B Waldmann and R Wiederkehr (n 10) ch 1, fns 25 ff.

[121] A Griffel, *Allgemeines Verwaltungsrecht* (n 3) fn 18; A Griffel, 'Dynamik und Stillstand' (n 3) 14.

[122] Botschaft über eine neue Bundesverfassung (BBl 1997 I 1) 28 ff, 43 f.

[123] A Koller, 'Ein neues Reformkonzept für die Totalrevision der Bundesverfassung (1993–1999)' (2013) 2 *LeGes* 365, 367, 372; A Koller, 'Zur Entstehung der neuen Bundesverfassung' in P Gauch and D Thürer (eds), *Die neue Bundesverfassung, Analysen, Erfahrungen, Ausblick* (Zurich, Schulthess, 2002) 4, 8.

[124] A Koller, 'Ein neues Reformkonzept' (n 123) 367.

[125] eg, Vote of Büttiker, Bundesverfassung. Reform (AB S 1998 3) 12.

initiative and that the Federal Supreme Court has no choice but to continue to further concretise the Constitution so that it remains a 'living instrument'.[126] This must apply all the more so to the legislative process because of the lower requirements. The total revision of the Constitution was carried out according to the so-called 'Baukastensystem' (modular system) – ie, in parallel to the 'updating process' of the Constitution, larger partial reform packages were developed, which were put to the vote after the adoption of the constitutional revision. In this way, major substantive reforms could be co-ordinated without jeopardising the overall project;[127] this procedure could probably also be transferred to the legislation process. In fact, as Barkhuysen, Schuurmans and den Ouden report for the Netherlands, the General Administrative Law Act is designed as a 'modular Act' and was enacted in tranches.[128]

Nevertheless, there have been interventions by the legislator. However, the legislator has typically focused on a relatively narrow field of administrative law or even on a single problem.[129] It is therefore difficult to draw conclusions as to what the effects of a larger codification could be. The few examples point in different directions.

The APA has certainly stabilised administrative procedure and has not been subjected to substantial critique. Still, one could notice some signs of the petrification of administrative law in certain areas. The concentration on the administrative decision (not only but in particular) has long been standing in the way of any protection in public procurement and was only remedied when the legislator transposed the GPA into national law.[130] Similarly, the notion of the administrative decision was stretched to the limit in order to offer sufficient legal protection. Still, it could not cover cases where real acts clearly fall outside the scope of an administrative decision.[131] Again, it was the legislator correcting this lack and redeeming the constitutional guarantee of access to the courts (Article 29a of the Constitution). One might wonder whether without the Act, general administrative law would have been more flexible in this respect, of course possibly

[126] Botschaft über eine neue Bundesverfassung (BBl 1997 I 1) 117.

[127] Botschaft über eine neue Bundesverfassung (BBl 1997 I 1) 32; A Koller, 'Ein neues Reformkonzept' (n 123) 367; A Koller, 'Zur Entstehung der neuen Bundesverfassung' (n 123) 4.

[128] See in this book Y Schuurmans, T Barkhuysen and W den Ouden, 'Codification of Administrative Law in the Netherlands', section III.C.

[129] eg, the liability of the Confederation and its civil servants is regulated in the Bundesgesetz über die Verantwortlichkeit des Bundes sowie seiner Behördemitglieder und Beamten (Verantwortlichkeitsgesetz, VG) vom 14. März 1958 (SR 170.32), while the expropriation by the federal government is regulated in the Bundesgesetz über die Enteignung (EntG) vom 20. Juni 1930 (SR 711). See also the Federal Act on Subsidies (above, n 67).

[130] Botschaft zu den für die Ratifizierung der GATT/WTO-Übereinkommen (Uruguay-Runde) notwendigen Rechtsanpassungen (GATT-Botschaft 2) (BBl 1994 IV 950), 1252.

[131] See generally S Giacomini, 'Vom „Jagdmachen auf Verfügung" Ein Diskussionsbeitrag' (1993) *Schweizerisches Zentralblatt für Staats- und Verwaltungsrecht* 237, 237; M Müller, 'Rechtsschutz gegen Verwaltungsrealakte' in P Tschannen (ed), *Neue Bundesrechtspflege – Auswirkungen der Revision auf den kantonalen und eidgenössischen Rechtsschutz, Berner Tage für die juristische Praxis BTJP 2006* (Bern, Stämpfli, 2007) 333 ff; F Uhlmann (n 102) 225 f.

leaving many other questions unanswered that were now obvious from the APA. Interestingly, Costa reports for France that the Council of State considered in an important judgment 'that some administrative acts are not decisions, but can still be controlled by the administrative judge'.[132]

It has been mentioned that in the area of public procurement, the legislator has created extensive regulation. It may have done so under the impression of international examples, not the least from the EU. Public procurement law has become an area of specialisation. One might speculate whether this has to do with the legislation in place or whether even in the absence of detailed rules, the complexity and importance of the subject would have led to a similar outcome. It is very possible.

Perhaps the only areas where the legislator introduced a code with the clear intention to supersede general administrative law and to streamline special legislation are the areas of subsidies and social insurance, as has been repeatedly mentioned above. Here we see a deliberate attempt to improve the legal landscape by stipulating some basic rules to make these areas more coherent. Indeed, the Acts have clarified important questions on subsidies and social insurance, and have, in my opinion, simplified the application of the law. It would be certainly worthwhile to further analyse this area, but it cannot excluded that it could serve as a role model for other areas of administrative law. The discussion is wide open.

[132] See in this book D Costa, 'Codification of Administrative Law: A French Oxymoron', section III.B.

# 12

# Codification of Administrative Law in the United Kingdom

## *Beyond the Common Law*

SARAH NASON

## I. Introduction

In the UK there had historically been only sporadic interest in codifying administrative law. Procedures and remedies on judicial review specifically have been rationalised and statutorily recognised, but it is the judges who are said to have crafted the substantive common law principles of general administrative law. Nevertheless, many areas of administrative policy and decision-making are subject to significantly 'codified' statutory regimes, such as immigration, procurement, town and country planning, and environmental law, and the tribunals system (with a caseload some orders of magnitude higher than that of the Administrative Court) has undergone structural and procedural codification.[1]

From 2019 onwards, the notion of codifying administrative law moved from relative obscurity to the forefront of constitutional debate, with seeds sown in a Conservative and Unionist Party election manifesto seeking to update both administrative law (in fact only judicial review) and the Human Rights Act 1998 (which incorporated the European Convention on Human Rights (ECHR)[2] into domestic law).[3] The manifesto committed to focus on balancing between the rights of individuals and effective government, based on the premise that judicial review may have been 'abused to conduct politics by other means'.[4] On the one hand, this was just the latest salvo in long-running debates about the constitutional foundations

[1] In the Tribunals, Courts and Enforcement Act (TCEA) 2007.

[2] European Convention on Human Rights, Convention for the Protection of Human Rights and Fundamental Freedoms 1950.

[3] Conservative and Unionist Party Manifesto (2019), assets-global.website-files.com/5da42e2cae7eb d3f8bde353c/5dda924905da587992a064ba_Conservative%202019%20Manifesto.pdf.

[4] ibid 48.

of judicial review; on the other hand, the premise of rebalancing through potential wholesale statutory reform was novel. It is against this backdrop that the UK Government set up an Independent Review of Administrative Law (IRAL). The IRAL Panel was tasked to consider the following issues: 'Should substantive public law be placed on a statutory footing? Would such legislation promote clarity and accessibility in the law and increase public trust and confidence in JR [judicial review]?' And specifically: 'Whether the amenability of public law decisions to judicial review by the courts and the grounds of public law illegality should be codified in statute.'[5] IRAL ultimately concluded that little significant advantage would be obtained by statutory codification of the grounds of judicial review, but left the matter of broader administrative law reform open.

Against this backdrop, in this chapter I outline administrative law and administrative organisation in the UK, focusing primarily on England and Wales as the largest jurisdiction. I discuss what codification has generally meant in England and Wales, explaining the role played by the Law Commission. I then analyse historical and contemporary proposals to codify aspects of administrative law, including structural tribunal reform. I explain IRAL's conclusions on codification and subsequent reforms proposed by the UK Government. I then identify three issues that warrant further investigation: first, that IRAL did not specifically consider the potential to codify developing principles of administrative rule-making, principles that have been codified in some other jurisdictions with a largely common law lineage; second, that in the light of devolution, the growing divergence in administrative laws between the UK nations requires close monitoring, particularly given the Welsh experiment with a more 'cosmetic' form of codification, also based on improving the accessibility of existing legal sources; and, finally, that emphasising judicial review of administrative action has obscured the broader compass of administrative law sources and norms, and other mechanisms of administrative law adjudication (including statutory appeals and applications in various tribunals and courts). I close by noting the similarities in the issues raised by the codification of administrative law, regardless of legal tradition and culture.

## II. Administrative Law

Across the UK, administrative law can be seen as covering the institutional framework of public administration, as well as principles of administrative law developed by the courts, principles of good administration developed by ombudsmen, other norms such as those developed in various delegated legislation and rules made by administrative bodies, and mechanisms for holding administrators to account.[6]

[5] 'Terms of Reference – Independent Review of Administrative Law', 2020, assets.publishing.service.gov.uk/government/uploads/system/uploads/attachment_data/file/915624/independent-review-admin-law-terms-of-reference.pdf (hereinafter 'IRAL Report').

[6] P Cane, *Administrative Law* (Oxford, Oxford University Press, 2011).

This wide compass of sources and institutions is also variously referred to as the 'administrative justice system', with the term 'administrative law' reserved for the general legal principles applied primarily by the Administrative Court on judicial review. The Administrative Court, so named in 2000 but with a much longer history, forms part of the 'supervisory jurisdiction' of the Queen's Bench Division of the High Court whose origins can be traced back to the late twelfth and early thirteenth centuries. In this volume Edward Rubin provides a detailed account of the development of English common law,[7] and both Rubin and Pierre Issalys[8] analyse the influence of such law on American and Canadian administrative law, respectively.

The chapters in this volume, including those relating to common law systems, also discuss the variable and sometimes competing conceptions of administrative law: as concerned with controlling and constraining government through law, as facilitating good administration, and as protecting citizens' rights and elaborating the so-called will of the people. In England and Wales the narrative of control has been significant, particularly the Latin tag 'ultra vires' (beyond the powers), which many still see as the central organising principle of administrative law. Reference is often made to the period beginning around the mid-1960s, where, according to Lord Diplock, judicial intervention, largely to control the executive, led to the 'rapid development in England [and Wales] of a rational and comprehensive system of administrative law'.[9] By way of rationalisation (a codification of sorts), Lord Diplock's judgment in the case of *Council of Civil Service Unions v Minister for the Civil Service*[10] confirmed three principles: that administrative decisions must be in accordance with the law (illegality), that they must be rational (reasonableness) and that they must be procedurally fair. These principles remain central; however, any codification of them as general statements is arguably little more than 'cosmetic'[11] or even 'banal'.[12]

Despite common perceptions, legislation is central to UK administrative law. Enabling legislation granting powers to administrative decision-makers is often specific as to the limits of those powers and how they should be exercised, but courts have also expanded the principle of 'illegality' to include implied limitations: powers should not be used for improper purposes, relevant considerations must be taken into account, and irrelevant considerations should be excluded. Other illegality subprinciples include that administrative bodies must not develop

[7] See in this book EL Rubin, 'The United States: Systematic But Incomplete Codification', section II.

[8] See in this book P Issalys, 'A Persistent Taste for Diversity: Codification of Administrative Law in Canada', section II.

[9] *Re Racal Communications Ltd* [1981] AC 374 at 382, per Lord Diplock; see also *IRC v National Federation of Self-Employed and Small Businesses Ltd* [1982] AC 617 at 641.

[10] *Council of Civil Service Unions v Minister for the Civil Service* [1985] AC 374.

[11] M Elliott, 'The Judicial Review II: Codifying Judicial Review – Clarification or Evisceration?', publiclawforeveryone.com/2020/08/10/the-judicial-review-review-ii-codifying-judicial-review-clarification-or-evisceration.

[12] TH Jones, 'Judicial Review and Codification' (2000) 20(4) *Legal Studies* 517, 533.

over-rigid policies dispensing with consideration of individual circumstances, and that there should be no improper delegation. These subprinciples run to such an extent that it would be practically impossible to codify them and, in any case, many function as principles of statutory interpretation that cannot be properly understood abstracted from the context (planning, education, welfare benefits, immigration etc) in which they fall to be applied.

More recently, a so-called principle of 'legality' has emerged. This is an interpretive presumption that the Westminster Parliament does not intend to legislate in a way that violates constitutional rights or principles. Courts have relied on this presumption to narrowly interpret a range of legislation, often in the name of protecting so-called common law constitutional rights, such as the right of access to the courts, the principle of open justice, universal suffrage and the right to seek judicial review itself.[13] The significance to administrative law of constitutional principles that are either explicit or implicit in common law, whether also codified in some way (including in human rights legislation of a constitutional character), seems to be an attribute shared by Anglo-influenced legal systems.[14]

## III. Administrative Organisation

In the UK, much of the general organisation of the state is also not codified law, and there are few special legal principles applying to public servants. Public authorities, including Ministers of the Crown, are subject to ordinary civil obligations and the ordinary contract law, unless they are given special statutory dispensation. Failure to exercise a statutory power might also constitute negligence in some contexts. Public authorities are subject to the master-servant rule, whereby the employer is liable for tortious activities committed by the employee in the course of their employment, and where the employee may also be personally liable. In practice, as opposed to the situation in formal legal rules, there are many aspects of public authorities' contracts which, though interpreted and enforced according to ordinary contract law, have tended to coalesce as a distinctive body of principles. Government departments have drawn up various guides to common form clauses for particular contracts to ensure a degree of consistency.

Much of tort and contract law remains founded in common law, with tweaks that apply to public bodies. For example, an authority will not be liable in tort

[13] *R v Secretary of State for the Home Department ex p Pierson* [1998] AC 539, 573 (Lord Browne-Wilkinson); *R v Secretary of State for the Home Department ex p Simms* [2002] 2 AC 115, 131 (Lord Hoffmann); *Kennedy v The Charity Commission* [2014] UKSC 20; *Lee-Hirons v Secretary of State for Justice* [2016] UKSC 46.

[14] See, for example, in this book P Issalys (n 8) section II and also in this book J Boughey, 'The "Codification" of Administrative Law in Australia, section III.B. With similar experiences in South Africa, see C Hoexter, 'The Constitutionalisation and Codification of Judicial Review in South Africa' in CF Forsyth, M Elliott, S Jhaveri, M Ramsden and A Scully-Hill (eds), *Effective Judicial Review: A Cornerstone of Good Governance* (Oxford, Oxford University Press, 2010).

where the injury is the inevitable consequence of what Parliament has authorised through statute. Similarly, there is no liability for nuisance which is necessarily implied by an empowering Act. Rights over property can be over-ridden where a public body acquires land which is subject to some third-party right of way, these rights cannot prevent a public body from exercising its statutory powers, though individuals affected may be able to claim compensation.

There are some circumstances where if a statute imposes a duty on a public body, breach of this duty causing injury enables the person injured to seek damages. Even when there is no ministerial duty and no recognised tort, public authorities and officers may still be liable in damages for malicious, deliberate or injurious wrongdoing, through a specific tort known as misfeasance in public office, which includes malicious abuse of power and deliberate maladministration. An example of this is the suggestion that Prime Minister Boris Johnson could have been liable for this tort after it was argued that he had given misleading advice to the monarch about his reasons for seeking to prorogue Parliament.[15]

A specific area of law that has been largely codified is freedom of information. The Freedom of Information Act 2000 came into force in 2005 for England, Wales and Northern Ireland. Alongside corresponding legislation in Scotland, it applies to almost every public authority in the UK. It introduced a presumption of mandatory disclosure for information held by a public authority, with some absolute and some qualified exclusions and exemptions. An independent Commissioner rules on complaints of non-disclosure, with both sides having a right of appeal to specialist tribunals and then to the courts.

In addition to traditional branches of state, there are agencies and non-departmental public bodies that can be difficult to classify. The main distinction seems to be between 'executive agencies' on the one hand and 'non-departmental public bodies' (NDPBs) on the other. Executive agencies are effectively part of the Crown, they operate under powers delegated from ministers, usually without statutory foundation, and they do not have independent legal status.[16] Their functions and responsibilities are set out in Framework Documents. In terms of accountability to the courts under general administrative law, any legal action would likely be brought against the relevant Minister under whose aegis the agency operates.

Executive NDPBs have a separate legal identity and will normally have their origins in statute or, in some instances, under prerogative powers. Most require legislation to confer functions on them and also for Government accountancy

[15] *Ball v Johnson* (May 2019), www.judiciary.uk/wp-content/uploads/2019/05/Ball-v-Johnson-FV-290519.pdf.

[16] Cabinet Office, *Classification of Public Bodies: Guidance for Departments* (April 2016), assets.publishing.service.gov.uk/government/uploads/system/uploads/attachment_data/file/519571/Classification-of-Public_Bodies-Guidance-for-Departments.pdf; Cabinet Office, *Executive Agencies: A Guide for Departments* (March 2018), assets.publishing.service.gov.uk/government/uploads/system/uploads/attachment_data/file/690636/Executive_Agencies_Guidance.PDF.

reasons. The staff of these bodies do not have Crown status and will not be civil servants. There are also advisory NDPBs that will normally be set up administratively rather than by statute, but legislation may be necessary if their activities require continuing Government funding. Here it is up to the Government department to decide if the body will be set up as part of the Crown or as an incorporated/unincorporated body with a separate legal personality. In general, this 'agencification' of central government tends to occur with little need for legislation. The establishing of framework agreements and setting performance targets for the Government more generally is largely a matter of internal self-regulation in which the Treasury plays a key role.

The contracting-out of public administration was extended specifically by the Deregulation and Contracting Out Act 1994, which provides that any statutory function of a Minister which is exercisable by an officer of theirs (either by statute or by rule of law) may, if an order of the Minister so provides, be made exercisable by any person (or employee) authorised by either the officer or the Minister. The 1994 Act was supplemented as regards local authorities by the Local Government (Contracts) Act 1997. In addition, the Localism Act 2011 gives local authorities a general power to do anything that individuals may do. As other commentators in this volume note, there has been much transformation in the institutions and norms of administrative law, with more traditional distinctions between public and private actors (and modes of operation) becoming outmoded, and the emergence of newer hybrid forms based on negotiation, self-management, contractual standards and guidelines.[17]

## IV. Codification

Statutory law-making in England and Wales generally begins from the bedrock of accumulated common law wisdom. Legislation passed by the Westminster Parliament tends to be detailed, seeking to cover as many eventualities as possible, but still subject to authoritative exposition by the judiciary, who will interpret each provision as it comes to be litigated in largely adversarial proceedings. This is often contrasted with broader general principles of continental codes, but the distinction can be overstated, as Delphine Costa's chapter in this volume on administrative law in France, the so-called birthplace of codification, goes to show.[18] Reconstructing the historical record, Gunther Weiss explains that far from being completely alien to the development of the English and Welsh common law legal system, the idea of codification has been a persistent presence, often beginning with a desire to consolidate a large body of case law (and/or statute)

[17] See in this book P Issalys (n 8) section IV.
[18] See in this book D Costa, 'Codification of Administrative Law: A French Oxymoron', section II.D.

and sometimes linked to distrust of judges. Rarely have objections to codification been based on what he calls genuine jurisprudential reasons, eg, that the relevant law was not sufficiently systematised and conceptualised and therefore not yet ripe for codification; rather, the stumbling blocks have tended to be matters of political will, conservativism, traditionalism and parliamentary process.[19] The same is true today. Weiss also discusses various theses about the role of codification in the common law world: that codification is simply distinct from common law method and therefore largely irrelevant to it; a more sophisticated account where codification is relevant to common law systems, but in a way that is distinctive from how codification operates in civil law systems; a convergence thesis which suggests a tendency towards codification in major common law systems and civil law judges being less inclined to conform to a passive role; an equivalence thesis which appears to suggest that convergence has already been reached and that both common law and civil law systems already function successfully using codification-based law; and, finally, a reversal thesis, such that entrenched systems of codification and common law are reversing their original preference for one approach over another (giving the example of the US turn towards codification). Weiss' view is that something approaching a sophisticated distinctiveness thesis is likely the most accurate, namely that codification is not an idea historically confined to the European continent, but that approaches to codification and its nature and extent of enactment remain different across common law and civil law jurisdictions. This is a conclusion with which I tend to agree.

Codification of sorts is highly relevant to many areas of administrative law in the UK, including planning and immigration, where the field is largely occupied by statute as the first source of information, often governing most aspects of administrative decision-making. As Harlow and Rawlings note in practice:

> Far from the Victorian prototype of the common law 'supplying the omission of the legislature' in sparse statutes, it is commonly a case of the judges navigating, evaluating, and commenting on, whole thickets of legislatively sanctioned administrative procedures.[20]

Codifying legislation is understood to involve bringing together statutory law on a single subject into one legal instrument without substantially changing the boundaries between statute law and case law. If this is done without any changes, or at least without any substantial changes, then it can properly be referred to as consolidation rather than codification. On the other hand, statutory codification is a distinctive activity since it tends to be associated with substantive reform of the

[19] G Weiss, 'The Enchantment of Codification' (2000) 25 *Yale Journal of International Law* 435.

[20] C Harlow and R Rawlings, 'Proceduralism and Automation: Challenges to the Values of Administrative Law' in E Fisher, J King and AL Young (eds), *The Foundations and Future of Public Law (in Honour of Paul Craig* (Oxford, Oxford University Press, 2019) 11. The centrality of legislation to administrative law adjudication is a point also made in J Bell, *The Anatomy of Administrative Law* (Oxford, Hart Publishing, 2020).

subject matter, as well as having potential longer-term implications for the form of the law. The starting point for legislative codification is often that the collection of statutes is considered to be flawed, both because existing law is scattered over a range of sources and also because each source is reflective of policy choices that might no longer be compatible with contemporary circumstances, and where the content of the law must be modernised, as well as simplified and more rationally ordered.

The Law Commission of England and Wales has sought to develop codes as comprehensive statements of particular areas of law. However, much more common are what Harlow and Rawlings refer to as 'statutory mini-codifications' in specialist subject areas. They consider such to be 'a key space for contextualisation, influenced to a greater or lesser extent by judicial precepts and typically designed in pragmatic fashion for particular policy domains'.[21] In this volume, Issalys refers to similar developments in Canada as 'small-scale' codes, whilst noting that this might seem something of an oxymoron if the very definition of a code entails systematic development and comprehensiveness.[22] Mini-codifications could also relate to a small number of statutory sections rather than a statute as a whole – for example, codification of a particular procedural requirement (such as standing or permission), time-limits and remedies in the case of judicial review.

## A. Codification and the Law Commission

The Law Commission of England and Wales was created under the Law Commission Act 1965, section 3(1) of which lists the following aims:

> Keep under review all of the law … with a view to its systematic development and reform, including in particular the codification of such law, the elimination of anomalies, the repeal of obsolete and unnecessary enactments, the reduction of the number of separate enactments and generally the simplification and modernisation of the law.

Establishing the Law Commission was preceded by the book *Law Reform Now*, which was published in 1963. Its two editors, Gerald Gardiner QC and Andrew Martin, laid out their vision for what would become the Law Commission. Later Gerald Gardiner QC, by then Lord Gardner, became Lord Chancellor and responsible for the Law Commission Act 1965.

The Law Commission published its First Programme of Law Reform in 1965 with proposals to codify the law of contract, the law of landlord and tenant, and family law. From the outset, the Commission noted that consolidation and codification should both be seen as a means to simplify the law rather than ends in

[21] C Harlow and R Rawlings (n 20) 3.
[22] See in this book P Issalys (n 8) section IV.

their own right. In *Law Reform Now*, the issue of codification was discussed as follows:

> The unwieldiness of English [and Welsh] law has reached a degree which raises one of the more agonising problems of democracy: the question whether the citizen is placed in a position to ascertain the law by which he lives without incurring unreasonable trouble and disproportionate expense. The answer, we fear, is in the negative.[23]

Writing in 2017 on the success of the Law Commission, the then Lord Chief Justice, Lord Thomas, noted:

> The problem highlighted [by *Law Reform Now*] was that both common law and statute needed fundamental overhaul, which was a consequence of their historic and incremental development. Developments over the centuries had not, with some very notable exceptions, been systematised or rationalised. Inconsistencies had arisen, and had been left uncorrected. Obsolete laws remained on the statute book.[24]

In *Law Reform Now*, Gardiner and Martin argued that there was a strong case for codification, by which they meant reducing the whole of the law on any particular subject to one statute or a small collection of statutes. However, they also suggested that the more pressing need was for substantive law reform.

The first Chairman of the Law Commission, Sir Leslie (later Lord) Scarman, defined codes as 'a species of enacted law which purports so to formulate the law that it becomes within its field the authoritative, comprehensive and exclusive source of that law'. However, he also appreciated that the 1965 Act did not stipulate exactly what sort of codification it promoted. In 1966 Sir Scarman delivered a speech seeking to match codification to the realities of England and Wales as a legal jurisdiction, noting that the habit of codification could spread were it to succeed in making law more manageable and easier to understand; on the other hand, if codes failed in achieving these aims, judges would ultimately look back to the common law. Sir Scarman was also doubtful whether codification in England and Wales would diminish the importance of the courts as law-makers, suggesting that 'the code will ultimately mean what the judge says it means. Already our courts spend most of their time interpreting statute law'.[25]

A 2017 Law Commission Report examining the *Form and Accessibility of the Law Applicable in Wales* reiterates Sir Scarman's aim: 'The law was to be reformed in a series of codes, of varying size and form. This was to be a continuous activity, the codes being effectively maintained by Parliament working with the Law

[23] G Gardiner and A Martin (eds), *Law Reform Now*, 2nd edn (London, V Gollancz, 1963) 10 ff.

[24] Speech by the Lord Chief Justice, '"Law Reform Now" in 21st Century Britain – Brexit and Beyond' (June 2017), https://www.lawcom.gov.uk/lectures-talks/law-reform-now-in-21st-century-britain-brexit-and-beyond, para 3.

[25] L Scarman, 'Codification and Judge-Made Law: A Problem of Co-existence' (1967) 42 *Indiana Law Journal* 361.

Commission', in a model which 'preserved the role of the judges, but as authoritative interpreters of the code, not oracles of the common law'.[26]

This ambitious approach of fully codifying particular areas of law was short-lived, and by 1980, the then Chairman of the Law Commission, Sir Michael Kerr, announced that codification had failed. His reasons included the sheer scale of the task. A developing codification of common law principles of contract had reached some 500 articles in partial draft,[27] and the landlord and tenant code looked to require some 880 articles. Reaching agreement on the formulation of various rules and propositions to replace an immense body of case law appeared to be an insurmountable task.[28]

Although the complete codification of large areas of civil law has so far remained an unobtainable goal, the Law Commission has had more success in simplifying particular subject areas, leading to the enactment of rationalised and modernised statutes. The Law Commission also remains committed to the codification of criminal law, with the Sentencing Act 2020 consolidating certain enactments relating to sentencing. However, the lack of success of the grander scheme for codification of large areas of civil law is instructive in relation to some of the difficulties encountered when seeking to codify judge-made law. Codification is seen as a practice quite alien to the Westminster legislative process, particularly because Parliament is concerned with legislating so far as possible for every foreseeable situation, whereas codes are seen as being formed of a series of general rules. Government departments have shown little interest in codification; the parliamentary timetable is overcrowded, so securing space for a large-scale codification process would require significant political enthusiasm. This is particularly difficult to establish when there was, and still is, no single government department with overall responsibility for the shape or health of the law as a whole.[29]

In designing is 10th Programme of Law Reform, which was published in 2008, the Law Commission stressed that it 'continues to believe that codification is desirable, but considers that it needs to redefine its approach to make codification more achievable'.[30] That redefined approach still adopts Gardiner's definition of codification, namely that it involves 'reducing to one statute, or a small collection of statutes, the whole of the law on any particular subject'. However, the Commission restates that its first priority is to reform an area of law sufficiently to enable it to return and codify the law at a subsequent stage.[31]

[26] *Form and Accessibility of the Law Applicable in Wales*; Consultation Paper (Law Com No 223, 2016) 8.41.

[27] PM North, 'Problems of Codification in a Common Law System' (1982) 46 *Rabel Journal of Comparative and International Private Law* 490, 494.

[28] M Kerr, 'Law Reform in Changing Times' (1980) 96 *Law Quarterly Review* 515, 528 f.

[29] D Greenberg, 'Dangerous Trends in Modern Legislation' (2015) 2 *Public Law* 96.

[30] Law Commission, *10th Programme of Law Reform*, Law Com No 311, https://s3-eu-west-2.amazonaws.com/lawcom-prod-storage-11jsxou24uy7q/uploads/2015/03/lc311_10th_Programme.pdf, para 1.5.

[31] ibid.

In her analysis of the work of the England and Wales, and Scottish Law Commissions, Shona Wilson-Stark suggests that the impetus for codification has passed and that a more gradual approach of simplification as a prelude to codification is preferable. Codification is a task that requires extensive resources, and despite increasing discussion, its nature and purpose in England and Wales is still not sufficiently certain. She goes further in suggesting that codification should no longer be referred to explicitly in the Law Commission Act 1965, which sets out the Commission's duties.[32]

## B. Codification of Administrative Law

In the UK there has been a long history of specialised non-judicial bodies (once called administrative tribunals) determining disputes between administrators and the public. In 1932, the Donoughmore Committee was established to determine if the proliferation of administrative tribunals, following industrialisation and the growth of the welfare state, had undermined the rule of law in bypassing the ordinary judiciary. It found that there was no principled concern with the operation of tribunals so long as appeal to the High Court on a point of law remained available. The 1957 Franks Report concluded that 'tribunals should properly be regarded as machinery provided by Parliament for adjudication rather than as part of the machinery of administration'.[33] Various pieces of evidence to the Franks Committee stressed the need for a more extensive review of administrative law. In their discussion of the 'curious origins of judicial review', TT Arvind and Lindsay Stirton[34] point out that many submissions to the Franks Committee showed an appetite for broader reform.

The Law Commission took an early interest in administrative law; its First Programme, published in October 1965, drew attention 'to the problems which arise in the reconciliation of the rule of law with the administrative techniques of a highly developed industrial society'.[35] In July 1967 the Commission published an *Exploratory Working Paper on Administrative Law*. It noted in particular the need for the rationalisation of remedies; at the time, there were procedural complexities and anomalies such that each different type of remedy available against the decision-making of administrative bodies had to be sought through different procedures, and sometimes through a range of separate proceedings in different courts. This need to rationalise procedures and remedies has also been experienced by other Anglo-American jurisdictions with legacy issues dating back to the

[32] S Wilson-Stark, *The Work of the British Law Commissions: Law Reform ... Now?* (Oxford, Hart Publishing, 2019) ch 5.

[33] Report of the Committee on Administrative Tribunals and Enquiries (Cmnd 218, 5s, 1957) 40.

[34] TT Arvind and L Stirton, 'The Curious Origins of Judicial Review' (2017) 133 *Law Quarterly Review* 91.

[35] Law Commission, *Exploratory Working Paper on Administrative Law* [1967] EWLC C13.

English common law. In the 1960s, the Law Commission also noted concerns that general administrative law lacked a sufficiently developed and coherent body of substantive legal rules (where codification might have been a potential solution), but recognised that views on the issue varied.[36]

In 1969, the Government rejected the Law Commission's broader proposal to establish a Royal Commission to examine administrative law. Arvind and Stirton lay responsibility for the refusal to conduct a wider review and the narrow terms of reference of a later Law Commission project (which reported in 1976) on the shoulders of Lord Diplock,[37] for apparently persuading the then Lord Chancellor (still Lord Gardiner, who was influential in establishing the Law Commission) not to take a more substantive look.

The Law Commission's *Report on Remedies in Administrative Law* examined court organisation and procedure, but did not consider principles of administrative law or their relationship to private law. The Law Commission's main recommendation was the development of an Application for Judicial Review (AJR), harmonising ancient procedures with modern civil claims for declarations and injunctions, in order to improve access to justice and the efficiency of the courts.

The resulting AJR under Order 53 of the Rules of the Supreme Court[38] put in place in 1977 was in effect a codification (rationalisation, reform, simplification and bringing together) of a set of disparate procedures and remedies. The Order also introduced a leave criterion, nowadays known as a permission stage, and specific time limits for issuing claims. The procedure was revised in 1980 and is now contained in section 31 of the Senior Courts Act 1981 and Part 54 of the Civil Procedure Rules.

In the absence of broader Law Commission work, a 1978 committee of experts (JUSTICE-All Souls) began a review into administrative law.[39] It made wide-ranging recommendations; specifically in terms of legislative change, it recommended the enactment of a duty to provide reasons for administrative decisions, and a duty to provide financial remedies where a person suffers loss as a result of wrongful administrative action not involving negligence. At the time of writing, neither duty has been enacted in legislation or is yet recognised under common law.

The AJR was not designed to replace other avenues for challenging the legality of administration; such purported unlawfulness could still be raised collaterally where relevant in other civil and criminal proceedings. However, in a single case, with the leading judgment delivered by Lord Diplock,[40] a rule of procedural

[36] Law Commission, *Report on Remedies in Administrative Law* [1976] EWLC 73.

[37] TT Arvind and L Stirton (n 34).

[38] Rules of the Supreme Court 1997.

[39] JUSTICE-All Souls, *Administrative Justice: Some Necessary Reforms* (Oxford, Clarendon Press, 1988).

[40] *O'Reilly v Mackman* [1983] UKHL 1.

exclusivity was instituted such that remedies against the unlawful acts and omissions of public bodies should generally be sought only via the AJR procedure in the High Court in London. This vision of procedural exclusivity went against the traditional plurality of the common law with its emphasis on flexible procedures and remedies. Part of the case for exclusivity was that the judicial review procedure incorporates safeguards to protect the administration from vexatious claims and to ensure the swift progress of litigation. It is these procedural elements that continue to be the main site of statutory intervention.

In the early 1990s the Law Commission considered further proposals to improve the efficiency of the AJR. It recommended new tests to be applied at the permission stage, but these were not taken forward. The proposed test was a two-part one: claims involving private rights would immediately be granted permission; and those involving public interest matters in which no private rights were specifically and directly affected would have to overcome further hurdles.[41]

Further reforms to the permission stage were recommended by a Conservative–Liberal Democrat Coalition Government in 2012 and 2013, but these were not progressed. However, a new category of Totally Without Merit claims was introduced through the Civil Procedure Rules. If a judge determines a claim to be Totally Without Merit, a claimant is barred from seeking to renew their permission application, in particular being prevented from asking that a permission decision on the papers is reconsidered orally. The category was introduced by Procedural Rules (a mini-codification of sorts), but the judiciary have been left to determine the contents of the legal test, and they appear to have done so with little consistency.

Another example of restrictive 'mini-codification' is section 84 of the Criminal Justice and Courts Act 2015, under which permission to seek review must be declined if 'it appears to the court to be highly likely that the outcome for the applicant would not have been substantially different if the conduct complained of had not occurred'. Section 84 is another of the Conservative–Liberal Democrat Coalition Government reforms, seeking to ensure that judicial review is not abused for political gain. Previous case law, which recognised a discretion on the part of the courts to refuse relief if they were satisfied that a particular outcome was inevitable, continues to apply in the context of other procedural routes to challenging administration which are the functional equivalent of judicial review.[42] This peculiarity is particularly evident in planning law, where claims are brought to the Administrative Court's attention through a variety of different routes.

Administrative Court judicial review is in fact only a small element of administrative law practice in England and Wales; numerically more significant is the

[41] Law Commission, *Administrative Law: Judicial Review and Statutory Appeals* [1994] EWLC 226, [5.20]–[5.22].

[42] *Simplex GE (Holdings) Ltd v Secretary of State for the Environment* [1988] 3 PLR 25.

caseload of the tribunals system, that was consolidated and reformed in the early to mid-2000s. Almost all existing tribunals with England and Wales, Great Britain or UK jurisdiction were transferred into a single system by the Tribunals, Courts and Enforcement Act (TCEA) 2007.

The First-Tier Tribunal and Upper Tribunal are both split into Chambers. Each Chamber comprises similar jurisdictions or brings together similar types of experts to hear appeals. The Upper Tribunal primarily (but not exclusively) reviews and decides appeals arising from the First-Tier Tribunal. Like the High Court, it is a superior court of record. As well as having the existing specialist judges of the senior tribunal judiciary at its disposal, it can also call on the services of High Court judges. The First-Tier Tribunal primarily hears appeals from citizens against decisions made by Government departments or agencies. Alongside rights of appeal from the First-Tier to the Upper Tribunal, the TCEA provides opportunities for both tiers to review their own decisions. There are provisions for second-tier appeals to the Court of Appeal (and Court of Session in Scotland).

The rationalisation of an estimated more than 1,000 existing tribunals into a single structure governed by a central statute and distinct procedural rules could be seen as a major codification of the procedures and institutions that form the mainstay of the judicial part of the administrative justice system. Whilst at its busiest the Administrative Court dealt with approximately 15,000 AJRs per annum (some 80 per cent of which related to immigration), the rationalised tribunals system handles many hundreds of thousands of cases.

In this new structure, the Upper Tribunal has been given a specific statutory power to determine judicial review applications on the same legal grounds and with the power to award the same remedies as the Administrative Court. Particular classes of judicial review claim, most notably immigration cases, have been transferred to the jurisdiction of specific Upper Tribunal Chambers (the vast majority of immigration judicial reviews are now determined by the Upper Tribunal (Immigration and Asylum Chamber). Whilst there has as yet been no systematic study of the case law emanating from the Upper Tribunal or its particular Chambers, Lord Justice Sedley has suggested the institution has the 'potential to develop a legal culture which is not in all respects one of lawyers' law – a system, in other words, of administrative law'.[43]

The Supreme Court grappled with the relationship between the Administrative Court and the Upper Tribunal, concluding that certain decisions of the Upper Tribunal to refuse permission to appeal (either to itself or to the Court of Appeal) might be subject to an AJR in the Administrative Court if it raises an important matter of legal principle or practice, or otherwise compelling case (such as a serious miscarriage of justice). This test was 'codified' in the Civil Procedure Rules; however, IRAL recommended its reversal and the UK Government agreed.

[43] *R (Cart) v Upper Tribunal* [2010] EWCA Civ 859, [2011] 2 WLR 36 [42].

Section 2 of the Judicial Review and Courts Act 2022, 'Exclusion of review of Upper Tribunal's permission-to-appeal decisions', seeks to reverse the Supreme Court's decision by statutorily excluding judicial review of particular Upper Tribunal permission to appeal decisions, a so-called 'ouster clause'.

## C. Codification of Judicial Review

In its Report, IRAL made clear that it did not conduct a wide-ranging assessment of administrative law, but rather focused on the Government's priorities in relation to judicial review. Motivating the Government's focus were two high-profile Supreme Court defeats relating to judicial supervision of prerogative powers: the first finding it unlawful for the Prime Minister to give notice of the UK's intention to withdraw from the EU without parliamentary involvement;[44] and the second ruling that Prime Ministerial advice to the Queen giving rise to a lengthy prorogation at a time of great constitutional importance unlawfully frustrated the legislative supervision of the executive, resulting in a judicial order for Parliament to reconvene immediately.[45] Despite this background, IRAL largely rejected the instruction to see judicial review as a contest between the executive and the courts where rules of the game require rebalancing. As the IRAL Panel report noted, the codification of judicial review gives rise to at least two separate issues: the first is amenability to judicial review, which the Panel understood to mean some kind of statutory formulation of a jurisdictional test delineating the boundaries of judicial review; and the second is codifying the grounds of judicial review.[46]

In various precedents, the judiciary have affirmed that the source of the jurisdiction to conduct judicial review remains the common law, despite statutory statements about the rules of court procedure. According to Lord Kerr in *Michalak v General Medical Council*,[47] 'judicial review is not a procedure which arises "by virtue of" any statutory source. Its origins lie in common law'. In its consultation on further reforms, the UK Government proposed that judicial review is, alternatively, as much a creature of statute (due to the codification of court jurisdiction and procedure) as it is of common law, focusing on characterising courts as 'servants of Parliament'.[48] There is no real suggestion on any side that Parliament cannot reform judicial review through statutes; the debate is over the scope of judicial power to interpret statutory provisions on the basis of common law principle.

[44] *R (Miller) v Secretary of State for Exiting the European Union* [2017] UKSC 5.
[45] *R (Miller) v The Prime Minister* [2019] UKSC 41.
[46] IRAL Report (n 5) ch 1.
[47] *Michalak v General Medical Council* [2017] 1 WLR 4193 [32].
[48] Ministry of Justice, *Judicial Review Reform: The Government Response to the Independent Review of Administrative Law* (CP 408, 2021) paras 18 and 26.

Returning to IRAL, the Panel did not reach a distinct conclusion on the matter of amenability to judicial review, but rather blended the issue into a discussion of whether a codifying statute runs an unacceptable risk of allowing Parliament (or sometimes even the executive) to abrogate or oust both amenability to judicial review and/or the substantive content of judicial review's grounds from the purview of the common law. The Panel went on to note that if a codifying statute were silent as to its effect on common law, then ordinary principles of statutory interpretation apply, and on this basis: 'Everything points to the conclusion that statutory silence would not be enough for modification of the common law rules of judicial review to be implied.'[49] If enacted as a primary statute, a judicial review code would likely be treated as a 'constitutional statute' and as such could only be repealed, or amended in a way that significantly affects its provisions as concerns citizens' rights, by unambiguous words on the face of a later statute. The courts would also likely imply the interpretive provision of legality, again requiring an express statement of intent in primary legislation before accepting that Parliament intends to override recognised common law rights.

Much of the above discussion proceeds on the assumption – unsurprisingly, given the political background to IRAL – that statutory codification might seek to abolish the common law of judicial review, replacing it with a code that both restricts amenability to judicial review and narrows down the substantive grounds. A further concern is that even if this were not the original formulation: 'The code effectively crowds out the more flexible common law, making it easy and perhaps even a routine matter to change the rules of the game.'[50] This ease is further illustrated by a practice that has grown up, and which has been extensively used post-Brexit, of parent Acts providing that relevant Ministers (members of the executive) can amend primary legislation by way of secondary legislation. As the IRAL Panel notes, these so-called Henry VIII clauses 'would put judicial review grounds into the powers of the executive'.[51]

A codifying statute that seeks to abolish some or all provisions of the common law of judicial review is characteristic of more specific ouster clauses aimed at preventing particular institutions and/or areas of decision-making from review on some or all grounds. IRAL noted that the case law here is complex. With some judgments described variously as either a 'pragmatic' judicial case-management decision or as founded on the constitutional principle of access to justice,[52] others appear to have been decided on more routine grounds of statutory interpretation.[53]

[49] IRAL Report (n 5) para 1.28.
[50] ibid para 1.32.
[51] ibid para 1.25.
[52] *R (Cart) v The Upper Tribunal* and *R (MR (Pakistan)) (FC) v The Upper Tribunal (Immigration & Asylum Chamber) and Secretary of State for the Home Department* [2011] UKSC 28, [2012] 1 AC 663.
[53] *R (Privacy International) v Investigatory Powers Tribunal* [2020] AC 491 [31], per Sales LJ.

The IRAL Panel determined that 'no conclusive answer can be given as to whether and when there can be a statutory abrogation of judicial review'.[54] Some evidence to IRAL supported the view that in a state which espouses parliamentary sovereignty, the legislature has a legitimate role in setting out the grounds of review, if only to give imprimatur to the judiciary to flesh out the detailed principles whilst concurrently emphasising that this role is not exclusive to them. Nevertheless, the inconsistency in case law over ouster clauses and abrogation likely informed IRAL's conclusion that statutory codification runs too great a risk of total parliamentary, or even executive, repeal of common law.

In addressing codification of the grounds of review, IRAL noted two main approaches: either a statement of general principles or a detailed list of the main grounds. A 'light touch' general formulation may be valued by those who support leaving interpretation and development to the judiciary. For example, back in the 1990s, James Goudie QC argued that codification could be used to broaden the grounds for judicial review in a way that might further increase judicial discretion to develop substantive principle. For Goudie, codification is based on the need to bring greater clarity and accessibility to the law as a means to facilitate development. This expansive approach can be contrasted with John Griffith's early 1980s argument for codification as a means to curb what he saw as excessive judicial discretion in the development of common law principles. He argued that codified grounds of review should be restricted to ultra vires in the narrow sense of being within the powers of enabling legislation, the rules of fair procedure, and bad faith or corruption. For him, codification of more substantive principles such as unreasonableness potentially allowed for judicially introduced inconsistency, risking injustice in complex areas of legislation.[55] The fact that both Griffith's and Goudie's positions, from around 40 and 30 years ago, respectively, are represented in responses to IRAL serves to emphasise the perennial nature of this discourse. IRAL's observation on general statements was that they bring:

> [T]ogether the traditional grounds for judicial review in one place, stamping them with the authority of Parliament and restating basic principle in simple language accessible to the general public. They therefore bestow the legitimacy of democratic approval on the judicial process and are educative, while retaining the flexibility of the common law.[56]

In terms of the alternative option to list judicial review grounds more specifically, the IRAL panel drew on the experiences of South Africa and Australia. The South African Constitution enshrines a right to administrative justice, and the subsequent Promotion of Administrative Justice Act (PAJA)[57] lists more than

[54] IRAL Report (n 5) para 1.39.

[55] J Griffith, 'Constitutional and Administrative Law' in P Archer and A Martin (eds), *More Law Reform Now: A Collection of Essays on Law Reform* (London, Rose, 1983) 49 ff.

[56] IRAL Report (n 5) para 1.11.

[57] Promotion of Administrative Justice Act 3 of 2000.

15 specific grounds of review intended to give practical effect to that right. The PAJA is not regarded as an exhaustive statement of legal principles, and this has given rise to complexity. For example, the PAJA states that an administrative action is one that must 'adversely affect the rights of any person', whereas the courts have interpreted this as meaning that the decision must 'have the capacity to affect legal rights'. Use of the word 'adversely' also appears to have been no barrier for finding that a decision which conferred a benefit on an individual qualified as administrative action under the PAJA.[58]

The PAJA definition of 'administrative action' also seems to be inconsistent with the meaning attributed to the same concept by the South African Constitutional Court prior to the enactment of the PAJA.[59] In addition, the judicially crafted principle of legality, echoing a similar constitutional principle in the UK, has developed as a means to replicate many grounds within the PAJA. The principle of legality has the advantage of broader application and less onerous procedural requirements than the PAJA, and arguably its basis in common law parallels or even supplants the PAJA's legislative democratic pedigree.[60] This sets up a conflict with constitutional law, and a phenomenon (also experienced in other jurisdictions such as Australia, as discussed by Janina Boughey in this volume)[61] of a judicial review landscape including the Constitution, relevant codified administrative law/administrative justice statute and also (in the case of Australia) other statutes that apply to specific areas of administrative activity withdrawn from the coverage of the main codification Act.

Since the UK does not have a written constitution, there is a double risk that statutory codification could conflict with the common law supervisory jurisdiction and/or seek to supplant or 'oust' that jurisdiction entirely. This is coupled with concerns that the extent of government power in a Westminster-style parliamentary democracy, as well as uncertainty over concepts such as legality and constitutional statutes, provides the executive with significant unchecked power to fashion judicial review as it wishes.

IRAL drew on the Australian Administrative Decisions (Judicial Review) Act 1977 (ADJR Act), analysed in Boughey's chapter in this book, noting how it contains a codified statement of grounds of review and provides an additional species of judicial review proceedings as a supposedly simple alternative to the route already extant under the Australian Constitution.[62] The ADJR Act sets out 17 specific grounds of judicial review and a further two open-ended grounds.

[58] G Penfold, 'Substantive Reasoning and the Concept of "Administrative Action"' (2019) 36 *South African Law Journal* 84, 109.

[59] C Hoexter (n 14) 55 f.

[60] C Hoexter, 'A Rainbow of One Colour? Judicial Review on Substantive Grounds in South African Law' in M Elliott and H Wilberg (eds) *The Scope and Intensity of Substantive Review: Traversing Taggart's Rainbow* (Oxford, Hart Publishing, 2015) 178 ff.

[61] See in this book J Boughey (n 14) section IV.C.i.

[62] See in this book J Boughey (n 14) section IV.C.i.

As Boughey explains, whether setting out such precise grounds has stunted further judicial development of common law in Australia remains open to debate.[63] Whilst it is often argued that common law development has been slowed by the Act, Boughey concludes that limited development (in comparison to England and Wales as one example) may be as much due to the specific constitutional separation of powers in Australia, and the Australian High Court's interpretation of this constitutional principle, as it is to explicit statement of grounds in the Act. In particular, the judiciary have the power to craft new common law developments under the umbrella of the two open-ended grounds should they so wish.[64]

A related concern is that the extensive list of grounds led provisions of the ADJR Act to become buried under technical interpretive problems, which have little impact on improving administrative decision-making and practice.[65] On the other hand, whilst the grounds are lengthy, they are far from comprehensive. As TH Jones puts it, 'the bare text of the 1977 Act does not even provide an accurate guide to the grounds of judicial review, let alone the details of their application'.[66]

The UK IRAL Panel concluded that academic opinion varies as to the impact of the ADJR Act. Among the themes identified were that whilst some see it as providing a reasonable model for codification of judicial review and an important milestone in development, many are concerned about the largely formulaic restatement of common law and the technical interpretive case law that has arisen, alongside criticism that it lacks general themes on which to shape principled development.

The IRAL Panel noted that a UK Act of Parliament seeking to codify judicial review could either make a specific provision intending to preserve the common law or could take the Australian approach of having an open-ended clause that permits any other ground of judicial review. It concluded that both approaches would lead to the same practical results:

> The Panel consider that the chief advantage of such an approach is flexibility. It would allow judicial review to change and expand in line with the changing times, leaving space for new grounds to be introduced. The statute might have an inhibiting effect on judicial creativity, and specifically to authorise retention of the common law would create uncertainty, decrease clarity and might have the effect of reducing the statutory formulation to a largely educative function. In these circumstances, it would achieve very little.[67]

In total, the IRAL Secretariat logged 149 responses on the matter of codification: the largest number of responses were from pressure groups/charities (26 per cent

[63] See in this book ibid section IV.C.iii.
[64] In this book ibid section IV.B.
[65] M Groves, 'Federal Constitutional Influences on State Judicia Review' (2011) 39 *Federal Law Review* 399.
[66] TH Jones (n 12) 533.
[67] IRAL Report (n 5) para 1.27.

of responses), with other main categories of respondents being legal associations, law firms, lawyers and academics. Controversially, whereas 14 Government Departments responded to IRAL, the majority of these submissions were never published in full; the decision to withhold the submissions was challenged under the Freedom of Information Act 2000, with the Information Commission eventually accepting that the decision to withhold was justified under section 36(2)(c) (prejudice to the effective conduct of public affairs).

Overall, of those IRAL respondents answering questions on codification, six were fully in favour of codification, 22 supported partial codification and 110 were opposed. Those in favour cited the following benefits: enhancing legislative clarity, including as to the purpose of judicial review; increasing accessibility including for unrepresented litigants and the potential for improved efficiency; and, tellingly, at different ends of the claimant–defendant spectrum, legislating for remedies to be available as of right rather than judicial discretion (improving claimant prospects), with others citing the potential of codification to prevent the Supreme Court from confirming proportionality as a general ground (codification here would arguably entrench a more defendant-friendly position). The arguments against included the following: that rigidity could undermine the rule of law; that legislative changes might lead to less certainty and a resulting reduction in accessibility; that a rise in litigation, especially on technical issues that would have little impact on improving the quality of administration or access to justice for individuals, would result; and that the perception, or indeed reality, that the Government has too great a hand in crafting the grounds on which it is to be held accountable undermines confidence in the public sector, including confidence in regulatory oversight potentially impacting investment. Weighing up all these matters, IRAL concluded: 'On balance, little significant advantage would be obtained by statutory codification, as the grounds of review are well established and accessibly stated in the leading textbooks. But codification might make judicial review more accessible to non-lawyers.'[68] This has likely put to bed the idea of wholesale codification in a general Act of Parliament for some time.

The Government's subsequent Judicial Review and Courts Act 2022 does not address the grounds of review, but amends available remedies.[69] Section 1 introduces so-called 'suspended quashing orders' allowing the court to make a quashing order that would only come into effect at a predetermined point in the future, thus enabling an unlawful administrative provision to be treated as valid until that time. The aim is that where a case might raise significant constitutional issues, including potential national security issues, Parliament would be allowed time to clarify or amend the law before the quashing order took effect. Section 1

[68] ibid para 1.43.

[69] Judicial Review and Courts Bill, House of Commons Session 2021–22, bills.parliament.uk/bills/3035.

also provides for prospective-only quashing orders that would limit or remove any retrospective effect that a particular quashing order might have. It is suggested that these provisions give the judiciary more flexibility in granting remedies; however, it can also be argued that they encourage the limitation of judicial discretion and improperly influence proceedings and outcomes in favour of public authorities being challenged, as against doing justice for aggrieved individuals.

Historically the judiciary have used their control of various principles at permission stage (such as determining the meaning of an 'arguable case' and 'sufficient interest') and their remedial discretion as means to manage caseloads alongside developing a particular judicial vision of the nature and purpose of administrative law. Successive governments have then sought to respond, both to procedural interpretation and substantive judgments in particular areas, through methods Harlow and Rawlings describe this as 'striking back' and 'clamping down'. 'Striking back' is an 'official response to court rulings that are deliberately negative in the sense that government or administration sets out to rid itself of a judicial decision that it finds inconvenient or otherwise dislikes'. Tactics include ouster clauses, delaying tactics and retaking annulled decisions. A subset of 'striking back' is 'clamping down', which occurs where the Government attempts to 'protect itself against future judicial "interference" by changing the rules of the game in a restrictive fashion' such as through procedural and costs reforms.[70] It remains to be seen how much the Judicial Review and Courts Act 2022 enhances, or in fact or 'clamps down', on judicial remedial discretion, but what is clear is that applications for civil (non-immigration and asylum) judicial review in the early 2020s have fallen to their lowest number per annum in over two decades.

# V. Issues for Further Research

## A. Administrative Rule-Making

In his chapter in this volume on codification of administrative law in the US, Edward Rubin explains how the American Administrative Procedure Act enacted in 1946 divides administrative action into two categories: rule-making and adjudication.[71] It is important to recognise that in the UK too, administration is conducted not only through individualised adjudication but also through the application of predetermined rules which can strongly influence or even be determinative of an issue. A primary statute which empowers ministers to make rules will normally specify whether these rules are to be regarded as statutory

[70] C Harlow and R Rawlings, '"Striking Back" and "Clamping Down": An Alternative Perspective on Judicial Review' in J Bell, M Elliott, JNE Varuhas and P Murray (eds), *Public Law Adjudication in Common Law Systems: Process and Substance* (Oxford, Hart Publishing, 2016) ch 13.

[71] See in this book EL Rubin (n 7) section III.

instruments for the purposes of the Statutory Instruments Act 1946, which contains provisions for publication and legislative controls. Rules that are not specifically expressed to be statutory instruments fall outside the control of this regime. Delegated legislative rules come with a wide variety of labels, such as Orders in Council, rules, regulations, bylaws and directions; however, in practice nothing really turns upon the labelling. Authority to make Orders in Council derives from statute; these tend to be the most important piece of secondary legislative rule-making and are drafted by the executive and enacted as an Order of the Privy Council. This is a body of senior politicians of both Houses of Parliament (Commons and Lords) who act as an advisory council to the monarch, who then exercises Royal Prerogative powers to make the Orders. Prerogative powers are a unique constitutional source of law-making power, and are subject to judicial supervision operating under various common law limitations – for example, prerogative powers cannot be used to remove rights granted to individuals by primary statutes.

In most cases statutory instruments or other subordinate legislation (subordinate rules) will be subject to some parliamentary scrutiny, through simply being laid before the Houses of Parliament, through the requirement of an affirmative resolution by each House or through a negative resolution procedure whereby a private Member must secure parliamentary time to attack the instrument; there is no provision for amendment in the latter procedure, only outright rejection.

The various sources of parliamentary procedure are brought together in a collection, Erskine May, which is described as treatise on the law, privileges, proceedings and usage of Parliament. It is not a legal source or code in its own right, but covers a wide range of sources such as Standing Orders, prerogatives, common law and constitutional conventions.[72] The observance of some provisions of some of these sources might potentially be subject to judicial review, but often on more limited grounds than applies to other sources of state power due to their more political nature.

Delegated rule-making is also subject to scrutiny through consultation. In some areas the legislation will be specific as to which bodies should be consulted, whereas in others there may be a general duty to consult such interests as appear to be appropriate. There are various Codes of Practice on Consultation that are adhered to as a matter of convention. There is no common law duty to consult where the order is of a legislative character, and any right to a reasoned decision specifically does not apply where the order is of a legislative character. Consultation rights have been accorded in particular circumstances under common law, such as where a representation has been made to an individual that they will be consulted before an instrument altering policy is made, that instruments seeking to depart from established policy might require reasons to be given to affected individuals, and where a legitimate expectation of consultation arises.

[72] Erskine May's *Treatise on the Law, Privileges, Proceedings and Usage of Parliament* (25th edn, 2019): erskinemay.parliament.uk.

Outside of the above circumstances of delegated and subdelegated legislation, there is a further category where there is no express legislative mandate to make rules, but where the administration nonetheless makes rules of a legislative character. Such rules are of general application and would be indistinguishable if juxtaposed to true statutory instruments (eg, the latter having been made on behalf of a Minister and having undergone some form of parliamentary scrutiny). There are various types of such 'rules' including codes of practice, circulars, directions, rules and regulations; some are procedural rules, while others are interpretive guides, instructions to officials, prescriptive/evidential rules, commentary codes, voluntary codes, rules of practice, management and operation, and so on. The precise legal status of these 'rules' may vary, but some general points can be noted: first, the fact that an administrative body does not have express delegated power to make the rules does not automatically invalidate them; second, the precise legal status is likely to be found primarily by examining the relevant statutory background to the particular area of law; and, finally, even if a 'rule' is not specifically related to primary legislation, it can still have legal consequences by being dispositive of an individual person's case, and the rule's existence may generate a common law right to consultation if the administrative body seeks to depart from applying that rule in particular circumstances.

A court will be able to decide first if the specific 'rule' is subject to judicial review and, if so, it will also be the judiciary that provides an authoritative meaning of the substance of the 'rule' itself. It is likely that the existence of a 'rule' will generate a general administrative law (common law) obligation that there should be a degree of consistency in its application, which may go as far as creating a legitimate expectation that the 'rule' will not be departed from.

There seems to be a perceptible trend across jurisdictions, referred to as the proceduralisation of administration (and, with it, administrative law), that allows conceptual space for potentially less contentious codification. In the UK this proceduralisation is most often associated with so-called 'New Public Management' (NPM), which is designed to re-impose political control over public administration and to reorganise bureaucracy and push it into self-control through the use of managerialist methodology. NPM emphasises procedural tools at various stages of the administrative process: from standard setting, benchmarking and the setting of targets and performance indicators, to cost-effectiveness analysis, multiple impact assessments and consultations, compliance codes, measuring impact and monitoring and supervision techniques such as inspections and value-for-money audits. Harlow and Rawlings then note that the combined effect of these developments could lead to increased calls for something like the American Administrative Procedure Act that provides a more generalised statement of principles applying to administrative rule-making and regulatory-type activity. An England and Wales or broader UK code here could avoid some of the difficulties of the American Administrative Procedure Act by expressly only applying to rule-making as opposed to adjudication, with IRAL having concluded that the codification of the latter would not bring sufficient benefits. This rule-making code could also apply to so-called 'integrity' institutions which sometimes do not have a high level of independence from government (in effect bureaucratic regulation of government by other bodies with varying degrees of connection to government). As Harlow and Rawlings conclude:

> [S]tatutory public regulators are themselves in an ambiguous position, acting on the one hand as enforcers of good governance standards and fair procedures, on the other as targets for them. There have, for example, been complaints that regulators are insufficiently open and suggestions that the UK should adopt an equivalent to the American Administrative Procedures Act.[73]

Aileen McHarg has argued that case law governing administrative rule-making and other forms of soft law is becoming more extensive and that it could potentially be more coherently rationalised.[74] This could perhaps pave the way for agreed codification of general principles, although this is not McHarg's proposal. McHarg argues that judicial regulation of rule-making is becoming increasingly elaborate and that judges have sometimes gone as far as mandating the adoption of rules. She believes that judges should prima facie accept that administrative decision-makers can adopt rules (something of a grey area in current case law) and focus their attention instead on the latter questions of regulating those rules.

The American Administrative Procedure Act is not without its own controversies. As Rubin notes in this volume, it can be seen as a compromise between New Deal and Anti-New Deal, Democratic and Republican positions which arguably made more political than legal sense. Some of its provisions were deliberately left ambiguous, with each side hoping the courts might later resolve them in their favour. As TH Jones notes: 'The statute does not – and could not – settle the ideological disputes which accompanied its gestation.'[75] Shapiro has similarly noted that judicial interpretation of the APA has changed radically over the years, most likely driven by political considerations and forces.[76]

## B. Devolution

The debate over administrative law reform in the UK has also highlighted divergence between the UK Government and the devolved nations (Scotland, Northern Ireland and Wales). The IRAL Panel only considered judicial review of powers that may be exercised across the whole of the UK, excluding powers in respect of matters that are devolved or transferred under one of the UK's devolution settlements.

[73] C Harlow and R Rawlings (n 20) 11.

[74] A McHarg, 'Administrative Discretion, Administrative Rule-Making and Judicial Review' (2017) 70(1) *Current Legal Problems* 267.

[75] TH Jones (n 12) 523.

[76] M Shapiro, 'Codification of Administrative Law: The US and the Union' (1996) 2 *European Law Journal* 26.

As IRAL only examined judicial review of the central UK Government powers, its analysis excluded swathes of day-to-day judicial review and administrative law activity. This is particularly concerning for the legal jurisdiction of England and Wales, as IRAL's procedural and remedial recommendations, and the latter recommendations of the UK Government, necessarily also apply to English local and regional authorities, Welsh local authorities and even Welsh Government Ministers. Scotland and Northern Ireland have their own separate administrative law jurisdictions, albeit with general principles under supervision of the UK Supreme Court. The UK Government considers that its further judicial review reforms proposed after IRAL should act to strengthen the Union,[77] though it has not explained how.

The UK could learn from federal nations in terms of developing diverse administrative justice systems across its four nations. Substantive administrative law differs across these nations in devolved areas such as housing, health, education and planning. The UK's devolved nations are adopting broader general principles of administrative law inspired by a different approach to human rights, equality, sustainable development and the nature of good administration when compared to the UK Government. As Issalys notes of Quebec, there is a relationship between distinct social values and the flavour of administrative law.[78] Issalys also notes the relevance of distinct legal traditions, and one UK nation, Wales, is experimenting with a new form of codification, in some ways looking back to the codification of the laws of the native Welsh princes in the tenth century by Hywel Ap Cadell (known as Hywel Dda, Hywel the Good). As with Quebec and most other Canadian provinces, Welsh law is drafted bilingually, which gives it a distinctive character among UK legislation.

The Welsh Government and the Senedd Cymru/Welsh Parliament have embarked on a project to codify the majority of applicable law, the background being fragmentation over many years of sources of law applicable in Wales. The Law Commission recommended bringing together legislation whose subject matter is within Welsh competence, but which is scattered across various sources, and reforming that law where appropriate. In a process since described as 'groundbreaking' for a UK jurisdiction, it proposed the end goal as the organisation of primary and secondary legislation into a series of codes dealing comprehensively with particular areas of Welsh law.

The Welsh Government's first step towards implementing the Law Commission recommendations was to propose, and enact through the Senedd, the Legislation (Wales) Act 2019. This places the Counsel General for Wales under a duty to keep the accessibility of Welsh law under review. For each Senedd term, the Welsh Ministers and the Counsel General must prepare a programme of what they intend to do to improve the accessibility of Welsh law. This must include proposed

[77] Ministry of Justice (n 48) 9.
[78] See in this book P Issalys (n 8) section I.

activities 'to – (a) contribute to an ongoing process of consolidating and codifying Welsh law' and '(b) maintain the form of Welsh law (once codified)'.

Codification here is then related to the felt need to crystallise an emerging legal identity that is distinctive from England, alongside the goal of rationalising (primarily through consolidation) a plethora of sources of devolved and non-devolved law that are often impenetrable for lawyers, let alone the public. As Bargenda and Wilson-Stark have put it: 'In Wales, the case for codification to carve out a national identity is more compelling because it could be said that Wales now has its own "living system of law" after losing its legal identity centuries ago.'[79]

Although the Law Commission recommended an approach to codification for Wales closely resembling that of continental jurisdictions, with code discipline built into the legislative process, the method adopted by the Welsh Government so far is more presentational or cosmetic; one of consolidation with reform (although some degree of code discipline is built into the Legislation (Wales) Act 2019 and in Senedd Standing Orders). As the Welsh Government states:

> [A] 'Code' is the label we will use to describe legislation that has been classified under a particular topic, for example for a 'Housing Code' or a 'Public Health Code'. In this guise it is essentially a publication tool and we should stress that a Code will not be a formal legal instrument in its own right. We use the term 'Code' as the term for a collection of enactments on a particular subject – it is not intended to have a separate legal status to those enactments.[80]

The Welsh Government has consulted on a Draft Taxonomy of Codes of Welsh Law, which includes a proposed Public Administration Code. Wales has also notably enacted the Well-being of Future Generations (Wales) Act 2015, which establishes a legal duty on public bodies to practice sustainable development by fostering various well-being goals and seeking to act in five particular ways (collaboration, integration, long-termism, prevention and involvement). Interestingly, in this volume Issalys suggests that sustainable development might be a beneficial guiding concept for organising the spread of explicitly principled legislation as an appropriate basis for executive action.[81]

## C. Administrative Law Norms, Sources and Procedures

Emphasis on judicial review of administrative action in the UK has tended to obscure the importance of other sources of administrative law principles and

[79] A Bargenda and S Wilson-Stark, 'The Legal Holy Grail? German Lessons on Codification for a Fragmented Britain' (2018) 22(2) *Edinburgh Law Review* 183.

[80] Welsh Government Consultation Document (WG39203), *The Future of Welsh Law: Classification, Consolidation, Codification* (October 2019), gov.wales/sites/default/files/consultations/2019-10/the-future-of-welsh-law-consultation-document_1.pdf.

[81] See in this book P Issalys (n 8) section III.

other forms of administrative law adjudication (including statutory appeals and applications in various tribunals and courts).[82] As discussed above, reforms to remedial discretion on judicial review do not affect other forms of administrative law adjudication, such as statutory appeals in the Administrative Court and in the Upper Tribunal that can be functionally equivalent to judicial review. Additionally, the Upper Tribunal, which itself has a statutory judicial review jurisdiction, has the potential to develop a body of, as Lord Justice Sedley referred to it, 'not quite lawyers' law', given its specialist areas of work and the presence in some instances of non-judicial expert members.

In addition to through various forms of adjudication, administrative law norms can also be found in other categories of public law. For example, the Human Rights Act 1998, which was a codification of sorts as it incorporated the ECHR into domestic legislation. The ECHR, and particularly domestic incorporation, has had significant implications for UK administrative law, and various chapters in this volume show this effect is also true for other European countries. Specifically, the interpretation of ECHR rights by the European Court of Human Rights (ECtHR) such as to render them 'practical and effective' rather than 'theoretical and illusory' has led to the development of implied procedural rights that have no analogue in domestic UK common law. For example, where an interference with a particular right is found to be in accordance with the law, it may still be considered not 'necessary in a democratic society' if the individual is not 'involved in the decision-making process, seen as a whole, to a degree sufficient to provide them with the requisite protection of their interests' under Article 8 ECHR.[83] The ECtHR has also implied a number of positive duties that are not found in common law: the duty to have in place laws and systems, and to take operational measures to protect rights. The common law does not, for example, contain specific duties to investigate, prosecute or to make available judicial remedies. At the time of writing, the UK Government intends to reform the Human Rights Act 1998, with the aim of developing a so-called 'modern British bill of rights'. This new Bill of Rights seeks to restrain the ability of the UK courts from using human rights to impose positive administrative obligations on public authorities without what is considered to be 'proper democratic oversight';[84] in effect, this new 'codification' will reverse common law judicial interpretation of the previous Human Rights Act 1998 and seek to further minimise domestic judicial references to so-called 'Strasbourg jurisprudence'.

[82] J Bell and S Nason, 'The Future of Judicial Review Scholarship and the Importance of an Expanding Legal Scholarly Imagination' in C Harlow (ed), *A Research Agenda for Administrative Law* (Cheltenham, Edward Elgar, forthcoming, 2023).

[83] *TP and KM v United Kingdom* (28945/95) 10 May 2001 ECtHR [GC] at [72].

[84] Ministry of Justice, *Human Rights Act Reform: A Modern Bill of Rights* (CP588, 2021) paras 229 ff.

## VI. Concluding Reflections

On the whole, UK administrative law scholarship has shown a recent and marked increase in investigating and understanding the centrality of legislation to various forms of administrative law adjudication, including judicial review.[85] The Welsh experiment has also ignited renewed interest in the nature and processes of codification more generally, as well as the role of the Law Commission. These are valuable developments that will help in establishing a wider and more reliable picture of the subject area, dispelling myths that administrative law is purely a creature of common law.

The relationship between codes and judicially developed principles is clearly a general theme of this volume. As Delphine Costa notes in her chapter, despite France being widely acknowledged as the birthplace of codification, in fact the Conseil d'Etat (Council of State) is the main producer of general administrative law and the origin of many principles. Each chapter in this volume also demonstrates how codification might be seen as clarifying legal principles and rendering them more accessible to the broader public, but that this also risks ossification of a particular vision of the function and values of administrative law, and invites litigation over technical matters that might have little relevance to good administrative practice. Thus, this volume clearly shows that these matters are pervasive and perennial, regardless of particular legal cultures and traditions, and that there is much scope for cross-jurisdictional learning.

[85] J Bell and E Fisher, 'Exploring a Year of Administrative Law Adjudication in the Administrative Court' [2021] *Public Law* 505.

# 13

# The United States

## *Systematic but Incomplete Codification*

EDWARD L RUBIN

The process of codifying administrative law in the US began less than a century ago. However, the meaning of codification for Americans and the contours of the resulting legislation cannot be grasped without an understanding of the nation's common law background, which goes back 800 years. This chapter begins with a definition of administrative law in the US (section I), discusses the original and development of common law (section II), and then proceeds (section III) to give a description of the basic American codification, the Administrative Procedure Act of 1946 (APA).[1] It then discusses the gaps or lacunae in this codification (section IV) and the continued reliance on common law within this statutory framework to fill those gaps and serve related purposes (section V). The chapter concludes with a brief assessment of American administrative law codification and some thoughts about its future (section VI).

## I. The Definition of American Administrative Law

The functional definition of administrative law in the US is 'the law concerning the powers and procedures of administrative agencies'.[2] For the purpose of discussing codification, this is clearly an adequate definition because the primary codification of American administrative law – the APA – applies to administrative agencies and only to administrative agencies. The statute defines an agency as 'each authority of the Government of the United States', which is broad enough to encompass virtually everything we describe as an agency in ordinary language, but it specifically excludes (inter alia) Congress, the courts and military authorities, which we generally do not describe as agencies.[3] In other words, the statute's boundaries

[1] Pub L 79-404, 60 Stat 237 (1946), codified at 5 USC §§ 551 ff.
[2] K Culp Davis, *Administrative Law* (St Paul, West Publishing, 1951) 1.
[3] 5 USC § 551 (1).

correspond to our ordinary language definition of an agency. Thus, American administrative law, as determined by the prevailing codification, is the law that agencies enforce.

However, this is a somewhat mechanical definition (like defining humans as featherless bipeds) that fails to illuminate the character of administrative law. An alternative is to define administrative law as the legal rules governing the process by which the government takes action that is articulated in two senses of the term: first, that it is carried out by distinct (ie, articulated) governmental units that operate in a particular subject area; and, second, that it implements conscious (ie, articulated) social policies designed to benefit the public.[4] These features have long been recognised,[5] and can be readily derived from two elements of Weber's sociology. The specialisation of subject area is central to his definition of bureaucracy,[6] while conscious social policies designed to benefit the public are a type of instrumental rationality.[7] In other words, administrative law applies to governmental action that reflects the structure of knowledge in modern, technological society where special expertise is required to govern effectively, and also reflects the political structure of modern government, specifically democracies, which no longer view law as a declaration of norms, but rather as a means of carrying out the desires of a sovereign populace.[8] Contrary to prevailing jurisprudential theories,[9] this action includes not only the regulation of private behaviour, but also the entire range of positive enactments designed to achieve social purposes, including benefits distribution, science and arts grants, industrial development subsidies, and the creation of operation of institutions such as national parks, prisons and universities. Even if this more conceptual definition of administrative law is used, it remains fair to say that the APA, rather than the Federal Rules of Civil Procedure or the Federal Rules of Criminal Procedure, is the primary means by which the legal actions of the national government in the US are controlled.[10]

[4] For a fuller explication, see EL Rubin, *Beyond Camelot: Rethinking Politics and Law for the Modern State* (Princeton, Princeton University Press, 2005) 22 ff.

[5] Report of the Attorney General's Committee on Administrative Procedure, Jan 24, 1941, 15 ff, available at www.regulationwriters.com/downloads/apa1941.pdf. This was a committee established by President Franklin Roosevelt to study the status of federal administration and offer recommendations for what ultimately became the APA. See below, section IV.

[6] M Weber, *Economy and Society*, G Roth and C Wittich (eds) (Berkeley, University of California Press, 1978) 956 and generally 956 ff.

[7] ibid 24.

[8] See EL Rubin, 'From Coherence to Effectiveness: A Legal Methodology for the Modern World' in R van Gestel, H-W Micklitz and EL Rubin (eds), *Rethinking Legal Scholarship: A Transatlantic Dialogue* (New York, Cambridge University Press, 2017) 310.

[9] See, eg, R Dworkin, *Law's Empire* (Cambridge, MA, Belknap Press, 1986); L Fuller, *The Morality of Law*, revised edn (New Haven, Yale University Press, 1969); HLA Hart, *The Concept of Law* (Oxford, Oxford University Press, 1961).

[10] Federal Rules of Civil Procedure, Comm Print No 8, 115th Cong, 2nd Sess 2018 (updated version of the Rules prepared for the Committee on the Judiciary, House of Representatives); Federal Rules of Criminal Procedure, Comm Print No 9, 113th Cong, 2nd Sess 2014 (updated version of the Rules prepared for the Committee on the Judiciary, House of Representatives).

## II. The Common Law Background to Administrative Codification

As Sarah Nason notes, the legal system that prevails in Great Britain to the present day is common law.[11] Britain's North American colonies retained this system even after they rebelled and formed the US, in part because it was perceived as emerging from the people, and thus an element of the English liberty that the new republic wanted to preserve.[12] Although displaced by administrative law in many areas, common law retains authority in certain others. Even more importantly, common law continues to be viewed as the basis, or conceptual foundation, of the American legal system. In essence, it is judge-made law, judges being public officials who resolve disputes by applying legal principles. They make new law by extending prior doctrine incrementally, relying on analogical arguments.[13] By this means, common law achieves an impressive level of flexibility and creativity while retaining political legitimacy through the assertion that it does not create new law, but only extends the law's in-dwelling principles to new situations. However, the common law is limited by the institutional structure of dispute resolution. It is reactive rather than proactive, dependent on the issues presented by the contending parties, incapable of making new rules globally as opposed to incrementally, restricted to remedies imposed on the contesting parties, and unable to allocate government resources.

The historical origins of the common law not only provide an understanding of the way in which it became dominant in the Anglo-American legal system, but also shed light on its subsequent status and its influence on administrative law. When King Henry I of England died without an heir in 1135, a civil war broke out between the two claimants to the throne: his daughter Matilda and his nephew Stephen of Blois. Each attempted to gain adherents by the standard means of doing so in medieval times, which was to offer grants of land. The war was finally resolved and Henry of Anjou, a compromise candidate, acceded to the throne as Henry II (r 1154–89). He wanted to settle the conflicting land grants in order to re-establish civil order, but he could not rely on the existing legal structure to do so, since each leading nobleman had his own court, which imposed the customary law within his own lands. Instead, Henry decided to establish a uniform or common law on the entire realm (hence the odd name for judge-made law).[14]

[11] See in this book S Nason, 'The Codification of Administrative Law in the United Kingdom: Beyond the Common Law', section I. For historical accounts of common law, see AR Hogue, *Origins of the Common Law* (Indianapolis, Liberty Press, 1966); T Plucknett, *A Concise History of the Common Law* (Rochester, NY, Lawyers Co-operative, 1936). The classic summary of the doctrine is W Blackstone, *Commentaries on the Laws of England*, vol 4 (Oxford, Oxford University Press, 2016) 1765 ff.

[12] See L Friedman, *A History of American Law*, 4th edn (New York, Oxford University Press, 2019); OW Holmes, *The Common Law* (Boston, Little, Brown, 1881).

[13] M Eisenberg, *The Nature of the Common Law* (Cambridge, MA, Harvard University Press, 1991) ch 3. See in this book S Nason (n 11) section III.

[14] WL Warren, *Henry II* (Berkeley, University of California Press, 1977) 301 ff.

He enacted several assizes – essentially statutes – the best known being the Assize of Clarendon (1166), which declared that seizing someone's landed property by force (*disseisen*) was not merely a private wrong, but also a breach of the King's peace. He then decreed a uniform procedure for resolving such cases and appointed royal judges to implement it.[15] He was less concerned about the particular content of the legal rules by which the cases would be resolved and was thus willing to allow such rules to be developed by his appointed judges; what he wanted was a resolution of the conflicts. The common law courts did so with great success, so much so that a few decades later, when rebellious barons forced Henry's son and second successor King John to sign the Magna Carta, they demanded that he judge them by the 'law of the land', by which they meant the common law.[16] From that point on, the scope and prestige of the common law administered by royal judges grew apace.

After James I (r 1603–25), the Stuart King of Scotland (as James VI),[17] became King of England, he quickly fell into a political conflict with the common law judges, most notably Lord Edward Coke.[18] In several decisions, including the famous *Dr Bonham's Case*,[19] Coke argued that the common law was superior to the King's decrees. His argument was that the common law was the customary law of England, whose origins stretched back into England's Anglo-Saxon past. It was thus much older than the monarchy, which only dated from the Norman Conquest (1066).[20] The argument could be maintained because, strangely enough, everyone in England had forgotten the real origin of common law. It was buttressed by a more conceptual and persuasive argument, akin to what we now describe as 'the wisdom of crowds', which went back at least as far as Thomas Aquinas. In the *Summa Theologica*,[21] Aquinas argued that customary law (and by extension common law), having developed gradually over a long period of time, cancelled out the idiosyncrasies of individual decision-makers and reflected the underlying regularity of human reason. Thus, it was likely to be superior to any act of positive law, which was necessarily an act of will by the law-maker. In addition, due to its gradual development, it is well understood by those who are subject to it,

[15] F Pollock and F Maitland, *A History of English Law before the Time of Edward I*, vol 1 (Cambridge, Cambridge University Press, 1988) 136 ff.

[16] JC Holt, *Magna Carta* (Cambridge, Cambridge University Press, 1992) 9 ff.

[17] James I was not only a strong believer in the divine right of kings, but the author of a book setting forth this doctrine. James I, *The True Law of Free Monarchies*, D Fischlin and M Fortier (eds) (Toronto, Centre for Reformation and Renaissance Studies, 1996).

[18] R Lockyer and P Gaunt, *Tudor and Stuart Britain*, 4th edn (New York, Routledge, 2019) 319 ff; JR Stoner, *Common Law and Liberal Theory: Coke, Hobbes and the Origin of American Constitutionalism* (Lawrence, University Press of Kansas, 1992) 11 ff. He also fell into conflict with Parliament, of course. See below section IV.

[19] *Dr Bonham's Case* 77 Eng Rep 638 (1610).

[20] See JGA Pocock, *The Ancient Constitution and the Feudal Law: A Study of English Historical Thought in the Seventeenth Century* (Cambridge, Cambridge University Press, 1987) 30 ff.

[21] T Aquinas, *Summa Theologica*, translated by Fathers of the English Dominican Province (Notre Dame, Christian Classics, 1981) (IaIIae Q 97) 1022 ff.

whereas positive law can implement an abrupt and unexplained change in settled expectations.

Although Pollack and Maitland revealed the statutory origin of common law in the 1890s,[22] the American legal system remained dominated, or one might even say transfixed, by the concept of common law that Lord Coke had articulated. American legal education was built upon this concept. It began at Harvard in the 1870s (American lawyers having trained as apprentices before then), spread to other established universities and then rode the crest of the tidal wave of new law schools that resulted from the enormous growth of American higher education generally. The curriculum of these law schools, and most importantly the compulsory first-year courses, consisted entirely of common law (torts, contracts, property, crimes), largely ignoring the dramatic growth of statutory law that was occurring at the time.[23] Students did not learn the common law of any particular state, but rather a generalised version incorporating what the law professors regarded as the modal or preferable decisions. Professors also wrote treatises presenting the generalised versions of each common law subject, and these were regarded as the pinnacle of scholarly achievement at the time.[24]

Similar beliefs led to the founding of the American Law Institute in 1923, a private organisation of prominent attorneys. It issued treatises, called Restatements, presenting the same sort of generalised or idealised version of the common law subjects, and encouraged state courts to rely on these treatises when deciding cases.[25] The overarching influence of common law affected constitutional law as well. During this same period (the first third of the twentieth century), the US Supreme Court struck down a good deal of Progressive Era regulatory legislation on the basis of economic due process.[26] This was, in essence, the use of the Due Process Clause of the Fourteenth Amendment to require that a statute that

[22] F Pollock and F Maitland (n 15).

[23] See L Friedman, *A History of American Law*, 2nd edn (New York, Oxford University Press, 2005) 466 ff; W LaPiana, *Logic and Experience: The Origin of Modern Legal Education* (New York, Oxford University Press, 1994) 55 ff; R Stevens, *Law School: Legal Education in America from the 1850s to the 1980s* (Chapel Hill, University of North Carolina Press, 1983) 35 ff.

[24] See, eg, A Corbin, *A Comprehensive Treatise on the Rules of Contract Law* (St Paul, West Publishing, 1874); W Prosser, *Handbook on the Law of Torts* (St Paul, West Publishing, 1941); JH Wigmore, *A Treatise on the System of Evidence in Trials at Common Law Including the Statutes and Judicial Decisions of All Jurisdictions of the United States* (Boston, Little, Brown, 1904); S Williston, *The Law of Contracts* (New York, Baker, Voorhis, 1927); A Prowancher, *John Henry Wigmore and the Rules of Evidence: The Hidden Origins of Modern Law* (Columbia, University of Missouri Press, 2016); KS Abraham and EG White, 'Prosser and His Influence' (2013) 6 *Journal of Tort Law* 27.

[25] See DP Currie, 'The Federal Courts and the American Law Institute' (1969) 36(2) *University of Chicago Law Review* 268; NEH Hull, 'A New Perspective on the Origins of the American Law Institute' (1990) 8(1) *Law and History Review* 55; JR Macey, 'The Transformation of the American Law Institute' (1992) 61 *George Washington Law Review* 1212; GE White, 'The American Law Institute and the Triumph of Modernist Jurisprudence' (2011) 15(1) *Law and History Review* 1.

[26] For descriptions of this legislation, see JW Chambers II, *The Tyranny of Change: America in the Progressive Era, 1890–1920*, 2nd edn (New Brunswick, NJ, Rutgers University Press, 1992) 132 ff; LL Gould, *America in the Progressive Era, 1890–1914* (London, Routledge, 2001) 38 ff; RH Wiebe, *The Search for Order, 1877–1920* (New York, Hill & Wang, 1967) 164 ff.

displaced common law possess a higher level of justification than other types of statutes.[27] At the same time, the federal courts were deciding diversity cases (that is, cases where the litigants came from different states) on the grounds of 'general common law', roughly the same body of decisional law that was being taught in law schools, presented in treatises and promulgated in the Restatements.[28]

American lawyers thus had extensive experience of developing new doctrine through the common law when administrative cases began appearing in the federal courts during the Progressive Era, that is, during the same time that American law schools were proliferating, common law treatises were being written and the first Restatements were issued. Administrative governance in the US pre-dates this period,[29] but during the first third of the twentieth century, it expanded rapidly, and the procedures that governed it became a matter of attention and concern. Judges were confronted with cases where an administrative agency was attempting to impose a penalty on a private party by using a statutory authorisation, or where a private party was challenging, on statutory or constitutional grounds, a rule or order issued by the agency. Because these cases were based on positive law, they could sometimes be resolved by the direct application of that law, as interpreted according to developed principles of statutory or constitutional interpretation. Quite often, however, there were gaps that needed to be filled or novel issues that needed to be addressed. The federal courts responded by developing a common law of administration. They articulated, for example, principles to determine whether an agency possessed rule-making authority when the statute was silent on this matter,[30] and what the effect of agency guidelines that were not issued as rules should be.[31] They fashioned rules of evidence for administrative hearings based on the analogy to bench trials and diverging from the rules that prevailed in jury trials,[32] and determined when an agency adjudicator could take judicial

[27] The leading case, which gave its name to this whole period of Supreme Court decision-making, is *Lochner v New York* 198 US 45 (1905) (striking down maximum hours legislation). See generally H Gillman, *The Constitution Besieged: The Rise and Demise of Lochner* (Durham, NC, Duke University Press, 1993); P Kens, *Lochner v New York: Economic Regulation on Trial* (Lawrence, University Press of Kansas, 1998). For other significant examples of the doctrine, see, eg, *New State Ice Co v Liebmann* 285 US 262 (1932) (striking down law requiring ice manufacturers to be licensed); *Jay Burns Baking Co v Bryan* 264 US 504 (1924) (striking down law requiring standardised weight for bread loaves); *Adair v United States* 208 US 161 (1908) (striking down prohibition on employers hiring only non-union workers).

[28] *Black & White Taxicab Co v Brown & Yellow Taxicab Co* 276 US 518 (1928); *Baltimore & Ohio Railroad Co v Bough* 149 US 368 (1893); *Swift v Tyson* 41 US 18 (1842).

[29] Recent scholarship has emphasised the earlier origins of American administrative governance; see B Balogh, *A Government out of Sight: The Mystery of National Authority in Nineteenth Century America* (New York, Cambridge University Press, 2009); JL Mashaw, *Creating the Administrative Constitution: The Lost One Hundred Years of American Administrative Law* (New Haven, Yale University Press, 2012).

[30] *Columbia Broadcasting System, Inc v United States* 316 US 407 (1942).

[31] *Skidmore v Swift & Co* 323 US 134 (1944); *United States v American Trucking Association* 310 US 534 (1940).

[32] eg, *Opp Cotton Mills v Administrator* 312 US 126 (1941); *Spiller v Atchison Topeka & Santa Fe Railway* 253 US 117 (1920); *ICC v Baird* 194 US 25 (1904).

notice of factual information.[33] They established the substantial evidence standard for review of agency fact-finding[34] developed the doctrine that the agency must state a valid legal basis for its decision,[35] and defined areas of agency discretion where the courts would give deference to agency interpretations of their authorising statutes[36] or of their own regulations.[37] Quite soon thereafter, the treatises for common law subjects that law professors were producing were joined by treatises summarising and categorising administrative decisions as well.[38] Courses on administrative law were introduced into the upper-class curriculum, using collections of decided cases as their teaching materials in the same way that the common law courses did.[39]

In 1937, the Supreme Court repudiated the economic due process cases, holding, in effect, that statutes displacing common law required no special justification, but need only meet the very low standard of minimal rationality that applies to democratically enacted statutes in general.[40] The next year, the Court held, in *Erie RR v Tompkins*,[41] that diversity cases must be decided according to the law of the relevant state. Writing for the Court, Justice Brandeis declared that that 'is no federal general common law'. The belief that there is, he said (quoting Justice Holmes) 'rests upon the assumption that there is "a transcendental body of law outside of any particular State but obligatory within it unless and until changed by statute" … The common law so far as it is enforced in a State, whether called common law or not, is not the common law generally but the law of that State existing by the authority of that State'.[42] In other words, Justices Brandeis and Holmes were reflecting the historical reality that English common law began with positive law, and represented a delegation of law-making authority to courts.[43] They were denying that common law was customary law, arising from the people and reflecting general principles of rationality or legality that could be applied apart from any specific legal authorisation.

[33] *Pacific States Box & Basket Co v White* 296 US 176 (1935); *Norwegian Nitrogen Products Co v United States* 288 US 294 (1933); *ICC v Louisville & Nashville RR* 227 US 88 (1913).

[34] *Consolidated Edison Co v NLRB* 395 US 197 (1938).

[35] *SEC v Chenery Corp* 315 US 80 (1943) (*Chenery I*).

[36] *NLRB v Hearst Publications* 322 US 111 (1944); *Dobson v Commissioner* 320 US 489 (1943).

[37] *Bowles v Seminole Rock & Sand Co* 325 US 4110 (1945).

[38] See, eg, W Gellhorn, *Federal Administrative Proceedings* (Baltimore, Johns Hopkins University Press, 1941); B Wyman, *The Principles of Administrative Law Governing the Relations of Public Officers* (Clark, NJ, The Lawbook Exchange, 2014).

[39] See, eg, F Frankfurter, *Cases and Other Materials on Administrative Law* (Chicago, Foundation Press, 1935); RA Maurer, *Cases and Other Materials on Administrative Law* (Rochester, NY, Lawyers Cooperative, 1937); KC Sears, *Cases and Materials on Administrative Law* (St Paul, West Publishing, 1938).

[40] *West Coast Hotel v Parrish* 300 US 379 (1937); see generally B Cushman, *Rethinking the New Deal Court: The Structure of a Constitutional Revolution* (New York, Oxford University Press, 1998).

[41] *Erie RR v Tompkins* 304 US 64 (1938).

[42] ibid, quoting *Black & White Taxicab Co v Brown & Yellow Taxicab Co* 276 US 518 (1928).

[43] They were thus adopting the standard positivist view of law. See H Kelsen, *General Theory of Law and the State*, A Wedberg (trans) (Cambridge, MA, Harvard University Press, 1945); H Kelsen, *Pure Theory of Law* (Berkeley, University of California Press, 1967).

## III. Codification: The Administrative Procedure Act

The definitive repudiation of general common law by the Supreme Court, and the closely allied rejection of economic due process, occurred at the same time as the beginning of the efforts to codify administrative law in the US. One might assume that these two events were directly related, but there is little evidence of any such connection. In fact, the demotion of common law as a constitutional and procedural doctrine did little to diminish its continuing influence on the American legal system. Law schools retained the common law curriculum for the first year and, while gradually acknowledging the existence of administrative law in upper class electives, failed to draw any more general conclusions from its increasing prominence. Law professors continued to produce treatises on common law subjects and the Reinstatements continued to be issued from the American Law Institute. Rather than emerging from any repudiation of common law, the codification effort of the late 1930s was motivated by discomfort regarding the common law's displacement by New Deal legislation and the concomitant development of new legal procedures and remedies, unknown to common law, that were needed to implement this legislation.[44] Within a relatively short time – less than a decade – American government had been transformed; new agencies had been created, new functions established and new responsibilities assumed. Most significantly, from a purely pragmatic point of view, a new philosophy of governance had become dominant. Needless to say, changes of this magnitude produced concern among many law-trained people, particularly when the changes were perceived as disadvantageous to the business corporations who employed a large proportion of the leading lawyers.

These concerns were gathered and galvanised by the American Bar Association, which established a committee chaired by Roscoe Pound, the recently retired Dean of Harvard Law School. The committee's report was harshly critical of the New Deal administrative apparatus, going so far as to compare it to the Soviet Union.[45] Inspired by the ABA report, Congress passed the Walter-Logan Act in 1940.[46] The Act's basic strategy was to subject agency action to extensive procedural rules that would be enforced by the courts. President Roosevelt vetoed the Act; although he added the argument that it would encumber national defence efforts as war approached, his main concern was the effectiveness of the administrative process. 'Great interests … which desire to escape regulation', he wrote, 'rightly see that if they can strike at the heart of modern reform by sterilising the administrative tribunal which administers them they will have effectively destroyed the reform

[44] GE Metzger, 'The Supreme Court, 2016 Term: Foreword: 1930s Redux: The Administrative State under Siege' (2017) 131 *Harvard Law Review* 1.

[45] 63 ABA Rep 331, 339–40 (1938). See also 59 ABA Rep 539 (1934) (arguing that all controversies should be decided by the judiciary and not adjudicated by agencies).

[46] S 915, HR 6324, 75th Cong, 3d Sess, 1939. See JM Landis, 'Critical Issues in Administrative Law: The Walter-Logan Bill' (1940) 53(7) *Harvard Law Review* 1077.

itself.'[47] The House of Representatives came close to over-riding his veto, thus indicating the strength of the concerns about the rapidly expanding administrative state.[48]

In response, Roosevelt charged his own committee, which he had recently established under the leadership of the Attorney General, with crafting an alternative bill.[49] The result, submitted the following year, was predictably lenient towards recent administrative innovations, but a minority report was issued that reiterated many of the concerns, and recommended many of the proposals, of the ABA Committee.[50] This report became the focus of Congressional debate during the succeeding years, a debate which ultimately led to the APA.[51] The APA, like nearly all legislation, represented a compromise between the contesting forces.[52] New Dealers, mainly Democrats, wanted to preserve the administrative agencies' freedom of action, while their opponents, mainly Republicans, wanted to impose legal limits on agency decision-making. The general view is that the Democrats got their way regarding administrative rule-making, which was left largely unregulated, while the Republicans triumphed regarding administrative adjudication, which was subjected to fairly elaborate requirements.[53]

However political this compromise may have been – and it certainly represented some sort of political equilibrium, since the APA was enacted without a single negative vote in either House of Congress! – its specific contours corresponded to broadly accepted notions about law and government. Legislation, on which administrative rule-making was modelled, is supposed to be open-ended and informal, while adjudication is supposed to be formal and subject to strict rules. There are two powerful rationales that support this distinction. First, legislators are elected by the people and are thus authorised to act in accordance with their own best judgement, while judges are appointed and expected to be constrained by law. Second, legislation is directed towards groups, which compete in a robust and relatively unstructured political forum, while adjudication involves the imposition of legal rules on individuals, who generally do not have access to the political process and thus need the protection of formal rules of evidence and

[47] 84 Cong Rec 13942–43; Message from the President of the United States, Providing for the Expeditious Settlement of Disputes with the United States, HR Doc No 986, 76th Cong, 3d Sess (1940).

[48] H Doc 986, 75th Cong, 3d Sess 1939 (failing to over-ride veto).

[49] Report of the Attorney General's Committee (n 5) 191 ff. The Report stated: 'If administrative agencies did not exist in the Federal Government, Congress would be limited to a technique of legislation primarily designed to correct evils after they have arisen rather than to prevent them from arising' (at 13).

[50] ibid 203 ff.

[51] See GE Metzger (n 44).

[52] For general histories of the Act, see GE White, *The Constitution and the New Deal* (Cambridge, MA, Harvard University Press, 2002) 117–21; McNollgast, 'The Political Origins of the Administrative Procedure Act' (1999) 15 *Journal of Law, Economics & Organization* 180; R Rabin, 'Federal Regulation Historical Perspective' (1986) 38(5) *Stanford Law Review* 1189. See also M Tushnet, 'Administrative Law in the 1930s: The Supreme Court's Accommodation of Progressive Legal Theory' (2011) 60 *Duke Law Journal* 1565.

[53] See M Shapiro, 'APA: Past, Present, Future' (1986) 72(2) *Virginia Law Review* 447.

proof. Given these features of the American legal and political system, it is almost inconceivable that the political compromise would have operated in reverse, that is, that the rule-making process would have been specified in great detail and the adjudicatory process loosely delineated.

The APA is a relatively brief statute, almost constitutional in its scope and concision.[54] It has two basic components: the first is to specify the procedures that agencies must follow when they act;[55] and the second is to provide for judicial review of agency action and specify the standards that courts should apply.[56] It is possible to describe the statute as designed entirely to establish and channel judicial review, with the procedural provisions simply providing the basis on which review is to occur. However, that would be an excessively positivist perspective; as HLA Hart points out, it ignores the normative force of law.[57] The Act is better viewed as specifying the procedures that agencies are expected to follow, and then providing judicial review to correct errors or occasional malfeasance. That is in fact the way it has functioned. For the most part, with the notable exception of the recent Trump Administration, agencies treat the APA's procedural provisions as an obligatory prescription.[58]

As the history of the legislation indicates, the APA divides administrative action into two categories: rule-making and adjudication. The statute's definition of these terms is idiosyncratic, a reflection of doubts about the legal status of rate-making and licensing at the time of enactment.[59] For practical purposes, all the participants in the system understand that rules are provisions of generalised application, while adjudications are determinations of a particular private party's legal status according to the statute or its implementing rules.[60] However,

[54] See WN Eskridge and J Ferejohn, *A Republic of Statutes: The New American Constitution* (New Haven, Yale University Press, 2010).

[55] 5 USC §§ 553–57.

[56] 5 USC §§ 701–06.

[57] HLA Hart (n 9).

[58] This has been less true during the Trump Administration. As a result, the rate of reversal of administrative actions by the federal courts seems to have increased. See, eg, *Department of Homeland Security v Regents of the University of California* 591 US _____ (2020) (rescission of the Deferred Action for Childhood Arrivals program by the Attorney General violated the APA); *Clean Air Council v Pruitt* 852 F3d 1 (DC Cir, 2017) (EPA grant of reconsideration of Obama Administration greenhouse gas regulations was invalid under the APA); *Sierra Club v Pruitt* 293 F Supp 3d (ND Cal, 2013) (delay in implementation of the Obama Administration regulations regarding formaldehyde in wood products using the APA reconsideration violates the authorising statute).

[59] 5 USC § 551(4): '"rule" means the whole or a part of an agency statement of general or particular applicability and future effect … and includes the approval or prescription for rates, wages … While the result of rulemaking is called a rule, the result of adjudication is called an "order", which is unhelpfully defined as "the whole or part of a factual disposition … other than rulemaking but including licensing"'. 5 USC § 551(6).

[60] The leading case which establishes this principle is *Bi-Metallic Investment Corp v State Board* 239 US 441 (1915). See Ronald M Levin, 'The Case for (Finally) Fixing the APA's Definition of "Rule"' (2004) 56 *Administrative Law Review* 1077. For a general analysis, see EL Rubin, 'The Mistaken Idea of Regulatory Takings' (2019) *Michigan State Law Review* 225; EL Rubin, 'Lochner and Property' in NR Parillo (ed), *Administrative Law from the Inside Out: Essays on Themes in the Work of Jerry L Mashaw* (New York, Cambridge University Press, 2017) 308; EL Rubin, 'The Illusion of Property as a Right and its Reality as an Imperfect Alternative' (2013) *Wisconsin Law Review* 573.

rather than providing separately specified procedures for these two defined categories of action, the APA establishes a second distinction between formal and informal procedures that overlaps with the distinction between rule-making and adjudication.

One way to understand the relationship between the two is that the APA establishes two tracks for administrative action: the formal track and the informal track. If the agency wants to act by rule, then it begins with section 553. It follows the prescriptions of that section by giving '[g]eneral notice of the proposed rulemaking'. If it is permitted or required to use 'informal' rule-making, then it must comply with the remaining section 553 requirements. It must publish a preliminary version of a proposed rule, 'give interested persons an opportunity to participate in the rulemaking' through the comment process specified in subsection (c), and incorporate in the final rule a 'concise statement of [its] basis and purpose'. There is no requirement that the agency respond to any of the comments, and no specification of what the statement of basis and purpose should contain.

However, if the agency is required to use 'formal' rule-making (which is rare in practice), it shifts from the section 553 track to the sections 556–57 track after complying with the notice requirement. The operative language is the last sentence of subsection (c): 'When rules are required by statute to be made on the record after opportunity for an agency hearing, sections 556 and 557 apply instead of this subsection.' Section 556 specifies a trial-type hearing and section 557 contains specifications about the identity of the decision-maker, the appeal process, post-hearing procedure and *ex parte* contacts. Having followed this sections 556–57 procedure, the agency must then publish the resulting rule in accordance with section 553(d), which can be regarded as a return to the original track.

By contrast, if the agency decides to act by order – that is, to conduct an adjudication – it begins with section 554 rather than section 553. This section contains basic provisions regarding the adjudicatory process. The agency then proceeds (via section 555, which is entitled 'Ancillary Matters' and deals with topics such as service of process and the right to counsel) to sections 556 and 557. This is the only track permitted for adjudications; the APA does not offer any alternatives. Since adjudication under the Act must conform to sections 556 and 557, the 'formal' procedural provisions, it is known as 'formal adjudication'. Thus, all adjudications under the APA are formal. The presiding officer for such adjudications is an administrative law judge, and a series of statutory provisions provide a level of judicial independence for these officers that is essentially equivalent to that of a federal judge.[61] Typically, the substantive statute will specify whether the agency is required to follow the APA's formal adjudication process when applying the law to a private party.

[61] 5 USC §§ 1305, 3105, 3344, 5372. See generally JS Lubbers, 'Federal Administrative Law Judges: A Focus on Our Invisible Judiciary' (1981) 33 *Administrative Law Review* 109; J Zwerdling, 'Reflections on the Role of an Administrative Law Judge' (1973) 25(1) *Administrative Law Review* 9.

Judicial review, the other component of the APA, is codified according to its scope and its standards. The scope is notably broad. According to section 702, entitled 'Right of Review': 'A person suffering legal wrong because of agency action, or adversely affected or aggrieved by agency action within the meaning of the relevant statute, is entitled to judicial review thereof.' Certain exceptions are stated, but these tend to be narrowly construed by the courts.[62] This broad authorisation is effectuated in section 702 by a general waiver of sovereign immunity, a provision that was clarified in subsequent legislation.[63] The standards for review are stated in general and notably vague terms in section 706. All actions, a category which most significantly include rules or regulations, are to be 'set aside' if they are 'arbitrary, capricious, and abuse of discretion, or otherwise not in accordance with law'. Adjudications (that is, formal adjudications) are subject to an additional rule that they are to be set aside if they are 'unsupported by substantial evidence'.

## IV. The Gaps in the APA's Codification

As soon as the APA became law, observers realised that there was another way to view its procedural prescriptions. These prescriptions, instead of being treated as two separate but sometimes overlapping tracks, could be seen as based upon two independent variables – the first being whether the agency was using 'rule-making' or 'adjudication' and the second being whether the agency was required to use 'informal' or 'formal' procedures.[64] This naturally suggests that the statute's procedural provisions can be placed on the social scientist's famous four-box grid, the four cells being formal rule-making, informal rule-making, formal adjudication and informal adjudication.[65] One might speculate that the framers of the APA were thinking in terms of the track analogy and that it was outside observers who first became aware of the dual variable or four-box grid analogy. The reason is that the four-box grid reveals a curious lacuna in the statute. Procedural requirements are specified for both formal and informal rule-making, but only for formal

[62] See, eg, *Bowen v Michigan Academy of Family Physicians* 476 US 667, 680–81 (1986); *Citizens to Preserve Overton Park v Volpe* 401 US 402, 410–13 (1971); *Abbott Laboratories v Gardner* 387 US 136, 140–41 (1967). This general approach in fact pre-dates the APA. See *Stark v Wickard* 321 US 288, 307–10 (1944). *Shields v Utah Idaho Central RR* 305 US 177 (1938).

[63] PubL 94–574, 90 Stat 2721 (1976).

[64] See Note, 'The Federal Administrative Procedure Act: Codification or Reform' (1947) 56(4) *Yale Law Journal* 670.

[65] Such a grid appeared in ibid 705. Here is a simplified version:

| | Rule-making | Adjudication |
|---|---|---|
| Informal | § 553 | |
| Formal | §§ 553, 556, 557 | §§ 554, 556, 557 |

adjudication. Nothing is said about informal adjudication and, in fact, the term never appears in the statute at all.

But the category of informal adjudication is not merely an artifact of the APA's structure, a theoretically generated but pragmatically non-existent combination like feathered quadrupeds. It is more like the particles predicted by the Standard Model of Particle Physics that turned out to actually exist and play important roles in shaping physical reality. Informal adjudication encompasses all agency action that does not produce a final or definitive effect on a private party's status, and thus does not fall within the definitions of a rule or an order. This category, which might also be called executive action,[66] includes advice, suggestions, threats, pleas, promises to act, promises not to act, plans, ideas, inquiries, speculations, educational materials, most guidance documents, inspections, demands for information, requests for information and a vast range of other actions.[67] In addition, it includes any adjudication of a private party's status where the substantive statute does not require formal adjudication under the APA. Thus, many proceedings that seem as formal in practice as formal adjudications under the APA, such as deportation hearings and nuclear plant licensing hearings, fall within the category of informal adjudications.[68] As is apparent from the list, the overwhelming majority of the agency's activities also fall within this category; they are what the staff does on a daily basis.[69] Yet the APA imposes no rules on informal adjudications at all and does not even identify it as a category. For these reasons, to go back to the physics metaphor, informal adjudication has been called the dark matter of the administrative process.

Why did the drafters of the APA fail to address executive action and why did they ignore the category of informal adjudication that emerges from the framework they devised? Any answer to this question is necessarily speculative, but it is far from idle speculation. Rather, it provides a crucial insight into the underlying conceptual framework of the codification of American administrative law. One possibility is that the drafters were unaware of executive action as a category of agency operations, but this seems unlikely. They had no lack of practical experience with agencies, and a clear identification of the category had been articulated by Bruce Wyman in the first administrative law treatise, which was published

[66] See in this book P Issalys, 'A Persistent Taste for Diversity: Codification of Administrative Law in Canada', section II, who uses this term for essentially this same purpose.

[67] See EL Rubin, 'Executive Action: Its History, its Dilemmas and its Potential Remedies' (2016) 8(1) *Journal of Legal Analysis* 1.

[68] *Vermont Yankee Nuclear Power Corp v NRDC* 435 US 519 (1978) (describing process for licensing nuclear plants and holding that courts may not require additional procedures not required by statute or the APA); *Marcello v Bonds* 349 US 302 (1955) (holding that formal adjudication is only required when specified by Congress).

[69] This is a feature of many administrative systems and is sometimes referred to as 'soft law'. See in this book J Boughley, 'The "Codification" of Administrative Law in Australia', fn 58; K Lachmayer, 'Codification of Administrative Law in Austria', sections II.B and III.B; JCF Nordrum, 'Codification of Norwegian Administrative Law', section IV; R Caranta, 'Administrative Proceedings in Italy', fns 72–76.

in 1903.[70] A more plausible explanation, suggested by the distinction of Pierre Issalys between anglophone and francophone Canada, is that a common law approach, as exists in anglophone Canada and the US, tends to focus on particular techniques and protections rather than a comprehensive and systematic overview of administrative practice.[71] Starting from this more limited perspective, the drafters based the procedural rules that they established in the statute on the familiar models of legislation and judicial decisions. Administrative rule-making was analogised to legislation, and administrative adjudication was analogised to judicial procedure, specifically civil procedure. But the drafters had no model for executive action, the vast, diffuse category of government operations that fell into its residual category of informal adjudication. As a result, they not only failed to prescribe procedural rules for any of these actions, but they also seem to have failed to notice their existence.

It is worthwhile to go one step further and ask why there was no model for executive action. All our structures of government – legislatures, courts in their current form, even administrative agencies – date back to the Middle Ages. At that time, what we now call executive action was part of the king's prerogative.[72] Legislators were supposed to represent, and be answerable to, their constituents, and were thus subject to political control; judges were supposed to follow the law and were thus subject to legal control. But the king, who ruled by divine right, was not subject to any control, at least not in this world. He certainly had moral obligations – a medieval monarch was far from being an absolute ruler – but he was answerable only to God.[73]

However, as time passed, two institutions were created that began to limit the English king's authority. Both were initially established by the kings themselves. The first were the common law courts. As described above, these were established by King Henry II in the latter part of the twelfth century to resolve conflicting land grants. The second institution was Parliament, which evolved from the king's council, a standard medieval institution. Feudal law granted the king various sources of revenue, sufficient for buying furniture and hunting dogs, but inadequate for waging sustained warfare. War, however, was exactly what the English kings wanted to wage in their efforts to conquer places such as Wales, Scotland or

[70] B Wyman (n 38) 294. Wyman observed that this area had 'a common law of its own – its customs'. For commentary on this aspect of the treatise, see KM Stack, 'Introduction' in B Wyman (ed), *The Principles of Administrative Law Governing the Relations of Public Officers* (Clark, NJ, The Lawbook Exchange, 2014) i.

[71] See in this book P Issalys (n 66) section I.

[72] See N Cox, *The Royal Prerogative and Constitutional Law: A Search for the Quintessence of Executive Power* (Abingdon, Routledge, 2020); M McGlynn, *The Royal Prerogative and the Learning of the Inns of Court* (Cambridge, Cambridge University Press, 2003).

[73] T Aquinas, *On Kingship: To the King of Cyprus*, GB Phelan (trans) (Toronto, Pontifical Institute of Medieval Studies, 1949). There is some doubt among modern scholars that this book was written by Aquinas. See A Black, *Political Thought in Europe* (Cambridge, Cambridge University Press, 1992) 136 ff; J Dubabin, 'Government' in JH Burns (ed), *The Cambridge History of Medieval Political Thought, c. 350–c. 1450* (Cambridge, Cambridge University Press, 1988) 477, 482 ff.

France. To impose additional taxes, perhaps according to feudal law, and clearly as a matter of political viability, they needed the permission of those on whom the new taxes would be imposed.[74] It was easy enough to ask the leaders of the Church or the small number of leading noblemen (earls and barons) directly, but by the end of the thirteenth century, commerce was reviving and much of the taxable wealth was held by commoners. They were a diffuse and widespread group, with no hierarchical structure. By gradual steps, beginning with small landowners who happened to be included among the group of leading noblemen, then by organising elections among the larger group of landowners who attended meetings of the county courts, representatives of the common people (the future House of Commons) were assembled and consulted (or intimidated)[75] Here too, the institution proved effective, gradually expanded its authority and asserted an increasing independence from the king.

When James I became King at the beginning of the seventeenth century, he took exception to the growing independence of England's common law courts, as described above. He also took exception to the increasing authority of Parliament.[76] Parliament ultimately rebelled against James' equally imperious but less politically skilful son Charles I, executed him and established a dictatorship.[77] The Stuart monarchy was restored in 1660 but was deposed by Parliament in the Glorious Revolution of 1688.[78] Over the course of the next century, Parliament's authority steadily increased, particularly under the skilful leadership of Robert Walpole, and the common law courts became increasingly revered and independent.[79] By the time George III went insane around 1810, the monarch's political authority had been reduced to a virtual nullity and Britain had become a full democracy with fully an independent judiciary.

[74] A Monahan, *Consent, Coercion and Limit: The Medieval Origins of Parliamentary Democracy* (Kingston, McGill-Queen's University Press, 1987) 97 ff; JB Morrall, *Political Thought in Medieval Times* (New York, Harper & Row, 1958) 59 ff; G Post, *Studies in Medieval Legal Thought: Public Law and the State, 1100–1322* (Princeton, Princeton University Press, 1964); G Post, 'A Roman Legal Theory of Consent: *Quod Omnes Tagit*' (1950) Wisconsin Law Review 66.

[75] W Churchill, *A History of the English Speaking Peoples, Vol 1: The Birth of Britain* (New York, Dodd, Mead, 1956) 273 ff; JR Maddicott, *The Origins of the English Parliament, 924–1327* (Oxford, Oxford University Press, 2010); M Morris, *Edward I: A Great and Terrible King* (New York, Pegasus Books, 2009); WM Ormrod, *The Reign of Edward III: Crown and Political Society in England, 1327–1377* (New Haven, Yale University Press, 1990).

[76] F Wormuth, *The Royal Prerogative 1603–1649: A Study in English Political and Constitutional Ideas* (Ithaca, NY, Cornell University Press, 1939).

[77] See W Churchill, *A History of the English Speaking Peoples, Vol 2: The New World* (New York, Dodd, Mead, 1956) 183 ff (Petition of Right), 211 ff (Civil War); P Ackroyd, *Rebellion: A History of England from James I to the Glorious Revolution* (New York, St Martin's Press, 2014); M Braddick, *God's Fury, England's Fire: A New History of the English Civil Wars* (New York, Penguin, 2009).

[78] W Churchill (n 77) 396 ff; S Pincus, *1688: The First Modern Revolution* (New Haven, Yale University Press, 2009); E Vallance, *The Glorious Revolution: 1688: Britain's Fight for Liberty* (New York, Pegasus Books, 2008).

[79] W Churchill, *A History of the English Speaking Peoples, Vol 3: The Age of Revolution* (New York, Dodd, Mead, 1957) 113 ff; BW Hill, *Sir Robert Walpole: Sole and Prime Minister* (New York, Penguin, 1989); JH Plumb, *Sir Robert Walpole* (New York, Houghton Mifflin Harcourt, 1973).

What is notable about this process is that the royal prerogative was gradually reduced and ultimately eliminated by restricting its scope, not by imposing legal rules upon the way in which the prerogative was exercised. The two institutions that increased their authority at the king's expense – the common law courts and the legislature – both operated according to defined procedures, which in essence determined the legality of their actions. The drafters of the US Constitution, of course, replaced the king with an elected President, thus imposing the same kind of constraint on the new chief executive as was placed on the legislators, that is, the political constraint of standing for election. But they did not place any specific, substantive constraints on presidential action, perhaps because they had no basis in the English governmental tradition from which such constraints could be derived. For the same reason, perhaps, they did not place any constraints on the President's agents, that is, the executive departments; in fact, they did not even specify those departments.[80]

When independent agencies were created, beginning with the Interstate Commerce Commission in the late 1870s, they were, in part, conceptualised as mini-governments – that is, self-contained institutions that would regulate (ie, govern) all aspects of a particular industry or subject matter.[81] Thus, they had rule-making functions, analogous to legislative action, and adjudicatory functions, analogous to judicial action. They also had executive functions, of course, but the same vagueness, the same lack of specification and constraints that had been a feature of the Anglo-American legal tradition for more than half a millennium was perpetuated.[82] This is reflected in the organic statutes for these agencies, and also in the Supreme Court's 1935 decision in *Humphrey's Executor v United States*,[83] which declared that independent agencies, whose presidential appointees could not then be dismissed by the President at will, were not unconstitutional because

[80] The Committee on Detail proposed a clause that gave the President the power to 'inspect Departments of foreign Affairs – War – Treasury – Admiralty'. M Farrand, *The Records of the Federal Convention*, vol 2 (New Haven, Yale University Press, 1966), vol 2, 158, vol 3, 111. In addition, a motion was made to create a 'Council of State' that would 'assist the President in conducting the Public Affairs'. It would consist, in addition to the Chief Justice of the Supreme Court, the Secretaries of domestic affairs, commerce and finance, foreign affairs, war and the marine, with each secretary's responsibilities being specified: ibid vol 2, 335 ff. But neither provision was incorporated into the final document. A vestige of the first appears in US Const Art II, Sec 2 cl 1: 'The President … may require the Opinion, in writing, of the principal Officer in each of the executive Departments, upon any subject relating to the Duties of their respective Offices.' The oddity of specifying this one relatively minor feature of presidential control is explained by the fact that it is a remnant of larger provision.

[81] See TK McCraw, *Prophets of Regulation: Charles Francis Adams, Louis D. Brandeis, James M. Landis and Alfred E. Kahn* (Cambridge, MA, Belknap Press, 1984) 57 ff.

[82] This same mechanism, with a similarly ambiguous status, can now be found in nations with legal traditions distinct from those of the US. See in this book K Lachmayer (n 69) section II (Austria); JCF Nordrum (n 69) section V; R Caranta (n 69) fns 46–48 (Italy).

[83] *Humphrey's Executor v United States* 295 US 602 (1935); S Skowronek, *Building a New American State: The Expansion of National Administrative Capacities, 1877–1920* (New York, Cambridge University Press, 1982) 121 ff; RD Stone, *The Interstate Commerce Commission and the Railroad Industry: A History of Regulatory Policy* (New York, Praeger, 1991).

they were 'quasi-legislative or quasi-judicial' in character. Here again, the bulk of their activities, which were executive in nature, went unmentioned.

The same conceptual lacuna appears in the APA. Once again, action that resembles legislation (rule-making) and action that resembles judicial decision-making (adjudication) are subjected to procedural constraints, while executive action – the mode of action in which a chief executive engages – is not constrained or even identified. It remains a residual category that emerges from the structure of the Act, but has only been christened by the Act's observers. By now, of course, there is a vast academic literature – generally in the field of political science, but increasingly in legal scholarship as well – describing and analysing this obviously crucial mode of governmental action. Yet there is still no systematic characterisation of it, and any legal constraints must be improvised by using collateral considerations. This situation may be contrasted with nations that have developed comprehensive administrative codes, as Delphine Costa describes regarding France,[84] Marcus Heintzen describes regarding Germany,[85] and Ymre Schuurmans, Tom Barkhuysen and Willemien den Ouden describe regarding the Netherlands.[86] However, given the complexity of administrative law, even these codifications are not complete, and other nations with code law traditions, such as Switzerland, have concluded that such codifications are too daunting to attempt, as Felix Uhlmann reports.[87]

## V. The Persistence of Common Law in American Administrative Law

The intended vagueness of the APA's provisions regarding rule-making, the negotiated vagueness of its provisions regarding judicial review, and the unintended or at least unnoticed absence of any provisions in all governing executive actions have motivated the federal judges to supply greater specificity in all these areas. As Gillian Metzger has discussed at length, they have done so through a process that can be fairly described as common law, that is, the common law of federal administrative process.[88] This is hardly surprising. Common law, although displaced in many areas by statutory enactments enforced by administrative agencies, retains its conceptual influence on virtually all law-trained Americans. It is, after all, an 800-year-long tradition in the Anglo-American world and continues to be the

[84] See in this book D Costa, 'Codification of Administrative Law: A French Oxymoron', section II.B.

[85] See in this book M Heintzen, 'Codification of Administrative Law in Germany and the European Union', section I.C.

[86] See in this book YE Schuurmans, T Barkhuysen and W den Ouden, 'Codification of Administrative Law in the Netherlands', section II.A.

[87] See in this book F Uhlmann, 'Codification of Administrative Law in Switzerland', fns 109–15.

[88] GE Metzger, 'Embracing Administrative Common Law' (2012) 80 *George Washington Law Review* 1293.

central theme of American legal education. All American judges know both the mythology and methodology of common law, and when confronted with statutory uncertainties and lacunae, they will instinctively rely on it. A similar pattern prevails in other common law jurisdictions. Pierre Issalys notes the 'massive reliance on the common law' in Canadian administrative decisions,[89] Janine Boughey observes that in Australia 'principles and presumptions of statutory interpretation are sourced in common law',[90] and Sarah Nason documents the same phenomenon in Great Britain.[91]

Concededly, the general common law that federal courts applied in diversity cases was declared invalid –indeed, non-existent – in 1938 on the ground that law must be the enactment, directly or by delegation, of a legal authority.[92] But this does not preclude federal courts from developing common law within the ambit of a statutory grant of authority (that is, in cases that come to the courts on the basis of a federal question rather than diversity of citizenship). The Supreme Court has explicitly held, for example, that federal courts have the authority to fashion common law rules governing the commercial paper of the US,[93] and it is well understood that they have done so in other areas as well, such as labour, antitrust and bankruptcy.

The APA, of course, is a procedural rather than a substantive statute, specifically a statute governing the procedures that agencies are required to follow when issuing rules and conducting adjudications. This could have been viewed as precluding a common law approach and requiring that uncertainties be resolved on the basis of the instructions in the Act,[94] which is the way a judge might deal with uncertainties in a code law jurisdiction.[95] But as Delphine Costa points out, even in France, 'which imagines that it is the birthplace of codification', judges exercise extensive discretion.[96] The vagueness of language, combined with the scope and velocity of technological and social change, asserts powerful pressures against fixed rules and insistently demands judicial flexibility and innovation. The process parallels the development of the common law itself when viewed in its historical context.

[89] See in this book P Issalys (n 66) section II.

[90] See in this book J Boughley (n 69) fn 25.

[91] In this book S Nason (n 11) sections II and IV.

[92] *Erie RR v Tompkins* 304 US 64 (1938). See above, section II.

[93] *Clearfield Trust v United States* 318 US 363 (1943).

[94] For an argument to this effect, see JF Duffy, 'Administrative Common Law in Judicial Review' (1998) 77 *Texas Law Review* 113.

[95] See generally R David, *French Law: Its Structure, Sources and Methodology* (Baton Rouge, Louisiana State University Press, 1972); CM Germain, 'Approaches to Statutory Interpretation and Legislative History in France' (2003) 13 *Duke Journal of Comparative and International Law* 195; K Zweigert and H-J Puttfarken, 'Statutory Interpretation – Civilian Style' (1969) 44 *Tulane Law Review* 704. For comparisons in nations where the two systems are used in different jurisdictions, see JL Dennis, 'Interpretation and Application of the Civil Code and the Evaluation of Judicial Precedent' (1993) 54 *Louisiana Law Review* 1; W Friedmann, 'Stare Decisis at Common Law and under the Civil Code of Quebec' (1951) 31(7) *Canadian Bar Review* 723.

[96] See in this book D Costa (n 84) section III.E.

Like common law, the APA was established when the supreme legislator (Congress in this case and the king previously) granted a group of judges the authority to decide litigated cases in a particular area (administrative law in this case and property disputes previously). Like common law, that grant of authority was vague, leaving the judges with a great deal of discretion in fashioning the particularised rules. And like common law, the judges felt an insistent need to develop rules in response to changing circumstances that had not been anticipated when the process began. Thus, it seems fair to say that American administrative law is only partially or incompletely codified, and that a common law of administrative action, embodied in judicial precedents, determines a significant proportion of the nation's administrative law doctrine.

Quite strikingly, some of the most significant judicial decisions in American administrative law in the three-quarters of a century since the APA's enactment address the issue of common law decision-making under the statute. They do not do so explicitly, but rather frame their analysis in terms of statutory interpretation. This would appear to be a rejection of the common law approach and, in fact, two of the earlier cases effectively declare that rejection. In *Universal Camera Corp v NLRB*,[97] the Supreme Court reversed a decision written by Learned Hand, who many regarded as the leading American jurist at the time. Hand had devised a per se rule for reviewing appeals from adjudicatory decisions by an agency, arguing that the reviewing court should essentially ignore the findings of the hearing officer (an Administrative Law Judge in modern parlance) when the agency had reversed those findings.[98] The Court, per Felix Frankfurter, admonished Hand that this was a departure from the statutory language. Section 706 APA states that reviewing courts must 'review the whole record' in making its determination, a provision that, as Frankfurter noted, had attracted much attention and debate during the drafting process. The Court declared that this language must be faithfully applied and precluded Hand's highly practical modification.[99] Similarly, in *Vermont Yankee Nuclear Power Corp v NRDC*,[100] the Court reversed a decision by the District of Columbia Court of Appeals, generally regarded as the leading court for administrative law because of the volume of cases it decides. The DC Court had invalidated a rule promulgated by the Nuclear Regulatory

[97] *Universal Camera Corp v NLRB* 340 US 474 (1951).

[98] *National Labor Relations Board v. Universal Camera* 179 F2d 749 (2nd Cir, 1950). He reached this conclusion because the statutory standard of review, which was to reverse if the decision was 'unsupported by substantial evidence' (5 USC § 706(F)) was understood to be more lenient that the clear error standard by which a trial judge would reverse a special master that the judge had appointed. Hand wrote: 'it is practically impossible for a court, upon review of those findings which the Board itself substitutes, to consider the Board's reversal as a factor in the court's own decision. This we say, because we cannot find any middle ground between doing that and treating such a reversal as error, whenever it would be such, if done by a judge to a master in equity'.

[99] In an earlier, pre-APA decision, Justice Frankfurter had declared: 'There is no such thing as a common law of judicial review in the federal courts.' *Stark v Wickard* 321 US 288, 312 (1944).

[100] *Vermont Yankee Nuclear Power Corp v NRDC* 435 US 519 (1978).

Commission on the grounds that the Commission had failed to provide sufficient evidence to justify the rule. The Supreme Court, per William Rehnquist, admonished the DC Circuit that it was demanding additional procedures beyond those specified in section 553, and that this was an invalid departure from the statutory language.[101]

These decisions are widely cited but they have not proved to be as influential as they might appear.[102] During the same period that they were decided, the Supreme Court also handed down several major decisions that went in essentially the opposite direction. In *Citizens to Preserve Overton Park v Volpe*,[103] the Court gave an expansive reading of the APA's provision for judicial review, and then used that reading to fashion rules governing an informal adjudication, that is, an adjudication that fell within the missing category of the APA scheme. This was, in effect, an extension of a pre-APA (and thus arguably common law) decision to the informal adjudication context.[104] Similarly, in *Abbot Laboratories v Gardner*,[105] the Court gave the reviewability provisions an extensive reading and developed a doctrine to allow private parties to obtain judicial review of agency rules, in certain circumstances, before the rule had been applied to them.[106] The language of the subsequently decided *Vermont Yankee* case might appear to have overruled decisions such as these, but that is not the way the case has been interpreted.

Following quickly after *Vermont Yankee*, the Supreme Court handed down two of most important decisions of the last half century, *Motor Vehicle Manufacturers Association v. State Farm Mutual Automobile Insurance Co*[107] and *Chevron, USA v NRDC*.[108] Professor Metzger identifies these decisions as exemplifying and in fact embodying the common law approach of federal courts in

[101] See also *Darby v Cisneros* 509 US 137 (1993), which overturned the judicially crafted doctrine of exhaustion of administrative remedies on the basis of the statutory language in the APA: 5 USC § 704.

[102] See GE Metzger (n 88) 1305 ('despite its stern language, Vermont Yankee has not prevented substantial judicial expansion of § 553's minimal procedural demands. The Court appears to have sanctioned these developments, or, at a minimum, has made no effort to rebuff them') (footnotes omitted).

[103] *Citizens to Preserve Overton Park v Volpe* 401 US 402 (1971).

[104] *SEC v Chenery Corp* 315 US 80 (1943) (*Chenery I*). However, it is possible that the decision has a stronger foundation than administrative common law. See KM Stack, 'The Constitutional Foundations of *Chenery*' (2007) 116 *Yale Law Journal* 952.

[105] *Abbot Laboratories v Gardner* 387 US 186 (1967).

[106] Consistent with the common law method, the Court also recognised other circumstances where pre-enforcement review would be denied: *Toilet Goods Association v Gardner* 387 US 158 (1967). The Court's expansive approach to reviewability follows a long-established tradition, as noted above; see above, n 62. Kenneth Culp Davis, commenting on the state of the law prior to the APA, stated: 'Whether common law or not, nearly all the law concerning reviewability of administrative action is judge made.' K Culp Davis (n 2) 814. In *Dabry v Cisneros* 509 US 137 (1993), the Court invalidated judicial precedent on the basis of statutory language, an anti-common law decision, but did so in favour of expanded reviewability, a common law development in other contexts.

[107] *Motor Vehicle Manufacturers Association v State Farm Mutual Automobile Insurance Co* 463 US 29 (1983).

[108] *Chevron, USA v NRDC* 467 US 837 (1984).

modern administrative law.[109] At issue in *State Farm* was the basic standard of review under section 706 APA, which provides that any agency action is to be set aside if it is 'arbitrary [or] capricious'. This language is not easy to interpret. It is clearly old-fashioned and can be traced back at least as far as the discussion of judgement in Rousseau's *Emile*.[110] These terms may be useful for delineating good judgement for an individual like Emile, but they convey very little when applied to agency rule-making. An arbitrary action is an act of will and a capricious action is an act of whim; agency rules, whatever else they may be, are planned actions developed by professional staff members. Instead of attempting to parse the APA's language, the *State Farm* opinion interpreted it by fashioning a four-part test that focused on the scope of the substantive statute that the agency was implementing, the evidence obtained by the agency, and the plausibility of its conclusions.[111] The decision was unanimous on this point, and it has been followed literally thousands of times by lower courts without significant disagreement.

The second of these important decisions, *Chevron*, made two major conceptual advances in administrative law. First, the Court, per Justice John Paul Stevens, identified a lacuna in the APA, one that is perhaps as significant as the statute's failure to address executive action. This is the recognition that when an agency takes either of the two types of actions whose procedures are addressed in the statute, that is, rule-making or adjudication, on the basis of a statutory authorisation, it is necessarily interpreting the statute as the first step in the process. Remarkably, no one had focused on this as a separate mode of administrative action.[112] As soon as the Court did so, it became apparent that the APA was silent on the subject. Since then, commentators have recognised and elaborated on this insight.[113]

The Court then made its second conceptual advance, which was to recognise that reviewing a statutory interpretation by an agency is not the same as reviewing an interpretation by a lower court. If the appellate court is reviewing an

[109] GE Metzger (n 88) 1298 ff.

[110] J-J Rousseau, *Emile, or On Education*, C Kelly and A Bloom (trans) (Hanover, NH, Dartmouth College Press, 2010) 295: vanity 'is a work of men subject to caprice and to all sorts of abuses' and a person of judgement 'will not worry about arbitrary evaluations whose only law is fashion or prejudice' (at 511).

[111] The Court's language is as follows: 'Normally, an agency rule would be arbitrary and capricious if the agency has relied on factors which Congress has not intended it to consider, entirely failed to consider an important aspect of the problem, offered an explanation for its decision that runs counter to the evidence before the agency, or is so implausible that it could not be ascribed to a difference in view or the product of agency expertise' (*State Farm* 463 US 29 (1983) at 43).

[112] One partial exception is HP Monaghan, 'Marbury and the Administrative State' (1983) 83 *Columbia Law Review* 1.

[113] See J Mashaw, 'Norms, Practices, and the Paradox of Deference: A Preliminary Inquiry into Agency Statutory Interpretation' (2005) 57 *Administrative Law Review* 501; KM Stack, 'Purposivism in the Executive Branch: How. Agencies Interpret Statutes' (2014) 109(4) *Northwestern Law Review* 871.

interpretation by a lower court – that is, a trial court – it is because the judiciary is charged with enforcing the statute and the reviewing court is acting in a direct supervisory capacity over the trial court. In that case, the reviewing court will defer to the trial court on findings of fact, but it will decide questions of statutory interpretation de novo. The rationale is that the trial court is in a better position to evaluate evidence that it directly examined, but that the appellate court is in as good a position as the trial court to read the law. Moreover, the appellate court is charged with direct supervision of the trial court. In contrast, if the appellate court is reviewing an interpretation by an agency, the agency is charged with enforcing the statute, and the reviewing court is acting in a collateral capacity, after the initial decision has already been reviewed, or supervised, within the agency. When the statutory language is clear, or unambiguous, the reviewing court, as a specialist in law, is still in a better position than the agency to interpret the statutory terms. But if the language is ambiguous (or, to use a better term, open-ended), then Congress has signalled that it wants the agency, in its role as subject-matter specialist, to interpret the statute. Thus, *Chevron* holds that the reviewing court should defer to agency interpretations of law when the statute is ambiguous as well as agency findings of fact. Since this is not specified in the APA, *Chevron*, like the *State Farm* test, is federal common law.[114]

Given the vagueness of the APA and the complexity of the modern administrative system, it is possible to question the characterisation of these leading decisions as common law. After all, the APA establishes a broad right to judicial review by statutory command, thus obligating courts to decide frequent challenges to administrative action. If the statute does not provide sufficient guidance, the courts must decide one way or another, and that decision must go beyond the statute's incomplete coverage and sketchy language, no matter what methodology the court is using. Such a decision could be consistent with a code law approach; it is certainly not unusual for comprehensive legal codes to contain fairly open-ended language.[115] What renders so many of the leading decisions common law are two specific features of their methodology and mood. First, the deciding judges have been willing to take the initiative to develop rules in areas that the APA leaves unregulated, such as the *Overton Park* decision on informal adjudication or the

[114] *Chevron* has been the source of a vast academic debate. Some criticisms of the case focus on the mechanics of the decision: see, eg, JM Beermann, 'End the Failed *Chevron* Experiment Now: How *Chevron* Has Failed and Why it Can and Should Be Overruled' (2010) 42 *Connecticut Law Review* 779, 832 ff; MC Stephenson and A Vermeule, '*Chevron* Has Only One Step' (2009) 95(3) *Virginia Law Review* 597. Many argue that the basic theory of the decision is wrong because ambiguous statutory language should not be interpreted as a delegation of interpretive authority to the agency. See, eg, DJ Barron and E Kagan, '*Chevron*'s Nondelegation Doctrine' (2001) *Supreme Court Review* 201, 212; TW Merrill, 'Judicial Deference to Executive Precedent' (1992) 101 *Yale Law Journal* 969, 998; M Seidenfeld, 'Chevron's Foundation' (2001) 86 *Notre Dame Law Review* 273, 278; RL Weaver, 'The Emperor Has No Clothes: Christenson, Mead and Dual Deference Standards' (2002) 54 *Administrative Law Review* 173, 175.

[115] BW Frier, 'Interpreting Codes' (1990) 89(8) *Michigan Law Review* 2201.

*Chevron* decision on interpretation of the law. Second, when explaining their decisions, the judges have tended to analogise and distinguish prior judicial decisions rather than parsing the statutory language.[116] This is inevitable for the *Chevron* doctrine, where there is no statutory language for the Court to invoke.[117] But it is also true for judicial review of administrative rule-making under the arbitrary and capricious standard, where the Court often refers to the *State Farm* test rather than trying to discern the meaning of the (admittedly Delphic) statutory terms.

The Court's approach in these federal common law cases may be contrasted with interpretations of other statutes, where the Supreme Court has reached its decision by focusing on the language of the statute itself.[118] A notable example is its recent decision in *Bostock v Clayton County*, where the Court, employing a detailed analysis of the relevant statutory term (which was 'sex'), concluded that gay, lesbian and transgender people were protected from discrimination under the Civil Rights Act of 1964.[119] The same contrast appears within the *Chevron* doctrine itself because the doctrine holds that the courts should only defer to agency interpretations of the statute when the statutory language is ambiguous. Thus, in the typical *Chevron* case, judicial analysis begins with a close reading of the substantive

[116] Consistent with a common law approach, administrative lawyers in the US must be fully familiar with these judicial precedents. With respect to the *Chevron* doctrine, leading decisions include *City of Arlington v FCC* 133 S Ct 1863 (2013); *Barnhart v Walton* 535 US 212 (2002) (further discussed below in section V); *United States v Mead Corp* 533 US 218 (2001) (further discussed below in section V); *SWANCC v US Army Corps of Engineers* 531 US 159 (2001); *MCI Telecomm Corp v AT&T Co* 512 US 218 (1994). With respect to *State Farm*, leading decisions include *Department of Homeland Security v Regents of the University of California* 591 US _____ (2020); *FCC v Fox Television Stations, Inc* 556 US 502 (2009); *National Cable & Telcomm Association v Brand X International Services* 545 US 967 (2005) (also following *Chevron*); *AT&T Corp v Iowa Utilities Board* 525 US 366 (1999). There are, of course, innumerable lower court decisions applying and assessing these two precedents.

[117] Some of *Chevron*'s many critics assert that the statutory language in fact precludes its result because s 706 APA instructs reviewing courts to decide 'all relevant questions of law'. See, eg, JF Duffy (n 94); T Merrill, 'Capture Theory and the Courts: 1967–1983' (1997) 72 *Chicago-Kent Law Review* 1039; G Lawson and S Kam, 'Making Law out of Nothing at All: The Origins of the *Chevron* Doctrine' (2013) 65b *Administrative Law Review* 1; J Molot, 'Reexamining *Marbury* in the Administrative State: A Structural and Institutional Defense of Judicial Power over Statutory Interpretation' (2002) 96(4) *Northwestern University Law Review* 1239. This is in effect a rejection of *Chevron* as federal common law on the basis of statutory language. However, it is not a convincing argument. First, the sentence in the APA that contains this language begins: 'To the extent necessary to decision.' Second, it is hard to argue that the statutory language addressed this issue when no one was aware of it at the time of enactment.

[118] See, eg, *Milner v Department of the Navy* 562 US 562 (2011) (interpretation of the word 'personnel' in the Freedom of Information Act, which is further discussed below in section VI); *Muscarello v United States* 524 US 125 (1998) (interpretation of the word 'carry' in the federal criminal code); *Babbitt v Sweet Home* 515 US 687 (19950 (interpretation of the word 'take' in the Endangered Species Act).

[119] *Bostock v Clayton County* 590 US ____ (2020) (construing Pub L 88-352, 78 Stat 241, codified at 42 USC § 2000a ff). This decision exemplifies the doctrine of textualism, an approach strongly championed by Justice Scalia. See A Scalia, *A Matter of Interpretation: Federal Courts and the Law* (Princeton, Princeton University Press, 1997) 21 ff. See also, eg, RA Rossum, *Anton Scalia's Jurisprudence: Text and Tradition* (Lawrence, University Press of Kansas, 2016); WN Eskridge, 'The New Textualism' (1990) 37 *UCLA Law Review* 621, 625; JF Manning, 'Textualism and Legislative Intent' (2005) 91(2) *Virginia Law Review* 419, 419 ff.

statute, often in terms that would resemble the approach that judges use in a code law jurisdiction.

While the *Chevron* doctrine is itself federal common law, it has the interesting effect of closing off the development of federal common law in many substantive areas. The simple way to state this is that *Chevron* clearly limits the scope of judicial review by holding that courts should defer to agencies in situations where they might previously have exercised their own judgment. From a more structural perspective, *Chevron* at least suggests that the process of legal development – the way that applicable rules evolve under the pressure of circumstances – should be determined by the agency rather than the judiciary. In other words, the administrative system contains a new category of legal rules that has no equivalent in pre-administrative government: agency-made law. This new type of law, *Chevron* might be seen as declaring, obviates the need for common or judge-made law; the agency responds to circumstances and the judiciary should defer to the agency unless the agency has misinterpreted the statute that authorises it to engage in the law-creation process. Note that the agency, in responding to circumstances, has the capacities of the entire government, that is, the capacity to act through positive law (rule-making) as well as judge-made law (adjudication).

A question that flows from this understanding of *Chevron* involves the status of the law that the agency is creating, and to which the federal courts are now instructed to defer. To answer this question, it is necessary to distinguish between agency rule-making and agency adjudication. With respect to adjudication, *United States v Mead Corp* held that federal courts should only defer to agency decisions that possess the force of law. On this basis, the Supreme Court denied *Chevron* deference to tariff classification rulings by the Customs Service, concluding that these were low-level decisions with no precedential effect.[120] The Court stated: 'Any suggestion that rulings intended to have the force of law are being churned out at a rate of 10,000 a year at an agency's 46 scattered offices is simply self-refuting.'[121] While the decision is not easy to make sense of, as Justice Scalia argued forcefully in dissent, it is perhaps best viewed as authorising the agency to create law by adjudication only if it follows recognised common law methodology – that is, if the decision in question is based on stated reasons and carries precedential effect.

With respect to rule-making, the situation seems to be different. *Chevron*'s major significance involves deference to agency interpretation in rule-making, not adjudication, in part because rules have much more impact than particular adjudications and in part because interpretation typically plays a larger role in making new rules than it does in deciding a fact-specific dispute. Any rule promulgated in accordance with the notice and comment rule-making procedure of section 553 will be eligible for *Chevron* deference under the *Mead* decision.

[120] *United States v Mead Corp* 533 US 218 (2001).
[121] ibid 233.

In *Barnhart v Walton*,[122] the Supreme Court, per Justice Stephen Breyer, held that agency interpretations were entitled to *Chevron* deference even if those interpretations seemed to suffer from the same informality that precluded *Chevron* deference in *Mead*. He relied on the fact that 'the Agency's interpretation is of long standing … [T]he interstitial nature of the legal question, the related expertise of the Agency, the importance of the question to administration of the statute, the complexity of that administration, and the careful consideration the Agency has given the question over a long period of time all indicate that *Chevron* provides the appropriate lens through which to view the legality of the Agency interpretation here at issue'.[123] In contrast to *Mead*, the methodology of such an informal rule-making process cannot be called common law. If the concept of common law is to have any meaning, it must be restricted to law made by judges. They need not be federal judges, but must at least be officials who are engaged in resolving disputes. The *Barnhart* decision grants interpretive authority to executive policy-makers. Their decisions are thus more accurately described as customary law, in that they emerge from the ongoing arrangements and understandings of an interacting community.

However, this sort of administrative customary law is the product of trained professionals, not of the ordinary (and at the time uneducated) common folk of Aquinas' era[124] or the semi-mystical *volk* of the German historical school of jurisprudence.[125] Consequently, it is often written down in official documents that might conceivably be regarded as codifications. The primary document, in many cases, would be the employee manual that states the procedures that officials are expected to follow in carrying out their regular activities. If the courts are being instructed, by the common administrative law embodied in *Chevron* and *Barnhart*, to defer to the statutory interpretations embodied in these manuals, then the manuals are in effect customary law. Although they are internal documents, and are not regarded as being binding on the public, they may well affect the public by controlling the behaviour of agency officials who interact with private parties. This issue surfaced in a pre-*Chevron* decision, *Morton v Ruiz*,[126] where the Supreme Court held that instructions in such a manual could not control a rule regarding benefit distribution that conflicted with Congressional intent. But the result might be different under *Chevron* and *Barnhart*. In any case, as a practical matter, employee manuals and other internal documents represent a vast body of rules and practices that might be reasonably regarded as the codified customary law of the agency.

[122] *Barnhart v Walton* 535 US 212 (2002).

[123] ibid 221–22.

[124] See above, n 21.

[125] See FK von Savigny, *Possession, or the Jus Possessionis of the Civil Code*, 6th edn, E Perry (trans) (Clark, The Lawbook Exchange, 2003). Savigny argued specifically against codification on the grounds that customary law is superior. See FK von Savigny, *Of the Vocation of Our Age for Legislation and Jurisprudence*, A Hayward (trans) (New York, Arno Press, 1975).

[126] *Morton v Ruiz* 415 US 199 (1974). See *Auer v Robbins* 519 US, 452 (1997), which also involved interpretation of the language in an employee manual, in this case by a federal agency.

## VI. An Assessment of American Administrative Law Codification

Apart from a few minor clarifications in 1976, the APA has not been amended since its original enactment three-quarters of a century ago. Its resilience can be attributed to its limited scope and to the common law process by the courts that have filled in a number of the statute's significant lacuna. However, there has been one significant addition to the procedural law governing American administrative agencies: the Freedom of Information Act (FOIA).[127] It is codified in section 552 of the APA, yet it is in fact an entirely separate statute, which does not displace any of the APA's provisions, but rather adds a new procedural modality. This reflects the relatively recent development of concerns about administrative transparency; even in the Netherlands, whose comprehensive codification of administrative law is described by Schuurmans, Barkhuysen and den Ouden in this volume, the issue has been addressed by separate legislation.[128]

The FOIA grants 'any person' the right to obtain any agency records on demand, and at modest cost, subject to nine specific exceptions. While some of these are fairly broad, they render most agency records eligible for disclosure. In *Milner v Department of the Navy*,[129] the Supreme Court held that the FOIA exceptions are to be narrowly construed. They had been gradually expanded by the federal courts since the statute's enactment through what can be fairly described as the common law method. At issue in the case was the exception for matters 'related solely to internal personnel rules and practices of an agency'. The Navy invoked this exception to deny a request that it disclose the locations where explosives were stored on one of its military bases, and it had relied on several appellate court precedents that read the statutory language as applying to a broad range of internal agency records. The Supreme Court, per Justice Elena Kagan, reversed by going back to the original statutory language, and interpreting it to refer only to personnel matters such as employee records – a code law mode of interpretation that, as Professor Metzger notes, contrasts with the Court's common law approach in many APA decisions.[130] Justice Breyer, the strongest proponent of common law decision-making on the Court, dissented. Quoting Justice Stevens, he said that 'once "a statute has been construed, either by this Court or by a consistent course of decision by other

[127] Pub L No 89-487, 80 Stat 250 (1967).

[128] See in this book YE Schuurmans, T Barkhuysen and W den Ouden (n 86) n 10. Other nations with separate enactments include: Australia – see in this book J Boughley (n 69) n 7 (at the state and territorial level); Belgium – see in this book S De Somer and I Opdebeek, 'Codification of Belgian Administrative Law: "Nothing is Written"', section III.F.i (Flemish legislature); and Norway – see in this book JCF Nordrum (n 69) sections II.C and VII.A–VII.C. See also in this book R Caranta (n 69) section II (application of the Aarhus Convention of 1998 to Italy); and J Reichel and M Ribbing, 'Codification of Administrative Law in Sweden', section V.D (the same issue in relation to Sweden).

[129] *Milner v Department of the Navy* 562 US 562 (2011).

[130] GE Metzger (n 88) 1305 ff.

federal judges and agencies" it can acquire a clear meaning that this Court should hesitate to change'.[131] The decision suggests that the Court's reliance on common law decision-making is driven by policy. It relies on this approach when construing the APA's procedural specifications because it perceives the APA as a broad framework statute that contains many gaps that need to be filled and uncertainties that need to be resolved. But it adopts a narrow, positive law approach for the APA's limits on judicial review and the FOIA's exceptions to agency disclosure because it believes that the underlying policy of these statutes supports extensive disclosure.

The FOIA represents an important addition to the codification of American administrative law, but it also highlights another way in which this codification is incomplete. The statute is quite different from the APA, in that it requires that information should flow from agencies to private parties rather than having information flow from private parties to the agencies in the form of comments to proposed rules, testimony in adjudicatory proceedings, or claims of illegality in demands for judicial review. But the two statutes possess an underlying similarity. Both empower private parties to intervene in the administrative process and both use that intervention as the primary means of exercising control over the process and preventing abuses. The FOIA does so by enabling private parties to discover and, if they so choose, publicise the actions that the agency has taken, pursuant to Louis Brandeis' observation that 'sunlight is said to be the best of disinfectants'.[132] The APA grants private parties the right to participate in rule-making through the notice and comment process, the right to participate in adjudications through its various procedural rules such as the right to be heard, the right to be represented by counsel and the right to petition the agency for reconsideration. It also grants private parties a right to judicial review, which can only be triggered, according to standard adversarial procedures, if a private party chooses to bring suit.

What is clearly missing from these codifications of American administrative law is the other basic means of controlling administrative behaviour, which is in internal supervision rather than external monitoring.[133] There is no general law that speaks to the way in which agency hierarchies are established or agency policies are set, no law that governs the research that agencies should carry out or the range of alternatives that they should consider, and no law that requires them to evaluate their strategies or measure the behaviour or reactions of their subject populations. Substantive statutes may contain legal controls of this nature, but they

[131] *Milner v Department of the Navy* 562 US 586 (2011) (quoting *Shearson/American Express Inc v McMahon* 482 US 220, 268 (1987) (concurring in part and dissenting in part).

[132] L Brandeis, *Other People's Money and How Bankers Use it* (New York, Frederick A Stokes, 1914) 92. This line is so well known that it was undoubtedly on the minds of the statute's drafters and proponents; indeed, a follow-up statute that requires agency decision-making meetings to be open to the public is called the Government in the Sunshine Act, Pub L 94–409, 90 Stat 1241 (1976), codified in 5 USC § 552.

[133] For an argument that this should be the focus of administrative law, see EL Rubin, 'It's Time to Make the Administrative Procedure Act Administrative' (2003) 89(1) *Cornell Law Review* 95.

typically do not do so, or do so only for a few matters that become salient during the legislative process. Internal documents such as employee manuals undoubtedly specify some controls, and they may count as customary law of the agency, but they are entirely within the agency's control and generally are not systematic in their coverage.

Perhaps it would be best to follow the inclination of the New Dealers and leave these matters to the agency's discretion. However, the absence of any such provisions from the codification of administrative law distorts that law and potentially creates certain difficulties that a law might remedy. First, it leaves legally defined supervision in the control of private parties. Such parties may be motivated by attitudes and interests that provide no benefit to the general public, such as the desire to delay implementation of a valid and beneficial regulation. In addition, the members of the public who will take advantage of these supervisory rights are likely to be those who have substantial knowledge and resources. Anyone can file a FOIA request or a comment to a rule-making proposal, but one must be quite knowledgeable to make the request to the proper agency or be aware that the proposal has been promulgated, and even more knowledgeable to know whether the request has been adequately addressed by the agency, or to write a comment that agency or a reviewing court will take seriously. It is somewhat expensive to obtain a lawyer's representation in even a simple administrative adjudication, and very expensive to bring suit against an agency in a federal court. Special interest groups, such as trade associations, have the knowledge and resources to take advantage of their APA and FOIA rights. Some public interests, such as environmentalism, have managed to generate the necessary support, but others are weak or absent from the process.

Second, leaving supervision in the hands of private parties produces distortions in the overall pattern of agency behaviour. It is relatively easy for private parties to frame objections to agency action, but difficult for them to frame objections to agency inaction. People who have applied for and obtained benefits and then been terminated for ineligibility will often object, and thereby discipline the agency's decision. People who do not know about the benefit, or are intimidated about applying for it, will be invisible to the agency, which might then indulge its natural tendency to save money and reduce hassle by ignoring them.[134] Third, and perhaps most important, private party supervision is likely to be effective in curbing abuse, but not in eliciting efficiency, creativity and foresight, three crucial virtues for administrative agencies in this complex modern world.

One codified provision in American law that represents a tentative but far from optimal beginning in his direction is Executive Order 12866.[135] It requires

[134] See DA Super, 'Privatization, Policy Paralysis, and the Poor' (2008) 96 *California Law Review* 324; DA Super, 'Offering an Invisible Hand: The Rise of the Personal Choice Model for Rationing Public Benefits' (2003) 113 *Yale Law Journal* 815.

[135] 56 Fed Reg 51735 (1993).

all executive (but not independent agencies) to carry out a cost-benefit analysis of new regulations and all agencies to submit a plan of the major initiatives they expect to undertake in the coming fiscal year. Originally part of Ronald Reagan's ill-considered deregulatory programme, this provision has been renewed by every successive President, probably because it provides a mechanism for exerting policy control over the agencies.[136] Its obvious weakness is that it employs a controversial methodology, one that depends, among other things, on establishing the monetary value of a human life.[137] Even more seriously, cost-benefit analysis addresses only a small set of the potential difficulties, inefficiencies and limitations to which agencies are subject. The 'horrible' that it is designed to combat is the regulation that imposes huge costs on industry to save a handful of lives, and that was enacted on the basis of a dramatic incident or impassioned press coverage. However, this problem is relatively rare, and those disadvantaged by it, namely regulated industries, generally have other means of redress. But the Executive Order does highlight the limits of American administrative law codification, and perhaps will point the way towards future efforts to subject administrative agencies to law without impairing their ability to act.

America's political leaders are enthusiastic legislators but reluctant codifiers. They do not hesitate to implement their policies through legal enactments; in fact, they generally prefer massive statutes, with sweeping impact, to alternative approaches such as subsidies, threats or corporativist negotiation. Codification efforts, in contrast, have generally been initiated and carried forward by lawyers, often organised in expert committees. These efforts address substantive issues when the need is insistent, as in the case of the Uniform Commercial Code, but more often focus on the lawyer's home territory of procedure, such as the Federal Rules of Civil Procedure and the Federal Rules of Criminal Procedure. The APA shares this origin and focus. As described above, its development was initiated by the American Bar Association, then implemented by a committee formed by Franklin Roosevelt's Attorney General. Its provisions tell administrative agencies how to enact rules and conduct adjudications, then grant federal courts the authority to determine whether the agencies have complied with these procedural requirements. Substantive codification, designed to make the administrative process more systematic and effective, would probably be desirable, but it may need to wait until Americans come to terms with the reality that they live in a complex regulatory state, not a bucolic frontier whose denizens can rely on common law.

[136] See E Kagan, 'Presidential Administration' (2001) 114 *Harvard Law Review* 2245.

[137] See F Ackerman and L Heinzerling, 'Pricing the Priceless: Cost-Benefit Analysis of Environmental Protection' (2002) 150 *University of Pennsylvania Law Review* 1553; MA Livermore and RL Revesz, 'Regulatory Review, Capture, and Agency Inaction' (2013) 101 *Georgetown Law Journal* 1337.

# 14

# Science Codification for the European Union: The ReNEUAL Network

## *On the Limits of Legal Control of Innovation and Technology*

ARIANE BERGER

## I. Introduction

You can only regulate what you understand. Obtaining this expertise has always been a central challenge for all legislative institutions and bodies within the EU and its Member States. The more complex and fast-moving the subject matter to be regulated, the more likely it is that the usual legal instruments will reach their limits. This is currently particularly evident in cross-cutting issues such as climate protection and sustainability, as well as innovation- and technology-driven regulatory issues such as digitisation. The legal control of digitisation is reaching its limits at both the national and the EU levels. Adapting the creation of law to the requirements of an extremely complex, fast-moving and time-critical regulatory matter and achieving better regulation without relinquishing the claim to the shaping and steering power of state law is a central challenge for the EU and its Member States.

Law-making can be accompanied organisationally, procedurally and scientifically. The EU, the German legislature and academia are working on possible instruments for improving law-making intensively. This always involves the appropriate integration of external technical expertise from society or industry and science. Science can provide support here, as can other stakeholders. This chapter first presents the European scientific codification project ReNEUAL (Research Network on EU Administrative Law) as a prominent example of the contribution of science to law-making (see below, section II). A special focus will be on the second expansion stage of the ReNEUAL project (ReNEAUL 2.0). A particular challenge for administrative law in the Member States is the digitisation of public administration. The ReNEAUL project is looking for solutions for this area of regulation in particular. On the basis of the ReNEUAL project, the practical effectiveness and limits of a scientific codification project are to be examined. The approach of science codification will be mirrored under section III with further instruments for improving the legal framework on the basis of prominent regulatory challenges at the level of EU and German digital administrative law.

This mirroring of two codification materials that at first glance appear to stand next to each other – EU administrative law and subject-specific codification approaches in the field of digitisation – has a function. On the one hand, the reasons for the success or failure of the respective codification projects are identical in each case; in all case studies, the traditional instruments of law-making reach their limits, and both EU and state law-making bodies deal with this realisation differently. Here it is worthwhile to wander back and forth. On the other hand, the various codification approaches and case studies have a factual and substantive connection, since in all cases it is a matter of reforming and redefining – analogue and digital – decision-making processes in public administration. The digitisation of the state and society is the driver of national and EU reform considerations, as it highlights the need for reform as if through a magnifying glass. It is therefore not surprising that new forms of law-making are being tested, especially in the area of digitisation. In this respect too, it is worth taking a comparative look, which – as far as can be anticipated at this point – can also promote the political effectiveness of the ReNEAUL project, which has so far failed to materialise.

## II. The Research Network on EU Administrative Law (ReNEUAL)

Recently, it has been discussed whether EU self-administration law[1] should be codified, since such a codification has not yet taken place and the administrative procedure of the institutions of the EU – apart from written regulations existing only in certain areas – is governed by general procedural principles developed in the case law of the European Court of Justice (ECJ).[2] Specific regulations on tasks, competences and instruments can only be found in the technical provisions of EU primary and secondary law, and if such provisions are lacking, general procedural principles must be applied.[3] This has resulted in a 'wildly grown' and

[1] A Hatje in U Becker, A Hatje, J Schoo and J Schwarze (eds), *EU-Kommentar* (Baden-Baden, Nomos, 2019), art 298 AEUV, n 22.

[2] A Guckelberger, 'Gibt es bald ein unionsrechtliches Verwaltungsverfahrensgesetz?' (2013) *Neue Zeitschrift für Verwaltungsrecht* 601; U Ramsauer in F Kopp and U Ramsauer (eds), *VwVfG-Kommentar*, Einf II fn 36a.

[3] *cf* M Böhm, 'Grundlagen und Rechtsquellen der Europäischen Union – Teil 1' (2008) *Juristische Ausbildung* 838, 838.

non-transparent network of norms that is – from the point of view of science – no longer comprehensible.[4]

ReNEUAL, a network of European legal and administrative scholars,[5] has developed a first draft proposal for an EU self-government law to solve this problem.[6] Consisting of approximately 150 members[7] from legal research and practice,[8] it was founded in 2009[9] and aims to investigate the potential and need for simplification of EU administrative law, ie, the rules and principles governing the implementation of EU policies by EU institutions and Member States. This simplification is to be achieved by streamlining and improving the structures and methods used in all EU policies, and to develop an understanding of the EU public sphere that ensures that the constitutional values of the EU are present and respected in all instances of the exercise of public authority.[10]

## A. ReNEUAL 1.0

### i. *ReNEUAL Model Rules*

From 2009 to 2014, ReNEUAL developed a set of model rules intended as draft binding legislation. They contain a conceivable legal framework for the non-legislative implementation of European law, bringing together, systematising and in some cases innovatively updating the various sector-specific procedural rules of European law.[11] The ReNEUAL Model Rules on EU Administrative Procedure aim to improve the administrative implementation of European law – on the basis of comparative research[12] – by transforming the EU's constitutional principles of the rule of law and democracy into a general codification of administrative procedural law with sufficiently specific rules through a legislative act, thus reinforcing the general principles of European law and identifying best practices in various specific European policy areas.[13]

[4] W Kahl, 'Kodifizierung des Verwaltungsverfahrensrechts in Deutschland und in der EU' (2018) *Juristische Schulung* 1025, 1030.

[5] www.reneual.eu/organization.

[6] www.reneual.eu/projects-and-publications/reneual-1-0.

[7] For the full list, see: www.reneual.eu/members.

[8] A Guckelberger (n 2) 601; W Kahl (n 4) 1031.

[9] Joint Statement of the European Law Institute (ELI) and the Research Network on EU Administrative Law (ReNEUAL), available at: www.reneual.eu/images/Home/ReneualELI_joint_statement.pdf.

[10] www.reneual.eu.

[11] B Schmidt am Busch, 'Der ReNEUAL-Musterentwurf für ein Europäisches Verwaltungsverfahrensrecht in der Diskussion' (2016) *Gewerbearchiv* 236, 236.

[12] www.reneual.eu/projects-and-publications/reneual-1-0.

[13] F Schoch, 'Einleitung' in F Schoch and J-P Schneider (eds), *Verwaltungsrecht, Bd 2 (VwVfG)* (Munich, CH Beck, 2022), Einl fn 724.

The ReNEUAL Model Rules are divided into six books with a total of 132 articles.[14] The scope of application of the draft model is delimited and defined in Book I.[15] According to this, the draft is basically limited to measures of the EU authorities in so-called direct enforcement and only extends to Member State authorities in the case of the so-called 'Verbundverwaltung' (interconnection procedure).[16]

Book II[17] regulates 'administrative law making', ie, law-making procedures other than the formal legislative procedures, which means all non-legislative acts – especially delegated acts and implementing acts according to Article 290f of the Treaty on the Functioning of the European Union (TFEU)[18] – as well as legal acts based on other competences.[19] The consultation and participation of the citizens of the EU is central, with the aim of ensuring a comprehensive and impartial examination of all relevant circumstances in administrative law-making. In this way, the legitimacy of the administration's legislative activity is to be increased in accordance with Article 11 of the Treaty on European Union (TEU),[20] which obliges the EU institutions to guarantee participatory democracy in their actions.[21]

The provisions of Book III[22] – which regulates the most important administrative single case decisions in practice[23] – serve to implement the right to good administration enshrined in Article 41 of the Charter of Fundamental Rights of the European Union (CFR).[24] The scope of application extends to all administrative procedures aimed at issuing a legally binding decision with external effect and, in addition to general requirements such as scope of application and definitions, all procedural steps of an individual case decision procedure are dealt with, ie, the initiation of the procedure, the determination of the facts, access to the file, the hearing and participation of third parties and other authorities, the conclusion of the procedure and the official revocation of decisions.[25]

Book IV[26] contains comprehensive rules on the law of administrative contracts of the EU's own administration, which concern both the conclusion and the

[14] W Kahl (n 4) 1031.

[15] www.reneual.eu/images/Home/BookI-general_provision_2014-09-03_individualized_final.pdf.

[16] B Schmidt am Busch (n 11) 236.

[17] www.reneual.eu/images/Home/BookII-AdministrativeRulemaking_individualized_final_2014_09_03.pdf.

[18] Consolidated Version of the Treaty on the Functioning of the European Union [2012] OJ C326/47.

[19] S Lenz, 'Der ReNEUAL-Musterentwurf für ein Europäisches Verwaltungsverfahrensrecht in der Diskussion' (2016) *Neue Zeitschrift für Verwaltungsrecht* 38, 39.

[20] Consolidated Version of the Treaty on European Union [2012] OJ C326/13.

[21] B Bievert in U Becker et al (n 1), art 11 EUV, n 1.

[22] www.reneual.eu/images/Home/BookIII-Single_CaseDecision-Making_individualized_final_2014-09-03.pdf.

[23] F Schoch (n 13) Einl fn 731.

[24] Charter of Fundamental Rights of the European Union [2012] OJ C326/391. *cf* M Ruffert in C Calliess and M Ruffert (eds), *EUV/AEUV* (Munich, CH Beck, 2022), art 41, GrCH fn 1.

[25] B Schmidt am Busch (n 11) 236.

[26] www.reneual.eu/images/Home/BookIV-Contracts_online_version_individualized_final__2014-09-03.pdf.

execution of contracts and is based on the distinction between those EU administrative contracts to which only European law applies and those contracts whose performance is governed exclusively by Member State (private) law.[27] Book IV is structured according to the 'life phases' of a contract: conclusion, performance and termination.[28] Book III applies as a subsidiary to Book IV.[29]

Books V[30] and VI[31] – which are closely related to each other[32] – deal with vertical and horizontal interactions between EU authorities and Member State authorities, and, unlike Books II–IV, concern not only EU authorities but also Member State authorities insofar as they enforce European law.[33]

Book V regulates vertical administrative assistance between EU authorities and Member State authorities as well as horizontal administrative assistance, especially between different Member States, and focuses on classic administrative assistance. Such a general regulation on administrative assistance, which would cover both the vertical aspect (ie, the relationship between EU institutions and national authorities) and the horizontal aspect (in particular, administrative assistance between Member State authorities in EU matters), does not yet exist, except in certain areas of secondary law such as cartel law,[34] tax law[35] and agricultural law.[36] It is also doubtful whether Article 114 TFEU would suffice for a general regulation of administrative assistance or whether the path via Article 352 TFEU would have to be taken.[37]

Book VI, on the other hand, concerns special forms of inter-administrative information management activities, which form the basis for the administrative measures regulated in Books II–IV.[38]

[27] U Stelkens in P Stelkens, H Bonk and M Sachs (eds), *Verwaltungsverfahrensgesetz* (Munich, CH Beck, 2018), § 54 fn 177.

[28] W Abromeit, 'Der ReNEUAL-Musterentwurf für ein Europäisches Verwaltungsverfahrensrecht' (2016) *Die Öffentliche Verwaltung* 345, 347.

[29] S Lenz (n 19) 40.

[30] www.reneual.eu/images/Home/BookV-mutual_assistance_online_publication_individualized_final_2014-09-03.pdf.

[31] www.reneual.eu/images/Home/BookVI-information_management_online_publication_individualized_final_2014-09-03.pdf.

[32] F Schoch (n 13) Einl fn 733.

[33] S Lenz (n 19) 40.

[34] *cf* art 105, para 1, sentence 2 TFEU.

[35] *cf* Directive 2011/16/EU of the Council on administrative cooperation in the field of taxation [1977] OJ L336/15 and repealing Directive 77/799/EEC of the Council of 19 December 1977 concerning mutual assistance by the competent authorities of the Member States in the field of direct taxation [1977] OJ L336/15.

[36] *cf* Regulation 1468/81/EEC of the Council of 19 May 1981on mutual assistance between the administrative authorities of the Member States and cooperation between the latter and the Commission to ensure the correct application of the law on customs or agricultural matters [1979] OJ L54/136; Regulation 359/79/EEC of the Council of 5 February 1979 on direct cooperation between the bodies designated by Member States to verify compliance with Community and national provisions in the wine sector [1979] OJ L54/136.

[37] R Stettner, 'Verwaltungsvollzug' in M Dauses and M Ludwigs (eds), *Handbuch des EU-Wirtschaftsrechts* (Munich, CH Beck 2021), B. III. Verwaltungsvollzug n 81.

[38] B Schmidt am Busch (n 11) 237.

Due to the discussion following the translation of the model rules into several European languages,[39] an updated English version of the model rules was published in 2015.[40]

### ii. *The Evaluation and Practical Significance of ReNEUAL 1.0*

On the fringes of a symposium held on 5 and 6 November 2015 at the Bundesverwaltungsgericht[41] in Leipzig,[42] where the ReNEUAL Model Rules were presented, an assessment was also made by various lawyers from academia, administrative and judicial practice.[43] As a result, it was agreed that the ReNEUAL Model Rules will find an elevated level of acceptance among experts and legal scholars due to the high scientific standard and the diverse composition of the group of authors consisting of academics and practitioners from across the EU.[44]

However, although in 2013 the European Parliament (EP) called on the Commission to draft an administrative procedure law dealing with individual case decisions by the EU authorities,[45] the ReNEUAL Model Rules have little prospect of success as a codification project, even though the EP has since decided[46] to push ahead with its own draft.[47] Compared to the ReNEUAL model draft, the EP's draft is significantly less extensive and limited to the administrative activities of the EU institutions, bodies, offices and agencies (Article 2, paragraphs 1 and 3 of the draft) and covers only individual decisions taken unilaterally by an EU authority.[48]

However, in the Commission's view, there is already no competence[49] for such a far-reaching codification of European administrative procedural law and without a solution to the question of the scope of the EU's norm-setting competence in the area of administrative procedural law in interconnected procedures, neither the ReNEUAL model draft nor the EP proposal will have a chance of

[39] Unlike the English and Spanish translation, the French, German, Italian, Polish and Romanian versions are unfortunately only obtainable at a charge: *cf* www.reneual.eu/projects-and-publications/reneual-1-0.

[40] Available at: www.reneual.eu/images/Home/ReNEUAL--Model-Rules-update-2015_rules-only-2017.PDF.

[41] The German Federal Administrative Court.

[42] www.bverwg.de/das-gericht/veranstaltungen.

[43] B Stüer, 'ReNEUAL-Musterentwurf für ein EU-Verwaltungsverfahrensrecht' (2016) *Deutsches Verwaltungsblatt* (*DVBl*) 100, 101.

[44] S Lenz (n 19) 40.

[45] www.europarl.europa.eu/doceo/document/A-7-2012-0369_DE.html.

[46] www.europarl.europa.eu/meetdocs/2014_2019/plmrep/COMMITTEES/JURI/DV/2016/01-28/1083272EN.pdf.

[47] www.europarl.europa.eu/meetdocs/2014_2019/plmrep/COMMITTEES/JURI/DV/2016/01-11/1081253DE.pdf.

[48] W Kahl (n 4) 1032.

[49] B Stüer (n 44) 101 f.

realisation.[50] Also, the areas of self-administration are very technical, highly specialised and have hardly any commonalities, so that sector-specific regulations are always necessary and codification would not bring any added value, as EU administration is not the rule but the exception.[51] As the Commission's right of initiative[52] requires its involvement in such a project and it does not see any added value in it, an implementation of the EP proposal is not conceivable any time soon.[53]

No support could be expected from Member States either, as national politicians would have nothing to gain from investing their energy in a long-term project that would attract little attention from the electorate.[54] Nevertheless, the project could be an inspiration for EU Member States that do not yet have an administrative procedure law or only have a very new one.[55]

If, contrary to expectations, it does come to be implemented, Book III would be preferable from the point of view of science because of the importance of individual case decisions – as the EP's attempted proposal also shows.[56]

## B. ReNEUAL 2.0

Following the completion of the ReNEUAL 1.0 project, the ReNEUAL Steering Committee decided to refocus its research away from a codification exercise and towards an evaluation of issues of major importance for EU administrative law from 2018 onwards.[57] The ReNEUAL 2.0 working groups focus on Common European Principles of Administrative Law and Good Administration (work group 2.1), Digitalised Public Administration (work group 2.2) and International and Transnational Administrative Law (work group 2.3):

### *i. Common European Principles of Administrative Law and Good Administration (ReNEUAL 2.1)*

Consisting of two externally funded projects, this working group focuses on certain basic principles of administrative law common to the national administrative laws of EU Member States, the legal order of the EU and the law of the Council of Europe (CoE).[58]

[50] F Schoch (n 13) Einl fn 737.
[51] B Schmidt am Busch (n 11) 237.
[52] J Schoo in U Becker et al (n 1), art 293 AEUV, fns 1, 5.
[53] W Kahl (n 4) 1032.
[54] S Lenz (n 19) 49.
[55] W Abromeit (n 30) 348.
[56] B Stüer (n 44) 102.
[57] www.reneual.eu/projects-and-publications/reneual-2-0.
[58] ibid.

The Common Core of European Administrative Law (CoCEAL)[59] examines the procedural norms applied by European legal systems and the content of procedural protections based on a factual method.

'The development of pan-European general principles of good administration by the Council of Europe and their impact on the administrative law of its Member States'[60] deals with the principles of administrative law common to the national administrative law of the European states.

The results will later be linked and merged with the results of other research projects and working groups of ReNEUAL, thus leading to a 'European Administrative Law Toolbox', which will show the deeper meaning of legal instruments that are considered necessary or at least helpful to ensure central democratic principles in constitutional states, such as the protection of individual rights by the administration, transparency and the democratic legitimacy of the administration and its actions.[61]

#### a. The Common Core of European Administrative Law (CoCEAL)

This (comparative)[62] law project examines whether and to what extent there is a common basis or a 'common core' of European administrative law in the administrative procedure of the various legal systems of the European countries, ie, whether behind the countless differences there are also some 'common and unifying elements' that can be legally formulated in the form of general legal principles and mechanisms for their application.[63]

In this context, administrative procedure was chosen as the object of study because the emergence of procedural law has shaped all European legal systems, the concept of administrative procedure is of increasing legal importance, and the concept of procedure has not just one but a multitude of functions (protection against the abuse of discretionary powers, instrument for the functioning of complex administrative apparatuses, as an instrument of political control over the administration).[64]

To examine the nature and scope of a common core of administrative law, several hypothetical cases are formulated that can be understood and resolved in all legal systems.[65] In addition to legal provisions and general legal principles,

[59] Funded by the European Research Council (ERC) under the Horizon 2020 – Research and Innovation – Advanced Grant – Excellent Science programme (grant agreement no 694697: www.cordis.europa.eu/project/id/694697), organised by Giacinto della Cananea and Mauro Bussani.

[60] Funded by the German Research Foundation (gepris.dfg.de/gepris/projekt/274964159?language=en) and organised by Ulrich Stelkens.

[61] www.reneual.eu/projects-and-publications/reneual-2-0.

[62] www.coceal.it/index.php?option=com_content&view=article&id=12&Itemid=101.

[63] G della Cananea, 'The "Common Core" of Administrative Laws in Europe: A Research Agenda', www.coceal.it/pdf/1.dellaCananea_AResearchAgenda.pdf, 2.

[64] www.coceal.it/index.php?option=com_content&view=article&id=13&Itemid=109.

[65] Della Cananea (n 64) 28.

legal theories and judicial law – ie, all factors that contribute to the resolution of cases – will be taken into account.[66]

### b. Pan-European General Principles of Good Administration

This project examines the development, content, and effectiveness of the written and unwritten standards of good administration developed within the framework of the CoE – called 'Pan-European General Principles of Good Administration'.[67] The legal sources of these principles are the Statute of the Council of Europe (SCoE) (in particular Article 3 of the Statute), the European Convention on Human Rights (ECHR), 'Council of Europe Conventions', the recommendations of the Committee of Ministers of the Council of Europe and finally the recommendations, resolutions, opinions and reports issued by the Parliamentary Assembly and other Council of Europe institutions.[68]

In a first phase, the project measured the effectiveness of the general principles of good governance applicable throughout Europe, in order to draw conclusions on their overall effectiveness in a second step. Following the completion of the first phase, a second phase of the project now follows in which the various Europe-wide general principles of good governance are placed in a framework to 'specify' them.

*Phase 1*: Researchers from 28 selected Member States[69] of the Council of Europe were asked to prepare country reports to clarify whether and to what extent the pan-European general principles of good administration shape the respective national administrative law systems and whether the pan-European general principles of good administration have a harmonising effect in the Member States.[70]

Based on these different country reports, the interaction between national administrative law and the pan-European general principles of good administrative practice was analysed with the result that the adaptation of national administrative law to the pan-European general principles of good administrative practice is a process that has progressed to different degrees in the different Member States and is therefore effective to different degrees in each Member State.[71]

[66] www.coceal.it/index.php?option=com_content&view=article&id=13&Itemid=109.

[67] www.reneual.eu/projects-and-publications/reneual-2-0.

[68] A Andrijauskaitė and U Stelkens, 'Added Value of the Council of Europe to Administrative Law: The Development of Pan-European General Principles of Good Administration by the Council of Europe and their Impact on the Administrative Law of its Member States' (2016) *Deutsches Forschungsinstitut für öffentliche Verwaltung Discussion Papers (FÖV 86)* 1, 8 ff.

[69] The 28 states are: Albania, Armenia, Austria, Belgium, Bulgaria, Croatia, the Czech Republic, Estonia, Finland, France, Georgia, Germany, Hungary, Italy, Latvia, Lithuania, the Netherlands, Norway, Poland, Portugal, Romania, Serbia, Slovenia, Spain, Sweden, Switzerland, Turkey and the UK.

[70] U Stelkens, 'Die paneuropäischen allgemeinen Rechtsgrundsätze guter Verwaltung des Europarats: Ein Europäisches Verwaltungsrecht jenseits der Europäischen Union?' (2021) *Verwaltungsarchiv* 309, 328 f.

[71] www.reneual.eu/projects-and-publications/reneual-2-0/2-uncategorised/15-good-administration.

The project therefore concluded that the pan-European general principles of good administrative behaviour can be used by Council of Europe bodies and institutions and by the European Court of Human Rights (ECtHR) as normative assessment benchmarks for assessing the compliance of national administrative law of Council of Europe Member States with Council of Europe law.[72]

In this context, 'genuine' compliance with the general European principles of good administrative behaviour is only possible if they are implemented, applied and enforced in sufficient numbers in various 'manifestations' and 'flexible combinations'. Only then can national administrative law provide checks, balances and limits on powers so that the 'administrative law component' of the Council of Europe's fundamental values is effectively implemented.[73]

Based on these findings, the project developed the so-called building block theory, according to which various pan-European general principles constitute 'building blocks' (public service, local self-government, individual rights, administrative procedures, administrative justice, transparency etc) for the construction of a 'tower of good administration'. Council of Europe experts, national experts, academics and also others can then use the stability of the 'tower' to examine how the individual state has put the building blocks together and how functional this composition is.[74] In this way, the building block theory ultimately represents a 'good governance test'.[75]

*Phase 2*: The finding of the first project phase that the pan-European general principles of good administration are not a loose bundle of different rules in administrative matters, but form a 'coherent whole' reflecting the common experience of the Member States of the Council of Europe and are thus part of the 'common heritage' of the peoples of these states in the sense of the preambles of the SCoE and the ECHR serves as the basis for further investigation in the second project phase.[76]

To examine the background, functions and meaning of these principles, as well as the experiences that led to their adoption, the project will organise the various pan-European general principles of good administration in terms of their 'specification' in a 'thematic framework' to further develop the 'building block theory', which as a result should be an analytical tool for structuring the 'test of good administration'.[77]

Anyone with sufficient expertise to handle it should be able to use this tool so that it can be used not only for academic research on the conformity of national administrative law with the Europe-wide general principles of good administration, but also in control procedures in the intergovernmental framework of the

[72] ibid.
[73] U Stelkens (n 71) 333.
[74] ibid 335.
[75] A Andrijauskaitė and U Stelkens (n 69) 70.
[76] www.reneual.eu/projects-and-publications/reneual-2-0/2-uncategorised/18-good-administration-phase-2.
[77] ibid.

Council of Europe, in proceedings before the ECtHR or as a tool in the EU's 'rule of law toolbox' and by national courts or control bodies to check the alignment of national administrative law with the standard of Article 3 SCoE.[78]

To further develop the building block theory, a detailed explanation of the content, purpose and rationale of the different EU-wide principles of good administration with their different 'specifications' is needed, which is the main aim of the second phase of the project.[79]

### *ii. Digitalised Public Administration in the European Union (ReNEUAL 2.2)*

The working group Digitalised Public Administration in the European Union (ReNEUAL 2.2) will investigate how new technologies especially digitalised information and communication technologies (ICT) affect the way in which public administrations work and interact with each other. Drawing on traditional administrative law concepts and building on earlier research activities and findings of ReNEUAL 1.0 Working Group 4 on Information Management, the research will mainly focus on the following topics:[80]

- the administrative process and the influence of ICT on its functioning and internal structure;
- discretionary decision-making and ICT (machine learning, algorithmic decision-making and deep learning algorithms);
- databases and interoperability in different areas of EU activity (internal market cooperation, police and justice cooperation, and financial market regulation);
- public services and ICT (eg, smart cities);
- legal language, legal translation and ICT.

### *iii. International and Transnational Administrative Law (ReNEUAL 2.3)*

Against the backdrop of ever-increasing globalisation, this working group is looking at the legal effects of administrative cooperation on the structure of legal systems. It examines the gaps in the legal systems that regulate cross-border and functional cooperation, and explores the question of which law is to be applied when no legal system comes into question without dispute. This involves both horizontal interaction between legal systems (cross-border cooperation) and vertical interaction (regulatory cooperation).[81]

[78] ibid.
[79] ibid.
[80] www.reneual.eu/projects-and-publications/reneual-2-0.
[81] ibid.

### iv. *The Evaluation and Practical Significance of ReNEUAL 2.0*

According to Article 10, paragraph 3 TEU, all citizens of the EU have the right to take part in the democratic life of the Union. Under Article 10, paragraph 3 TEU, decisions shall be taken as openly as possible and as closely as possible to the citizen. The EU institutions shall, in an appropriate manner, give Union citizens and representative associations the opportunity to make known and exchange their views publicly in all policy areas falling within the competence of the EU, through an open, transparent and regular dialogue with representative associations and civil society.[82] A specific consultation obligation regarding compliance with the principles of subsidiarity and proportionality arises for the Commission from Article 5, Protocol No 2 on the application of the principles of subsidiarity and proportionality.[83]

In addition to these legal requirements from primary law, the EU is pursuing a 'better regulation' agenda with the aim of putting EU action on an evidence-based footing and making EU legislation simpler and better, involving citizens, businesses and stakeholders in the decision-making process.[84] To achieve these goals, a Better Regulation Guideline[85] and the Better Regulation Toolbox[86] were created. The Guideline sets out the requirements for the key steps in the policy cycle, while the Better Regulation Toolbox supplies practical guidance and operational details for staff in the EU institutions.[87]

Due to these requirements, the Commission currently uses a so-called stakeholder consultation[88] in legislative procedures. Stakeholders are all interested parties who are not EU legislators or EU institutions (private individuals, lobby groups, municipal associations etc).[89] Before a legislative proposal is made, these stakeholders are consulted by the Commission.[90] This consultation leads – at least so far – to a purely quantitative and not to a qualitative evaluation by the Commission.[91]

From the point of view of a municipal central association – such as the Deutscher Landkreistag (German County Association) – it is therefore most successful as a 'stakeholder' to assert its concerns and criticisms in the legislative process if it can bring them to the attention of the Commission in a pre-legislative

[82] T Kröll and G Lienbacher in U Becker et al (n 1), art 10 EUV, n 20.

[83] www.eur-lex.europa.eu/legal-content/DE/TXT/HTML/?uri=CELEX:12008E/PRO/02&from=DE.

[84] www.ec.europa.eu/info/law/law-making-process/planning-and-proposing-law/better-regulation-why-and-how_de.

[85] www.ec.europa.eu/info/sites/default/files/swd2021_305_en.pdf.

[86] www.ec.europa.eu/info/sites/default/files/br_toolbox-nov_2021_en_0.pdf.

[87] www.ec.europa.eu/info/sites/default/files/swd2021_305_en.pdf, 4.

[88] *cf* 'Chapter 7 – Stakeholder Consultation' in the Toolbox: www.ec.europa.eu/info/sites/default/files/br_toolbox_-_nov_2021_-_chapter_7.pdf.

[89] www.ec.europa.eu/social/main.jsp?catId=1192&langId=en.

[90] www.ec.europa.eu/social/main.jsp?catId=333&langId=de.

[91] M Schmitz, 'Stärkung der Kommunen im Gesetzgebungsverfahren' (2019) 1 *EUROPA kommunal* 17, 19.

procedure (eg, work in expert groups[92] or participation in consultations) and thus be heard early in the legislative process. Once the legislative proposal leaves the Commission's sphere of influence, it is only possible to exert influence by lobbying the EP and the Council (ie, 'post-legislative'), which is much more difficult. From the point of view of an Kommunaler Spitzenverband (association for municipalities and regions), it is pleasing that the Commission intends to make the feedback it receives from local and regional authorities on its proposals more visible to the EP and the Council in each legislative procedure in future.[93]

The experience of the ReNEUAL 1.0 project, on the other hand, shows that it is difficult to get the Commission excited about a (scientific) codification of legislation in which the latter is not actively involved. Earlier experience also shows that the Commission does not actively approach the scientific community for new laws to be enacted. Rather, the scientific community must make its voice heard in a general consultation – in which all other stakeholders are also involved – if research findings are to be reflected in the legislative process. Also, the fact that the EP – which has been trying since 2001 to persuade the Commission to regulate EU self-governance in the form of a regulation[94] – is working on its own proposal[95] for an EU self-governance law and is not simply adopting the ReNEUAL model rules shows that the science codification approach currently has no chance of success within the framework of the EU.

As a result, a codification project such as ReNEUAL can only succeed and be effective if it involves the Commission in its project from the outset, or if, analogous to associations for municipalities and regions and other stakeholders, it contributes its findings in the context of consultations with the Commission on already planned legislation.

## C. Summary and Result: Science Codification as a Building Block for Better Regulation

Science codification is a building block for better law-making that must prove its political weight. This instrument must prove its worth in the subject matters of technology and innovation in particular. EU and national legislators increasingly share the realisation that this task is extremely demanding due to the technical and organisational complexity of the subject matter and that it cannot always be adequately mastered with the approaches used to date. It is becoming increasingly difficult to reflect the ever more dynamic technological challenges in the law.

[92] For example, in the European Committee of the Regions (CoR): cor.europa.eu/de.
[93] www.ec.europa.eu/info/sites/default/files/communication-principles-subsidiarity-proportionality-strengthening-role-policymaking_de.pdf 9.
[94] F Schoch (n 13) Einl fn 723.
[95] *cf* above n 46.

ReNEAUL 2.0 addresses this issue, but concrete results are not yet available. The European Commission and German legislators also see the limits of legal control and are trying to improve the quality of legislation in these areas with their own instruments. The following section deals with other instruments for improving legislation besides science codification, the interaction of these codification instruments and the limits of legal steering.

## III. The Digital State: Codification *Quo Vadis*?

In the following, prominent regulatory challenges and selected regulatory instruments in the field of European and German law will be described, which can be summarised under the topos 'digital state'. They include data protection, the establishment of a digital administration and the regulation of artificial intelligence (AI) – areas that are also the focus of the ReNEUAL 2.0 science codification project.

First, however, the (German) judiciary should have its say, which for its part is also an agent of law-making alongside the legislature and academia. The German Federal Constitutional Court has repeatedly and recently dealt with the constitutional requirements for good or better law-making. The Court does not release the German legislator from its duty to steer correctly under constitutional law, even in the case of complex issues. Most recently, the Court had to deal prominently with the appropriateness of the respective statutory regulations both in its two decisions on the constitutionality of the so-called 'Corona-Bundesnotbremse' (federal emergency brake)[96] and in its decision on the constitutionality of the Bundes-Klimaschutzgesetz (Federal Climate Protection Act).[97] The three decisions are united by the finding that neither the complexity of the underlying regulatory area nor its crisis-like character is capable of releasing the legislature from its responsibility to steer. However, the complexity of the facts of life is accompanied by greater scope for decision-making in the creation of statutory law, which in turn finds its limits in constitutional court control and the creation of statutory law by judges, as was the case in particular with the much-noted new 'intertemporale Freiheitssicherung' (intertemporal safeguarding of freedom)[98] derived from fundamental rights.

The relationship between legislative and judicial law-making will not be discussed further at this point. However, the question that arises in the present

[96] German Federal Constitutional Court decision 1 BvR 986/21 et al (sales area restrictions) of 20 May 2021 and decision 1 BvR 781/21 et al (night-time exit restrictions) of 5 May 2021.

[97] Bundes-Klimaschutzgesetz (KSG) vom 12 Dezember 2019 (BGBl I, 2513), zuletzt geändert durch Artikel 1 des Gesetzes vom 18 August 2021 (BGBl I, 3905); German Federal Constitutional Court decision 1 BvR 2656/18 et al of 24 March 2021.

[98] ibid Leitsatz 4.

case is how the legislature can be enabled to create appropriate law if it does not want to rely primarily on the element of judicial law-making.

The Federal Constitutional Court has repeatedly emphasised the abstract danger posed by the complex regulatory subject of digitisation to fundamental freedoms and has demanded appropriate safeguards from the legislature. This was true, for example, as early as 1983 in the census ruling (Volkszählungsurteil)[99] with its Recht auf informationelle Selbstbestimmung (right to informational self-determination) and the danger of so-called profiling through the state collection of personal data. The abstract danger of state profiling that impairs freedom and its appropriate legal handling were also the subject of the most recent parliamentary debate on the Registermodernisierungsgesetz (Federal Register Modernisation Act).[100]

These examples, which are by no means exhaustive, are intended to give an impression of the breadth of digitally related regulatory matters in the most diverse fields of action. In view of this and against the backdrop of the dynamics of technological developments at both the national and the EU levels, we have a legal framework for the digital state that is still in the process of being created or is constantly changing, and which has a number of deficits. These will also be presented only by way of an example. Following this, selected instruments for overcoming these deficits will be presented.

## A. Regulatory Challenges Based on Current Examples

Regulatory works on the subject of digitisation at both the national and EU levels can be distinguished first of all according to whether and to what extent they make abstract-general full regulations of a codificatory nature or use a sector-specific approach involving further standard generators (government, authorities and standardisation bodies). The European Commission is currently leaning towards an abstract-general codificatory approach with the existing General Data Protection Regulation (GDPR)[101] adopted by the EU legislative bodies and with the recently presented comprehensive draft Artificial Intelligence Regulation. In contrast, the German legislature is taking a more sectoral, work-sharing approach with the Onlinezugangsgesetz (Federal Online

[99] German Federal Constitutional Court decision 1 BvR 209/83, 1 BvR 269/83 of 13 April 1983.

[100] Gesetz zur Einführung und Verwendung einer Identifikationsnummer in der öffentlichen Verwaltung und zur Änderung weiterer Gesetze (Registermodernisierungsgesetz – RegMoG) vom 28 März 2021 (BGBl I, 591), zuletzt geändert durch Artikel 11 des Gesetzes vom 9 Juli 2021 (BGBl I, 2467).

[101] Regulation (EU) 2016/679 of the European Parliament and of the Council of 27 April 2016 on the protection of natural persons with regard to the processing of personal data and on the free movement of such data, and repealing Directive 95/46/EC (General Data Protection Regulation) [2016] OJ L119/1.

Access Act),[102] the Registermodernisierungsgesetz (Federal Register Modernisation Act),[103] the eGovernment-Gesetze des Bundes[104] und der Länder (Federal- and Länder-eGovernment Acts), other subject-specific individual regulations and, not least, a wide variety of data protection law standardisations. Both approaches show dysfunctionalities, which will be briefly outlined here.

### *i. Evaluation of the General Data Protection Regulation*

The 2016 GDPR pursues an ambitious approach by subjecting the processing of personal data by public and private entities to comprehensive EU-wide regulation and by claiming to be a codification. Article 97, paragraph 1 GDPR provides for an evaluation to be repeated every four years. According to paragraph 5 of this provision, the European Commission must submit 'if necessary, appropriate proposals for amending' the GDPR in its report and 'shall take into account, in particular, developments in information technology and progress in the information society'. The Commission presented its first evaluation in mid-2020,[105] which did not identify any need for change. However, in the view of many critics, technological changes are forcing adjustments to the GDPR, and the Commission has simply not adequately addressed this evolutionary requirement.[106]

The evaluation was preceded by extensive stakeholder and expert group participation, which included interested parties from all over Europe, including the Council, the Member States and, in relation to Germany, the Federal Government, the Bundesrat, the Conference of Independent Data Protection Authorities (DSK) and many associations, organisations and initiatives.[107] Almost all of the comments demanded that the EU Commission respond to new technical developments. It should examine the challenges posed by emerging technologies such as the collection and analysis of large amounts of data (Big Data), AI, the Internet of Things, blockchain, facial recognition, profiling and seemingly authentic video or audio material modified by AI (so-called deep fakes). Above all, it should review protection gaps created by the increasing concentration of data among individual providers and platforms, as well as by the use of scoring and profiling, and should close them through additional regulations. Particularly in the face

[102] Gesetz zur Verbesserung des Onlinezugangs zu Verwaltungsleistungen (Onlinezugangsgesetz – OZG) vom 14 August 2017 (BGBl I, 3122, 3138), zuletzt geändert durch Artikel 16 des Gesetzes vom 28 Juni 2021 (BGBl I, 2250).

[103] See above n 104.

[104] Gesetz zur Förderung der elektronischen Verwaltung (E-Government-Gesetz – EGovG) vom 25 Juli 2013 (BGBl I, 2749), zuletzt geändert durch Artikel 1 des Gesetzes vom 16 Juli 2021 (BGBl I, 2941).

[105] ec.europa.eu/info/law/law-topic/data-protection/communication-two-years-application-general-data-protection-regulation_en.

[106] A Roßnagel, 'Die Evaluation der Datenschutz-Grundverordnung' (2020) *MMR – Zeitschrift für IT-Recht und Recht der Digitalisierung* 657, 657.

[107] ibid.

of new challenges posed by digitisation, protection gaps have emerged that give rise to fears that existing data protection law is not suitable for ensuring adequate protection of fundamental rights in the future. In addition, the GDPR contains technical errors, inconsistencies, inconsistencies in values, regulatory gaps and over-regulation, which cause incomprehension, legal uncertainties, investment backlogs, enforcement obstacles, barriers to action and protection gaps.

The evaluation required under Article 97 GDPR would have been a good opportunity to discuss and address this need for improvement.[108] In contrast, the evaluation report of the EU Commission is limited to selected questions of the implementation of the regulation, not to needs in relation to the regulation itself. Rather, reference was made to pending and future legislative projects within the framework of the so-called European Data Strategy, such as the Data Governance Act on the use of data from public bodies[109] or the Data Act on the regulation of platform service providers,[110] as well as to the planned Regulation on Artificial Intelligence,[111] whose relationship to the GDPR is, however, still unclear.

It can be observed after all that abstract-generic, codificatory full regulations find their limits in the dynamics of the facts to be regulated and obviously tend to a dysfunctional resistance to change, which does not withstand the dynamics of technological developments.

### *ii. Draft for an European Regulation on Artificial Intelligence*

The Commission is taking a similar codificatory 'full approach' with its draft regulation on AI presented at the beginning of 2021.[112] The normative foundation of the proposal is formed in particular by the preliminary work of the independent expert group on AI mandated by the EU Commission. In its final report, this group had previously presented core requirements derived from ethical principles for the creation of trustworthy AI.[113] The proposed regulation, which now comprises 120 pages, is based on this report. The aim of the planned regulation is

[108] ibid.

[109] Proposal for a Regulation of the European Parliament and of the Council on European data governance (Data Governance Act), eur-lex.europa.eu/legal-content/EN/TXT/HTML/?uri=CELEX:52020PC0767&from=EN.

[110] Proposal for a Regulation of the European Parliament and of the Council on harmonised rules on fair access to and use of data (Data Act), digital-strategy.ec.europa.eu/en/library/data-act-proposal-regulation-harmonised-rules-fair-access-and-use-data.

[111] See above, section II.Aii.

[112] Proposal for a Regulation of the European Parliament and of the Council laying down harmonised rules on Artificial Intelligence (Artificial Intelligence Act) and amending certain Union legislative acts, eur-lex.europa.eu/resource.html?uri=cellar:e0649735-a372-11eb-9585-01aa75ed71a1.0001.02/DOC_1&format=PDF; and Annexes to the Proposal for a Regulation of the European Parliament and of the Council laying down harmonised rules on Artificial Intelligence (Artificial Intelligence Act) and amending certain Union legislative acts, eur-lex.europa.eu/resource.html?uri=cellar:e0649735-a372-11eb-9585 01aa75ed71a1.0001.02/DOC_2&format=PDF.

[113] digital-strategy.ec.europa.eu/en/library/ethics-guidelines-trustworthy-ai.

to strengthen trust in AI practices, to ensure that the use of technology complies with fundamental rights and to increase the competitiveness of the EU in the field of AI.

The draft of the Artificial Intelligence Regulation subjects AI to a holistic regulatory regime. In the future, a comprehensive catalogue will be used to preventively assess whether AI applications can pose risks to certain legal interests and, depending on the findings, protective measures will be taken. For this purpose, the draft distinguishes between four different risk levels: unacceptable risk, high risk, low risk and minimal risk, whereby the last two levels are not further differentiated in the draft.[114] AI with unacceptable risk is completely prohibited by the draft, with one exception; systems with high risk are subject to high regulatory and technological requirements. In contrast, implementation of draft requirements for AI with low and minimal risk is voluntary. Pursuant to Article 59, paragraph 1 of the Artificial Intelligence Regulation, Member States shall establish those authorities which shall supervise the application and implementation of the Regulation, including a national supervisory authority (Article 59, paragraph 2). Comparable to the European Data Protection Board (EDSA), Article 56, paragraph 1 of the Artificial Intelligence Regulation provides for the establishment of a European Artificial Intelligence Committee, consisting of the competent supervisory authorities of the Member States and the European Data Protection Supervisor (Article 57, paragraph 1 of the Artificial Intelligence Regulation).

In terms of codification, the draft Artificial Intelligence Regulation is thus largely based on the structure of the GDPR, but is also subject to comparable risks of bureaucracy and fossilisation.[115] The abstract-general assignment of applications to risk groups in the annex to the Regulation also provokes the question of delimitation and assignment in individual cases. The subdivision according to the risk of certain applications poses significant forecasting problems for developers and entrepreneurs with regard to the legal classification of their products.[116] For example, AI products can serve multiple application areas. A simple image processing AI would be classified as low risk, while its use for biometric recognition would be classified as high risk up to prohibited unacceptable risk.[117]

As a counterproposal to this abstract-general risk-based approach, the international engineering association IEEE (I Triple E) (Institute of Electrical and

[114] digital-strategy.ec.europa.eu/en/policies/regulatory-framework-ai.

[115] M Herberger, 'Künstliche Intelligenz und Recht' (2018) *Neue Juristische Wochenschrift* 2825; A Eber and I Spiecker genannt Döhmann, 'Der Kommissionsentwurf für eine KI Verordnung der EU' (2021) *Neue Zeitschrift für Verwaltungsrecht* 1188; M Valta and J Vasel, 'Kommissionsvorschlag für eine Verordnung über Künstliche Intelligenz' (2021) *Zeitschrift für Rechtspolitik* 142.

[116] P Hacker, 'Europäische und nationale Regulierung von Künstlicher Intelligenz' (2020) *Neue Juristische Wochenschrift* 2142.

[117] M Herberger (n 116); M Valta and J Vasel (n 116).

Electronic Engineers) drew up a so-called Code of Ethics, a guideline for ethical coding, in June 2020, which is intended to anchor freedom protection already one stage before the legal risk classification, namely already in the design of the respective AI software.[118] Data protection is treated here – albeit by an interest group that is not democratically legitimised in this respect – through software design as a countermodel to a subsequent official regulation of risks.

### *iii. The Draft for a German Online Access Law 2.0*

In contrast to the regulatory frameworks described at the EU level, the national legislature has so far tended towards subject-specific individual regulations with extensive powers to issue ordinances, ie, a sectoral regulatory regime based on the division of labour. Regulations on digital administration are spread across federal and state administrative procedural law (eg, paragraphs 35a and 71e of the Administrative Procedure Act (VwVfG)),[119] eGovernment laws, data protection laws, specialised laws, the Onlinezugangsgesetz (Online Access Act) and the Registermodernisierungsgesetz (Register Modernisation Act).

So far, these regulations have not had an effective effect on the degree of digitisation of public administration. The deadline set in the Online Access Act for creating a cross-federal-state network of administrative access portals with universally accessible applications, so-called online services, by the end of 2022 will not be met.[120] The Online Access Act has not yet proven its worth or, to put it another way, it is dysfunctional. One of the reasons for this is that the federal legislature misjudged the ability of the federal, state (Länder) and local governments to act in a technically coordinated manner, the lack of domestic interoperability due to inadequate standardisation, and the persistence of state and local IT service providers.

Sharing this finding, the new German government is currently preparing a so-called Online Access Act 2.0. The specific content of this legislation is still open, and a draft bill has not yet been presented. However, the Federal Ministry of the Interior, which is in charge of the project, has for the first time informally announced the involvement of the federal states and local authorities in the drafting of the bill, independently of the formal participation procedures, in the constitutionally established federal-state committee of the IT Planning Council (IT-Planungsrat). This will involve a comprehensive reform of the written form requirements and

[118] www.ieee.org/about/corporate/governance/p7-8.html.

[119] Verwaltungsverfahrensgesetz in der Fassung der Bekanntmachung vom 23 Januar 2003 (BGBl I, 102), zuletzt geändert durch Artikel 24 Absatz 3 des Gesetzes vom 25 Juni 2021 (BGBl I, 2154).

[120] Prüfungsmitteilung des Bundesrechnungshofs vom 17 September 2021 (www.bundesrechnungshof.de/de/veroeffentlichungen/produkte/pruefungsmitteilungen/2021/umsetzung-des-ozg-in-den-ressorts) sowie dessen Bemerkung vom 5.3.2022 (www.bundesrechnungshof.de/de/veroeffentlichungen/produkte/bemerkungen-jahresberichte/jahresberichte/2021-ergaenzungsband/einzelplanbezogene-pruefungsergebnisse/bundesministerium-des-innern-und-fuer-heimat/2021-43).

thus also a reform of the Administrative Procedure Act, which many have been requesting for a long time. In addition, Article 91c of the Grundgesetz (Basic Law) does not answer the question of whether and to what extent certain procedural and organisational standards for digital administration in the federal states can be unilaterally prescribed by the federal government. There is also the question of whether a constitutional amendment might be necessary in this respect.

Regarding the relevant question of the regulatory approach, it can be stated independently of this: even sector-specific legislation based on the division of labour does not protect the legislator from regulatory blunders. Only what is understood in the subject matter and can be regulated at all can be regulated. The question therefore arises as to how the legislator can achieve a better understanding of the subject matter to be regulated.

## B. Selected Instruments for Improving the Regulatory Framework.

Law-making can be supported organisationally, scientifically and procedurally.

### *i. Constitutional Approach to Digital Governance through Article 91c GG*

One way to support the legislature in understanding the facts to be regulated is to introduce cooperative elements and institutionalise a distributed knowledge base.

Article 91c, paragraph 1 of the Basic Law and the state treaty between the Federal Government and the Länder based on it install the IT-Planungsrat (IT Planning Council)[121] as an instrument of state organisation for improving the practicability of legislation in the area of digitisation. The starting point here is the assumption that the prerequisite for digital administrative processes in a federal state with decentralised administrative organisation is cross-level information technology cooperation between the federal and state governments. This assumption is largely undisputed, but there is still no consensus on the specific form this information technology cooperation should take. In its 2021 annual report, for example, the Nationaler Normenkontrollrat (National Standards Control Council) noted with regard to the functioning of the IT Planning Council that 'complicated structures and regulations' bring the principle of cooperative law and standard setting based on the division of labour 'to its limits – also with regard to future development requirements'.[122]

[121] www.it-planungsrat.de.

[122] Jahresbericht des Nationalen Normenkontrollrats, www.normenkontrollrat.bund.de/resource/blob/300864/1959268/dfbaf1cf4066255b7c902e4000bb56c9/210916-jahresbericht-data.pdf.

In its initial considerations for a so-called Onlinezugangsgesetz (OZG) 2.0 (Single Digital Gateway), the new federal government took this finding as an opportunity to raise the constitutional question once again of whether the organisational sovereignty of the Länder might need to be restricted more strongly and Article 91c of the Basic Law adapted in this respect. In the view of the federal government, the constitutional instrument of voluntary cooperation has proven to be inadequate.

### *ii. A Scientific Approach to Systematisation*

In addition to the constitutional and organisational framework to be created by the legislature, legal science can also make a contribution to the appropriate regulation of digitisation. Its very own task is to systematise the law. Legal science can and should support law-makers by identifying layers of data processing law and systematising the specialised law that has been dispersed to date. Various attempts have been made to describe a 'system of digital administrative law' or 'building blocks of digital administrative law'. Three regulatory areas can be considered in a layered model:

- public data processing law;
- digital infrastructure law; and
- the law governing the regulation of the digital economy.

These layers build on each other and overlap in parts. To varying degrees, they are determined by EU law and have been shaped by constitutional law. Preparing these layers or overarching fields of regulatory action could help prevent singular legislative additions and incomplete partial regulations.

To the extent that science identifies regulatory gaps and proposes specific additions, scientific system building becomes scientific codification. The ReNEAUL project described above is a prominent example here.

### *iii. The Toolbox Approach: Proceduralisation and Dynamisation*

Not in conflict with, but clearly distinct from, the above-mentioned overarching organisational and systematisation approaches are considerations that focus on a more participatory, procedural and dynamic generation of law.

#### a. Approaches at the EU Level

The European Commission, as a legal harmonisation body accustomed to dealing with different legal cultures, has been addressing the issue of good law-making for years. The Regulatory Fitness and Performance Programme (REFIT)[123]

[123] ec.europa.eu/info/law/law-making-process/evaluating-and-improving-existing-laws/refit-making-eu-law-simpler-less-costly-and-future-proof_en.

was launched in 2012 to simplify European law and reduce enforcement costs. The Commission provides an overview of its simplification and administrative burden reduction efforts through an annual effort survey. REFIT is complemented by the 'Fit for Future' platform,[124] a high-level group of experts from the Member States, the Committee of the Regions and the European Economic and Social Committee, as well as other stakeholders representing businesses and non-governmental organisations. Their purpose is to support the Commission in improving EU law.

One outcome of these participatory efforts is the 'Better Regulation' guidelines published by the EU Commission in 2021.[125] According to these guidelines, the aim is to create legislation that achieves its objectives and at the same time is easy to comply with and can be implemented with as little effort as possible. The Commission proposes a comprehensive toolbox for this purpose:[126] impact assessments address the problems to be addressed, the objectives to be achieved and the trade-offs to be considered, the options for action and their potential impacts. Stakeholder engagement supports this work throughout the legislative cycle. Compliance tools support Member States in implementation. Comprehensive evaluations and so-called fitness checks involve a thorough analysis of the way in which existing legislation has been implemented to verify that it is effective, coherent and actually adds value.

This so-called toolbox approach is increasingly finding its way into national discussions on better regulation in the area of digitisation.[127]

### b. Approaches at the National Level

At the national (German) level, the Nationaler Normenkontrollrat has long called for greater involvement of external expertise in legislation (practice-oriented legislation and 'better legislation').[128] The discussion about integrating expertise via expert commissions, experimentation rooms, digitisation labs and now digitisation checks has a long tradition in Germany, without the legislative process having actually undergone any significant institutional development to date.

German legislation is only slowly beginning to make structured use of the instruments of participation and evaluation in particular. In this respect, the regulatory subject of digitisation and, not least, data protection law are drivers of development. This also applies to innovation and crisis topics such as the COVID-19

[124] ec.europa.eu/info/law/law-making-process/evaluating-and-improving-existing-laws/refit-making-eu-law-simpler-less-costly-and-future-proof/fit-future-platform-f4f_en.

[125] ec.europa.eu/info/law/law-making-process/planning-and-proposing-law/better-regulation-why-and-how/better-regulation-guidelines-and-toolbox_de.

[126] ec.europa.eu/info/law/law-making-process/planning-and-proposing-law/better-regulation-why-and-how/better-regulation-guidelines-and-toolbox_de.

[127] O Lepsius, 'Gesetzesstruktur im Wandel' (2019) *Juristische Schulung* 14.

[128] www.normenkontrollrat.bund.de/nkr-de/bessere-rechtsetzung-buerokratieabbau.

pandemic and climate protection. By way of an example, we should again recall the Federal Constitutional Court in its decisions on the Bundesnotbremse I und II (Federal Emergency Brake I and II)[129] and the Federal Climate Protection Act,[130] in which the question of the degree of participatory involvement of third parties in the legislative process was raised. In its assessment of the so-called Federal Emergency Brake, the Federal Constitutional Court stipulated the involvement of virological expertise.[131] In the case of the Climate Protection Act, the federal legislature was required to conduct a much more comprehensive fact-finding process.[132] However, there is no uniform concept for the involvement of external expertise that goes beyond previous legislative practice.

So far, the involvement of municipal, local enforcement experts has also not been sufficiently institutionalised, at least at the federal level. A well-known deficit with regard to the quality of legislative procedures, but one that has become much more pronounced in the past two legislative periods, is the inadequate participation of the German Kommunalen Spitzenverbände (associations for municipalities and regions) in practice. In contrast to the rights of participation of the German municipal associations at the state (Länder) level, which are regularly anchored in state constitutional law or statute, as well as additional constitutionally established consultation procedures in various federal states, the rights of participation of the German associations for municipalities and regions at the federal level result normatively only from paragraphs 41, 44 and 47 of the Joint Rules of the Gemeinsame Geschäftsordnung der Bundesministerien (GGO) (Procedure of the Federal Ministries), as well as from paragraph 66, section 2, paragraph 69, section 5 and paragraph 70 of the Geschäftsordnung des Deutschen Bundestages (GO BT) (Rules of Procedure of the German Bundestag).[133] In view of the vast majority of administrative contacts at the local level, which have already implemented a wide variety of individual digital solutions, this lack of attention to municipal, local expertise justifies considerable regulatory deficits.

In addition to the issue of stakeholder and expert group participation, the instrument of evaluation is also coming more into focus in German legislation. In its 2010 decision on the Sozialgesetzbuch II – SGB II (Social Code),[134] the Federal Constitutional Court commented for the first time on so-called evidence-based

[129] German Federal Constitutional Court decision 1 BvR 986/21 et al (sales area restrictions) of 20 May 2021 and decision 1 BvR 781/21 et al (night-time exit restrictions) of 5 May 2021.

[130] German Federal Constitutional Court decision 1 BvR 781/21 et al (night-time exit restrictions) of 24 March 2021, 1 BvR 2656/18 et al.

[131] German Federal Constitutional Court decision 1 BvR 986/21 et al (sales area restrictions) of 20 May 2021 and decision 1 BvR 781/21 et al (night-time exit restrictions) of 5 May 2021.

[132] German Federal Constitutional Court decision 1 BvR 2656/18 et al of 24 March 2021.

[133] Geschäftsordnung des Deutschen Bundestages vom 25 Juni 1980 (BGBl I, 1237), zuletzt geändert durch den Beschluss d Bundestages vom 8 Juli 2022.

[134] Das Zweite Buch Sozialgesetzbuch – Grundsicherung für Arbeitsuchende – in der Fassung der Bekanntmachung vom 13 Mai 2011 (BGBl I S 850, 2094), zuletzt geändert durch Artikel 1 des Gesetzes vom 19 Juni 2022 (BGBl I S. 921).

legislation. The legislator had to take precautions to react promptly to changes in the economic framework conditions, such as price increases or increases in excise taxes, in order to ensure that current needs are met at all times.[135] In this respect, the SGB II legislation marks a watershed in German legislative technique by enshrining legislative evaluation in law for the first time.[136] Subsequently, the Federal Constitutional Court has imposed an obligation on the legislature to monitor and amend many areas of law, from telecommunications to criminal law. Many specialised laws dealing with information technology and data privacy now contain evaluation obligations.

However, evidence-based legislation is a double-edged sword:[137] on the one hand, it aims to ensure the effectiveness of laws; on the other hand, monitoring and improvement obligations cause an effort that does not always seem affordable. In practice, therefore, evaluation obligations often run dry.[138]

## IV. Summary and Results: The Limits of Legal Control

The era of abstract-general codifications designed to be resistant to change seems to be over with regard to the extremely dynamic development of digitisation.[139] Codificatory full regulations are increasingly being replaced by a regulatory strategy that uses laws in interaction with sublegislative norms as a form of law-making based on the mutual division of responsibilities and involves other norm creators – government, authorities and courts.

For legal technology, this means a greater differentiation between final and conditional programming with an emphasis on final-oriented, outcome-based law-making.

Particularly in the area of innovation and technology, the importance of participatory, procedural and dynamic law-making will increase. The participation of stakeholders and external experts, as well as the binding evaluation of legislation, will be driven not least by European law – despite all its shortcomings to date.

Furthermore, the relationship between state regulation and private standardisation work will have to be re-examined, especially in technology-driven areas of regulation. This concerns possible cooperation between public and private standardisation bodies, such as the IT Planning Council and the German Institute

[135] German Federal Constitutional Court decision 1 BvL 10/09 et al of 9 February 2010.
[136] A Steinbach, 'Rationale Gesetzgebung' (2020) *Zeitschrift für Rechtspolitik* 91.
[137] ibid.
[138] ibid.
[139] O Lepsius (n 128).

for Standardisation (DIN),[140] as well as the binding effect of private norms and standards and liability issues.

As a result, it is always a question of legal culture as to whether law-makers tend towards abstract-general approaches to standardisation or selective, procedural and dynamic regulation. For the European legal area, at any rate, the first signs of a cultural change towards more proceduralisation and dynamisation are emerging.[141] And a clear trend can be observed to attach greater importance to the multi-stakeholder approach in law-making. Especially in volatile and complex legal matters, law-making can no longer be organised purely by the state, but is dependent on the structured involvement of external private and – depending on the state organisation – municipal expertise.

In contrast, the ReNEUAL project – the starting point of this study – was and is a purely scientific codification project, which initially made the EU's administrative law and now, within the framework of the continuation project ReNEUAL 2.0, administrative law in the Member States the subject of reform proposals. In view of the lack of political effectiveness of the reform considerations so far, there is much to be said for making the multi-stakeholder approach fruitful here as well and moving away from a purely scientific codification towards an evidence-based open law-making process.

[140] www.din.de/de.
[141] O Lepsius (n 128).

# 15

# Comparative Analysis

FELIX UHLMANN

## I. Introduction

Every modern legal order needs a set of general rules to enforce administrative law. These rules are 'general' because they apply regardless of the specific subject area. They impose principles of action, of procedure and of organisation of the authorities, and form the core of administrative law.

The legal basis of such rules may be quite diverse. Common law is obviously an important legal source in countries with a common law tradition, but, despite general perceptions, legislation is central to administrative law, too.[1] In typical civil law countries – for the sake of this chapter we also use the term 'civil law countries' for countries with a Nordic law tradition, for which there is some debate as to how well they fit into the dichotomy of civil law and common law countries[2] – but also in the EU,[3] there is a mixture of judicial development and selective interventions by the legislator. In Switzerland, for example, substantive principles of administrative action are strongly influenced by the case law of the Federal Supreme Court and other courts, while procedural law has largely been codified, both at the federal level and the cantonal (state) level.[4] There are also countries in which principles of general administrative law have been converted

[1] For the UK, see in this book S Nason, 'Codification of Administrative Law in the United Kingdom: Beyond the Common Law', sections I and II; for the US, see EL Rubin, 'The United States: Systematic But Incomplete Codification', section II.

[2] See U Bernitz, 'What is Scandinavian Law? Concept, Characteristics, Future' in P Wahlgren (ed), *Scandinavian Studies in Law Volume 50 – What is Scandinavian Law? – Social Private Law* (Stockholm, Stockholm University, 2007) especially 17 ff, 28 f.

[3] See in this book M Heintzen, 'Codification of Administrative Law in Germany and the European Union', section II.

[4] See in this book F Uhlmann, 'Codification of Administrative Law in Switzerland', sections II.A, II.B and II.E.

into a comprehensive codification, in particular the Netherlands (Algemene wet bestuursrecht or General Administrative Law Act (GALA)).[5]

Which rules are codified at which level depends partly on a conscious systematic decision. As we see in the chapters of this volume, in many countries fundamental principles that (also) bind the administration are laid down in the constitution.[6] Different settings will be discussed below in section IV.B. What is codified and on which level can be explained in part by tradition, but in some cases, it appears rather random. For example, in Switzerland the institute of revocation of administrative law decisions has largely been developed on the basis of court practice, while the related institute of revisions has been regulated in procedural Acts;[7] still, there are also cantons which have expressly legislated on the revocation of administrative law decisions, and a right to a revision is accepted by courts under specific conditions even in the absence of an expressive legal provision. The boundaries between uncodified and codified are not drawn with precision. Similar examples can be found for Switzerland in the areas of state liability for false official information or for the delegation of administrative tasks to private persons.[8] Also, in the area of administrative organisation, the scope and level of legislative details vary considerably between Swiss cantons and the Confederation. There are similar findings in many other countries – for example, in Austria there are mainly procedural laws on administrative decisions and court proceedings, while other areas such as administrative ordinances and other forms of action are far less codified, as Lachmayer reports.[9]

To date, there has been little comparative research on the practical consequences that arise from the different degrees of codification of general administrative law. Does codification increase predictability and legal certainty? Does codification lead to an 'ossification' of general administrative law? To what degree does the

[5] The GALA (English translation) can be found on the websites of various public authorities with a partly international audience, such as the tax authorities (www.belastingdienst.nl). The version in English contains all tranches, but is not totally up to date. All Dutch legislation and regulation can be found on the governmental website: wetten.overheid.nl. One can find all parliamentary papers on the codification of the GALA at: www.pgawb.nl. See in this book Y Schuurmans, T Barkhuysen and W den Ouden, 'Codification of Administrative Law in the Netherlands', section II.A.

[6] For Austria, see in this book K Lachmayer, 'Codification of Administrative Law in Austria', section III.A.i; for Belgium, see S De Somer and I Opdebeek, 'Codification of Belgian Administrative Law: "Nothing is Written"', section II.C; for France, see D Costa, 'Codification of Administrative Law: A French Oxymoron', section II.A; for Germany, see M Heintzen (n 3) section I.B.i; for Italy, see R Caranta, 'Administrative Proceedings in Italy', section II; for Norway, see JCF Nordrum, 'Codification of Norwegian Administrative Law', section III.A; for Sweden, see J Reichel and M Ribbing, 'Codification of Administrative Law in Sweden', sections II.B and V.C; for Switzerland, see F Uhlmann (n 4) section II.A.

[7] See U Häfelin, G Müller and F Uhlmann, *Allgemeines Verwaltungsrecht* (Zurich, Dike, 2020) fns 1226 ff.

[8] For the doctrine of legitimate expectations, see F Uhlmann, 'Administrative Law' in M Thommen (ed), *Introduction to Swiss Law* (Zurich, Sui Generis, 2022) 167 ff; U Häfelin, G Müller and F Uhlmann (n 7) fns 624 ff. For the delegation of administrative tasks to private persons, see U Häfelin, G Müller and F Uhlmann (n 7) fns 1817 ff.

[9] K Lachmayer (n 6) sections III.B and III.E.

Constitution shape administrative law? Which areas of general administrative law are suitable for codification, which are not, and why not?

# II. The Definition of General Administrative Law

## A. Approaches to General Administrative Law

The chapters in this book show how different administrative law is understood from country to country.[10] There are also a variety of ways how to address the very question.[11] This following question is also telling in terms of how administrative law is approached: *as (positive) rules for (good) governmental action or as (negative) behaviour warranting court intervention*?

De Somer and Opdebeek have taken the path of defining general administrative law in Belgium through one of the *trias politica*, namely the executive. As they explain, this is a good starting point, but has its flaws. They see the weaknesses of the definition in the following aspects: first, it presupposes that the definition and the demarcation of 'the executive' is evident, second, administrative law (in most of the countries) may in specific circumstances also regulate activities of the legislator and judiciary; thirdly, administrative law sometimes may not apply to the executive when it contributes to the legislative or judicial function; and, finally, the executive assumes a large variety of tasks that go far beyond 'executing' statutory law.[12]

As Costa explains for France, general administrative law can be defined by an *organic*, a *purposive* and a *material criterion*. The organic criterion is fulfilled if a person in charge of the national or local government is involved. This criterion is very similar to the definition of De Somer and Opdebeek. In addition, the purposive criterion is fulfilled if the intended purpose of an action is a 'public service or a mission of general interest'. Lastly, it can be defined by the material criterion

[10] For Australia, see in this book J Boughey, 'The "Codification" of Administrative Law in Australia', section II; for Austria, see K Lachmayer (n 6) section II; for Belgium, see S De Somer and I Opdebeek (n 6) section I; for Canada, see P Issalys, 'A Persistent Taste for Diversity: Codification of Administrative Law in Canada', section I; for France, see D Costa (n 6) section I; for Germany, see M Heintzen (n 3) section I.A; for Italy, see R Caranta (n 6) section I; for the Netherlands, see Y Schuurmans, T Barkhuysen and W den Ouden (n 5) section I; for Norway, see JCF Nordrum (n 6) section I; for Sweden, see J Reichel and M Ribbing (n 6) section II; for Switzerland, see F Uhlmann (n 4) section I; for the UK, see S Nason (n 1) section II; for the US, see EL Rubin (n 1) section I.

[11] Does one look at what is done by (the lower level of) the executive branch, concentrating on the particularities to be found, does one analyse court decisions dealing with the subject matter of administrative law or turn to government publications or legal scholarship – or, of course, to a code as we see in the Netherlands, which is the sole country to have a code explicitly regulating general administrative law as an object?.

[12] S De Somer and I Opdebeek (n 6) section I. A similar approach defining administrative law over the organic criterion of the administration is known in Austria (see K Lachmayer (n 6) section II.A.ii), Germany (see M Heintzen (n 3) section I.A.i) and the US (see EL Rubin (n 1) section I).

of public authority, such as taxing power, enforcement authority, public policy or unilateral action.[13]

This shows the difficulties of defining general administrative law in a positive way. However, circumscribing it via court intervention is not easier either, as the example of Australia shows. As Boughey reports, there is no consensus in Australia as to what constitutes administrative law besides the four central components: judicial review, merits review, ombudsmen and freedom of information laws: 'All additions are defensible, as each of these laws and institutions contributes to the administrative law enterprise of government accountability and transparency. However, if administrative law is defined as broadly as any law or institution concerned with government accountability and transparency, then this list should be even broader – indeed, endless.' Therefore, it is impossible to neatly map the boundaries of administrative law in Australia.[14]

It is noteworthy that one can find these different approaches in one sole country, as in Canada. The common law approach in the Anglophone provinces and at the federal level follows a logic of a '"defensive", "red-light" approach to the subject, emphasising the protection of individual rights and a degree of diffidence in the face of government intervention'. The civilian approach, prevalent in Quebec 'suggests sensitivity to the need for government intervention on behalf of the public interest and therefore a "positive", "green-light" approach to "le droit administratif" that includes confidence in the ability of rules to prevent abuse or misfeasance by power-holders'.[15]

For the sake of completeness, it should be noted that it is not only in Canada that we find different administrative laws in one country. Generally, federal countries like Australia, Austria, Belgium, Canada, Germany, Switzerland and the US know administrative law both on the federal level and the state level.[16] The differences vary. In Switzerland, federal administrative law often serves as an example and the Swiss Supreme Court has derived administrative principles from the Constitution that are also the law of the land in the cantons.[17] In Germany some laws of the Länder are literally in accordance with the federal law, and some of the laws even contain dynamic references to the federal law.[18] However, it is not only in federal states and especially in Canada that there are different systems of administrative

[13] D Costa (n 6) section I.A. A similar approach to the material criterion using the hierarchical principle is also known in Austria (K Lachmayer (n 6) section II.A.iii) and Germany (M Heintzen (n 3) section I.A.i). Lachmayer mentions that this criteria is only of limited use because of the EU's tendency to set up independent (regulatory) agencies (K Lachmayer (n 6) section II.A.iii; see also below, section II.B).

[14] J Boughey (n 10) section II.

[15] P Issalys (n 10) section I.

[16] For Australia, see J Boughey (n 10) section I; for Austria, see K Lachmayer (n 6) sections III.C and IV.A.ii; for Belgium, see S De Somer and I Opdebeek (n 6) sections I and II; for Canada, see P Issalys (n 10) sections I–IV; for Germany, see M Heintzen (n 3) section I.B.iv; and for Switzerland, see F Uhlmann (n 4) section I.B.

[17] F Uhlmann (n 4) section I.B.

[18] M Heintzen (n 3) section I.A.iii.

law in one country. For example, in Norway there exists a distinction between central secondary legislation and local secondary legislation. The later applies only to a limited geographical area and is often enacted by municipalities.[19] Also worth mentioning is the fact that the EU adds another level for its Member States, which makes the system more complex and can lead to difficulties.[20]

Under many aspects, the understanding of administrative law will shape the legal landscape of this topic. For this reason, the question *who* defines the term 'general administrative law' or, in other words, how one approaches the question is of great importance. A simple way to find out is to turn to textbooks and manuals. Indeed, in all countries covered in this book, general administrative law is part of the curriculum for students. Again, the subjects are different, but there seems to be a need for general rules before approaching more special subjects of administrative law.

Obviously, especially the legislator's – and in the case of common law the court's – understanding of administrative law will shape the legal landscape. As such, the focus can be placed on the courts and tribunals (in the following, the term 'court' is used for both courts and tribunals)[21] – as we see it extensively in the common law world. In the UK, codification of judicial review raises at least the question of amenability to judicial review and the question of the grounds of judicial review, as Nason describes. To date, the source of jurisdiction for conducting most judicial reviews in the UK is common law, despite the statutory provisions on procedural rules.[22]

Another approach tries to create a good administration as we see it in Nordic and other countries. In Sweden, for example, the legislator included in the new Swedish Administrative Procedures Act (APA) 2017[23] several provisions with principles of good administration.[24] Of course, this does not exclude the idea that the legislator deals with legal remedies. The Dutch GALA contains substantial sections on administrative appeals.[25] Yet it is not the starting point of administrative law, but a consequence. The house is built, but it needs caretakers. In the common law system, you start with the caretakers that are also carpenters of the house of administrative law.

Nevertheless, the contradiction is perhaps less strong than it first appears, as the example of Australia shows. As Boughey reports, in Australia there are some common principles, such as the duty to afford procedural fairness and the obligation to act reasonably, which generally apply to administrative powers unless a statute expressly or impliedly limits them. They are often referred to as 'grounds'

[19] JCF Nordrum (n 6) section IV.
[20] K Lachmayer (n 6) section IV.A.ii.
[21] As the distinction between court and tribunal, which is known in some countries, is not relevant for this analysis, it is not made.
[22] S Nason (n 1) section IV.C.
[23] 2017 APA (2017:900).
[24] J Reichel and M Ribbing (n 6) section II.B.
[25] Y Schuurmans, T Barkhuysen and W den Ouden (n 5) section III.C.ii.

of judicial review, although the term 'ground' is misleading as they are not free-standing causes of action. 'They are, in fact, simply common express and implied legal limits on administrative power which interact and overlap with one another, and are highly context-specific … These common limits are listed in sections 5 and 6 of the ADJR Act'.[26]

With this in mind, it is also worth looking at different legal sources. They do not define *general* administrative law – of course, the Netherlands is the exception that confirms the rule[27] – but already the term 'administrative law' is far from obvious. Legal sources may be systematically published in categories such as civil law, penal law and administrative law (as in Switzerland). Rules on enforcement may indirectly qualify administrative law, being part of the duties of an agency ('administration'). Even in countries that do not have the dichotomy between private and public law, there might be a need for classification. In federations, if there is a federal power to enact rules on civil law, the residuum will form public law, including administrative law of the federated units (see below, section VI.B). And obviously, if one introduces administrative courts, the term 'administrative' also includes a legal meaning in defining the competence of the court.

For all these reasons, we will further explore the notion of 'general administrative law' and highlight as far as possible some common ground of the different counties in the next section.

## B. Typical Areas of General Administrative Law

If one tries to boil down general administrative law to one idea, it defines how the administration shall act (if one comes from a positive point) or how it should not act, ie, what is forbidden (if one comes from a negative point; see above, section II.A). The basis for such rules may vary greatly and will be subject of the second part of this analysis. The rail guards of administrative action may come from the constitution, other legal sources, court practice, legal scholarship etc.

Typically, the idea of proper administrative action is concretised by different *principles*, again positive (good administration etc), negative (ultra vires etc) or hybrid in the sense that they are enforced by courts, but also rooted in the understanding of the agency itself (proportionality etc).[28] In the European context it

[26] Administrative Decisions (Judicial Review) Act 1979 (Cth) ('ADJR Act'); J Boughey (n 10) section III.

[27] Y Schuurmans, T Barkhuysen and W den Ouden (n 5) section I.A.

[28] For Australia, see J Boughey (n 10) sections II, III, IV.C and V; for Austria, see K Lachmayer (n 6) section III.A; Belgium, see S De Somer and I Opdebeek (n 6) section II.C; for Canada, see P Issalys (n 10) sections II and III; for France, see D Costa (n 6) sections I.B and II; for Germany, see M Heintzen (n 3) section I.B.i; for Italy, see R Caranta (n 6) section IV; for the Netherlands, see Y Schuurmans, T Barkhuysen and W den Ouden (n 5) sections II–IV; for Norway, see JC Fløysvik Nordrum (n 6) section III; for Sweden, see J Reichel and M Ribbing (n 6) section II.B; for Switzerland, see F Uhlmann (n 4) sections I.A, II.A, II.C and II.D; for the UK, see S Nason (n 1) sections II–IV; for the US, see EL Rubin (n 1) section II.

is interesting to see some trends towards the conversion of these principles, due to the decisions of the European Court of Human Rights (ECtHR) as well as the European Court of Justice (ECJ) (see below, section IV.A).

Distinctive differences are still seen as far as *administrative action* is concerned.[29] Many countries have rules concerning the forms of administrative action.[30] The cornerstone of this logic is the administrative decision (*acte administratif*, Verwaltungsakt, Verfügung etc).[31] It is both a privilege and a burden. It is a privilege as the agency may enforce administrative rules unilaterally. It is a burden as an administrative decision comes with a rat tail of obligations of the agency, most notably the duty to hear a private party before an administrative decision is taken and the duty to give reasons (both typical part of a right to be heard). The very idea of legal protection is often built around the instrument of administrative action, leaving other forms of administrative action underdeveloped as far legal protection is concerned.[32]

Interestingly, Rubin highlights a similar finding for the US, where the Administrative Procedure Act of 1946 (APA) lacks provisions concerning informal adjudications. According to him, this could be explained by the American tendency to focus on particular techniques and protections rather than a comprehensive and systematic overview of administrative practice. Unlike administrative rule-making and administrative adjudication, informal adjudication had no

[29] For Australia, see J Boughey (n 10) sections II–IV; for Austria, see K Lachmayer (n 6) section III.B; Belgium, see S De Somer and I Opdebeek (n 6) section II.B; for Canada, see P Issalys (n 10) section III; for France, see D Costa (n 6) section II; for Germany, see M Heintzen (n 3) section I.B.ii; for Italy, see R Caranta (n 6) section V; for the Netherlands, see Y Schuurmans, T Barkhuysen and W den Ouden (n 5) sections II.A and II.G; for Norway, see JC Fløysvik Nordrum (n 6) section IV; for Sweden, see J Reichel and M Ribbing (n 6) section IV.B; for Switzerland, see F Uhlmann (n 4) sections II.B and II.C; for the UK, see S Nason (n 1) sections IV and V; for the US, see EL Rubin (n 1) sections III and IV. For a comparative analysis of administrative action in Europe, see T Gross, 'Grundelemente eines handlungsformbezogenen Verwaltungsrechtsvergleichs in Europa' (2021) *Archiv des öffentlichen Rechts* 543.

[30] See, eg, Germany: Verwaltungsverfahrensgesetz in der Fassung der Bekanntmachung vom 23 Januar 2003 (BGBl I, 102), zuletzt geändert durch Artikel 24 Absatz 3 des Gesetzes vom 25. Juni 2021 (BGBl I, 2154); for Italy, see l 7 agosto 1990, n 241 *Nuove norme in materia di procedimento amministrativo e di diritto di accesso ai documenti amministrativi*; for the Netherlands, see the GALA (n 5); for Norway, see Lov 10. Februar 1967 om behandlingsmåten i forvaltningssaker (forvaltningsloven); for Sweden, see Förvaltningslagen (2017:900); for Switzerland, see Bundesgesetz über das Verwaltungsverfahren (Verwaltungsverfahrensgesetz, VwVG) vom 20 Dezember 1968 (SR 172.021) (Federal Act on Administrative Procedure (Administrative Procedure Act, APA) (text available in English)); for the US, see Administrative Procedure Act of 1946 Pub L 79-404, 60 Stat 237 (1946), codified at 5 USC §§ 551 ff.

[31] For Austria, see K Lachmayer (n 6) section III.B.i; for Belgium, see S De Somer and I Opdebeek (n 6) section II.C; for Canada, see P Issalys (n 10) section III; for France, see D Costa (n 6) section II.D; for Germany, see M Heintzen (n 3) section I.B.ii; for Italy, see R Caranta (n 6) section V; for the Netherlands, see Y Schuurmans, T Barkhuysen and W den Ouden (n 5) sections I.A and III.C.ii; for Norway, see JCF Nordrum (n 6) section IV; for Sweden, see J Reichel and M Ribbing (n 6) section IV.B.ii; for Switzerland, see F Uhlmann (n 4) section II.B; for the US, see EL Rubin (n 1) sections III–IV.

[32] For the Swiss context, see F Uhlmann (n 8) 171 ff; F Uhlmann, 'Administrative Procedure' in M Thommen (ed), *Introduction to Swiss Law* (Zurich, Sui Generis, 2022) 188 ff.

model to follow. This can be explained historically, since executive action in the Middle Ages belonged to the prerogatives of the king, who was subject to neither political nor legal control. According to Rubin, the drafters of the US Constitution perhaps 'did not place any specific, substantive constraints on presidential action … because they had no basis in the English governmental tradition from which such constraints could be derived'. In his opinion the same is probably true for the President's agents, that is, the executive departments.[33] This historical view could perhaps also help to explain some legal deficits in other countries.

Still, newer rules on administrative law often include administrative rule-making, real (factual) acts (eg, information for the public), private law contracts, administrative law contracts etc.[34] The alternative to administrative decisions, mostly seen in common law countries but also before the ECtHR, is to concentrate on the *substance* of the administrative action, and hence typically turn to the question of whether individual rights have been infringed.[35]

Another major topic, which is dealt with by almost all jurisdictions as part of general administrative law, is *administrative organisation*.[36] An exception to this is the Netherlands; as Schuurmans, Barkhuysen and den Ouden report, 'the organisation of the administration mainly falls outside the scope of administrative law'.[37] The administrative organisation is in many countries traditionally ruled by the hierarchy principle.[38] But, as Lachmayer points out for the EU Member States, the hierarchical characteristic of administration lost much of its importance and influence due to the more and more independent (regulatory) agencies established by EU law.[39]

Apart from these three areas (principles, administrative action versus rights, and administrative organisation), it is difficult to find common ground for what constitutes general administrative law. Some countries include administrative procedure and appeals (rather than just administrative action) state liability, data protection and access to public records, civil servants, state monopolies and state

[33] EL Rubin (n 1) section III.

[34] For France, see D Costa (n 6) section III.C; for Norway, see JCF Nordrum (n 6) section IV; for the US, see EL Rubin (n 1) sections III and IV; see also Austria and Sweden, where some forms of administrative actions are determined by the constitution: K Lachmayer(n 6) section III.B.i; and J Reichel and M Ribbing (n 6) section IV.B.i.

[35] For the UK, see S Nason (n 1) section III.C; for the US, see EL Rubin (n 1) section III.

[36] Austria: K Lachmayer (n 6) sections II.C and III.C; for Belgium, see S De Somer and I Opdebeek (n 6) sections I and II.D; for Canada, see P Issalys (n 10) sections II and III; for France, see D Costa (n 6) section II; for Germany, see M Heintzen (n 3) sections I.A.i and I.B.iv; for Italy, see R Caranta (n 6) section III; for Norway, see JCF Nordrum (n 6) section V; for Sweden, see J Reichel and M Ribbing (n 6) sections II.A, IV.A and VI; for Switzerland, see F Uhlmann (n 4) section I.B; for the UK, see S Nason (n 1) section III.

[37] Y Schuurmans, T Barkhuysen and W den Ouden (n 5) section II.G.

[38] For Austria, see K Lachmayer (n 6) section II.A.iii; Belgium, see S De Somer and I Opdebeek (n 6) section II.D; for France, see D Costa(n 6) section II.D; for Italy, see R Caranta (n 6) section I; for Norway, see JCF Nordrum (n 6) section V; for Switzerland, see F Uhlmann (n 4) section I.B.

[39] K Lachmayer (n 6) section II.A.iii.

enterprises, public procurement (and other private law contracts), expropriation, (spatial) planning etc, while others do not. The choice is often explained by tradition and rarely follows a distinctive plan or concept. This should be borne in mind if one turns to the question of codification.

# III. Forms of Codification

## A. Codes

There is no generally accepted definition of a code in legislative theory. In the UK, codifying 'is understood to involve bringing together statutory law on a single subject into one legal instrument without substantially changing the boundaries between statute law and case law'. Within this scope, it can be distinguished between codification which comes with a substantial reform of the codified area and a mere consolidation.[40] In Canada and similarly in Belgium the word 'codification' has other meanings besides the following two: first, 'formulating in a single, orderly, systematic and coherent enactment all the essential rules forming a fairly extensive branch of the legal system'; and, second, 'formulating in a legislative enactment some rule or set of rules previously recognised in the common law'.[41] The second meaning is also the common understanding of 'codification' in Australia.[42] As Issalys points out, the first meaning describes the defining feature of so-called 'civilian' legal orders.[43] In line with this understanding, many countries with a long tradition of civil codes use codification as a tool to streamline and systemise a certain area of law.[44] In this understanding, codes need a 'vision' and are not just a pragmatic approach to solve problems on a day-to day basis. As Costa points out, in France the pedagogic aim of making law more accessible and intelligible is what distinguishes codification from ordinary legislative writing.[45] The same holds true for Italy, where it is not the practice of codification that is new, but the word 'code'.[46] Both in France and in Italy, codification can mean on the one hand a mere consolidation of existing rules or on the other hand an innovative substantial reform, as in the UK.[47]

Regardless, a common feature of codification in all countries that it is an instrument of Parliament, notwithstanding that the process may be initiated,

[40] S Nason (n 1) section IV.

[41] For Canada, see P Issalys (n 10) section III; for Belgium, see S De Somer and I Opdebeek (n 6) section III.A.

[42] J Boughey (n 10) section II.A.

[43] For Canada, see P Issalys (n 10) section III.

[44] For Austria, see K Lachmayer (n 6) section IV.A; for France, see D Costa (n 6) section III.C; for Italy, see R Caranta (n 6) section VI.

[45] D Costa (n 6) section III.C.

[46] R Caranta (n 6) section VI. Previously the expression 'testi unici' was used in Italy.

[47] For France, see D Costa (n 6) section III.C; for Italy, see R Caranta (n 6) section VI.

executed and even dominated by government or some other state actor. It is a deliberate choice to create and shape administrative law. It is an 'abstract' approach to administrative law, an *approach of rules* in contrast to an *approach by cases*. It is interesting to see that even in the civil law countries, administrative law often forms some sanctuary for a case-based approach to law (see below, section IV.D). On a very general level, one may state that general administrative law is clearly less codified than other areas of law – of course again, the Netherlands being the exception in this pattern requiring codification of general administrative law even on the basis of the Constitution.[48]

## B. Legislation by Parliament (Primary Legislation)

If codes are the abstract approach to administrative law, it is quite obvious that they come not from the courts, but from the legislator. We understand 'legislation by Parliament' to be any legislation formally enacted by Parliament. However, this does not mean that Parliament must be the initiator, drafter or author of the legislative text. On the contrary, the government, legal scholarship or private actors often play an important role in the process of legislation by Parliament, as will be explained below in sections III.B.i and III.B.ii. It should be noted that the very concept and extent of general administrative law, as a distinct part of administrative law as a whole, are quite fluid. The legislator does not enact 'general' administrative law (outside the Netherlands)[49] by using the very term, but in every country one can find rules enacted by the legislator that can qualify as general administrative law, depending on the very diverse definition of the subject. This holds especially true for administrative procedure, including the organisation of administrative courts and such. Here, we often find legislative interventions (and it needs to be discussed why this might be the case; see below, section V.B).[50] Similarly, Acts on state liability, access to public records, civil servants etc will not be labelled as 'general' by the legislator, but may fall under the notion of general administrative law as used by the courts, agencies and legal scholarship in this country (or certainly in others).

It may also be the case that an important area of 'special' administrative law also gains widespread acceptance for other situations, such as by analogy, so it becomes 'general' in the sense that it leaves the subject matter (scope) it was originally designed for (see below, section IV.E). The original source of such a

[48] Y Schuurmans, T Barkhuysen and W den Ouden (n 5) section III.A.

[49] ibid section I.

[50] For Australia, see J Boughey (n 10) section IV; for Austria, see K Lachmayer (n 6) sections IV.C and IV.D; for France, see D Costa (n 6) section II.B; for Germany, see M Heintzen (n 3) section I.B.iii; for Italy, see R Caranta (n 6) section I; for Norway, see JCF Nordrum (n 6) section VI; for Sweden, see J Reichel and M Ribbing (n 6) section IV.C; for Switzerland, see F Uhlmann (n 4) section II.B; for the UK, see S Nason (n 1) section III; for the US, see EL Rubin (n 1) section III.

rule is legislative, but it has become at least hybrid, because the expanse must come from other actors, namely courts. One cannot speak of codification in the sense that it was designed by the legislator as general rule on administrative law. Codification, in the sense defined in this work, is an *intentional intervention of the legislator* to support or change a certain practice or an older rule on general administrative law, not necessarily using the term 'general'.

Legislative interventions may be in favour of or in contrast to what was the legal situation beforehand. The question of codification can be studied in its 'purest' form when no changes in substance are intended by the legislator. Here, the intervention can only be justified by some sort of 'technical' improvement of the legal basis. The accessibility and readability for citizens are typical suspects (see below, section V.A), but others (eg, legitimacy) also come to mind (see below, section V.C). There are also possible drawbacks (eg, ossification), which are often neglected (see below, section V.B). Such questions may also play a role when the legislator intends to change the rules in place, but, of course, here the intent to codify is overlaid by intentions in substance. It is not the form that matters – the legislator merely uses its preferred instrument, the law – but the content. Of course, we also find reforms that contain both, ie, the intent of strengthening the legal basis (form), but also to introduce selected amendments (substance). All would qualify as 'codification' in the sense of the word used in this text.

### *i. Influence on the Primary Legislation by the Government*

If one speaks of the legislator, one must bear in mind that it often acts on the proposition of government or with the support of the government. Primary legislation in this area is rarely the outcome of Parliament acting of its own motion. This is not a defect, but is inherently built into the parliamentary system. Parliament must concentrate on the politically sensitive issues. It is also the government that has typically more resources than Parliament and is maybe also closer to the agencies affected by such reforms. This holds especially true for 'technical' areas that often form the bulk of administrative law – which does not mean that administrative law is not 'political'. The reforms of many countries show the contrary.[51] Still, a typical minor reform of the administrative procedure will pass unnoticed by the political parties.

[51] See eg, the effects of the Aarhus Convention for Sweden (J Reichel and M Ribbing (n 6) section V.D). See also the popular initiatives in Switzerland regarding highly disputed administrative matters (see below, section IV.B).

### *ii. Impact on the Primary Legislation by Legal Scholarship and Other Actors*

In Switzerland, it is not only the government that has a big influence on the primary legislation, but also the legal scholarship and private actors. Some codifications were only initiated at the insistence of the legal scholarship and/or private actors; in some cases they even prepared a draft which was eventually passed by the Parliament. For example, the impulse for the codification of administrative procedure at the federal level came from the legal scholarship. In the Zurich canton, different authorities, private organisations and the Zurich law association were pushing for a codification of the administrative procedure on the cantonal level because of a lack of sufficient legal protection. And as a last example, the Schweizerische Gesellschaft für Versicherungssecht (Swiss Society of Insurance Law) prepared a preliminary draft which acted as a basis for the Federal Act on the General Part of Social Insurance Law.[52,53]

In France the legislation process 'is coordinated by the Superior Codification Commission, which is composed of senior officials, including magistrates, parliamentarians (deputies and senators) and scholars, in close contact with the government's General Secretariat'. Further, the process is often facilitated by ministerial or interministerial working groups to which some scholars can, less frequently, participate.[54]

Finally, it should be noted that an influence of legal scholarship or other actors on the legislative process can also result from the appointment of professors or other actors to the position of high-ranking civil servants. This will be discussed below in section IV.D.

## C. Secondary Legislation

One should not overlook the mass of secondary legislation, either expressly delegated or an implicit governmental power to implement and concretise primary legislation. It is possible that the bulk of codification is a task for the government or that the government can be given the power to amend Acts of Parliament, as is the case, for example, in Italy and the UK.[55] For the sake of this text, this does not have to be more specific. It will matter when one analyses the legitimacy of a codification and when one looks at the institutional question, ie, the relationship between Parliament, the government and the courts (see below, section V.C). For most of the other aspects (legal certainty, ossification etc), it is the contrast between case law and abstract rules that is relevant.

[52] Bundesgesetz über den Allgemeinen Teil des Sozialversicherungsrechts (ATSG) vom 6 Oktober 2000 (SR 830.1).

[53] F Uhlmann (n 4) section II.B.

[54] D Costa (n 6) section III.C.

[55] For Italy, see R Caranta (n 6) section VI; for the UK, see S Nason (n 1) section IV.C.

# IV. Other Sources of Administrative Law

## A. European Law

Almost all contributions from European countries emphasise the increasing importance of international law in the recent decades.[56] For EU Member States, EU legislation is most influential. Lachmayer reports: 'However, the greatest impact on Austrian administrative law occurred with the accession to the European Union in 1995. The following 25 years led to a steady and substantial change in administrative organisation, tools and procedures.'[57] Reichel and Ribbing state that 'substantive administrative law has been identified as the fastest-developing legal area in Sweden, at a pace determined mainly by the development within the EU'.[58]

What is especially worth noting in relation to the EU are the right to good administration (Article 41 of the Charter of Fundamental Rights of the European Union (CFR))[59] and the right of access (Article 42 CFR) which apply to all EU institutions, bodies, offices and agencies. The case law of the ECJ has developed a number of general principles pertaining specifically to administrative law.[60]

Besides the EU legislation, the human rights guaranteed in the ECHR also have an impact on administrative law in European countries – in some countries more, in others less.[61] The ECHR has intervened in typical fields of administrative law such as the right to reply, criminal tax proceedings and state liability.[62]

[56] For Austria, see K Lachmayer (n 6) sections I, II.A.iii, II.B, IV.A.ii and IV.E; Belgium, see S De Somer and I Opdebeek (n 6) sections II and III.D.ii; for France, see D Costa (n 6) section II.D; for Germany, see M Heintzen (n 3) section II; for Italy, see R Caranta (n 6) section II; for the Netherlands, see Y Schuurmans, T Barkhuysen and W den Ouden (n 5) section II.F; for Norway, see JCF Nordrum (n 6) sections II.B and VII.D; for Sweden, see J Reichel and M Ribbing (n 6) sections II.A and V.B; for the UK, see S Nason (n 1) section V.C. Switzerland is here the exception to the rule – neither human rights nor contracts with the EU had a major impact on general administrative law (F Uhlmann (n 4) sections II.6 and II.7). See also P Issalys (n 10) section V.

[57] K Lachmayer (n 6) section I.

[58] J Reichel and M Ribbing (n 6) section II.A.

[59] Charter of Fundamental Rights of the European Union [2012] OJ C326/391.

[60] See A Berger, 'Science Codification for the European Union – The ReNEUAL-Network: On the Limits of Legal Control of Innovation and Technology', section II.A.i; R Caranta (n 6) section II; M Heintzen (n 3) sections I.B.iii and II.B; K Lachmayer (n 6) section III.A.ii.

[61] On (national and international) human rights generally: for Austria, see K Lachmayer (n 6) sections III.A.i, IV.A.i and IV.C; Belgium, see S De Somer and I Opdebeek (n 6) section II.C; for France, see D Costa (n 6) sections II.A and II.D; for Italy, see R Caranta (n 6) section II; for the Netherlands, see Y Schuurmans, T Barkhuysen and W den Ouden (n 5) section II.F; for Norway, see JCF Nordrum (n 6) sections II.B, II.C, VII.B and VII.D; for Sweden, see J Reichel and M Ribbing (n 6) section I; for Switzerland, see F Uhlmann (n 4) section II.F; for the UK, see S Nason (n 1) section V.C.

[62] On the influence of the ECHR generally: for Belgium, see S De Somer and I Opdebeek (n 6) section II.C; for France, see D Costa (n 6) section II.D; for Italy, see R Caranta (n 6) section II; for the Netherlands, see Y Schuurmans, T Barkhuysen and W den Ouden (n 5) section II.F; for Norway, see JCF Nordrum (n 6) section VII.D; for Sweden, see J Reichel and M Ribbing (n 6) section V.B; for Switzerland, see F Uhlmann (n 4) section II.F; for the UK, see S Nason (n 1) section V.C.

## B. Constitutional Law

Constitutional and administrative law form what many countries denominate as public law. The divide between the two areas of law is quite different from country to country. We see countries that draw a strict line, often supplemented by institutional arrangements, such as special constitutional courts, in contrast to administrative courts. France and the Netherlands, for example, have such a divide.[63] In others, the common denominator 'public law' is at the forefront, in contrast to civil and penal law, and courts applying public law will not subtly distinguish between the simple application of administrative law and a 'constitutional question'. This goes often hand in hand with the element of 'constitutional interpretation' or 'interpretation in the best meaning of the Constitution'. Administrative law is 'concretised constitutional law'.[64] Here, a boundary between administrative and constitutional law is hard to locate, although at least in the curriculum of law students, we usually see the distinction.[65] On the other side of the spectrum, we see administrative law that is widely untouched if not immune to constitutional law. To use another famous quote from Germany: 'Constitutional law fades away, administrative law stays.'[66] It is easy to see the meaning of this quote at the dusk of the Weimar Republic. The 'good' administrative law is not (and should not be) troubled by the political arbitrariness of constitutional changes. It is a sad irony that even under the worst atrocities in Nazi Germany, administrative authorities were still concerned with administrative details of disenfranchised Jews. The face, rather the mirage of the Rechtsstaat, still stood.

In modern times, we see hardly any fears of detrimental constitutional influence on administrative law; on the contrary. 'Sanctuaries of arbitrariness'[67] are criticised, meaning that the administrative authorities must be subjected to (constitutional) review for all their action. In this context, it is worth noting that in the UK a so-called principle of legality[68] has emerged. This principle states a

[63] For France, see D Costa (n 6) section III.A; for the Netherlands, see Y Schuurmans, T Barkhuysen and W den Ouden (n 5) section I.B.

[64] This quote reads 'Verwaltungsrecht ist konkretisiertes Verfassungsrecht' in the German original and is taken from F Werner, 'Verwaltungsrecht als konkretisiertes Verfassungsrecht' (1959) *Deutsches Verwaltungsblatt* 527.

[65] ForAustria, see K Lachmayer (n 6) sections IV.A.i and IV.B; Belgium, see S De Somer and I Opdebeek (n 6) section II; for Germany, see M Heintzen (n 3) section I.B.i; for Italy, see R Caranta (n 6) sections II and III; for Norway, see JCF Nordrum (n 6) section II.B; for Switzerland, see F Uhlmann (n 4) section II.A; for the UK, see S Nason (n 1) section II.

[66] This quote reads 'Verfassungsrecht vergeht, Verwaltungsrecht besteht' in the German original and stems from O Mayer, *Deutsches Verwaltungsrecht*, 3rd edn (Berlin, Duncker & Humbolt, 1924) v.

[67] This quote reads 'Reservate staatlicher Willkür' in the German original and stems from G Müller; 'Reservate staatlicher Willkür – Grauzone zwischen Rechtsfreiheit, Rechtsbindung und Rechtskontrolle' in *Recht als Prozess und Gefüge: Festschrift für Hans Huber zum 80. Geburtstag* (Bern, Stämpfli, 1981) 109.

[68] It is important to note that the principle of legality according to this understanding is different from the common understanding of the principle of legality in civil law countries.

presumption that a parliamentary Act does not intend to violate common law constitutional rights.[69] The aforementioned 'constitutional interpretation' is a similar approach in civil law countries.[70] Nason points out that the significance to administrative law of explicit and implicit constitutional principles seems to be an attribute shared by Anglo-influenced legal systems.[71] Again, there is a parallel with some civil law countries, as in countries with written constitutions, the courts use openly formulated constitutional provisions in a 'creative' way to implement further 'unwritten constitutional guarantees' via their case law. For example, the Swiss Supreme Court formulated several procedural guarantees and the prohibition of arbitrariness based on the equal protection clause.[72]

In any case, it is quite clear from the chapters in this book that the constitutional influence,[73] including human rights,[74] on administrative law has grown in the last few decades. In Switzerland one might add the particularity that popular initiatives may directly regulate administrative law, such as protecting marshlands (Article 78, paragraph 5 of the Constitution), immigration policy (Article 121a of the Constitution), the expulsion of criminal foreigners (Article 121, paragraphs 3–6 of the Constitution), the prohibition on building minarets (Article 72 para 3 Constitution) etc, but of course these political charged areas mirror only a very small percentage of administrative law (and are rarely 'general'). Much more influential are administrative principles and rights of private individuals that forge legitimate administrative action.[75]

## C. Common Law

Common law is the most obvious alternative to codified (legislated) administrative law, and it is found in the UK, Australia, Canada and the US.[76] Rubin characterises common law as follows:

> In essence, it is judge-made law, judges being public officials who resolve disputes by applying legal principles. They make new law by extending prior doctrine incrementally,

[69] S Nason (n 1) section II.

[70] eg, in Switzerland it is known as *verfassungskonforme Auslegung* (U Häfelin, G Müller and F Uhlmann (n 7) fns 194 ff).

[71] S Nason (n 1) section II.

[72] F Uhlmann (n 4) section II.B.

[73] For Australia, see J Boughey (n 10) section III.B; for Canada, see P Issalys (n 10) section II; for the UK, see S Nason (n 1) section II.

[74] See n 63.

[75] For Austria, see K Lachmayer (n 6) section III.A.i; for Belgium, see S De Somer and I Opdebeek (n 6) section II.C; for France, see D Costa (n 6) section II.B; for Germany, see M Heintzen (n 3) section I.B.i; for Italy, see R Caranta (n 6) section II; for Norway, see JCF Nordrum (n 6) sections II.B and III; for Sweden, see J Reichel and M Ribbing (n 6) section II.B; for Switzerland, see F Uhlmann (n 4) section II.A; for the UK, see S Nason (n 1) section II.

[76] For Canada, see P Issalys (n 10) section II; for the UK, see S Nason (n 1) section II; for the US, see EL Rubin (n 1) section II.

> relying on analogical arguments. By this means, common law achieves an impressive level of flexibility and creativity while retaining political legitimacy through the assertion that it does not create new law, but only extends the law's in-dwelling principles to new situations. However, the common law is limited by the institutional structure of dispute resolution. It is reactive rather than proactive, dependent on the issues presented by the contending parties, incapable of making new rules globally as opposed to incrementally, restricted to remedies imposed on the contesting parties, and unable to allocate government resources.[77]

Common law includes, besides many other things, some procedural requirements which give effect to natural justice, as Boughey notes for Australia. As she reports further, in Australia in asylum matters, the court's review often clashes with administrative procedures restricting these requirements provoking counteraction by national legislators.[78] Here, obviously, it is not the technical question of codifying but the subject matter that is at the centre of attention, including institutional questions such as the relationship between the legislator and the courts.

In all common law countries, one can note two general developments. First, administrative law comes quite late in the legal development. In the US in the first third of the twentieth century, administrative law expanded rapidly.[79] In the UK frequent reference is made to the mid-1960s, when a rational, comprehensive administrative law system was developed.[80] Second, the common law basis has been superseded to quite an extent by codified law.[81] Judges have become 'interpreters of the code, not oracles'.[82] Even so, codification in common law countries has a different meaning from that in civil law countries. Common law is always there and will be always there. It might need some legislative intervention, but not a new construct eliminating what was before or was missing. Outside the common law world, a typical legislator will design an area from scratch, being in a way more abstract than a common law legislator that improves the whole system, creating some sort of hybrid between common law and legislative sources. The gap between the systems has become smaller, but there is still a fundamental contrast in approach.[83]

## D. Administrative Practice and Legal Scholarship

It has already been said that even outside the common law world, the logic of judge-made rules is most tangible in the area of general administrative law

[77] EL Rubin (n 1) section II.
[78] J Boughey (n 10) section IV.
[79] EL Rubin (n 1) section II.
[80] S Nason (n 1) section II.
[81] For Canada, see P Issalys (n 10) section II; for the UK, see S Nason (n 1) sections I and II; for the US, see EL Rubin (n 1) section II.
[82] S Nason (n 1) section IV.A.
[83] ibid section IV.

(see above, section III.A). The rules to be found are often an amalgam from administrative practice,[84] court decisions[85] and legal scholarship,[86] generally accepted but not easily classified. For example, in Switzerland, the prohibition of retroactivity was first brought up in a textbook on administrative law, more or less neutrally quoted by the Swiss Supreme Court, requoted by the next edition of the handbook in the sense that it was referred to the Swiss Supreme Court, copied and used by other doctrinal sources and in other decisions of the court, and slowly but steadily became a generally accepted – and quite powerful – administrative law principle for both the Swiss Supreme Court and legal scholarship. Its foundation in Swiss constitutional law or any other source is still unclear to this very day.[87]

It is also not easy to qualify administrative practice. It often comes in the form of manuals edited by the government. It can be binding to agencies in the sense that it has been put into force by their superiors. If this is the case, its quality gets quite close to what has been described as codified rules.[88] It is comparable to other forms of secondary legislation, even if it is still less formal (no official publication etc).

On the other side of the spectrum, administrative practice can be developed on a case-by-case basis, just as is done by courts. This may go together with following court decisions or being an administrative practice in its own name. The latter typically occurs in areas that are left to administrative discretion. Here, courts are reluctant to intervene making administrative practice highly relevant. This practice can be described in manuals, bringing it again within the scope of codified rules.[89] Still, as long as it is mainly a description of what is decided, it is not normative and binding on the agencies. It cannot qualify as a codified source. Not surprisingly, the transition is quite fluid.

Administrative practice and doctrinal influence often go hand in hand. This is best seen when higher-ranking civil servants become university teachers and vice versa. Similar exchanges take place in respect to judges.[90] Larger countries such as Germany and France tend to have fixed careers for judges and civil

[84] See especially Norway (JCF Nordrum (n 6) section II.E) and Switzerland (F Uhlmann (n 4) section II.E).

[85] See especially France (D Costa (n 6) section II.D), Sweden (J Reichel and M Ribbing (n 6) section III.B) and Switzerland (F Uhlmann (n 4) section II.E).

[86] See especially Sweden (J Reichel and M Ribbing (n 6) section III.D) and Switzerland (F Uhlmann (n 4) section II.E).

[87] F Uhlmann and R Trümpler, '"Das Rückwirkungsverbot ist im Bereich der Amtshilfe nicht von Bedeutung" – Überlegungen zum Urteil des Bundesverwaltungsgerichts vom 15. Juli 2010 betreffend den UBS-Staatsvertrag' (2011) 1 *Zeitschrift für schweizerisches Recht* 139, 142 f, 153, 155.

[88] On administrative rule-making: for Austria, see K Lachmayer (n 6) section III.B.i; Belgium, see S De Somer and I Opdebeek (n 6) section II.B; for Canada, see P Issalys (n 10) sections II and III; for Germany, see M Heintzen (n 3) section I.B.ii; for Norway, see JCF Nordrum (n 6) section IV; for Sweden, see J Reichel and M Ribbing (n 6) section IV.B.i; for the UK, see S Nason (n 1) section V.A; for the US, see EL Rubin (n 1) section III.

[89] F Uhlmann (n 4) section II.E.

[90] For the Netherlands, see Y Schuurmans, T Barkhuysen and W den Ouden (n 5) section III.B; for Sweden, see J Reichel and M Ribbing (n 6) section III.D.

servants, whereas in smaller countries, possibly to enlarge the pool of applicants, universities, courts and agencies seem to be more permeable. In either system, legal scholarship plays quite an important role.[91] This seems quite plausible as the element 'general' in general administrative law requires some distance from the day-to-day business of administrative adjudication. However, this is not to say that the latter has not strongly influenced administrative law as well.

## E. Analogy from Private Law and from Special Legislation

In the logic of administrative law as an amalgam, derived from the constitution by courts, agencies and scholars, one should not forget other legal sources that may serve as bricks to build the house of general administrative law.[92]

The first of these is private law. In both common and civil law countries, it is older than administrative law and it comes as no surprise that it was used to find practical solutions for administrative law questions. Private law still serves this purpose. In many countries, the administration may conclude private law contracts.[93] State liability may be subject to or imitate civil litigation.[94] The idea of good faith often binds both private individuals and state actors.[95] Hence, private law was and still is an important part of administrative law, of course to a varying degree from country to country. How it is introduced into administrative law is of lesser importance. It may be directly applicable as private law (and the agency may be subject to civil court competence) or it may be used by analogy, becoming part of public law (and administered by administrative courts). In any case, it serves to resolve a legal dispute in administrative matters and generates rules of general administrative law.[96]

Special legislation can play a similar role. It has been already pointed out that special legislation may extend its scope by way of example or, again, by analogy

[91] For the Netherlands, see Y Schuurmans, T Barkhuysen and W den Ouden (n 5) section III.B; for Sweden, see J Reichel and M Ribbing (n 6) section III.D; for Switzerland, see F Uhlmann (n 4) section II.E.

[92] F Uhlmann (n 4) sections II.C and II.D.

[93] For Austria, see K Lachmayer (n 6) section III.B.ii; for the Netherlands, see Y Schuurmans, T Barkhuysen and W den Ouden (n 5) section I.C; for Norway, see JCF Nordrum (n 6) section IV; for Switzerland, see F Uhlmann (n 4) section I.B. Canada is an exception here. Although the basic concepts of the law of (private) contracts do apply to contracts, this is so heavily supplemented or modified by public law rules that such contracts hardly qualify as 'private law contracts' (P Issalys (n 10) section III).

[94] On liability generally: for Austria, see K Lachmayer (n 6) section III.A.i; for the EU, see A Berger (n 60) section IV; for France, see D Costa (n 6) section I.B; for Germany, see M Heintzen (n 3) sections I.A.iii and I.B.v; for Norway, see JCF Nordrum (n 6) section III.E; for Switzerland, see F Uhlmann (n 4) section II.D.

[95] On good faith generally: for Belgium, see S De Somer and I Opdebeek (n 6) section II.C; for Italy, see R Caranta (n 6) sections II, IV.D; for Norway, see JCF Nordrum (n 6) section III.D; for Switzerland, see F Uhlmann (n 4) section II.D. Pointing out that good faith contains for individuals not only rights but also duties, for Belgium:, seeS De Somer and I Opdebeek (n 6) section II.C; for Switzerland, see F Uhlmann (n 4) section II.D.

[96] For Switzerland, see, eg, U Häfelin, G Müller and F Uhlmann (n 7) fns 245 ff.

(see above, section III.B). In stark contrast to what the mass of special legislation might suggest, administrative law always has gaps, typically relying on general administrative law.[97] In the absence of clear answers in general administrative law, there is little more to do than to turn to other areas of special administrative law in the hope that the rules there may be transposed into the area in question (of course, always respecting deliberate omissions of the legislator not to regulate a question and, by doing so, answering it in the negative).

# V. The Effects of Codification

## A. Simplification and Access

From the previous observations, it is quite obvious that general administrative law is a highly complex legal topic (and often feared by law students, at least in Switzerland). One element of its complexity is the legal sources. These often form an intriguing compound from the Constitution, private law, special legislation, handbooks and manuals etc, moulded together by courts, agencies and legal scholarship. Administrative law is not readily accessible for private individuals. Legal protection suffers if parties have little knowledge of their rights. Advice is costly. Hence, codification offers itself as a simplification to the existing legal order. It may enhance access for private individuals. Codification may even be a result of international policy-benchmarking. As Nordrum reports, in Norway there is an 'ongoing discussion on whether to codify administrative practice to conform to ideas of good regulation, prompted by assessments of the Norwegian regulatory systems in country reports by the World Bank and the Organisation for Economic Co-operation and Development'.[98]

Indeed, many chapters in this volume highlight the goal of simplification and increasing accessibility.[99] Heintzen takes a more pragmatic point of view when he says codification 'is never really about what might motivate professors, namely perfecting the legal system. The motives are partly of a sectoral political nature and partly of a general political nature'.[100] Nevertheless, many initiatives on codification exactly target the goal of simplification.

[97] For Belgium, see S De Somer and I Opdebeek (n 6) section II.C; for Switzerland, see F Uhlmann (n 4) section I.A.

[98] JCF Nordrum (n 6) section VII.E.

[99] For Australia, see J Boughey (n 10) sections IV.A and IV.C.i; for the EU, see A Berger (n 60) sections II.A.i, III.B.i, III.B.ii and IV; for France, see D Costa (n 6) section III.C; for Italy, see R Caranta (n 6) section VI; for the Netherlands, see Y Schuurmans, T Barkhuysen and W den Ouden (n 5) section III.C; for Norway, see JCF Nordrum (n 6) section VII.G; for Sweden, see J Reichel and M Ribbing (n 6) section III.A; for the UK, see S Nason (n 1) sections IV.A and IV.C; for the US, see EL Rubin (n 1) section VI.

[100] M Heintzen (n 3) section I.C.

In the Netherlands, the most important objective of codification for the Scheltema Commission, which was preparing a preliminary draft which evolved into the GALA, was the promotion of uniformity of administrative legislation. Furthermore, administrative law should be systematised and simplified.[101] Something similar can be observed in France, where 'nowadays codification is an integral part of a bigger process – the simplification of law – the objectives of which are both the accessibility and intelligibility of law required by constitutional law', as Costa puts it.[102] Also in Norway, there have been many initiatives and proposals to improve the accessibility of the law and to facilitate a good legislative structure.[103]

In the UK 'the simplification and modernisation of the law' is listed as an aim for the Law Commission in the Law Commission Act 1965. The importance of simplification is nicely pointed out by Sir Scarman in a speech from 1962 when he said that 'if codified law succeeds in becoming more manageable and easier to understand than the law which it supersedes, the habit of codification will spread. If it fails … judges will look through and beyond them to the judge-made law'.[104] In addition, the answers in favour of codification of administrative law handed to the UK Independent Review of Administrative Law (IRAL) cited the benefit of enhancing legislative clarity. This could also help to make judicial review more accessible to non-lawyers. But on the other hand, the majority of the answers were against the codification of administrative law, with the argument that legislative changes might lead to less certainty resulting in a reduction in accessibility. The negative answers further argued that codification could cause a rise in litigation, especially on technical issues. The UK IRAL concluded: 'On balance, little significant advantage would be obtained by statutory codification, as the grounds of review are well established and accessibly stated in the leading textbooks. But codification might make judicial review more accessible to non-lawyers'.[105]

For some other codification/legislative projects, the practical effects of codification are rarely discussed. There seems to be a tacit consensus that non-codified administrative law is complex and codified administrative law is preferable in this respect. There is little scientific support in the process of codification. Many questions are left open – for example, how do private individuals know about the law before the codification and what is their understanding after the reform? Do private individuals read codified administrative law? Do they understand it? How do they fare with sources of general administrative law in connection with

[101] Y Schuurmans, T Barkhuysen and W den Ouden (n 5) section III.C.

[102] D Costa (n 6) section III.C.

[103] JCF Nordrum (n 6) section VII.G.

[104] L Scarman, 'Codification and Judge-Made Law: A Problem of Co-existence' (1967) 42 *Indiana Law Journal* 361; for further information on this, see S Nason (n 1) section IV.A.

[105] 'Terms of Reference – Independent Review of Administrative Law', 2020, assets.publishing.service.gov.uk/government/uploads/system/uploads/attachment_data/file/915624/independent-review-admin-law-terms-of-reference.pdf, para 1.43; for further information on this, see S Nason (n 1) section IV.C.

new or pre-existing special legislation? How are these questions to be answered if asked to the courts, civil servants and lawyers? Such benchmarks of legislative theory remain unanswered.

This is not to say that codification does not improve access to general administrative law; rather, it formulates some scepticism on the hypothesis of an automatic improvement by codification. There is no doubt that non-codified administrative law is often a jungle. Still, it is far from obvious that the jungle disappears at the advent of legislation, as the British comments show. First, the quality of legislation may be doubtful, for example, for which Caranta harshly criticises Italy.[106] It may also be that the relationship between the codified and uncodified sources are not properly determined by the legislator – or cannot be easily determined because it is unclear what part of administrative law is constitutional in nature and hence pre-empts legislative intervention. And even if the codification is perfect in all these respects, it lies in the very nature of the law that new questions will always emerge which are not covered by the legal source and need interpretation. The paradise does not exist.

What one sees from the chapters in this volume is that the *discussion on codification* is often beneficial for the understanding of general administrative law.[107] The abstract thinking on rules forces us to categorise and structure administrative law, to compare different areas of special legislation and assess the differences on general issues, to formulate general ideas to catch the essence of an administrative practice etc. This seems to be an important element of the success of the GALA in the Netherlands.[108] The European initiative ReNEUAL 1.0[109] has not been taken up by the political actors, but its influence might be very well felt in courts and practice.[110] Hence, one positive effect of codification is the process itself. It helps to better understand and master general administrative law.

## B. Less Flexibility: Ossification

Common law systems – and with them any (administrative) court or agency practice – work on the incremental logic to build up a legal order step by step. This offers a unique flexibility to adjust the system. The constant reform is inherent to this approach, whereas fundamental changes are more difficult in such a system and typically require a legislator's intervention.

'[C]odes evoke … fixed, stable and typified institutions under which may be exhaustively subsumed the diversity of actual instances.'[111] This raises the question

[106] R Caranta (n 6) section VI.
[107] eg, as pointed out by S De Somer and I Opdebeek (n 6) section III.E.i.
[108] Y Schuurmans, T Barkhuysen and W den Ouden (n 5) sections IV.A and V.
[109] A Berger (n 60) section II.A.i.
[110] ibid section II.A.ii.
[111] P Issalys (n 10) section IV.

whether codification reduces flexibility and in the worst-case scenario will ossify the law. The question is usually not posed in this fundamental way, but there are clear traces that the legislator is worried about it. The UK IRAL reflected two main approaches to codification: 'either a statement of general principles or a detailed list'.[112] Indeed, the question is not only *whether* one codifies, but also *how* one codifies. A statement of principles will trigger the need for concretisation, either by secondary legislation (ordinances, decrees) or, again, by judicial decisions and administrative practice. Here, ossification and flexibility should not be a problem, but of course one must critically assess whether the goal of simplification and access will be attained. Still, detailed regulation is no guarantee of a better understanding of administrative law by the public. Only legislation of good quality may realistically improve the situation.

More often than a fundamental discussion of the advantages and disadvantages of codification and thus different legislative techniques of codification, we find different approaches that will preserve the flexibility of the law. In the Netherlands the GALA offers flexibility as it consists of four kinds of rules: first, mandatory provisions which cannot be overruled by the secondary legislator; second, rules which are considered as the 'best solution' for normal cases which can be overruled by the secondary legislator; third, rules as a 'residual provision' which in the main are supposed to fill in gaps in the event that special legislation fails to include a provision; and, fourth, 'optional rules' which are applicable if it is so provided by the special legislator.[113] In Australia the ADJR Act contains two open-ended or catch-all grounds due to concern expressed by Professor Wade that specifying the grounds of review could result in excluding the possibility of judicial development of additional grounds. Interestingly, to date, the Australian courts have not found it necessary to rely on these two catch-all grounds.[114] In contrast, in Switzerland, legal protection is initially linked to the requirement of an administrative decision. This led to problems with legal protection. Some of the problems could be solved by the courts through case law, but the main problem – the lack of legal protection against real acts – could only be solved through further legislative intervention.[115] Perhaps these problems could have been prevented if, like Australia, the legislature had introduced a catch-all clause for hardship cases from the beginning and thus prevented ossification.

These remarks urge the conclusion that the aforementioned question of *how* something is codified determines whether ossification occurs. This thesis is also supported by Nordrum's comments. As he explains, in Norway codification has not led to ossification, first, because 'Norwegian legislative language is typically short and leaves interpretative room and room for discretion, and there is in general a pragmatic approach to law, where the intention of the legislator is

[112] S Nason (n 1) section IV.C.
[113] Y Schuurmans, T Barkhuysen and W den Ouden (n 5) section II.B.
[114] J Boughey (n 10) sections IV.B, IV.B.iii and IV.C.iii.
[115] F Uhlmann (n 4) section III.

given considerable weight' and, second, because '[c]odification of administrative law seems to provide an *anchor* for case law rather than fully replacing it as a source of law.'[116] In addition, other contributors to this volume have pointed out that codification does not have to lead to a lesser importance of case law or to an ossification.[117] The question posed at the beginning can be answered as follows: insofar as a code is used as a flexible instrument that provides a framework and leaves space for case law, it neither leads to ossification nor comes into conflict with innovations – a concern pointed out by Issalys.[118]

There is another point that should not be underestimated: 'Codification is a task that requires extensive resources.'[119] This is obvious for the preparatory works, but it is not over once the code has been enacted. Codification needs maintenance. The GALA in the Netherlands has been reformed and extended in recent years.[120] If enough flexibility is built into the code, this may happen after several years. Of course, this need not be to the disadvantage of codification. It has been suggested that the discussion on codification has a value of its own and is beneficial for the understanding of general administrative law (see above, section V.A). It may be safely assumed that this also holds true for the works involved in keeping a code up to date.

## C. Legitimacy

Codification is at the crossroads of three powers: the legislator, the courts and administrative agencies, and possibly also the government itself. How does codification square in this equation?

It depends on what the legislator finds before enacting a code. If the administrative law is basically built on administrative practice, codification will typically strengthen the legitimacy of the sources. In some countries, the principle of legality encompasses a duty of Parliament to make a decision on all important issues.[121] Parliament may not delegate such questions. If indeed in administrative law the agencies act on their own legal sources (if any), one may rightly put in question the legitimacy. The agencies become the legislator and courts in their own right, a possible source of the old lament of an overpowering administration. It seems sensible that codification confirms and reinforces the sources. A parliamentary discourse may also help to drag some submerged 'technical' aspects of administrative law into the public realm. Of course, one may differently assess whether a politicisation of general administrative law is desirable or not.

[116] JCF Nordrum (n 6) section VII.A.
[117] For Belgium, see S De Somer and I Opdebeek (n 6) section III.F.iii; for France, see D Costa (n 6) section III.B.
[118] P Issalys (n 10) section IV.
[119] S Nason (n 1) section IV.A.
[120] Y Schuurmans, T Barkhuysen and W den Ouden (n 5) section III.C.
[121] For Switzerland, see, eg, F Uhlmann (n 8) 164 f.

These thoughts are not only found on the national level, but are also invoked for the EU. An important argument for the codification of ReNEUAL 1.0 was the strengthening of the political rights of EU citizens.[122] However, Heintzen critically notes:

> The fact that European codification efforts, such as the ReNEUAL project, start with the rights of the citizen in the administrative procedure, might be tactically motivated. Citizens' procedural rights are standard in many EU Member States and do not cost a lot (as opposed to state liability, which is a codificatory 'no-go' area). It will be difficult to find severe deficiencies concerning the rule of law in Germany that justify European regulations with regard to administrative procedures, with the exception of the topic of excessively long administrative procedures. On the other hand, politically, strengthening citizens' rights is always easy to sell.[123]

The picture is different if administrative law is mainly built on court decisions. Here, codification will hardly enhance legitimacy. Courts often enjoy the same authority as the legislator – if not even a higher one. There are concerns that Parliament gains supremacy in an unhealthy way.[124] Of course, this question very much depends on the greater constitutional design, namely the question of constitutional review. A strong constitutional court such as the US Supreme Court or the German Bundesverfassungsgericht will hardly be intimidated by sweeping reforms of the legislator as long as these reforms will be subject to constitutional scrutiny. It has already been suggested that the influence of the constitution (and of human rights) on general administrative law is growing (see above, sections IV.A and IV.B), and this also increases the power of the courts. Again, one may embrace such a development, but one should not overlook the fact that the question of sources is often a question of power. Codification is the sword of Parliament. How sharp it is depends on the constitution.

These constitutional aspects introduce a more general, political view on codification. Where political institutions are functioning well, one can be more optimistic that an administrative reform will also produce positive results. On the other hand, very little good will come out of a dysfunctional political system.[125] In the Italian case, both the political system as well as the quality of codification are criticised, which may be best condensed in the following quote: 'The burden to develop general principles from these utterly chaotic legislative materials fell squarely upon the case law of the Consiglio di Stato'.[126] Indeed, if this is the case,

[122] A Berger (n 60) section II.A.i.

[123] M Heintzen (n 3) section III.

[124] As Nason explains, especially in the UK, there exists a double risk 'that statutory codification could conflict with the common law supervisory jurisdiction and/or seek to supplant or "oust" that jurisdiction entirely' because the UK does not have a written constitution. This is coupled with the concern that the executive has significant unchecked power to fashion judicial review as it wishes (S Nason (n 1) section IV.C).

[125] This applies not only to a crisis in a political system, but also to a crisis within the doctrinal and judicial opinion. In this regard, '[a]s a Belgian writer perceptively observed 70 years ago, codification cannot be carried out successfully in an area of the law that is in a state of crisis' (P Issalys (n 10) n 148).

[126] R Caranta (n 6) section II.

one may abstain from codification with good reason. On the other side of the spectrum, the GALA from the Netherlands serves as an example of a rather successful reform under a relatively stable political system.[127]

## D. Contradictions and Conflicts

It has been already analysed that codification offers a more sweeping, general approach than the incremental steps of common law or administrative practice. Such a general approach may be needed if the goal of 'general' rules seems difficult to reach. If one speaks of administrative practice, the singular may be deceptive. In most countries, the implementation of administrative law lies in many hands. Specialised agencies, different courts or the chambers thereof may develop diverse solutions to the very same problem of general administrative law. Professionalism and specialisation may come with the cost that no entity will develop a more general picture – this may also be true for universities, where 'classical' administrative law is often superseded by specialised fields such as energy law, data protection, public procurement and migration law.

The same effect may be produced by a legislator that answers general questions in different fields of administrative law differently. Here, the legal sources command a specific rule for each question. General administrative law becomes superfluous, but contradictions of values are likely to occur. It may also be assumed that the application of different rules in different fields is more challenging than relying on general administrative rules.

Codification may offer a solution. It may accomplish uniformity. A great example of this is the enactment of the GALA in the Netherlands. The legislator 'needed to amend special laws, to bring them into line with the provisions of the GALA, comprises thousands of amendments spread across hundreds of statutes'. Therefore, the impact of the GALA on Dutch administrative law has been great. It has been even called a cultural revolution in the field of administrative law.[128] This process led to the uniformity that makes it such a success.[129]

Uniformity could also be reached by reforms of administrative procedure in several countries, as the chapters in this volume show.[130] In Switzerland, another area of general administrative law that has been streamlined both by the federal legislator and many cantonal legislators is that of subsidies. The regulation

[127] Y Schuurmans, T Barkhuysen and W den Ouden (n 5) sections IV and V.
[128] ibid section III.C.iii.
[129] ibid sections IV.A and V.
[130] For Austria, see K Lachmayer (n 6) section IV.C (see also the reservations in section IV.D); for Canada, see P Issalys (n 10) section III; for the Netherlands, see Y Schuurmans, T Barkhuysen and W den Ouden (n 5) section IV.A; for Norway, see JCF Nordrum (n 6) section VII.A; for Sweden, see J Reichel and M Ribbing (n 6) sections V.D and VI; for Switzerland, see F Uhlmann (n 4) section III; for the US, see EL Rubin (n 1) section VI.

of subsidies was confusing to say the least. An Act on the general questions of subsidies such as form (administrative act versus administrative contract) revocation helped to improve access to this legal topic. The special Acts still existed and provided the basis for subsidies, but the existing Acts were denuded of all general questions covered by the (general) Federal Act on Subsidies.[131] The idea was copied by many cantons and the reform was considered a success.[132] Hence, uniformity may offer a good reason to codify.

On the other hand, codification can also lead to new difficulties. As Boughey reports for Australia, the codification of judicial review in the ADJR has led to a complex, *dual system of review* because the narrow jurisdictional formula has meant that common law and the Constitution remain important sources of judicial review.[133] Similar concerns exist in the UK. As mentioned above (see section V.B), there are two opposing stereotypes of codification: a codification in the form of a detailed list or in the form of general principles. The first bears the risk of an ossification or, in common law countries, of a parliamentary, or even executive, displacement of the common law (see above, sections V.B and V.C). Further it could result in *technical interpretive problems*, which would undermine the idea of simplification (see above, section V.A). The later could lead, as in Australia, to a conflict between the statutory judicial review and the common law supervisory jurisdiction.[134] For these reasons, the UK IRAL concluded that there would be little benefit to either form of codification.[135] One or the other problem is discussed in all common law country chapters in this book.[136]

## E. Banality

It is interesting to see that many countries have codified administrative procedure, whereas the main principles of administrative action are often left untouched. This even holds true for the Dutch GALA, where, on a very general note, one can observe that procedural rules predominate. Codification in substance is rare. According to Schuurmans, Barkhuysen and den Ouden, this sometimes gives the impression that the GALA legislator sticks to provisions of a more procedural and technical nature in order to avoid the need to make difficult material choices.[137] Why is that so?

[131] Bundesgesetz über Finanzhilfen und Abgeltungen (Subventionsgesetz, SuG) vom 5 Oktober 1990 (SR 616.1).
[132] F Uhlmann (n 4) section II.C.
[133] J Boughey (n 10) sections I, IV.C.i and V.
[134] S Nason (n 1) section IV.C.
[135] See above n 106.
[136] For Australia, see J Boughey (n 10) section IV.C.i; for Canada, see P Issalys (n 10) section III; for the UK, see S Nason (n 1) sections II and IV.C; for the US, see EL Rubin (n 1) section IV and V.
[137] Y Schuurmans, T Barkhuysen and W den Ouden (n 5) section III.C.ii.

One explanation relates to the term 'general' in general administrative law. The substance of administrative law does not lie in the principles, but in special legislation. Indeed, general administrative law without a specific area is often bloodless if not without any proper meaning by its own, whereas administrative procedure works well on a more abstract level. A rule on substantive general administrative law often sounds trivial, and even in the GALA some articles seem so self-evident that they beg the question of banality.

In this regard, Nason states that a codification of the three central principles 'that administrative decisions must be in accordance with the law (illegality), that they must be rational (reasonableness) and that they must be procedurally fair' would be 'arguably little more than "cosmetic" or even "banal"'.[138]

Still, one may contend that there are (and indeed need to be) more detailed rules on substantive general administrative law. The principle of proportionality is usually disassembled in subparts and sub-subparts, generating a fully operational standard of action and review.[139] If courts, agencies and legal scholarship can add precision to the system, why is it so hard for the legislator to do so?

Indeed, it may well be that it is more difficult to find common denominators for the enormously diverse administrative action, whereas the procedures may be more alike. It is also possible that the description of a process is merely simpler and hence more tempting for the legislator than the Herculean task of catching the essence of good administrative decisions. There are also many examples on administrative procedure, but few on substance. Furthermore, the Constitution may play a role. Different procedures can be used in different systems to achieve the same outcome (eg, to respect the right to be heard), whereas it is hard to see how proportionality can be implemented in different ways. A decision of an agency is either proportional or it is not, which means that the legislator may specify rules of procedure but not (further) determine proportionality. Finally, any rule in substance will raise the question of *administrative discretion*. The stricter the rules, the less administrative discretion remains. This may be quite acceptable for questions of procedure, whereas in substance it is commonly accepted that agencies must have a certain leeway, either because they are more knowledgeable than courts or because they must be given some margin of appreciation to be able to include all aspects of a case and, by that, reaching a just and fair decision.

Still, codification on procedure but not in substance is not self-evident. One should duly also consider codifying principles, organisation and other typical topics of general administrative law. The discussion on the subject alone may be rewarding.

[138] S Nason (n 1) section II.
[139] For Switzerland, see, eg, F Uhlmann (n 8) 166 f.

# VI. Hurdles to Codification

## A. Extensive Resources

As Nason points out: 'Codification is a task that requires extensive resources.'[140] This applies both to the maintenance of an Act (see above, section V.B) and to the codification process itself. As a result, it is important to show good reasons for codification on the one hand and possible solutions that reduce resource consumption on the other hand. The reasons for a codification have already been discussed above in section V.

De Somer and de Opdebeek consider a thorough revision of the whole of general administrative law to be preferable.[141] In our opinion, a general revision has the advantage, as Lachmayer[142] and De Somer and Opdebeek point out, that it 'would force all those involved to face inconsistencies in prevailing law and to update and simplify the body of rules and principles where this is possible'.[143] This would serve the aforementioned goals of simplification and eliminating contradictions (see above, sections V.A and V.D). Consequently, the legislator should not settle for the uncoordinated enactment of special decrees to save resources. This would further increase the lack of coherence and complexity of administrative law, which would eventually turn administrative law into an impervious 'jungle' (if this has not already happened). Issalys states something similar when he calls 'small-scale codes – something of an oxymoron'.[144] However, as the example of the Netherlands shows, this does not mean that a codification of administrative law must be undertaken at one time. As Schuurmans, Barkhuysen and den Ouden report, the GALA is designed as a 'modular Act' and was enacted in stages.[145] This approach is also known in Switzerland and was successfully used for the constitutional revision. In this way, major material reforms can be co-ordinated without jeopardising the overall project.[146] Of course, the need for 'big tranches' to achieve uniformity has to be weighed against the need to reduce the resources to be able to realise the project itself. This will be no easy task.

Finally, it should be emphasised that codification also has the potential to save resources after its adoption by systematising complex, contradictory or scattered rules and clarifying outstanding questions, thereby reducing the administrative workload. This will at the same time relieve the administrative courts and private parties.

[140] S Nason (n 1) section IV.A; see also M Heintzen (n 3) section I.C.
[141] S De Somer and I Opdebeek (n 6) section IV.
[142] K Lachmayer (n 6) section V.
[143] S De Somer and I Opdebeek (n 6) section IV.
[144] P Issalys (n 10) section IV; see also S Nason (n 1) section IV.
[145] Y Schuurmans, T Barkhuysen and W den Ouden (n 5) section III.C.
[146] F Uhlmann (n 4) section III.

## B. Federalism

Serious challenges for codifications could arise from federalism. In this regard, Issalys points out that 'Canadian federalism has led to the development of different political cultures, and political culture exerts a strong influence on the development of administrative law'. The federalism and the resulting differences cause a codification to consume more time, expertise and other resources. Furthermore, a codification evokes the concept of unity. 'One might say, then, that codification is intrinsically centripetal: a code is the centre of some legal universe.' Federal states are by definition centrifugal. 'In such a context, "code", with its strong connotations of unity, is a loaded word.'[147]

This highlights a central discrepancy of codification in a federal state, which should be carefully analysed in every federal state. The underlying basic problem can also be seen in the German contribution, in which Heintzen states that 'in Germany, a comprehensive codification of general administrative law is practically impossible. This applies especially to administrative organisation and public service law'.[148] Also, in Switzerland, it is rather unlikely that a constitutional amendment giving the federal government the competence for codifying general administrative law for the state and the cantons would be successful. It would be a far-reaching intervention in the cantonal autonomy and there is hardly a need as the cantons often follow the federal example. Likewise, it is feasible that the constitutional influence on administrative law is increasing in some countries because it is easier to introduce material principles of general administrative law through constitutional based case-law instead of taking the arduous path of legislation to address federal issues with the associated democratic and federal hurdles.

The same basic problem can be observed in the EU. As Heintzen explains, a codification of general administrative law could be viewed 'as an attempt by a central authority to gain influence, if not dominance, over decentralised administrations. If this central authority is the EU Commission, the "octopus of competences", it can be certain of resistance from Germany'.[149] For this reason, the EU Commission was convinced that without a solution to the question of the scope of the EU's norm-setting competence in the area of administrative procedural law in interconnected procedures, the ReNEUAL 1.0 project would have no chance of being realised.[150]

As far as it is not possible to realise a codification of general administrative law in certain federal countries or the EU due to federal reasons, a remaining option would be to codify general administrative law at the subfederal level or at the level

[147] P Issalys (n 10) section IV.
[148] M Heintzen (n 3) section I.A.iii.
[149] ibid section I.C.
[150] A Berger (n 60) section II.A.ii.

of the EU Member States respectively. But, as Issalys highlights, this leads to a higher consumption of resources.[151]

### C. The Wrong Moment: A Lack of Euphoria?

Another question which is raised by Lachmayer is if codification is still 'a concept which seems attractive in the twenty-first century'. As he points out, the nineteenth century was the century of codification and now in the twenty-first century, international law and the privatisation of law have decreased the power of codification. For this reason, Lachmayer calls the twenty-first century a 'post-codification era'. Nevertheless, he highlights – and I fully agree – that the potential of codification still exists with the same benefits as was the case 100 years ago: legal certainty, efficient administration and effective legal protection.[152] I would like to add two things. First, Lachmayer's description of our time as a 'post-codification era' reflects the lack of enthusiasm not only in the politics but also in the academy for codifications. Perhaps a successful codification could reawaken the enthusiasm and turn the 'post-codification era' into a second codification era. Second, in my opinion, it seems even more important in today's more complex and multi-layered legal landscape to improve the clarity and accessibility of the law.

## VII. Summary and Recommendations

As has been shown, there are a variety of different understandings not only on what is meant by general administrative law, but also on what is meant by codification. However, a common feature of codification in all countries is it is an instrument of Parliament to create and shape administrative law. It is an 'abstract' approach to administrative law, an *approach of rules* in contrast to an approach by *cases*. As the chapters in this volume have shown, it can be said (except for the Netherlands) that general administrative law is clearly less codified than other areas of law. The means of choice for codification is thus a parliamentary Act combined with the necessary secondary legislation.

As shown by the chapters in this book, to date there are considerable differences in the sources of administrative law from country to country. However, what all countries have in common is that different sources are relevant for administrative law. In both civil and common law countries, primary and secondary legislation is of great importance for administrative law. For the latter, the main source remains common law, which can lead to delimitation difficulties. But also, for civil law counties, judge-made rules are of great importance. They are often an

[151] P Issalys (n 10) section IV.
[152] K Lachmayer (n 6) section V.

amalgam of administrative practice, court decision and legal scholarship that is generally accepted but not easy to classify. In this context, private law and special legislation are also made available for analogies. Almost all countries highlight, besides the main sources, the increasing importance and influence of international law. This especially holds true for the EU Member States. Lastly, depending on the constitutional system, the Constitution can be of outstanding importance or almost meaningless for administrative law as a source.

Against the backdrop of this variety of sources, which have usually evolved randomly, and in view of the complexity of general administrative law, it is hardly surprising that simplification and systematisation are basic concerns to be achieved by codification. The question depends less on whether codification is done and more on how it is done. There are several things to bear in mind.

First, the codification must be carefully fitted into the existing system, which means that the relationship between the codification and the other sources of law must be resolved, and provisions must be made for any contradictions or gaps. This is especially true for common law countries.

Second, it is important that realistic expectations are set for codification. A codification can simplify administrative law through systematisation and standardisation, and by eliminating contradictions. However, it is neither possible nor sensible to answer every question in advance in a detailed manner. Rather, a balance must be struck between clear rules that provide legal certainty by establishing a framework and open provisions that allow for appropriate decision-making by leaving room for interpretation, common law or judicial discretion. Only such a balance can ensure that the provisions in a codification survive the rapid change of the legal landscape over time, that adequate decisions can also be made in cases of hardship, and that codification does not lead to an undesirable ossification of administrative law.

Third, it should be noted that the question of source and method is also a question of the power of the institutions. The first question to be asked is to whom the constitution gives this power. Insofar as the answer is not clear, what the legislator finds before codification should be examined. In general, it can be said that codification increases legitimacy if the administrative law is basically built on administrative practice. If general administrative law is mainly built on court practices or common law, things are more difficult. In some civil law countries, codification would be constitutionally required by the principle of legality. In some common law countries – especially the UK, which has no written constitution – there is a legitimate concern that Parliament may use detailed Westminster-style legislation to displace the common law of judicial review, thereby upsetting the prevailing system of separation of powers.[153]

Fourth, even if some rules expose themselves to the accusation of banality, the investigation should not be neglected. First of all, there are general principles

[153] S Nason (n 1) section IV.C.

that are anything but banal and, further, the discussion on the topic already seems worthwhile.

Fifth, it should be kept in mind that codification consumes lots of resources, not only for its creation but even more so for its maintenance. In order to achieve the goal of simplification and systematisation, it seems advisable to tackle a major reform and not limit oneself to many uncoordinated small revisions. Nevertheless, it is also important to bear in mind that this goal must be reconciled with the politically achievable. A possible solution to this problem could be a 'modular Act', as was successfully used in the Netherlands and in Switzerland, which allows for a co-ordinated step-by-step revision.

Sixth, in federal states and the EU, the distribution of legislative powers is of central importance. Where the federal or EU authorities are not empowered to enact an overall codification of administrative law, the alternative approach would consist in codifying general administrative law separately at the federal/EU level and in each of the federated states/Member States. This solution has two major disadvantages: on the one hand, the goal of simplification and standardisation is achieved far less well or, in the worst case, not at all; on the other hand, resource consumption increases significantly.

Lastly, it should be borne in mind that codification is heavily dependent on political will. Even in a 'post-codification era', codification still has its justification. In any case, the political will to codify is essential for such a project. A constitutional provision in this direction might help. Of course, this does not exempt a political debate from the advantages and disadvantages of codification; on the contrary, it presupposes such a debate. However, it can counter-act a deadlock due to difficulties or declining political interest. The example of the Netherlands shows that such a basis can be promising.[154]

In summary, it can be said that the right balance between clear rules that provide legal certainty by establishing a framework and open provisions that allow for appropriate decision-making by leaving room for interpretation, common law or judicial discretion is crucial for the success of a codification. Whether it can be realised depends on the constitutional order, the available resources and, above all, the political will.

Even all these recommendations are followed, the task of codification remains challenging. The diversity of approaches to define administrative law, which do not draw sharp boundaries, and the disagreement about what should fall within the scope of general administrative law pose considerable difficulties for the legislator in codifying it. How should the legislator establish general rules or principles without knowing what he is regulating?[155] There are basically two opposing solutions to this problem, each with its advantages and disadvantages.

[154] Y Schuurmans, T Barkhuysen and W den Ouden (n 5) section III.A.

[155] The importance to understand the subject matter for regulating it is pointed out by Berger (A Berger (n 60) sections I and III.A.iii).

The first and often used approach is to analyse the 'common understanding' in the country and to use it as a guide for legislation without defining administrative law in the Act itself. This leaves it to the legal scholarship and the courts to circumscribe the scope of application of general administrative law and to draw the boundaries. The advantage of this approach is that it gives courts the flexibility to judge borderline cases appropriately, but it lacks clarity.

The second approach defines general administrative law in the Act itself. This is possible through an abstract definition, which in turn brings with it room for interpretation and thus uncertainty. Another way is to apply administrative law only if the statute regulates as such, which is the case in the Netherlands.[156] This presupposes that there is a generally applicable law for the remaining cases. In the Netherlands, civil law assumes this role.[157] In other jurisdictions, perhaps constitutional law could do the same. This approach comes with the disadvantage that uncodified areas remain underdeveloped, as is reported by Schuurmans, Barkhuysen and den Ouden in this volume.[158]

Still, the Dutch example highlights the many positive effects codification of general administrative law may have. Legislators and scholars should think about it.

[156] Y Schuurmans, T Barkhuysen and W den Ouden (n 5) section I.A.
[157] ibid sections I.A and I.C.
[158] ibid section IV.A.

# INDEX

www.ingramcontent.com/pod-product-compliance
Ingram Content Group UK Ltd.
Pitfield, Milton Keynes, MK11 3LW, UK
UKHW020228290926
15470UKWH00001B/420

9 781509 954926